philosophy
of religion:
selected readings

philosophy
selected readings

under the general editorship of **robert ferm**
middlebury college

# of religion:

edited by
william l. rowe
purdue university

william j. wainwright
university of wisconsin

ᴴᴮᴶ

harcourt brace jovanovich, inc.
new york / chicago / san francisco / atlanta

Philosophy of Religion: Selected Readings

ISBN: 0–15–570580–6

Library of Congress Catalog Card Number: 72–93725

Printed in the United States of America

PREFACE

The aim of this volume is to introduce students to the philosophy of religion by acquainting them with the writings of some of the thinkers who have made substantial contributions to this area. The text covers many topics that are central to the philosophy of religion, and, for each topic it considers, we have sought to provide a group of readings that reflects various philosophical viewpoints and pursues them in some depth without a loss of clarity.

There are several special features of the book. First, a substantial number of selections are included in a section that deals solely with the nature and attributes of God, treating such fundamental concepts as *omniscience* and *omnipotence*. Along with several discussions of these concepts by contemporary philosophers of religion, the section also offers pertinent readings from such classical sources as Augustine, Boethius, and Aquinas. We believe that a study of the readings in this section will deepen the student's understanding of the concept of God that has been dominant in Western thought. Second, in the section devoted to arguments for the existence of God, lesser known arguments have been avoided in favor of pursuing the three traditional arguments more thoroughly than is customary in works of this sort. The thoroughness of the selections thus provided should lead each reader to an understanding of the ontological, cosmological, and teleological arguments for the existence of God. Finally, wherever possible, we have tried to include selections that relate the philosophical topic being discussed to some current issue. There is, for example, a selection on the question of whether hallucinogenic drugs can produce mystical states of consciousness.

The editorial material includes an introduction to each major topic, with suggestions for further reading presented at the end of each section. The student may also benefit from the brief biographical footnotes that identify the authors of the selections.

We appreciate the help and encouragement given us on this book by Professors Robert Ferm of Middlebury College, Rem B. Edwards of the University of Tennessee, and Monroe and Elizabeth Beardsley of Temple University. We wish also to thank our wives, Betty Rowe and Eleanor S. Wainwright, for their help in the preparation of the manuscript, and to express our gratitude to the staff members of Harcourt Brace Jovanovich, for their cooperation and helpful suggestions.

W. L. R.

W. J. W.

CONTENTS

KNOWLEDGE

POWER

THE METAPHYSICAL ATTRIBUTES

II
ARGUMENTS FOR THE EXISTENCE OF GOD

THE ONTOLOGICAL ARGUMENT

III
OBJECTIONS
TO THEISM

IV
MYSTICISM
AND RELIGIOUS
EXPERIENCE

THE NATURE AND TYPES OF RELIGIOUS AND MYSTICAL EXPERIENCE

THE COGNITIVE STATUS OF RELIGIOUS AND MYSTICAL EXPERIENCE

V
REVELATION, FAITH, AND MIRACLES

FAITH AND REVELATION

MIRACLES

VI
RELIGIOUS
LANGUAGE

MEANING AND VERIFICATION

THE ANALOGY THEORY

THE SYMBOL THEORY

philosophy
of religion:
selected readings

THE NATURE
AND ATTRIBUTES
OF GOD

T he theistic concept of God is the concept of a purely spiritual being who is perfectly good, omnipotent, and omniscient. A number of important theologians—Augustine, Anselm, and Aquinas—have held that the concept of God also requires that He be necessary, timeless, immutable, and simple (without parts). The readings in this section serve two general aims. First, they clarify and explain some of the very basic attributes of the theistic God. Second, they examine some of the fundamental problems that have arisen in connection with the theistic concept of God.

The idea that God is a necessary being is a fundamental theme of theism. But what is meant by the expression "necessary being"? Proponents of the eighteenth-century form of the cosmological argument used the expression to mean a *logically* necessary being, one whose nonexistence is a logical impossibility. Certain remarks by Anselm and Aquinas suggest that they had also thought of God as a logically necessary being. John Hick, however, challenges this interpretation of Anselm and Aquinas, and points out—particularly in Aquinas—a different sense of "necessary being" according to which God is necessary provided that He is incorruptible, indestructible, without beginning or end, and not dependent on anything for His existence. In Hick's view, God is a *factually* necessary being, not a logically necessary being. Like other beings, God's nonexistence is a logical possibility, but unlike other beings, God has no beginning or end and does not depend for His existence on any other thing.

Hick accepts without criticism the view of many modern philosophers that logical necessity applies only to propositions and that no propositions affirming the existence of something can be logically necessary. But it is doubtful that either feature of this view is acceptable as it stands. For, in the first place, we can define the notion of a logically necessary being in terms of some proposition being logically necessary—for example, "God is a logically necessary being just in case some proposition affirming the existence of the being who is God is logically necessary." And, in the second place, it is not true that no proposition affirming the existence of something can be logically necessary. "There exists a prime number between 1 and 3" affirms the existence of something and is generally admitted to be logically necessary.

Two general problems are discussed in the readings on God's knowledge. First, there is the problem of whether Divine Foreknowledge is consistent with future contingency and human freedom. Second, there is the problem of whether God's omniscience is consistent with one or more of His other attributes. The selections from Boethius, Aquinas, and Anthony Kenny touch on the first of these two problems, and the selection from Norman Kretzmann discusses the compatibility of omniscience and immutability. The following discussion will concern only the first of these two problems.

One traditional theistic belief is that God knows everything that has happened, everything that is now happening, and everything that will happen in the future. It is the last of these, the concept of Divine Foreknowledge, that has been thought to lead to a difficulty. For if God has foreknowledge of everything that happens, then it seems to follow that whatever happens happens of necessity, could not have failed to happen. Whatever we may believe about Divine Foreknowledge, most of us believe that not everything that happens happens of necessity. For example, consider such events as the election of Richard Nixon to the Presidency or the invasion of Cambodia. These events have happened, but they could have failed to happen. We think that at some time before their occurrence it was in the power of some person or group to have prevented them from happening—they were not bound to happen. It was, in the months preceding their occurrence, possible for them to occur and possible for them not to occur. They were then what the medievals called future contingent events. They were then still in the future, and they were then contingent: it was possible for them to be and possible for them not to be. Of course, once they had occurred they were no longer future, nor were they any longer contingent—for it was no longer possible for them not to be. Thus to believe, as we do, that many events that occur are such that in the time preceding their occurrence it is equally possible for them to occur or not to occur, that their occurrence or nonoccurrence can be determined by some individual or group, is to believe that not everything that happens is bound to happen, happens of necessity. Most of us believe, in short, that there are future contingent events. But many people have thought that Divine Foreknowledge is inconsistent with future contingency. In their view, for example, if in the year 5000 B.C. God knew that Nixon would be elected in 1968, then it follows that in the months and years preceding the election, his election to the Presidency was future, but not contingent, for it was then not possible for it not to be. Given God's Foreknowledge, the election of Nixon was (in the months preceding the election) bound to happen, it was then (at that time) not possible for it not to happen.

Why should the fact that God knew in 5000 B.C. that Nixon would be elected in 1968 lead us to think that in 1967 Nixon's election in 1968 was bound to happen, that in the months preceding the presidential election no person or group had the power to prevent Nixon's winning? Of course, given what God knew in 5000 B.C., it follows that in 1967 no one was to successfully exercise his power to prevent Nixon's election. But does it follow that in 1967 no one even had it in his power to do so? In support of the claim that it does follow, various reasons have been given, but the most forceful is the following: given the fact of what God knew in 5000 B.C.—namely, that Nixon would be elected in 1968—to say that in 1967 some person or group had the power to prevent Nixon's election seems to imply that some person or group had the power to alter a fact about the past—that is, the fact of what God knew in 5000 B.C. But surely no one ever has it in his power to alter a fact about the past. The past is beyond our power. God's foreknowledge, therefore, is inconsistent with the idea of the future being contingent.

A theist might challenge the reasoning in support of the inconsistency between Divine Foreknowledge and future contingency or admit the inconsistency and conclude either that God does not, properly speaking, have foreknowledge or that future events are not really contingent. Boethius and Aquinas choose the second course, appealing to God's timelessness as grounds for denying that God can be said to know the future before it happens. Kenny, however, takes the first course and suggests that perhaps the past is not altogether out of our power. Some theists, among them the American theologian Jonathan Edwards, take the last alternative and deny that there are any future contingent events. They also argue, however, that when rightly understood, human freedom does not require this sort of future contingency.

How are we to understand the attribute of omnipotence as applied to God? Suppose we say that

1. God is omnipotent = God can do anything.

But, as Aquinas points out, even God cannot create things which are absolutely impossible (contradictory)—for example, an object that is both perfectly round and perfectly square. God's power extends only to those things which are possible. Following Aquinas' suggestion we have

2. God is omnipotent = God can do anything that is logically possible.

Difficulties remain, however. Although making an object both round and square is impossible, self-destruction and evil are things which clearly can be done. But many theologians have denied that God's power extends to self-destruction and evil. For the doing of such things, as Samuel Clarke argues, is inconsistent with God's nature (His infinity and perfect goodness). It might be argued that God's perfections imply only that God will not destroy Himself or do evil, not that He cannot—He has the power to do evil, but because He is supremely perfect it is a power He will never exercise. What this objection overlooks is that to attribute to God the power to do evil is to attribute to Him the power to cease to have an attribute (perfection) which is part of His very essence or nature. For since "God does evil" entails "God is not supremely perfect," if God has the power to do evil then He has the power to become not supremely perfect. And it is doubtful that any being has the power to remove from itself an attribute essential to it. Perhaps, then, we should replace definition 2 with

3. God is omnipotent = God can do anything that is logically possible and that is not inconsistent with any of His essential attributes.

Is "creating a stone so heavy He cannot lift it" something which God can or cannot do? Even if He can, there is still something He cannot do—lift the stone in question. C. Wade Savage endeavors to answer this dilemma by arguing that given the fact that a being cannot create such a stone, it does not follow that the being is limited in any way. If Savage is right, then the fact that God cannot create such a stone is not inconsistent with His omnipotence. Another possible solution to the paradox is to argue that the existence of a stone God cannot lift is inconsistent with one of His attributes (omnipotence). Hence, according to definition 3, God's omnipotence does not imply that He can create such a stone.

Plato argued that God must be unchangeable, for to change is to change either for the worse or for the better. But God, being perfect, cannot change for the worse. Nor can He change for the better since only what is less than supremely perfect can be improved. In his discussion of God's unchangeableness (immutability), Anselm presupposes a distinction between essential and accidental attributes of a thing. An essential attribute is a quality that a thing cannot lose and remain the thing that it is—for example, being human is an essential attribute of Plato, whereas being a philosopher is accidental to Plato. Among accidental properties Anselm distinguishes those which, if lost, result in a real change in a thing and those which do not. If one thing has the property of being taller than a second and, as a result of a change in the second thing, comes to have the property of being shorter than the second, no change need have occurred in it; whereas if a thing is red, but later becomes blue, a real change has occurred in it. God's immutability, in Anselm's view, implies that no change whatever can occur in God, either accidental or essential. God may, however, acquire the property of being worshiped by someone without undergoing any change. The implication of the foregoing is that God cannot be subject to feelings and emotions—for if a being comes to feel joy and then remorse, it has undergone change. Finally, immutability, as Anselm understands it, relates closely to timelessness. A being in time changes in virtue of the fact that, with each passing moment, it becomes older. But, as Anselm claims, God is completely outside of time: He does not endure through any period of time nor is He located at any point in time.

The selection by Charles Hartshorne raises serious objections to the metaphysical attributes of God described by Anselm and Aquinas. In his view, these attributes, as traditionally understood, seem to render God indifferent to the sufferings of His creatures.

W. L. R.

NECESSARY BEING

ST. ANSELM
The Divine Nature Exists through Itself

CHAPTER IV.

. . . There is, therefore, a certain Nature, or Substance, or Essence, which is through itself good and great, and through itself is what it is; and through which exists whatever is truly good, or great, or has any existence at all; and which is the supreme good being, the supreme great being, being or subsisting as supreme, that is, the highest of all existing beings.

CHAPTER V.   Just as this Nature exists through itself, and other beings through it, so it derives existence from itself, and other beings from it.

Seeing, then, that the truth already discovered has been satisfactorily demonstrated, it is profitable to examine whether this Nature, and all things that have any existence, derive existence from no other source than it, just as they do not exist except through it.

But it is clear that one may say, that what derives existence from some-

St. Anselm (1033–1109), consecrated Archbishop of Canterbury in 1093, was the most important philosopher and theologian of the eleventh century. His major works include *Monologium, Proslogium,* and *Cur Deus Homo.*

THE DIVINE NATURE EXISTS THROUGH ITSELF   From *Monologium* by St. Anselm, translated by Sidney N. Deane. Reprinted by permission of The Open Court Publishing Co., La Salle, Illinois.

thing exists through the same thing; and what exists through something also derives existence from it. For instance, what derives existence from matter, and exists through the artificer, may also be said to exist through matter, and to derive existence from the artificer, since it exists through both, and derives existence from both. That is, it is endowed with existence by both, although it exists through matter and from the artificer in another sense than that in which it exists through, and from, the artificer.

It follows, then, that just as all existing beings are what they are, through the supreme Nature, and as that Nature exists through itself, but other beings through another than themselves, so all existing beings derive existence from this supreme Nature. And therefore, this Nature derives existence from itself, but other beings from it.

> CHAPTER VI.   This Nature was not brought into existence with the help of any external cause, yet it does not exist through nothing, or derive existence from nothing.—How existence through self, and derived from self, is conceivable.

Since the same meaning is not always attached to the phrase, "existence through" something, or, to the phrase, "existence derived from" something, very diligent inquiry must be made, in what way all existing beings exist through the supreme Nature, or derive existence from it. For, what exists through itself, and what exists through another, do not admit the same ground of existence. Let us first consider, separately, this supreme Nature, which exists through self; then these beings which exist through another.

Since it is evident, then, that this Nature is whatever it is, through itself, and all other beings are what they are, through it, how does it exist through itself? For, what is said to exist through anything apparently exists through an efficient agent, or through matter, or through some other external aid, as through some instrument. But, whatever exists in any of these three ways exists through another than itself, and it is of later existence, and, in some sort, less than that through which it obtains existence.

But, in no wise does the supreme Nature exist through another, nor is it later or less than itself or anything else. Therefore, the supreme Nature could be created neither by itself, nor by another; nor could itself or any other be the matter whence it should be created; nor did it assist itself in any way; nor did anything assist it to be what it was not before.

What is to be inferred? For that which cannot have come into existence by any creative agent, or from any matter, or with any external aids, seems either to be nothing, or, if it has any existence, to exist through nothing, and derive existence from nothing. And although, in accordance with the observations I have already made, in the light of reason, regarding the supreme Substance, I should think such propositions could in no wise be true in the case of the supreme Substance; yet, I would not neglect to give a connected demonstration of this matter.

For, seeing that this my meditation has suddenly brought me to an important and interesting point, I am unwilling to pass over carelessly even any simple or almost foolish objection that occurs to me, in my argument; in order that by leaving no ambiguity in my discussion up to this point, I may have the better assured strength to advance toward what follows; and in order that if, perchance, I shall wish to convince any one of the truth of my speculations, even one of the slower minds, through the removal of every obstacle, however slight, may acquiesce in what it finds here.

That this Nature, then, without which no nature exists, is nothing, is as false as it would be absurd to say that whatever is is nothing. And, moreover, it does not exist through nothing, because it is utterly inconceivable that what is something should exist through nothing. But, if in any way it derives existence from nothing, it does so through itself, or through another, or through nothing. But it is evident that in no wise does anything exist through nothing. If, then, in any way it derives existence from nothing, it does so either through itself or through another.

But nothing can, through itself, derive existence from nothing, because if anything derives existence from nothing, through something, then that through which it exists must exist before it. Seeing that this Being, then, does not exist before itself, by no means does it derive existence from itself.

But if it is supposed to have derived existence from some other nature, then it is not the supreme Nature, but some inferior one, nor is it what it is through itself, but through another.

Again: if this Nature derives existence from nothing, through something, that through which it exists was a great good, since it was the cause of good. But no good can be understood as existing before that good, without which nothing is good; and it is sufficiently clear that this good, without which there is no good, is the supreme Nature which is under discussion. Therefore, it is not even conceivable that this Nature was preceded by any being, through which it derived existence from nothing.

Hence, if it has any existence through nothing, or derives existence from nothing, there is no doubt that either, whatever it is, it does not exist through itself, or derive existence from itself, or else it is itself nothing. It is unnecessary to show that both these suppositions are false. The supreme Substance, then, does not exist through any efficient agent, and does not derive existence from any matter, and was not aided in being brought into existence by any external causes. Nevertheless, it by no means exists through nothing, or derives existence from nothing; since, through itself and from itself, it is whatever it is.

Finally, as to how it should be understood to exist through itself, and to derive existence from itself: it did not create itself, nor did it spring up as its own matter, nor did it in any way assist itself to become what it was not before, unless, haply, it seems best to conceive of this subject in the way in which one says that *the light lights* or is *lucent*, through and from itself.

For, as are the mutual relations of *the light* and *to light* and *lucent* (*lux, lucere, lucens*), such are the relations of *essence*, and *to be* and *being*, that is, *existing* or *subsisting*. So the supreme *Being*, and *to be* in the highest degree, and *being* in the highest degree, bear much the same relations, one to another, as *the light* and *to light* and *lucent*.

ST. THOMAS AQUINAS
God's Nature Cannot Be Separated from His Existence

FIRST ARTICLE.   WHETHER THE EXISTENCE OF GOD IS SELF-EVIDENT?

. . . A thing can be self-evident in either of two ways: on the one hand, self-evident in itself, though not to us; on the other, self-evident in itself, and to us. A proposition is self-evident because the predicate is included in the essence of the subject: *e.g., Man is an animal,* for animal is contained in the essence of man. If, therefore, the essence of the predicate and subject be known to all, the proposition will be self-evident to all; as is clear with regard to the first principles of demonstration, the terms of which are certain common notions that no one is ignorant of, such as being and non-being, whole and part, and the like. If, however, there are some to whom the essence of the predicate and subject is unknown, the proposition will be self-evident in itself, but not to those who do not know the meaning of the predicate and subject of the proposition. Therefore, it happens, as Boethius says, that there are some notions of the mind which are common and self-evident only to the learned, as that incorporeal substances are not in space.[1] Therefore I say that this proposition, *God exists,* of itself is self-evident, for the predicate is the same as the subject, because God is His own existence as will be hereafter shown.[2] Now because we do not know the essence of God, the propo-

St. Thomas Aquinas (1225–1274) was a Dominican friar and, in the opinion of many, the greatest medieval philosopher and theologian. His writings, which attempt to adapt Aristotle's philosophy to a Christian setting, are the basis for modern Thomism and constitute the semiofficial philosophy of the Roman Catholic Church. His principal works are *Summa Theologica* and *Summa Contra Gentiles.*

GOD'S NATURE CANNOT BE SEPARATED FROM HIS EXISTENCE   From *Summa Theologica*, Part I, Questions 2 and 3, in *Basic Writings of Saint Thomas Aquinas*, edited by Anton C. Pegis. Copyright 1945 by Random House, Inc. Reprinted by permission of the publisher and St. Dominic's Priory, London.

[1] *De Hebdom.* (PL 64, 1311).
[2] Q. 3, a. 4 [in *Philosophy of Religion: Selected Readings,* pp. 12–13].

sition is not self-evident to us, but needs to be demonstrated by things that are more known to us, though less known in their nature—namely, by His effects. . . .

THIRD ARTICLE.   WHETHER GOD IS THE SAME AS HIS ESSENCE OR NATURE?

We proceed thus to the Third Article:—

Objection 1. It seems that God is not the same as His essence or nature. For nothing is in itself. But the essence or nature of God—*i.e.,* the Godhead—is said to be in God. Therefore it seems that God is not the same as His essence or nature.

Obj. 2. Further, the effect is assimilated to its cause; for every agent produces its like. But in created things the *suppositum* is not identical with its nature; for a man is not the same as his humanity. Therefore God is not the same as His Godhead.

On the contrary, It is said of God that He is life itself, and not only that He is a living thing: *I am the way, the truth, and the life (Jo.* xiv. 6). Now the relation between Godhead and God is the same as the relation between life and a living thing. Therefore God is His very Godhead.

I answer that, God is the same as His essence or nature. To understand this, it must be noted that in things composed of matter and form, the nature or essence must differ from the *suppositum,* for the essence or nature includes only what falls within the definition of the species; as humanity includes all that falls within the definition of man, for it is by this that man is man, and it is this that humanity signifies, that, namely, whereby man is man. Now individual matter, with all the individuating accidents, does not fall within the definition of the species. For this particular flesh, these bones, this blackness or whiteness, etc., do not fall within the definition of a man. Therefore this flesh, these bones, and the accidental qualities designating this particular matter, are not included in humanity; and yet they are included in the reality which is a man. Hence, the reality which is a man has something in it that humanity does not have. Consequently, humanity and a man are not wholly identical, but humanity is taken to mean the formal part of a man, because the principles whereby a thing is defined function as the formal constituent in relation to individuating matter. The situation is different in things not composed of matter and form, in which individuation is not due to individual matter—that is to say, to *this* matter—but the forms themselves are individuated of themselves. Here it is necessary that the forms themselves should be subsisting *supposita.* Therefore *suppositum* and nature in them are identified. Since, then, God is not composed of matter and form, He must be His own Godhead, His own Life, and whatever else is so predicated of Him.

Reply Obj. 1. We can speak of simple things only as though they were like the composite things from which we derive our knowledge. Therefore, in speaking of God, we use concrete nouns to signify His subsistence, because with us only those things subsist which are composite, and we use abstract nouns to signify His simplicity. In speaking therefore of Godhead, or life, or the like as being in God, we indicate the composite way in which our intellect understands, but not that there is any composition in God.

Reply Obj. 2. The effects of God do not imitate Him perfectly, but only as far as they are able. It pertains to defect in imitation that what is simple and one can be represented only by a multiplicity. This is the source of composition in God's effects, and therefore in them *suppositum* is not the same as nature.

FOURTH ARTICLE.   WHETHER ESSENCE AND BEING
ARE THE SAME IN GOD?

We proceed thus to the Fourth Article:—

Objection 1. It seems that essence and being [*esse*] are not the same in God. For if it be so, then the divine being has nothing added to it. Now being to which no addition is made is the being-in-general which is predicated of all things. Therefore it follows that God is being-in-general which can be predicated of everything. But this is false: *For men gave the incommunicable name to stones and wood* (Wisd. xiv. 21). Therefore God's being is not His essence.

Obj. 2. Further, we can know *whether* God exists, as was said above,[3] but we cannot know *what* He is. Therefore God's being is not the same as His essence—that is, as His quiddity or nature.

On the contrary, Hilary says: *In God being is not an accidental quality, but subsisting truth.*[4] Therefore what subsists in God is His being.

I answer that, God is not only His own essence, as has been shown, but also His own being. This may be shown in several ways. First, whatever a thing has besides its essence must be caused either by the constituent principles of that essence (like a proper accident that necessarily accompanies the species—as the faculty of laughing is proper to a man—and is caused by the constituent principles of the species), or by some exterior agent,—as heat is caused in water by fire. Therefore, if the being of a thing differs from its essence, this being must be caused either by some exterior agent or by the essential principles of the thing itself. Now it is impossible for a thing's being to be caused only by its essential constituent principles, for nothing can be the sufficient cause of its own being, if its being is caused. Therefore that thing, whose being differs from its essence, must have its being caused by another. But this cannot be said of God, because we call God the first efficient cause. Therefore it is impossible that in God His being should differ from His essence.

---

[3] Q. 2, a. 2.   [4] *De Trin.,* VII (PL 10, 208).

Second, being is the actuality of every form or nature; for goodness and humanity are spoken of as actual, only because they are spoken of as being. Therefore, being must be compared to essence, if the latter is distinct from it, as actuality to potentiality. Therefore, since in God there is no potentiality, as shown above, it follows that in Him essence does not differ from being. Therefore His essence is His being. Third, just as that which has fire, but is not itself fire, is on fire by participation, so that which has being, but is not being, is a being by participation. But God is His own essence, as was shown above. If, therefore, He is not His own being, He will be not essential, but participated, being. He will not therefore be the first being—which is absurd. Therefore, God is His own being, and not merely His own essence.

Reply Obj. 1. A thing-that-has-nothing-added-to-it can be understood in two ways. Either its essence precludes any addition (thus, for example, it is of the essence of an irrational animal to be without reason), or we may understand a thing to have nothing added to it, inasmuch as its essence does not require that anything should be added to it (thus the genus animal is without reason, because it is not of the essence of animal in general to have reason; but neither is it of the essence of animal to lack reason). And so the divine being has nothing added to it in the first sense; whereas being-in-general has nothing added to it in the second sense.

Reply Obj. 2. To be can mean either of two things. It may mean the act of being, or it may mean the composition of a proposition effected by the mind in joining a predicate to a subject. Taking *to be* in the first sense, we cannot understand God's being (or His essence); but only in the second sense. We know that this proposition which we form about God when we say *God is*, is true; and this we know from His effects, as was said above.[5]

[5] Q. 2, a. 2.

JOHN HICK
Necessary Being

'Necessary being' is one of the terms by means of which Christian thought has sought to define the difference between God and man. The notion of necessary being, applied to God and withheld from man, indicates that God and man differ not merely in the characteristics which they possess but more fundamentally, in their modes of being, or in the fact that they exist in different senses of the word 'exist'.

That such a distinction, however it may be best expressed, is essential to the Christian concept of God is agreed virtually on all hands. Paul Tillich in our own day emphasises the distinction to the extent of using different terms to refer to the reality of God and of man respectively. Human beings and other created things exist; God, on the other hand, does not exist, but is Being-itself. This is the most recent way of formulating a discrimination which has been classically expressed in the history of Christian thought by the idea of the necessary being of God in contrast to the contingent being of man and of the whole created order.

There are, however, two importantly different concepts which may be, and which have been, expressed by the phrase 'necessary being'. 'Necessity', in a philosophical context, usually means logical necessity, and gives rise in theology to the concept of a being such that it is logically impossible that this being should not exist. But this is not the only kind of necessity referred to in philosophical literature. The non-logical concepts of causal, empirical and material necessity can be grouped together as forms of *factual* necessity. The distinction between logical and factual necessity first appears, so far as I know, in the *Critique of Pure Reason*, where Kant treats of the three modal categories of possibility, existence and necessity. The category of necessity is derived by him from the necessary or analytic proposition in formal logic. But its schema in time is the existence of an object throughout all time [1]; and the corresponding 'postulate of empirical thought' is called by Kant *die materiale Notwendigkeit* and is equivalent to what is often described as causal neeessity, i.e. being part of the universal causal system of nature.[2] The schema of necessity as existence throughout all time suggests the notion

---

John Hick (1922–   ), born in England, has taught philosophy of religion at Cornell University and Princeton Theological Seminary. He is now a professor of theology at Birmingham University in England. Among his major publications are *Faith and Knowledge* and *Evil and the God of Love*.

NECESSARY BEING   From *Scottish Journal of Theology*, December, 1961, published by Cambridge University Press. Reprinted by their permission.

[1] [Second Edition] 184.   [2] [Second Edition] 279–80.

of a temporally unlimited being, and this is an important part, though not the whole, of the concept of God as a factually necessary being. I shall argue that the notion of factual necessity, when appropriately spelled out, is an essential element in the Christian doctrine of God, but that the notion of logical necessity is both philosophically and religiously profitless, and indeed even dangerous, to theology.

It is important to distinguish explicitly between logical and factual necessity, not only for the elucidation of the doctrine of God within the Church, but also in the interests of apologetics. For a number of contemporary philosophers of the analytical school have assumed that Christian theology requires the notion of logically necessary being, and having noted that this idea is rendered meaningless by the modern understanding of the nature of logical necessity, have rejected what they suppose to be the Christian concept of God. They are, however, I believe, mistaken in their initial assumption. My thesis thus has a threefold bearing. I wish to suggest, as a matter of theology, that the idea of the divine being as factually necessary is more adequate to the data of Christian faith than the idea of God's being as logically necessary; and as a matter of philosophy, that the idea of factually necessary being is immune from the criticisms which have rightly been levelled against the notion of logically necessary being; and as a matter of history, that the notion of God's being as factually necessary has a stronger claim to be regarded as the normative Christian use of the term 'necessary being' than has its interpretation in terms of logical necessity.

Let us begin with the idea of logically necessary being. To say that God has logically necessary being, or that His existence is logically necessary, is to say that it is logically impossible that God should not exist; or that the concept of God is such that the proposition 'God exists' is a logical, analytic or *a priori* truth; or again that the proposition 'God does not exist' is a self-contradiction, a statement of such a kind that it is logically impossible for it to be true. Such a claim, however, contravenes one of the fundamental positions of empiricist philosophy—that an existential proposition (i.e. a proposition asserting existence) cannot be logically necessary. For modern empiricism is largely founded upon the distinction between, in Hume's phrases, 'the relations between ideas' on the one hand, and 'matters of fact and existence' on the other. Given this distinction, logical necessity clearly belongs exclusively to the sphere of the relations between ideas. The ideas of 'larger' and 'smaller' for example, are such that it is a logically necessary truth that if A is larger than B, then B is smaller than A, the necessity arising from the meanings which we have given to the words 'larger' and 'smaller'. On the same principle, such propositions as 'God is omniscient' and 'God is omnipotent' express necessary truths, if 'God' has been defined as 'a being who is omniscient and omnipotent' or, compendiously, as 'unlimited Being'. Given this definition, it is not only a truth but an analytic truth that God is omniscient and omnipotent; for the definition renders it incorrect to call a Being 'God' who is other than omniscient and omnipotent. But, on the other hand, 'God exists' cannot be treated in the same way. God cannot be *defined* as existing. For, in the familiar slogan which has emerged from the critiques of the Ontological Argument, existence is not a predicate. To say that x exists is not to define, or to expand the definition of, the term 'x', but is to assert that this term refers to some object. And whether a given description has a referent or, to use another terminology, whether a given term has denotation, is a question of fact which cannot be settled *a priori*.

The logical doctrine involved, which had been previously clearly delineated by Hume and Kant, has been formulated definitively in our own time by Bertrand Russell in his theory of descriptions.[3] Russell showed that the question 'Does x exist?' does not imply that in some prior sense the x of which we speak is, or subsists, or has being; and further, that the assertion that x exists is not an attribution to a subsisting x of the further characteristic of existence. It is rather the assertion, with regard to a certain description (or name as standing for a description) that this description has a referent. Thus 'horses exist' has the logical structure: 'there are x's such that "x is a horse" is true'. Such an analysis exorcises the puzzle which has tended since the time of Plato to haunt negative existential propositions. 'Unicorns do not exist' does not entail that unicorns must first in some mysterious sense *be* in order that we may then say of them that they do not exist; it means simply that 'there are no x's such that "x is a unicorn" is true'. And 'God exists' means 'there is one (and only one) x such that "x is omniscient, omnipotent, etc." is true'. This Russelian analysis makes plain the logical structure of propositions asserting existence. Their structure is such that they cannot be true by definition, nor therefore by *a priori* necessity. Hence the concept of a being such that the proposition asserting its existence is a logically necessary truth, is a self-contradictory concept. There cannot—logically cannot—be a being whose nonexistence is logically impossible. I conclude then that we must on philosophical grounds repudiate all talk of God as having necessary being, when the necessity in question is construed as logical necessity.

Granting then that the notion of God's existence as *logically* necessary has to be ruled out as untenable, it is perhaps worth asking, as a matter of history, whether this notion has in fact figured at all prominently in Christian thought.[4] The first great thinker of the Church who comes to mind in this connexion is Anselm. The ontological argument, to the effect that the concept of God, as the concept of the greatest conceivable being, entails the existence of God, appears to be an attempt to show that the proposition

[3] *Introduction to Mathematical Philosophy,* 2nd edn. (1920), ch. 16.
[4] Whether or not this notion occurs prominently in Christian thought it does apparently have a place in Muslim theology. Apparently the *pons asinorum* which the theological novice must cross is the distinction between the necessary, the possible and the impossible; and the necessary is defined as that the non-existence of which cannot be thought. (D. B. Macdonald, *Aspects of Islam* (London, 1911), p. 121.)

'God exists' is a logically necessary truth. Certainly Descartes' version of the ontological argument has this character. According to Descartes, as the concept of a triangle entails the truth that its internal angles are jointly equal to two right angles, so the concept of God entails the truth that God exists.[5] But in Anselm himself there is another line of thought which stands in conflict with such an interpretation. In the second formulation of the ontological argument, in the third chapter of the *Proslogium*, we read that 'it is possible to conceive of a being which cannot be conceived not to exist (*potest cogitari esse aliquid, quod non possit cogitari non esse)*'. On the face of it this statement would seem to confirm the view that Anselm has in mind what we would today call the notion of logically necessary being. For the most natural interpretation of his words, at any rate by a twentieth-century reader, is that a being which cannot be conceived not to exist means a being whose nonexistence is logically inconceivable, that is to say, logically impossible. However, when we turn to Anselm's reply to Gaunilo we find that he states explicitly what he means by the notion of beings which can and which cannot be conceived not to exist. 'All those objects, and those alone,' he says, 'can be conceived not to exist, which have a beginning or end or composition of parts: also . . . whatever at any place or at any time does not exist as a whole. That being alone, on the other hand, cannot be conceived not to exist, in which any conception discovers neither beginning nor end nor composition of parts (*nec initium nec finem nec partium conjunctionem*), and which any conception finds always and everywhere as a whole.'[6]

Here we have something quite different from the claim that 'God exists' is a logically necessary truth. We have instead the essence of the contrasting notion of factual necessity—the notion, that is, of God as sheer, ultimate, unconditioned reality, without origin or end. Another aspect of the concept of factual necessity, namely *aseity*, is contributed by Anselm in the *Monologion*, where he draws the distinction between existence *a se* and existence *ab alio*. He says of God: 'The supreme Substance, then, does not exist through any efficient agent, and does not derive existence from any matter, and was not aided in being brought into existence by any external causes. Nevertheless, it by no means exists through nothing, or derives existence from nothing; since, through itself and from itself, it is whatever it is (*per seipsam et ex seipsa est quidquid est*).'[7] The relation between this aspect of Anselm's thought and his ontological argument is another and difficult question into which I do not propose to enter; I only wish, for the present purpose, to point to the presence, often I think unnoticed, of the notion of factually necessary being in his discussions.

Let us now turn the centuries to Thomas Aquinas, who explicitly uses the term 'necessary being'.[8] The conclusion of his Third Way argument is that

[5] *Meditations*, V.   [6] *Responsio editoris*, ch. IV. Cf. *Proslogium*, ch. XXII.   [7] Ch. VI.
[8] *Summa Theologica*, bk. I, q. 2, art. 3.

'there must exist something the existence of which is necessary (*oportet aliquid esse necessarium in rebus*).[9] But he also, I believe, like Anselm, uses the idea of necessary existence in the sense of factually, and not logically, necessary existence. For in the Third Way passage the mark of contingency is transciency, or temporal finitude—having a beginning and an end in time. And by contrast the mark of non-contingency, or of the necessary being of God, must be not having a beginning or an end in time—in other words, *eternal* being.

Can we then perhaps equate contingent with transient existence, and necessary with eternal existence? The answer that must be given, which is also the answer implicit in Thomas, is No. Eternity is one of the ingredients of the necessary being of the Godhead, but is not by itself sufficient. For it is possible to conceive of something existing eternally, not because it is such that there is and could be no power capable of abolishing it, but only because, although there are powers capable of abolishing it, they always refrain from doing so. Such a being would be eternal by courtesy of the fact that it is never destroyed but not by the positive virtue or power of being indestructible. And it is surely integral to the Christian concept of God that God, as the ultimate Lord of all, is not capable of being destroyed.

We must add at this point that, as the ultimate Lord of all, God is also incorruptible, in the sense of being incapable of ceasing either to exist or to possess His divine characteristics by reason of an inner decay or discerption. God can neither be destroyed from without nor suffer dissolution from within.

Indestructibility and incorruptibility, however, even taken together, cannot replace but must supplement the notion of eternal being. For it is possible to conceive of something being both indestructible and incorruptible and yet not eternal in the sense of being without beginning or end. Such a being would exist only if created, but once created would be indissoluble and indestructible.

In Thomist theology angels and human souls are held to have precisely this character, on the ground that they are simple substances. They have a beginning by divine creation, but once created they exist for ever, unless of course destroyed by omnipotent divine action. As incorruptible, such beings are described as necessary beings, and it is presumably these, and perhaps especially angels, that Thomas has in mind when he distinguishes in the Third Way passage between necessary beings which have their necessary existence caused by another and ultimately necessary being which does not have its necessary existence caused by another, but which is uncreated and is God. Some Thomist theologians describe these two kinds of necessary being as, in the one case, intrinsically but not extrinsically necessary, and in the other case, both intrinsically and extrinsically necessary. These definitional refinements do not concern us here except as emphasising that in Thomist

---

[9] cf. Norman Malcolm, 'Anselm's Ontological Arguments', *Philosophical Review*, January 1960.

thought the notion of necessary being is not an all-or-nothing logical concept but is a factual notion, capable of degrees and qualifications; so that the distinction between necessary and contingent being is not to be correlated with the distinction between logically necessary and contingent truths. Necessity is for Thomas a factual or ontic and not a logical characteristic.

I conclude then, concerning Thomas, that whilst he does not explicitly make the distinction between logical and factual necessity, in practice he cleaved so consistently to one side of the distinction that he was not led into any important ambiguity or confusion by the lack of an explicit separation of the two notions. However, some Thomist writers of our own day do fall into the ambiguity which their master avoided. M. Maritain, for example,[10] uses an instance of logical necessity to illustrate the idea of existence *a se*, thereby revealing that he is not conscious of the difference between these two notions. He first defines necessary existence in these terms: 'a thing is necessary when it *cannot* be prevented, contingent when it *can* be prevented. A thing is *absolutely necessary* when nothing can prevent it from being.' This is a clear enough account of the notion of existence *a se*. But in the next sentence Maritain offers an example from mathematics. 'Thus the properties of the sphere,' he says, 'are absolutely necessary'. Now the properties of a sphere—for example, the fact that every point on its surface is equidistant from the centre—are indeed absolutely necessary; that is to say, there could not possibly be a sphere which lacked these properties. But the reason for this is not that there is nothing that can *prevent* a sphere from having these properties, but simply that these properties belong to the definition of 'sphere'. There is nothing to prevent there being objects which approximate in varying degrees to this particular set of properties, but such objects would not be called spheres for the simple reason that we have chosen to confine the name 'sphere' to objects which fit certain specifications, which thus constitute the defining and necessary properties of a sphere.

II

If a skilled theologian can suppose that the Christian concept of God requires the notion of logically necessary existence, we can hardly blame secular philosophers if they make the same assumption and proceed to draw damaging conclusions from it. I should like in this connexion to refer to the much discussed article by Professor J. N. Findlay of London University, entitled 'Can God's existence be disproved?' [11] in which he derives from the self-contradictory nature of the idea of logically necessary being what he regards as a strict disproof of divine existence. To see what is amiss with Findlay's

[10] 'Necessity and Contingency' in *Essays in Thomism*, edited by Robert E. Brennan (New York, 1942).

[11] *Mind*, 1948. Reprinted in *New Essays in Philosophical Theology*, edited by Flew and MacIntyre (London, 1955).

argument is by contrast to see a little more clearly the outlines of a religiously and philosophically acceptable account of the unique mode of being of the Godhead.

Professor Findlay is, so far as I know, the first philosopher to have proposed an *a priori* proof of the non-existence of God. He puts the ontological argument into reverse by contending that the concept of deity, so far from guaranteeing the existence of an object corresponding to it, is such as to guarantee that no object corresponds to it.

Findlay defines the concept of God as that of the adequate object of religious attitudes, a religious attitude being described as one in which we tend 'to abase ourselves before some object, to defer to it wholly, to devote ourselves to it with unquestioning enthusiasm, to bend the knee before it, whether literally or metaphorically',[12] such an attitude is rationally adopted only by one who believes that the object to which he relates himself as worshipper has certain very remarkable characteristics. Findlay lists the most important of these characteristics. First, an adequate object of religious attitudes must be conceived as being infinitely superior to ourselves in value or worth. (Accordingly Findlay refers to this object as 'he' rather than as 'it'.) Second, he must be conceived as being unique: God must not merely be one of a class of beings of the same kind, but stand in an asymmetrical relationship to all other objects as the source of whatever value they may have. Third, says Findlay, the adequate objects of religious attitudes must be conceived as not merely happening to exist, but as existing necessarily; if he merely happened to exist he would not be worthy of the full and unqualified attitude of worship. And fourth, this being must be conceived as not merely happening to possess his various characteristics, but as possessing them in some necessary manner. For our present purpose we may conflate these two necessities, necessary existence and the necessary possession of properties, and treat them as one. It should be borne in mind throughout that in Findlay's argument 'necessary' means 'logically necessary'.

It is the last two in his list of requirements that provide the ground for Findlay's ontological disproof of theism. 'For if God is to satisfy religious claims and needs, he must be a being in every way inescapable, One whose existence and whose possession of certain excellencies we cannot possibly conceive away. And modern views make it self-evidently absurd (if they don't make it ungrammatical) to speak of such a Being and attribute existence to him.'[13] For, as we have already noted, post-Humean empiricism can assign no meaning to the idea of necessary existence, since nothing can be conceived to exist that cannot also be conceived not to exist. No propositions of the form 'x exists' can be analytically true. Hence, Findlay argues, the concept of an adequate object of religious attitudes, involving as it does the notion of a necessarily existent being who possesses his characteristic in some neces-

---

[12] *New Essays*, p. 49.   [13] op. cit., p. 55.

sary manner, is a self-contradictory concept. We can know *a priori*, from inspection of the idea itself, that there is and can be no such being.

We may distinguish in Findlay's argument a philosophical premise to the effect that no existential propositions can be necessary truths, and a theological premise to the effect that an adequate object of religious worship must be such that it is logically necessary that he exists. Of these two premises I wish to accept the former and reject the latter. I deny, that is to say, the theological doctrine that God must be conceived, if at all, in such a way that 'God exists' is a logically necessary truth. I deny this for precisely the same reason as Findlay, namely that the demand that 'God exists' should be a necessary truth is, like the demand that a circle should be square, not a proper demand at all, but a misuse of language. Only, whereas Findlay concludes that the notion of an adequate object of religious attitude is an absurdity, I conclude that that of which the idea is an absurdity cannot be an adequate object of religious attitudes; it would on the contrary be an unqualifiedly *in*adequate object of worship.

Let us then ask the question, which seems highly appropriate at this point, as to how religious persons actually think of the Being whom they regard as the adequate object of their worship. What aspect of the Christian experience of God lies behind the idea of necessary being?

The concept of God held by the biblical writers was based upon their experience of God as awesome power and holy will confronting them and drawing them into the sphere of His ongoing purpose. God was known as a dynamic will interacting with their own wills; a sheer given reality, as inescapably to be reckoned with as destructive storm and life-giving sunshine, or the fixed contours of the land, or the hatred of their enemies and the friendship of their neighbours; indeed even more ineluctably so, as the Book of Jonah emphasises. God was not for them an inferred entity; He was an experienced reality. The biblical writers were (sometimes, though doubtless not at all times) as vividly conscious of being in God's presence as they were of living in a material environment. Their pages resound and vibrate with the sense of God's presence, as a building might resound and vibrate from the tread of some great being walking through it. They thought of this holy presence as unique—as the maker and ruler of the Universe, the sole rightful sovereign of men and angels, as eternal and infinite, and as the ultimate reality and determining power, in relation to whom His creatures have no standing except as the objects of His grace. But nowhere in the biblical thought about God is use made of the idea of logical necessity. The notion is quite foreign to the characteristically Hebraic and concrete utterances found in the Bible, and forms no part of the biblical concept or concepts of God.

But, it might be said, was it not to the biblical writers inconceivable that God should *not* exist, or that he should cease to exist, or should lose His divine powers and virtues? Would it not be inconceivable to them that God might one day go out of existence, or cease to be good and become evil? And does not this attitude involve an implicit belief that God exists necessarily, and possesses His divine characteristics in some necessary manner? The answer, I think, is that it was to the biblical writers psychologically inconceivable—as we say colloquially, unthinkable—that God might not exist, or that His nature might undergo change. They were so vividly conscious of God that they were unable to doubt His reality, and they were so firmly reliant upon His integrity and faithfulness that they could not contemplate His becoming other than they knew Him to be. They would have allowed as a verbal concession only that there might possibly be no God; for they were convinced that they were at many times directly aware of His presence and of His dealings with them. But the question whether the non-existence of God is *logically* inconceivable, or *logically* impossible, is a purely philosophical puzzle which could not be answered by the prophets and apostles out of their own first-hand religious experience. This does not of course represent any special limitation of the biblical figures. The logical concept of necessary being cannot be given in religious experience. It is an object of philosophical thought and not of religious experience. It is a product—as Findlay argues, a malformed product—of reflection. A religious person's reply to the question, Is God's existence logically necessary? will be determined by his view of the nature of logical necessity; and this is not part of his religion but of his system of logic. The biblical writers in point of fact display no view of the nature of logical necessity, and would doubtless have regarded the topic as of no religious significance. It cannot reasonably be claimed then, that necessary existence was part of their conception of the adequate object of human worship.

What, we must therefore ask, has led Findlay to hold so confidently that logically necessary existence is an essential element in the religious man's concept of God? His process of thought is revealed in these words: 'We can't help feeling that the worthy object of our worship can never be a thing that merely *happens* to exist, nor one on which all other objects merely *happen* to depend.' [14] The reasoning here is that if a being does not exist by logical necessity, He merely happens to exist; and in this case He ought not to be worshipped as God. But in presenting the dilemma, either God exists necessarily, or He merely happens to exist, Findlay makes the very mistake for which he has criticised the theologians. Findlay should be the last person to use this dichotomy, since he has himself rendered it inoperative by pointing out that one half of the dichotomy is meaningless. And to remove half a dichotomy is to remove the dichotomy. If for example it is said that all human beings are either witches or non-witches, and it is then discovered that there is no such thing as a witch, it becomes pointless, and indeed misleading, to describe everyone as a non-witch. Likewise, having concluded that the notion of necessary existence has no meaning, to continue to

[14] ibid., p. 52.

speak of things merely *happening* to exist, as though this stood in contrast to some other mode of existing, no longer has any validity. From an empiricist standpoint, there are not two different ways of existing, existing by logical necessity and merely happening to exist. A thing either exists or does not exist; or to be more exact a description either has or does not have a referent. But Findlay, after ruling out the notion of necessary existence, in relation to which alone the contrasting idea of 'merely happening to exist' has any meaning, continues to use the latter category, and what is more, to use it as a term of reproach! This is a very advanced form of the method of having it both ways.

Our conclusion must be that Findlay has only disproved the existence of God if we mean by God a being whose existence is a matter of logical necessity. Since, however, we do not mean this, we may take Findlay's argument instead as emphasising that we must either abandon the traditional phrase 'necessary being', or else be very clear that the necessary being of God is not to be construed as *logically* necessary being.

III

We have arrived thus far at an identification of the necessary being of the Godhead with incorruptible and indestructible being without beginning or end. These characteristics, however, can properly be regarded as different aspects of the more fundamental characteristic which the Scholastics termed aseity, or being *a se*. The usual English translation, 'self-existence', is strictly a meaningless phrase, but for the lack of a better we must continue to use it. The core of the notion of aseity is independent being. That God exists *a se* means that He is not dependent upon anything for His existence. In contrast to this the created Universe and everything in it exist *ab alio*. For it is true of each distinguishable item composing the Universe that its existence depends upon some factor or factors beyond itself. Only God exists in total non-dependence; He alone exists absolutely as sheer unconditioned, self-existent being.

From God's aseity, or ontic independence, His eternity, indestructibility and incorruptibility can be seen to follow. A self-existent being must be eternal, i.e. without temporal limitation. For if He had begun to exist, or should cease to exist, He must have been caused to exist, or to cease to exist, by some power other than Himself; and this would be inconsistent with His aseity. By the same token He must be indestructible, for to say that He exists in total ontic independence is to say that there is and could be no reality with the capacity to constitute or to destroy Him; and likewise He must be incorruptible, for otherwise His aseity would be qualified as regards its duration. The question might however be asked at this point: Although it is incompatible with the idea of a self-existent being that He should ever be destroyed from without, yet is there any contradiction in the thought of such a being destroying Himself? Is it not possible in principle that God might 'commit suicide'? The question perhaps deserves more than the brief discussion that is possible within the limits of this paper. I am inclined, however, to think that the query itself is as logically improper as it is obviously religiously improper; and this for three reasons. First, the expression 'commit suicide' is highly misleading in this context. The 'suicide' of the absolute self-existent being would not be like a human suicide though on a much grander scale. For the concept of divine death is not analogous to that of human death. The death of a human being means the destruction or the cessation of function of his physical body; but God has no physical body to be destroyed, whether by Himself or by another. We have to try to think instead of a purely 'mental suicide'; but so far as I can see this is a completely empty phrase, to which we are able to attach no positive meaning. Second, an absolute end is as inconceivable as is an absolute beginning. Third, there is an additional contradiction in the notion of sheer, unqualified *being* ceasing to exist. Specific modifications of being may alter or cease, but to speak of being itself ceasing to exist is apparently to speak without meaning. I cannot then accept the question as to whether God might commit suicide as a genuine question posing intelligible alternatives.

Finally, to refer back to Findlay's discussion, it is meaningless to say of the self-existent being that He might not have existed or that He merely happens to exist. For what could it mean to say of the eternal, uncreated Creator of everything other than Himself that He 'merely happens to exist'? When we assert of a dependent and temporally finite being, such as myself, that I only happen to exist, we mean that if such-and-such an event had occurred in the past, or if such-and-such another event had failed to occur, I should not now exist. But no such meaning can be given to the statement, 'A self-existent being only happens to exist', or 'might not have existed'. There is no conceivable event such that if it had occurred, or failed to occur, a self-existent being would not have existed; for the concept of aseity is precisely the exclusion of such dependence. There is and could be nothing that would have prevented a self-existent being from coming to exist, for it is meaningless even to speak of a self-existent being as *coming* to exist.

What may properly be meant, then, by the statement that God is, or has, necessary as distinguished from contingent being is that God *is*, without beginning or end, and without origin, cause or ground of any kind whatsoever. He *is*, as the ultimate, unconditioned, absolute, unlimited being.

On the one hand, the fact that God is, is not a logically necessary truth; for no matter of fact can be logically necessary. The reality of God is a sheer datum. But on the other hand this is an utterly unique datum. That God is, is not one fact amongst others, but is related asymmetrically to all other facts as that which determines them. This is the ultimate given circumstance behind which it is not possible to go with either question or explanation. For to explain something means either to assign a cause to it or to show its place within some wider context in relation to which it is no longer puzzling to us. But the idea of the self-existent Creator of everything other than Himself is the idea of a reality which is beyond the scope of these explanatory procedures. As self-existent, such a being is uncaused, and is therefore not susceptible to the causal type of explanation; and as the Creator of all things other than Himself He stands in no wider context—on the contrary, His creative action constitutes the context in which all else stands. He is the ultimate reality, about which it is no longer meaningful to ask the questions which can be asked concerning other realities. For this reason God cannot but be mysterious to us. He is mysterious, not merely because there are questions about Him to which we do not know the answers, but because we frame questions about Him to which there are no answers since the questions themselves can have meaning only in relation to that which is not ultimate. As the final unconditioned, all-conditioning reality God cannot be included within any system of explanation. This is not to say that we cannot know any truths about Him, but that such truths are not logically deduced conclusions but sheer incorrigible facts disclosed within human experience. We may express this by saying that God has no characterising name; He is not of any kind, or for any reason, or from any cause He just *is*, and is what He is. When He reveals His nature to man He says to Moses 'I shall be what I shall be' [15]; and the fulfilment of that prolepsis is in the fact, the given historical fact, of Jesus Christ.

IV

A further step remains to be taken. For there are two respects in which the concept of aseity is less than adequate to the Christian understanding of God, or at least there are two dangers to be guarded against in speaking of God's aseity. One is the danger of understanding aseity in a purely static sense; and the other is the readiness of aseity to be construed in merely negative terms, simply as independence. The next major original treatment of the subject since Aquinas, that of Karl Barth in our own time, would appear to have been undertaken with these two dangers in mind; and it is accordingly to Barth that we now turn.

In his great dogmatic work Barth has a section on the *aseitas Dei* under the heading, *The Being of God in Freedom*.[16] As against any tendency to think of God as static, self-existent substance, the term 'freedom' reminds us that God is the living God, the Life which is the source of all life, and that He is Life not only as an Agent in human time, but also in His own hidden being, apart from and prior to that which is other than Himself. This is an important aspect of the Christian concept of God. The Scholastic '*actus purus*', and the more biblical term 'life', both point to it; and Paul Tillich,

---

[15] Exodus 3. 14.   [16] *Church Dogmatics,* vol. II, pt. I, ch. VI, § 28, 3.

in his own theological system, seeks to introduce the same dynamic note when he refers to God as 'the power of Being'. All these terms—pure act, divine life, freedom, and power—are of course symbolic in Tillich's sense of being expressions whose ordinary meaning is partially negated by that to which they point. That is to say (speaking more prosaically) even as we use them we are conscious of certain respects in which they would be misleading if taken literally. However, granting the symbolic character of all these words, the term 'freedom', as Barth uses it, does appear to have special appositeness as supplementing the notion of aseity.

Barth draws a distinction between what he calls the primary, or ontic, and the secondary, or neotic, absoluteness or freedom of God. The former refers to God's absoluteness in Himself, the latter to His absoluteness or Lordship in relation to His creation. This secondary absoluteness is characterised by Barth as total independence; God does not depend for His existence upon any factor external to Himself. From this point of view, He is 'the One who is free from all origination, conditioning or determination from without, by that which is not Himself'.[17] But, Barth insists, we must not think of God's unique mode of being only or even primarily in negative terms, as the absence of dependence upon His creation. God's absoluteness in relation to the world is secondary and derivative. Behind it there lies the primary absoluteness or freedom which is prior to and outside of all relations. God is free, says Barth, 'quite apart from His relation to another from whom He is free'.[18] God, in His own inner being, entirely apart from His creative action, is intrinsically free, and 'the freedom to exist which He exercises in His revelation is the same which He has in the depths of His eternal being, and which is proper to Him quite apart from His exercise of it ad extra'.[19] This insight of Barth's provides an important balancing note to the traditional discussion of aseity. Instead of being thought of primarily in His relation to the world, even though that relation be one of unqualified independence, God is to be conceived in the first instance as positive self-existence in infinite richness and plenitude. The ultimate Being should not be defined negatively as the One who does not depend upon other beings; on the contrary, His independence of the world is a corollary of His own sheer unique Godness, His infinite and absolute uncreated self-sustaining life.

Barth's doctrine of the primary absoluteness or freedom of God also provides the resources for his response to the question, How can we think of the absolute, self-existent Being as creating a universe and bestowing upon it a relative autonomy over against Himself, and yet remaining unimpaired in His own absolute self-sufficiency and freedom?[20] This however is a distinct, though adjacent, topic which cannot be taken up in the present article.

---

[17] op. cit., p. 307.   [18] ibid., p. 307.   [19] ibid., p. 305.

[20] It should be noted that Barth has developed his position further, in IV/1, ch. XIV, § 59, 1, in the direction of holding that the self-other relationship is already present within the triune Godhead, so that creation does not involve the problem of the inherently unrelated entering into relations.

Finally, a brief summary of conclusions. If we continue (as I think we properly may) to use the expression 'necessary being', we must explicitly interpret it in terms of the concept of factual, as distinguished from logical, necessity.[21] So interpreted, the necessary being of the Godhead is His aseity, understood primarily, however, not as non-dependence upon His creation, but positively, as absolute and unlimited being in infinite plenitude and freedom.

[21] cf. Terrence Penelhum, 'Divine Necessity', *Mind,* April 1960.

KNOWLEDGE

BOETHIUS
Divine Foreknowledge and Freedom of the Will

Boethius contends that divine foreknowledge and freedom of the human will are incompatible.

"Now I am confused by an even greater difficulty," I said.

"What is it?" Philosophy answered, "though I think I know what is bothering you."

"There seems to be a hopeless conflict between divine foreknowledge of all things and freedom of the human will. For if God sees everything in advance and cannot be deceived in any way, whatever his Providence foresees will happen, must happen. Therefore, if God foreknows eternally not only all the acts of men, but also their plans and wishes, there cannot be freedom of will; for nothing whatever can be done or even desired without its being known beforehand by the infallible Providence of God. If things could somehow be accomplished in some way other than that which God foresaw, his

Boethius (480–524) was a Roman scholar who translated into Latin a number of Aristotle's major works, and wrote important commentaries on Aristotle and Cicero. He is the author of *The Consolation of Philosophy* and several books on logic.

DIVINE FOREKNOWLEDGE AND FREEDOM OF THE WILL   From Boethius: *The Consolation of Philosophy,* translated by Richard Green, copyright © 1962, by the Bobbs-Merrill Company, Inc., reprinted by permission of the publisher.

foreknowledge of the future would no longer be certain. Indeed, it would be merely uncertain opinion, and it would be wrong to think that of God.

"I cannot agree with the argument by which some people believe that they can solve this problem. They say that things do not happen because Providence foresees that they will happen, but, on the contrary, that Providence foresees what is to come because it will happen, and in this way they find the necessity to be in things, not in Providence. For, they say, it is not necessary that things should happen because they are foreseen, but only that things which will happen be foreseen—as though the problem were whether divine Providence is the cause of the necessity of future events, or the necessity of future events is the cause of divine Providence. But our concern is to prove that the fulfillment of things which God has foreseen is necessary, whatever the order of causes, even if the divine foreknowledge does not seem to make the occurrence of future events necessary. For example, if a man sits down, the opinion that he is sitting must be true; and conversely, if the opinion that someone is sitting be true, then that person must necessarily be sitting. Therefore, there is necessity in both cases: the man must be sitting and the opinion must be true. But the man is not sitting because the opinion is true; the opinion is true because the sitting came before the opinion about it. Therefore, even though the cause of truth came from one side, necessity is common to both.

"A similar line of reasoning applies to divine foreknowledge and future events. For even though the events are foreseen because they will happen, they do not happen because they are foreseen. Nevertheless, it is necessary either that things which are going to happen be foreseen by God, or that what God foresees will in fact happen; and either way the freedom of the human will is destroyed. But of course it is preposterous to say that the outcome of temporal things is the cause of eternal foreknowledge. Yet to suppose that God foresees future events because they are going to happen is the same as supposing that things which happened long ago are the cause of divine Providence. Furthermore, just as when I know that a thing is, that thing must necessarily be; so when I know that something will happen, it is necessary that it happen. It follows, then, that the outcome of something known in advance must necessarily take place.

"Finally, if anyone thinks that a thing is other than it actually is, he does not have knowledge but merely a fallible opinion, and that is quite different from the truth of knowledge. So, if the outcome of some future event is either uncertain or unnecessary, no one can know in advance whether or not it will happen. For just as true knowledge is not tainted by falsity, so that which is known by it cannot be otherwise than as it is known. And that is the reason why knowledge never deceives; things must necessarily be as true knowledge knows them to be. If this is so, how does God foreknow future possibilities whose existence is uncertain? If He thinks that things will inevitably happen which possibly will not happen, He is deceived. But it is wrong to say that, or even to think it. And if He merely knows that they may or may not happen, that is, if He knows only their contingent possibilities, what is such knowledge worth, since it does not know with certainty? Such knowledge is no better than that expressed by the ridiculous prophecy of Tiresias: 'Whatever I say will either be or not be.' [1] Divine Providence would be no better than human opinion if God judges as men do and knows only that uncertain events are doubtful. But if nothing can be uncertain to Him who is the most certain source of all things, the outcome is certain of all things which He knows with certainty shall be.

"Therefore, there can be no freedom in human decisions and actions, since the divine mind, foreseeing everything without possibility of error, determines and forces the outcome of everything that is to happen. Once this is granted, it is clear that the structure of all human affairs must collapse. For it is pointless to assign rewards and punishment to the good and wicked since neither are deserved if the actions of men are not free and voluntary. Punishment of the wicked and recognition of the good, which are now considered just, will seem quite unjust since neither the good nor the wicked are governed by their own will but are forced by the inevitability of predetermination. Vice and virtue will be without meaning, and in their place there will be utter confusion about what is deserved. Finally, and this is the most blasphemous thought of all, it follows that the Author of all good must be made responsible for all human vice since the entire order of human events depends on Providence and nothing on man's intention.

"There is no use in hoping or praying for anything, for what is the point in hope or prayer when everything that man desires is determined by unalterable process? Thus man's only bonds with God, hope and prayer, are destroyed. We believe that our just humility may earn the priceless reward of divine grace, for this is the only way in which men seem able to communicate with God; we are joined to that inaccessible light by supplication before receiving what we ask. But if we hold that all future events are governed by necessity, and therefore that prayer has no value, what will be left to unite us to the sovereign Lord of all things? And so mankind must, as you said earlier, be cut off from its source and dwindle into nothing.[2]

POEM III

"What cause of discord breaks the ties which ought to bind this union of things? What God has set such conflict between these two truths? Separately each is certain, but put together they cannot be reconciled. Is there no discord between them? Can they exist side by side and be equally true?

"The human mind, overcome by the body's blindness, cannot discern by its dim light the delicate connections between things. But why does the mind

[1] Horace, *Satires* II. 5. 59.   [2] See Book IV, Poem 6.

burn with such desire to discover the hidden aspects of truth? Does it know what it is so eager to know? Then why does it go on laboriously trying to discover what it already knows? And if it does not know, why does it blindly continue the search? For who would want something of which he is unaware, or run after something he does not know? How can such a thing be found, or, if found, how would it be recognized by someone ignorant of its form?

"When the human mind knew the mind of God, did it know the whole and all its parts? Now the mind is shrouded in the clouds of the body, but it has not wholly forgotten itself; and, although it has lost its grasp of particulars, it still holds fast to the general truth. Therefore, whoever seeks the truth knows something: he is neither completely informed nor completely ignorant. He works with what he remembers of the highest truth, using what he saw on high in order to fill in the forgotten parts."

PROSE IV

> Philosophy begins her argument that divine Providence does not preclude freedom of the will by stressing the difference between divine and human knowledge.

"This is an old difficulty about Providence," Philosophy answered. "It was raised by Cicero in his book on divination,[3] and has for a long time been a subject of your own investigation, but so far none of you has treated it with enough care and conviction. The cause of the obscurity which still surrounds the problem is that the process of human reason cannot comprehend the simplicity of divine foreknowledge. If in any way we could understand that, no further doubt would remain. I shall try to make this clear after I have explained the things which trouble you.

"First, let me ask why you regard as inconclusive the reasoning of those who think that foreknowledge is no hindrance to free will because it is not the cause of the necessity of future things. For do you have any argument for the necessity of future events other than the principle that things which are known beforehand must happen? If, as you have just now conceded, foreknowledge does not impose necessity on future events, why must the voluntary outcome of things be bound to predetermined results? For the sake of argument, so that you may consider what follows from it, let us suppose that there is no foreknowledge. Then would the things which are done by free will be bound by necessity in this respect?"

"Not at all."

"Then, let us suppose that foreknowledge exists but imposes no necessity on things. The same independence and absolute freedom of will would remain.

[3] *De divinatione* II. 8ff.

"But you will say that even though foreknowledge does not impose necessity on future events, it is still a sign that they will necessarily happen. It must follow then that even if there were no foreknowledge the outcome of these future things would be necessary. For signs only show what is, they do not cause the things they point to. Therefore we must first prove that nothing happens other than by necessity, in order to demonstrate that foreknowledge is a sign of this necessity. Otherwise, if there is no necessity, then foreknowledge cannot be a sign of something that does not exist. Moreover, it is clear that firmly based proof does not rest on signs and extrinsic arguments but is deduced from suitable and necessary causes. But how can it be that things which are foreseen should not happen? We do not suppose that things will not happen, if Providence has foreknowledge that they will; rather we judge that, although they will happen, they have nothing in their natures which makes it necessary that they should happen. For we see many things in the process of happening before our eyes, just as the chariot driver sees the results of his actions as he guides his chariot; and this is true in many of our activities. Do you think that such things are compelled by necessity to happen as they do?"

"No. For the results of art would be vain if they were all brought about by compulsion."

"Then, since they come into being without necessity, these same things were not determined by necessity before they actually happened. Therefore, there are some things destined to happen in the future whose outcome is free of any necessity. For everyone, I think, would say that things which are now happening were going to happen before they actually came to pass. Thus, these things happen without necessity even though they were known in advance. For just as knowledge of things happening now does not imply necessity in their outcomes, so foreknowledge of future things imposes no necessity on their outcomes in the future.

"But, you will say, the point at issue is whether there can be any foreknowledge of things whose outcomes are not necessary. For these things seem opposed to each other, and you think that if things can be foreseen they must necessarily happen, and that if the necessity is absent they cannot be foreseen, and that nothing can be fully known unless it is certain. If uncertain things are foreseen as certain, that is the weakness of opinion, not the truth of knowledge. You believe that to judge that a thing is other than it is departs from the integrity of knowledge. Now the cause of this error lies in your assumption that whatever is known, is known only by the force and nature of the things which are known; but the opposite is true. Everything which is known is known not according to its own power but rather according to the capacity of the knower.

"Let me illustrate with a brief example: the roundness of a body is known in one way by the sense of touch and in another by the sight. The sight, remaining at a distance, takes in the whole body at once by its reflected rays;

but the touch makes direct contact with the sphere and comprehends it piecemeal by moving around its surface. A man himself is comprehended in different ways by the senses, imagination, reason, and intelligence. The senses grasp the figure of the thing as it is constituted in matter; the imagination, however, grasps the figure alone without the matter. Reason, on the other hand, goes beyond this and investigates by universal consideration the species itself which is in particular things. The vision of intelligence is higher yet, and it goes beyond the bounds of the universe and sees with the clear eye of the mind the pure form itself.

"In all this we chiefly observe that the higher power of knowing includes the lower, but the lower can in no way rise to the higher. For the senses achieve nothing beyond the material, the imagination cannot grasp universal species, reason cannot know simple forms; but the intelligence, as though looking down from on high, conceives the underlying forms and distinguishes among them all, but in the same way in which it comprehends the form itself which cannot be known to any other power. The intelligence knows the objects of the lower kinds of knowledge: the universals of the reason, the figures of the imagination, the matter of the senses, but not by using reason, or imagination, or senses. With a single glance of the mind it formally, as it were, sees all things. Similarly, when reason knows a universal nature, it comprehends all the objects of imagination and the senses without using either. For reason defines the general nature of her conception as follows: man is a biped, rational animal. This is a universal idea, but no one ignores the fact that man is also an imaginable and sensible object which reason knows by rational conception rather than by the imagination and senses. Similarly, although the imagination begins by seeing and forming figures with the senses, nevertheless it can, without the aid of the senses, behold sensible objects by an imaginative rather than a sensory mode of knowing.

"Do you see, then, how all these use their own power in knowing rather than the powers of the objects which are known? And this is proper, for since all judgment is in the act of the one judging, it is necessary that everyone should accomplish his own action by his own power, not by the power of something other than himself.

PROSE VI

Philosophy solves the problem of Providence and free will by distinguishing between simple and conditional necessity.

"Since, as we have shown, whatever is known is known according to the nature of the knower, and not according to its own nature, let us now consider as far as is lawful the nature of the Divine Being, so that we may discover what its knowledge is. The common judgment of all rational creatures holds that God is eternal. Therefore let us consider what eternity is, for this will reveal both the divine nature and the divine knowledge.

"Eternity is the whole, perfect, and simultaneous possession of endless life. The meaning of this can be made clearer by comparison with temporal things. For whatever lives in time lives in the present, proceeding from past to future, and nothing is so constituted in time that it can embrace the whole span of its life at once. It has not yet arrived at tomorrow, and it has already lost yesterday; even the life of this day is lived only in each moving, passing moment. Therefore, whatever is subject to the condition of time, even that which—as Aristotle conceived the world to be—has no beginning and will have no end in a life coextensive with the infinity of time, is such that it cannot rightly be thought eternal. For it does not comprehend and include the whole of infinite life all at once, since it does not embrace the future which is yet to come. Therefore, only that which comprehends and possesses the whole plenitude of endless life together, from which no future thing nor any past thing is absent, can justly be called eternal. Moreover, it is necessary that such a being be in full possession of itself, always present to itself, and hold the infinity of moving time present before itself.

"Therefore, they are wrong who, having heard that Plato held that this world did not have a beginning in time and would never come to an end,[4] suppose that the created world is coeternal with its Creator. For it is one thing to live an endless life, which is what Plato ascribed to the world, and another for the whole of unending life to be embraced all at once as present, which is clearly proper to the divine mind. Nor should God be thought of as older than His creation in extent of time, but rather as prior to it by virtue of the simplicity of His nature. For the infinite motion of temporal things imitates the immediate present of His changeless life and, since it cannot reproduce or equal life, it sinks from immobility to motion and declines from the simplicity of the present into the infinite duration of future and past. And, since it cannot possess the whole fullness of its life at once, it seems to imitate to some extent that which it cannot completely express, and it does this by somehow never ceasing to be. It binds itself to a kind of present in this short and transitory period which, because it has a certain likeness to that abiding, unchanging present, gives everything it touches a semblance of existence. But, since this imitation cannot remain still, it hastens along the infinite road of time, and so it extends by movement the life whose completeness it could not achieve by standing still. Therefore, if we wish to call things by their proper names, we should follow Plato in saying that God indeed is eternal, but the world is perpetual.[5]

"Since, then, every judgment comprehends the subjects presented to it according to its own nature, and since God lives in the eternal present, His knowledge transcends all movement of time and abides in the simplicity of its immediate present. It encompasses the infinite sweep of past and future,

---

[4] *Timaeus* 28ff.   [5] *Timaeus* 37d ff.

and regards all things in its simple comprehension as if they were now taking place. Thus, if you will think about the foreknowledge by which God distinguishes all things, you will rightly consider it to be not a foreknowledge of future events, but knowledge of a never changing present. For this reason, divine knowledge is called providence, rather than prevision, because it resides above all inferior things and looks out on all things from their summit.

"Why then do you imagine that things are necessary which are illuminated by this divine light, since even men do not impose necessity on the things they see? Does your vision impose any necessity upon things which you see present before you?"

"Not at all," I answered.

"Then," Philosophy went on, "if we may aptly compare God's present vision with man's, He sees all things in his eternal present as you see some things in your temporal present. Therefore, this divine foreknowledge does not change the nature and properties of things; it simply sees things present before it as they will later turn out to be in what we regard as the future. His judgment is not confused; with a single intuition of his mind He knows all things that are to come, whether necessarily or not. Just as, when you happen to see simultaneously a man walking on the street and the sun shining in the sky, even though you see both at once, you can distinguish between them and realize that one action is voluntary, the other necessary; so the divine mind, looking down on all things, does not disturb the nature of the things which are present before it but are future with respect to time. Therefore, when God knows that something will happen in the future, and at the same time knows that it will not happen through necessity, this is not opinion but knowledge based on truth.

"If you should reply that whatever God foresees as happening cannot help but happen, and that whatever must happen is bound by necessity—if you pin me down to this word 'necessity'—I grant that you state a solid truth, but one which only a profound theologian can grasp. I would answer that the same future event is necessary with respect to God's knowledge of it, but free and undetermined if considered in its own nature. For there are two kinds of necessity: one is simple, as the necessity by which all men are mortals; the other is conditional, as is the case when, if you know that someone is walking, he must necessarily be walking. For whatever is known, must be as it is known to be; but this condition does not involve that other, simple necessity. It is not caused by the peculiar nature of the person in question, but by an added condition. No necessity forces the man who is voluntarily walking to move forward; but as long as he is walking, he is necessarily moving forward. In the same way, if Providence sees anything as present, that thing must necessarily be, even though it may have no necessity by its nature. But God sees as present those future things which result from free will. Therefore, from the standpoint of divine knowledge these things are necessary because of the condition of their being known by God; but, considered only in themselves, they lose nothing of the absolute freedom of their own natures.

"There is no doubt, then, that all things will happen which God knows will happen; but some of them happen as a result of free will. And, although they happen, they do not, by their existence, lose their proper natures by which, before they happened, they were able not to happen. But, you may ask, what does it mean to say that these events are not necessary, since by reason of the condition of divine knowledge they happen just as if they were necessary? The meaning is the same as in the example I used a while ago of the sun rising and the man walking. At the time they are happening, they must necessarily be happening; but the sun's rising is governed by necessity even before it happens, while the man's walking is not. Similarly, all the things God sees as present will undoubtedly come to pass; but some will happen by the necessity of their natures, others by the power of those who make them happen. Therefore, we quite properly said that these things are necessary if viewed from the standpoint of divine knowledge, but if they are considered in themselves, they are free of the bonds of necessity. In somewhat the same way, whatever is known by the senses is singular in itself, but universal as far as the reason is concerned.

"But, you may say, if I can change my mind about doing something, I can frustrate Providence, since by chance I may change something which Providence foresaw. My answer is this: you can indeed alter what you propose to do, but, because the present truth of Providence sees that you can, and whether or not you will, you cannot frustrate the divine knowledge any more than you can escape the eye of someone who is present and watching you, even though you may, by your free will, vary your actions. You may still wonder, however, whether God's knowledge is changed by your decisions, so that when you wish now one thing, now another, the divine knowledge undergoes corresponding changes. This is not the case. For divine Providence anticipates every future action and converts it to its own present knowledge. It does not change, as you imagine, foreknowing this or that in succession, but in a single instant, without being changed itself, anticipates and grasps your changes. God has this present comprehension and immediate vision of all things not from the outcome of future events, but from the simplicity of his own nature. In this way, the problem you raised a moment ago is settled. You observed that it would be unworthy of God if our future acts were said to be the cause of divine knowledge. Now you see that this power of divine knowledge, comprehending all things as present before it, itself constitutes the measure of all things and is in no way dependent on things that happen later.

"Since this is true, the freedom of the human will remains inviolate, and laws are just since they provide rewards and punishments to human wills which are not controlled by necessity. God looks down from above, knowing all things, and the eternal present of his vision concurs with the future character of our actions, distributing rewards to the good and punishments to the evil. Our hopes and prayers are not directed to God in vain, for if they are just they cannot fail. Therefore, stand firm against vice and cultivate virtue. Lift up your soul to worthy hopes, and offer humble prayers to heaven. If you will face it, the necessity of virtuous action imposed upon you is very great, since all your actions are done in the sight of a Judge who sees all things."

ST. THOMAS AQUINAS
The Knowledge of God

FIFTH ARTICLE.   WHETHER GOD KNOWS THINGS OTHER THAN HIMSELF?

We proceed thus to the Fifth Article:—

Objection 1. It seems that God does not know other things besides Himself. For all other things but God are outside of God. But Augustine says that *God does not behold anything out of Himself.*[1] Therefore He does not know things other than Himself.

Obj. 2. Further, the object understood is the perfection of the one who understands. If therefore God understands other things besides Himself, something else will be the perfection of God, and will be nobler than He; which is impossible.

Obj. 3. Further, the act of understanding is specified by the intelligible object, as is every other act from its own object. Hence the intellectual act is so much the nobler, the nobler the object understood. But God is His own intellectual act, as is clear from what has been said. If therefore God understands anything other than Himself, then God Himself is specified by something other than Himself; which cannot be. Therefore He does not understand things other than Himself.

On the contrary, It is written: *All things are naked and open to His eyes* (*Heb.* iv. 13).

I answer that, God necessarily knows things other than Himself. For it is manifest that He perfectly understands Himself; otherwise His being would

---

THE KNOWLEDGE OF GOD   From *Summa Theologica*, Part I, Question 14, in *Basic Writings of Saint Thomas Aquinas*, edited by Anton C. Pegis. Copyright 1945 by Random House, Inc. Reprinted by permission of the publisher and St. Dominic's Priory, London.

[1] *Lib. 83 Quaest.*, q. 46 (PL 40, 30).

not be perfect, since His being is His act of understanding. Now if anything is perfectly known, it follows of necessity that its power is perfectly known. But the power of anything can be perfectly known only by knowing to what that power extends. Since, therefore, the divine power extends to other things by the very fact that it is the first effective cause of all things, as is clear from the aforesaid,[2] God must necessarily know things other than Himself. And this appears still more plainly if we add that the very being of the first efficient cause—viz., God—is His own act of understanding. Hence whatever effects pre-exist in God, as in the first cause, must be in His act of understanding, and they must be there in an intelligible way: for everything which is in another is in it according to the mode of that in which it is.

Now in order to know how God knows things other than Himself, we must consider that a thing is known in two ways: in itself, and in another. A thing is known *in itself* when it is known by the proper species adequate to the knowable object itself; as when the eye sees a man through the species of a man. A thing is seen *in another* through the species of that which contains it; as when a part is seen in the whole through the species of the whole, or when a man is seen in a mirror through the species of the mirror, or by any other way by which one thing is seen in another.

So we say that God sees Himself in Himself, because He sees Himself through His essence; and He sees other things, not in themselves, but in Himself, inasmuch as His essence contains the likeness of things other than Himself.

Reply Obj. 1. The passage of Augustine in which it is said that God *sees nothing outside Himself* is not to be taken in such a way, as if God saw nothing that was outside Himself, but in the sense that what is outside Himself He does not see except in Himself, as was explained above.

Reply Obj. 2. The object understood is a perfection of the one understanding, not by its substance, but by its species, according to which it is in the intellect as its form and perfection. For, as is said in *De Anima* iii,[3] *a stone is not in the soul, but its species.* Now those things which are other than God are understood by God inasmuch as the essence of God contains their species, as was explained above; and hence it does not follow that anything is the perfection of the divine intellect other than the divine essence.

Reply Obj. 3. The intellectual act is not specified by what is understood in another, but by the principal object understood in which other things are understood. For the intellectual act is specified by its object inasmuch as the intelligible form is the principle of the intellectual operation, since every operation is specified by the form which is its principle of operation, as heating by heat. Hence the intellectual operation is specified by that intelligible form which makes the intellect to be in act. And this is the species of the

[2] Q. 2 a. 3 [in *Philosophy of Religion: Selected Readings,* pp. 117–19].
[3] Aristotle, *De An.,* III, 8 (431b 29).

principal thing understood, which in God is nothing but His own essence in which all the species of things are comprehended. Hence it does not follow that the divine intellectual act, or rather God Himself, is specified by anything other than the divine essence itself.

EIGHTH ARTICLE.   WHETHER THE KNOWLEDGE OF GOD IS THE CAUSE OF THINGS?

We proceed thus to the Eighth Article:—
   Objection 1. It seems that the knowledge of God is not the cause of things. For Origen says (in *Rom.* viii. 30): *A thing will not happen, because God knows it as future, but because it is future, it is on that account known by God before it exists.*[4]
   Obj. 2. Further, given the cause, the effect follows. But the knowledge of God is eternal. Therefore if the knowledge of God is the cause of created things, it seems that creatures are eternal.
   Obj. 3. Further, *The knowable thing is prior to knowledge, and is its measure,* as the Philosopher says.[5] But what is posterior and measured cannot be a cause. Therefore the knowledge of God is not the cause of things.
   On the contrary, Augustine says, *Not because they are, does God know all creatures spiritual and temporal, but because He knows them, therefore they are.*[6]
   I answer that, The knowledge of God is the cause of things. For the knowledge of God is to all creatures what the knowledge of the artificer is to things made by his art. Now the knowledge of the artificer is the cause of the things made by his art from the fact that the artificer works through his intellect. Hence the form in the intellect must be the principle of action; as heat is the principle of heating. Nevertheless, we must observe that a natural form, being a form that remains in that to which it gives being, denotes a principle of action according only as it has an inclination to an effect; and likewise, the intelligible form does not denote a principle of action in so far as it resides in the one who understands unless there is added to it the inclination to an effect, which inclination is through the will. For since the intelligible form has a relation to contraries (inasmuch as the same knowledge relates to contraries), it would not produce a determinate effect unless it were determined to one thing by the appetite, as the Philosopher says.[7] Now it is manifest that God causes things by His intellect, since His being is His act of understanding; and hence His knowledge must be the cause of things, in so far as His will is joined to it. Hence the knowledge of God as the cause of things is usually called the *knowledge of approbation.*

[4] *In Rom.,* VII, super VIII, 30 (PG 14, 1126).
[5] Aristotle, *Metaph.,* IX, 1 (1053a 33).
[6] *De Trin.,* XV, 13 (PL 42, 1076); VI, 10 (PL 42, 931).
[7] Aristotle, *Metaph.,* VIII, 5 (1048a 11).

Reply Obj. 1. Origen [8] spoke in reference to that aspect of knowledge to which the idea of causality does not belong unless the will is joined to it, as is said above.

But when he says that the reason why God foreknows some things is because they are future, this must be understood according to the cause of consequence, and not according to the cause of being. For if things are in the future, it follows that God foreknows them; but the futurity of things is not the cause why God knows them.

Reply Obj. 2. The knowledge of God is the cause of things according as things are in His knowledge. But that things should be eternal was not in the knowledge of God; hence, although the knowledge of God is eternal, it does not follow that creatures are eternal.

Reply Obj. 3. Natural things are midway between the knowledge of God and our knowledge: for we receive knowledge from natural things, of which God is the cause by His knowledge. Hence, just as the natural things that can be known by us are prior to our knowledge, and are its measure, so the knowledge of God is prior to them, and is their measure; as, for instance, a house is midway between the knowledge of the builder who made it, and the knowledge of the one who gathers his knowledge of the house from the house already built.

NINTH ARTICLE.   WHETHER GOD HAS KNOWLEDGE
OF THINGS THAT ARE NOT?

We proceed thus to the Ninth Article:—

Objection 1. It seems that God has not knowledge of things that are not. For the knowledge of God is of true things. But *truth* and *being* are convertible terms. Therefore the knowledge of God is not of things that are not.

Obj. 2. Further, knowledge requires likeness between the knower and the thing known. But those things that are not cannot have any likeness to God, Who is very being. Therefore what is not, cannot be known by God.

Obj. 3. Further, the knowledge of God is the cause of what is known by Him. But it is not the cause of things that are not, because a thing that is not has no cause. Therefore God has no knowledge of things that are not.

On the contrary, The Apostle says: *Who . . . calleth those things that are not as those that are* (Rom. iv. 17).

I answer that, God knows all things whatsoever that in any way are. Now it is possible that things that are not absolutely should be in a certain sense. For, absolutely speaking, those things are which are actual; whereas things, which are not actual, are in the power either of God Himself or of a creature, whether in active power, or passive; whether in the power of thought or of imagination, or of any other kind whatsoever. Whatever therefore can be

---

[8] *In Rom.,* VII, super VIII, 30 (PG 14, 1126).

made, or thought, or said by the creature, as also whatever He Himself can do, all are known to God, although they are not actual. And to this extent it can be said that He has knowledge even of things that are not.

Now, among the things that are not actual, a certain difference is to be noted. For though some of them may not be in act now, still they have been, or they will be; and God is said to know all these with the *knowledge of vision:* for since God's act of understanding, which is His being, is measured by eternity, and since eternity is without succession, comprehending all time, the present glance of God extends over all time, and to all things which exist in any time, as to objects present to Him. But there are other things in God's power, or the creature's, which nevertheless are not, nor will be, nor have been; and as regards these He is said to have the knowledge, not of vision, but of *simple intelligence.* This is so called because the things we see around us have distinct being outside the seer.

Reply Obj. 1. Those things that are not actual are true in so far as they are in potentiality, for it is true that they are in potentiality; and as such they are known by God.

Reply Obj. 2. Since God is very being, everything is in so far as it participates in the likeness of God; as everything is hot in so far as it participates in heat. So, things in potentiality are known by God, even though they are not in act.

Reply Obj. 3. The knowledge of God is the cause of things when the will is joined to it. Hence it is not necessary that whatever God knows should be, or have been or is to be; but this is necessary only as regards what He wills to be, or permits to be. Further, it is not in the knowledge of God that these things be, but that they be possible.

ELEVENTH ARTICLE.   WHETHER GOD KNOWS
SINGULAR THINGS?

We proceed thus to the Eleventh Article:—

Objection 1. It seems that God does not know singular things. For the divine intellect is more immaterial than the human intellect. Now the human intellect, by reason of its immateriality, does not know singular things; but as the Philosopher says, *reason has to do with universals, sense with singular things.*[9] Therefore God does not know singular things.

Obj. 2. Further, in us those powers alone know the singular, which receive the species not abstracted from material conditions. But in God things are in the highest degree abstracted from all materiality. Therefore God does not know singular things.

Obj. 3. Further, all knowledge comes about through some likeness. But the likeness of singular things, in so far as they are singular, does not seem

[9] *De An.,* II, 5 (417b 22).

to be in God; for the principle of singularity is matter, which, since it is in potentiality only, is altogether unlike God, Who is pure act. Therefore God cannot know singular things.

On the contrary, It is written (*Prov.* xvi. 2), *All the ways of a man are open to His eyes.*

I answer that, God knows singular things. For all perfections found in creatures pre-exist in God in a higher way, as is clear from the foregoing.[10] Now to know singular things is part of our perfection. Hence God must know singular things. Even the Philosopher considers it incongruous that anything known by us should be unknown to God; and thus against Empedocles he argues that *God would be most ignorant if He did not know discord.*[11] Now the perfections which are found divided among inferior beings exist simply and unitedly in God; hence, although by one power we know the universal and immaterial, and by another we know singular and material things, nevertheless God knows both by His simple intellect.

Now some, wishing to show how this can be, said that God knows singular things through universal causes.[12] For nothing exists in any singular thing that does not arise from some universal cause. They give the example of an astronomer who knows all the universal movements of the heavens, and can thence foretell all eclipses that are to come. This, however, is not enough; for from universal causes singular things acquire certain forms and powers which, however they may be joined together, are not individuated except by individual matter. Hence he who knows Socrates because he is white, or because he is the son of Sophroniscus, or because of something of that kind, would not know him in so far as he is this particular man. Hence, following the above explanation, God would not know singular things in their singularity.

On the other hand, others have said that God knows singular things by the application of universal causes to particular effects.[13] But this will not hold; for no one can apply a thing to another unless he first knows that other thing. Hence the said application cannot be the reason of knowing the particular; it rather presupposes the knowledge of singular things.

Therefore we must propose another explanation. Since God is the cause of things by His knowledge, as was stated above, His knowledge extends as far as His causality extends. Hence, as the active power of God extends not only to forms, which are the source of universality, but also to matter, as we shall prove further on, the knowledge of God must extend to singular things, which are individuated by matter.[14] For since He knows things other than Himself by His essence, as being the likeness of things, or as their active principle, His essence must be the sufficing principle of knowing all

[10] Q. 4, a. 2.   [11] *De An.,* I, 5 (410b 4); *Metaph.,* II, 4 (1000b 3).
[12] Cf. Avicenna, *Metaph.,* VIII, 6 (100rb).   [13] Cf. Averroes, *Destruct. Destruct.,* XI (IX, 47rb).
[14] Q. 44, a. 2.

things made by Him, not only in the universal, but also in the singular. The same would apply to the knowledge of the artificer, if it were productive of the whole thing, and not only of the form.

Reply Obj. 1. Our intellect abstracts the intelligible species from the individuating principles; hence the intelligible species in our intellect cannot be the likeness of the individual principles, and on that account our intellect does not know the singular. But the intelligible species in the divine intellect, which is the essence of God, is immaterial not by abstraction, but of itself, being the principle of all the principles which enter into the composition of the thing, whether these be principles of the species or principles of the individual; hence by it God knows not only universals, but also singular things.

Reply Obj. 2. Although the species in the divine intellect has no material conditions in its being like the species received in the imagination and sense, yet it extends to both immaterial and material things through its power.

Reply Obj. 3. Although matter, because of its potentiality, recedes from likeness to God, yet, even in so far as it has being in this wise, it retains a certain likeness to the divine being.

TWELFTH ARTICLE.   WHETHER GOD CAN KNOW
INFINITE THINGS?

We proceed thus to the Twelfth Article:—

Objection 1. It seems that God cannot know infinite things. For the infinite, as such, is unknown, since the infinite is that which, *to those who measure it, leaves always something more to be measured,* as the Philosopher says.[15] Moreover, Augustine says that *whatever is comprehended by knowledge is bounded by the comprehension of the knower.*[16] Now infinite things have no boundary. Therefore they cannot be comprehended by the knowledge of God.

Obj. 2. Further, if it be said that things infinite in themselves are finite in God's knowledge, against this it may be urged that the essence of the infinite is that it is untraversable, and of the finite that it is traversable, as is said in *Physics* iii.[17] But the infinite is not traversable either by the finite or by the infinite, as is proved in *Physics* vi.[18] Therefore the infinite cannot be bounded by the finite, not even by the infinite; and so the infinite cannot be finite in God's knowledge, which is infinite.

Obj. 3. Further, the knowledge of God is the measure of what is known. But it is contrary to the essence of the infinite that it be measured. Therefore infinite things cannot be known by God.

On the contrary, Augustine says, *Although we cannot number the infinite,*

---

[15] *Phys.,* III, 6 (207a 7).   [16] *De Civit. Dei,* XII, 18 (PL 41, 368).
[17] Aristotle, *Phys.,* III, 4 (204a 3).   [18] *Op. cit.,* VI, 7 (238b 17).

nevertheless it can be comprehended by Him whose knowledge has no number.[19]

I answer that, Since God knows not only things actual but also things possible to Himself or to created things, as was shown above, and since these must be infinite, it must be held that He knows infinite things. Although the *knowledge of vision,* which has relation only to things that are, or will be, or have been, is not of infinite things, as some say,[20] for we do not hold that the world is eternal, nor that generation and movement will go on for ever, so that individuals be infinitely multiplied; yet, if we consider more attentively, we must hold that God knows infinite things even by the knowledge of vision. For God knows even the thoughts and affections of hearts, which will be multiplied to infinity since rational creatures will endure forever.

The reason of this is to be found in the fact that the knowledge of every knower is measured by the mode of the form which is the principle of knowledge. For the sensible species in the sense is the likeness of only one individual thing, and can give the knowledge of only one individual. But the intelligible species in our intellect is the likeness of the thing as regards its specific nature, which is participable by infinite particulars. Hence our intellect by the intelligible species of man in a certain way knows infinite men, not however as distinguished from each other, but as communicating in the nature of the species; and the reason is because the intelligible species of our intellect is the likeness of man, not as to the individual principles, but as to the principles of the species. On the other hand, the divine essence, whereby the divine intellect understands, is a sufficing likeness of all things that are, or can be, not only as regards the universal principles, but also as regards the principles proper to each one, as was shown above. Hence it follows that the knowledge of God extends to infinite things, even according as they are distinct from each other.

Reply Obj. 1. The idea of the infinite pertains to quantity, as the Philosopher says.[21] But the idea of quantity implies an order of parts. Therefore to know the infinite according to the mode of the infinite is to know part after part; and in this way the infinite cannot be known, for whatever quantity of parts be taken, there will always remain something else outside. But God does not know the infinite, or infinite things, as if He enumerated part after part; since He knows all things simultaneously and not successively, as was said above. Hence there is nothing to prevent Him from knowing infinite things.

Reply Obj. 2. Transition imports a certain succession of parts; and hence it is that the infinite cannot be traversed by the finite, nor by the infinite. But equality suffices for comprehension, because that is said to be comprehended which has nothing outside the comprehender. Hence, it is not against

[19] *De Civit. Dei,* XII, 18 (PL 41, 368).
[20] Cf. q. 7, a. 4; q. 46, a. 2, ad 8.
[21] *Phys.,* I, 2 (185a 33).

the idea of the infinite to be comprehended by the infinite. And so, what is infinite in itself can be called finite to the knowledge of God as comprehended; but not as if it were traversable.

Reply Obj. 3. The knowledge of God is the measure of things, not quantitatively, for the infinite is not subject to this kind of measure, but because it measures the essence and truth of things. For everything has truth of nature according to the degree in which it imitates the knowledge of God, as the thing made by art agrees with the art. Granted, however, an actually infinite number of things (for instance, an infinitude of men, or an infinitude in continuous quantity, as an infinite air, as some of the ancients held),[22] yet it is manifest that these would have a determinate and finite being, because their being would be limited to certain determinate natures. Hence they would be measurable as regards the knowledge of God.

THIRTEENTH ARTICLE.   WHETHER THE KNOWLEDGE

OF GOD IS OF FUTURE CONTINGENT THINGS?

We proceed thus to the Thirteenth Article:—

Objection 1. It seems that the knowledge of God is not of future contingent things. For from a necessary cause proceeds a necessary effect. But the knowledge of God is the cause of things known, as was said above. Since therefore that knowledge is necessary, what He knows must also be necessary. Therefore the knowledge of God is not of contingent things.

Obj. 2. Further, every conditional proposition, of which the antecedent is absolutely necessary, must have an absolutely necessary consequent. For the antecedent is to the consequent as principles are to the conclusion: and from necessary principles only a necessary conclusion can follow, as is proved in *Poster.* i.[23] But this is a true conditional proposition, *If God knew that this thing will be, it will be,*[24] for the knowledge of God is only of true things. Now, the antecedent of this conditioned proposition is absolutely necessary, because it is eternal, and because it is signified as past. Therefore the consequent is also absolutely necessary. Therefore whatever God knows is necessary; and so the knowledge of God is not of contingent things.

Obj. 3. Further, everything known by God must necessarily be, because even what we ourselves know must necessarily be; and, of course, the knowledge of God is much more certain than ours. But no future contingent thing must necessarily be. Therefore no contingent future thing is known by God.

---

[22] Attributed to Anaximenes and Diogenes by Aristotle, *Phys.,* III, 4 (203a 18); *Metaph.,* I, 3 (984a 5).

[23] Aristotle, *Post. Anal.,* I, 6 (75a 4).

[24] Cf. St. Anselm, *De Concord. Praesc. cum Lib. Arb.,* q. I, 1 (PL 158, 509); St. Augustine, *De Civit. Dei,* V, 9; XI, 21 (PL 41, 148; 334); *De Lib. Arb.,* III, 4 (PL 32, 1276); Boethius, *De Consol.,* V, prose 3; prose 6 (PL 63, 840; 860); Peter Lombard, *Sent.,* I, xxxviii, 2 (I, 244).

On the contrary, It is written (*Ps.* xxxii. 15), *He Who hath made the hearts of every one of them, Who understandeth all their works,* that is, of men. Now the works of men are contingent, being subject to free choice. Therefore God knows future contingent things.

I answer that, Since, as was shown above, God knows all things, not only things actual but also things possible to Him and to the creature, and since some of these are future contingent to us, it follows that God knows future contingent things.

In evidence of this, we must observe that a contingent thing can be considered in two ways. First, in itself, in so far as it is already in act, and in this sense it is not considered as future, but as present; neither is it considered as contingent to one of two terms, but as determined to one; and because of this it can be infallibly the object of certain knowledge, for instance to the sense of sight, as when I see that Socrates is sitting down. In another way, a contingent thing can be considered as it is in its cause, and in this way it is considered as future, and as a contingent thing not yet determined to one; for a contingent cause has relation to opposite things: and in this sense a contingent thing is not subject to any certain knowledge. Hence, whoever knows a contingent effect in its cause only, has merely a conjectural knowledge of it. Now God knows all contingent things not only as they are in their causes, but also as each one of them is actually in itself. And although contingent things become actual successively, nevertheless God knows contingent things not successively, as they are in their own being, as we do, but simultaneously. The reason is because His knowledge is measured by eternity, as is also His being; and eternity, being simultaneously whole, comprises all time, as was said above.[25] Hence, all things that are in time are present to God from eternity, not only because He has the essences of things present within Him, as some say,[26] but because His glance is carried from eternity over all things as they are in their presentiality. Hence it is manifest that contingent things are infallibly known by God, inasmuch as they are subject to the divine sight in their presentiality; and yet they are future contingent things in relation to their own causes.

Reply Obj. 1. Although the supreme cause is necessary, the effect may be contingent by reason of the proximate contingent cause; just as the germination of a plant is contingent by reason of the proximate contingent cause, although the movement of the sun, which is the first cause, is necessary. So, likewise, things known by God are contingent because of their proximate causes, while the knowledge of God, which is the first cause, is necessary.

Reply Obj. 2. Some say that this antecedent, *God knew this contingent to be future,* is not necessary, but contingent; because, although it is past, still it imports a relation to the future.[27] This, however, does not remove necessity

---

[25] Q. 10, a. 2, ad 4.   [26] Avicenna, *Metaph.,* VIII, 6 (100rb).

[27] St. Bonaventure, *In I Sent.,* d. xxxviii, a. 2, q. 2 (I, 678); St. Albert, *In I Sent.,* d. xxxviii, a. 4 (XXVI, 290).

from it, for whatever has had relation to the future, must have had it, even though the future sometimes is not realized. On the other hand, some say that this antecedent is contingent because it is a compound of the necessary and the contingent; [28] as this saying is contingent, *Socrates is a white man.* But this also is to no purpose; for when we say, *God knew this contingent to be future,* contingent is used here only as the matter of the proposition, and not as its principal part. Hence its contingency or necessity has no reference to the necessity or contingency of the proposition, or to its being true or false. For it may be just as true that I said a man is an ass, as that I said Socrates runs, or God is: and the same applies to necessary and contingent.

Hence it must be said that this antecedent is absolutely necessary. Nor does it follow, as some say, that the consequent is absolutely necessary because the antecedent is the remote cause of the consequent, which is contingent by reason of the proximate cause.[29] But this is to no purpose. For the conditional would be false were its antecedent the remote necessary cause, and the consequent a contingent effect; as, for example, if I said, *if the sun moves, the grass will grow.*

Therefore we must reply otherwise: when the antecedent contains anything belonging to an act of the soul, the consequent must be taken, not as it is in itself, but as it is in the soul; for the being of a thing in itself is other than the being of a thing in the soul. For example, when I say, *What the soul understands is immaterial,* the meaning is that it is immaterial as it is in the intellect, not as it is in itself. Likewise if I say, *If God knew anything, it will be,* the consequent must be understood as it is subject to the divine knowledge, that is, as it is in its presentiality. And thus it is necessary, as is also the antecedent; *for everything that is, while it is, must necessarily be,* as the Philosopher says in *Periherm.* i.[30]

Reply Obj. 3. Things reduced to actuality in time are known by us successively in time, but by God they are known in eternity, which is above time. Whence to us they cannot be certain, since we know future contingent things only as contingent futures; but they are certain to God alone, Whose understanding is in eternity above time. Just as he who goes along the road does not see those who come after him; whereas he who sees the whole road from a height sees at once all those traveling on it. Hence, what is known by us must be necessary, even as it is in itself; for what is in itself a future contingent cannot be known by us. But what is known by God must be necessary according to the mode in which it is subject to the divine knowledge, as we have already stated, but not absolutely as considered in its proper causes. Hence also this proposition, *Everything known by God must necessarily be,*

---

[28] Robert Grosseteste, *De Lib. Arb.,* VI (p. 170).
[29] Alex of Hales, *Summa Theol.,* I, no. 171 (I, 255); no. 184 (I, 270); Alain of Lille, *Theol. Reg.,* LXVI (PL 210, 653).
[30] Aristotle, *Perih.,* I, 9 (19a 23).

is usually distinguished,[31] for it may refer to the thing or to the saying. If it refers to the thing, it is divided and false; for the sense is, *Everything which God knows is necessary*. If understood of the saying, it is composite and true, for the sense is, *This proposition, 'that which is known by God is' is necessary*.

Now some urge an objection and say that this distinction holds good with regard to forms that are separable from a subject.[32] Thus if I said, *It is possible for a white thing to be black*, it is false as applied to the saying, and true as applied to the thing: for a thing which is white can become black; whereas this saying, *a white thing is black*, can never be true. But in forms that are inseparable from a subject, this distinction does not hold: for instance, if I said, *A black crow can be white*; for in both senses it is false. Now to be known by God is inseparable from a thing; for what is known by God cannot be not known. This objection, however, would hold if these words *that which is known* implied any disposition inherent in the subject; but since they import an act of the knower, something can be attributed to the known thing in itself (even if it always be known) which is not attributed to it in so far as it falls under an act of knowledge. Thus, material being is attributed to a stone in itself, which is not attributed to it inasmuch as it is intelligible.

FIFTEENTH ARTICLE.   WHETHER THE KNOWLEDGE OF GOD IS VARIABLE?

We proceed thus to the Fifteenth Article:—

Objection 1. It seems that the knowledge of God is variable. For knowledge is related to what is knowable. But whatever imports relation to the creature is applied to God from time, and varies according to the variation of creatures. Therefore, the knowledge of God is variable according to the variation of creatures.

Obj. 2. Further, whatever God can make He can know. But God can make more things than He does. Therefore, He can know more than He knows. Thus, His knowledge can vary according to increase and diminution.

Obj. 3. Further, God knew that Christ would be born. But He does not know now that Christ will be born, because Christ is not to be born in the future. Therefore God does not know everything He once knew; and thus the knowledge of God is variable.

On the contrary, It is said, that in God *there is no change nor shadow of alteration* (*Jas.* i. 17).

I answer that, Since the knowledge of God is His substance, as is clear from the foregoing, just as His substance is altogether immutable, as was shown above,[33] so His knowledge likewise must be altogether invariable.

---

[31] Cf. Wm. of Sherwood, *Introd. in Logicam* (p. 89); St. Albert, *In Prior. Anal.,* I, tr. 4, ch. 16 (I, 562).
[32] Cf. St. Thomas, *In I Sent.,* d. xxxviii, q. 1, a. 5, ad 5–6; *De Ver.,* II, 12, ad 4.
[33] Q. 9, a. 1.

Reply Obj. 1. *Lord, Creator,* and the like, import relations to creatures in so far as they are in themselves. But the knowledge of God imports relation to creatures in so far as they are in God; because everything is actually understood according as it is in the one who understands. Now created things are in God in an invariable manner; while they exist variably in themselves. —Or we may say that *Lord, Creator,* and the like, import the relations consequent upon the acts which are understood as terminating in the creatures themselves as they are in themselves; and thus these relations are attributed to God variously, according to the variation of creatures. But *knowledge* and *love,* and the like, import relations consequent upon the acts which are understood to be in God; and therefore these are predicated of God in an invariable manner.

Reply Obj. 2. God knows also what He can make, and does not make. Hence from the fact that He can make more than He makes, it does not follow that He can know more than He knows, unless this be referred to the *knowledge of vision,* according to which He is said to know those things which actually exist in some period of time. But from the fact that He knows that some things can be which are not, or that some things can not-be which are, it does not follow that His knowledge is variable, but rather that He knows the variability of things. If, however, anything existed which God did not previously know, and afterwards knew, then His knowledge would be variable. But this is impossible, for whatever is, or can be in any period of time, is known by God in His eternity. Therefore, from the fact that a thing is said to exist in some period of time, we must say that it is known by God from all eternity. Therefore it cannot be granted that God can know more than He knows; because such a proposition implies that first of all He did not know, and then afterwards knew.

Reply Obj. 3. The ancient Nominalists said that it was the same thing to say *Christ is born* and *will be born,* and *was born;* because the same thing is signified by these three—viz., the nativity of Christ.[34] Therefore it follows, they said, that whatever God knew, He knows; because now He knows that Christ is born, which means the same thing as that Christ will be born. This opinion, however, is false, both because the diversity in the parts of a sentence causes a diversity in enunciations, and because it would follow that a proposition which is true once would always be true; which is contrary to what the Philosopher lays down when he says that this sentence, *Socrates sits,* is true when he is sitting, and false when he stands up.[35] Therefore, it must be conceded that this proposition, *Whatever God knew He knows,* is not true if referred to what is enunciated. But because of this, it does not follow that the knowledge of God is variable. For as it is without variation in the divine knowledge that God knows one and the same thing sometime

---

[34] Cf. Abelard, *Introd. ad Theol.,* III, 5 (PL 178, 1102); Peter Lombard, *Sent.,* I, xli, 3 (I, 258).
[35] *Cat.,* V (4a 23).

to be, and sometime not, so it is without variation in the divine knowledge that God knows that an enunciation is sometime true, and sometime false. The knowledge of God, however, would be variable if He knew enunciations according to their own limitations, by composition and division, as occurs in our intellect. Hence our knowledge varies either as regards truth and falsity, for example, if when a thing is changed we retained the same opinion about it; or as regards diverse opinions, as if we first thought that someone was sitting, and afterwards thought that he was not sitting; neither of which can be in God.

ANTHONY KENNY
Divine Foreknowledge and Human Freedom [1]

In this paper I intend to discuss whether belief in God's foreknowledge of the future is compatible with belief in the freedom of human actions. Before stating the problem in further detail, I must make clear which problems I do *not* intend to consider. I shall not discuss whether there is a God, nor whether it is the case that some human actions are free. I shall not try to show that an action which is causally determined is not free, nor that God knows the future free actions of men. It might be thought, indeed that this last at least needs no proving: surely, if there is a God at all, He knows all that is to come; a God who did not know the future would not be a real God. But this is not so. It is indeed the case that any God worthy of the name knows everything that there is to be known; but it does not follow from this alone that He knows the future free actions of men. For many philosophers have maintained, and some do maintain, that statements about as yet undecided free actions, such as the statement "The United States will declare war on China", are as yet neither true nor false. Since only what is true can be known, then if it is not yet true either that the U.S. will declare war on China nor that the U.S. will not declare war on China, then not even God can know whether the U.S. will do so or not. Again, as a matter of history there have been philosophers who have believed that God was omniscient without thereby believing that God knew the future free actions of

Anthony Kenny (1931–) has been a fellow and tutor in philosophy at Balliol College, Oxford, since 1964. His writings include *Action, Emotion and Will* and *The Five Ways*.

DIVINE FOREKNOWLEDGE AND HUMAN FREEDOM   From *Aquinas: A Collection of Critical Essays* by Anthony Kenny, copyright © 1969 by Anthony Kenny. Reprinted by permission of the author.

[1] Revised version of a paper read at Liverpool in 1960. In the original preparation of the paper I had the advantage of discussions with Miss G. E. M. Anscombe and Mr. A. N. Prior.

men. Indeed, as we shall see, even a philosopher so orthodox as St. Thomas Aquinas denied, in one important sense, that God knows the future when the future is not already determined by causal necessity. Even to theists, therefore, it needs to be proved that God knows what is going to take place through the free action of his creature. As I have said, I do not intend to argue for this. I intend merely to investigate whether there is or is not compatibility between two statements, namely, "God knows beforehand everything that men will do" and "Some actions of men are free". Even in this restricted area I intend to examine only two arguments which have been brought up to show that the statements are incompatible. The question of incompatibility retains its interest for philosophers even if both statements are in fact false.

It is necessary, as a final preamble, to insist that the problem to be discussed concerns only foreknowledge and not foreordaining. Just as people have believed that God knows beforehand all that happens in the world, so also they have believed that He ordains beforehand all that happens in the world. Just as no human action escapes God's prescience, so no human action escapes His providence. Accordingly, just as there is a problem how God's foreknowledge may be reconciled with human freedom, so also there is a problem how human freedom may be reconciled with God's providence. In particular, since according to traditional Christian belief, no-one is saved who is not predestined by God to be saved, those who accept that belief have a special problem in reconciling it with the belief that those who are damned are damned through their own fault. These further problems are interesting, complicated and difficult; but they will not be our concern in this paper.

The problem may be stated as follows. God's foreknowledge appears to be incompatible with human freedom. It does not seem to be possible both that God should know what I shall do in the future, and that I shall do freely whatever it is that I shall do. For in order for me to be able to do an action freely, it is necessary that it should be within my power not to do that action. But if God knows what my action is going to be before I do it, then it does not seem to be within my power not to do it. For it cannot be the case both that God knows that I shall do such and such an action, and that I shall not in fact do it. For what God knows must be true: and indeed what anybody knows must be true, since it is impossible to know what is false. But if what God knows is true, and God knows that I will do such and such an action, then it must be true that I will do it. And if it is true that I will do it, then it seems that nothing I can do can prevent it coming true that I am doing it. And if nothing I can do can prevent it coming true that I am doing it, then I cannot prevent myself doing it. And if I cannot prevent myself doing a certain action, then that action cannot be free. Therefore, either God cannot know what I shall do tomorrow, or else whatever I shall do tomorrow will not be done freely.

For example: if God knows now that I will tell a lie this time tomorrow, then it seems that I cannot be free not to tell a lie this time tomorrow. For it cannot be the case both that God knows that I will tell a lie tomorrow, and that I will not in fact tell a lie tomorrow. For what God knows must be true: so that if God knows that I will tell a lie tomorrow, it must be ture that I will tell a lie tomorrow. But if it must be true that I will tell a lie tomorrow, then I cannot be free not to tell a lie tomorrow. But if I am not free not to tell a lie tomorrow, then when tomorrow I tell a lie, I shall not do so freely. A similar argument appears to hold, no matter what human action we consider instead of telling lies. Therefore it seems that if God foresees all human actions, no human action can be free.

This difficulty is a very old one. It is stated, for instance, in St. Thomas Aquinas' *Summa Theologiae*, Ia 14, 3, 3. Aquinas' statement of the difficulty is as follows: "Whatever is known by God must be; for whatever is known by us must be, and God's knowledge is more certain than ours. But nothing which is future and contingent *must* be. Therefore, nothing which is future and contingent is known by God." This difficulty is recognizably the same as the one which I have just stated more verbosely. The only difference of importance is that while I spoke of future free actions, St. Thomas speaks of future contingent events. St. Thomas uses the word "contingent" as equivalent to "not causally determined". Assuming that no causally determined action is a free action, a free human action would be a contingent event within the meaning of St. Thomas' phrase. Indeed St. Thomas expressly states (ibid, *Sed contra*) that free human actions are contingent events. He thought also that there were other contingent events besides free human actions: the budding of a tree, for instance. Whether he was correct in thinking this is an interesting question, but not to our purpose.

To the difficulty which he has set, St. Thomas provides a long answer. Part of his answer runs as follows. "The proposition 'whatever is known by God must be' can be analysed in two ways. It may be taken as a proposition *de dicto* or as a proposition *de re*; in other words, it may be taken either *in sensu composito* or *in sensu diviso*. As a *de re* proposition, it means:

Of everything which is known by God, it is true that that thing must be.

So understood the proposition is false. As a proposition *de dicto* it means:

The proposition 'whatever God knows is the case' is necessarily true.

So understood, the proposition is true."

There is much more in St. Thomas' answer than this paragraph, but this argument, as it stands, seems to me an adequate answer to the difficulty. In order to understand it one must know something about the medieval distinction between propositions *de dicto* and propositions *de re*. Consider the following proposition.

(1) If there is a University at Oxford, then necessarily there is a University at Oxford.

Someone who asserts that proposition may be taken to assert

(2) "If there is a University at Oxford, then there is a University at Oxford" is a necessary truth.

Or he may be taken to assert

(3) If there is a University at Oxford, then "there is a University at Oxford" is a necessary truth.

The medievals would have called proposition (1), if interpreted in the sense of proposition (2), a proposition *de dicto*; if interpreted in the sense of proposition (3) they would call it a proposition *de re*. The difference between the two interpretations is obviously of crucial importance. For (2), which merely states that a certain conditional—whose consequent is a repetition of its antecedent—is necessarily true, is itself true. But (3) is false, since its antecedent is true (there is a University at Oxford), and its consequent is false (it is not a necessary truth that there is a University at Oxford, since there has not always been a University at Oxford).

It is not difficult to see how to apply this to the problem in hand. The proposition "Whatever is known by God is necessarily true" if taken *de dicto* means

(4) "Whatever is known by God is true" is a necessary truth.

Interpreted *de re*, however, it means

(5) Whatever is known by God is a necessary truth.

Proposition (4) is true, but it has no tendency to show that acts foreseen by God are not free. For, it is equally a necessary truth that if I will tell a lie this time tomorrow, then I will tell a lie this time tomorrow: but this necessary truth has no tendency to show that my telling of a lie tomorrow will not be free. On the other hand, (5) if true would rule out the possibility of free action. If it is a necessary truth that I will tell a lie tomorrow, then I have no choice in the matter. But this need not trouble us, for proposition (5) is simply false. If God knows everything, then God knows that I am now writing this paper; but "I am writing this paper" is not a necessary truth, since it was in fact false ten days ago. We might bring out the difference between the two interpretations of "whatever is known by God is necessarily true" by punctuation, as follows.

(4a) Whatever is known by God is, necessarily, true.
(5a) Whatever is known by God is necessarily-true.

It seems to me, therefore, that St. Thomas' answer to this particular difficulty is entirely satisfactory. But he puts to himself a further, and more persuasive, difficulty; and his answer to this second difficulty does not appear satisfactory at all.

The further difficulty runs as follows. In any true conditional proposition whose antecedent is necessarily true, the consequent is also necessarily true. That is to say, whatever is implied by a necessary proposition is itself a necessary proposition. The following is clearly a true conditional proposition: "If it has come to God's knowledge that such and such a thing will happen, then such and such a thing will happen." The antecedent of the conditional, if it is true at all, appears to be necessarily true: for it is in the past tense, and what is past cannot be changed. What has been the case cannot now not have been the case. Therefore, the consequent is also necessarily true. Therefore, whatever is known by God is a necessary truth.

This is a powerful argument: it appears, at least at first sight, impossible to deny any of its premises. St. Thomas himself treated it with great respect: before putting forward his own solution he considered and rejected three attempts to deny one or other premise. In the end, he could find no alternative to accepting the argument, while trying to show that the conclusion is not, as it appears to be, incompatible with the occurrence of contingent events.

His solution runs as follows. God, he says, is outside time: God's life is measured not by time, but by eternity. Eternity, which has no parts, overlaps the whole of time; consequently, the things which happen at different times are all present together to God. An event is known *as future* only when there is a relation of future to past between the knowledge of the knower and the happening of the event. But there is no such relation between God's knowledge and any contingent event: the relation between God's knowledge and any event in time is always one of simultaneity. Consequently, a contingent event, as it comes to God's knowledge, is not future but present; and as present it is necessary; for what is the case, is the case, and is beyond anyone's power to alter. Hence, we can admit that what is known to God is a necessary truth; for as known by God it is no longer future but present. But this necessity does not destroy contingency: for the fact that an event is necessary when it happens does not mean that it was predetermined by its causes.

St. Thomas adds plausibility to his solution with a famous illustration. "To us, because we know future contingent events as future, there can be no certainty about them; but only to God, whose knowing is in eternity, above time. A man who is walking along a road cannot see those who are coming after him; but a man who looks down from a hill upon the whole length of the road can see at the same time all those who are travelling along it. So it is with God . . . Future events which are in themselves contingent cannot be known to us. What is known to God is necessary in the way in which it lies open to God's knowledge (namely, in its presentness); it is not necessary in regard to its own causes." [2]

---

[2] *Summa Theologiae*, 14, 13 ad 3 (words in parentheses from the body of the article). The preceding paragraph is a mosaic of translations from *De Veritate* 2, 12.

This explanation of St. Thomas has become the classic solution of the problem raised by God's foreknowledge. It is still sometimes presented in popular expositions of Christian theology, for instance in *Theology and Sanity* by F. J. Sheed. "If God knew last Tuesday what you were going to do next Tuesday, what becomes of your free will? . . . God did *not* know *last* Tuesday. Tuesday is a period of time and part of the duration in which I act. But God acts in eternity which has no Tuesdays. God acts in the spacelessness of his immensity and the timelessness of his eternity: we receive the effects of his acts in space and time" (p. 117).

Despite the authority of St. Thomas, the solution seems fundamentally misconceived. In the first place, it forces one to deny that it is true, in any strict sense, that God knows future free actions. St. Thomas insists repeatedly that no-one, not even God, can know contingent events *qua* future: he says of such events that we should rather say "if God knows something, then it *is*" than "if God knows something, then it *will be*" (*De Veritate* 2, 12 ad 7). Strictly speaking, then, God has no *fore*knowledge of contingent events: as He knows them, they are not still future but already present. A defender of St. Thomas might reply that this does not matter: when we say that God knows future events we mean merely that (a) God knows all events (b) some events are future *to us*. Of any event which is future to us it will be true to say that God knows it, though he will not know it *qua* future. Thus, let us suppose that at some future date a man will land on Mars. The event which is the landing on Mars is, so far as we are concerned, in the future; but to God it is already present. Thus, although we cannot say that God knows that a man *will* land on Mars (for this would be to make God know it *qua* future) we can say that God knows, timelessly, the event which is the landing on Mars. And this event is future to us, that is to say, it comes later in the time series than e.g. your reading this.

But this reply does not meet the objection. If "to know the future" means know more than "to know a fact which comes later in the time series than some other fact" then we, no less than God, can know the future. For we know about the Wars of the Roses which *were* future when Cleopatra was a girl. If we were to take St. Thomas' suggestion seriously, we should have to say that God knows that a man *is landing* on Mars; but we cannot say this, since the statement that a man is landing on Mars, being false, cannot be known, even by God, to be true.

St. Thomas' solution then, is not so much a defence as a denial of God's foreknowledge. But it forces us to deny not only God's foreknowledge, but also God's omniscience. For the statement that God's foreknowledge is outside time must mean, if anything, that no temporal qualifications can be attached to God's knowledge. Where God is the subject, verbs of knowing cannot have adverbs of time affixed to them. We cannot, therefore, say that God knows now that Brutus killed Caesar; nor that God will know tomorrow what time I went to bed tonight. But as A. N. Prior has remarked, it seems an extraordinary way of affirming God's omniscience if a person, when asked what God knows *now*, must say "Nothing", and when asked what he knew *yesterday*, must again say "Nothing", and must yet again say "Nothing" when asked what God will know *tomorrow*.

An argument *ad hominem* against St. Thomas' position may be drawn from the notion of prophecy. St. Thomas believed that God could foretell, and had foretold, future contingent events. He believed, for example, that God, as the principal author of the Epistle to the Romans, had foretold the conversion of the Jewish people to Christianity. On the view that God's knowledge is timeless, such prediction becomes inexplicable. For, if God's knowledge is timeless, then we cannot attach to statements about God's knowledge such adverbial clauses as "at the time when the Epistle to the Romans was written". We cannot, for example, say "At the time when the Epistle to the Romans was written God already knew that the Jews would finally be converted". But if God did not then know it, how could he then foretell it? To put it bluntly: if God did not then *know* that the Jews would be converted, he had no right then to *say* that they would.

Indeed, the whole concept of a timeless eternity, the whole of which is simultaneous with every part of time, seems to be radically incoherent. For simultaneity as ordinarily understood is a transitive relation. If A happens at the same time as B, and B happens at the same time as C, then A happens at the same time as C. If the BBC programme and the ITV programme both start when Big Ben strikes ten, then they both start at the same time. But, on St. Thomas' view, my typing of this paper is simultaneous with the whole of eternity. Again, on his view, the great fire of Rome is simultaneous with the whole of eternity. Therefore, while I type these very words, Nero fiddles heartlessly on.

If St. Thomas' solution to the difficulty is unacceptable, is it possible to give a different one? The objection ran thus. What is implied by a necessary proposition is itself necessarily true. But from "it has come to God's knowledge that such and such will be the case" it follows that "such and such will be the case". But "it has come to God's knowledge that such and such will be the case" is necessarily true; therefore "such and such will be the case" is necessarily true. Therefore, if God knows the future, the future is not contingent.[3]

The premises of the argument appear difficult to deny; yet if its conclusion is true there is no freedom or else no foreknowledge. For if it must be the case that I will murder my grandfather, then I am not free not to murder my grandfather; and conversely, if I am free not to murder my grandfather, then God cannot know that I will murder him even if in fact I will do so.

Let us examine each premise in turn. It appears incontrovertible that what

---

[3] Using *"Lp"* for "Necessarily *p*", *"Gp"* for "It has come to God's knowledge that *p*", and *"Cpq"* for "If *p*, then *q*", we could symbolise the argument thus: *LCLCGppLCLGpLp; LCGpp; LGp;* ergo, *Lp.*

follows from a necessary proposition is itself necessary.[4] Moreover, it cannot be denied that "it is the case that p" follows from "It has come to God's knowledge that p": this is true *ex vi termini* "know". So, for any substitution for "p", if "It has come to God's knowledge that p" is necessarily true, then "it is the case that p" is also necessarily true.

But is it true, for all substitutions for "p", that it must be the case that it has come to God's knowledge that p? St. Thomas accepted it without question. "It has come to God's knowledge that p" is a proposition in the past tense, and for St. Thomas as for Aristotle all propositions in the past tense are necessary. Now let us first notice that even if this doctrine were true, there has occurred a significant change in the sense of "necessary". Hitherto, "necessarily" has been used in such a way that in every case it could have been replaced by "it is a logical truth that . . ." But if an Aristotelian claims that "Cesare Borgia was a bad man" is now necessarily true, he must be using "necessarily" in a different sense. For he cannot claim that it is a logical truth that Cesare Borgia was a bad man. Again, let us notice, that the necessity of past propositions, if they are necessary, is not something that is *eo ipso* incompatible with freedom. If it is now necessary that Cesare Borgia was a bad man, it does not follow from this alone that it was, when he was born, necessary that he *would* be a bad man. For, according to Aristotle, necessity applies only to true past and present propositions, not to future propositions of contingent fact. But, when Cesare Borgia was born, the proposition "Cesare Borgia will be a bad man" was a future-tensed proposition of contingent fact—as indeed it still is.

It is clear, then, that if present- and past-tensed propositions are, as Aristotle thought, necessary in a way in which future-tensed propositions are not, they are not necessary in the way in which logical truths are necessary; and they are not necessary in a way which excludes the freedom of the action they report, if they report an action at all.

But is there any sense at all in which past- and present-tensed propositions have a necessity which is not shared by future-tensed propositions? The very least which seems to be demanded of a proposition if it is to be called "necessary" is that it is, always has been, and always will be, true. In this sense of "necessary" the proposition "there is a God" is necessarily true if it is true at all; but of course the proposition "there is a God" is not a logical truth, as critics of the ontological argument, from Gaunilo to Russell, have frequently pointed out. Now the proposition "Queen Anne is dead", which is a true present-tensed proposition if ever there was one, is not a necessary truth in this sense at all, since before 1714 it was not true. The past-tensed proposition "Queen Anne has died" will indeed never cease to be true; but it *was* not true in King Alfred's day. So, even if "necessary" is given the weak interpretation of "true at all times", there seems no reason to believe

---

[4] $LCLCpqLCLpLq$ is a law in every standard modal system.

the Aristotelian doctrine that past- and present-tensed propositions *in materia contingenti* are necessary.

Yet is it not true that what has happened cannot now not have happened, and that which is happening cannot now not be happening? We have a very strong inclination to think that there is some way in which we can change the future, in which we cannot change the past. But this inclination appears to be a delusion. There appears to be no sense in which we can change the future in which we cannot change the past. As A. N. Prior has pointed out, whatever changes of plan we may make, the future is whatever takes place after all the changes are made; what we alter is *not* the future, but our plans; the real future can no more be altered than the past. The sort of case which we have in mind when we are tempted to say that we can change the future is this: suppose that I have no intention of typing "elephant" backwards; then I decide I will do so; and finally I do so. Does not my decision change the future, since without my decision the word would never have been typed backwards? No, for even when I had no intention of doing so, e.g. ten years ago, it *was* true that I would, ten years later, type "elephant" backwards; and so my decision altered nothing except my own intentions. There is, indeed, a sense in which we can change the future: we can change the truth-value of a future-tensed proposition. Suppose that it is true that I will commit suicide: then the proposition "A.K. will commit suicide" now has the truth-value "true". I can change this truth-value by committing suicide; for once I have committed suicide the proposition "A.K. will commit suicide" ceases to be true and the quite different proposition "A.K. has committed suicide" becomes true instead. But if "to change the future" means merely "to change the truth-value of a future-tensed proposition" then in a corresponding sense I can change the past no less than the future. Nothing is easier. Tnahpele. The past-tensed proposition "A.K. has typed 'elephant' backwards" which *was* false, is now true; and so I have changed the past.

It seems, then, that there is no sense in which we can change the future in which we cannot change the past. Still, it does seem true that we can bring about the future, but cannot bring about the past; our present activity may have a causal effect on the future but cannot have a causal effect on the past. Consequently deliberation about the future is sensible, deliberation about the past absurd; so if God's knowledge of what I will do tomorrow is already a thing of the past, deliberation about what I will do tomorrow appears already pointless, and once again there appears to be an incompatibility between foreknowledge and freedom.

However, in certain cases, it does seem that present actions can affect the past. By begetting a son, I make my grandfather, long dead, into a great-grandfather; by becoming Poet Laureate I make my late grandmother's belief that I would one day be Poet Laureate into a true belief. In such cases, of course, what we are doing is establishing new relations between past things and events and present or future things or events. But the truth of a belief, and the question of whether a certain belief does or does not constitute knowledge, involve relationships between those beliefs and the events they concern. So it is possible that it is precisely by telling a lie today that I bring it about that God knew yesterday that I would tell a lie today. Of course, I do not bring it about by today's lie that God yesterday *believed* that I would lie; but it is my current lie which makes his belief then true.

Even so, it might be retorted, this does not make it possible for God to have *known* yesterday without curtailment of my freedom; because knowledge is not true belief, but justified true belief; and the justification of a past belief would have to be past grounds for the belief; and nothing in the past could be adequate grounds for a belief about my current action unless it necessitated that action. To this the reply is open that even in non-theological contexts there seem to be cases where true belief, without grounds, constitutes knowledge. One such case is our knowledge of our own actions. Commonly, we know what we are doing with our hands, and we do not know this on the basis of any evidence or grounds. Of course, we can be mistaken: I may think I am typing "piece" and in fact be typing "peice". But when I am not mistaken, my belief about what I am doing constitutes knowledge. It does not seem unreasonable to suggest that in this respect a Creator's knowledge of his creature's actions might resemble a human agent's knowledge of his own actions.

There seems, then, no reason to maintain that "It has come to God's knowledge that *p*" is a necessary truth, in any of the senses we have suggested, merely because it is past-tensed. Might it not be argued, however, that it is a necessary truth for a different reason: namely, that it is a truth about God's knowledge, which is the knowledge of a necessarily omniscient necessary being? If God is omniscient, it might be argued, then whatever we substitute for "*p*", "it has come to God's knowledge that *p*" will be true. But "if it has come to God's knowledge that *p*" is true no matter what we substitute for "*p*", then it must be something like a logical truth, and so a necessary truth in the sense in which necessity is incompatible with freedom.

It does not take a moment to detect the fallacy in this argument. God's omniscience does not at all imply that whatever we substitute for "*p*" in "God knows that *p*" is true. For instance, if we substitute "$2 + 2 = 3$" we get not a necessary truth but the falsehood "God knows that $2 + 2 = 3$". It is indeed a logical truth that if *p* is true, then *p* is known by any omniscient being; but this is insufficient to provide the premise needed by St. Thomas' objector.[5] A sentence such as "God knows that I am sitting down" expresses not a necessary, but a contingent truth: it may be true now, but it was not true last night and it will cease to be true as soon as I stand up. In fact, God's knowledge will only be necessary where what He knows is necessary: "$2 + 2 = 4$" is a necessary truth, so "God knows that $2 + 2 = 4$" is a necessary truth.[6] But, by definition, a contingent proposition—such as a proposition reporting or predicting a free action—is never a necessary truth. Hence,

---

[5] We have not LGp but $LCpGp$. [6] We have not $LCpLGp$, but $LCLpLGp$.

the argument that we have been considering has no tendency to show that human freedom and divine foreknowledge are incompatible.

There are other arguments to prove this incompatibility: Aquinas alone gives thirteen of which we have considered only two. None, however, are as initially plausible, or as complicated to unravel, as the two we have considered.

NORMAN KRETZMANN
Omniscience and Immutability

It is generally recognized that omniscience and immutability are necessary characteristics of an absolutely perfect being. The fact that they are also incompatible characteristics seems to have gone unnoticed.

In the main body of this paper I will present first an argument that turns on the incompatibility of omniscience and immutability and, secondly, several objections to that argument with my replies to the objections.

(1) A perfect being is not subject to change.[1]
(2) A perfect being knows everything.[2]

Norman Kretzmann (1928–   ), a professor of philosophy at Cornell University, has written extensively on medieval philosophy and logic. He is the author of the article on semantics in *The Encyclopedia of Philosophy* and has translated and edited *William of Sherwood's Introduction to Logic* and *William of Sherwood's Treatise on Syncategorematic Words*.

OMNISCIENCE AND IMMUTABILITY   From *The Journal of Philosophy*, Volume LXIII, No. 14, July 14, 1966. Copyright 1966 by The Journal of Philosophy, Inc. Reprinted by permission of *The Journal of Philosophy* and the author.

[1] This principle of immutability is regularly supported by one of two arguments. (i) *From Supreme Excellence:* A perfect being is a supremely excellent being; thus any change in such a being would constitute corruption, deterioration, loss of perfection. (See Plato, *Republic*, II, 381B.) (ii) *From Complete Actualization:* A perfect being is a being whose capacities for development are all fully realized. A being subject to change, however, is in that respect and to that extent a being with an unrealized capacity for development, a being merely potential and not fully actualized, a being in a state of process and not complete; hence not perfect. (See Aristotle, *Metaphysics*, XII, 9; 1074b26.) The principle of immutability is a thesis of orthodox Christian theology, drawn from Greek philosophy and having among its credentials such biblical passages as Malachi 3.6 and James 1.17. (See Aquinas, *Summa theologica*, I, Q. 9, art. 1.)

[2] Being incapable of knowing all there is to know or being capable of knowing all there is to know and knowing less than that are conditions evidently incompatible with absolute perfection. Hence (2), which seems even more familiar and less problematic than (1).

(3) A being that knows everything always knows what time it is.[3]

(4) A being that always knows what time it is is subject to change.[4]

∴ (5) A perfect being is subject to change.

∴ (6) A perfect being is not a perfect being.

Finally, therefore,

(7) There is no perfect being.[5]

In discussing this argument with others [6] I have come across various objections against one or another of its premises. Considering such objections here helps to clarify the line taken in the argument and provides an opportunity to anticipate and turn aside several natural criticisms of that line.

Because premises (1) and (2) present the widely accepted principles of immutability and omniscience, objections against them are not so much criticisms of the line taken in the argument as they are attempts to modify the concept of a perfect being in the light of the argument. And since premise (3) gives every impression of being an instance of a logical truth, premise (4) is apparently the one most vulnerable to attacks that are genuinely attacks on the argument. The first four of the following seven objections are all directed against premise (4), although Objection D raises a question relevant to premise (3) as well.

---

[3] Part of what is meant by premise (3) is, of course, that a being that knows everything always knows what time it is in every time zone on every planet in every galaxy; but it is not quite in that horological sense that its knowledge of what time it is is most plainly relevant to considerations of omniscience and immutability. The relevant sense can be brought out more easily in the consideration of objections against the argument.

[4] Adopting 'it is now t_n' as a convenient standard form for propositions as to what time it is, we may say of a being that always knows what time it is that the state of its knowledge changes incessantly with respect to propositions of the form 'it is now t_n'. First such a being knows that it is now t_1 (and that it is not now t_2), and then it knows that it is now t_2 (and that it is not now t_1). To say of any being that it knows something different from what it used to know is to say that it has changed; hence (4).

[5] [1f] $(x)(Px \supset \sim Cx)$; [2f] $(x)(Px \supset (p)(p \equiv Kxp))$ [K: . . . knows that . . .]; [3f] (x) $((p) (p \equiv Kxp) \supset (p) (Tp \supset (p \equiv Kxp)))$ [T: . . . is of the form 'it is now t_n']; [4f] (x) $((p)(Tp \supset (p \equiv Kxp)) \supset Cx)$; [5f] $(x)(Px \supset Cx)$ [entailed by 2f, 3f, 4f]; [6f] $(x)(Px \supset \sim Px)$ [entailed by 1f, 5f]; [7f] $(x) \sim Px$ [equivalent to 6f]. The formalization [3f] is an instance of a logical truth; nevertheless, premise (3) is not one of the established principles in philosophical or theological discussions of the nature of a perfect being. Not only is it not explicitly affirmed, but it seems often to be implicitly denied. This circumstance may arouse a suspicion that the formalization [3f] is inaccurate or question-begging. Any such suspicion will, I think, be dissipated in the course of considering the objections to the argument, but it may be helpful in the meantime to point out that the validity of the argument does not depend on this formalization. It is of course possible to adopt less detailed formalizations that would not disclose the special logical status of premise (3) and would nevertheless exhibit the validity of the argument. For example, [2f'] $(x)(Px \supset Ox)$; [3f'] $(x)(Ox \supset Nx)$ together with a similarly imprecise formalization of premise (4) would serve that purpose.

[6] I am indebted especially to Miss Marilyn McCord and to Professors H. N. Castañeda, H. G. Frankfurt, C. Ginet, G. B. Matthews, G. Nakhnikian, W. L. Rowe, S. Shoemaker, and W. Wainwright.

Objection A. It must be granted that a being that always knows what time it is knows something that is changing—say, the state of the universe. But change in the object of knowledge does not entail change in the knower.

The denial that a change in the object necessitates a change in the knower depends on imprecise characterizations of the object. For example, I know that the Chrysler Building in Manhattan is 1,046 feet tall. If it is said that the Chrysler Building is the object of my knowledge, then of course many changes in it—in its tenants or in its heating system, for example—do not necessitate changes in the state of my knowledge. If, however, it is more precisely said that the object of my knowledge is the *height* of the Chrysler Building, then of course a change in the object of my knowledge does necessitate a change in me. If a 40-foot television antenna is extended from the present tip of the tower, either I will cease to know the height of the Chrysler Building or I will give up believing that its height is 1,046 feet and begin believing that its height is 1,086 feet. In the case of always knowing what time it is, if we are to speak of an object of knowledge at all it must be characterized not as the state of the universe (which might also be said to be the object of, for example, a cosmologist's knowledge), but as the *changing* of that state. To know the changing of anything is to know first that *p* and then that not-*p* (for some particular instance of *p*), and a knower that knows first one proposition and then another is a knower that changes.

Objection B. The beliefs of a being that always knows what time it is are subject to change, but a change in a being's beliefs need not constitute a change in the being itself. If last year Jones believed the Platonic epistles to be genuine and this year he believes them to be spurious, then Jones has changed his mind; and that sort of change in beliefs may be considered a change in Jones. But if last year Jones believed that it was 1965 and this year he believes that it is 1966, he has not changed his mind, he has merely taken account of a calendar change; and that sort of change in beliefs should not be considered a change in Jones. The change in beliefs entailed by always knowing what time it is is that taking-account sort of change rather than a change of mind, the sort of change in beliefs that might reasonably be said to have been at least in part initiated by the believer and that might therefore be reasonably attributed to him.

It seems clear, first of all, that the sort of change in beliefs entailed by knowing the changing of anything is the taking-account sort of change rather than a change of mind. But once that much has been allowed, Objection B seems to consist in no more than an expression of disappointment in the *magnitude* of the change necessitated by always knowing what time it is. The entailed change in beliefs is not, it is true, sufficiently radical to qualify as a change of character or of attitude, but it is no less incompatible with immutability for all that. If Jones had been immutable from December 1965 through January 1966 he could no more have taken account of the calendar change than he could have changed his mind.

It may be worth noting that just such small-scale, taking-account changes in beliefs have sometimes been recognized by adherents of the principle of immutability as incompatible with immutability. Ockham, for example, argues at length against the possibility of a change in the state of God's foreknowledge just because God's changelessness could not be preserved through such a change. In Question Five of his *Tractatus de praedestinatione et de praescientia Dei et de futuris contingentibus* Ockham maintains that "if 'God knows that A' (where A is a future contingent proposition) and 'God does not know that A' *could* be true successively, it *would* follow that God was changeable," and the principle on which Ockham bases that claim is in no way restricted to future contingents. (As an adherent of the principle of immutability Ockham of course proceeds to deny that God could first know that A and then not know that A, but his reasons for doing so involve considerations peculiar to future contingent propositions and need not concern us here.) [7]

Objection C. For an omniscient being always to know what time it is is to know the state of the universe at every instant, but it is possible for an omniscient being to know the state of the universe at every instant all at once rather than successively. Consequently it is possible for an omniscient being always to know what time it is without being subject to change.

The superficial flaw in this objection is the ambiguity of the phrase 'to know the state of the universe at every instant', but the ambiguity is likely to be overlooked because the phrase is evidently an allusion to a familiar, widely accepted account of omniscience, according to which omniscience regarding contingent events is nothing more nor less than knowledge of the entire scheme of contingent events from beginning to end at once. I see no reason for quarreling here with the ascription of such knowledge to an omniscient being; but the underlying flaw in Objection C is the drastic *incompleteness* of this account of omniscience regarding contingent events.

The kind of knowledge ascribed to an omniscient being in this account is sometimes characterized as "seeing all time at a glance," which suggests that if one sees the entire scheme of contingent events from beginning to end at once one sees all there is to see of time. The totality of contingent events,

---

[7] The most interesting historical example of this sort that I have seen was called to my attention by Professor Hugh Chandler after I had submitted this paper for publication. It is Problem XIII in the *Tahāfut al-Falāsifah* of al-Ghazali (d. ca. 1111): "REFUTATION OF THEIR [i.e., the philosophers', but principally Avicenna's] DOCTRINE THAT GOD (MAY HE BE EXALTED ABOVE WHAT THEY SAY) DOES NOT KNOW THE PARTICULARS WHICH ARE DIVISIBLE IN ACCORDANCE WITH THE DIVISION OF TIME INTO 'WILL BE', 'WAS', AND 'IS' " (tr. S. A. Kamali; Lahore, Pakistan Philosophical Congress, 1963; pp. 153–162). This work was not known to medieval Christian philosophers. [See Etienne Gilson, *History of Christian Philosophy in the Middle Ages* (New York: Random House, 1955), p. 216.]

we are to suppose, may be known either simultaneously or successively, and an omniscient being will of course know it not successively but simultaneously. In his *Summa contra gentiles* (Book I, Ch. 55, sects. [6]–[9]) Aquinas presents a concise version of what seems to be the standard exposition of this claim.

> . . . the intellect of one considering *successively* many things cannot have only one operation. For since operations differ according to their objects, the operation by which the first is considered must be different from the operation by which the second is considered. But the divine intellect has only one operation, namely, the divine essence, as we have proved. Therefore God considers all that he knows not successively, but *together*. Moreover, succession cannot be understood without time nor time without motion . . . But there can be no motion in God, as may be inferred from what we have said. There is, therefore, no succession in the divine consideration. . . . Every intellect, furthermore, that understands one thing after another is at one time *potentially* understanding and at another time *actually* understanding. For while it understands the first thing actually it understands the second thing potentially. But the divine intellect is never potentially but always actually understanding. Therefore it does not understand things successively but rather understands them together.

On this view an omniscient being's knowledge of contingent events is the knowledge that event *e* occurs at time *t* (for every true instance of that form). Thus an omniscient being knows that my birth occurs at t_n, that my writing these words occurs at t_{n+x}, that my death occurs at t_{n+x+y}. This omniscient being also knows what events occur simultaneously with each of those events—knows, for example, that while I am writing these words my desk calendar lies open at the page bearing the date "Friday, March 4, 1966," and the watch on my wrist shows 10:15. Moreover, since an omniscient being by any account knows all necessary truths, including the truths of arithmetic, this omniscient being knows how much time elapses between my birth and my writing these words and between my writing these words and my death. But I *am* writing these words just *now*, and on this view of omniscience an omniscient being is incapable of knowing that that is what I am now doing, and for all this omniscient being knows I might just as well be dead or as yet unborn. That is what knowing everything amounts to if knowing "everything" does not include always knowing what time it is. Alternatively, that is what knowing the state of the universe at every instant comes to if that phrase is interpreted in the way required by the claim that it is possible to have that sort of knowledge all at once.

According to this familiar account of omniscience, the knowledge an omniscient being has of the entire scheme of contingent events is in many relevant respects exactly like the knowledge you might have of a movie you had written, directed, produced, starred in, and seen a thousand times. You would know its every scene in flawless detail, and you would have the length of each scene and the sequence of scenes perfectly in mind. You would know, too, that a clock pictured in the first scene shows the time to be 3:45, and that a clock pictured in the fourth scene shows 4:30, and so on. Suppose, however, that your movie is being shown in a distant theater today. You know the movie immeasurably better than do the people in the theater who are now seeing it for the first time, but they know one big thing about it you don't know, namely, what is now going on on the screen.

Thus the familiar account of omniscience regarding contingent events is drastically incomplete. An omniscient being must know not only the entire scheme of contingent events from beginning to end at once, but also *at what stage of realization that scheme now is.* It is in this sense of knowing what time it is that it is essential to claim in premise (3) that a being that knows everything always knows what time it is, and it is in this sense that always knowing what time it is entails incessant change in the knower, as is claimed in premise (4).

In orthodox Christianity the prevalence of the incomplete account of omniscience regarding contingent events effectively obscures the incompatibility of omniscience and immutability. Aquinas, for example, is not content with proving merely that "it is impossible for God to change in any way." He goes on in the *Summa theologica* (Book I, Q. 14, art. 15) to argue that "since God's knowledge is his substance, as is clear from the foregoing, just as his substance is altogether immutable, as was shown above, so *his knowledge likewise must be altogether invariable.*" What Aquinas, Ockham, and others *have* recognized is that God's knowledge cannot be variable if God is to remain immutable. What has *not* been seen is that God's knowledge cannot be altogether invariable if it is to be perfect, if it is to genuine omniscience.

Objection D. A perfect being transcends space and time. Such a being is therefore not subject to change, whether as a consequence of knowing what time it is or for any other reason.

The importance of this objection lies in its introduction of the pervasive, mysterious doctrine of the transcendence of space and time, a doctrine often cited by orthodox Christians as if it were both consistent with their theology and explanatory of the notion that God sees all time at a glance. It seems to me to be neither.

In *Proslogium* Chapters XIX and XX Anselm apostrophizes the being transcendent of space and time as follows:

> Thou wast not, then, yesterday, nor wilt thou be tomorrow; but yesterday and today and tomorrow thou art; or, rather, neither yesterday nor today nor tomorrow thou art, but simply *thou art, outside all time.* For yesterday and today and tomorrow have no existence except in time, but thou, although nothing exists without thee, nevertheless dost not exist in space or time, but all things exist in thee. For nothing contains thee, but thou containest all.

For present purposes the spatial aspect of this doctrine may be ignored. What is meant by the claim that an entity transcends time? The number 2 might, I suppose, be said to transcend time in the sense that it does not age, that it is no older now than it was a hundred years ago. I see no reason to quarrel with the doctrine that a perfect being transcends time in *that* sense, since under that interpretation the doctrine is no more than a gloss on the principle of immutability. But under that interpretation the doctrine begs the question of premise (4) rather than providing a basis for objecting to it.

Only one other interpretation of the doctrine of the transcendence of time suggests itself, and that is that from a God's-eye point of view there is no time, that the passage of time is a universal human illusion. (Whatever else may be said of this interpretation, it surely cannot be considered compatible with such essential theses of Christian doctrine as the Incarnation and the Resurrection.) Under this interpretation the doctrine of the transcendence of time does have a devastating effect on the argument, since it implies either that there are no true propositions of the form 'it is now t_n' or that there is exactly one (eternally) true proposition of that form. Thus under this interpretation premise (3) either is vacuous or has a single trivializing instance, and premise (4) is false. But this interpretation preserves the immutability of a perfect being by imposing immutability on everything else, and that is surely an inconceivably high price to pay, in the view of Christians and non-Christians alike.

The remaining three objections are directed against premise (1) or (2) and may, therefore, be considered not so much criticisms of the argument as attempts to revise the principle of immutability or the principle of omniscience in the light of the argument. Objections E and F have to do with premise (2), Objection G with premise (1).

Objection E. Since a perfect being transcends time it is logically impossible that a perfect being know what time it is and hence logically impossible that such a being know everything. But it is no limitation on a perfect being that it cannot do what is logically impossible. Therefore, its not knowing absolutely everything (in virtue of not knowing what time it is) does not impair its perfection.

Objections E and F are attempts to hedge on omniscience as philosophers and theologians have long since learned to hedge on omnipotence. In Objection E this attempt depends on directly invoking one of the standard limitations on omnipotence, but the attempt does not succeed. Perhaps the easiest way of pointing up its failure is to produce analogous inferences of the same form, such as this: since I am a human being and a human being is a mortal rational animal, it is logically impossible that I should live forever; therefore it is no limitation on me that I must die—or this: since I am a creature of limited power, it is logically impossible that I be capable of doing whatever is logically possible; therefore it is no limitation on me that I cannot do whatever is logically possible. What is wrong with all these inferences is that the crucial limitation is introduced in the initial description of the being in question, after which it does of course make sense to deny that mere consequences of the limiting description are to be introduced as if they constituted additional limitations. It is not an *additional* limitation on a legless man that he cannot walk, or on a mortal being that it must die, or on a creature of limited power that it cannot do whatever it might choose to do. No more is it an *additional* limitation on a being that is *incapable* of knowing what time it is that it *does not* know what time it is. But any claim to perfection that might have been made on behalf of such a being has already been vitiated in the admission that its transcendence of time renders it incapable of omniscience.

Objection F. Just as in explicating the concept of omnipotence we have been forced to abandon the naive formula 'a perfect being can do anything' and replace it with 'a perfect being can do anything the doing of which does not impair its perfection', so the argument suggests that the naive formula 'a perfect being knows everything' must be revised to read 'a perfect being knows everything the knowing of which does not impair its perfection'. Thus, since the argument does show that knowing what time it is impairs the perfection of the knower, it cannot be a part of the newly explicated omniscience to know what time it is.

Even if Objection F could be sustained, this particular grasping of the nettle would surely impress many as just too painful to bear, for in deciding whether or not to try to evade the conclusion of the argument in this way it is important to remember that in the context of the argument 'knowing what time it is' means knowing *what is going on*. Objection F at best thus provides an exceptionally costly defense of absolute perfection, emptying it of much of its content in order to preserve it; for under the newly explicated notion of omniscience Objection F commits one to the view that it is impossible for a *perfect, omniscient* being to know what is going on.

Objection F attempts to draw an analogy between an explication of omnipotence and a proposed explication of omniscience, borrowing strength from the fact that in the case of omnipotence such an explication has long since been recognized as a necessary condition of the coherence of the notion. In evaluating this attempt it is helpful to note that there are at least three types of provisos that may be inserted into formulas of omnipotence for that purpose. The first is relevant to omnipotence generally, the second specifically to eternal omnipotence, and the third specifically to eternal omnipotence as one perfect characteristic of a being possessed of certain other perfect characteristics. (For present purposes it is convenient to say simply that the third is relevant specifically to eternal omnipotence as one aspect of an absolutely perfect being.) These three types of provisos may be exemplified in the following three formulas of omnipotence:

I. A being that is omnipotent (regardless of its other characteristics) can do anything provided that (a) the description of what is to be done does not involve a logical inconsistency.

II. A being that is eternally omnipotent (regardless of its other characteristics) can do anything provided that (a) . . . and (b) the doing of it does not constitute or produce a limitation on its power.

III. A being that is absolutely perfect (and hence eternally omnipotent) can do anything provided that (a) . . . and (b) . . . and (c) the doing of it does not constitute a violation of some aspect of its perfection other than its power.

Provisos of type (c) only are at issue in Objection F, no doubt because provisos of types (a) and (b) have no effective role to play in the explication of omniscience. No being knows anything that *is not* the case; *a fortiori* no omniscient being knows anything that *cannot be* the case. So much for type (a). As for type (b), since certain things the description of which involves no logical inconsistency would if done incapacitate the doer—committing suicide, for example, or creating another omnipotent being—there is good reason for such a proviso in the explication of eternal omnipotence. It might likewise be claimed that an omniscient being knows everything except things that would if known limit the being's *capacity for knowledge,* the formal justification for this claim being just the same as that for the corresponding omnipotence-claim. The significant difference between these two claims is that the omniscience-claim is evidently vacuous. There is no reason to suspect that there *are* things that would if known limit the knower's capacity for knowledge. More directly to the point at issue in the argument, there is no reason whatever to think that knowing what is going on is a kind of knowing that limits the knower's capacity for knowledge. Thus although a type (b) proviso is needed in the explication of eternal omnipotence in order to preserve the coherence of the notion of eternal omnipotence, no such proviso need be inserted into the formula of omniscience in order to preserve the coherence of that notion.

The putative analogy in Objection F presupposes that a proviso of type (c) will preserve omniscience as it preserves omnipotence in such a (Cartesian) argument as the following. It is impossible for an absolutely perfect being to lie, for although such a being, as omnipotent, has the power to lie, the exercise of that power would violate the perfect goodness of the being. To say that it is impossible for an absolutely perfect being to lie is not to say that it lacks the power to lie but rather that its absolute perfection in another aspect—perfect goodness—necessitates its refraining from the exercise of that power. Whether or not this line of argument succeeds in doing what it is designed to do, it seems clear that there is no genuine analogue for it in the case of omniscience. Consider the following candidate. It is impossible for an absolutely perfect being to know what is going on, for although such a being, as omniscient, has the power to know what is going on, the exercise of that power would violate the immutability of the being. To say that it is impossible for an absolutely perfect being to know what is going on is not to say that it lacks the power to know what is going on but rather that its absolute perfection in another aspect—immutability—necessitates its refraining from the exercise of that power. A being that has the power to do something that it refrains from doing may not thereby even jeopardize its omnipotence. All the same, a being that has the power to know something that it refrains from knowing does thereby forfeit its omniscience. Omniscience is not the *power to know* everything; it is the *condition of knowing* everything, and that condition cannot be preserved through even a single instance of omitting to exercise the power to know everything.

Therefore, whatever strength Objection F seems to derive from its appeal to the putative analogy between omnipotence and omniscience in this respect is illusory, and this attempted evasion of the argument's conclusion reduces to an arbitrary decision to sacrifice omniscience to immutability.

Objection G. The traditional view of philosophers and theologians that absolute perfection entails absolute immutability is mistaken, founded on the misconception that in a perfect being any change would have to be for the worse. In particular the kind of change entailed by always knowing what time it is is a kind of change that surely cannot be construed as deterioration, even when it is ascribed to an absolutely perfect being. No doubt an absolutely perfect being must be immutable in most and perhaps in all other respects, but the argument shows that absolute perfection *entails* mutability in at least this one respect.

Objection G proceeds on the assumption that immutability is ascribed to a perfect being for only one reason—namely, that all change in such a being must constitute deterioration. There is, however, a second reason, as has been indicated at several points in the discussion so far—namely, that any change in a "perfect" being must indicate that the being was in some respect not in the requisite state of completion, actualization, fixity. The aspect of absolute completion is no less essential an ingredient in the concept of absolute perfection than is the aspect of absolute excellence. Moreover, those such as Aquinas and Ockham who argue against the mutability of a perfect being's *knowledge* would surely agree that the change they are intent on ruling out would not constitute *deterioration*, since they regularly base their arguments on the inadmissibility of *process* in an absolutely perfect being.

An absolutely perfect being may be described as a being possessing all logically compossible perfections. Thus if the argument had shown that omniscience and immutability were logically incompossible, it would have called for no more than an adjustment in the concept of absolute perfection, an adjustment of the sort proposed in Objection G. The proposition 'things change' is, however, not necessarily but only contingently true. If as a matter of fact nothing else ever did change, an omniscient being could of course remain immutable. In Objection G, however, an absolutely perfect being has been confused with a being possessing all *really* compossible perfections, the best of all *really* possible beings. Perhaps, as the objection implies, the most *nearly* absolutely perfect being in the circumstances that happen to prevail *would* be mutable in the respect necessitated by always knowing what time it is. But that is of no consequence to the argument, which may be taken as showing that the prevailing circumstances do not admit of the existence of an absolutely perfect being.

This concluding section of the paper is in the nature of an appendix. It might be subtitled "Omniscience and Theism"; for it may be shown that the doctrine that God knows everything is incompatible also with theism, the doctrine of a personal God distinct from other persons.[8]

Consider these two statements.

S_1. Jones knows that he is in a hospital.
S_2. Jones knows that Jones is in a hospital.

S_1 and S_2 are logically independent. It may be that Jones is an amnesia case. He knows perfectly well that he is in a hospital, and after reading the morning papers he knows that Jones is in a hospital. An omniscient being surely must know all that Jones knows. Anyone can know what S_2 describes Jones as knowing, but no one other than Jones can know what S_1 describes Jones as knowing. (A case in point: Anyone could have proved that Descartes existed, but that is not what Descartes proved in the Cogito, and what he proved in the Cogito could not have been proved by anyone else.) The kind of knowledge S_1 ascribes to Jones is, moreover, the kind of knowledge characteristic of every self-conscious entity, of every person. Every person knows certain propositions that no *other* person *can* know. Therefore, if God is omniscient, theism is false; and if theism is true, God is not omniscient.

It may fairly be said of God, as it once was said of William Whewell, that "omniscience [is] his foible."

---

[8] The following argument was suggested to me by certain observations made by Professor Hector Castañeda in a paper entitled "He," presented at the Wayne State University philosophy colloquium in the fall of 1964.

POWER

ST. THOMAS AQUINAS
The Omnipotence of God

THIRD ARTICLE.   WHETHER GOD IS OMNIPOTENT?

We proceed thus to the Third Article:—

Objection 1. It seems that God is not omnipotent. For movement and passiveness belong to everything. But this is impossible for God, since He is immovable, as was said above.[1] Therefore He is not omnipotent.

Obj. 2. Further, sin is an act of some kind. But God cannot sin, nor *deny Himself*, as it is said 2 *Tim.* ii. 13. Therefore He is not omnipotent.

Obj. 3. Further, it is said of God that He manifests His omnipotence *especially by sparing and having mercy.*[2] Therefore the greatest act possible to the divine power is to spare and have mercy. There are things much greater, however, than sparing and having mercy; for example, to create another world, and the like. Therefore God is not omnipotent.

Obj. 4. Further, upon the text, *God hath made foolish the wisdom of this world* (1 *Cor.* i. 20), the *Gloss* says: *God hath made the wisdom of this world foolish* by showing those things to be possible which it judges to be impossi-

THE OMNIPOTENCE OF GOD   From *Summa Theologica*, Part I, Question 25, in *Basic Writings of Saint Thomas Aquinas*, edited by Anton C. Pegis. Copyright 1945 by Random House, Inc. Reprinted by permission of the publisher and St. Dominic's Priory, London.

[1] Q. 2, a. 3; q. 9, a. 1 [in *Philosophy of Religion: Selected Readings*, pp. 117–19; 85–86].
[2] *Collect* of Tenth Sunday after Pentecost.

ble.[3] Whence it seems that nothing is to be judged possible or impossible in reference to inferior causes, as the wisdom of this world judges them; but in reference to the divine power. If God, then, were omnipotent, all things would be possible; nothing, therefore, impossible. But if we take away the impossible, then we destroy also the necessary; for what necessarily exists cannot possibly not exist. Therefore, there would be nothing at all that is necessary in things if God were omnipotent. But this is an impossibility. Therefore God is not omnipotent.

On the contrary, It is said: *No word shall be impossible with God* (Luke i. 37).

I answer that, All confess that God is omnipotent; but it seems difficult to explain in what His omnipotence precisely consists. For there may be a doubt as to the precise meaning of the word "all" when we say that God can do all things. If, however, we consider the matter aright, since power is said in reference to possible things, this phrase, *God can do all things,* is rightly understood to mean that God can do all things that are possible; and for this reason He is said to be omnipotent. Now according to the Philosopher a thing is said to be possible in two ways.[4] First, in relation to some power; thus whatever is subject to human power is said to be possible to man. Now God cannot be said to be omnipotent through being able to do all things that are possible to created nature; for the divine power extends farther than that. If, however, we were to say that God is omnipotent because He can do all things that are possible to His power, there would be a vicious circle in explaining the nature of His power. For this would be saying nothing else but that God is omnipotent because He can do all that He is able to do.

It remains, therefore, that God is called omnipotent because he can do all things that are possible absolutely; which is the second way of saying a thing is possible. For a thing is said to be possible or impossible absolutely, according to the relation in which the very terms stand to one another: possible, if the predicate is not incompatible with the subject, as that Socrates sits; and absolutely impossible when the predicate is altogether incompatible with the subject, as, for instance, that a man is an ass.

It must, however, be remembered that since every agent produces an effect like itself, to each active power there corresponds a thing possible as its proper object according to the nature of that act on which its active power is founded; for instance, the power of giving warmth is related, as to its proper object, to the being capable of being warmed. The divine being, however, upon which the nature of power in God is founded, is infinite; it is not limited to any class of being, but possesses within itself the perfection of all being. Whence, whatsoever has or can have the nature of being is numbered among the absolute possibles, in respect of which God is called omnipotent.

---

[3] *Glossa ordin., super I Cor.* I, 20 (VI, 34E).—Cf. St. Ambrose, *In I Cor.,* super I, 20 (PL 17, 199).
[4] *Metaph.,* IV, 12 (1019b 34).

Now nothing is opposed to the notion of being except non-being. Therefore, that which at the same time implies being and non-being is repugnant to the notion of an absolute possible, which is subject to the divine omnipotence. For such cannot come under the divine omnipotence; not indeed because of any defect in the power of God, but because it has not the nature of a feasible or possible thing. Therefore, everything that does not imply a contradiction in terms is numbered among those possibles in respect of which God is called omnipotent; whereas whatever implies contradiction does not come within the scope of divine omnipotence, because it cannot have the aspect of possibility. Hence it is more appropriate to say that such things cannot be done, than that God cannot do them. Nor is this contrary to the word of the angel, saying: *No word shall be impossible with God* (*Luke* i. 37). For whatever implies a contradiction cannot be a word, because no intellect can possibly conceive such a thing.

Reply Obj. 1. God is said to be omnipotent in respect to active power, not to passive power, as was shown above. Whence the fact that He is immovable or impassible is not repugnant to His omnipotence.

Reply Obj. 2. To sin is to fall short of a perfect action; hence to be able to sin is to be able to fall short in action, which is repugnant to omnipotence. Therefore it is that God cannot sin, because of His omnipotence. Now it is true that the Philosopher says that *God can deliberately do what is evil.*[5] But this must be understood either on a condition, the antecedent of which is impossible—as, for instance, if we were to say that God can do evil things if He will. For there is no reason why a conditional proposition should not be true, though both the antecedent and consequent are impossible: as if one were to say: *If man is an ass, he has four feet.* Or he may be understood to mean that God can do some things which now seem to be evil: which, however, if He did them, would then be good. Or he is, perhaps, speaking after the common manner of the pagans, who thought that men became gods, like Jupiter or Mercury.

Reply Obj. 3. God's omnipotence is particularly shown in sharing and having mercy, because in this it is made manifest that God has supreme power, namely, that He freely forgives sins. For it is not for one who is bound by laws of a superior to forgive sins of his own free choice. Or, it is thus shown because by sparing and having mercy upon men, He leads them to the participation of an infinite good; which is the ultimate effect of the divine power. Or it is thus shown because, as was said above, the effect of the divine mercy is the foundation of all the divine works.[6] For nothing is due anyone, except because of something already given him gratuitously by God. In this way the divine omnipotence is particularly made manifest, because to it pertains the first foundation of all good things.

Reply Obj. 4. The absolute possible is not so called in reference either to higher causes, or to inferior causes, but in reference to itself. But that which

[5] *Top.,* IV, 5 (126a 34).   [6] Q. 21, a. 4.

is called possible in reference to some power is named possible in reference to its proximate cause. Hence those things which it belongs to God alone to do immediately—as, for example, to create, to justify, and the like—are said to be possible in reference to a higher cause. Those things, however, which are such as to be done by inferior causes, are said to be possible in reference to those inferior causes. For it is according to the condition of the proximate cause that the effect has contingency or necessity, as was shown above.[7] Thus it is that the wisdom of the world is deemed foolish, because what is impossible to nature it judges to be impossible to God. So it is clear that the omnipotence of God does not take away from things their impossibility and necessity.

SAMUEL CLARKE
Can God Do Evil?

. . . The self-existent being, the supreme cause of all things, must of necessity have infinite power. This proposition is evident and undeniable. For since nothing (as has been already proved) can possibly be self-existent besides himself, and consequently all things in the universe were made by him, and are entirely dependent upon him, and all the powers of all things are derived from him and must therefore be perfectly subject and subordinate to him; it is manifest that nothing can make any difficulty or resistance to the execution of his will, but he must of necessity have absolute power to do everything he pleases, with the perfect ease, and in the perfect manner, at once and in a moment, whenever he wills it. . . . The only question is, what the true meaning of what we call infinite power is, and to what things it must be understood to extend, or not to extend.

Now in determining this question, there are some propositions about which there is no dispute. Which therefore I shall but just mention. First, infinite power reaches to all possible things, but cannot be said to extend to

Samuel Clarke (1675–1729) was an important exponent of rational theology as well as an early supporter of Newtonian physics. He is best known for his correspondence with Leibniz in which he defended Newton's views on space and time. His principal philosophical works are *A Discourse Concerning the Being and Attributes of God* and *The Obligations of Natural Religion and the Truth and Certainty of the Christian Revelation.*

CAN GOD DO EVIL?   From *Discourse Concerning the Being and Attributes of God,* ninth edition. (Selections are from Propositions X and XII. Punctuation, use of capitals, etc. have been modernized by the editors.)

[7] Q. 14, a. 13, ad 1 [in *Philosophy of Religion: Selected Readings,* pp. 45, 46].

the working of any thing which implies a *contradiction:* as that a thing should be and not be at the same time; that the same thing should be made and not be made, or have been and not have been; that twice two should not make four, or that that which is necessarily false should be true. The reason whereof is plain. Because the power of making a thing to be, at the same time that it is not, is only a power of doing that which is nothing, that is, no power at all. Second, infinite power cannot be said to extend to those things which imply *natural* imperfection in the being to whom such power is ascribed—as that it should destroy its own being, weaken itself, or the like. These things imply natural imperfection, and are by all men confessed to be such as cannot possibly belong to the necessary, self-existent being. There are also other things which imply imperfection in another kind, viz., *moral* imperfection.

. . . Though nothing, I say, is more certain than that God acts not necessarily, but voluntarily; yet it is nevertheless as truly and absolutely impossible for God not to do (or to do any thing contrary to) what his moral attributes require him to do, as if he was really not a free but a necessary agent. And the reason hereof is plain: because infinite knowledge, power, and goodness in conjunction may, notwithstanding the most perfect freedom and choice, act with altogether as much certainty and unalterable steadiness as even the necessity of fate can be supposed to do. Nay, these perfections cannot possibly but so act. Because free choice in a being of infinite knowledge, power and goodness can no more choose to act contrary to these perfections than knowledge can be ignorance, power be weakness, or goodness malice. So that free choice in such a being may be as certain and steady a principle of action as the necessity of fate. We may therefore as certainly and infallibly rely upon the moral, as upon the natural attributes of God—it being as absolutely impossible for him to act contrary to the one as to divest himself of the other; and as much a contradiction to suppose him choosing to do anything inconsistent with his justice, goodness and truth as to suppose him divested of infinity, power, or existence.

From hence it follows, that though God is both perfectly free and also infinitely powerful, yet he cannot possibly do anything that is evil. The reason of this is also evident. Because, as it is manifest infinite power cannot extend to natural contradictions which imply a destruction of that very power by which they must be supposed to be effected, so neither can it extend to moral contradictions which imply a destruction of some other attributes as necessarily belonging to the divine nature as power. I have already shown that justice, goodness and truth are necessarily in God, even as necessarily as power and understanding, and knowledge of the nature of things. It is, therefore, as impossible and contradictory to suppose his will should choose to do anything contrary to justice, goodness or truth as that his power should be able to do anything inconsistent with power. It is no diminution of power not to be able to do things which are no object of power. And it is in like manner no diminution either of power or liberty to have such a perfect and unalterable rectitude of will as never possibly to choose to do anything inconsistent with that rectitude.

C. WADE SAVAGE
The Paradox of the Stone

A. (1) Either God can create a stone which He cannot lift, or He cannot create a stone which He cannot lift.

(2) If God can create a stone which He cannot lift, then He is not omnipotent (since He cannot lift the stone in question).

(3) If God cannot create a stone which He cannot lift, then He is not omnipotent (since He cannot create the stone in question).

(4) Therefore, God is not omnipotent.

Mr. Mavrodes has offered a solution to the familiar paradox above;[1] but it is erroneous. Mavrodes states that he assumes the existence of God,[2] and then reasons (in pseudo-dilemma fashion) as follows. God is either omnipotent or He is not. If we assume that He is not omnipotent, the task of creating a stone which He cannot lift is not self-contradictory. And we can conclude that God is not omnipotent on the grounds that both His ability and His inability to perform this task imply that He is not omnipotent. But to prove His non-omnipotence in this way is trivial. "To be significant [the paradoxical argument] must derive this same conclusion *from the assumption that God is omnipotent;* that is, it must show that the assumption of the omnipotence of God leads to a *reductio.*" However, on the assumption that God is omnipotent, the task of creating a stone which God cannot lift is self-contradictory. Since inability to perform a self-contradictory task does not imply a limitation on the agent, one of the premises of the paradoxical argument—

C. Wade Savage (1932–   ) has taught philosophy at Harpur College and at the University of California at Los Angeles. He is currently a member of the Department of Philosophy and the Minnesota Center for the Philosophy of Science of the University of Minnesota.

THE PARADOX OF THE STONE   From *The Philosophical Review*, Volume 76, No. 1, January 1967. Reprinted by permission of *The Philosophical Review* and the author.

[1] George I. Mavrodes, "Some Puzzles Concerning Omnipotence," *Philosophical Review,* LXXII (1963), 221–223. The heart of his solution is contained in pars. 6, 7, and 11.

[2] See n. 2, p. 221.

premise A(3)—is false. The argument is, in consequence, either insignificant or unsound.

There are many objections to this solution. First, the paradoxical argument need not be represented as a *reductio*; in A it is a dilemma. Mavrodes' reasoning implies that the paradoxical argument must either assume that God is omnipotent or assume that He is not omnipotent. This is simply false: neither assumption need be made, and neither is made in A. Second, "a stone which God cannot lift" is self-contradictory—on the assumption that God is omnipotent—only if "God is omnipotent" is necessarily true. "Russell can lift any stone" is a contingent statement. Consequently, if we assume that Russell can lift any stone we are thereby committed only to saying that creating a stone which Russell cannot lift is a task which *in fact* cannot be performed by Russell or anyone else. Third, if "God is omnipotent" is necessarily true—as Mavrodes must claim for his solution to work—then his assumption that God exists begs the question of the paradoxical argument. For what the argument really tries to establish is that the existence of an omnipotent being is logically impossible. Fourth, the claim that inability to perform a self-contradictory task is no limitation on the agent is not entirely uncontroversial. Descartes suggested that an omnipotent God must be able to perform such self-contradictory tasks as making a mountain without a valley and arranging that the sum of one and two is not three.[3] No doubt Mavrodes and Descartes have different theories about the nature of contradictions; but that is part of the controversy.

Mavrodes has been led astray by version A of the paradox, which apparently seeks to prove that *God is not omnipotent*. Concentration on this version, together with the inclination to say that God is by definition omnipotent, leads straight to the conclusion that the paradox is specious. For if God is by definition omnipotent, then, obviously, creating a stone which God (an omnipotent being who can lift any stone) cannot lift is a task whose description is self-contradictory. What the paradox of the stone really seeks to prove is that the notion of an omnipotent being is logically inconsistent—that is, that *the existence of an omnipotent being, God or any other, is logi-*

---

[3] Harry G. Frankfurt, "The Logic of Omnipotence," *Philosophical Review*, LXXIII (1964), 262–263. The relevant passage from Descartes is quoted by Frankfurt in a long footnote.

Mavrodes assumes (on his "significant" interpretation of the paradox) that creating a stone which God cannot lift is a self-contradictory task, and contends that God therefore cannot perform it. This forces him onto the second horn of dilemma A, which he tries to break by arguing that inability to perform a self-contradictory task does not imply a limitation on the agent. Frankfurt also assumes that creating a stone which God cannot lift is a self-contradictory task, but contends with Descartes (for the sake of argument) that God can nevertheless perform it. This forces him onto the first horn of the dilemma, which he tries to break with the following argument. If God can perform the self-contradictory task of creating a stone which He cannot lift, then He can just as easily perform the additional self-contradictory task of lifting the stone which He (creates and) cannot lift. Frankfurt's fundamental error is the same as Mavrodes': both suppose that on any significant interpretation the paradox sets for God the self-contradictory task of creating a stone which God (an omnipotent being who can lift any stone) cannot lift.

cally impossible. It tries to do this by focusing on the perfectly consistent task of creating a stone which the creator cannot lift. The essence of the argument is that an omnipotent being must be able to perform this task and yet cannot perform the task.

Stated in its clearest form, the paradoxical argument of the stone is as follows. Where x is any being:

B. (1) Either x can create a stone which x cannot lift, or x cannot create a stone which x cannot lift.

   (2) If x can create a stone which x cannot lift, then, necessarily, there is at least one task which x cannot perform (namely, lift the stone in question).

   (3) If x cannot create a stone which x cannot lift, then, necessarily, there is at least one task which x cannot perform (namely, create the stone in question).

   (4) Hence, there is at least one task which x cannot perform.

   (5) If x is an omnipotent being, then x can perform any task.

   (6) Therefore, x is not omnipotent.

Since x is any being, this argument proves that the existence of an omnipotent being, God or any other, is logically impossible.

It is immediately clear that Mavrodes' solution will not apply to this version of the paradox. B is obviously a significant, nontrivial argument. But since it does not contain the word "God," no critic can maintain that B assumes that God is omnipotent. For the same reason, the point that "a stone which God cannot lift" is self-contradictory is simply irrelevant. Notice also that B is neutral on the question of whether inability to perform a self-contradictory task is a limitation on the agent's power. We can, however, replace every occurrence of "task" with "task whose description is not self-contradictory" without damaging the argument in any way.

The paradox does have a correct solution, though a different one from that offered by Mavrodes. The two solutions are similar in that both consist in arguing that an agent's inability to create a stone which he cannot lift does not entail a limitation on his power. But here the similarity ends. For, as we shall see presently, the basis of the correct solution is not that creating a stone which the creator cannot lift is a self-contradictory task (which it is not). Consequently, the correct solution side-steps the question of whether an agent's inability to perform a self-contradictory task is a limitation on his power.

The fallacy in the paradox of the stone lies in the falsity of the second horn—B(3)—of its dilemma: "x can create a stone which x cannot lift" does indeed entail that there is a task which x cannot perform and, consequently, does entail that x is not omnipotent. However, "x cannot create a stone which x cannot lift" does not entail that there is a task which x cannot perform and, consequently, does not entail that x is not omnipotent. That the entailment *seems* to hold is explained by the misleading character of the statement "*x* cannot create a stone which *x* cannot lift." The phrase "cannot create a stone" seems to imply that there is a task which *x* cannot perform and, consequently, seems to imply that *x* is limited in power. But this illusion vanishes on analysis: "*x* cannot create a stone which *x* cannot lift" can only mean "If *x* can create a stone, then *x* can lift it." It is obvious that the latter statement does not entail that *x* is limited in power.

A schematic representation of B(1)–B(3) will bring our point into sharper focus. Let S = stone, C = can create, and L = can lift; let *x* be any being; and let the universe of discourse be conceivable entities. Then we obtain:

C. (1) $(\exists y)(Sy \cdot Cxy \cdot -Lxy)$ v $-(\exists y)(Sy \cdot Cxy \cdot -Lxy)$.

(2) $(\exists y)(Sy \cdot Cxy \cdot -Lxy) \supset (\exists y)(Sy \cdot -Lxy)$.

(3) $-(\exists y)(Sy \cdot Cxy \cdot -Lxy) \supset (\exists y)(Sy \cdot -Cxy)$.

That the second alternative in C(1) is equivalent to "$(y)[(Sy \cdot Cxy) \supset Lxy]$" schematically explains our interpretation of "*x* cannot create a stone which *x* cannot lift" as meaning "If *x* can create a stone, then *x* can lift it." It is now quite clear where the fallacy in the paradoxical argument lies. Although C(2) is logically true, C(3) is not. "$(\exists y)(Sy \cdot Cxy \cdot -Lxy)$" logically implies "$(\exists y)$ $(Sy \cdot -Lxy)$." But "$-(\exists y)(Sx \cdot Cxy \cdot -Lxy)$" does not logically imply "$(\exists y)$ $(Sy \cdot -Cxy)$"; nor does it logically imply "$(\exists y)(Sy \cdot -Lxy)$." In general, "*x* cannot create a stone which *x* cannot lift" does not logically imply "There is a task which *x* cannot perform."

For some reason the above analysis does not completely remove the inclination to think that an agent's inability to create a stone which he himself cannot lift does entail his inability to perform some task, does entail a limitation on his power. The reason becomes clear when we consider the task of creating a stone which someone *other than* the creator cannot lift. Suppose that *y* cannot lift any stone heavier than seventy pounds. Now if *x* cannot create a stone which *y* cannot lift, then *x* cannot create a stone heavier than seventy pounds, and is indeed limited in power. But suppose that *y* is omnipotent and can lift stones of any poundage. Then *x*'s inability to create a stone which *y* cannot lift does not necessarily constitute a limitation on *x*'s power. For *x* may be able to create stones of any poundage, although *y* can lift any stone which *x* creates. If *y* can lift stones of any poundage, and *x* cannot create a stone heavier than seventy pounds, then *x* cannot create a stone which *y* cannot lift, and *x* is limited in power. But if *x* can create stones of any poundage, and *y* can lift stones of any poundage, then *x* cannot create a stone which *y* cannot lift, and yet *x* is not thereby limited in power. Now it is easy to see that precisely parallel considerations obtain where *x* is both stone-creator and stone-lifter.

The logical facts above may be summarized as follows. Whether *x* = *y* or *x* ≠ *y*, *x*'s inability to create a stone which *y* cannot lift constitutes a limitation on *x*'s power only if (i) *x* is unable to create stones of any poundage, or

(ii) y is unable to lift stones of any poundage. And, since either (i) or (ii) may be false, "x cannot create a stone which y cannot lift" does not entail "x is limited in power." This logical point is obscured, however, by the normal context of our discussions of abilities and inabilities. Since such discussions are normally restricted to beings who are limited in their stone-creating, stone-lifting, and other abilities, the inability of a being to create a stone which he himself or some other being cannot lift *normally* constitutes a limitation on his power. And this produces the illusion that a being's inability to create a stone which he himself or some other being cannot lift *necessarily* constitutes a limitation on his power, the illusion that "x cannot create a stone which y cannot lift" (where either $x = y$ or $x \neq y$) entails "x is limited in power."

Since our discussions normally concern beings of limited power, the erroneous belief that "x cannot create a stone which x cannot lift" entails "x is limited in power" will normally cause no difficulty. But we must beware when the discussion turns to God—a being who is presumably unlimited in power. God's inability to create a stone which He cannot lift is a limitation on His power only if (i) He is unable to create stones of any poundage, or (ii) He is unable to lift stones of any poundage—that is, only if He is limited in His power of stone-creating or His power of stone-lifting. But until it has been proved otherwise—and it is difficult to see how this could be done—we are free to suppose that God suffers neither of these limitations. On this supposition God's inability to create a stone which He cannot lift is nothing more nor less than a necessary consequence of two facets of His omnipotence.[4] For if God is omnipotent, then He can create stones of any poundage and lift stones of any poundage. And "God can create stones of any poundage, and God can lift stones of any poundage" entails "God cannot create a stone which He cannot lift."

---

[4] Mavrodes apparently sees this point in the last three paragraphs of his article. But his insight is vitiated by his earlier mistaken attempt to solve the paradox.

THE METAPHYSICAL ATTRIBUTES

ST. ANSELM
God Is Timeless, Immutable, and Impassible

CHAPTER XIX.   He does not exist in place or time, but all things exist in him.

But if through thine eternity thou hast been, and art, and wilt be; and to have been is not to be destined to be; and to be is not to have been, or to be destined to be; how does thine eternity exist as a whole forever? Or is it true that nothing of thy eternity passes away, so that it is not now; and that nothing of it is destined to be, as if it were not yet?

Thou wast not, then, yesterday, nor wilt thou be to-morrow; but yesterday and to-day and to-morrow thou art; or, rather, neither yesterday nor to-day nor to-morrow thou art; but simply, thou art, outside all time. For yesterday and to-day and to-morrow have no existence, except in time; but thou, although nothing exists without thee, nevertheless dost not exist in space or time, but all things exist in thee. For nothing contains thee, but thou containest all.

GOD IS TIMELESS, IMMUTABLE, AND IMPASSIBLE   From *Proslogium* (Chapters VIII and XIX) and *Monologium* (Chapter XXV) by St. Anselm, translated by Sidney N. Deane. Reprinted by permission of The Open Court Publishing Co., La Salle, Illinois.

CHAPTER XXV.   It cannot suffer change by any accidents.[1]

But does not this Being, which has been shown to exist as in every way substantially identical with itself, sometimes exist as different from itself, at any rate, accidentally? But how is it supremely immutable, if it can, I will not say, *be*, but, be conceived of, as variable by virtue of accidents? And, on the other hand, does it not partake of accident, since even this very fact that it is greater than all other natures and that it is unlike them seems to be an accident in its case (*illi accidere*)? But what is the inconsistency between susceptibility to certain facts, called *accidents*, and natural immutability, if from the undergoing of these accidents the substance undergoes no change?

For, of all the facts, called accidents, some are understood not to be present or absent without some variation in the subject of the accident—all colors, for instance—while others are known not to effect any change in a thing either by occurring or not occurring—certain relations, for instance. For it is certain that I am neither older nor younger than a man who is not yet born, nor equal to him, nor like him. But I shall be able to sustain and to lose all these relations toward him, as soon as he shall have been born, according as he shall grow, or undergo change through divers qualities.

It is made clear, then, that of all those facts, called accidents, a part bring some degree of mutability in their train, while a part do not impair at all the immutability of that in whose case they occur. Hence, although the supreme Nature in its simplicity has never undergone such accidents as cause mutation, yet it does not disdain occasional expression in terms of those accidents which are in no wise inconsistent with supreme immutability; and yet there is no accident respecting its essence, whence it would be conceived of, as itself variable.

Whence this conclusion, also, may be reached, that it is susceptible of no accident; since, just as those accidents, which effect some change by their occurrence or non-occurrence, are by virtue of this very effect of theirs regarded as being true *accidents*, so those facts, which lack a like effect, are found to be improperly called accidents. Therefore, this Essence is always, in every way, substantially identical with itself; and it is never in any way different from itself, even accidentally. But, however it may be as to the proper signification of the term *accident*, this is undoubtedly true, that of the supremely immutable Nature no statement can be made, whence it shall be conceived of as mutable.

CHAPTER VIII.   How he is compassionate and passionless. God is compassionate, in terms of our experience, because we experience the

---

[1] *Accidents,* as Anselm uses the term, are facts external to the essence of a being, which may yet be conceived to produce changes in a mutable being.

effect of compassion. God is not compassionate, in terms of his own being, because he does not experience the feeling (*affectus*) of compassion.

But how art thou compassionate, and, at the same time, passionless? For, if thou art passionless, thou dost not feel sympathy; and if thou dost not feel sympathy, thy heart is not wretched from sympathy for the wretched; but this it is to be compassionate. But if thou art not compassionate, whence cometh so great consolation to the wretched? How, then, art thou compassionate and not compassionate, O Lord, unless because thou art compassionate in terms of our experience, and not compassionate in terms of thy being.

Truly, thou art so in terms of our experience, but thou art not so in terms of thine own. For, when thou beholdest us in our wretchedness, we experience the effect of compassion, but thou dost not experience the feeling. Therefore, thou art both compassionate, because thou dost save the wretched, and spare those who sin against thee; and not compassionate, because thou art affected by no sympathy for wretchedness.

ST. THOMAS AQUINAS
The Simplicity and Immutability of God

SEVENTH ARTICLE.   WHETHER GOD IS ALTOGETHER SIMPLE?

We proceed thus to the Seventh Article:—

Objection 1. It seems that God is not altogether simple. For whatever is from God imitates Him. Thus from the first being are all beings, and from the first good are all goods. But in the things which God has made, nothing is altogether simple. Therefore neither is God altogether simple.

Obj. 2. Further, whatever is better must be attributed to God. But with us that which is composite is better than that which is simple: thus, chemical compounds are better than elements, and elements than the parts that compose them. Therefore it cannot be said that God is altogether simple.

On the contrary, Augustine says, *God is truly and absolutely simple.*[1]

THE SIMPLICITY AND IMMUTABILITY OF GOD   From *Summa Theologica,* Part I, Questions 3 and 9, in *Basic Writings of Saint Thomas Aquinas,* edited by Anton C. Pegis. Copyright 1945 by Random House, Inc. Reprinted by permission of the publisher and St. Dominic's Priory, London.

[1] *De Trin.,* VI, 6 (PL 42, 928).

I answer that, The absolute simplicity of God may be shown in many ways. First, from the previous articles of this question. For there is neither composition of quantitative parts in God, since He is not a body; nor composition of form and matter; nor does His nature differ from His *suppositum;* nor His essence from His being; neither is there in Him composition of genus and difference, nor of subject and accident. Therefore, it is clear that God is in no way composite, but is altogether simple. Secondly, because every composite is posterior to its component parts, and is dependent on them; but God is the first being, as has been shown above.[2] Thirdly, because every composite has a cause, for things in themselves diverse cannot unite unless something causes them to unite. But God is uncaused, as has been shown above,[3] since He is the first efficient cause. Fourthly, because in every composite there must be potentiality and actuality (this does not apply to God) for either one of the parts actualizes another, or at least all the parts are as it were in potency with respect to the whole. Fifthly, because nothing composite can be predicated of any one of its parts. And this is evident in a whole made up of dissimilar parts; for no part of a man is a man, nor any of the parts of the foot, a foot. But in wholes made up of similar parts, although something which is predicated of the whole may be predicated of a part (as a part of the air is air, and a part of water, water), nevertheless certain things are predicable of the whole which cannot be predicated of any of the parts; for instance, if the whole volume of water is two cubits, no part of it can be two cubits. Thus in every composite there is something which is not it itself. But, even if this could be said of whatever has a form, viz., that it has something which is not it itself, as in a white object there is something which does not belong to the essence of white, nevertheless, in the form itself there is nothing besides itself. And so, since God is absolute form, or rather absolute being, He can be in no way composite. Hilary touches upon this argument when he says: *God, Who is strength, is not made up of things that are weak; nor is He, Who is light, composed of things that are dark.*[4]

Reply Obj. 1. Whatever is from God imitates Him, as caused things imitate the first cause. But it is of the essence of a thing caused to be in some way composite; because at least its being differs from its essence, as will be shown hereafter.[5]

Reply Obj. 2. With us composite things are better than simple things, because the perfection of created goodness is not found in one simple thing, but in many things. But the perfection of divine goodness is found in one simple thing, as will be shown hereafter. . . .[6]

---

[2] Q. 2, a. 3 [in *Philosophy of Religion: Selected Readings,* pp. 117–19].
[3] *Ibid.*
[4] *De Trin.,* VII (PL 10, 223).
[5] Q. 50, a. 2.
[6] Q. 4, a. 1; Q. 6, a. 3.

FIRST ARTICLE.   WHETHER GOD IS
ALTOGETHER IMMUTABLE?

We proceed thus to the First Article:—

Objection 1. It seems that God is not altogether immutable. For whatever moves itself is in some way mutable. But, as Augustine says, *The Creator Spirit moves Himself neither by time, nor by place.*[7] Therefore God is in some way mutable.

Obj. 2. Further, it is said of Wisdom that *it is more mobile than all active things* (Wis. vii. 24). But God is wisdom itself; therefore God is movable.

Obj. 3. Further, to approach and to recede signify movement. But these are said of God in Scripture: *Draw nigh to God, and He will draw nigh to you* (Jas. iv. 8). Therefore God is mutable.

On the contrary, It is written, *I am the Lord, and I change not* (Mal. iii. 6).

I answer that, From what precedes, here is the proof that God is altogether immutable. First, because it was shown above that there is some first being, whom we call God,[8] and that this first being must be pure act, without the admixture of any potentiality, for the reason that, absolutely, potentiality is posterior to act.[9] Now everything which is in any way changed, is in some way in potentiality. Hence it is evident that it is impossible for God to change in any way. Secondly, because everything which is moved remains in part as it was, and in part passes away, as what is moved from whiteness to blackness remains the same as to substance; and thus in everything which is moved there is some kind of composition to be found. But it has been shown above that in God there is no composition, for He is altogether simple.[10] Hence it is manifest that God cannot be moved. Thirdly, because everything which is moved acquires something by its movement, and attains to what it had not attained previously. But since God is infinite, comprehending in Himself all the plenitude of the perfection of all being, He cannot acquire anything new, nor extend Himself to anything whereto He was not extended previously. Hence movement in no way belongs to Him. So it is that some of the ancients, constrained, as it were, by the truth, held that the first principle was immovable.[11]

Reply Obj. 1. Augustine there [12] speaks in a similar way to Plato, who said that the first mover moves Himself,[13] thus calling every operation a movement, according to which even the acts of understanding, and willing, and loving, are called movements. Therefore, because God understands and loves Himself, in that respect they said that God moves Himself; not, however, as

---

[7] *De Genesis ad Litt.,* VIII, 20 (PL 34, 388).   [8] Q. 2, a. 3.   [9] Q. 3, a. 3.   [10] Q. 3, a. 7.
[11] Parmenides and Melissus, according to Aristotle, *Phys.,* I, 2 (184b 16).
[12] *De Genesi ad Litt.,* VIII, 20 (PL 34, 388).
[13] Aristotle, *Metaph.,* XI, 6 (1071b 37); cf. Plato, *Timaeus* (pp. 30a, 34b); *Phaedrus* (p. 245c).—Cf. also Averroes, *In Phys.,* VIII, comm. 40 (IV, 173r).

movement and change belong to a thing existing in potentiality, as we now speak of change and movement.

Reply Obj. 2. Wisdom is called mobile by way of similitude, according as it diffuses its likeness even to the outermost of things, for nothing can exist which does not proceed from the divine wisdom, by way of some kind of imitation, as from the first effective and formal principle; as also works of art proceed from the wisdom of the artist. And so in the same way, inasmuch as the similitude of the divine wisdom proceeds in degrees from the highest things, which participate more fully of its likeness, to the lowest things which participate of it in a lesser degree, there is said to be a kind of procession and movement of the divine wisdom to things; as if we should say that the sun proceeds to the earth, inasmuch as a ray of its light reaches the earth. In this way Dionysius expounds the matter, saying that every procession of the divine manifestation comes to us from the movement of the Father of lights.[14]

Reply Obj. 3. These things are said of God in Scripture metaphorically. For as the sun is said to enter a house, or to go out, according as its rays reach the house, so God is said to approach to us, or to recede from us, when we receive the influx of His goodness or fall away from Him.

CHARLES HARTSHORNE
The Divine Relativity

RELIGIOUS MEANING OF ABSOLUTE

Why is it religiously significant that God be supposed absolute? The reason is at least suggested by the consideration that absoluteness is requisite for complete reliability. What is relative to conditions may fail us if the conditions happen to be unfavorable. Hence if there is to be anything that *cannot* fail, it must be nonrelative, absolute, in those respects to which "reliability" and "failure" have reference. But it is often not noted that this need not be every respect or aspect from which God's nature can be regarded. For there may be qualities in God whose relativity or variability would be neutral to his

Charles Hartshorne (1897–), a professor of philosophy at the University of Texas, is a leading advocate of the metaphysics of Alfred N. Whitehead. Among his important writings are *Reality as Social Process, Anselm's Discovery,* and *The Logic of Perfection.*

THE DIVINE RELATIVITY   From *The Divine Relativity* by Charles Hartshorne. Copyright © 1948 by Yale University Press. Reprinted by their permission.

[14] *De Cael. Hier.,* I, 1 (PG 3, 120).

reliability. To say of a man that (as human affairs go) his reliability is established refers not to every quality of the man, but only to certain principles exhibited in his otherwise highly variable behavior. We do not mean that if something comes close to his eye he will not blink, or that if he is given bad-tasting food he will enjoy it as much as better fare. We mean that his fixed intention to act according to the requirements of the general welfare will not waver, and that his wisdom and skill in carrying out this aim will be constant. But in all this there is not only no implication that conditions will not have effect upon the man, but the very plain implication that they will have plenty of effect. Skill in one set of circumstances means one form of behavior, in another set another form, and the same is true of the intention to serve the general good. Of course, one may argue that complete fixity of good intention and complete constancy of skill imply every other sort of fixity as well. But this has never yet been definitely shown by careful, explicit reasoning, and anything less is inappropriate in as difficult a subject as we are dealing with. General hunches will not do.

A typically invalid argument in this connection is that unless God surveys at once the whole of time and thus is independent of change, he cannot be relied upon to arrange all events with due regard to their relations to all that has gone before and all that is to come after. This argument either rests on an equivocation or it destroys all religious meaning for the divine reliability. For, if it is meant in any clear sense, it implies that every event has been selected by deity as an element in the best of all possible worlds, the ideal total pattern of all time and all existence. But this ideal pattern includes all acts of sin and the most hideous suffering and catastrophe, all the tragedies of life. And what then becomes of the ideas of human responsibility and choice, and of the notion that some deeds ought not to have taken place? These are only the beginning of the absurdities into which the view thrusts us. To mitigate these absurdities theologians introduce various more or less subtle equivocations. Would they not do better to take a fresh start (as indeed many have done) and admit that we have no good religious reason for positing the notion of providence as an absolute contriving of all events according to a completely detailed plan embracing all time? The religious value of such a notion is more negative than positive. It is the mother of no end of chicanery (see the book of Job for some examples), of much deep feeling of injustice (the poor unfortunate being assured that God has deliberately contrived everything as exactly the best way events could transpire), and of philosophical quagmires of paradox and unmeaning verbiage. The properly constituted man does not want to "rely" upon God to arrange all things, including our decisions, in accordance with a plan of all events which fixes every least detail with reference to every other that ever has happened or ever "is to" happen. How many atheists must have been needlessly produced by insistence upon this arbitrary notion, which after all is invariably softened by qualifications surreptitiously introduced *ad hoc* when certain problems are stressed! We shall see later that the really usable meaning of divine reliability is quite different and is entirely compatible with a profound relativity of God to conditions and to change. For the present, I suggest that all we can assert to have obvious religious value is the faith that God is to be relied upon to do for the world all that ought to be done for it, and with as much survey of the future as there ought to be or as is ideally desirable, leaving for the members of the world community to do for themselves and each other all that they ought to be left to do. We cannot assume that what ought to be done for the world by deity is everything that ought to be done at all, leaving the creatures with nothing to do for themselves and for each other. Nor can we assume that the ideal survey of what for us at least constitutes the future is one which fully defines it in every detail, leaving no open alternatives of possibility. So far from being self-evidently of religious value, these assumptions, viewed in the light of history, seem clearly of extreme disvalue. Yet they are often either asserted, or not unequivocally denied or avoided, in the intemperate insistence upon the total absoluteness of deity.

GOD AS SOCIAL

We have also to remember that if there is religious value in the absoluteness of God, as requisite for his reliability, there is equally manifest religious value in another trait which seems unequivocally to imply relativity rather than absoluteness. This is the social or personal nature of God. What is a person if not a being qualified and conditioned by social relations, relations to other persons? And what is God if not the supreme case of personality? Those who deny this have yet to succeed in distinguishing their position from atheism, as Hume pointedly noted. Either God really does love all beings, that is, is related to them by a sympathetic union surpassing any human sympathy, or religion seems a vast fraud. The common query Can the Absolute or Perfect Being be personal or social? should really run In what sense, if any, can a social being be absolute or perfect? For God is conceived socially before he is conceived absolutely or as perfect. God is the highest ruler, judge, benefactor; he knows, loves, and assists man; he has made the world with the design of sharing his bliss with lesser beings. The world is a vast society governed by laws instituted by the divine monarch—the supreme personal power to whom all other persons are subject. These are all, more or less clearly, social conceptions—if you like, metaphors (though aimed, as we shall see, at a literal, intuited meaning) drawn from the social life of man. They constitute the universal, popular meaning of "God," in relation to which descriptions such as "absolute," "perfect," "immutable," "impassive," "simple," and the like, are technical refinements aimed at logical precision. They seek to define the somewhat vague ideas of *highest* ruler, *supreme* power, or *author of all*, himself without author or origin. "Immutable," for example, is an attempted definition of the superiority of deity with respect to death and degeneration, and also with respect to vacillation of will due to fear, or other weakness. Earthly rulers are all brought low by death; and their promises and protection and execution of justice must always be discounted somewhat in anticipation of the effect upon them of changing circumstances and the development of their own motives, the growth of good and evil in their own hearts. God is not under sentence of death, cannot decay; and his convenant abides, nor is his wisdom ever clouded by storms of blind passion, the effects of strong drink or of disease.

The future of theology depends, I suggest, above all upon the answer to this question: can technically precise terms be found which express the supremacy of God, among social beings, without contradicting his social character? To say, on the one hand, that God is love, to continue to use popular religious terms like Lord, divine will, obedience to God, and on the other to speak of an absolute, infinite, immutable, simple, impassive deity, is either a gigantic hoax of priestcraft, or it is done with the belief that the social connotations of the popular language are ultimately in harmony with these descriptions. Merely to speak of the "mysteriousness" of God is not sufficient. If he escapes all the resources of our language and analysis, why be so insistent upon the obviously quite human concepts, absolute, infinite, perfect, immutable? These too are our conceptions, our terms, fragments of the English or Latin languages. Perhaps after all it is not correct to say God is absolute. How shall we know, if the subject is utterly mysterious and beyond our powers? . . .

COMPLETE INDEPENDENCE NOT ADMIRABLE

But, supposing that God is to be conceived worthy of utter respect, and in that sense "perfect," it may not follow that God is quite everything that has customarily been associated with this adjective. For it is entirely possible that theologians have sometimes respected things which, when more carefully considered, are seen not to be suitable objects of this respect. The being in the highest degree admirable will have, in the highest degree or manner, all properties that deserve admiration. But even tyrants and scoundrels have actually been admired and, it rather seems, admired sometimes for their very tyranny and rascality. To some of us, nothing is more deeply shocking than certain directions frequently taken by theological admiration. What is the ideal of the tyrant? Is it not that, while the fortunes of all should depend upon the tyrant's will, he should depend as little as possible, ideally not at all, upon the wills and fortunes of others? This one-sided independence, in ideally complete or "absolute" form, was held the crowning glory of deity! Sheer independence in every respect whatsoever, while all else in every respect depended upon him, was regarded as essential to God's perfection. There are those, including Berdyaev and many other good and wise men, who find no stimulus to admiration or respect in this doctrine.

Of course there are modes of independence which are admirable. But is it any less true that there are modes of dependence which we all admire, and of independence which we detest? The father that as little as possible depends upon the will and welfare of his child is an inhuman monster. Let the child—say, a daughter—be happy, let her be miserable, let her deeply desire this or deeply detest that, let her develop in a moral or in a vicious direction, it is all one to the independent parent, who goes his way in complete neutrality to all such alternatives (this neutrality being the exact meaning of absoluteness or independence) wholly uninfluenced by weal or woe, love or hate, preference or detestation, in the unlucky child that, in such a one-sided way, depends upon the parent. Is this really an ideal? Is not the correct ideal rather this, that the parent should be influenced in appropriate, and only in appropriate, ways by the child's desires and fortunes? One should not simply agree to every whim of the child, or strive always to save her from pain or furnish her with pleasure. Nor should one be sunk in misery with her every sorrow, or fantastically elated with her every triumph. But neither should one try to act and think and feel just as one would have acted or thought or felt had the child's joy been sorrow, or her sorrow joy, or her likes dislikes. Yet God, we are told, is impassive and immutable and without accidents, is just as he would be in his action and knowledge and being had we never existed, or had all our experiences been otherwise. Instead of attributing to God an eminently appropriate dependence upon us, the majority of theologians simply denied dependence of any and every sort. This seems plainly an idealization of the tyrant-subject relationship, as Whitehead, a critic as fair and moderate as he is profound, has reminded us.

THE INDEPENDENCE WHICH IS ADMIRABLE

Suppose a man says, I can be a good man, do my duty, only so long as a certain friend continues to live and to encourage me. Our feeling will surely be that, while it is natural and human to lean upon friends for moral assistance, still a man should do his duty whatever anyone else may do. In ethical character one should be as independent as possible of other contingent beings. Thus to depend for doing one's duty upon others is inappropriate, unadmirable dependence. God then, as object of piety, will be in highest degree, or utterly, independent of our actions and fortunes for the preservation of his holiness of will. That is, he will promote the highest cosmic good, come what may. But it does not in the least follow that what God will do to promote the cosmic good will be uninfluenced by our actions and fortunes, or that how he will think and feel about the world will in no way reflect what is going on in the world. The man who does his duty regardless of what happens will not have the same specific duties regardless of what happens.

And with different duties he will perform different acts with different specific intentions, ideas, and feelings.

Suppose, on the other hand, a man says, I can be equally happy and serene and joyous regardless of how men and women suffer around me. Shall we admire this alleged independence? I think not. Why should we admire it when it is alleged of God? I have yet to learn a good answer to this question. On the other hand, if we see a person who is dragged down into helpless misery by the sight of suffering in others, we feel that this response is as inappropriate as the opposite one of gay serenity would be in the same circumstances. And there is no inconsistency in condemning both responses, for a clear logical principle can be applied to both. This is that we should respond to the total situation appropriately, not just to a part of it, or inappropriately. The suffering of the world is not the world; there is also the joy of the world. If the one should sadden us, the other should delight us. He who refuses to rejoice with the joy of others is as selfish as he who refuses to grieve with their sorrows. Indeed, as has been often remarked, it is if anything a rarer unselfishness to be really inspired by the happiness of our friends than to be saddened by their unhappiness. For the happiness of others may inspire us with envy instead of sympathetic pleasure. Such neutralization by envy of sympathetic dependence for our own happiness upon that of others is scarcely admirable!

PROPORTIONAL DEPENDENCE

The notion that total emotional independence is admirable seems, then, to be without foundation in experience. There *is* an admirable independence, but it is independence in basic ethical purpose, not in specific concrete experience and happiness. There is also admirable dependence, which is appropriate response, duly proportionate to the balance of factors in the world known to us, of sympathetic rejoicing and sorrowing. Why not attribute to the divine response the ideal of such appropriateness, or proportionality, of dependence? The requirement of piety seems entirely compatible with such attribution.

To depend upon others emotionally through sympathy is to change when they change—for example, to grow in joy when they do. But if God changes, it is often argued, then he changes either for the worse or for the better. If the former, how can we admire him without stint? If the latter, then it seems he must previously have lacked something, and been incomplete and imperfect. The first horn of the dilemma need not concern us, unless it can be proved that there is ever more sorrow than joy in the world. For if there is always more satisfaction than dissatisfaction, then God should always have more reason to rejoice than to grieve over the world, and since he can retain the consciousness of past joys, there will always be a *net increment* of value accruing to God at each moment. Now if life were not more satisfying than otherwise, could it go on? Is there anything to maintain the will to live save satisfaction in living? I do not see that there is. Hence I shall confine my attention to the second horn of the dilemma, that a God who increases in value must previously have lacked some value, and therefore have been imperfect. My reply is that, as we are here using the term, perfect means completely worthy of admiration and respect, and so the question becomes, is such complete admirableness infringed by the possibility of enrichment in total value? I say it is not. We do not admire a man less because we know he would be a happier man if his son, who is wretched, became well and happy, or because we anticipate that when a child is born to him it will enrich his life with many new joys. Admiration is not directed to happiness, except so far as we feel that a person does or does not attain the happiness appropriate to the state of the world as known to him. We admire not the amount but the appropriateness of the joy. We rejoice in another's happiness, we grieve over his misfortune, but we do not praise or blame or admire on this account, unless we think the good or bad fortune is the person's own doing. So far as it is due rather to the decisions of others, which were their responsibility, not his, then it determines not our respect, but only the tone of our sympathy or participatory feeling, toward the person. Why should it be otherwise in relation to God? If God rejoices less today than he will tomorrow, but ideally appropriately at both times, our reverence for him should in no way be affected by the increase in joy. Indeed, if he were incapable of responding to a better world with greater satisfaction, this should infringe upon our respect; for it would imply a lack of proportionality in the divine awareness of things.

Gratitude is the appropriate expression of genuine indebtedness, of really having received benefit from others. Conceited men would perhaps like to avoid occasions for gratitude, so that they might boast of their independence. But no good man blessed with a beloved wife is sorry to feel that without her he could not have been so happy. To God each of us is dearer than wife to husband, for no human being knows the inner experiences of another human being so intimately as they are known to God. And to know experiences is to appreciate them; for the value of experience is just the experience itself. As we are indebted to a few persons for the privilege of feeling something of the quality of their experiences, so God is indebted to *all* persons for the much fuller enjoyment of the same privilege. God is not conceited or envious; therefore he has no motive for wishing to escape or deny this indebtedness. It is envious men, priests, theologians, guardians—in some cases one could almost say watchdogs—of the divine majesty, who attribute such an attitude, such unbridled will to independence, to God. (No doubt God's sense of indebtedness to us lacks some of the connotations of "gratitude," such as the sense of a common moral frailty, almost miraculously overcome in a certain case.)

SYMPATHETIC DEPENDENCE

I have been contending that there are appropriate forms of dependence, in relation to certain terms. To this an opponent may object that the appropriateness is not determined solely by the nature of the entities toward which the dependence obtains, but involves also the nature of that which is thus made dependent. It is appropriate for man to depend upon man, not for the supreme being to depend upon anything. But my proposition is that the higher the being the more dependence of certain kinds will be appropriate for it. One does not expect an oyster to depend for its joy or sorrow upon my joy or sorrow, as such, or even upon that of other oysters to any great extent. Sympathetic dependence is a sign of excellence and waxes with every ascent in the scale of being. Joy calls for sympathetic joy, sorrow for sympathetic sorrow, as the most excellent possible forms of response to these states. The eminent form of sympathetic dependence can only apply to deity, for this form cannot be less than an omniscient sympathy, which depends upon and is exactly colored by every nuance of joy or sorrow anywhere in the world. It would certainly not be appropriate for man to even try to sympathize with all life. How could he hope to do such a thing? Thus I grant to the opponent that what is "appropriate dependence" varies with the subject as well as the object of the dependence relation. But I deny that zero dependence for happiness is ever appropriate, and I assert that the closest to such zero dependence would occur at the bottom, not the top of the scale of beings, while the top, the most eminent form of dependence for happiness, would be maximal dependence, dependence upon all life even to its least nuance for the exact happiness of the eminent individual.

I invite you to perform with me a mental experiment. Imagine someone to read aloud an eloquent poem, in the presence of: (A) a glass of water, (B) an ant, (C) a dog, (D) a human being unacquainted with the language of the poem, (E) a human being knowing the language but insensitive to poetry, (F) a person sensitive to poetry and familiar with the language. Now I submit that each member of this series is superior, in terms of the data, to its predecessors, and that each is more, not less, dependent upon or relative to the poem as such, including its meanings as well as its mere sounds. The molecules of water will be utterly "impassible" (the theological term) to the words of the poem as words, and not even much affected by the mere physical sounds. The ant, since it has hearing, will be affected by the physical sounds more drastically, it seems probable, than the water. The dog will not only hear and be influenced by the sound, as such, but will have some sense of the emotional tones of voice, and may be quite excited by these. It may also have a feeling of familiarity concerning some of the words. The human being not knowing the language will receive more varied influences of this kind and will enjoy some sense of the verbal music of the poem, which may furnish a rather absorbing experience. The insensitive, but comprehending, listener will be given a variety of images and ideas, even though without intense esthetic feeling or adequate integration. The adequate listener may go through a deep and thousandfold adventure of thought and feeling. Thus we see that the simple correlation of inferior with dependent or relative is anything but a report upon experience. The identification of "absolute" and "supreme" has to be proved, not blandly assumed, and it is in the teeth of the experiences without which we could not know what either absolute or supreme could reasonably mean.

Suggestions for Further Reading

A good collection of writings dealing with various concepts of God is Charles Hartshorne and William L. Reese, eds., *Philosophers Speak of God* * (The University of Chicago Press, 1953). E. O. James provides a helpful, historical study of the major views on God in *The Concept of Deity* (Hutchinson, 1950). An excellent account of the philosophical importance of the Judeo-Christian idea of God can be found in Etienne Gilson, *God and Philosophy* * (Yale University Press, 1941). Recent discussions of the idea of God as a necessary being are included in Alvin Plantinga, *God and Other Minds* (Cornell University Press, 1967) and in James F. Ross, *Philosophical Theology* (Bobbs-Merrill, 1969).

Important discussions of foreknowledge and future contingents include: William Ockham, *Predestination, God's Foreknowledge and Future Contingents*, translated by Marilyn Adams and Norman Kretzmann (Appleton-Century-Crofts, 1969); Nelson Pike, "Divine Omniscience and Voluntary Action," *Philosophical Review*, 74 (1965); John Turk Saunders, "Of God and Freedom," *Philosophical Review*, 75 (1966); Marilyn Adams, "Is the Existence of God a Hard Fact?" *Philosophical Review*, 76 (1967); and Arthur Prior, "The Formalities of Omniscience," *Philosophy*, 38 (1963).

Notable among the recent discussions of omnipotence are G. B. Keene, "A Simpler Solution to the Paradox of Omnipotence," *Mind*, 69, No. 273 (January 1960); B. Mayo, "Mr. Keene on Omnipotence," *Mind*, 70, No. 278 (April 1961); George Mavrodes, "Some Puzzles Concerning Omnipotence," *Philosophical Review*, 72 (1963); and James Cargile, "On Omnipotence," *Nous*, 1, No. 2 (May 1967).

For a penetrating study of timelessness and some of the other metaphysical attributes of God, see Nelson Pike, *God and Timelessness* (Schocken, 1970).

* Available in paperback.

ARGUMENTS
FOR THE EXISTENCE
OF GOD

For centuries, philosophers and theologians have sought to justify theism by advancing arguments for the existence of the theistic God. The most important of these arguments can be classified as ontological, cosmological, or teleological. An ontological argument endeavors to show that given our concept of God, it follows that God actually exists. An argument that is cosmological reasons that God exists in order to account for the fact that a world exists. And a teleological argument reasons that God exists in order to account for the fact that a world which exhibits order and design exists.

The most well known ontological argument is presented in Anselm's *Proslogium II*. Anselm understands the concept God to be the concept of a being than which none greater is possible. He argues that such a God actually exists because if He did not exist—that is, if God were nonexistent like, for example, the Fountain of Youth—then, since He, like the Fountain of Youth, might (logically) have existed, He might (logically) have been greater than He in fact is. But this is impossible. For although there is no contradiction in thinking that the Fountain of Youth might have been a greater being than it is, there does seem to be a contradiction in the idea that the being than which none greater is possible is a being that might have been greater. Hence, given our concept of God, we are driven to the conclusion that He actually exists.

The fundamental idea on which Anselm's reasoning rests is that if a being does not exist, but might have existed, then it might have been greater than it in fact is. This idea implies that existence is a perfection, a quality which enhances the greatness of a being: a being that has existence is greater than it would have been had it lacked existence. Many philosophers object to this idea on the grounds that existence, unlike such qualities as wisdom and power, is not a quality a being may have or lack; others question Anselm's reasoning on the grounds that the concept of a being than which none greater is possible may be an incoherent concept, like the concept of an integer than which none larger is possible. C. D. Broad raises both these objections to the argument. Yet another objection which some philosophers make is that if the reasoning in the argument were correct, we could use it to prove the existence of things we know do not exist—for example, the island than which none greater is possible. This last objection, if correct, shows that Anselm's argument contains a mistake, but does not tell us what the mistake is.

René Descartes offers an argument that is similar in important ways to Anselm's. Hartshorne, however, advances an ontological argument—also found in Anselm—that differs in important ways from the one discussed above. The key idea in the argument discussed by Hartshorne is that *necessary existence* —as opposed to *contingent existence*—is a perfection. A being has contingent existence provided that it exists but might (logically) not have existed. A being has necessary existence provided that it exists and could not (logically) have not existed. Some philosophers reject the idea that existence is a perfection but accept the idea that necessary existence is a perfection.

Cosmological arguments have been advanced since antiquity but received considerable attention in the thirteenth and eighteenth centuries. Among the following selections, the thirteenth-century form of the cosmological argument is represented by Aquinas and Duns Scotus; the eighteenth-century form is presented by the character Demea in the selection from Hume. Both forms of the argument are also discussed and criticized by Edwards.

The key idea in the thirteenth-century form of the cosmological argument is that it is impossible for there to be an infinite regress in an *essentially ordered* series of efficient causes. Duns Scotus gives an account of an essentially ordered series of causes, and Patterson Brown endeavors to explain why the proponents of the argument rejected an infinite regress in such a series.

The eighteenth-century form of the argument is based on the Principle of Sufficient Reason, which maintains that there must be an explanation of the existence of any being and of any positive fact whatever. Using this principle, it is easy to see that not every being could have the explanation of its existence in other beings and their activities. For if every being were of this sort, then there would be something lacking an explanation. Of course, no particular being would lack an explanation since each being would be explained by the causal activities of some other being or beings. What would be left unexplained is not some particular being but the positive fact that there are beings rather than no beings at all. For if every being is explained by other beings, then the fact that there are beings would lack an explanation—we could not explain why there are beings rather than not by appealing to the causal activity of some being. Therefore, if the Principle of Sufficient Reason is true, there must exist some being whose existence is not explained by any other beings. Does this being, then, just happen to exist, without any explanation? But this is impossible since the Principle of Sufficient Reason requires that it too must have an explanation. The conclusion we must draw is that its existence is explained by its own nature, that there exists at least one being whose nature accounts for its existence. Such a being, it is argued, would be a necessary being and possess the perfections of God. Therefore, God exists.

We need to question this argument first by asking whether the idea of a being having the explanation of its existence within its own nature is a coherent idea. Some facts about a thing can, perhaps, be explained by referring to the thing's nature—for example, we might explain why a triangle has three angles by referring to the nature of a triangle, to what it is for something to be a triangle—but is the existence of a thing a fact about that thing, and even if it is, does it make sense to think of it being explained by the nature of that thing? Secondly, we need to question the Principle of Sufficient

Reason itself. Do we have any reasons for thinking it to be true? Is it, as some philosophers have claimed, a principle that cannot be proved or disproved, one which is simply presupposed by us in our dealings with the world in which we live? Finally, we need to ask whether a necessary being, if there is one, would have to be God. As Hume's character Cleanthes suggests, why couldn't the necessary being be something less than God, such as matter?

In the section on the teleological argument for the existence of God, Paley compares the universe to a watch and Hume's character Cleanthes compares it to a machine. The point of these comparisons is to suggest an analogy between the universe and things known to be produced by intelligent beings, thereby to justify the conclusion that the universe was probably produced by an intelligent being. We may represent Cleanthes' version of the teleological argument as follows:

1. Machines are produced by intelligent design.
2. The universe is like a machine. Therefore—
3. Probably the universe was produced by intelligent design. Therefore—
4. Probably God exists and created the universe.

Concerning this argument, we need to ask first in what ways the entire universe can be said to resemble a machine. Paley assures us that every manifestation of design which exists in a watch also exists in the works of nature. And Cleanthes affirms that there is a "curious adapting of means to ends" throughout all nature. Apparently they hold that the parts of nature are related to one another in a manner similar to the way in which the parts of a machine are related to one another. If we introduce the idea of a *teleological system* to mean any system of parts in which the parts are so arranged that under proper conditions they work together to serve a certain end or purpose, it is clear that machines are teleological systems. For example, a watch is a system of parts in which the parts work together so that the watch will tell the time of day. Moreover, machines with complex parts, like automobiles, are teleological systems and also systems of teleological systems —for many of their parts, like the carburetor in an automobile, are themselves teleological systems. It is also clear that many parts of living organisms are teleological systems. The human eye, for example, no less than a camera, is a teleological system. Can the same be said of the universe itself? Of course, if theism is true and God has created the universe and arranged its parts so that they work together for some far-off divine purpose, then the universe is indeed a teleological system. But, if we follow Cleanthes and limit ourselves to empirical observation of the universe and its parts, we cannot say with any degree of certainty that the universe is a teleological system. For we are not in a position to observe what the purpose of the universe is and how the parts of the universe are so arranged that they work together for the attainment of that purpose. Nevertheless, it may be reasonable to believe that the universe is a vast system of parts which are themselves teleological systems. And this concept may be all that is required to justify the conclusion that the universe probably was produced by intelligent design. But, as Hume has Philo point out, we observe at best only a small fraction of the total universe—perhaps elsewhere in the universe chaos reigns. Hence, we may be justified only in claiming that a small fraction of the universe contains a number of teleological systems. And if that is so, we may not be justified by empirical observation in thinking that the entire universe is, like a complex machine, a system of teleological systems. We must, then, seriously question whether the universe is sufficiently like a machine to warrant the conclusion that it was produced by intelligent design.

Even if the inference from points 1 and 2 of Cleanthes' argument to point 3 is acceptable, it is doubtful that the teleological argument can do much to establish theism. For there are several questions to be raised concerning the inference from point 3 to point 4. In the first place, since there are numerous instances of evil in the universe, the intelligent producer of the universe, for all we know, may be morally indifferent to his handiwork. Secondly, since many intricate teleological systems have resulted from the cooperative work of many architects, we cannot reasonably infer the unity of the Deity—many intelligent beings may have cooperated in the production of the universe. These and other objections are raised by Philo against Cleanthes' attempt to found theism on a teleological argument.

W. L. R.

THE ONTOLOGICAL ARGUMENT

ST. ANSELM
The Ontological Argument

CHAPTER II.   Truly there is a God, although the fool hath said in his heart, There is no God.

And so, Lord, do thou, who dost give understanding to faith, give me, so far as thou knowest it to be profitable, to understand that thou art as we believe; and that thou art that which we believe. And, indeed, we believe that thou art a being than which nothing greater can be conceived. Or is there no such nature, since the fool hath said in his heart, there is no God? (Psalms xiv. 1). But, at any rate, this very fool, when he hears of this being of which I speak—a being than which nothing greater can be conceived—understands what he hears, and what he understands is in his understanding; although he does not understand it to exist.

For, it is one thing for an object to be in the understanding, and another to understand that the object exists. When a painter first conceives of what he will afterwards perform, he has it in his understanding, but he does not yet understand it to be, because he has not yet performed it. But after he has made the painting, he both has it in his understanding, and he understands that it exists, because he has made it.

Hence, even the fool is convinced that something exists in the under-

THE ONTOLOGICAL ARGUMENT   From *Proslogium* by St. Anselm, translated by Sidney N. Deane. Reprinted by permission of The Open Court Publishing Co., La Salle, Illinois.

standing, at least, than which nothing greater can be conceived. For, when he hears of this, he understands it. And whatever is understood, exists in the understanding. And assuredly that, than which nothing greater can be conceived, cannot exist in the understanding alone. For, suppose it exists in the understanding alone: then it can be conceived to exist in reality; which is greater.

Therefore, if that, than which nothing greater can be conceived, exists in the understanding alone, the very being, than which nothing greater can be conceived, is one, than which a greater can be conceived. But obviously this is impossible. Hence, there is no doubt that there exists a being, than which nothing greater can be conceived, and it exists both in the understanding and in reality.

> CHAPTER III.   God cannot be conceived not to exist.—God is that, than which nothing greater can be conceived.—That which can be conceived not to exist is not God.

And it assuredly exists so truly, that it cannot be conceived not to exist. For, it is possible to conceive of a being which cannot be conceived not to exist; and this is greater than one which can be conceived not to exist. Hence, if that, than which nothing greater can be conceived, can be conceived not to exist, it is not that, than which nothing greater can be conceived. But this is an irreconcilable contradiction. There is, then, so truly a being than which nothing greater can be conceived to exist, that it cannot even be conceived not to exist; and this being thou art, O Lord, our God.

So truly, therefore, dost thou exist, O Lord, my God, that thou canst not be conceived not to exist; and rightly. For, if a mind could conceive of a being better than thee, the creature would rise above the Creator; and this is most absurd. And, indeed, whatever else there is, except thee alone, can be conceived not to exist. To thee alone, therefore, it belongs to exist more truly than all other beings, and hence in a higher degree than all others. For, whatever else exists does not exist so truly, and hence in a less degree it belongs to it to exist. Why, then, has the fool said in his heart, there is no God (Psalms xiv. 1), since it is so evident, to a rational mind, that thou dost exist in the highest degree of all? Why, except that he is dull and a fool?

> CHAPTER IV.   How the fool has said in his heart what cannot be conceived.—A thing may be conceived in two ways: (1) when the word signifying it is conceived; (2) when the thing itself is understood. As far as the word goes, God can be conceived not to exist; in reality he cannot.

But how has the fool said in his heart what he could not conceive; or how is it that he could not conceive what he said in his heart? since it is the same to say in the heart, and to conceive.

But, if really, nay, since really, he both conceived, because he said in his heart; and did not say in his heart, because he could not conceive; there is more than one way in which a thing is said in the heart or conceived. For, in one sense, an object is conceived, when the word signifying it is conceived; and in another, when the very entity, which the object is, is understood.

In the former sense, then, God can be conceived not to exist; but in the latter, not at all. For no one who understands what fire and water are can conceive fire to be water, in accordance with the nature of the facts themselves, although this is possible according to the words. So, then, no one who understands what God is can conceive that God does not exist; although he says these words in his heart, either without any, or with some foreign, signification. For, God is that than which a greater cannot be conceived. And he who thoroughly understands this, assuredly understands that this being so truly exists, that not even in concept can it be non-existent. Therefore, he who understands that God so exists, cannot conceive that he does not exist.

I thank thee, gracious Lord, I thank thee; because what I formerly believed by thy bounty, I now so understand by thine illumination, that if I were unwilling to believe that thou dost exist, I should not be able not to understand this to be true.

RENÉ DESCARTES
The Supremely Perfect Being Must Exist

But now, if just because I can draw the idea of something from my thought, it follows that all which I know clearly and distinctly as pertaining to this object does really belong to it, may I not derive from this an argument demonstrating the existence of God? It is certain that I no less find the idea of God, that is to say, the idea of a supremely perfect Being, in me, than that of any figure or number whatever it is; and I do not know any less clearly and distinctly that an [actual and] eternal existence pertains to this nature

René Descartes (1596–1650) marks the beginning of the modern period in philosophy and is also celebrated as a mathematician for his development of the principles of analytic geometry. He is best known in philosophy for seeking the foundation of knowledge in the certainty of one's own existence. Among his major writings are *Discourse on Method, Meditations on First Philosophy,* and *Principles of Philosophy.*

THE SUPREMELY PERFECT BEING MUST EXIST   From *Meditations on First Philosophy* by René Descartes, in *The Philosophical Works of Descartes,* translated by Elizabeth S. Haldane and G. R. T. Ross. Reprinted by permission of Cambridge University Press.

than I know that all that which I am able to demonstrate of some figure or number truly pertains to the nature of this figure or number, and therefore, although all that I concluded in the preceding Meditations were found to be false, the existence of God would pass with me as at least as certain as I have ever held the truths of mathematics (which concern only numbers and figures) to be.

This indeed is not at first manifest, since it would seem to present some appearance of being a sophism. For being accustomed in all other things to make a distinction between existence and essence, I easily persuade myself that the existence can be separated from the essence of God, and that we can thus conceive God as not actually existing. But, nevertheless, when I think of it with more attention, I clearly see that existence can no more be separated from the essence of God than can its having its three angles equal to two right angles be separated from the essence of a [rectilinear] triangle, or the idea of a mountain from the idea of a valley; and so there is not any less repugnance to our conceiving a God (that is, a Being supremely perfect) to whom existence is lacking (that is to say, to whom a certain perfection is lacking), than to conceive of a mountain which has no valley.

But although I cannot really conceive of a God without existence any more than a mountain without a valley, still from the fact that I conceive of a mountain with a valley, it does not follow that there is such a mountain in the world; similarly although I conceive of God as possessing existence, it would seem that it does not follow that there is a God which exists; for my thought does not impose any necessity upon things, and just as I may imagine a winged horse, although no horse with wings exists, so I could perhaps attribute existence to God, although no God existed.

But a sophism is concealed in this objection; for from the fact that I cannot conceive a mountain without a valley, it does not follow that there is any mountain or any valley in existence, but only that the mountain and the valley, whether they exist or do not exist, cannot in any way be separated one from the other. While from the fact that I cannot conceive God without existence, it follows that existence is inseparable from Him, and hence that He really exists; not that my thought can bring this to pass, or impose any necessity on things, but, on the contrary, because the necessity which lies in the thing itself, i.e. the necessity of the existence of God determines me to think in this way. For it is not within my power to think of God without existence (that is of a supremely perfect Being devoid of a supreme perfection) though it is in my power to imagine a horse either with wings or without wings.

And we must not here object that it is in truth necessary for me to assert that God exists after having presupposed that He possesses every sort of perfection, since existence is one of these, but that as a matter of fact my original supposition was not necessary, just as it is not necessary to consider that all quadrilateral figures can be inscribed in the circle; for supposing I thought this, I should be constrained to admit that the rhombus might be inscribed in the circle since it is a quadrilateral figure, which, however, is manifestly false. [We must not, I say, make any such allegations because] although it is not necessary that I should at any time entertain the notion of God, nevertheless whenever it happens that I think of a first and a sovereign Being, and, so to speak, derive the idea of Him from the storehouse of my mind, it is necessary that I should attribute to Him every sort of perfection, although I do not get so far as to enumerate them all, or to apply my mind to each one in particular. And this necessity suffices to make me conclude (after having recognised that existence is a perfection) that this first and sovereign Being really exists; just as though it is not necessary for me ever to imagine any triangle, yet, whenever I wish to consider a rectilinear figure composed only of three angles, it is absolutely essential that I should attribute to it all those properties which serve to bring about the conclusion that its three angles are not greater than two right angles, even although I may not then be considering this point in particular. But when I consider which figures are capable of being inscribed in the circle, it is in no wise necessary that I should think that all quadrilateral figures are of this number; on the contrary, I cannot even pretend that this is the case, so long as I do not desire to accept anything which I cannot conceive clearly and distinctly. And in consequence there is a great difference between the false suppositions such as this, and the true ideas born within me, the first and principal of which is that of God. For really I discern in many ways that this idea is not something factitious, and depending solely on my thought, but that it is the image of a true and immutable nature; first of all, because I cannot conceive anything but God himself to whose essence existence [necessarily] pertains; in the second place because it is not possible for me to conceive two or more Gods in this same position; and, granted that there is one such God who now exists, I see clearly that it is necessary that He should have existed from all eternity, and that He must exist eternally; and finally, because I know an infinitude of other properties in God, none of which I can either diminish or change.

For the rest, whatever proof or argument I avail myself of, we must always return to the point that it is only those things which we conceive clearly and distinctly that have the power of persuading me entirely. And although amongst the matters which I conceive of in this way, some indeed are manifestly obvious to all, while others only manifest themselves to those who consider them closely and examine them attentively; still, after they have once been discovered, the latter are not esteemed as any less certain than the former. For example, in the case of every right-angled triangle, although it does not so manifestly appear that the square of the base is equal to the squares of the two other sides as that this base is opposite to the greatest angle; still, when this has once been apprehended, we are just as certain of its truth as of the truth of the other. And as regards God, if my mind were not pre-occupied with prejudices, and if my thought did not find itself on all hands diverted by the continual pressure of sensible things, there would be nothing which I could know more immediately and more easily than Him. For is there anything more manifest than that there is a God, that is to say, a Supreme Being, to whose essence alone existence pertains? [1]

CHARLES HARTSHORNE
The Logic of the Ontological Argument

The logical structure of the Anselmian argument, in its mature or "Second" form, may be partially formalized as follows:

'q' for '$(\exists x)Px$' There is a perfect being, or perfection exists
'N' for 'it is necessary (logically true) that'
'$\sim$' for 'it is not true that'
'v' for 'or'
'$p \rightarrow q$' for 'p strictly implies q' or '$N \sim (p\& \sim q)$'

(1) $q \rightarrow Nq$	"Anselm's Principle": perfection could not exist contingently
(2) $Nq \vee \sim Nq$	Excluded Middle
(3) $\sim Nq \rightarrow N \sim Nq$	Form of Becker's Postulate: modal status is always necessary
(4) $Nq \vee N \sim Nq$	Inference from (2, 3)
(5) $N \sim Nq \rightarrow N \sim q$	Inference from (1): the necessary falsity of the consequent implies that of the antecedent (Modal form of modus tollens)
(6) $Nq \vee N \sim q$	Inference from (4, 5)
(7) $\sim N \sim q$	Intuitive postulate (or conclusion from other theistic arguments): perfection is not impossible
(8) Nq	Inference from (6, 7)
(9) $Nq \rightarrow q$	Modal axiom
(10) q	Inference from (8, 9)

Those who challenge the Argument should decide which of these 10 items or inferential steps to question. Of course one may reject one or more of the

THE LOGIC OF THE ONTOLOGICAL ARGUMENT   From *The Logic of Perfection* by Charles Hartshorne. Reprinted by permission of The Open Court Publishing Co., La Salle, Illinois.

[1] 'In the idea of whom alone necessary or eternal existence is comprised.' French version.

assumptions (1, 3, 7); but reject is one thing, refute or show to be a mere sophistry is another. To me at least, the assumptions are intuitively convincing, provided perfection is properly construed, a condition Anselm did not fulfill. Moreover, no absurd consequence seems derivable from them by valid reasoning.

Concerning (1). Note that we do not take as initial assumption that $\sim q$ is directly contradictory, or that a nonexistent being must therefore be imperfect. Non-existent subjects cannot be said to have predicates, even inconsistent ones. Rather we reason that by virtue of (1) and certain principles of modal logic,

$$((\exists x)Px\ \&\ \sim N(\exists x)Px) \to\ \sim Px$$

and thus the antecedent is necessarily false, since it both asserts and by implication denies perfection, not of a supposed non-existent but of a supposed contingently-existent subject. Such a subject can very well have predicates, and indeed all ordinary subjects are precisely of this kind. Thus we make contingency and its negation, not existence or non-existence, the predicates with which the argument is concerned, in connection with the predicate perfection.

The postulate of logical possibility (7) is in my view the hardest to justify. One way of doing this is to employ one or more of the other theistic proofs, some forms of which demonstrate that perfection must be at least conceivable. . . .

VII.   IS EXISTENCE A PREDICATE?

Logicians, including some who would rather be seen in beggars' rags than in the company of the Ontological Argument, have held that existence is, after all, a sort of predicate, even of ordinary things.[1] But for our purpose this is unimportant, since the Argument does not depend upon the treatment of ordinary existence. The status which Anselm and Descartes (when, as in the quotations with which this essay begins, they are being most careful) deduce from "conceived as perfect" is not "conceived as existent," but rather "conceived as existentially non-contingent," i.e., conceived as that which "cannot be conceived not to exist." It is the existential modality which is taken as part of the meaning of the conceived property perfection. But whereas, in the ordinary or contingent case, neither "existent" nor "non-existent" can be inferred from the modal status, from "non-contingent" one may infer "necessarily existent unless impossible." (To exclude impossibility, the Argument as it stands does not suffice, except for one who grants that "the fool's" or non-theist's idea of God is self-consistent. But here the other theistic arguments may help.) . . .

---

[1] See H. Reichenbach, *Elements of Symbolic Logic* (New York: The Macmillan Company, 1947), pp. 333–334.

The pertinent question is not, is the fact of non-existence, but is the bare possibility of non-existence, a defect, and one which, being admitted, must infect the thing *"even if it exists"*? (Anselm's use of this phrase makes it quite clear that he saw the point, even though he did not hold onto it tightly enough.) To repeat, the pertinent question is not, is non-existence a defect, but is the contingency which is deducible from the mere possibility of non-existence a defect? To exist contingently is to exist precariously, or by chance (for to say, by cause or intention is to prompt the query, is the cause or intention necessary—achieving its result necessarily?—or non-necessary?). But to exist precariously or by chance is an imperfection, appropriate only to imperfect individuals. That "humanity" might not have been at all means that each of us exists, and has any particular excellence, thanks to accidental factors only. This total dependence on the way things happen to be, this radical "iffyness" or precariousness of our existence and nature (how easily it could all have been, or could yet be, indefinitely otherwise!) is a defect in principle from which various limitations follow, for instance, having a temporal beginning of existence. If, then, an individual of a kind which can only exist contingently is necessarily imperfect, no such individual could exemplify perfection. Perfection either could not possibly exist, or it exists necessarily. And the necessarily true is true. The existence of divine perfection is a question not of contingent fact, but of necessity, positive or negative. Logical analysis, not observation of nature, alone can settle it.

C. D. BROAD
A Critique of the Ontological Argument

II.   THE ONTOLOGICAL ARGUMENT

This argument presupposes the notion of degrees of 'reality' or 'perfection'. This notion is never clearly defined, but it seems to amount roughly to the following. A would be said to have 'more reality' or 'a higher degree of perfection' than B, if either of the two following conditions were fulfilled.

C. D. Broad (1887–1971) was for many years a professor of moral philosophy at Cambridge University. He is noted for his careful analyses of philosophical problems and for his contributions to psychical research. His major works include *The Mind and Its Place in Nature* and *Five Types of Ethical Theory*.

A CRITIQUE OF THE ONTOLOGICAL ARGUMENT   From *Religion, Philosophy and Psychical Research* by C. D. Broad. Reprinted by permission of Routledge & Kegan Paul Ltd.

(i) A has all the positive powers and qualities which B has and, in addition, it has some which B lacks. (When this condition is fulfilled we will say that A is '*extensively* superior to B'.) (ii) A is either extensively equal or extensively superior to B; some of the positive qualities or powers which are common to both are present in A with a higher degree of intensity than in B; and none of them are present in B with a higher degree of intensity than in A. (When this condition is fulfilled we will say that A is '*intensively* superior to B'.)

Now the first thing to notice is that these two criteria do not allow us, even in theory, to arrange everything in a single scale of perfection. Plainly the following cases are logically possible. (i) It might be that A has some powers or qualities which B lacks, and that B has some which A lacks. Cats, e.g., can climb trees, whilst dogs cannot; but dogs can track by scent, whilst cats cannot. In that case A is neither extensively superior, nor equal, nor inferior, to B. Now the criterion for intensive superiority presupposes extensive equality or superiority between the terms to be compared. Therefore, in the case supposed, there can be no comparison between A and B in respect of either extensive or intensive perfection. (ii) A might be extensively superior to B and intensively inferior. (iii) A and B might be extensively equal. But some of their common powers or qualities might be present in A with greater intensity than in B, whilst others of them might be present in B with greater intensity than in A. Let us suppose, e.g., that the minds of any two human beings are extensively equal. How are we to compare, in respect of intensive perfection, a mathematical genius of very slight musical capacity with a musical genius of very slight mathematical capacity?

These considerations are highly relevant to the Ontological Argument; for it uses the phrase 'most perfect being', and it presupposes that this is not meaningless verbiage like the phrase 'greatest integer'. In accounts of the Ontological Argument one finds the phrase 'most perfect being' translated in two different ways, one comparative and the other positive. The comparative interpretation makes it equivalent to the phrase 'a being such that nothing more perfect than it is logically possible'. The positive interpretation makes it equivalent to the phrase 'a being which has all positive powers and qualities to the highest possible degree'. Now, as Leibniz noted, it becomes very important at this point to consider whether all positive characteristics are mutually compatible, i.e. whether it is possible for them all to co-inhere in a common subject. Let us consider how this affects the two interpretations of the phrase 'most perfect being'.

(i) Evidently, unless all positive characteristics are mutually compatible, the positive interpretation becomes meaningless verbiage. Suppose, e.g., that it is impossible for an extended substance to be conscious and impossible for a conscious substance to be extended, then it is impossible that there should be a substance which has all the positive properties that there are. The phrase 'a being which has all positive powers and qualities' would be meaningless verbiage like the phrase 'a surface which is red and blue all over at the same time'.

(ii) How would the comparative interpretation of the phrase 'most perfect being' fare on the same supposition, viz. that not all positive properties are compatible with each other? Let us suppose, e.g., that there were just three positive properties X, Y, and Z; that any two of them are compatible with each other; but that the presence of any two excludes the remaining one. Then there would be *three* possible beings, viz. one which combines X and Y, one which combines Y and Z, and one which combines Z and X, *each* of which would be such that nothing extensively superior to it is logically possible. For the only kind of being which would be extensively superior to any of these would be one which had all three properties, X, Y, and Z; and, by hypothesis, this combination is logically impossible. Moreover, these three beings, each of which answers to the comparative definition of a 'most perfect being' so far as concerns extensive perfection, would be incomparable with each other in this respect. For, if you take any two of them, e.g., XY and YZ, each has a positive property which the other lacks. Now the Ontological Argument talks, not merely of 'most perfect beings', but of '*the* MOST PERFECT BEING'. It is now plain that, unless all positive properties be compatible with each other, this phrase is just meaningless verbiage like the phrase 'the greatest integer'.

(iii) Let us now make the opposite supposition, viz. that all positive properties are mutually compatible. Then it is easy to see that nothing could answer to the comparative definition of 'most perfect being' unless it answered to the positive definition of that phrase. For consider any substance which had some but not all of the positive properties. Since all positive properties are now assumed to be compatible with each other, it is logically possible that there should be a substance which should have all the properties which the one under consideration *has*, together with the remaining ones which it *lacks*. This would be extensively superior to the one under consideration, and therefore the latter would not answer to the comparative definition of a 'most perfect being'.

(iv) I have now shown (*a*) that the phrase 'the most perfect being' is meaningless unless all positive properties be compatible with each other; and (*b*) that, if they be all mutually compatible, nothing could answer to the comparative interpretation of the phrase unless it answered to the positive interpretation thereof. The next point to notice is that, even if all positive properties be mutually compatible, the phrase 'most perfect being' may still be meaningless verbiage. For we have now to attend to that part of the positive interpretation of the phrase which we have hitherto ignored, viz. that each positive property is to be present in the highest possible degree. Now this will be meaningless verbiage unless there is some *intrinsic* maximum or upper limit to the possible intensity of every positive property which is capable of degrees. With some magnitudes this condition is fulfilled. It is, e.g., logically impossible that any proper fraction should exceed the ratio 1/1; and again, on a certain definition of 'angle', it is logically impossible for any angle to exceed four right angles. But it seems quite clear that there are other positive properties, such as length or temperature or pain, to which there is no intrinsic maximum or upper limit of degree.

For these reasons it seems to me fairly certain that the Ontological Argument is wrecked before ever it leaves port. However, we will waive these objections and consider the argument itself. I will try to state it as plausibly as I can. It might be put as follows: 'Anything that lacked existence would lack a positive property which it might conceivably have had. Nothing which lacked a positive property which it might conceivably have had would be a most perfect being; for it is logically possible that there should be something superior to it, viz. a being which resembled it in all other respects but had the additional property of existence. Therefore no most perfect being would lack existence. Therefore all most perfect beings exist'.

Let us now consider this argument. It has two steps, viz. a syllogism followed by an immediate inference. There is nothing wrong with the syllogism in respect of its verbal form. It is verbally of the form 'Anything that lacked P would lack M. Nothing that lacked M would be S. Therefore no S would lack P.' This breaks none of the rules; it is in fact a slightly disguised form of the valid fourth-figure syllogism *Camenes*. The second step looks like a generally accepted form of immediate inference, viz. Obversion. But at this point there is a serious risk of a fallacy. The verbal form 'All S is P' is ambiguous. It may mean simply 'If anything were S it would be P', or, what is equivalent, 'Anything that was S would be P'. Interpreted in this way, it leaves the question whether anything *in fact is* S quite open. We will call this the 'conditional' interpretation. On the other hand, it is much more often taken to mean 'There are some S's and none of them lack P'. This may be called the 'instantial' interpretation. Now it is a general principle of logic that it is always illegitimate to draw an instantial conclusion from premisses which are wholly conditional. Let us now apply these principles to the second step of the argument.

The two premisses of the syllogism are purely conditional. Therefore the conclusion must be interpreted purely conditionally if the syllogism is to be valid. So the conclusion of the syllogism must be taken to be 'If anything were a most perfect being it would not lack existence'. Now all that can be legitimately inferred from this by obversion is the conditional proposition 'If anything were a most perfect being it would exist'. If you interpret the sentence 'All most perfect beings exist' in this way, the conclusion follows from the premisses but is completely trivial and useless. If, on the other hand, you interpret it instantially, i.e. take it to mean 'There are most perfect beings and none of them lack existence', there are two fatal criticisms to be made. (i) You are attempting to draw an instantial conclusion from purely conditional premisses and therefore are committing a logical fallacy. (ii) The sentence as a whole is pleonastic. It is idle to add 'none of them lack existence' to 'there are so-and-so's', whether the so-and-so's be most perfect beings or potatoes or dragons.

Let us now consider the syllogism itself. As I have said, it is correct in verbal form. Nevertheless, as I shall now proceed to show, it is radically vicious. Its defect is, not that its premisses are false, but that they are meaningless. They are sentences which seem, from their verbal form, to express propositions; but in fact they express nothing whatever. The argument presupposes that existence is a quality or power, like extension or consciousness or life; it assumes that there is sense in talking of a comparison between a non-existent term and an existent term; and it produces the impression that this is like comparing two existing terms, e.g., a corpse and a living organism, one of which lacks life and the other of which has it.

Now all this is nonsensical verbiage. It is intelligible to make a *categorical* comparison between two actual existents, e.g., Hitler and Stalin, in respect of their qualities and powers. It is intelligible to take a description of a merely possible existent, e.g., a creature with a horse's body and a man's head, and to make a *conditional* comparison with an actual existent. It is, e.g., intelligible to say 'If a centaur existed (or, if there were a centaur), it would be swifter than any actual man and more rational than any actual horse'. Lastly, it is intelligible to take descriptions of two merely possible existents, and to make a doubly conditional comparison. It is, e.g., intelligible to say 'If centaurs existed and unicorns existed (or, if there were centaurs and unicorns), the former would be superior (or inferior) to the latter in such and such respects'. Now the Ontological Argument professes to make a *categorical* comparison between a non-existent and an existent in respect of the presence or absence of *existence*. The objection is twofold. (i) No comparison can be made between a non-existent term and anything else except on the hypothesis that it exists. And (ii) on this hypothesis it is meaningless to compare it with anything in respect of the presence or absence of *existence*.

It is evident, then, that the Ontological Argument must be rejected. Probably most people feel that there is something wrong with it; but the important and interesting and not too easy task is to put one's finger on the precise points at which it goes wrong. When a fallacious argument has seemed cogent to many people of the highest intelligence, such as St. Anselm, Descartes, and Leibniz, it is desirable to supplement the refutation of it by an attempt to explain the causes of its plausibility. I believe that there are two causes, in the present case; and I will now proceed to exhibit them.

(i) The first and most important cause of the illusion is the fact that existential propositions and characterizing propositions are expressed by sentences which have the same grammatical form. Thus, e.g., existential propositions are expressed by such sentences as 'S exists' or 'S is real', while characterizing propositions are expressed by such grammatically similar sentences as 'S eats' or 'S is red'. This linguistic fact tempts people to assume uncritically that existential propositions are *logically* of the same form as characterizing propositions. This uncritical assumption makes the Ontological Argument seem plausible. But it is certainly false, as can easily be shown. The demonstration of this fact may be put as follows.

Let us begin with the two negative propositions *Cats do not bark* and *Dragons do not exist*. It is obvious that the first is about cats. But, if the second be true, it is certain that it cannot be about dragons; for there will be no such things as dragons for it to be about. The first might be expressed, on the conditional interpretation, by the sentence 'If there were any cats, none of them would bark'. On the instantial interpretation it might be expressed by the sentence 'There are cats, and none of them bark'. Suppose you try to express the negative existential proposition in the same way. On the first alternative it would be expressed by the sentence 'If there were any dragons, none of them would exist'. On the second alternative it would be expressed by the sentence 'There are dragons, and none of them exist'. Both these sentences are self-contradictory and meaningless. So, if you try to analyse negative existential propositions in the same way as negative characterizing propositions, you will find that they are all self-contradictory. But it is plain that *Dragons do not exist* is *not* self-contradictory. It is not only logically possible but is almost certainly true.

Now consider the two affirmative propositions *Cats scratch* and *Cats exist*. On the conditional interpretation the former would be expressed by the sentence 'If there were any cats, none of them would fail to scratch'. On the instantial interpretation it would be expressed by the sentence 'There are cats, and none of them fail to scratch'. Suppose you try to express the affirmative existential proposition in the same way. On the first alternative it would be expressed by the sentence 'If there were any cats, none of them would fail to exist'. On the second alternative it would be expressed by the sentence 'There are cats, and none of them fail to exist'. Now both these sentences are mere platitudes. So, if you try to analyse affirmative existential propositions in the same way as affirmative characterizing propositions, you will find that they are all platitudes. But it is plain that *Cats exist* is not a mere platitude. It is a substantial proposition which might very well be doubted by a person who had never seen a cat. So it is certain that existential propositions need a different kind of analysis.

The right analysis, as is now well known, is somewhat as follows. These propositions are not about cats or dragons, i.e. about *things* which have the cat-characteristics or the dragon-characteristics. They are about these *characteristics* themselves. What they assert is that these characteristics do apply to something or that they do not apply to anything, as the case may be. 'Cats exist' is equivalent to 'The defining characteristics of the word "cat" apply to something'. Again 'Dragons do not exist' is equivalent to 'The defining characteristics of the word "dragon" do not apply to anything'. Suppose, e.g., that a 'dragon' is defined as a reptile which flies and breathes fire. Then the statement that dragons do not exist is equivalent to the statement that nothing combines the three properties of being a reptile, of flying, and of breathing fire. Such statements are neither tautologies nor contradictions.

It only remains to apply this analysis to statements about the existence or non-existence of a most perfect being. To say that a most perfect being exists is equivalent to saying that something has all positive characteristics to the highest possible degree. For reasons which I have given, it seems likely that this is not only false but also self-contradictory and nonsensical. To say that a most perfect being does not exist is equivalent to saying that nothing has all positive characteristics to the highest possible degree. For the same reasons it seems likely that this is not only true but a truism.

(ii) I strongly suspect that another linguistic fact about the use of the word 'exist' has helped to make the Ontological Argument seem evident truth instead of meaningless nonsense. It is not uncommon to say, of a person or animal who has died, that he has 'ceased to exist'. Now in this case there is something visible and tangible left, viz. the corpse, which can be compared with the person or animal as he was before he died. Moreover, it is obvious that a living organism is more perfect than a corpse. This leads people to think of existence as a positive characteristic which can be added to or substracted from a thing, and whose presence makes a thing more perfect than it would have been without it. But, in the sense of 'existence' required for the Ontological Argument, a corpse exists as much as a living organism. So this linguistic fact does nothing to *justify* the speculations which it *encourages*.

THE COSMOLOGICAL ARGUMENT

ST. THOMAS AQUINAS
The Existence of God and the Beginning of the World

THIRD ARTICLE.   WHETHER GOD EXISTS?

We proceed thus to the Third Article:—

Objection 1. It seems that God does not exist; because if one of two contraries be infinite, the other would be altogether destroyed. But the name God means that He is infinite goodness. If, therefore, God existed, there would be no evil discoverable; but there is evil in the world. Therefore God does not exist.

Obj. 2. Further, it is superfluous to suppose that what can be accounted for by a few principles has been produced by many. But it seems that everything we see in the world can be accounted for by other principles, supposing God did not exist. For all natural things can be reduced to one principle, which is nature; and all voluntary things can be reduced to one principle, which is human reason, or will. Therefore there is no need to suppose God's existence.

On the contrary, It is said in the person of God: *I am Who am* (*Exod.* iii. 14).

THE EXISTENCE OF GOD AND THE BEGINNING OF THE WORLD   From *Summa Theologica*, Part I, Questions 2 and 46, in *Basic Writings of Saint Thomas Aquinas*, edited by Anton C. Pegis. Copyright 1945 by Random House, Inc. Reprinted by permission of the publisher and St. Dominic's Priory, London.

I answer that, The existence of God can be proved in five ways.

The first and more manifest way is the argument from motion. It is certain, and evident to our senses, that in the world some things are in motion. Now whatever is moved is moved by another, for nothing can be moved except it is in potentiality to that towards which it is moved; whereas a thing moves inasmuch as it is in act. For motion is nothing else than the reduction of something from potentiality to actuality. But nothing can be reduced from potentiality to actuality, except by something in a state of actuality. Thus that which is actually hot, as fire, makes wood, which is potentially hot, to be actually hot, and thereby moves and changes it. Now it is not possible that the same thing should be at once in actuality and potentiality in the same respect, but only in different respects. For what is actually hot cannot simultaneously be potentially hot; but it is simultaneously potentially cold. It is therefore impossible that in the same respect and in the same way a thing should be both mover and moved, *i.e.,* that it should move itself. Therefore, whatever is moved must be moved by another. If that by which it is moved be itself moved, then this also must needs be moved by another, and that by another again. But this cannot go on to infinity, because then there would be no first mover, and, consequently, no other mover, seeing that subsequent movers move only inasmuch as they are moved by the first mover; as the staff moves only because it is moved by the hand. Therefore it is necessary to arrive at a first mover, moved by no other; and this everyone understands to be God.

The second way is from the nature of efficient cause. In the world of sensible things we find there is an order of efficient causes. There is no case known (neither is it, indeed, possible) in which a thing is found to be the efficient cause of itself; for so it would be prior to itself, which is impossible. Now in efficient causes it is not possible to go on to infinity, because in all efficient causes following in order, the first is the cause of the intermediate cause, and the intermediate is the cause of the ultimate cause, whether the intermediate cause be several, or one only. Now to take away the cause is to take away the effect. Therefore, if there be no first cause among efficient causes, there will be no ultimate, nor any intermediate, cause. But if in efficient causes it is possible to go on to infinity, there will be no first efficient cause, neither will there be an ultimate effect, nor any intermediate efficient causes; all of which is plainly false. Therefore it is necessary to admit a first efficient cause, to which everyone gives the name of God.

The third way is taken from possibility and necessity, and runs thus. We find in nature things that are possible to be and not to be, since they are found to be generated, and to be corrupted, and consequently, it is possible for them to be and not to be. But it is impossible for these always to exist, for that which can not-be at some time is not. Therefore, if everything can not-be, then at one time there was nothing in existence. Now if this were true, even now there would be nothing in existence, because that which does not exist begins to exist only through something already existing. Therefore, if at one time nothing was in existence, it would have been impossible for anything to have begun to exist; and thus even now nothing would be in existence—which is absurd. Therefore, not all beings are merely possible, but there must exist something the existence of which is necessary. But every necessary thing either has its necessity caused by another, or not. Now it is impossible to go on to infinity in necessary things which have their necessity caused by another, as has been already proved in regard to efficient causes. Therefore we cannot but admit the existence of some being having of itself its own necessity, and not receiving it from another, but rather causing in others their necessity. This all men speak of as God.

The fourth way is taken from the gradation to be found in things. Among beings there are some more and some less good, true, noble, and the like. But *more* and *less* are predicated of different things according as they resemble in their different ways something which is the maximum, as a thing is said to be hotter according as it more nearly resembles that which is hottest; so that there is something which is truest, something best, something noblest, and, consequently, something which is most being, for those things that are greatest in truth are greatest in being, as it is written in *Metaph*. ii.[1] Now the maximum in any genus is the cause of all in that genus, as fire, which is the maximum of heat, is the cause of all hot things, as is said in the same book.[2] Therefore there must also be something which is to all beings the cause of their being, goodness, and every other perfection; and this we call God.

The fifth way is taken from the governance of the world. We see that things which lack knowledge, such as natural bodies, act for an end, and this is evident from their acting always, or nearly always, in the same way, so as to obtain the best result. Hence it is plain that they achieve their end, not fortuitously, but designedly. Now whatever lacks knowledge cannot move towards an end, unless it be directed by some being endowed with knowledge and intelligence; as the arrow is directed by the archer. Therefore some intelligent being exists by whom all natural things are directed to their end; and this being we call God.

Reply Obj. 1. As Augustine says: *Since God is the highest good, He would not allow any evil to exist in His works, unless His omnipotence and goodness were such as to bring good even out of evil.*[3] This is part of the infinite goodness of God, that He should allow evil to exist, and out of it produce good.

Reply Obj. 2. Since nature works for a determinate end under the direction of a higher agent, whatever is done by nature must be traced back to God as to its first cause. So likewise whatever is done voluntarily must be traced back to some higher cause other than human reason and will, since these can change and fail; for all things that are changeable and capable of defect must be traced back to an immovable and self-necessary first principle, as has been shown. . . .

[1] *Metaph.* Ia, 1 (993b 30).   [2] *Ibid.* (993b 25).   [3] *Enchir.*, XI (PL 40, 236).

SECOND ARTICLE.   WHETHER IT IS AN ARTICLE
OF FAITH THAT THE WORLD BEGAN?

We proceed thus to the Second Article:—

Objection 1. It would seem that it is not an article of faith but a demonstrable conclusion that the world began. For everything that is made has a beginning of its duration. But it can be proved demonstratively that God is the producing cause of the world; indeed this is asserted by the more approved philosophers. Therefore it can be demonstratively proved that the world began.[4]

Obj. 2. Further, if it is necessary to say that the world was made by God, it must have been made from nothing, or from something. But it was not made from something, or otherwise the matter of the world would have preceded the world; and against this are the arguments of Aristotle who held that the heavens are ungenerated. Therefore it must be said that the world was made from nothing; and thus it has being after non-being. Therefore it must have begun to be.[5]

Obj. 3. Further, *everything which works by intellect works from some principle,*[6] as is revealed in all works of human art. But God acts by intellect, and therefore His work has a principle, from which to begin. The world, therefore, which is His effect, did not always exist.

Obj. 4. Further, it appears manifestly that certain arts have developed, and certain parts of the world have begun to be inhabited at some fixed time. But this would not be the case if the world had always been in existence. Therefore it is manifest that the world did not always exist.

Obj. 5. Further, it is certain that nothing can be equal to God. But if the world had always been, it would be equal to God in duration. Therefore it is certain that the world did not always exist.[7]

Obj. 6. Further, if the world always was, the consequence is that an infinite number of days preceded this present day. But it is impossible to traverse what is infinite. Therefore we should never have arrived at this present day; which is manifestly false.[8]

Obj. 7. Further, if the world was eternal, generation also was eternal. Therefore one man was begotten of another in an infinite series. But the father is the efficient cause of the son.[9] Therefore in efficient causes there could be an infinite series; which however is disproved in *Metaph.* ii.[10]

---

[4] Alex. of Hales, *Summa Theol.,* I, no. 64 (I, 95); St. Bonaventure, *In II Sent.,* d. 1, pt. 1, a. 1, q. 3 (II, 22).

[5] Alex. of Hales, *Summa Theol.,* I, no. 64 (I, 93).

[6] Aristotle, *Phys.,* III, 4 (203a 31).   [7] Alex. of Hales, *Summa Theol.,* I, no. 64 (I, 93).

[8] Argument of Algazel in Averroes, *Destruct. Destruct.,* I (IX, 9rb; 10rb); and of the Mutakallimin, found in Maimonides, *Guide,* I, 74 (p. 138).

[9] Aristotle, *Phys.,* II, 3 (194b 30).

[10] Aristotle, *Metaph.,* Ia, 2 (994a 5)—For the use of this argument, cf. the Mutakallimin in Averroes, *Destruct. Destruct.,* I (IX, 12vab).

Obj. 8. Further, if the world and generation always were, there have been an infinite number of men. But man's soul is immortal. Therefore an infinite number of human souls would now actually exist, which is impossible. Therefore it can be known with certainty that the world began: it is not held by faith alone.[11]

On the contrary, The articles of faith cannot be proved demonstratively, because faith is of things *that appear not.* But that God is the Creator of the world in such a way that the world began to be is an article of faith; for we say, *I believe in one God,* etc.[12] And again, Gregory says that Moses prophesied of the past, saying, *In the beginning God created heaven and earth:* in which words the newness of the world is stated.[13] Therefore the newness of the world is known only by revelation, and hence it cannot be proved demonstratively.

I answer that, That the world did not always exist we hold by faith alone: it cannot be proved demonstratively; which is what was said above of the mystery of the Trinity.[14] The reason for this is that the newness of the world cannot be demonstrated from the world itself. For the principle of demonstration is the essence of a thing. Now everything, considered in its species, abstracts from *here* and *now*; which is why it is said that *universals are everywhere and always.*[15] Hence it cannot be demonstrated that man, or the heavens, or a stone did not always exist.

Likewise, neither can the newness of the world be demonstrated from the efficient cause, which acts by will. For the will of God cannot be investigated by reason, except as regards those things which God must will of necessity; and what He wills about creatures is not among these, as was said above.[16] But the divine will can be manifested by revelation, on which faith rests. Hence that the world began to exist is an object of faith, but not of demonstration or science. And it is useful to consider this, lest anyone, presuming to demonstrate what is of faith, should bring forward arguments that are not cogent; for this would give unbelievers the occasion to ridicule, thinking that on such grounds we believe the things that are of faith.

Reply Obj. 1. As Augustine says, the opinion of philosophers who asserted the eternity of the world was twofold.[17] For some said that the substance of the world was not from God, which is an intolerable error; and therefore it is refuted by proofs that are cogent. Some, however, said that the world was eternal, although made by God. *For they hold that the world has a beginning, not of time, but of creation; which means that, in a scarcely intelligible way, it was always made. And they try to explain their meaning thus: for just as, if a foot were always in the dust from eternity, there would always be a foot-*

---

[11] Argument of Algazel, found in Averroes, *Destruct. Destruct.,* I (IX, 12vab); and of the Mutakallimin in Maimonides, *Guide,* I, 73 (p. 132).

[12] *Symb. Nicaenum* (Denzinger, no. 54).   [13] *In Ezech.,* hom. 1, bk. 1 (PL 76, 786).

[14] Q. 32, a. 1.   [15] Aristotle, *Post. Anal.,* I, 31 (87b 33).

[16] Q. 19, a. 3.   [17] *De Civit. Dei,* XI, 4 (PL 41, 319).

print which without doubt was caused by him who trod on it, so also the world always was, because its Maker always existed.[18] To understand this we must consider that an efficient cause which acts by motion of necessity precedes its effect in time; for the effect exists only in the end of the action, and every agent must be the beginning of action. But if the action is instantaneous and not successive, it is not necessary for the maker to be prior in duration to the thing made, as appears in the case of illumination. Hence it is held that it does not follow necessarily that if God is the active cause of the world, He must be prior to the world in duration [19]; because creation, by which He produced the world, is not a successive change, as was said above.[20]

Reply Obj. 2. Those who would hold that the world was eternal, would say that the world was made by God from nothing; not that it was made after nothing, according to what we understand by the term *creation*, but that it was not made from anything. And so some of them even do not reject the term creation, as appears from Avicenna.[21]

Reply Obj. 3. This is the argument of Anaxagoras as reported in *Physics* iii.[22] But it does not lead to a necessary conclusion, except as to that intellect which deliberates in order to find out what should be done; which procedure is like movement. Such is the human intellect, but not the divine intellect.[23]

Reply Obj. 4. Those who hold the eternity of the world hold that some region was changed an infinite number of times from being uninhabitable to being inhabitable and *vice versa*.[24] They also hold that the arts, by reason of various corruptions and accidents, were subject to an infinite succession of discovery and decay.[25] Hence Aristotle says that it is absurd to base our opinion of the newness of the whole world on such particular changes.[26]

Reply Obj. 5. Even supposing that the world always was, it would not be equal to God in eternity, as Boethius says [27]; for the divine Being is all being simultaneously without succession, but with the world it is otherwise.

Reply Obj. 6. Passage is always understood as being from term to term. Whatever by-gone day we choose, from it to the present day there is a finite number of days which can be traversed. The objection is founded on the idea that, given two extremes, there is an infinite number of mean terms.

Reply Obj. 7. In efficient causes it is impossible to proceed to infinity *per se*. Thus, there cannot be an infinite number of causes that are *per se* required for a certain effect; for instance, that a stone be moved by a stick, the stick

---

[18] *Op. cit.,* X, 31 (PL 41, 311).
[19] Cf. Averroes, *Destruct. Destruct.,* I (IX, 13rb).
[20] Q. 45, a. 2, ad 3.
[21] *Metaph.,* IX, 4 (104va).
[22] Aristotle, *Phys.,* III, 4 (203a 31); VIII, 1 (250b 24).
[23] Q. 14, a. 7.
[24] Cf. St. Augustine, *De Civit. Dei,* XII, 10 (PL 41, 358); Aristotle, *Meteor.,* I, 14 (351a 19).
[25] Cf. St. Augustine, *De Civit. Dei,* XII, 10 (PL 41, 358); Averroes, *In Metaph.,* XII, comm. 50 (VIII, 156v).
[26] *Meteor.,* I, 14 (352a 26; 351b 8).
[27] *De Consol.,* V, prose 6 (PL 63, 859).

by the hand, and so on to infinity. But it is not impossible to proceed to infinity *accidentally* as regards efficient causes; for instance, if all the causes thus infinitely multiplied should have the order of only one cause, while their multiplication is accidental: *e.g.*, as an artificer acts by means of many hammers accidentally, because one after the other is broken. It is accidental, therefore, that one particular hammer should act after the action of another, and it is likewise accidental to this particular man as generator to be generated by another man; for he generates as a man, and not as the son of another man. For all men generating hold one grade in the order of efficient causes— viz., the grade of a particular generator. Hence it is not impossible for a man to be generated by man to infinity; but such a thing would be impossible if the generation of this man depended upon this man, and on an elementary body, and on the sun, and so on to infinity.

Reply Obj. 8. Those who hold the eternity of the world evade this argument in many ways. For some do not think it impossible for there to be an actual infinity of souls, as appears from the *Metaphysics* of Algazel, who says that such a thing is an accidental infinity.[28] But this was disproved above.[29] Some say that the soul is corrupted with the body.[30] And some say that of all souls only one remains.[31] But others, as Augustine says, asserted on this account a circulation of souls—viz., that souls separated from their bodies again return thither after a course of time.[32] A fuller consideration of this matter will be given later.[33] But be it noted that this argument considers only a particular case. Hence one might say that the world was eternal, or at least some creature, as an angel, but not man. But we are considering the question in general, namely, whether any creature can exist from eternity.

[28] *Metaph.*, I, tr. 1, div. 6 (p. 40).—Cf. Averroes, *Destruct. Destruct.*, I (IX, 12 vab).
[29] Q. 7, a. 4.
[30] Cf. Nemesius, *De Nat. Hom.*, II (PG 40, 537).
[31] Averroes, *Destruct. Destruct.*, I (IX, 10va).
[32] *Serm.* CCXLI, 4 (PL 38, 1135); *De Civit. Dei*, XII, 13 (PL 41, 361).—Cf. Plato *Timaeus* (p. 39a).
[33] Q. 75, a. 6; q. 76, a. 2; q. 118, a. 3.

JOHN DUNS SCOTUS
Proof of a First Efficient Cause

A. THE PRIMACY OF EFFICIENT CAUSALITY

Now the first of these nine conclusions is this: *Among beings which can produce an effect one is simply first,* in the sense that it neither can be produced by an efficient cause nor does it exercise its efficient causality in virtue of anything other than itself. Proof: Some being can be produced. Therefore, it is either produced by itself or by nothing or by something other than itself. Now it cannot be produced by nothing, for what is nothing causes nothing. Neither can it be produced by itself, for as Augustine points out in his work *De Trinitate,* BK. I, nothing ever makes itself or begets itself. Therefore it can only be produced by another. Now let this other be called A. If A is first in the way we have described, then I have what I seek to prove. But if it is not first, then it is some posterior agent—either because it can be produced by something else or because it is able to produce its effect only in virtue of something other than itself. To deny the negation is to assert the affirmation. Let us assume that this being is not first and call it B. Then we can argue of B as we did of A. And so we shall either go on *ad infinitum* so that each thing in reference to what precedes it in the series will be second; or we shall reach something that has nothing prior to it. However, an infinity in the ascending order is impossible; hence a primacy is necessary because whatever has nothing prior to itself is posterior to nothing prior, for a circle in causes is inadmissible.

Against this argument, it is objected, first, that the argument assumes an end in the series of causes; secondly, that it begins with contingent propositions and hence is not a demonstration. This second objection is argued in this way. The premises assume the existence of something that has been caused, and everything caused exists contingently. The first objection is confirmed from the admission of those who philosophise that an infinity is possible in an ascending order, as for instance, when they assume infinite generations, where no single one is first but each is second to some other. For they find nothing inconvenient about proceeding to infinity with productions of

John Duns Scotus (1266–1308) belonged to the Franciscan order and taught theology at Oxford University and at the University of Paris. Although his death left most of his important writings unfinished, he is considered a brilliant philosopher and theologian on the basis of such works as *Commentaries on the Sentences* (of Peter Lombard) and *Tractatus de primo principio* (a compendium of Scotus's natural theology).

PROOF OF A FIRST EFFICIENT CAUSE   From *Duns Scotus: Philosophical Writings,* edited and translated by Allan Wolter, published in 1962 by Thomas Nelson & Sons Ltd. Reprinted by their permission.

the same kind, where nothing is first and every member [of the series] is second [to some other member]. And still they assume no circle in causes.

To exclude this first objection, I say that the philosophers do not assume the possibility of an infinity in causes essentially ordered, but only in causes accidentally ordered, as is evident from Avicenna's *Metaphysics*, BK. VI, C. V, where he speaks of an infinity of individuals in a species. To understand better what we have in mind, one should know that some causes are essentially ordered and others accidentally ordered. Here it should be noted that it is one thing to speak of incidental causes (*causae per accidens*) as contrasted with those which are intended by their nature to produce a given effect (*causae per se*). It is quite another to speak of causes which are ordered to one another essentially or of themselves (*per se*) and those which are ordered only accidentally (*per accidens*). For in the first instance we have merely a comparison one-to-one, namely of the cause to that which is caused. A *per se* cause is one which causes a given effect by reason of its very nature and not by reason of something incidental to it. For instance, the subject is a *per se* cause of its proper attributes. Other such instances are "white dilating" or "a builder building". On the contrary, "Polycletus building" would be an incidental cause. In the second instance, two causes are compared with each other in so far as they are causes of the same thing.

Per se or essentially ordered causes differ from accidentally ordered causes in three respects. The first difference is that in essentially ordered causes, the second depends upon the first precisely in its act of causation. In accidentally ordered causes this is not the case, although the second may depend upon the first for its existence or in some other way. Thus a son depends upon his father for existence but is not dependent upon him in exercising his own causality, since he can act just as well whether his father be living or dead. The second difference is that in essentially ordered causes the causality is of another nature and order, inasmuch as the higher cause is more perfect. Such is not the case, however, with accidentally ordered causes. This second difference is a consequence of the first, since no cause in the exercise of its causality is essentially dependent upon a cause of the same nature as itself, for to produce anything one cause of a given kind suffices. The third difference is that all *per se* and essentially ordered causes are simultaneously required to cause the effect, for otherwise some causality essential to the effect would be wanting. In accidentally ordered causes this is not so, because there is no need of simultaneity in causing inasmuch as each possesses independently of the others the perfection of causality with regard to its own effect. For it is enough that one cause after the other exercises causality successively.

From all this we propose to show that an infinity of essentially ordered causes is impossible; secondly, that an infinity of accidentally ordered causes is also impossible unless we admit a terminus in an essentially ordered series; therefore an infinity in essentially ordered causes is impossible in any case; thirdly, even if we deny the existence of an essential order, an infinity of causes is still impossible. Consequently, in every instance, of necessity some first being able to cause exists. For the sake of brevity, let us call the first of these three assumptions A, the second B and the third C.

Proof of the first of these propositions, A (namely that an infinity of essentially ordered causes is impossible): I prove this first, because in essentially ordered causes where our opponent assumes an infinity, the second of the series depends upon the first. This is a consequence of the first difference between essentially and accidentally ordered causes. Now if these causes were infinite so that not only would each single cause be posterior to something but every other cause which precedes it would be dependent in turn upon the cause that goes before it, then whole series of effects would be dependent upon some prior cause. Now the latter cannot be a cause that is part of the series, for then it would be its own cause. The series as a whole, then, is dependent on something which does not pertain to the group that is caused, and this I call the first efficient cause. Even if the group of beings caused were infinite, they would still depend upon something outside the group.

Then, too, if an infinite number of essentially ordered causes concurred to produce some effect, it would follow that an infinite number would simultaneously cause this effect, for it follows from the third difference that essentially ordered causes must exist simultaneously. Now no philosopher assumes this.

Then, thirdly, to be prior, a thing must be nearer to the beginning. Consequently, where there is no beginning, nothing can be essentially prior to anything else.

Then, fourthly; by reason of the second difference, the higher cause is more perfect in its causality, therefore what is infinitely higher is infinitely more perfect, and hence of infinite perfection. Now nothing infinitely perfect can cause something only in virtue of another, because everything of this kind is imperfect in its causality since it depends on another in order to cause its effect.

Then, fifthly, inasmuch as to be able to produce something does not imply any imperfection, it follows that this ability can exist in something without imperfection, because that which implies no imperfection can be asserted of beings without imperfection. But if every cause depends upon some prior cause, then efficiency is never found without imperfection. Hence an independent power to produce something can exist in some nature, and this nature is *simply* first. Therefore, such an efficient power is possible, and this suffices, for later we shall prove that if such a first efficient cause is possible, then it exists in reality. And so A becomes evident from these five arguments.

Now B (namely, that an infinity of accidentally ordered causes is impossible unless we admit that the essentially ordered series has an end) is proved in this way. If we assume an infinity of accidentally ordered causes, it is clear that these causes do not exist simultaneously but only successively, one after the other, so that what follows flows in some way from what precedes. Still the succeeding cause does not depend upon the preceding for the exercise of its causality, for it is equally effective whether the preceding cause exists or not. A son in turn may beget a child just as well whether his father be dead or alive. But an infinite succession of such causes is impossible unless it exists in virtue of some nature of infinite duration from which the whole succession and every part thereof depends. For no change of form is perpetuated save in virtue of something permanent which is not a part of the succession. And the reason for this is that everything of this succession which is in flux, is of the same nature and no part thereof can be coexistent with the entire series for the simple reason that it would no longer be a part of the latter. Something essentially prior to the series then exists, for everything that is part of the succession depends upon it, and this dependence is of a different order from that by which it depends upon the immediately preceding cause where the latter is a part of the succession. Therefore, whatever depends upon an accidentally ordered cause depends more essentially upon an essentially ordered cause. Indeed, to deny the essential order is to deny the accidental order also, since accidents do not have any order save in virtue of what is fixed and permanent. Consequently, neither will an infinite multitude exist. B, then, is evident.

Proposition C (namely that if an essential order is denied, an infinity is still impossible), also is proved. Proof: From the first reason adduced here, viz. that nothing can come from nothing, it follows that some nature is capable of causing effectively. Now, if an essential order of agents be denied, then this nature capable of causing does not cause in virtue of some other cause, and even if we assume that in one individual it is caused, nevertheless in some other it will not be caused, and this is what we propose to prove to be true of this nature. For if we assume that in every individual this nature is caused, then a contradiction follows immediately if we deny the existence of an essential order, since no nature that is caused can be assumed to exist in each individual in such a way that it is included in an accidental order of causes without being at the same time essentially ordered to some other nature. This follows from proposition B.

Then we come to the second objection cited above, namely that when I argue: "Some nature is capable of producing an effect, therefore something is an efficient cause", the argument is not a demonstration, since it proceeds from contingent propositions. I reply that I could indeed argue that some nature is produced because some subject undergoes a change and therefore the term of the change comes into existence in the subject, and consequently this term or the composite [i.e. the subject and term] are produced or effected. Hence by the nature of the correlatives, some efficient cause exists. Formulated in this fashion, this first argument would be based upon a contingent but manifest proposition. However, to prove our conclusion the argument can be reformulated in such a way that it proceeds from necessary premises. Thus it is true that some nature is able to be produced, therefore something is able to produce an effect. The antecedent is proved from the fact that something can be changed, for something is possible ("possible" being defined as contrary to "necessary"). In this case, the proof for the first conclusion proceeds from what the thing is or from its possible existence, but not from its actual existence. The actual existence of this being which up to now we have shown to be merely possible, however, will be established in the third conclusion.

The *second conclusion* about the first possible efficient cause is this. *Among those things which can produce an effect that which is simply first is itself incapable of being caused.* Proof: Such a being cannot be produced and is independently able to produce an effect. This was proved above, for if such a being could cause only in virtue of something else or if it could be produced, then either a process *ad infinitum* or a circle in causes would result, or else the series would terminate in some being which cannot be produced and yet independently is able to produce an effect. This being I call "first", and from what you grant, it is clear that anything other than this is not first. Therefore, the further conclusion follows that if such a being cannot be produced, it has no causes whatsoever, for it cannot be the result of a final, material or formal cause. Proof of the first consequence, viz. that if such a being cannot be produced, neither can it have any final cause. A final cause does not cause at all unless in a metaphorical sense it moves the efficient cause to produce the effect. Only in this way does the entity of what exists for the sake of an end depend on the end as prior. Nothing, however, is a *per se* cause unless the thing caused depends upon it essentially as upon something prior. Now the other two consequences are proved simultaneously. If something cannot be produced, then it can be the result neither of a material nor of a formal cause. The reason is this. If something has no extrinsic cause, neither does it have an intrinsic cause, for while to be an extrinsic cause does not imply imperfection but perfection, to be an intrinsic cause necessarily includes some imperfection since the intrinsic cause is a part of the thing it causes. For this reason, the very notion of an extrinsic cause has a natural priority over that of intrinsic cause; to deny what is prior is to deny also what is posterior.

Another way of proving these same consequences is this. Intrinsic causes are caused by extrinsic causes either in their very being or in so far as they cause the composite, or in both of these ways, for the intrinsic causes of themselves and without the intervention of some agent cannot constitute the composite. This suffices to make the second conclusion evident.

The *third conclusion* about this being capable of exercising efficient causality is this. *Such a being actually exists and some nature actually existing is capable of such causality.* Proof: Anything to whose nature it is repugnant to receive existence from something else, exists of itself if it is able to exist at all. To receive existence from something else, however, is repugnant to the very notion of a being which is first in the order of efficiency, as is clear from the second conclusion. That it can exist, is also clear from the first conclusion [namely A], where the fifth argument, which seems to be less conclusive than the others, establishes this much at least. However, the other proofs of proposition A can also be used to establish the existence of this being as proposed by this third conclusion, but in this case they are based on contingent though manifest propositions. If A, however, is understood of the nature, the quiddity and the possibility, then the conclusions proceed from necessary premises. From all this it follows that an efficient cause which is first in the unqualified sense of the term can exist of itself. Consequently, it does exist of itself, for what does not actually exist of itself, is incapable of existing of itself. Otherwise a non-existent being would cause something to exist; but this is impossible, even apart from the fact that in such a case the thing would be its own cause and hence could not be entirely uncaused.

Another way to establish this last conclusion, viz. the existence of this first efficient cause, would be to argue from the impropriety of a universe that would lack the highest possible degree of being.

A kind of corollary contained, as it were, in these three conclusions concerning the first being able to exercise efficient causality, is the following. Not only is such a cause prior to all the others, but it would be contradictory to say that another is prior to it. And, in so far as such a cause is first, it exists. This is proved in the same way as the preceding. The very notion of such a being implies its inability to be caused (which is proved from the second conclusion). Therefore, if it can exist, owing to the fact that to be is not contradictory to it (as the first conclusion proves), then it follows that it can exist of itself, and consequently that it does exist of itself.

PATTERSON BROWN
Infinite Causal Regression

III

It is evident that we cannot hope to understand the argument against infinite causal regresses without first getting straight on the supposedly critical contrast between causal series ordered *per se* and those ordered *per accidens*. So let us examine the previously quoted explanation by Scotus that "in essentially ordered series, the second [that is, the posterior] depends upon the

Patterson Brown (1938–   ) has taught philosophy at the State University of New York at Binghamton. He is the author of several papers in the areas of philosophy of religion and medieval philosophy.

INFINITE CAUSAL REGRESSION   Sections III, V from *The Philosophical Review*, Volume LXXV, No. 4, October 1966. Reprinted by permission of *The Philosophical Review* and the author.

first [the prior] precisely in its act of causation." I assume that the entire argument would be laid bare if we fully understood this criterion and its application to the two paradigm cases, propulsion and genealogy.

The criterion delineated by Scotus seems straightforward enough; it is simply that each member of an essential series (except of course the first and last *if* there be such) is causally dependent upon its predecessor for its own causal efficacy regarding its successor. The members are each intermediate (secondary, instrumental, dependent) in the sense discussed above. In an accidental series, however, each member is not dependent upon its predecessor for its own causal efficacy—though it may be dependent in some other regard. Thus a causal series is *per se* ordered if and only if it is throughout of the form: w's being F causes x to be G, x's being G causes y to be H, y's being H causes z to be I, . . . (here $F\hat{x}$, $G\hat{x}$, $H\hat{x}$, and $I\hat{x}$ may be identical or differing functions). A causal series is ordered *per accidens*, however, if and only if it is throughout of the form: w's being F causes x to be G, x's being H causes y to be I, y's being J causes z to be K, . . . (here $G\hat{x} \neq H\hat{x}$ and $I\hat{x} \neq J\hat{x}$, but otherwise $F\hat{x}$, $G\hat{x}$, $H\hat{x}$, $I\hat{x}$, $J\hat{x}$, and $K\hat{x}$ may be identical or differing functions). In other words, the two functions of each individual variable must be identical in the essential case, but must differ in the accidental case.

Consider the paradigm case where one's hand pushes a stick which in turn pushes a stone. This causal series is *per se* because it is the same function of the stick (namely, its locomotion) which both is caused by the movement of the hand and causes the movement of the stone. Again, a series where the fire heats the pot and the pot in turn heats the stew, causing it to boil, is also essentially ordered; for the warmth of the pot is both caused by the warmth of the fire and cause of the warmth of the stew, while the warmth of the stew is both caused by the warmth of the pot and cause of the stew's boiling.

On the other hand, consider the paradigm case of Abraham's begetting Isaac, who in turn begets Jacob. Here the series is accidentally ordered because that function of Isaac (namely, his copulating) which causes Jacob's birth is not caused by Abraham's copulation; the latter results in Isaac's *birth*, whereas it is Isaac's *copulation* which causes Jacob to be born. Genealogical series like the following are thus *per accidens*: Abraham's copulation causes Isaac's birth, Isaac's copulation causes Jacob's birth, Jacob's copulation causes Joseph's birth. Each member has one attribute qua effect (being born) and quite another attribute qua cause (copulating).

Now Aristotle and his followers held as a critically important thesis that the constituent relations in an essentially ordered series are *transitive*. This is, I suggest, the point of Aristotle's statement that "everything that is moved is moved by the movement that is further back in the series as well as by that which immediately moves it." [1] If, to use the standard example, the

---

[1] *Physics*, 257a10–12. All quotations from Aristotle will be from R. McKeon (ed.), *The Basic Works of Aristotle* (New York, 1941).

hand propels the stick and the stick in turn propels the stone, then the hand propels the stone by means of the stick. Again, if the fire heats the pot, which heats the stew, which causes the stew to boil, then the fire causes the stew to boil. St. Thomas makes this point in the following passage:

> If that which was given as moved locally is moved by the nearest mover which is increased, and that again is moved by something which is altered, and that again is moved by something which is moved in place, then that which is moved with respect to place will be moved more by the first thing which is moved with respect to place than by the second thing which is altered or by the third thing which is increased.[2]

Here we have an undisguised claim that "x moves y" is a transitive causal relation. . . .

V

I want now to suggest a reading of the argument against infinite causal regresses on the basis of our earlier understanding of the contrast between *per se* and *per accidens* ordering of causal series. I think that the substance of the proof was as follows, again using moving causation as our paradigmatic example. Parallel arguments could obviously be constructed regarding Aristotle's other types of cause, and also regarding Avicennian efficient causes.

The Aristotelian scientific model stipulates that all motions are to be given causal explanations, and that such explanations are to be of the form "x moves y." (Compare the analogous Newtonian stipulation that all accelerations are to be explained in terms of equations of the form "$F = ma$.") Suppose then that we observe something, a, to be moving, and we wish to explain this phenomenon by means of the Aristotelian physics. The explanation must be of the form "x moves a." Suppose further that a is moved by b, b is in turn moved by c, c in turn by d, and so on indefinitely. The issue is whether this series can continue ad infinitum. We now ask, what moves a? Well, it has already been stated that b moves a; so it may be suggested that "b moves a" is the desired explanation of a's motion, the desired value of "x moves a." But this would be an inadequate account of the matter. For b is itself being moved by c, which—owing to the transitivity of "x moves y"—thus yields the implication that a is moved by c, with b serving merely as an instrument or intermediate. But in turn d moves c; and so d moves a. But e moves d; therefore e moves a. And so on indefinitely. Now, so long as this series continues, we have not found the real mover of a; that is to say, we have not found the *explaining* value of the function "x moves a." The regress is thus a vicious one, in that the required explanation of a's motion is deferred so long as the series continues. With regard to any x which moves a, if there is a y such that y moves x, then we must infer that y moves a. And if for any x such that

2 *On Physics*, Bk. VIII, lec. 9, #1047.

x moves *a* there were a *y* such that *y* moved *x* (and therefore moved *a* as well), then no explanation of *a*'s motion would be possible with the Aristotelian model. There would of course be any number of *true* statements of the form "*x* moves *a*"—namely, "*b* moves *a*," "*c* moves *a*," "*d* moves *a*," and so forth. But none of these is to count as the Aristotelian *explanation* of *a*'s motion. Nor, it must be noted, is any such explanation given merely by asserting that there is an infinite regress of movers of *a*. "An infinite regress of movers move *a*" is not a possible value of the function "*x* moves *a*," for the variable in the latter ranges over individuals, not classes (and a fortiori not over series, finite or infinite). An uncaused motion, however, is no motion at all; in other words, an inexplicable motion would be an unintelligible motion. There must be, therefore, an unmoved mover of *a*.

The foregoing case is to be contrasted with giving an explanation of, for example, Jacob's birth. Such an account is to be of the form "*x* begat Jacob." The complete and unique explanation of that form is that Isaac begat Jacob. We do not get a new value for the function on the grounds that Abraham in turn begat Isaac, since this does not imply that Abraham begat Jacob; on the contrary, it implies that he did not do so. So a full explanation of Jacob's birth can be given regardless of whether his family tree extends back to infinity. An explanation of Isaac's copulation is still required, of course; but that will center on his actions with Rebecca, rather than on his having been sired by Abraham. (The Aristotelians would contend that Isaac's copulation, being a locomotion, must be the termination of an essentially ordered *moving* series. This means that there indeed is a *per se* series which terminates in Jacob's birth, but it does not ascend through Isaac, Abraham, Terah, and so on; rather, it goes back through Isaac's copulation and thence instantaneously back through a series of contiguous movers reaching up to the celestial spheres. Aquinas writes that "whatever generates here below, moves to the production of the species as the instrument of a heavenly body. Thus the Philosopher says that 'man and the sun generate man.' " [3] God is then in turn causally responsible for the locomotion of the heavenly spheres—though not of course by himself changing.[4] In this way each man is supposed to be efficiently caused by God via an essentially ordered series of movers, regardless of whether he has an infinite regress of ancestors in an accidentally ordered genealogy series.)

---

[3] *ST*, I, Q. 115, Art. 3, Reply Obj. 2; the quotation from Aristotle is from *Physics*, 194b13. See also *ST*, I, Q. 118, Art. 1, Reply Obj. 3, where Aquinas asserts that the act of begetting is "concurrent with the power of a heavenly body."

[4] Aristotle held that God is merely the final cause of the celestial rotations; cf. *Metaphysics*, 1072a19 ff. The medievals tended to abuse Avicenna's distinction (n. 2, *supra*) by saying that God is somehow the efficient cause of that locomotion, though perhaps with the intelligences (angels) as intermediates; see E. Gilson, *The Elements of Christian Philosophy* (New York, 1963), pp. 71–74.

DAVID HUME
Some Objections to the Cosmological Argument

But if so many difficulties attend the argument *a posteriori*, said Demea, had we not better adhere to that simple and sublime argument *a priori*, which, by offering to us infallible demonstration, cuts off at once all doubt and difficulty? By this argument, too, we may prove the INFINITY of the Divine attributes, which, I am afraid, can never be ascertained with certainty from any other topic. For how can an effect, which either is finite, or, for aught we know, may be so; how can such an effect, I say, prove an infinite cause? The unity too of the Divine Nature, it is very difficult, if not absolutely impossible, to deduce merely from contemplating the works of nature; nor will the uniformity alone of the plan, even were it allowed, give us any assurance of that attribute. Whereas the argument *a priori* . . . . .

You seem to reason, Demea, interposed Cleanthes, as if those advantages and conveniences in the abstract argument were full proofs of its solidity. But it is first proper, in my opinion, to determine what argument of this nature you choose to insist on; and we shall afterwards, from itself, better than from its *useful* consequences, endeavour to determine what value we ought to put upon it.

The argument, replied Demea, which I would insist on, is the common one. Whatever exists must have a cause or reason of its existence; it being absolutely impossible for any thing to produce itself, or be the cause of its own existence. In mounting up, therefore, from effects to causes, we must either go on in tracing an infinite succession, without any ultimate cause at all; or must at last have recourse to some ultimate cause, that is *necessarily* existent: Now, that the first supposition is absurd, may be thus proved. In the infinite chain or succession of causes and effects, each single effect is determined to exist by the power and efficacy of that cause which immediately preceded; but the whole eternal chain or succession, taken together, is not determined or caused by any thing; and yet it is evident that it requires a cause or reason, as much as any particular object which begins to exist in time. The question is still reasonable, why this particular succession of causes existed from eternity, and not any other succession, or no succession at all. If there be no necessarily existent being, any supposition which can be formed is equally

David Hume (1711–1776), born in Scotland, was a philosopher and an historian, and also served for several years as a member of the British diplomatic corps. Along with such philosophers as Locke and Berkeley, he is considered one of the major exponents of Empiricism. His philosophical works include *Treatise of Human Nature, Enquiry Concerning Human Understanding,* and *Enquiry Concerning the Principles of Morals.*

SOME OBJECTIONS TO THE COSMOLOGICAL ARGUMENT   From *Dialogues Concerning Natural Religion,* Part IX. *The Philosophical Works of David Hume,* Volume II. Edinburgh, Adam Black and William Tait; and Charles Tait, 1876.

possible; nor is there any more absurdity in Nothing's having existed from eternity, than there is in that succession of causes which constitutes the universe. What was it, then, which determined Something to exist rather than Nothing, and bestowed being on a particular possibility, exclusive of the rest? *External causes*, there are supposed to be none. *Chance* is a word without a meaning. Was it *Nothing?* But that can never produce any thing. We must, therefore, have recourse to a necessarily existent Being, who carries the REASON of his existence in himself, and who cannot be supposed not to exist, without an express contradiction. There is, consequently, such a Being; that is, there is a Deity.

I shall not leave it to Philo, said Cleanthes, though I know that the starting objections is his chief delight, to point out the weakness of this metaphysical reasoning. It seems to me so obviously ill-grounded, and at the same time of so little consequence to the cause of true piety and religion, that I shall myself venture to show the fallacy of it.

I shall begin with observing, that there is an evident absurdity in pretending to demonstrate a matter of fact, or to prove it by any arguments *a priori*. Nothing is demonstrable, unless the contrary implies a contradiction. Nothing, that is distinctly conceivable, implies a contradiction. Whatever we conceive as existent, we can also conceive as non-existent. There is no being, therefore, whose non-existence implies a contradiction. Consequently there is no being, whose existence is demonstrable. I propose this argument as entirely decisive, and am willing to rest the whole controversy upon it.

It is pretended that the Deity is a necessarily existent being; and this necessity of his existence is attempted to be explained by asserting, that if we knew his whole essence or nature, we should perceive it to be as impossible for him not to exist, as for twice two not to be four. But it is evident that this can never happen, while our faculties remain the same as at present. It will still be possible for us, at any time, to conceive the non-existence of what we formerly conceived to exist; nor can the mind ever lie under a necessity of supposing any object to remain always in being; in the same manner as we lie under a necessity of always conceiving twice two to be four. The words, therefore, *necessary existence*, have no meaning; or, which is the same thing, none that is consistent.

But farther, why may not the material universe be the necessarily existent Being, according to this pretended explication of necessity? We dare not affirm that we know all the qualities of matter; and for aught we can determine, it may contain some qualities, which, were they known, would make its non-existence appear as great a contradiction as that twice two is five. I find only one argument employed to prove, that the material world is not the necessarily existent Being; and this argument is derived from the contingency both of the matter and the form of the world. 'Any particle of matter,' it is said,[1] 'may be *conceived* to be annihilated; and any form may be *conceived* to be altered. Such an annihilation or alteration, therefore, is not impossible.' But it seems a great partiality not to perceive, that the same argument extends equally to the Deity, so far as we have any conception of him; and that the mind can at least imagine him to be non-existent, or his attributes to be altered. It must be some unknown, inconceivable qualities, which can make his non-existence appear impossible, or his attributes un-alterable: And no reason can be assigned, why these qualities may not belong to matter. As they are altogether unknown and inconceivable, they can never be proved incompatible with it.

Add to this, that in tracing an eternal succession of objects, it seems absurd to inquire for a general cause or first author. How can any thing, that exists from eternity, have a cause, since that relation implies a priority in time, and a beginning of existence?

In such a chain, too, or succession of objects, each part is caused by that which preceded it, and causes that which succeeds it. Where then is the difficulty? But the WHOLE, you say, wants a cause. I answer, that the uniting of these parts into a whole, like the uniting of several distinct countries into one kingdom, or several distinct members into one body, is performed merely by an arbitrary act of the mind, and has no influence on the nature of things. Did I show you the particular causes of each individual in a collection of twenty particles of matter, I should think it very unreasonable, should you afterwards ask me, what was the cause of the whole twenty. This is sufficiently explained in explaining the cause of the parts.

Though the reasonings which you have urged, Cleanthes, may well excuse me, said Philo, from starting any farther difficulties, yet I cannot forbear insisting still upon another topic. It is observed by arithmeticians, that the products of 9 compose always either 9, or some lesser product of 9, if you add together all the characters of which any of the former products is composed. Thus, of 18, 27, 36, which are products of 9, you make 9 by adding 1 to 8, 2 to 7, 3 to 6. Thus, 369 is a product also of 9; and if you add 3, 6, and 9, you make 18, a lesser product of 9.[2] To a superficial observer, so wonderful a regularity may be admired as the effect either of chance or design: but a skilful algebraist immediately concludes it to be the work of necessity, and demonstrates, that it must for ever result from the nature of these numbers. Is it not probable, I ask, that the whole economy of the universe is conducted by a like necessity, though no human algebra can furnish a key which solves the difficulty? And instead of admiring the order of natural beings, may it not happen, that, could we penetrate into the intimate nature of bodies, we should clearly see why it was absolutely impossible they could ever admit of any other disposition? So dangerous is it to introduce this idea of necessity

---

[1] Dr Clarke.   [2] Republique des Lettres, Aout 1685.

into the present question! and so naturally does it afford an inference directly opposite to the religious hypothesis!

But dropping all these abstractions, continued Philo, and confining ourselves to more familiar topics, I shall venture to add an observation, that the argument *a priori* has seldom been found very convincing, except to people of a metaphysical head, who have accustomed themselves to abstract reasoning, and who, finding from mathematics, that the understanding frequently leads to truth through obscurity, and, contrary to first appearances, have transferred the same habit of thinking to subjects where it ought not to have place. Other people, even of good sense and the best inclined to religion, feel always some deficiency in such arguments, though they are not perhaps able to explain distinctly where it lies; a certain proof that men ever did, and ever will derive their religion from other sources than from this species of reasoning.

PAUL EDWARDS
The Cosmological Argument

I

The so-called 'cosmological proof' is one of the oldest and most popular arguments for the existence of God. It was forcibly criticized by Hume,[1] Kant,[2] and Mill,[3] but it would be inaccurate to consider the argument dead or even moribund. Catholic philosophers, with hardly any exception, appear to believe that it is as solid and conclusive as ever. Thus Father Copleston confidently championed it in his Third Programme debate with Bertrand Russell;[4] and in America, where Catholic writers are more sanguine, we are told by a Jesuit professor of physics that 'the existence of an intelligent being as the First Cause of the universe can be established by *rational scientific inference*'.[5]

Paul Edwards (1923–), a professor of philosophy at Brooklyn College, is an exponent of the analytic method in philosophy. He is the editor of the *Encyclopedia of Philosophy* and the author of *The Logic of Moral Discourse*.

THE COSMOLOGICAL ARGUMENT   From *The Rationalist Annual*, 1959. Reprinted by permission of The Pemberton Publishing Co. Ltd. and the author.

[1] *Dialogues Concerning Natural Religion*, Part IX.
[2] *The Critique of Pure Reason*, Transcendental Dialectic, Book II, Ch III.
[3] 'Theism', Part I, in *Three Essays on Religion*.
[4] Reprinted in the British edition of Russell's *Why I Am Not a Christian*.
[5] J. S. O'Connor, 'A Scientific Approach to Religion', *The Scientific Monthly*, 1940, p 369; my italics.

> I am absolutely convinced [the same writer continues] that any one who would give the same consideration to that proof (the cosmological argument), as outlined for example in William Brosnan's *God and Reason*, as he would give to a line of argumentation found in the *Physical Review* or the *Proceedings of the Royal Society* would be forced to admit that the cogency of this argument for the existence of God far outstrips that which is found in the reasoning which Chadwick uses to prove the existence of the neutron, which today is accepted as certain as any conclusion in the physical sciences.[6]

Mild theists like the late Professor Dawes Hicks[7] and Dr Ewing,[8] who concede many of Hume's and Kant's criticisms, nevertheless contend that the argument possesses a certain core of truth. In popular discussions it also crops up again and again—for example, when believers address atheists with such questions as 'You tell me where the universe came from!' Even philosophers who reject the cosmological proof sometimes embody certain of its confusions in the formulation of their own position. In the light of all this, it may be worth while to undertake a fresh examination of the argument with special attention to the fallacies that were not emphasized by the older critics.

II

The cosmological proof has taken a number of forms, the most important of which are known as the 'causal argument' and 'the argument from contingency', respectively. In some writers, in Samuel Clarke for example, they are combined, but it is best to keep them apart as far as possible. The causal argument is the second of the 'five ways' of Aquinas and roughly proceeds as follows: we find that the things around us come into being as the result of the activity of other things. These causes are themselves the result of the activity of other things. But such a causal series cannot 'go back to infinity'. Hence there must be a first member, a member which is not itself caused by any preceding member—an uncaused or 'first' cause.

It has frequently been pointed out that even if this argument were sound it would not establish the existence of *God*. It would not show that the first cause is all-powerful or all-good or that it is in any sense personal. Somebody believing in the eternity of atoms, or of matter generally, could quite consistently accept the conclusion. Defenders of the causal argument usually concede this and insist that the argument is not in itself meant to prove the existence of God. Supplementary arguments are required to show that the first cause must have the attributes assigned to the deity. They claim, however, that the argument, if valid, would at least be an important step towards a complete proof of the existence of God.

---

[6] *Ibid.* pp 369–70.   [7] *The Philosophical Bases of Theism*, Lecture V.
[8] *The Fundamental Questions of Philosophy*, Ch XI.

Does the argument succeed in proving so much as a first cause? This will depend mainly on the soundness of the premise that an infinite series of causes is impossible. Aquinas supports this premise by maintaining that the opposite belief involves a plain absurdity. To suppose that there is an infinite series of causes logically implies that nothing exists now; but we know that plenty of things do exist now; and hence any theory which implies that nothing exists now must be wrong. Let us take some causal series and refer to its members by the letters of the alphabet:

$$A \to B \ldots W \to X \to Y \to Z$$

Z stands here for something presently existing, e.g. Margaret Truman. Y represents the cause or part of the cause of Z, say Harry Truman. X designates the cause or part of the cause of Y, say Harry Truman's father, etc. Now, Aquinas reasons, whenever we take away the cause, we also take away the effect: if Harry Truman had never lived, Margaret Truman would never have been born. If Harry Truman's father had never lived, Harry Truman and Margaret Truman would never have been born. If A had never existed, none of the subsequent members of the series would have come into existence. But it is precisely A that the believer in the infinite series is 'taking away'. For in maintaining that the series is infinite he is denying that it has a first member; he is denying that there is such a thing as a first cause; he is in other words denying the existence of A. Since without A, Z could not have existed, his position implies that Z does not exist now; and that is plainly false.

This argument fails to do justice to the supporter of the infinite series of causes. Aquinas has failed to distinguish between the two statements:

(1) A did not exist, and
(2) A is not uncaused.

To say that the series is infinite implies (2), but it does not imply (1). The following parallel may be helpful here: Suppose Captain Spaulding had said, 'I am the greatest explorer who ever lived', and somebody replied, 'No, you are not'. This answer would be denying that the Captain possessed the exalted attribute he had claimed for himself, but it would not be denying his existence. It would not be 'taking him away'. Similarly, the believer in the infinite series is not 'taking A away'. He is taking away the privileged status of A; he is taking away its 'first causiness'. He does not deny the *existence* of A or of any particular member of the series. He denies that A or anything else *is the first member* of the series. Since he is not taking A away, he is not taking B away, and thus he is also not taking X, Y, or Z away. His view, then, does not commit him to the absurdity that nothing exists now, or more specifically, that Margaret Truman does not exist now. It may be noted in this connection that a believer in the infinite series is not necessarily denying the existence of supernatural beings. He is merely committed to denying that such a being, if it exists, is uncaused. He is committed to holding that whatever other impressive attributes a supernatural being might possess, the attribute of being a first cause is not among them.

The causal argument is open to several other objections. Thus, even if otherwise valid, the argument would not prove a *single* first cause. For there does not seem to be any good ground for supposing that all the various causal series in the universe ultimately merge. Hence even if it is granted that no series of causes can be infinite the possibility of a plurality of first members has not been ruled out. Nor does the argument establish the *present* existence of the first cause. It does not prove this, since experience clearly shows that an effect may exist long after its cause has been destroyed.

III

Many defenders of the causal argument would contend that at least some of these criticisms rest on a misunderstanding. They would probably go further and contend that the argument was not quite fairly stated in the first place—or at any rate that if it was fair to some of its adherents it was not fair to others. They would in this connection distinguish between two types of causes—what they call 'causes *in fieri*' and what they call 'causes *in esse*'. A cause *in fieri* is a factor which brought or helped to bring an effect into existence. A cause *in esse* is a factor which 'sustains' or helps to sustain the effect 'in being'. The parents of a human being would be an example of a cause *in fieri*. If somebody puts a book in my hand and I keep holding it up, his putting it there would be the cause *in fieri*, and my holding it would be the cause *in esse* of the book's position. To quote Father Joyce:

> If a smith forges a horse-shoe, he is only a cause *in fieri* of the shape given to the iron. That shape persists after his action has ceased. So, too, a builder is a cause *in fieri* of the house which he builds. In both these cases the substances employed act as causes *in esse* as regards the continued existence of the effect produced. Iron, in virtue of its natural rigidity, retains in being the shape which it has once received; and, similarly, the materials employed in building retain in being the order and arrangement which constitute them into a house.[9]

Using this distinction, a defender of the argument now reasons in the following way. To say that there is an infinite series of causes *in fieri* does not lead to any absurd conclusions. But Aquinas is concerned only with causes *in esse* and an infinite series of *such* causes is impossible. In the words of the contemporary American Thomist, R. P. Phillips:

> Each member of the series of causes possesses being solely by virtue of the actual present operation of a superior cause. . . . Life is dependent, *inter alia*, on a certain atmospheric pressure, this again on the continual operation of physical forces, whose being and operation depends on the position of the

[9] *The Principles of Natural Theology,* p 58.

earth in the solar system, which itself must endure relatively unchanged, a state of being which can only be continuously produced by a definite—if unknown—constitution of the material universe. This constitution, however, cannot be its own cause. That a thing should cause itself is impossible: for in order that it may cause it is necessary for it to exist, which it cannot do, on the hypothesis, until it has been caused. So it must *be* in order to cause itself. Thus, not being uncaused nor yet its own cause, it must be caused by another, which produces and preserves it. It is plain, then, that as no member of this series possesses being except in virtue of the actual present operation of a superior cause, if there be no first cause actually operating none of the dependent causes could operate either. We are thus irresistibly led to posit a first efficient cause which, while itself uncaused, shall impart causality to a whole series. . . .

The series of causes which we are considering is not one which stretches back into the past; so that we are not demanding a beginning of the world at some definite moment reckoning back from the present, but an actual cause now operating, to account for the present being of things.[10]

Professor Phillips offers the following parallel to bring out his point:

In a goods train each truck is moved and moves by the action of the one immediately in front of it. If then we suppose the train to be infinite, i.e. that there is no end to it, and so no engine which starts the motion, it is plain that no truck will move. To lengthen it out to infinity will not give it what no member of it possesses of itself, viz. the power of drawing the truck behind it. If then we see any truck in motion we know there must be an end to the series of trucks which gives causality to the whole.[11]

Father Joyce introduces an illustration from Aquinas to explain how the present existence of things may be compatible with an infinite series of causes *in fieri* but not with an infinite series of causes *in esse*.

When a carpenter is at work, the series of efficient causes on which his work depends is necessarily limited. The final effect, e.g. the fastening of a nail is caused by a hammer: the hammer is moved by the arm: and the motion of his arm is determined by the motor-impulses communicated from the nerve centres of the brain. Unless the subordinate causes were limited in number, and were connected with a starting-point of motion, the hammer must remain inert; and the nail will never be driven in. If the series be supposed infinite, no work will ever take place. But if there is question of causes on which the work is not essentially dependent, we cannot draw the same conclusion. We may suppose the carpenter to have broken an infinite number of hammers, and as often to have replaced the broken tool by a fresh one. There is nothing in such a supposition which excludes the driving home of the nail.[12]

The supporter of the infinite series of causes, Joyce also remarks, is

. . . asking us to believe that although each link in a suspended chain is prevented from falling simply because it is attached to the one above it, yet if only the chain be long enough, it will, taken as a whole, need no support, but will hang loose in the air suspended from nothing.[13]

[10] *Modern Thomistic Philosophy,* Vol II, pp 284–85.
[11] *Op. cit.* p 278.   [12] *Op. cit.* pp 67–8.   [13] *Op. cit.* p 82.

This formulation of the causal argument unquestionably circumvents one of the objections mentioned previously. If Y is the cause *in esse* of an effect, Z, then it must exist as long as Z exists. If the argument were valid in this form it would therefore prove the present and not merely the past existence of a first cause. In this form the argument is, however, less convincing in another respect. To maintain that all 'natural' or 'phenomenal' objects—things like tables and mountains and human beings—require a cause *in fieri* is not implausible, though even here Mill and others have argued that strictly speaking only *changes* require a causal explanation. It is far from plausible, on the other hand, to claim that all natural objects require a cause *in esse*. It may be granted that the air around us is a cause *in esse* of human life and further that certain gravitational forces are among the causes *in esse* of the air being where it is. But when we come to gravitational forces or, at any rate, to material particles like atoms or electrons it is difficult to see what cause *in esse* they require. To those not already convinced of the need for a supernatural First Cause some of the remarks by Professor Phillips in this connection appear merely dogmatic and question-begging. Most people would grant that such particles as atoms did not cause themselves, since, as Professor Phillips observes, they would in that event have had to exist before they began existing. It is not at all evident, however, that these particles cannot be uncaused. Professor Phillips and all other supporters of the causal argument immediately proceed to claim that there is something else which needs no cause *in esse*. They themselves admit thus, that there is nothing self-evident about the proposition that everything must have a cause *in esse*. Their entire procedure here lends substance to Schopenhauer's gibe that supporters of the cosmological argument treat the law of universal causation like 'a hired cab which we dismiss when we have reached our destination'.[14]

But waiving this and all similar objections, the re-statement of the argument in terms of causes *in esse* in no way avoids the main difficulty which was previously mentioned. A believer in the infinite series would insist that his position was just as much misrepresented now as before. He is no more removing the member of the series which is supposed to be the first cause *in esse* than he was removing the member which had been declared to be the first cause *in fieri*. He is again merely denying a privileged status to it. He is not denying the reality of the cause *in esse* labelled 'A'. He is not even necessarily denying that it possesses supernatural attributes. He is again merely taking away its 'first causiness'.

The advocates of the causal argument in either form seem to confuse an infinite series with one which is long but finite. If a book, Z, is to remain in its position, say 100 miles up in the air, there must be another object, say another book, Y, underneath it to serve as its support. If Y is to remain where

---

[14] *The Fourfold Root of the Principle of Sufficient Reason*, pp 42–3. My attention to this passage was drawn by Professor C. J. Ducasse. See his excellent discussion of the arguments for the existence of God in *A Philosophical Scrutiny of Religion*, Ch 15.

it is, it will need another support, X, beneath it. Suppose that this series of supports, one below the other, continues for a long time, but eventually, say after 100,000 members, comes to a first book which is not resting on any other book or indeed on any other support. In that event the whole collection would come crashing down. What we seem to need is a first member of the series, a first support (such as the earth) which does not need another member as *its* support, which in other words is 'self-supporting'.

This is evidently the sort of picture that supporters of the First Cause argument have before their minds when they rule out the possibility of an infinite series. But such a picture is not a fair representation of the theory of the infinite series. A *finite* series of books would indeed come crashing down, since the first or lowest member would not have a predecessor on which it could be supported. If the series, however, were infinite this would not be the case. In that event every member *would* have a predecessor to support itself on and there would be no crash. That is to say: a crash can be avoided either by a finite series with a first self-supporting member or by an infinite series. Similarly, the present existence of motion is equally compatible with the theory of a first unmoved mover and with the theory of an infinite series of moving objects; and the present existence of causal activity is compatible with the theory of a first cause *in esse* as much as with the theory of an infinite series of such causes.

The illustrations given by Joyce and Phillips are hardly to the point. It is true that a carpenter would not, *in a finite time-span*, succeed in driving in a nail if he had to carry out an infinite number of movements. For that matter, he would not accomplish this goal in a finite time if he broke an infinite number of hammers. However, to make the illustrations relevant we must suppose that he has infinite time at his disposal. In that case he would succeed in driving in the nail even if he required an infinite number of movements for this purpose. As for the goods train, it may be granted that the trucks do not move unless the train has an engine. But this illustration is totally irrelevant as it stands. A relevant illustration would be that of engines, each moved by the one in front of it. Such a train would move if it were infinite. For every member of this series there would be one in front capable of drawing it along. The advocate of the infinite series of causes does not, as the original illustration suggests, believe in a series whose members are not really causally connected with one another. In the series he believes in every member is genuinely the cause of the one that follows it.

IV

No staunch defender of the cosmological argument would give up at this stage. Even if there were an infinite series of causes *in fieri* or *in esse*, he would contend, this still would not do away with the need for an ultimate, a first cause. As Father Copleston put it in his debate with Bertrand Russell:

> Every object has a phenomenal cause, if you insist on the infinity of the series. But the series of phenomenal causes is an insufficient explanation of the series. Therefore, the series has not a phenomenal cause, but a transcendent cause.[15] . . .
>
> An infinite series of contingent beings will be, to my way of thinking, as unable to cause itself as one contingent being.[16]

The demand to find the cause of the series as a whole rests on the erroneous assumption that the series is something over and above the members of which it is composed. It is tempting to suppose this, at least by implication, because the word 'series' is a noun like 'dog' or 'man'. Like the expression 'this dog' or 'this man' the phrase 'this series' is easily taken to designate an individual object. But reflection shows this to be an error. If we have explained the individual members there is nothing additional left to be explained. Supposing I see a group of five Eskimos standing on the corner of Sixth Avenue and 50th Street and I wish to explain why the group came to New York. Investigation reveals the following stories:

Eskimo No. 1 did not enjoy the extreme cold in the polar region and decided to move to a warmer climate.

No. 2 is the husband of Eskimo No. 1. He loves her dearly and did not wish to live without her.

No. 3 is the son of Eskimos 1 and 2. He is too small and too weak to oppose his parents.

No. 4 saw an advertisement in the *New York Times* for an Eskimo to appear on television.

No. 5 is a private detective engaged by the Pinkerton Agency to keep an eye on Eskimo No. 4.

Let us assume that we have now explained in the case of each of the five Eskimos why he or she is in New York. Somebody then asks: 'All right, but what about the group as a whole; why is *it* in New York?' This would plainly be an absurd question. There is no group over and above the five members, and if we have explained why each of the five members is in New York we have *ipso facto* explained why the group is there. It is just as absurd to ask for the cause of the series as a whole as distinct from asking for the causes of individual members.

v

It is most unlikely that a determined defender of the cosmological line of reasoning would surrender even here. He would probably admit that the series is not a thing over and above its members and that it does not make sense to ask for the cause of the series if the cause of each member has

[15] *Why I Am Not a Christian*, pp 152–53.   [16] *Ibid*. p 151.

already been found. He would insist, however, that when he asked for the explanation of the entire series, he was not asking for its *cause*. He was really saying that a series, finite or infinite, is not 'intelligible' or 'explained' if it consists of nothing but 'contingent' members. To quote Father Copleston once more:

> What we call the world is intrinsically unintelligible apart from the existence of God. The infinity of the series of events, if such an infinity could be proved, would not be in the slightest degree relevant to the situation. If you add up chocolates, you get chocolates after all, and not a sheep. If you add up chocolates to infinity, you presumably get an infinite number of chocolates. So, if you add up contingent beings to infinity, you still get contingent beings, not a necessary being.[17]

This last quotation is really a summary of the 'contingency argument', the other main form of the cosmological proof and the third of the five ways of Aquinas. It may be stated more fully in these words: All around us we perceive contingent beings. This includes all physical objects and also all human minds. In calling them 'contingent' we mean that they might not have existed. We mean that the universe can be *conceived* without this or that physical object, without this or that human being, however certain their actual existence may be. These contingent beings we can trace back to other contingent beings—e.g. a human being to his parents. However, since these other beings are also contingent, they do not provide a real or full explanation. The contingent beings we originally wanted explained have not yet become intelligible, since the beings to which they have been traced back are no more necessary than they were. It is just as true of our parents, for example, as it is of ourselves, that they might not have existed. We can then properly explain the contingent beings around us only by tracing them back ultimately to some necessary being, to something which exists necessarily, which has 'the reason for its existence within itself'. The existence of contingent beings, in other words, implies the existence of a necessary being.

This form of the cosmological argument is even more beset with difficulties than the causal variety. In the first place, there is the objection, stated with great force by Kant, that it really commits the same error as the ontological argument in tacitly regarding existence as an attribute or characteristic. To say that there is a necessary being is to say that it would be a self-contradiction to deny its existence. This would mean that at least one existential statement is a necessary truth; and this in turn presupposes that in at least one case existence is contained in a concept. But only a characteristic can be contained in a concept and it has seemed plain to most philosophers since Kant that existence is not a characteristic, that it can hence never be contained in a concept, and that hence no existential statement can ever be a necessary truth. To talk about anything 'existing necessarily' is in their

---

[17] *Op. cit.* p 151.

view about as sensible as to talk about round squares, and they have concluded that the contingency-argument is quite absurd.

It would lead too far to discuss here the reasons for denying that existence is a characteristic. I will assume that this difficulty can somehow be surmounted and that the expression 'necessary being', as it is intended by the champions of the contingency-argument, might conceivably apply to something. There remain other objections which are of great weight. I shall try to state these by first quoting again from the debate between Bertrand Russell and Father Copleston:

> RUSSELL: . . . It all turns on this question of sufficient reason, and I must say you haven't defined "sufficient reason" in a way that I can understand—what do you mean by sufficient reason? You don't mean cause?
>
> COPLESTON: Not necessarily. Cause is a kind of sufficient reason. Only contingent being can have a cause. God is his own sufficient reason; and he is not cause of himself. By sufficient reason in the full sense I mean an explanation adequate for the existence of some particular being.
>
> RUSSELL: But when is an explanation adequate? Suppose I am about to make a flame with a match. You may say that the adequate explanation of that is that I rub it on the box.
>
> COPLESTON: Well for practical purposes—but theoretically, that is only a partial explanation. An adequate explanation must ultimately be a total explanation, to which nothing further can be added.
>
> RUSSELL: Then I can only say that you're looking for something which can't be got, and which one ought not to expect to get.
>
> COPLESTON: To say that one has not found it is one thing; to say that one should not look for it seems to me rather dogmatic.
>
> RUSSELL: Well, I don't know. I mean, the explanation of one thing is another thing which makes the other thing dependent on yet another, and you have to grasp this sorry scheme of things entire to do what you want, and that we can't do.[18]

Russell's main point here may be expanded in the following way. The contingency-argument rests on a misconception of what an explanation is and does, and similarly on what it is that makes phenomena 'intelligible'. Or else it involves an obscure and arbitrary redefinition of 'explanation', 'intelligible', and related terms. Normally, we are satisfied that we have explained a phenomenon if we have found its cause or if we have exhibited some other uniform or near-uniform connection between it and something else. Confining ourselves to the former case, which is probably the most common, we might say that a phenomenon, Z, has been explained if it has been traced back to a group of factors, a, b, c, d, etc., which are its cause. These factors are the full and real explanation of Z, quite regardless of whether they are pleasing or displeasing, admirable or contemptible, necessary or contingent. The explanation would not be adequate only if the factors listed are not really the cause of Z. If they are the cause of Z, the ex-

[18] *Op. cit.* p 150.

planation would be adequate, even though each of the factors is merely a 'contingent' being.

Let us suppose that we have been asked to explain why General Eisenhower won the elections of 1952. 'He was an extremely popular general', we might answer, 'while Stevenson was relatively little known; moreover there was a great deal of resentment over the scandals in the Truman Administration.' If somebody complained that this was only a partial explanation we might mention additional antecedents, such as the widespread belief that the Democrats had allowed communist agents to infiltrate the State Department, that Eisenhower was a man with a winning smile, and that unlike Stevenson he had shown the good sense to say one thing on race relations in the North and quite another in the South. Theoretically, we might go further and list the motives of all American voters during the weeks or months preceding the elections. If we could do this we would have explained Eisenhower's victory. We would have made it intelligible. We would 'understand' why he won and why Stevenson lost. Perhaps there is a sense in which we might make Eisenhower's victory even more intelligible if we went further back and discussed such matters as the origin of American views on Communism or of racial attitudes in the North and South. However, to explain the outcome of the election in any ordinary sense, loose or strict, it would not be necessary to go back to prehistoric days or to the amœba or to a first cause, if such a first cause exists. Nor would our explanation be considered in any way defective because each of the factors mentioned was a 'contingent' and not a necessary being. The only thing that matters is whether the factors were really the cause of Eisenhower's election. If they were, then it has been explained although they are contingent beings. If they were not the cause of Eisenhower's victory, we would have failed to explain it even if each of the factors were a necessary being.

If it is granted that, in order to explain a phenomenon or to make it intelligible, we need not bring in a necessary being, then the contingency-argument breaks down. For a series, as was already pointed out, is not something over and above its members; and every contingent member of it could in that case be explained by reference to other contingent beings. But I should wish to go further than this and it is evident from Russell's remarks that he would do so also. Even if it were granted, both that the phrase 'necessary being' is meaningful and that all explanations are defective unless the phenomena to be explained are traced back to a necessary being, the conclusion would still not have been established. The conclusion follows from this premise together with the additional premise that *there are* explanations of phenomena in the special sense just mentioned. It is this further premise which Russell (and many other philosophers) would question. They do not merely question, as Copleston implies, whether human beings can ever obtain explanations in this sense, but whether they *exist*. To assume without further ado that phenomena have explanations or an explanation in this sense is to beg the very point at issue. The use of the same word 'explanation' in two crucially different ways lends the additional premise a plausibility it does not really possess. It may indeed be highly plausible to assert that phenomena have explanations, whether we have found them or not, in the ordinary sense in which this usually means that they have causes. It is then tempting to suppose, because of the use of the same word, that they also have explanations in a sense in which this implies dependence on a necessary being. But this is a gross *non sequitur*.

VI

It is necessary to add a few words about the proper way of formulating the position of those who reject the main premise of the cosmological argument, in either of the forms we have considered. It is sometimes maintained in this connection that in order to reach a 'self-existing' entity it is not necessary to go beyond the universe: the universe itself (or 'Nature') is 'self-existing'. And this in turn is sometimes expanded into the statement that while all individual things 'within' the universe are caused, the universe itself is uncaused. Statements of this kind are found in Büchner, Bradlaugh, Haeckel, and other free-thinkers of the nineteenth and early twentieth century. Sometimes the assertion that the universe is 'self-existing' is elaborated to mean that *it* is the 'necessary being'. Some eighteenth-century unbelievers, apparently accepting the view that there is a necessary being, asked why Nature or the material universe could not fill the bill as well or better than God.

> Why, [asks one of the characters in Hume's *Dialogues*,] may not the material universe be the necessarily existent Being? . . . We dare not affirm that we know all the qualities of matter; and for aught we can determine, it may contain some qualities, which, were they known, would make its non-existence appear as great a contradiction as that twice two is five.[19]

Similar remarks can be found in Holbach and several of the Encyclopedists.

The former of these formulations immediately invites the question why the universe, alone of all 'things', is exempted from the universal sway of causation. 'The strong point of the cosmological argument', writes Dr Ewing, 'is that after all it does remain incredible that the physical universe should just have happened. . . . It calls out for some further explanation of some kind.'[20] The latter formulation is exposed to the criticism that there is nothing any more 'necessary' about the existence of the universe or Nature as a whole than about any particular thing within the universe.

I hope some of the earlier discussions in this article have made it clear that in rejecting the cosmological argument one is not committed to either of these propositions. If I reject the view that there is a supernatural first

[19] *Op. cit.* Part IX.   [20] *Op. cit.* p 225.

cause, I am not thereby committed to the proposition that there is a *natural* first cause, and even less to the proposition that a mysterious 'thing' called 'the universe' qualifies for this title. I may hold that there is no 'universe' over and above individual things of various sorts; and, accepting the causal principle, I may proceed to assert that all these things are caused by other things, and these other things by yet other things, and so on, *ad infinitum*. In this way no arbitrary exception is made to the principle of causation. Similarly, if I reject the assertion that God is a 'necessary being', I am not committed to the view that the universe is such an entity. I may hold that it does not make sense to speak of anything as a 'necessary being' and that even if there were such a thing as the universe it could not be properly considered a necessary being.

However, in saying that nothing is uncaused or that there is no necessary being, one is not committed to the view that everything, or for that matter anything, is merely a 'brute fact'. Dr Ewing laments that 'the usual modern philosophical views opposed to theism do not try to give any rational explanation of the world at all, but just take it as a brute fact not to be explained'. They thus fail to 'rationalize' the universe. Theism, he concedes, cannot completely rationalize things either since it does not show 'how God can be his own cause or how it is that he does not need a cause'.[21] Now, if one means by 'brute fact' something for which there *exists* no explanation (as distinct from something for which no explanation is in our possession), then the theists have at least one brute fact on their hands, namely God. Those who adopt Büchner's formulation also have one brute fact on their hands, namely 'the universe'. Only the position I have been supporting dispenses with brute facts altogether. I don't know if this is any special virtue, but the defenders of the cosmological argument seem to think so.

[21] *Op. cit.* p 225.

THE TELEOLOGICAL ARGUMENT

WILLIAM PALEY
The Evidence of Design

In crossing a heath, suppose I pitched my foot against a *stone*, and were asked how the stone came to be there, I might possibly answer, that, for any thing I knew to the contrary, it had lain there for ever: nor would it perhaps be very easy to shew the absurdity of this answer. But suppose I had found a *watch* upon the ground, and it should be enquired how the watch happened to be in that place, I should hardly think of the answer which I had before given, that, for any thing I knew, the watch might have always been there. Yet why should not this answer serve for the watch as well as for the stone? Why is it not as admissible in the second case, as in the first? For this reason, and for no other, viz. that, when we come to inspect the watch, we perceive (what we could not discover in the stone) that its several parts are framed and put together for a purpose, e.g. that they are so formed and adjusted as to produce motion, and that motion so regulated as to point out the hour of the day; that, if the several parts had been differently shaped from what they are, of a different size from what they are, or placed after any other manner, or in any other order, than that in which they are placed, either no motion at all would have been carried on in the machine, or none

William Paley (1743–1805) was an English theologian and a teacher of moral philosophy at Cambridge. His important writings include *Evidences of Christianity* and *Natural Theology*.

THE EVIDENCE OF DESIGN   From *Natural Theology* (ninth edition). London. Printed for R. Faulder, 1805.

which would have answered the use that is now served by it. To reckon up a few of the plainest of these parts, and of their offices, all tending to one result:—We see a cylindrical box containing a coiled, elastic spring, which, by its endeavour to relax itself, turns round the box. We next observe a flexible chain (artificially wrought for the sake of flexure) communicating the action of the spring from the box to the fusee. We then find a series of wheels, the teeth of which catch in, and apply to, each other, conducting the motion from the fusee to the balance, and from the balance to the pointer; and at the same time, by the size and shape of those wheels, so regulating that motion, as to terminate in causing an index, by an equable and measured progression, to pass over a given space in a given time. We take notice that the wheels are made of brass, in order to keep them from rust; the springs of steel, no other metal being so elastic; that over the face of the watch there is placed a glass, a material employed in no other part of the work, but in the room of which, if there had been any other than a transparent substance, the hour could not be seen without opening the case. This mechanism being observed (it requires indeed an examination of the instrument, and perhaps some previous knowledge of the subject, to perceive and understand it; but being once, as we have said, observed and understood), the inference, we think, is inevitable, that the watch must have had a maker: that there must have existed, at some time and at some place or other, an artificer or artificers who formed it for the purpose which we find it actually to answer; who comprehended its construction, and designed its use.

I

Nor would it, I apprehend, weaken the conclusion, that we had never seen a watch made; that we had never known an artist capable of making one; that we were altogether incapable of executing such a piece of workmanship ourselves, or of understanding in what manner it was performed; all this being no more than what is true of some exquisite remains of ancient art, of some lost arts, and, to the generality of mankind, of the more curious productions of modern manufacture. Does one man in a million know how oval frames are turned? Ignorance of this kind exalts our opinion of the unseen and unknown, artist's skill, if he be unseen and unknown, but raises no doubt in our minds of the existence and agency of such an artist, at some former time, and in some place or other. Nor can I perceive that it varies at all the inference, whether the question arise concerning a human agent, or concerning an agent of a different species, or an agent possessing, in some respects, a different nature.

II

Neither, secondly, would it invalidate our conclusion, that the watch sometimes went wrong, or that it seldom went exactly right. The purpose of the machinery, the design, and the designer, might be evident, and in the case supposed would be evident, in whatever way we accounted for the irregularity of the movement, or whether we could account for it or not. It is not necessary that a machine be perfect, in order to shew with what design it was made: still less necessary, where the only question is, whether it were made with any design at all.

III

Nor, thirdly, would it bring any uncertainty into the argument, if there were a few parts of the watch, concerning which we could not discover, or had not yet discovered, in what manner they conduced to the general effect; or even some parts, concerning which we could not ascertain, whether they conduced to that effect in any manner whatever. For, as to the first branch of the case; if, by the loss, or disorder, or decay of the parts in question, the movement of the watch were found in fact to be stopped, or disturbed, or retarded, no doubt would remain in our minds as to the utility or intention of these parts, although we should be unable to investigate the manner according to which, or the connection by which, the ultimate effect depended upon their action or assistance; and the more complex is the machine, the more likely is this obscurity to arise. Then, as to the second thing supposed, namely, that there were parts which might be spared, without prejudice to the movement of the watch, and that we had proved this by experiment,—these superfluous parts, even if we were completely assured that they were such, would not vacate the reasoning which we had instituted concerning other parts. The indication of contrivance remained, with respect to them, nearly as it was before.

IV

Nor, fourthly, would any man in his senses think the existence of the watch, with its various machinery, accounted for, by being told that it was one out of possible combinations of material forms; that whatever he had found in the place where he found the watch, must have contained some internal configuration or other; and that this configuration might be the structure now exhibited, viz. of the works of a watch, as well as a different structure.

V

Nor, fifthly, would it yield his enquiry more satisfaction to be answered, that there existed in things a principle of order, which had disposed the parts of the watch into their present form and situation. He never knew a watch made by the principle of order; nor can he even form to himself an idea of what is meant by a principle of order, distinct from the intelligence of the watch-maker.

VI

Sixthly, he would be surprised to hear, that the mechanism of the watch was no proof of contrivance, only a motive to induce the mind to think so.

VII

And not less surprised to be informed, that the watch in his hand was nothing more than the result of the laws of *metallic* nature. It is a perversion of language to assign any law, as the efficient, operative cause of any thing. A law presupposes an agent; for it is only the mode, according to which an agent proceeds: it implies a power; for it is the order, according to which that power acts. Without this agent, without this power, which are both distinct from itself, the *law* does nothing; is nothing. The expression, "the law of metallic nature," may sound strange and harsh to a philosophic ear, but it seems quite as justifiable as some others which are more familiar to him, such as "the law of vegetable nature"—"the law of animal nature," or indeed as "the law of nature" in general, when assigned as the cause of phænomena, in exclusion of agency and power; or when it is substituted into the place of these.

VIII

Neither, lastly, would our observer be driven out of his conclusion, or from his confidence in its truth, by being told that he knew nothing at all about the matter. He knows enough for his argument. He knows the utility of the end: he knows the subserviency and adaptation of the means to the end. These points being known, his ignorance of other points, his doubts concerning other points, affect not the certainty of his reasoning. The consciousness of knowing little, need not beget a distrust of that which he does know. . . .

Suppose, in the next place, that the person, who found the watch, should, after some time, discover, that, in addition to all the properties which he had hitherto observed in it, it possessed the unexpected property of producing, in the course of its movement, another watch like itself; (the thing is conceivable;) that it contained within it a mechanism, a system of parts, a mould for instance, or a complex adjustment of lathes, files, and other tools, evidently and separately calculated for this purpose; let us enquire, what effect ought such a discovery to have upon his former conclusion.

I

The first effect would be to increase his admiration of the contrivance, and his conviction of the consummate skill of the contriver. Whether he regarded the object of the contrivance, the distinct apparatus, the intricate, yet in many parts intelligible, mechanism, by which it was carried on, he would perceive, in this new observation, nothing but an additional reason for doing what he had already done; for referring the construction of the watch to design, and to supreme art. If that construction *without* this property, or, which is the same thing, before this property had been noticed, proved intention and art to have been employed about it; still more strong would the proof appear, when he came to the knowledge of this further property, the crown and perfection of all the rest.

II

He would reflect, that though the watch before him were, *in some sense*, the maker of the watch, which was fabricated in the course of its movements, yet it was in a very different sense from that, in which a carpenter, for instance, is the maker of a chair; the author of its contrivance, the cause of the relation of its parts to their use. With respect to these, the first watch was no cause at all to the second: in no such sense as this was it the author of the constitution and order, either of the parts which the new watch contained, or of the parts by the aid and instrumentality of which it was produced. We might possibly say, but with great latitude of expression, that a stream of water ground corn: but no latitude of expression would allow us to say, no stretch of conjecture could lead us to think, that the stream of water built the mill, though it were too ancient for us to know who the builder was. What the stream of water does in the affair is neither more nor less than this: by the application of an unintelligent impulse to a mechanism previously arranged, arranged independently of it, and arranged by intelligence, an effect is produced, viz. the corn is ground. But the effect results from the arrangement. The force of the stream cannot be said to be the cause or author of the effect, still less of the arrangement. Understanding and plan in the formation of the mill were not the less necessary, for any share which the water has in grinding the corn: yet is this share the same, as that which the watch would have contributed to the production of the new watch, upon the supposition assumed in the last section. Therefore,

III

Though it be now no longer probable, that the individual watch which our observer had found, was made immediately by the hand of an artificer, yet doth not this alteration in any wise affect the inference, that an artificer had been originally employed and concerned in the production. The argument from design remains as it was. Marks of design and contrivance are no more accounted for now, than they were before. In the same thing, we may ask for the cause of different properties. We may ask for the cause of the colour of a body, of its hardness, of its heat; and these causes may be all different. We are now asking for the cause of that subserviency to an use, that relation to an end, which we have remarked in the watch before us. No answer is given to this question by telling us that a preceding watch produced it. There cannot be design without a designer; contrivance without a contriver; order without choice; arrangement, without any thing capable of arranging; subserviency and relation to a purpose, without that which could intend a purpose; means suitable to an end, and executing their office in accomplishing that end, without the end ever having been contemplated, or the means accommodated to it. Arrangement, disposition of parts, subserviency of means to an end, relation of instruments to an use, imply the presence of intelligence and mind. No one, therefore, can rationally believe, that the insensible, inanimate watch, from which the watch before us issued, was the proper cause of the mechanism we so much admire in it; could be truly said to have constructed the instrument, disposed its parts, assigned their office, determined their order, action, and mutual dependency, combined their several motions into one result, and that also a result connected with the utilities of other beings. All these properties, therefore, are as much unaccounted for, as they were before.

IV

Nor is any thing gained by running the difficulty further back, i.e. by supposing the watch before us to have been produced from another watch, that from a former, and so on indefinitely. Our going back ever so far brings us no nearer to the least degree of satisfaction upon the subject. Contrivance is still unaccounted for. We still want a contriver. A designing mind is neither supplied by this supposition, nor dispensed with. If the difficulty were diminished the further we went back, by going back indefinitely we might exhaust it. And this is the only case to which this sort of reasoning applies. Where there is a tendency, or, as we increase the number of terms, a continual approach towards a limit, *there*, by supposing the number of terms to be what is called infinite, we may conceive the limit to be attained: but where there is no such tendency, or approach, nothing is effected by lengthening the series. There is no difference as to the point in question, (whatever there may be as to many points), between one series and another; between a series which is finite, and a series which is infinite. A chain, composed of an infinite number of links, can no more support itself, than a chain composed of a finite number of links. And of this we are assured, (though we never *can* have tried the experiment), because, by increasing the number of links, from ten for instance to a hundred, from a hundred to a thousand, &c. we make not the smallest approach, we observe not the smallest tendency, towards self-support. There is no difference in this respect (yet there may be a great difference in several respects), between a chain of a greater or less length, between one chain and another, between one that is finite and one that is infinite. This very much resembles the case before us. The machine, which we are inspecting, demonstrates, by its construction, contrivance and design. Contrivance must have had a contriver, design, a designer; whether the machine immediately proceeded from another machine or not. That circumstance alters not the case. That other machine may, in like manner, have proceeded from a former machine: nor does that alter the case: contrivance must have had a contriver. That former one from one preceding it: no alteration still: a contriver is still necessary. No tendency is perceived, no approach towards a diminution of this necessity. It is the same with any and every succession of these machines; a succession of ten, of a hundred, of a thousand; with one series as with another: a series which is finite, as with a series which is infinite. In whatever other respects they may differ, in this they do not. In all equally, contrivance and design are un-accounted for.

The question is not simply, How came the first watch into existence? which question, it may be pretended, is done away by supposing the series of watches thus produced from one another to have been infinite, and con-sequently to have had no such *first*, for which it was necessary to provide a cause. This, perhaps, would have been nearly the state of the question, if nothing had been before us but an unorganized, unmechanized, substance, without mark or indication of contrivance. It might be difficult to shew that such substance could not have existed from eternity, either in succession (if it were possible, which I think it is not, for unorganized bodies to spring from one another), or by individual perpetuity. But that is not the question now. To suppose it to be so, is to suppose that it made no difference whether we had found a watch or a stone. As it is, the metaphysics of that question have no place; for, in the watch which we are examining, are seen con-trivance, design; an end, a purpose; means for the end, adaptation to the pur-pose. And the question, which irresistibly presses upon our thoughts, is, whence this contrivance and design. The thing required is the intending mind, the adapting hand, the intelligence by which that hand was directed. This question, this demand, is not shaken off, by increasing a number or succession of substances, destitute of these properties; nor the more, by in-creasing that number to infinity. If it be said, that, upon the supposition of one watch being produced from another in the course of that other's move-ments, and by means of the mechanism within it, we have a cause for the watch in my hand, viz. the watch from which it proceeded. I deny, that for the design, the contrivance, the suitableness of means to an end, the adapta-tion of instruments to an use (all which we discover in the watch), we have any cause whatever. It is in vain, therefore, to assign a series of such causes, or to allege that a series may be carried back to infinity; for I do not admit that we have yet any cause at all of the phænomena, still less any series of causes either finite or infinite. Here is contrivance, but no contriver; proofs of design, but no designer.

V

Our observer would further also reflect, that the maker of the watch before him, was, in truth and reality, the maker of every watch produced from it; there being no difference (except that the latter manifests a more exquisite skill) between the making of another watch with his own hands, by the mediation of files, lathes, chisels, &c. and the disposing, fixing, and inserting of these instruments, or of others equivalent to them, in the body of the watch already made, in such a manner, as to form a new watch in the course of the movements which he had given to the old one. It is only working by one set of tools, instead of another.

The conclusion which the *first* examination of the watch, of its works, construction, and movement, suggested, was, that it must have had, for the cause and author of that construction, an artificer, who understood its mechanism, and designed its use. This conclusion is invincible. A *second* examination presents us with a new discovery. The watch is found, in the course of its movement, to produce another watch, similar to itself: and not only so, but we perceive in it a system of organization, separately calculated for that purpose. What effect would this discovery have, or ought it to have, upon our former inference? What, as hath already been said, but to increase, beyond measure, our admiration of the skill, which had been employed in the formation of such a machine? Or shall it, instead of this, all at once turn us round to an opposite conclusion, viz. that no art or skill whatever has been concerned in the business, although all other evidences of art and skill remain as they were, and this last and supreme piece of art be now added to the rest? Can this be maintained without absurdity? Yet this is atheism.

This is atheism: for every indication of contrivance, every manifestation of design, which existed in the watch, exists in the works of nature; with the difference, on the side of nature, of being greater and more, and that in a degree which exceeds all computation. I mean that the contrivances of nature surpass the contrivances of art, in the complexity, subtility, and curiosity of the mechanism; and still more, if possible, do they go beyond them in number and variety: yet, in a multitude of cases, are not less evidently mechanical, not less evidently contrivances, not less evidently accommodated to their end, or suited to their office, than are the most perfect productions of human ingenuity. . . .

DAVID HUME
Design and the Teleological Argument

PART II

. . . Look round the world: contemplate the whole and every part of it: You will find it to be nothing but one great machine, subdivided into an infinite number of lesser machines, which again admit of subdivisions to a degree beyond what human senses and faculties can trace and explain. All these various machines, and even their most minute parts, are adjusted to each other with an accuracy which ravishes into admiration all men who have ever contemplated them. The curious adapting of means to ends, throughout all nature, resembles exactly, though it much exceeds, the productions of human contrivance; of human design, thought, wisdom, and intelligence. Since therefore the effects resemble each other, we are led to infer, by all the rules of analogy, that the causes also resemble; and that the Author of Nature is somewhat similar to the mind of man, though possessed of much larger faculties, proportioned to the grandeur of the work which he has executed. By this argument *a posteriori*, and by this argument alone, do we prove at once the existence of a Deity, and his similarity to human mind and intelligence.

I shall be so free, Cleanthes, said Demea, as to tell you, that from the beginning I could not approve of your conclusion concerning the similarity of the Deity to men; still less can I approve of the mediums by which you endeavour to establish it. What! No demonstration of the Being of God! No abstract arguments! No proofs *a priori*! Are these, which have hitherto been so much insisted on by philosophers, all fallacy, all sophism? Can we reach no farther in this subject than experience and probability? I will not say that this is betraying the cause of a Deity: But surely, by this affected candour, you give advantages to Atheists, which they never could obtain by the mere dint of argument and reasoning.

What I chiefly scruple in this subject, said Philo, is not so much that all religious arguments are by Cleanthes reduced to experience, as that they appear not to be even the most certain and irrefragable of that inferior kind. That a stone will fall, that fire will burn, that the earth has solidity, we have observed a thousand and a thousand times; and when any new instance of this nature is presented, we draw without hesitation the accustomed inference. The exact similarity of the cases gives us a perfect assurance of a similar event; and a stronger evidence is never desired nor sought after. But wherever you depart, in the least, from the similarity of the cases, you

DESIGN AND THE TELEOLOGICAL ARGUMENT   From *Dialogues Concerning Natural Religion*, Parts II, V, and VII. *The Philosophical Works of David Hume*, Volume II. Edinburgh, Adam Black and William Tait; and Charles Tait, 1876.

diminish proportionably the evidence; and may at last bring it to a very weak *analogy,* which is confessedly liable to error and uncertainty. After having experienced the circulation of the blood in human creatures, we make no doubt that it takes place in Titius and Mævius: But from its circulation in frogs and fishes, it is only a presumption, though a strong one, from analogy, that it takes place in men and other animals. The analogical reasoning is much weaker, when we infer the circulation of the sap in vegetables from our experience that the blood circulates in animals; and those, who hastily followed that imperfect analogy, are found, by more accurate experiments, to have been mistaken.

If we see a house, Cleanthes, we conclude, with the greatest certainty, that it had an architect or builder; because this is precisely that species of effect which we have experienced to proceed from that species of cause. But surely you will not affirm, that the universe bears such a resemblance to a house, that we can with the same certainty infer a similar cause, or that the analogy is here entire and perfect. The dissimilitude is so striking, that the utmost you can here pretend to is a guess, a conjecture, a presumption concerning a similar cause; and how that pretension will be received in the world, I leave you to consider.

It would surely be very ill received, replied Cleanthes; and I should be deservedly blamed and detested, did I allow, that the proofs of a Deity amounted to no more than a guess or conjecture. But is the whole adjustment of means to ends in a house and in the universe so slight a resemblance? The economy of final causes? The order, proportion, and arrangement of every part? Steps of a stair are plainly contrived, that human legs may use them in mounting; and this inference is certain and infallible. Human legs are also contrived for walking and mounting; and this inference, I allow, is not altogether so certain, because of the dissimilarity which you remark; but does it, therefore, deserve the name only of presumption or conjecture?

Good God! cried Demea, interrupting him, where are we? Zealous defenders of religion allow, that the proofs of a Deity fall short of perfect evidence! And you, Philo, on whose assistance I depended in proving the adorable mysteriousness of the Divine Nature, do you assent to all these extravagant opinions of Cleanthes? For what other name can I give them? or, why spare my censure, when such principles are advanced, supported by such an authority, before so young a man as Pamphilus?

You seem not to apprehend, replied Philo, that I argue with Cleanthes in his own way; and, by showing him the dangerous consequences of his tenets, hope at last to reduce him to our opinion. But what sticks most with you, I observe, is the representation which Cleanthes has made of the argument *a posteriori;* and finding that that argument is likely to escape your hold and vanish into air, you think it so disguised, that you can scarcely believe it to be set in its true light. Now, however much I may dissent, in other respects, from the dangerous principles of Cleanthes, I must allow that he has fairly represented that argument; and I shall endeavour so to state the matter to you, that you will entertain no farther scruples with regard to it.

Were a man to abstract from every thing which he knows or has seen, he would be altogether incapable, merely from his own ideas, to determine what kind of scene the universe must be, or to give the preference to one state or situation of things above another. For as nothing which he clearly conceives could be esteemed impossible or implying a contradiction, every chimera of his fancy would be upon an equal footing; nor could he assign any just reason why he adheres to one idea or system, and rejects the others which are equally possible.

Again; after he opens his eyes, and contemplates the world as it really is, it would be impossible for him at first to assign the cause of any one event, much less of the whole of things, or of the universe. He might set his fancy a rambling; and she might bring him in an infinite variety of reports and representations. These would all be possible; but being all equally possible, he would never of himself give a satisfactory account for his preferring one of them to the rest. Experience alone can point out to him the true cause of any phenomenon.

Now, according to this method of reasoning, Demea, it follows, (and is, indeed, tacitly allowed by Cleanthes himself), that order, arrangement, or the adjustment of final causes, is not of itself any proof of design; but only so far as it has been experienced to proceed from that principle. For aught we can know *a priori*, matter may contain the source or spring of order originally within itself, as well as mind does; and there is no more difficulty in conceiving, that the several elements, from an internal unknown cause, may fall into the most exquisite arrangement, than to conceive that their ideas, in the great universal mind, from a like internal unknown cause, fall into that arrangement. The equal possibility of both these suppositions is allowed. But, by experience, we find, (according to Cleanthes), that there is a difference between them. Throw several pieces of steel together, without shape or form; they will never arrange themselves so as to compose a watch. Stone, and mortar, and wood, without an architect, never erect a house. But the ideas in a human mind, we see, by an unknown, inexplicable economy, arrange themselves so as to form the plan of a watch or house. Experience, therefore, proves, that there is an original principle of order in mind, not in matter. From similar effects we infer similar causes. The adjustment of means to ends is alike in the universe, as in a machine of human contrivance. The causes, therefore, must be resembling.

I was from the beginning scandalized, I must own, with this resemblance, which is asserted, between the Deity and human creatures; and must conceive it to imply such a degradation of the Supreme Being as no sound Theist could endure. With your assistance, therefore, Demea, I shall endeavour to defend what you justly call the adorable mysteriousness of the Divine Nature, and shall refute this reasoning of Cleanthes, provided he allows that I have made a fair representation of it.

When Cleanthes had assented, Philo, after a short pause, proceeded in the following manner.

That all inferences, Cleanthes, concerning fact, are founded on experience; and that all experimental reasonings are founded on the supposition that similar causes prove similar effects, and similar effects similar causes; I shall not at present much dispute with you. But observe, I entreat you, with what extreme caution all just reasoners proceed in the transferring of experiments to similar cases. Unless the cases be exactly similar, they repose no perfect confidence in applying their past observation to any particular phenomenon. Every alteration of circumstances occasions a doubt concerning the event; and it requires new experiments to prove certainly, that the new circumstances are of no moment or importance. A change in bulk, situation, arrangement, age, disposition of the air, or surrounding bodies; any of these particulars may be attended with the most unexpected consequences: And unless the objects be quite familiar to us, it is the highest temerity to expect with assurance, after any of these changes, an event similar to that which before fell under our observation. The slow and deliberate steps of philosophers here, if any where, are distinguished from the precipitate march of the vulgar, who, hurried on by the smallest similitude, are incapable of all discernment or consideration.

But can you think, Cleanthes, that your usual phlegm and philosophy have been preserved in so wide a step as you have taken, when you compared to the universe houses, ships, furniture, machines, and, from their similarity in some circumstances, inferred a similarity in their causes? Thought, design, intelligence, such as we discover in men and other animals, is no more than one of the springs and principles of the universe, as well as heat or cold, attraction or repulsion, and a hundred others, which fall under daily observation. It is an active cause, by which some particular parts of nature, we find, produce alterations on other parts. But can a conclusion, with any propriety, be transferred from parts to the whole? Does not the great disproportion bar all comparison and inference? From observing the growth of a hair, can we learn any thing concerning the generation of a man? Would the manner of a leaf's blowing, even though perfectly known, afford us any instruction concerning the vegetation of a tree?

But, allowing that we were to take the *operations* of one part of nature upon another, for the foundation of our judgment concerning the *origin* of the whole, (which never can be admitted), yet why select so minute, so weak, so bounded a principle, as the reason and design of animals is found to be upon this planet? What peculiar privilege has this little agitation of the brain which we call *thought*, that we must thus make it the model of the whole universe? Our partiality in our own favour does indeed present it on all occasions; but sound philosophy ought carefully to guard against so natural an illusion.

So far from admitting, continued Philo, that the operations of a part can afford us any just conclusion concerning the origin of the whole, I will not allow any one part to form a rule for another part, if the latter be very remote from the former. Is there any reasonable ground to conclude, that the inhabitants of other planets possess thought, intelligence, reason, or any thing similar to these faculties in men? When nature has so extremely diversified her manner of operation in this small globe, can we imagine that she incessantly copies herself throughout so immense a universe? And if thought, as we may well suppose, be confined merely to this narrow corner, and has even there so limited a sphere of action, with what propriety can we assign it for the original cause of all things? The narrow views of a peasant, who makes his domestic economy the rule for the government of kingdoms, is in comparison a pardonable sophism.

But were we ever so much assured, that a thought and reason, resembling the human, were to be found throughout the whole universe, and were its activity elsewhere vastly greater and more commanding than it appears in this globe; yet I cannot see, why the operations of a world constituted, arranged, adjusted, can with any propriety be extended to a world which is in its embryo-state, and is advancing towards that constitution and arrangement. By observation, we know somewhat of the economy, action, and nourishment of a finished animal; but we must transfer with great caution that observation to the growth of a fœtus in the womb, and still more to the formation of an animalcule in the loins of its male parent. Nature, we find, even from our limited experience, possesses an infinite number of springs and principles, which incessantly discover themselves on every change of her position and situation. And what new and unknown principles would actuate her in so new and unknown a situation as that of the formation of a universe, we cannot, without the utmost temerity, pretend to determine.

A very small part of this great system, during a very short time, is very imperfectly discovered to us; and do we thence pronounce decisively concerning the origin of the whole?

Admirable conclusion! Stone, wood, brick, iron, brass, have not, at this time, in this minute globe of earth, an order or arrangement without human art and contrivance; therefore the universe could not originally attain its order and arrangement, without something similar to human art. But is a part of nature a rule for another part very wide of the former? Is it a rule for the whole? Is a very small part a rule for the universe? Is nature in one situation, a certain rule for nature in another situation vastly different from the former?

And can you blame me, Cleanthes, if I here imitate the prudent reserve of Simonides, who, according to the noted story, being asked by Hiero, *What God was?* desired a day to think of it, and then two days more; and after that manner continually prolonged the term, without ever bringing in his definition or description? Could you even blame me, if I had answered at first, *that I did not know*, and was sensible that this subject lay vastly beyond the reach of my faculties? You might cry out sceptic and rallier, as much as you pleased: but having found, in so many other subjects much more familiar, the imperfections and even contradictions of human reason, I never should expect any success from its feeble conjectures, in a subject so sublime, and so remote from the sphere of our observation. When two *species* of objects have always been observed to be conjoined together, I can *infer*, by custom, the existence of one wherever I *see* the existence of the other; and this I call an argument from experience. But how this argument can have place, where the objects, as in the present case, are single, individual, without parallel, or specific resemblance, may be difficult to explain. And will any man tell me with a serious countenance, that an orderly universe must arise from some thought and art like the human, because we have experience of it? To ascertain this reasoning, it were requisite that we had experience of the origin of worlds; and it is not sufficient, surely, that we have seen ships and cities arise from human art and contrivance.

Philo was proceeding in this vehement manner, somewhat between jest and earnest, as it appeared to me, when he observed some signs of impatience in Cleanthes, and then immediately stopped short. What I had to suggest, said Cleanthes, is only that you would not abuse terms, or make use of popular expressions to subvert philosophical reasonings. You know, that the vulgar often distinguish reason from experience, even where the question relates only to matter of fact and existence; though it is found, where that *reason* is properly analyzed, that it is nothing but a species of experience. To prove by experience the origin of the universe from mind, is not more contrary to common speech, than to prove the motion of the earth from the same principle. And a caviller might raise all the same objections to the Copernican system, which you have urged against my reasonings. Have you other earths, might he say, which you have seen to move? Have . . . .

Yes! cried Philo, interrupting him, we have other earths. Is not the moon another earth, which we see to turn round its centre? Is not Venus another earth, where we observe the same phenomenon? Are not the revolutions of the sun also a confirmation, from analogy, of the same theory? All the planets, are they not earths, which revolve about the sun? Are not the satellites moons, which move round Jupiter and Saturn, and along with these primary planets round the sun? These analogies and resemblances, with others which I have not mentioned, are the sole proofs of the Copernican system; and to you it belongs to consider, whether you have any analogies of the same kind to support your theory.

In reality, Cleanthes, continued he, the modern system of astronomy is now so much received by all inquirers, and has become so essential a part even of our earliest education, that we are not commonly very scrupulous in examining the reasons upon which it is founded. It is now become a matter of mere curiosity to study the first writers on that subject, who had the full force of prejudice to encounter, and were obliged to turn their arguments on every side in order to render them popular and convincing. But if we peruse Galilæo's famous Dialogues concerning the system of the world, we shall find, that that great genius, one of the sublimest that ever existed, first bent all his endeavours to prove, that there was no foundation for the distinction commonly made between elementary and celestial substances. The schools, proceeding from the illusions of sense, had carried this distinction very far; and had established the latter substances to be ingenerable, incorruptible, unalterable, impassible; and had assigned all the opposite qualities to the former. But Galilæo, beginning with the moon, proved its similarity in every particular to the earth; its convex figure, its natural darkness when not illuminated, its density, its distinction into solid and liquid, the variations of its phases, the mutual illuminations of the earth and moon, ther mutual eclipses, the inequalities of the lunar surface, &c. After many instances of this kind, with regard to all the planets, men plainly saw that these bodies became proper objects of experience; and that the similarity of their nature enabled us to extend the same arguments and phenomena from one to the other.

In this cautious proceeding of the astronomers, you may read your own condemnation, Cleanthes; or rather may see, that the subject in which you are engaged exceeds all human reason and inquiry. Can you pretend to show any such similarity between the fabric of a house, and the generation of a universe? Have you ever seen nature in any such situation as resembles the first arrangement of the elements? Have worlds ever been formed under your eye; and have you had leisure to observe the whole progress of the phenomenon, from the first appearance of order to its final consummation? If you have, then cite your experience, and deliver your theory. . . .

PART V

But to show you still more inconveniences, continued Philo, in your Anthropomorphism, please to take a new survey of your principles. *Like effects prove like causes.* This is the experimental argument; and this, you say too, is the sole theological argument. Now, it is certain, that the liker the effects are which are seen, and the liker the causes which are inferred, the stronger is the argument. Every departure on either side diminishes the probability, and renders the experiment less conclusive. You cannot doubt of the principle; neither ought you to reject its consequences.

All the new discoveries in astronomy, which prove the immense grandeur and magnificence of the works of Nature, are so many additional arguments for a Deity, according to the true system of Theism; but, according to your hypothesis of experimental Theism, they become so many objections, by removing the effect still farther from all resemblance to the effects of human art and contrivance. For, if Lucretius,[1] even following the old system of the world, could exclaim,

> Quis regere immensi summam, quis habere profundi
> Indu manu validas potis est moderanter habenas?
> Quis pariter cœlos omnes convertere? et omnes
> Ignibus ætheriis terras suffire feraces?
> Omnibus inque locis esse omni tempore præsto?

If Tully [2] esteemed this reasoning so natural, as to put it into the mouth of his Epicurean: 'Quibus enim oculis animi intueri potuit vester Plato fabricam illam tanti operis, qua construi a Deo atque ædificari mundum facit? quæ molito? quæ ferramenta? qui vectes? quæ machinæ? qui minstri tanti muneris fuerunt? quemadmodum autem obedire et parere voluntati architecti aer, ignis, aqua, terra potuerunt?' If this argument, I say, had any force in former ages, how much greater must it have at present, when the bounds of Nature are so infinitely enlarged, and such a magnificent scene is opened to us? It is still more unreasonable to form our idea of so unlimited a cause from our experience of the narrow productions of human design and invention.

The discoveries by microscopes, as they open a new universe in miniature, are still objections, according to you, arguments, according to me. The farther we push our researches of this kind, we are still led to infer the universal cause of all to be vastly different from mankind, or from any object of human experience and observation.

And what say you to the discoveries in anatomy, chemistry, botany? . . . . . These surely are no objections, replied Cleanthes; they only discover new instances of art and contrivance. It is still the image of mind reflected on us from innumerable objects. Add, a mind *like the human*, said Philo. I know of no other, replied Cleanthes. And the liker the better, insisted Philo. To be sure, said Cleanthes.

Now, Cleanthes, said Philo, with an air of alacrity and triumph, mark the consequences. *First,* By this method of reasoning, you renounce all claim to infinity in any of the attributes of the Deity. For, as the cause ought only to be proportioned to the effect, and the effect, so far as it falls under our cognizance, is not infinite; what pretensions have we, upon your suppositions, to ascribe that attribute to the Divine Being? You will still insist, that, by removing him so much from all similarity to human creatures, we give in to the most arbitrary hypothesis, and at the same time weaken all proofs of his existence.

Secondly, You have no reason, on your theory, for ascribing perfection to the Deity, even in his finite capacity, or for supposing him free from every error, mistake, or incoherence, in his undertakings. There are many in-

---

[1] Lib. xi. 1094.   [2] De Nat. Deor. lib. i.

explicable difficulties in the works of Nature, which, if we allow a perfect author to be proved *a priori*, are easily solved, and become only seeming difficulties, from the narrow capacity of man, who cannot trace infinite relations. But according to your method of reasoning, these difficulties become all real; and perhaps will be insisted on, as new instances of likeness to human art and contrivance. At least, you must acknowledge, that it is impossible for us to tell, from our limited views, whether this system contains any great faults, or deserves any considerable praise, if compared to other possible, and even real systems. Could a peasant, if the Æneid were read to him, pronounce that poem to be absolutely faultless, or even assign to it its proper rank among the productions of human wit, he, who had never seen any other production?

But were this world ever so perfect a production, it must still remain uncertain, whether all the excellences of the work can justly be ascribed to the workman. If we survey a ship, what an exalted idea must we form of the ingenuity of the carpenter who framed so complicated, useful, and beautiful a machine? And what surprise must we feel, when we find him a stupid mechanic, who imitated others, and copied an art, which, through a long succession of ages, after multiplied trials, mistakes, corrections, deliberations, and controversies, had been gradually improving? Many worlds might have been botched and bungled, throughout an eternity, ere this system was struck out; much labour lost, many fruitless trials made; and a slow, but continued improvement carried on during infinite ages in the art of world-making. In such subjects, who can determine, where the truth; nay, who can conjecture where the probability lies, amidst a great number of hypotheses which may be proposed, and a still greater which may be imagined?

And what shadow of an argument, continued Philo, can you produce, from your hypothesis, to prove the unity of the Deity? A great number of men join in building a house or ship, in rearing a city, in framing a commonwealth; why may not several deities combine in contriving and framing a world? This is only so much greater similarity to human affairs. By sharing the work among several, we may so much farther limit the attributes of each, and get rid of that extensive power and knowledge, which must be supposed in one deity, and which, according to you, can only serve to weaken the proof of his existence. And if such foolish, such vicious creatures as man, can yet often unite in framing and executing one plan, how much more those deities or demons, whom we may suppose several degrees more perfect!

To multiply causes without necessity, is indeed contrary to true philosophy: but this principle applies not to the present case. Were one deity antecedently proved by your theory, who were possessed of every attribute requisite to the production of the universe; it would be needless, I own, (though not absurd), to suppose any other deity existent. But while it is still a question, Whether all these attributes are united in one subject, or dispersed among several independent beings, by what phenomena in nature can we pretend to decide the controversy? Where we see a body raised in a scale, we are sure that there is in the opposite scale, however concealed from sight, some counterpoising weight equal to it; but it is still allowed to doubt, whether that weight be an aggregate of several distinct bodies, or one uniform united mass. And if the weight requisite very much exceeds any thing which we have ever seen conjoined in any single body, the former supposition becomes still more probable and natural. An intelligent being of such vast power and capacity as is necessary to produce the universe, or, to speak in the language of ancient philosophy, so prodigious an animal exceeds all analogy, and even comprehension.

But farther, Cleanthes: Men are mortal, and renew their species by generation; and this is common to all living creatures. The two great sexes of male and female, says Milton, animate the world. Why must this circumstance, so universal, so essential, be excluded from those numerous and limited deities? Behold, then, the theogeny of ancient times brought back upon us.

And why not become a perfect Anthropomorphite? Why not assert the deity or deities to be corporeal, and to have eyes, a nose, mouth, ears, &c.? Epicurus maintained, that no man had ever seen reason but in a human figure; therefore the gods must have a human figure. And this argument, which is deservedly so much ridiculed by Cicero, becomes, according to you, solid and philosophical.

In a word, Cleanthes, a man who follows your hypothesis is able perhaps to assert, or conjecture, that the universe, sometime, arose from something like design: but beyond that position he cannot ascertain one single circumstance; and is left afterwards to fix every point of his theology by the utmost license of fancy and hypothesis. This world, for aught he knows, is very faulty and imperfect, compared to a superior standard; and was only the first rude essay of some infant deity, who afterwards abandoned it, ashamed of his lame performance: it is the work only of some dependent, inferior deity; and is the object of derision to his superiors: it is the production of old age and dotage in some superannuated deity; and ever since his death, has run on at adventures, from the first impulse and active force which it received from him. You justly give signs of horror, Demea, at these strange suppositions; but these, and a thousand more of the same kind, are Cleanthes's suppositions, not mine. From the moment the attributes of the Deity are supposed finite, all these have place. And I cannot, for my part, think that so wild and unsettled a system of theology is, in any respect, preferable to none at all.

These suppositions I absolutely disown, cried Cleanthes: they strike me, however, with no horror, especially when proposed in that rambling way in which they drop from you. On the contrary, they give me pleasure, when I see, that, by the utmost indulgence of your imagination, you never get rid of the hypothesis of design in the universe, but are obliged at every turn to have recourse to it. To this concession I adhere steadily; and this I regard as a sufficient foundation for religion.

PART VI

It must be a slight fabric, indeed, said Demea, which can be erected on so tottering a foundation. While we are uncertain whether there is one deity or many; whether the deity or deities, to whom we owe our existence, be perfect or imperfect, subordinate or supreme, dead or alive, what trust or confidence can we repose in them? What devotion or worship address to them? What veneration or obedience pay them? To all the purposes of life the theory of religion becomes altogether useless: and even with regard to speculative consequences, its uncertainty, according to you, must render it totally precarious and unsatisfactory.

To render it still more unsatisfactory, said Philo, there occurs to me another hypothesis, which must acquire an air of probability from the method of reasoning so much insisted on by Cleanthes. That like effects arise from like causes: this principle he supposes the foundation of all religion. But there is another principle of the same kind, no less certain, and derived from the same source of experience; that where several known circumstances are observed to be similar, the unknown will also be found similar. Thus, if we see the limbs of a human body, we conclude that it is also attended with a human head, though hid from us. Thus, if we see, through a chink in a wall, a small part of the sun, we conclude, that, were the wall removed, we should see the whole body. In short, this method of reasoning is so obvious and familiar, that no scruple can ever be made with regard to its solidity.

Now, if we survey the universe, so far as it falls under our knowledge, it bears a great resemblance to an animal or organized body, and seems actuated with a like principle of life and motion. A continual circulation of matter in it produces no disorder: a continual waste in every part is incessantly repaired: the closest sympathy is perceived throughout the entire system: and each part or member, in performing its proper offices, operates both to its own preservation and to that of the whole. The world, therefore, I infer, is an animal; and the Deity is the SOUL of the world, actuating it, and actuated by it.

You have too much learning, Cleanthes, to be at all surprised at this opinion, which, you know, was maintained by almost all the Theists of antiquity, and chiefly prevails in their discourses and reasonings. For though, sometimes, the ancient philosophers reason from final causes, as if they thought the world the workmanship of God; yet it appears rather their favourite notion to consider it as his body, whose organization renders it subservient to him. And it must be confessed, that, as the universe resembles more a human body than it does the works of human art and contrivance, if our limited analogy could ever, with any propriety, be extended to the whole of nature, the inference seems juster in favour of the ancient than the modern theory.

There are many other advantages, too, in the former theory, which recommended it to the ancient theologians. Nothing more repugnant to all their notions, because nothing more repugnant to common experience, than mind without body; a mere spiritual substance, which fell not under their senses nor comprehension, and of which they had not observed one single instance throughout all nature. Mind and body they knew, because they felt both: an order, arrangement, organization, or internal machinery, in both, they likewise knew, after the same manner: and it could not but seem reasonable to transfer this experience to the universe; and to suppose the divine mind and body to be also coeval, and to have, both of them, order and arrangement naturally inherent in them, and inseparable from them.

Here, therefore, is a new species of *Anthropomorphism*, Cleanthes, on which you may deliberate; and a theory which seems not liable to any considerable difficulties. You are too much superior, surely, to *systematical prejudices*, to find any more difficulty in supposing an animal body to be, originally, of itself, or from unknown causes, possessed of order and organization, than in supposing a similar order to belong to mind. But the *vulgar prejudice*, that body and mind ought always to accompany each other, ought not, one should think, to be entirely neglected; since it is founded on *vulgar experience*, the only guide which you profess to follow in all these theological inquiries. And if you assert, that our limited experience is an unequal standard, by which to judge of the unlimited extent of nature; you entirely abandon your own hypothesis, and must thenceforward adopt our Mysticism, as you call it, and admit of the absolute incomprehensibility of the Divine Nature.

This theory, I own, replied Cleanthes, has never before occurred to me, though a pretty natural one; and I cannot readily, upon so short an examination and reflection, deliver any opinion with regard to it. You are very scrupulous, indeed, said Philo: were I to examine any system of yours, I should not have acted with half that caution and reserve, in starting objections and difficulties to it. However, if any thing occur to you, you will oblige us by proposing it.

Why then, replied Cleanthes, it seems to me, that, though the world does, in many circumstances, resemble an animal body; yet is the analogy also defective in many circumstances the most material: no organs of sense; no seat of thought or reason; no one precise origin of motion and action. In short, it seems to bear a stronger resemblance to a vegetable than to an animal, and your inference would be so far inconclusive in favour of the soul of the world.

Excellent historical and contemporary essays on the ontological argument can be found in Alvin Plantinga, ed., *The Ontological Argument* * (Doubleday, 1965) and in John Hick and Arthur McGill, eds., *The Many-Faced Argument: Recent Studies on the Ontological Argument for the Existence of God* (Macmillan, 1967). For important but somewhat difficult discussions of the ontological argument, see David Lewis, "Anselm and Actuality," *Nous*, 4, No. 2 (May 1970) and Robert M. Adams, "The Logical Structure of Anselm's Arguments," *Philosophical Review*, 80 (January 1971).

Good discussions of the thirteenth-century form of the cosmological argument can be found in R. Garrigou-Lagrange, *God: His Existence and Nature*, Volume 1 (B. Herder, 1936), R. P. Phillips, *Modern Thomistic Philosophy*, Volume 2 (Burns, Oates & Washbourne, 1935), and Anthony Kenny, *The Five Ways* (Schocken, 1969). Samuel Clarke, *A Discourse Concerning the Being and Attributes of God* (W. Botham, 1738) is a primary source for the eighteenth-century form of the argument. Recent discussions of this later form of the cosmological argument include Richard Taylor, *Metaphysics* (Prentice-Hall, 1963) and William L. Rowe, "The Cosmological Argument," *Nous*, 5, No. 1 (February 1971). A valuable collection of essays on the cosmological argument is Donald R. Burrill, ed., *The Cosmological Arguments* * (Doubleday, 1967).

An excellent introduction to the teleological argument is the editor's commentary in Nelson Pike, ed., *Hume: Dialogues Concerning Natural Religion* * (Bobbs-Merrill, 1970). Also of major importance on this subject is F. R. Tennant, *Philosophical Theology*, Volume 2 (Cambridge University Press, 1969). For good evaluative studies of the teleological argument, see Alvin Plantinga, *God and Other Minds* (Cornell University Press, 1967) and R. G. Swinburne, "The Argument from Design," *Philosophy*, 43, No. 164 (July 1968). And the book by Burrill that is mentioned above as a source for the cosmological argument offers several good discussions of the teleological argument as well.

* Available in paperback.

OBJECTIONS
TO THEISM

A theodicy is an attempt to "justify the ways of God to men"—an attempt to explain how an all-good, all-powerful, and all-knowing God could justifiably permit evil. If theism is to be intellectually respectable, it must provide a theodicy (or, failing that, explain why the demand for a theodicy is inappropriate).

What is the most that can reasonably be expected of a theodicist? First, since *an omnipotent, omniscient, and all-good being exists* and *evil exists* are propositions that are essential to theism,[1] we expect the theodicist to show us that they are compatible (because all true propositions are logically compatible, he could establish the consistency of this pair of propositions by establishing the truth of each member of the pair), or that attempts to prove these propositions incompatible are themselves unsuccessful. Alvin Plantinga undertakes the second of these tasks in "The Free Will Defence." Second, it would appear to be necessarily true that if God exists—that is, if there is a being which is omnipotent, omniscient, and all-good—there is a justification for all the evil that exists (that is, there is either a good reason for any given evil or a good reason for God's permitting it to occur[2]). If this is so, any reason for thinking that God exists is a reason for thinking that all evil is justified. Hence, the theodicist can provide good reasons for believing that the evil which exists is justified by providing us with good reasons for believing that God exists. However, we would like more than this. If theism is true, it follows that evil is justified. Nevertheless, if the theist is to make his position credible, he must, if at all possible, show not only that evil is justified but how it is justified. One should not, however, expect more than partial explanations. Probably the most that can be done along these lines is to show how certain major evils or certain important kinds of evil are, or might be, justified. It is unrealistic to expect the theodicist to be able to show in any precise and detailed way just how all evil is justified. In particular, it is safe to assert that he will not be able to fully explain why our world contains as much evil as it does. (The theodicist might, for example, be able to show that suffering is a logically necessary condition of certain kinds of moral good. It is highly unlikely that he will be able to show how just that degree of suffering which in fact exists is a logically necessary condition of the number and kind of moral goods our world actually exhibits.)

Suppose that the theodicist is able to show that God and evil are compatible, that there are reasons for supposing that God exists, and that there are partial explanations of the evil that exists. Is this sufficient? Reasons are sometimes given for believing that it is not. Thus, some critics assert that as

---

[1] *Evil exists* is entailed by many propositions that are important to theism (for example, *God forgives sin*).

[2] Or both. If there is a good reason for an evil, then there is a good reason for God's permission of it. The converse may not be true. It is frequently argued that God might have good reasons for permitting an evil (for example, the free and deliberate choice of a morally bad course of action) that cannot itself be justified by the goods it makes possible or in any other way.

long as there is some evil which is not fully explained, there is a reason for supposing that theism is false, and that if there is a reason for supposing that theism is false, we should be doubtful of theism. Both of these propositions are suspect. If theism entails that human beings can discover a fully adequate explanation of all evil, then the failure to find such an explanation counts against it. However, there does not appear to be any reason to suppose that the entailment holds. And it is by no means clear that we should doubt a proposition just because something counts against it. For example, if the evidence in a crime overwhelmingly points to Jones' innocence, then the fact that a few things point away from it (Jones might have been present at the scene of the crime and had a motive for committing it) does not imply that one who is aware of all the evidence should doubt Jones' innocence or that he should be reluctant to say that he knows that Jones is innocent. Whether he should be doubtful or not depends upon the comparative strengths of the evidence that points to Jones' innocence and of the evidence that points to his guilt. If the theodicist fails to provide a complete explanation of evil, it is indeed true that our intellectual demands are not fully met. There are un-answered questions, obscurities which are not fully explained. It does not however follow that a complete explanation must be provided in order to protect the view that theism is rationally superior to alternative world views.

Whether the theodicist's response is adequate or not depends upon the success of his attempt to defend the consistency of *God exists* and *evil exists*, the strength of the grounds which he provides for theism, and the scope and plausibility of the partial explanations which he offers. If he successfully defends the consistency of the two propositions, offers good reasons for theism, and is able to plausibly explain many important kinds of evil, there does not seem to be a reason to fault him. If, on the other hand, he fails to rebut the charges of inconsistency, offers no grounds or very weak ones for theism, and is unable to plausibly explain many major kinds of evil, then his defense must be regarded as unsuccessful. There are obviously many inter-mediate possibilities. If, for example, the theodicist manages to dispose of the charge of inconsistency and provides good though not conclusive grounds for theism, but offers sketchy and rather implausible explanations of the evil that exists, then his attempt cannot be judged to be either wholly successful or wholly unsuccessful.

Various explanations of evil have been offered, and many of these are examined in the selections that follow. Historically, the aesthetic defense was of major importance. According to this view, evil contributes to the aesthetic value of the universe in a way analogous to that in which an intrinsically ugly portion of a painting contributes to the beauty of the whole picture. This position is frequently criticized on the grounds that such a good could only be enjoyed by God; hence, to suppose that evil is permitted by God in order that this aesthetic good may exist is to suppose that He permits wickedness and suffering to secure his own selfish pleasure. It is also argued that the disvalue of wickedness and suffering cannot be outweighed by the value of the aesthetic goods they make possible. These criticisms are not conclusive: the first claim forgets that traditional theism maintained that the redeemed would share in God's enjoyment; the second claim, though plausible, is not clearly self-evident or clearly the result of propositions which are self-evident. Nevertheless, the aesthetic defense is not as popular as it once was. The two explanations of evil that currently enjoy the most favor are the view that evil is justified by the moral goods it makes possible and the free will defense. It may be argued, for example, that the presence of evil is a logically necessary condition of certain kinds of moral activity. Thus, it is sometimes asserted that since compassionate activity is a response to suffering, it is possible only if suffering exists and that the value of compassionate activity is sufficiently great to outweigh the disvalue of the evil upon which it depends. Or it is argued that souls are morally and spiritually developed through suffering and confrontation with evil and that this fact is sufficient to justify much of the evil that exists. The free will defense suggests that much evil and perhaps all of it is due to the fact that creatures have made a bad use of their freedom. While God need not have created free creatures, it was impossible both for Him to do so and for Him to determine the use which they would make of their freedom. If the value of free agency and the good it makes possible outweighs the disvalue of the bad actions which creatures perform, and if certain other conditions obtain (that is, roughly, there is no alternative good which should have been produced instead), then God is justified in permitting moral evil.

In evaluating these explanations, we should remember that God is not subject to many of the limitations to which we are subject. Thus, for example, while God is bound by logical necessity, He is not constrained by natural laws. (He cannot make round squares, but He can raise the dead and turn water into wine.) Therefore, any explanation of evil which presupposes that God is limited in these ways rests on a mistake. This observation does not, I think, seriously affect the explanations of evil which have been described above. It does, however, dispose of many less important ones. For example, as Hume points out, there appears to be no reason why an omnipotent being could not have arranged things so that pleasure alone would have been sufficient "to excite all creatures to action, and make them vigilant in the great work of self-preservation." Hence, one cannot justify pain by arguing that it is necessary if that end is to be achieved. God could have devised other means to secure the same result.

While the problem of evil is perhaps the most difficult problem for the theist, it is not the only problem which he must face. Theism must be rejected, for example, if its concepts are incoherent. Kretzmann and Hartshorne (Section I) argued that traditional theism (which ascribes immutability, impassibility, and timelessness to God) is beset with insurmountable internal difficulties.

Flew and Alston (Section VI) seriously question whether theistic sentences are factually significant.

It is sometimes suggested that traditional theism makes its major mistake when it takes its imagery literally or (at a more sophisticated level) when it supposes that concepts which properly apply to finite things can be literally applied to the ground of the universe.[3] Thus, Paul Tillich rejects the notion of a being who is literally omnipotent, omniscient, creator of heaven and earth, and so on, arguing that the idea of such a being is at best a symbol of the creative reality which is the ground of the universe. John Robinson makes a similar point, adding that new ways—ways which depart in many respects from traditional theism—must be found for expressing that reality if it is to be made accessible to modern man.

Tillich and Robinson's criticisms of traditional theism must be seen in connection with their attempt to present us with what they regard as a more adequate alternative to traditional theism—an alternative which preserves what is of value in that view, but at the same time escapes the difficulties that surround it. In addition to the alternatives presented by Tillich, Robinson, and other Western thinkers who have found their own traditions to be either bankrupt or the victims of daemonic distortions, one should consider the alternatives provided by other living religions.

William James asserts that religious life includes the following three beliefs: "1. That the visible world is part of [or related to] a more spiritual universe from which it draws its chief significance; 2. That union or harmonious relation with that higher universe is our true end"; and "3. That prayer or inner communion with the spirit thereof—be that spirit 'God' or 'law'—is a process wherein work is really done, and spiritual energy flows in and produces effects, psychological or material, within the phenomenal world." [4]

This "higher universe" need not be conceived theistically. Indian non-dualists (Advaitans) identify the "higher universe" with the Nirguna Brahman. The Nirguna Brahman is beyond space, time, causality, and the subject-object relationship. It may be characterized as being-consciousness-bliss, but while it is an overwhelmingly positive reality (indeed it is the only thing that is not infected with unreality), it is in essence devoid of attributes or determinations and can ultimately only be referred to as "neti, neti"—"not this, not that." Hīnayāna Buddhists, on the other hand, believe that the "higher universe" is Nirvāna. Nirvāna (or its attainment) is the end of ignorant desire and the suffering which is its consequence. Positive terms are sometimes ascribed to it, such as "Safety," "Purity," "Peace," "The Island," "The Refuge," "The Opposite Shore"; but most often it is described negatively. Unlike the Brahman, Nirvāna cannot be construed as a transcendent substance. Trevor

---

[3] Even if this is a mistake, it is by no means clear that all classical theists make it. See, for example, the selection by Mascall (Section VI).

[4] W. James, *Varieties of Religious Experience* (The Modern Library, 1936), p. 475.

Ling has suggested that it is best thought of as a transcendent condition or state.[5]

These views—and others like them—are free from certain difficulties that beset theism (such as the problem of evil, conflicts between divine omniscience and human freedom, and conflicts between God's omniscience and His immutability), though they do have difficulties of their own. A completely adequate assessment of theism would include an attempt to determine which of these world views involves the fewest difficulties and does most justice to the relevant facts.

w. j. w.

---

[5] See "Buddhist Mysticism," *Religious Studies* (April 1966), pp. 166–67.

THE PROBLEM OF EVIL

GOTTFRIED LEIBNIZ
The Argument Reduced to Syllogistic Form

Some persons of discernment have wished me to make this addition. I have the more readily deferred to their opinion, because of the opportunity thereby gained for meeting certain difficulties, and for making observations on certain matters which were not treated in sufficient detail in the work itself.

OBJECTION I

Whoever does not choose the best course is lacking either in power, or knowledge, or goodness.

God did not choose the best course in creating this world.

Therefore God was lacking in power, or knowledge, or goodness.

ANSWER

I deny the minor, that is to say, the second premiss of this syllogism, and the opponent proves it by this

Gottfried Wilhelm Leibniz (1646–1716), a successful German jurist and diplomat, was also known as a logician and mathematician. He shares, with Newton, the honor of having discovered the calculus. His major philosophical works include the *Monadology* and the *Discourse on Metaphysics*.

THE ARGUMENT REDUCED TO SYLLOGISTIC FORM   From *Theodicy* by G. W. Leibniz, translated by E. M. Huggard, edited with an introduction by Austin Farrer. Reprinted by permission of Routledge & Kegan Paul Ltd.

Whoever makes things in which there is evil, and which could have been made without any evil, or need not have been made at all, does not choose the best course.

God made a world wherein there is evil; a world, I say, which could have been made without any evil or which need not have been made at all.

Therefore God did not choose the best course.

I admit the minor of this prosyllogism: for one must confess that there is evil in this world which God has made, and that it would have been possible to make a world without evil or even not to create any world, since its creation depended upon the free will of God. But I deny the major, that is, the first of the two premises of the prosyllogism, and I might content myself with asking for its proof. In order, however, to give a clearer exposition of the matter, I would justify this denial by pointing out that the best course is not always that one which tends towards avoiding evil, since it is possible that the evil may be accompanied by a greater good. For example, the general of an army will prefer a great victory with a slight wound to a state of affairs without wound and without victory. I have proved this in further detail in this work by pointing out, through instances taken from mathematics and elsewhere, that an imperfection in the part may be required for a greater perfection in the whole. I have followed therein the opinion of St. Augustine, who said a hundred times that God permitted evil in order to derive from it a good, that is to say, a greater good; and Thomas Aquinas says (in libr. 2, *Sent. Dist.* 32, qu. 1, art. 1) that the permission of evil tends towards the good of the universe. I have shown that among older writers the fall of Adam was termed *felix culpa*, a fortunate sin, because it had been expiated with immense benefit by the incarnation of the Son of God: for he gave to the universe something more noble than anything there would otherwise have been amongst created beings. For the better understanding of the matter I added, following the example of many good authors, that it was consistent with order and the general good for God to grant to certain of his creatures the opportunity to exercise their freedom, even when he foresaw that they would turn to evil: for God could easily correct the evil, and it was not fitting that in order to prevent sin he should always act in an extraordinary way. It will therefore sufficiently refute the objection to show that a world with evil may be better than a world without evil. But I have gone still further in the work, and have even shown that this universe must be indeed better than every other possible universe.

OBJECTION II

If there is more evil than good in intelligent creatures, there is more evil
than good in all God's work.
Now there is more evil than good in intelligent creatures.
Therefore there is more evil than good in all God's work.

ANSWER

I deny the major and the minor of this conditional syllogism. As for the
major, I do not admit it because this supposed inference from the part to
the whole, from intelligent creatures to all creatures, assumes tacitly and
without proof that creatures devoid of reason cannot be compared or taken
into account with those that have reason. But why might not the surplus of
good in the non-intelligent creatures that fill the world compensate for and
even exceed incomparably the surplus of evil in rational creatures? It is true
that the value of the latter is greater; but by way of compensation the others
are incomparably greater in number; and it may be that the proportion of
number and quantity surpasses that of value and quality.

The minor also I cannot admit, namely, that there is more evil than good
in intelligent creatures. One need not even agree that there is more evil
than good in the human kind. For it is possible, and even a very reasonable
thing, that the glory and the perfection of the blessed may be incomparably
greater than the misery and. imperfection of the damned, and that here the
excellence of the total good in the smaller number may exceed the total evil
which is in the greater number. The blessed draw near to divinity through
a divine Mediator, so far as can belong to these created beings, and make
such progress in good as is impossible for the damned to make in evil, even
though they should approach as nearly as may be the nature of demons. God
is infinite, and the Devil is finite; good can and does go on *ad infinitum*,
whereas evil has its bounds. It may be therefore, and it is probable, that there
happens in the comparison between the blessed and the damned the opposite
of what I said could happen in the comparison between the happy and the
unhappy, namely that in the latter the proportion of degrees surpasses that
of numbers, while in the comparison between intelligent and non-intelligent
the proportion of numbers is greater than that of values. One is justified in
assuming that a thing may be so as long as one does not prove that it is
impossible, and indeed what is here put forward goes beyond assumption.

But secondly, even should one admit that there is more evil than good in
the human kind, one still has every reason for not admitting that there is
more evil than good in all intelligent creatures. For there is an inconceivable
number of Spirits, and perhaps of other rational creatures besides: and an
opponent cannot prove that in the whole City of God, composed as much of

Spirits as of rational animals without number and of endless different kinds, the evil exceeds the good. Although one need not, in order to answer an objection, prove that a thing is, when its mere possibility suffices, I have nevertheless shown in this present work that it is a result of the supreme perfection of the Sovereign of the Universe that the kingdom of God should be the most perfect of all states or governments possible, and that in consequence what little evil there is should be required to provide the full measure of the vast good existing there.

OBJECTION III

If it is always impossible not to sin, it is always unjust to punish.
Now it is always impossible not to sin, or rather all sin is necessary.
Therefore it is always unjust to punish.
The minor of this is proved as follows.

FIRST PROSYLLOGISM

Everything predetermined is necessary.
Every event is predetermined.
Therefore every event (and consequently sin also) is necessary.
Again this second minor is proved thus.

SECOND PROSYLLOGISM

That which is future, that which is foreseen, that which is involved in causes
   is predetermined.
Every event is of this kind.
Therefore every event is predetermined.

ANSWER

I admit in a certain sense the conclusion of the second prosyllogism, which is the minor of the first; but I shall deny the major of the first prosyllogism, namely that everything predetermined is necessary; taking 'necessity', say the necessity to sin, or the impossibility of not sinning, or of not doing some action, in the sense relevant to the argument, that is, as a necessity essential and absolute, which destroys the morality of action and the justice of punishment. If anyone meant a different necessity or impossibility (that is, a necessity only moral or hypothetical, which will be explained presently) it is plain that we would deny him the major stated in the objection. We might content ourselves with this answer, and demand the proof of the proposition denied: but I am well pleased to justify my manner of procedure in the present work, in order to make the matter clear and to throw more light on this whole subject, by explaining the necessity that must be rejected and the determination that must be allowed. The truth is that the necessity contrary to morality, which must be avoided and which would render punishment unjust, is an insuperable necessity, which would render all opposition unavailing, even though one should wish with all one's heart to avoid the necessary action, and though one should make all possible efforts to that end. Now it is plain that this is not applicable to voluntary actions, since one would not do them if one did not so desire. Thus their prevision and predetermination is not absolute, but it presupposes will: if it is certain that one will do them, it is no less certain that one will will to do them. These voluntary actions and their results will not happen whatever one may do and whether one will them or not; but they will happen because one will do, and because one will will to do, that which leads to them. That is involved in prevision and predetermination, and forms the reason thereof. The necessity of such events is called conditional or hypothetical, or again necessity of consequence, because it presupposes the will and the other requisites. But the necessity which destroys morality, and renders punishment unjust and reward unavailing, is found in the things that will be whatever one may do and whatever one may will to do: in a word, it exists in that which is essential. This it is which is called an absolute necessity. Thus it avails nothing with regard to what is necessary absolutely to ordain interdicts or commandments, to propose penalties or prizes, to blame or to praise; it will come to pass no more and no less. In voluntary actions, on the contrary, and in what depends upon them, precepts, armed with power to punish and to reward, very often serve, and are included in the order of causes that make action exist. Thus it comes about that not only pains and effort but also prayers are effective, God having had even these prayers in mind before he ordered things, and having made due allowance for them. That is why the precept *Ora et labora* (Pray and work) remains intact. Thus not only those who (under the empty pretext of the necessity of events) maintain that one can spare oneself the pains demanded by affairs, but also those who argue against prayers, fall into that which the ancients even in their time called 'the Lazy Sophism'. So the predetermination of events by their causes is precisely what contributes to morality instead of destroying it, and the causes incline the will without necessitating it. For this reason the determination we are concerned with is not a necessitation. It is certain (to him who knows all) that the effect will follow this inclination; but this effect does not follow thence by a consequence which is necessary, that is, whose contrary implies contradiction; and it is also by such an inward inclination that the will is determined, without the presence of necessity. Suppose that one has the greatest possible passion (for example, a great thirst), you will admit that the soul can find some reason for resisting it, even if it were only that of displaying its power. Thus though one may never have complete indifference of equipoise, and there is always a predominance of inclination for the course adopted, that predominance does not render absolutely necessary the resolution taken.

Whoever can prevent the sin of others and does not so, but rather contributes to it, although he be fully apprised of it, is accessary thereto.
God can prevent the sin of intelligent creatures; but he does not so, and he
rather contributes to it by his co-operation and by the opportunities he
causes, although he is fully cognizant of it.
Therefore, etc.

I deny the major of this syllogism. It may be that one can prevent the sin,
but that one ought not to do so, because one could not do so without committing a sin oneself, or (when God is concerned) without acting unreasonably.
I have given instances of that, and have applied them to God himself. It may
be also that one contributes to the evil, and that one even opens the way to
it sometimes, in doing things one is bound to do. And when one does one's
duty, or (speaking of God) when, after full consideration, one does that
which reason demands, one is not responsible for events, even when one
foresees them. One does not will these evils; but one is willing to permit them
for a greater good, which one cannot in reason help preferring to other considerations. This is a *consequent* will, resulting from acts of *antecedent* will,
in which one wills the good. I know that some persons, in speaking of the
antecedent and consequent will of God, have meant by the antecedent that
which wills that all men be saved, and by the consequent that which wills, in
consequence of persistent sin, that there be some damned, damnation being
a result of sin. But these are only examples of a more general notion, and one
may say with the same reason, that God wills by his antecedent will that men
sin not, and that by his consequent or final and decretory will (which is always followed by its effect) he wills to permit that they sin, this permission
being a result of superior reasons. One has indeed justification for saying, in
general, that the antecedent will of God tends towards the production of
good and the prevention of evil, each taken in itself, and as it were detached
(*particulariter et secundum quid*: Thom., I, qu. 19, art. 6) according to the
measure of the degree of each good or of each evil. Likewise one may say
that the consequent, or final and total, divine will tends towards the production of as many goods as can be put together, whose combination thereby
becomes determined, and involves also the permission of some evils and the
exclusion of some goods, as the best possible plan of the universe demands.
Arminius, in his *Antiperkinsus*, explained very well that the will of God can
be called consequent not only in relation to the action of the creature considered beforehand in the divine understanding, but also in relation to other
anterior acts of divine will. But it is enough to consider the passage cited
from Thomas Aquinas, and that from Scotus (I, dist. 46, qu. 11), to see that

they make this distinction as I have made it here. Nevertheless if anyone will not suffer this use of the terms, let him put 'previous' in place of 'antecedent' will, and 'final' or 'decretory' in place of 'consequent' will. For I do not wish to wrangle about words.

OBJECTION V

Whoever produces all that is real in a thing is its cause.
God produces all that is real in sin.
Therefore God is the cause of sin.

ANSWER

I might content myself with denying the major or the minor, because the term 'real' admits of interpretations capable of rendering these propositions false. But in order to give a better explanation I will make a distinction. 'Real' either signifies that which is positive only, or else it includes also privative beings: in the first case, I deny the major and I admit the minor; in the second case, I do the opposite. I might have confined myself to that; but I was willing to go further, in order to account for this distinction. I have therefore been well pleased to point out that every purely positive or absolute reality is a perfection, and that every imperfection comes from limitation, that is, from the privative: for to limit is to withhold extension, or the more beyond. Now God is the cause of all perfections, and consequently of all realities, when they are regarded as purely positive. But limitations or privations result from the original imperfection of creatures which restricts their receptivity. It is as with a laden boat, which the river carries along more slowly or less slowly in proportion to the weight that it bears: thus the speed comes from the river, but the retardation which restricts this speed comes from the load. Also I have shown in the present work how the creature, in causing sin, is a deficient cause; how errors and evil inclinations spring from privation; and how privation is efficacious accidentally. And I have justified the opinion of St. Augustine (lib. I, *Ad. Simpl.*, qu. 2) who explains (for example) how God hardens the soul, not in giving it something evil, but because the effect of the good he imprints is restricted by the resistance of the soul, and by the circumstances contributing to this resistance, so that he does not give it all the good that would overcome its evil. 'Nec (*inquit*) ab illo erogatur aliquid quo homo fit deterior, sed tantum quo fit melior non erogatur.' But if God had willed to do more here he must needs have produced either fresh natures in his creatures or fresh miracles to change their natures, and this the best plan did not allow. It is just as if the current of the river must needs be more rapid than its slope permits or the boats themselves be less laden, if they had to be impelled at a greater speed. So the limitation or original imperfection of creatures brings it about that even the best plan of the universe cannot admit more good, and cannot be exempted from certain evils, these, however, being only of such a kind as may tend towards a greater good. There are some disorders in the parts which wonderfully enhance the beauty of the whole, just as certain dissonances, appropriately used, render harmony more beautiful. But that depends upon the answer which I have already given to the first objection.

OBJECTION VI

Whoever punishes those who have done as well as it was in their power to
  do is unjust.
God does so.
Therefore, etc.

ANSWER

I deny the minor of this argument. And I believe that God always gives sufficient aid and grace to those who have good will, that is to say, who do not reject this grace by a fresh sin. Thus I do not admit the damnation of children dying unbaptized or outside the Church, or the damnation of adult persons who have acted according to the light that God has given them. And I believe that, *if anyone has followed the light he had*, he will undoubtedly receive thereof in greater measure as he has need, even as the late Herr Hulsemann, who was celebrated as a profound theologian at Leipzig, has somewhere observed; and if such a man had failed to receive light during his life, he would receive it at least in the hour of death.

OBJECTION VII

Whoever gives only to some, and not to all, the means of producing effec-
  tively in them good will and final saving faith has not enough goodness.
God does so.
Therefore, etc.

ANSWER

I deny the major. It is true that God could overcome the greatest resistance of the human heart, and indeed he sometimes does so, whether by an inward grace or by the outward circumstances that can greatly influence souls; but he does not always do so. Whence comes this distinction, someone will say, and wherefore does his goodness appear to be restricted? The truth is that it would not have been in order always to act in an extraordinary way and to derange the connexion of things, as I have observed already in answering the first objection. The reasons for this connexion, whereby the one is placed in more favourable circumstances than the other, are hidden in the depths of God's wisdom: they depend upon the universal harmony. The best plan of the universe, which God could not fail to choose, required this. One concludes thus from the event itself; since God made the universe, it was not possible to do better. Such management, far from being contrary to goodness, has rather been prompted by supreme goodness itself. This objection with its solution might have been inferred from what was said with regard to the first objection; but it seemed advisable to touch upon it separately.

OBJECTION VIII

Whoever cannot fail to choose the best is not free.
God cannot fail to choose the best.
Therefore God is not free.

ANSWER

I deny the major of this argument. Rather is it true freedom, and the most perfect, to be able to make the best use of one's free will, and always to exercise this power, without being turned aside either by outward force or by inward passions, whereof the one enslaves our bodies and the other our souls. There is nothing less servile and more befitting the highest degree of freedom than to be always led towards the good, and always by one's own inclination, without any constraint and without any displeasure. And to object that God therefore had need of external things is only a sophism. He creates them freely: but when he had set before him an end, that of exercising his goodness, his wisdom determined him to choose the means most appropriate for obtaining this end. To call that a *need* is to take the term in a sense not usual, which clears it of all imperfection, somewhat as one does when speaking of the wrath of God.

Seneca says somewhere, that God commanded only once, but that he obeys always, because he obeys the laws that he willed to ordain for himself: *semel jussit, semper paret.* But he had better have said, that God always commands and that he is always obeyed: for in willing he always follows the tendency of his own nature, and all other things always follow his will. And as this will is always the same one cannot say that he obeys that will only which he formerly had. Nevertheless, although his will is always indefectible and always tends towards the best, the evil or the lesser good which he rejects will still be possible in itself. Otherwise the necessity of good would be geometrical (so to speak) or metaphysical, and altogether absolute; the contingency of things would be destroyed, and there would be no choice. But necessity of this kind, which does not destroy the possibility of the contrary, has the name by analogy only: it becames effective not through the mere essence of things, but through that which is outside them and above them, that is, through the will of God. This necessity is called moral, because for the wise what is necessary and what is owing are equivalent things; and when it is always followed by its effect, as it indeed is in the perfectly wise, that is, in God, one can say that it is a happy necessity. The more nearly creatures approach this, the closer do they come to perfect felicity. Moreover, necessity of this kind is not the necessity one endeavours to avoid, and which destroys morality, reward and commendation. For that which it brings to pass does not happen whatever one may do and whatever one may will, but because one desires it. A will to which it is natural to choose well deserves most to be commended; and it carries with it its own reward, which is supreme happiness. And as this constitution of the divine nature gives an entire satisfaction to him who possesses it, it is also the best and the most desirable from the point of view of the creatures who are all dependent upon God. If the will of God had not as its rule the principle of the best, it would tend towards evil, which would be worst of all; or else it would be indifferent somehow to good and to evil, and guided by chance. But a will that would always drift along at random would scarcely be any better for the government of the universe than the fortuitous concourse of corpuscles, without the existence of divinity. And even though God should abandon himself to chance only in some cases, and in a certain way (as he would if he did not always tend entirely towards the best, and if he were capable of preferring a lesser good to a greater good, that is, an evil to a good, since that which prevents a greater good is an evil) he would be no less imperfect than the object of his choice. Then he would not deserve absolute trust; he would act without reason in such a case, and the government of the universe would be like certain games equally divided between reason and luck. This all proves that this objection which is made against the choice of the best perverts the notions of free and necessary, and represents the best to us actually as evil: but that is either malicious or asburd.

DAVID HUME
God and the Problem of Evil

PART X

. . . And is it possible, Cleanthes, said Philo, that after all these reflections, and infinitely more, which might be suggested, you can still persevere in your Anthropomorphism, and assert the moral attributes of the Deity, his justice, benevolence, mercy, and rectitude, to be of the same nature with these virtues in human creatures? His power we allow is infinite: whatever he wills

GOD AND THE PROBLEM OF EVIL   From *Dialogues Concerning Natural Religion*, Parts X and XI. *The Philosophical Works of David Hume*, Volume II. Edinburgh, Adam Black and William Tait; and Charles Tait, 1876.

is executed: but neither man nor any other animal is happy: therefore he does not will their happiness. His wisdom is infinite: he is never mistaken in choosing the means to any end: but the course of Nature tends not to human or animal felicity: therefore it is not established for that purpose. Through the whole compass of human knowledge, there are no inferences more certain and infallible than these. In what respect, then, do his benevolence and mercy resemble the benevolence and mercy of men?

Epicurus's old questions are yet unanswered.

Is he willing to prevent evil, but not able? then is he impotent. Is he able, but not willing? then is he malevolent. Is he both able and willing? whence then is evil?

You ascribe, Cleanthes (and I believe justly), a purpose and intention to Nature. But what, I beseech you, is the object of that curious artifice and machinery, which she has displayed in all animals? The preservation alone of individuals, and propagation of the species. It seems enough for her purpose, if such a rank be barely upheld in the universe, without any care or concern for the happiness of the members that compose it. No resource for this purpose: no machinery, in order merely to give pleasure or ease: no fund of pure joy and contentment: no indulgence, without some want or necessity accompanying it. At least, the few phenomena of this nature are overbalanced by opposite phenomena of still greater importance.

Our sense of music, harmony, and indeed beauty of all kinds, gives satisfaction, without being absolutely necessary to the preservation and propagation of the species. But what racking pains, on the other hand, arise from gouts, gravels, megrims, toothaches, rheumatisms, where the injury to the animal machinery is either small or incurable? Mirth, laughter, play, frolic, seem gratuitous satisfactions, which have no farther tendency: spleen, melancholy, discontent, superstition, are pains of the same nature. How then does the Divine benevolence display itself, in the sense of you Anthropomorphites? None but we Mystics, as you were pleased to call us, can account for this strange mixture of phenomena, by deriving it from attributes, infinitely perfect, but incomprehensible.

And have you at last, said Cleanthes smiling, betrayed your intentions, Philo? Your long agreement with Demea did indeed a little surprise me; but I find you were all the while erecting a concealed battery against me. And I must confess, that you have now fallen upon a subject worthy of your noble spirit of opposition and controversy. If you can make out the present point, and prove mankind to be unhappy or corrupted, there is an end at once of all religion. For to what purpose establish the natural attributes of the Deity, while the moral are still doubtful and uncertain?

You take umbrage very easily, replied Demea, at opinions the most innocent, and the most generally received, even amongst the religious and devout themselves: and nothing can be more surprising than to find a topic like this, concerning the wickedness and misery of man, charged with no less than Atheism and profaneness. Have not all pious divines and preachers, who have indulged their rhetoric on so fertile a subject; have they not easily, I say, given a solution of any difficulties which may attend it? This world is but a point in comparison of the universe; this life but a moment in comparison of eternity. The present evil phenomena, therefore, are rectified in other regions, and in some future period of existence. And the eyes of men, being then opened to larger views of things, see the whole connection of general laws; and trace with adoration, the benevolence and rectitude of the Deity, through all the mazes and intricacies of his providence.

No! replied Cleanthes, No! These arbitrary suppositions can never be admitted, contrary to matter of fact, visible and uncontroverted. Whence can any cause be known but from its known effects? Whence can any hypothesis be proved but from the apparent phenomena? To establish one hypothesis upon another, is building entirely in the air; and the utmost we ever attain, by these conjectures and fictions, is to ascertain the bare possibility of our opinion; but never can we, upon such terms, establish its reality.

The only method of supporting Divine benevolence, and it is what I willingly embrace, is to deny absolutely the misery and wickedness of man. Your representations are exaggerated; your melancholy views mostly fictitious; your inferences contrary to fact and experience. Health is more common than sickness; pleasure than pain; happiness than misery. And for one vexation which we meet with, we attain, upon computation, a hundred enjoyments.

Admitting your position, replied Philo, which yet is extremely doubtful, you must at the same time allow, that if pain be less frequent than pleasure, it is infinitely more violent and durable. One hour of it is often able to outweigh a day, a week, a month of our common insipid enjoyments; and how many days, weeks, and months, are passed by several in the most acute torments? Pleasure, scarcely in one instance, is ever able to reach ecstasy and rapture; and in no one instance can it continue for any time at its highest pitch and altitude. The spirits evaporate, the nerves relax, the fabric is disordered, and the enjoyment quickly degenerates into fatigue and uneasiness. But pain often, good God, how often! rises to torture and agony; and the longer it continues, it becomes still more genuine agony and torture. Patience is exhausted, courage languishes, melancholy seizes us, and nothing terminates our misery but the removal of its cause, or another event, which is the sole cure of all evil, but which, from our natural folly, we regard with still greater horror and consternation.

But not to insist upon these topics, continued Philo, though most obvious, certain, and important; I must use the freedom to admonish you, Cleanthes, that you have put the controversy upon a most dangerous issue, and are unawares introducing a total scepticism into the most essential articles of natural and revealed theology. What! no method of fixing a just foundation for religion, unless we allow the happiness of human life, and maintain a continued existence even in this world, with all our present pains, infirmities, vexations, and follies, to be eligible and desirable! But this is contrary to every one's feeling and experience: It is contrary to an authority so established as nothing can subvert. No decisive proofs can ever be produced against this authority; nor is it possible for you to compute, estimate and compare, all the pains and all the pleasures in the lives of all men and of all animals: And thus, by your resting the whole system of religion on a point, which, from its very nature, must for ever be uncertain, you tacitly confess, that that system is equally uncertain.

But allowing you what never will be believed, at least what you never possibly can prove, that animal, or at least human happiness, in this life, exceeds its misery, you have yet done nothing: For this is not, by any means, what we expect from infinite power, infinite wisdom, and infinite goodness. Why is there any misery at all in the world? Not by chance surely. From some cause then. Is it from the intention of the Deity? But he is perfectly benevolent. Is it contrary to his intention? But he is almighty. Nothing can shake the solidity of this reasoning, so short, so clear, so decisive; except we assert, that these subjects exceed all human capacity, and that our common measures of truth and falsehood are not applicable to them; a topic which I have all along insisted on, but which you have, from the beginning, rejected with scorn and indignation.

But I will be contented to retire still from this intrenchment, for I deny that you can ever force me in it. I will allow, that pain or misery in man is *compatible* with infinite power and goodness in the Deity, even in your sense of these attributes: What are you advanced by all these concessions? A mere possible compatibility is not sufficient. You must *prove* these pure, unmixt, and uncontrollable attributes from the present mixt and confused phenomena, and from these alone. A hopeful undertaking! Were the phenomena ever so pure and unmixt, yet being finite, they would be insufficient for that purpose. How much more, where they are also so jarring and discordant!

Here, Cleanthes, I find myself at ease in my argument. Here I triumph. Formerly, when we argued concerning the natural attributes of intelligence and design, I needed all my sceptical and metaphysical subtilty to elude your grasp. In many views of the universe, and of its parts, particularly the latter, the beauty and fitness of final causes strike us with such irresistible force, that all objections appear (what I believe they really are) mere cavils and sophisms; nor can we then imagine how it was ever possible for us to repose any weight on them. But there is no view of human life, or of the condition of mankind, from which, without the greatest violence, we can infer the moral attributes, or learn that infinite benevolence, conjoined with infinite power and infinite wisdom, which we must discover by the eyes of faith alone.

It is your turn now to tug the labouring oar, and to support your philosophical subtilties against the dictates of plain reason and experience.

PART XI

I scruple not to allow, said Cleanthes, that I have been apt to suspect the frequent repetition of the word *infinite*, which we meet with in all theological writers, to savour more of panegyric than of philosophy; and that any purposes of reasoning, and even of religion, would be better served, were we to rest contented with more accurate and more moderate expressions. The terms, *admirable, excellent, superlatively great, wise,* and *holy*; these sufficiently fill the imaginations of men; and any thing beyond, besides that it leads into absurdities, has no influence on the affections or sentiments. Thus, in the present subject, if we abandon all human analogy, as seems your intention, Demea, I am afraid we abandon all religion, and retain no conception of the great object of our adoration. If we preserve human analogy, we must for ever find it impossible to reconcile any mixture of evil in the universe with infinite attributes; much less can we ever prove the latter from the former. But supposing the Author of Nature to be finitely perfect, though far exceeding mankind, a satisfactory account may then be given of natural and moral evil, and every untoward phenomenon be explained and adjusted. A less evil may then be chosen, in order to avoid a greater; inconveniences be submitted to, in order to reach a desirable end; and in a word, benevolence, regulated by wisdom, and limited by necessity, may produce just such a world as the present. You, Philo, who are so prompt at starting views, and reflections, and analogies, I would gladly hear, at length, without interruption, your opinion of this new theory; and if it deserve our attention, we may afterwards, at more leisure, reduce it into form.

My sentiments, replied Philo, are not worth being made a mystery of; and therefore, without any ceremony, I shall deliver what occurs to me with regard to the present subject. It must, I think, be allowed, that if a very limited intelligence, whom we shall suppose utterly unacquainted with the universe, were assured, that it were the production of a very good, wise, and powerful Being, however finite, he would, from his conjectures, form *beforehand* a different notion of it from what we find it to be by experience; nor would he ever imagine, merely from these attributes of the cause, of which he is informed, that the effect could be so full of vice and misery and disorder, as it appears in this life. Supposing now, that this person were brought into the world, still assured that it was the workmanship of such a sublime and benevolent Being; he might, perhaps, be surprised at the disappointment; but would never retract his former belief, if founded on any very solid argument; since such a limited intelligence must be sensible of his own blindness and ignorance, and must allow, that there may be many solutions of those phenomena, which will for ever escape his comprehension. But supposing, which is the real case with regard to man, that this creature is not anteced-ently convinced of a supreme intelligence, benevolent, and powerful, but is left to gather such a belief from the appearances of things; this entirely alters the case, nor will he ever find any reason for such a conclusion. He may be fully convinced of the narrow limits of his understanding; but this will not help him in forming an inference concerning the goodness of superior powers, since he must form that inference from what he knows, not from what he is ignorant of. The more you exaggerate his weakness and ignorance, the more diffident you render him, and give him the greater suspicion that such sub-jects are beyond the reach of his faculties. You are obliged, therefore, to reason with him merely from the known phenomena, and to drop every arbitrary supposition or conjecture.

Did I show you a house or palace, where there was not one apartment convenient or agreeable; where the windows, doors, fires passages, stairs, and the whole economy of the building, were the source of noise, confusion, fatigue, darkness, and the extremes of heat and cold; you would certainly blame the contrivance, without any farther examination. The architect would in vain display his subtilty, and prove to you, that if this door or that window were altered, greater ills would ensue. What he says may be strictly true: The alteration of one particular, while the other parts of the building remain, may only augment the inconveniences. But still you would assert in general, that, if the architect had had skill and good intentions, he might have formed such a plan of the whole, and might have adjusted the parts in such a man-ner, as would have remedied all or most of these inconveniences. His igno-rance, or even your own ignorance of such a plan, will never convince you of the impossibility of it. If you find any inconveniences and deformities in the building, you will always, without entering into any detail, condemn the architect.

In short, I repeat the question: Is the world, considered in general, and as it appears to us in this life, different from what a man, or such a limited being, would, *beforehand*, expect from a very powerful, wise, and benevolent Deity? It must be strange prejudice to assert the contrary. And from thence I conclude, that however consistent the world may be, allowing certain sup-positions and conjectures, with the idea of such a Deity, it can never afford us an inference concerning his existence. The consistence is not absolutely denied, only the inference. Conjectures, especially where infinity is excluded from the Divine attributes, may perhaps be sufficient to prove a consistence, but can never be foundations for any inference.

There seem to be *four* circumstances, on which depend all, or the greatest part of the ills, that molest sensible creatures; and it is not impossible but all these circumstances may be necessary and unavoidable. We know so little beyond common life, or even of common life, that, with regard to the economy of a universe, there is no conjecture, however wild, which may not be just; nor any one, however plausible, which may not be erroneous. All that belongs to human understanding, in this deep ignorance and obscurity, is to be sceptical, or at least cautious, and not to admit of any hypothesis whatever, much less of any which is supported by no appearance of probability. Now, this I assert to be the case with regard to all the causes of evil, and the circumstances on which it depends. None of them appear to human reason in the least degree necessary or unavoidable; nor can we suppose them such, without the utmost license of imagination.

The *first* circumstance which introduces evil, is that contrivance or economy of the animal creation, by which pains, as well as pleasures, are employed to excite all creatures to action, and make them vigilant in the great work of self-preservation. Now pleasure alone, in its various degrees, seems to human understanding sufficient for this purpose. All animals might be constantly in a state of enjoyment: but when urged by any of the necessities of nature, such as thirst, hunger, weariness; instead of pain, they might feel a diminution of pleasure, by which they might be prompted to seek that object which is necessary to their subsistence. Men pursue pleasure as eagerly as they avoid pain; at least, they might have been so constituted. It seems, therefore, plainly possible to carry on the business of life without any pain. Why then is any animal ever rendered susceptible of such a sensation? If animals can be free from it an hour, they might enjoy a perpetual exemption from it; and it required as particular a contrivance of their organs to produce that feeling, as to endow them with sight, hearing, or any of the senses. Shall we conjecture, that such a contrivance was necessary, without any appearance of reason? and shall we build on that conjecture as on the most certain truth?

But a capacity of pain would not alone produce pain, were it not for the *second* circumstance, viz. the conducting of the world by general laws; and this seems nowise necessary to a very perfect Being. It is true, if every thing were conducted by particular volitions, the course of nature would be perpetually broken, and no man could employ his reason in the conduct of life. But might not other particular volitions remedy this inconvenience? In short, might not the Deity exterminate all ill, wherever it were to be found; and produce all good, without any preparation, or long progress of causes and effects?

Besides, we must consider, that, according to the present economy of the world, the course of nature, though supposed exactly regular, yet to us appears not so, and many events are uncertain, and many disappoint our expectations. Health and sickness, calm and tempest, with an infinite number of other accidents, whose causes are unknown and variable, have a great influence both on the fortunes of particular persons and on the prosperity of public societies; and indeed all human life, in a manner, depends on such accidents. A being, therefore, who knows the secret springs of the universe, might easily, by particular volitions, turn all these accidents to the good of mankind, and render the whole world happy, without discovering himself in any operation. A fleet, whose purposes were salutary to society, might always meet with a fair wind. Good princes enjoy sound health and long life. Persons born to power and authority, be framed with good tempers and virtuous dispositions. A few such events as these, regularly and wisely conducted, would change the face of the world; and yet would no more seem to disturb the course of nature, or confound human conduct, than the present economy of things, where the causes are secret, and variable, and compounded. Some small touches given to Caligula's brain in his infancy, might have converted him into a Trajan. One wave, a little higher than the rest, by burying Cæsar and his fortune in the bottom of the ocean, might have restored liberty to a considerable part of mankind. There may, for aught we know, be good reasons why Providence interposes not in this manner; but they are unknown to us; and though the mere supposition, that such reasons exist, may be sufficient to *save* the conclusion concerning the Divine attributes, yet surely it can never be sufficient to *establish* that conclusion.

If every thing in the universe be conducted by general laws, and if animals be rendered susceptible of pain, it scarcely seems possible but some ill must arise in the various shocks of matter, and the various concurrence and opposition of general laws; but this ill would be very rare, were it not for the *third* circumstance, which I proposed to mention, viz. the great frugality with which all powers and faculties are distributed to every particular being. So well adjusted are the organs and capacities of all animals, and so well fitted to their preservation, that, as far as history or tradition reaches, there appears not to be any single species which has yet been extinguished in the universe. Every animal has the requisite endowments; but these endowments are bestowed with so scrupulous an economy, that any considerable diminution must entirely destroy the creature. Wherever one power is increased, there is a proportional abatement in the others. Animals which excel in swiftness are commonly defective in force. Those which possess both are either imperfect in some of their senses, or are oppressed with the most craving wants. The human species, whose chief excellency is reason and sagacity, is of all others the most necessitous, and the most deficient in bodily advantages; without clothes, without arms, without food, without lodging, without any convenience of life, except what they owe to their own skill and industry. In short, nature seems to have formed an exact calculation of the necessities of her creatures; and, like a *rigid master*, has afforded them little more powers or endowments than what are strictly sufficient to supply those necessities. An *indulgent parent* would have bestowed a large stock, in order to guard against accidents, and secure the happiness and welfare of the creature in the most unfortunate concurrence of circumstances. Every course of life would not have been so surrounded with precipices, that the least departure from the true path, by mistake or necessity, must involve us in misery and ruin. Some reserve, some fund, would have been provided to ensure happiness; nor would the powers and the necessities have been adjusted with so rigid an economy. The Author of Nature is inconceivably powerful: his force is supposed great, if not altogether inexhaustible: nor is there any reason, as far as we can judge, to make him observe this strict frugality in his dealings with his creatures. It would have been better, were his power extremely limited, to have created fewer animals, and to have endowed these with more faculties for their happiness and preservation. A builder is never esteemed prudent, who undertakes a plan beyond what his stock will enable him to finish.

In order to cure most of the ills of human life, I require not that man should have the wings of the eagle, the swiftness of the stag, the force of the ox, the arms of the lion, the scales of the crocodile or rhinoceros; much less do I demand the sagacity of an angel or cherubim. I am contented to take an increase in one single power or faculty of his soul. Let him be endowed with a greater propensity to industry and labour; a more vigorous spring and activity of mind; a more constant bent to business and application. Let the whole species possess naturally an equal diligence with that which many individuals are able to attain by habit and reflection; and the most beneficial consequences, without any allay of ill, is the immediate and necessary result of this endowment. Almost all the moral, as well as natural evils of human life, arise from idleness; and were our species, by the original constitution of their frame, exempt from this vice or infirmity, the perfect cultivation of land, the improvement of arts and manufactures, the exact execution of every office and duty, immediately follow; and men at once may fully reach that state of society, which is so imperfectly attained by the best regulated government. But as industry is a power, and the most valuable of any, Nature seems determined, suitably to her usual maxims, to bestow it on men with a very sparing hand; and rather to punish him severely for his deficiency in it, than to reward him for his attainments. She has so contrived his frame, that nothing but the most violent necessity can oblige him to labour; and she employs all his other wants to overcome, at least in part, the want of diligence, and to endow him with some share of a faculty of which she has thought fit naturally to bereave him. Here our demands may be allowed very humble, and therefore the more reasonable. If we required the endowments of superior penetration and judgment, of a more delicate taste of beauty, of a nicer sensibility to benevolence and friendship; we might be told, that we impiously pretend to break the order of Nature; that we want to exalt ourselves into a higher rank of being; that the presents which we require, not being suitable to our state and condition, would only be pernicious to us. But it is hard; I dare to repeat it, it is hard, that being placed in a world so full of wants and necessities, where almost every being and element is either our foe or refuses its assistance. . . . we should also have our own temper to struggle with, and should be deprived of that faculty which can alone fence against these multiplied evils.

The *fourth* circumstance, whence arises the misery and ill of the universe, is the inaccurate workmanship of all the springs and principles of the great machine of nature. It must be acknowledged, that there are few parts of the universe, which seem not to serve some purpose, and whose removal would not produce a visible defect and disorder in the whole. The parts hang all together; nor can one be touched without affecting the rest, in a greater or less degree. But at the same time, it must be observed, that none of these parts or principles, however useful, are so accurately adjusted, as to keep precisely within those bounds in which their utility consists; but they are, all of them, apt, on every occasion, to run into the one extreme or the other. One would imagine, that this grand production had not received the last hand of the maker; so little finished is every part, and so coarse are the strokes with which it is executed. Thus, the winds are requisite to convey the vapours along the surface of the globe, and to assist men in navigation: but how oft, rising up to tempests and hurricanes, do they become pernicious? Rains are necessary to nourish all the plants and animals of the earth: but how often are they defective? how often excessive? Heat is requisite to all life and vegetation; but is not always found in the due proportion. On the mixture and secretion of the humours and juices of the body depend the health and prosperity of the animal: but the parts perform not regularly their proper function. What more useful than all the passions of the mind, am-bition, vanity, love, anger? But how oft do they break their bounds, and cause the greatest convulsions in society? There is nothing so advantageous in the universe, but what frequently becomes pernicious, by its excess or defect; nor has Nature guarded, with the requisite accuracy, against all dis-order or confusion. The irregularity is never perhaps so great as to destroy any species; but is often sufficient to involve the individuals in ruin and misery.

On the concurrence, then, of these *four* circumstances, does all or the greatest part of natural evil depend. Were all living creatures incapable of pain, or were the world administered by particular volitions, evil never could have found access into the universe: and were animals endowed with a large stock of powers and faculties, beyond what strict necessity requires; or were the several springs and principles of the universe so accurately framed as to preserve always the just temperament and medium; there must have been very little ill in comparison of what we feel at present. What then shall we pronounce on this occasion? Shall we say that these circumstances are not necessary, and that they might easily have been altered in the contrivance of the universe? This decision seems too presumptuous for creatures so blind and ignorant. Let us be more modest in our conclusions. Let us allow, that, if the goodness of the Diety (I mean a goodness like the human) could be established on any tolerable reasons *a priori*, these phenomena, however un-toward, would not be sufficient to subvert that principle; but might easily, in some unknown manner, be reconcileable to it. But let us still assert, that as this goodness is not antecedently established, but must be inferred from the phenomena, there can be no grounds for such an inference, while there are so many ills in the universe, and while these ills might so easily have been remedied, as far as human understanding can be allowed to judge on such a subject. I am Sceptic enough to allow, that the bad appearances, notwithstanding all my reasonings, may be compatible with such attributes as you suppose; but surely they can never prove these attributes. Such a conclusion cannot result from Scepticism, but must arise from the phenomena, and from our confidence in the reasonings which we deduce from these phenomena.

Look round this universe. What an immense profusion of beings, animated and organized, sensible and active! You admire this prodigious variety and fecundity. But inspect a little more narrowly these living existences, the only beings worth regarding. How hostile and destructive to each other! How insufficient all of them for their own happiness! How contemptible or odious to the spectator! The whole presents nothing but the idea of a blind Nature, impregnated by a great vivifying principle, and pouring forth from her lap, without discernment or parental care, her maimed and abortive children!

Here the Manichæan system occurs as a proper hypothesis to solve the difficulty: and no doubt, in some respects, it is very specious, and has more probability than the common hypothesis, by giving a plausible account of the strange mixture of good and ill which appears in life. But if we consider, on the other hand, the perfect uniformity and agreement of the parts of the universe, we shall not discover in it any marks of the combat of a malevolent with a benevolent being. There is indeed an opposition of pains and pleasures in the feelings of sensible creatures: but are not all the operations of Nature carried on by an opposition of principles, of hot and cold, moist and dry, light and heavy? The true conclusion is, that the original Source of all things is entirely indifferent to all these principles; and has no more regard to good above ill, than to heat above cold, or to drought above moisture, or to light above heavy.

There may *four* hypotheses be framed concerning the first causes of the universe: *that* they are endowed with perfect goodness; *that* they have perfect malice; *that* they are opposite, and have both goodness and malice; *that* they have neither goodness nor malice. Mixt phenomena can never prove the two former unmixt principles; and the uniformity and steadiness of general laws seem to oppose the third. The fourth, therefore, seems by far the most probable.

What I have said concerning natural evil will apply to moral, with little or no variation; and we have no more reason to infer, that the rectitude of the Supreme Being resembles human rectitude, than that his benevolence resembles the human. Nay, it will be thought, that we have still greater cause to exclude from him moral sentiments, such as we feel them; since moral evil, in the opinion of many, is much more predominant above moral good than natural evil above natural good.

But even though this should not be allowed, and though the virtue which is in mankind should be acknowledged much superior to the vice, yet so long as there is any vice at all in the universe, it will very much puzzle you Anthropomorphites, how to account for it. You must assign a cause for it, without having recourse to the first cause. But as every effect must have a cause, and that cause another, you must either carry on the progression *in infinitum*, or rest on that original principle, who is the ultimate cause of all things. . . .

FYODOR DOSTOEVSKY
Rebellion

"I must make you one confession," Ivan began. "I could never understand how one can love one's neighbours. It's just one's neighbours, to my mind, that one can't love, though one might love those at a distance. I once read somewhere of John the Merciful, a saint, that when a hungry, frozen beggar came to him, he took him into his bed, held him in his arms, and began breathing into his mouth, which was putrid and loathsome from some awful disease. I am convinced that he did that from 'self-laceration,' from the self-laceration of falsity, for the sake of the charity imposed by duty, as a penance laid on him. For any one to love a man, he must be hidden, for as soon as he shows his face, love is gone."

"Father Zossima has talked of that more than once," observed Alyosha; "he, too, said that the face of a man often hinders many people not practised in love, from loving him. But yet there's a great deal of love in mankind, and almost Christ-like love. I know that myself, Ivan."

"Well, I know nothing of it so far, and can't understand it, and the innumerable mass of mankind are with me there. The question is, whether that's due to men's bad qualities or whether it's inherent in their nature. To my thinking, Christ-like love for men is a miracle impossible on earth. He was God. But we are not gods. Suppose I, for instance, suffer intensely. Another can never know how much I suffer, because he is another and not I. And what's more, a man is rarely ready to admit another's suffering (as though it were a distinction). Why won't he admit it, do you think? Because

Fyodor Dostoevsky (1821–1881), considered one of the greatest Russian novelists, was deeply concerned with theological questions and often presented philosophical arguments within his fictional works. Among his best known novels are *Crime and Punishment*, *The Idiot*, and *The Brothers Karamazov*.

REBELLION   Reprinted with permission of The Macmillan Company and William Heinemann Ltd. from *The Brothers Karamazov* by Fyodor Dostoevsky, translated by Constance Garnett. Printed in Great Britain. Published in the United States by Random House, Inc.

I smell unpleasant, because I have a stupid face, because I once trod on his foot. Besides there is suffering and suffering; degrading, humiliating suffering such as humbles me—hunger, for instance—my benefactor will perhaps allow me; but when you come to higher suffering—for an idea, for instance—he will very rarely admit that, perhaps because my face strikes him as not at all what he fancies a man should have who suffers for an idea. And so he deprives me instantly of his favour, and not at all from badness of heart. Beggars, especially genteel beggars, ought never to show themselves, but to ask for charity through the newspapers. One can love one's neighbours in the abstract, or even at a distance, but at close quarters it's almost impossible. If it were as on the stage, in the ballet, where if beggars come in, they wear silken rags and tattered lace and beg for alms dancing gracefully, then one might like looking at them. But even then we should not love them. But enough of that. I simply wanted to show you my point of view. I meant to speak of the suffering of mankind generally, but we had better confine our- selves to the sufferings of the children. That reduces the scope of my argu- ment to a tenth of what it would be. Still we'd better keep to the children, though it does weaken my case. But, in the first place, children can be loved even at close quarters, even when they are dirty, even when they are ugly (I fancy, though, children never are ugly). The second reason why I won't speak of grown-up people is that, besides being disgusting and unworthy of love, they have a compensation—they've eaten the apple and know good and evil, and they have become 'like god.' They go on eating it still. But the children haven't eaten anything, and are so far innocent. Are you fond of children, Alyosha? I know you are, and you will understand why I prefer to speak of them. If they, too, suffer horribly on earth, they must suffer for their fathers' sins, they must be punished for their fathers, who have eaten the apple; but that reasoning is of the other world and is incomprehensible for the heart of man here on earth. The innocent must not suffer for an- other's sins, and especially such innocents! You may be surprised at me, Alyosha, but I am awfully fond of children, too. And observe, cruel people, the violent, the rapacious, the Karamazovs are sometimes very fond of chil- dren. Children while they are quite little—up to seven, for instance—are so remote from grown-up people; they are different creatures, as it were, of a different species. I knew a criminal in prison who had, in the course of his career as a burglar, murdered whole families, including several children. But when he was in prison, he had a strange affection for them. He spent all his time at his window, watching the children playing in the prison yard. He trained one little boy to come up to his window and made great friends with him. . . . You don't know why I am telling you all this, Alyosha? My head aches and I am sad."

"You speak with a strange air," observed Alyosha uneasily, "as though you were not quite yourself."

"By the way, a Bulgarian I met lately in Moscow," Ivan went on, seeming not to hear his brother's words, "told me about the crimes committed by Turks and Circassians in all parts of Bulgaria through fear of a general rising of the Slavs. They burn villages, murder, outrage women and children, they nail their prisoners by the ears to the fences, leave them so till morning, and in the morning they hang them—all sorts of things you can't imagine. People talk sometimes of bestial cruelty, but that's a great injustice and insult to the beasts; a beast can never be so cruel as a man, so artistically cruel. The tiger only tears and gnaws, that's all he can do. He would never think of nailing people by the ears, even if he were able to do it. These Turks took a pleasure in torturing children, too; cutting the unborn child from the mother's womb, and tossing babies up in the air and catching them on the points of their bayonets before their mother's eyes. Doing it before the mother's eyes was what gave zest to the amusement. Here is another scene that I thought very interesting. Imagine a trembling mother with her baby in her arms, a circle of invading Turks around her. They've planned a diversion; they pet the baby, laugh to make it laugh. They succeed, the baby laughs. At that moment a Turk points a pistol four inches from the baby's face. The baby laughs with glee, holds out its little hands to the pistol, and he pulls the trigger in the baby's face and blows out its brains. Artistic, wasn't it? By the way, Turks are particularly fond of sweet things, they say."

"Brother, what are you driving at?" asked Alyosha.

"I think if the devil doesn't exist, but man has created him, he has created him in his own image and likeness."

"Just as he did God, then?" observed Alyosha.

"'It's wonderful how you can turn words,' as Polonius says in *Hamlet*," laughed Ivan. "You turn my words against me. Well, I am glad. Yours must be a fine God, if man created Him in His image and likeness. You asked just now what I was driving at. You see, I am fond of collecting certain facts, and, would you believe, I even copy anecdotes of a certain sort from newspapers and books, and I've already got a fine collection. The Turks, of course, have gone into it, but they are foreigners. I have specimens from home that are even better than the Turks. You know we prefer beating—rods and scourges—that's our national institution. Nailing ears is unthinkable for us, for we are, after all, Europeans. But the rod and the scourge we have always with us and they cannot be taken from us. Abroad now they scarcely do any beating. Manners are more humane, or laws have been passed, so that they don't dare to flog men now. But they make up for it in another way just as national as ours. And so national that it would be practically impossible among us, though I believe we are being inoculated with it, since the religious movement began in our aristocracy. I have a charming pamphlet, translated from the French, describing how, quite recently, five years ago, a murderer, Richard, was executed—a young man, I believe, of three and twenty, who repented and was converted to the Christian faith at the very scaffold. This Richard was an illegitimate child who was given as a child of six by his parents to some shepherds on the Swiss mountains. They brought him up to work for them. He grew up like a little wild beast among them. The shepherds taught him nothing, and scarcely fed or clothed him, but sent him out at seven to herd the flock in cold and wet, and no one hesitated or scrupled to treat him so. Quite the contrary, they thought they had every right, for Richard had been given to them as a chattel, and they did not even see the necessity of feeding him. Richard himself describes how in those years, like the Prodigal Son in the Gospel, he longed to eat of the mash given to the pigs, which were fattened for sale. But they wouldn't even give him that, and beat him when he stole from the pigs. And that was how he spent all his childhood and his youth, till he grew up and was strong enough to go away and be a thief. The savage began to earn his living as a day labourer in Geneva. He drank what he earned, he lived like a brute, and finished by killing and robbing an old man. He was caught, tried, and condemned to death. They are not sentimentalists there. And in prison he was immediately surrounded by pastors, members of Christian brotherhoods, philanthropic ladies, and the like. They taught him to read and write in prison, and expounded the Gospel to him. They exhorted him, worked upon him, drummed at him incessantly, till at last he solemnly confessed his crime. He was converted. He wrote to the court himself that he was a monster, but that in the end God had vouchsafed him light and shown grace. All Geneva was in excitement about him—all philanthropic and religious Geneva. All the aristocratic and well-bred society of the town rushed to the prison, kissed Richard and embraced him; 'You are our brother, you have found grace.' And Richard does nothing but weep with emotion, 'Yes, I've found grace! All my youth and childhood I was glad of pigs' food, but now even I have found grace. I am dying in the Lord.' 'Yes, Richard, die in the Lord; you have shed blood and must die. Though it's not your fault that you knew not the Lord, when you coveted the pig's food and were beaten for stealing it (which was very wrong of you, for stealing is forbidden); but you've shed blood and you must die.' And on the last day, Richard, perfectly limp, did nothing but cry and repeat every minute: 'This is my happiest day. I am going to the Lord.' 'Yes,' cry the pastors and the judges and philanthropic ladies. 'This is the happiest day of your life, for you are going to the Lord!' They all walk or drive to the scaffold in procession behind the prison van. At the scaffold they call to Richard: 'Die, brother, die in the Lord, for even thou hast found grace!' And so, covered with his brothers' kisses, Richard is dragged on to the scaffold, and led to the guillotine. And they chopped off his head in brotherly fashion, because he had found grace. Yes, that's characteristic. That pamphlet is translated into Russian by some Russian philanthropists of aristocratic rank and evangelical aspirations, and has been distributed gratis for the enlightenment of the people. The case of Richard is interesting because it's national. Though to us it's absurd to cut off a man's head, because he has become our brother and has found grace, yet we have our own specialty, which is all but worse. Our historical pastime is the direct satisfaction of inflicting pain. There are lines in Nekrassov describing how a peasant lashes a horse on the eyes, 'on its meek eyes,' every one must have seen it. It's peculiarly Russian. He describes how a feeble little nag had foundered under too heavy a load and cannot move. The peasant beats it, beats it savagely, beats it at last not knowing what he is doing in the intoxication of cruelty, thrashes it mercilessly over and over again. 'However weak you are, you must pull, if you die for it.' The nag strains, and then he begins lashing the poor defenceless creature on its weeping, on its 'meek eyes.' The frantic beast tugs and draws the load, trembling all over, gasping for breath, moving sideways, with a sort of unnatural spasmodic action—it's awful in Nekrassov. But that's only a horse, and God has given horses to be beaten. So the Tatars have taught us, and they left us the knout as a remembrance of it. But men, too, can be beaten. A well-educated, cultured gentleman and his wife beat their own child with a birch-rod, a girl of seven. I have an exact account of it. The papa was glad that the birch was covered with twigs. 'It stings more,' said he, and so he began stinging his daughter. I know for a fact there are people who at every blow are worked up to sensuality, to literal sensuality, which increases progressively at every blow they inflict. They beat for a minute, for five minutes, for ten minutes, more often and more savagely. The child screams. At last the child cannot scream, it gasps, 'Daddy! daddy!' By some diabolical unseemly chance the case was brought into court. A counsel is engaged. The Russian people have long called a barrister 'a conscience for hire.' The counsel protests in his client's defence. 'It's such a simple thing,' he says, 'an everyday domestic event. A father corrects his child. To our shame be it said, it is brought into court.' The jury, convinced by him, give a favourable verdict. The public roars with delight that the torturer is acquitted. Ah, pity I wasn't there! I would have proposed to raise a subscription in his honour! . . . Charming pictures.

"But I've still better things about children. I've collected a great, great deal about Russian children, Alyosha. There was a little girl of five who was hated by her father and mother, 'most worthy and respectable people, of good education and breeding.' You see, I must repeat again, it is a peculiar characteristic of many people, this love of torturing children, and children only. To all other types of humanity these torturers behave mildly and benevolently, like cultivated and humane Europeans; but they are very fond of tormenting children, even fond of children themselves in that sense. It's just their defencelessness that tempts the tormentor, just the angelic confidence of the child who has no refuge and no appeal, that sets his vile blood on fire. In every man, of course, a demon lies hidden—the demon of rage, the demon of lustful heat at the screams of the tortured victim, the demon of lawlessness let off the chain, the demon of diseases that follow on vice, gout, kidney disease, and so on.

"This poor child of five was subjected to every possible torture by those cultivated parents. They beat her, thrashed her, kicked her for no reason till her body was one bruise. Then, they went to greater refinements of cruelty—shut her up all night in the cold and frost in a privy, and because she didn't ask to be taken up at night (as though a child of five sleeping its angelic, sound sleep could be trained to wake and ask), they smeared her face and filled her mouth with excrement, and it was her mother, her mother did this. And that mother could sleep, hearing the poor child's groans! Can you understand why a little creature, who can't even understand what's done to her, should beat her little aching heart with her tiny fist in the dark and the cold, and weep her meek unresentful tears to dear, kind God to protect her? Do you understand that, friend and brother, you pious and humble novice? Do you understand why this infamy must be and is permitted? Without it, I am told, man could not have existed on earth, for he could not have known good and evil. Why should he know that diabolical good and evil when it costs so much? Why, the whole world of knowledge is not worth that child's prayer to 'dear, kind God'! I say nothing of the sufferings of grown-up people, they have eaten the apple, damn them, and the devil take them all! But these little ones! I am making you suffer, Alyosha, you are not yourself. I'll leave off if you like."

"Never mind. I want to suffer too," muttered Alyosha.

"One picture, only one more, because it's so curious, so characteristic, and I have only just read it in some collection of Russian antiquities. I've forgotten the name. I must look it up. It was in the darkest days of serfdom at the beginning of the century, and long live the Liberator of the People! There was in those days a general of aristocratic connections, the owner of great estates, one of those men—somewhat exceptional, I believe, even then— who, retiring from the service into a life of leisure, are convinced that they've earned absolute power over the lives of their subjects. There were such men then. So our general, settled on his property of two thousand souls, lives in pomp, and domineers over his poor neighbours as though they were dependents and buffoons. He has kennels of hundreds of hounds and nearly a hundred dog-boys—all mounted, and in uniform. One day a serf boy, a little child of eight, threw a stone in play and hurt the paw of the general's favourite hound. 'Why is my favourite dog lame?' He is told that the boy threw a stone that hurt the dog's paw. 'So you did it.' The general looked the child up and down. 'Take him.' He was taken—taken from his mother and kept shut up all night. Early that morning the general comes out on horseback, with the hounds, his dependents, dog-boys, and huntsmen, all mounted around him in full hunting parade. The servants are summoned for their edification, and in front of them all stands the mother of the child. The child is brought from the lock-up. It's a gloomy cold, foggy autumn day, a capital day for hunting. The general orders the child to be undressed; the child is stripped naked. He shivers, numb with terror not daring to cry. . . . 'Make him run,' commands the general. 'Run! run!' shout the dog-boys.

The boy runs. . . . 'At him!' yells the general, and he sets the whole pack of hounds on the child. The hounds catch him, and tear him to pieces before his mother's eyes! . . . I believe the general was afterwards declared incapable of administering his estates. Well—what did he deserve? To be shot? To be shot for the satisfaction of our moral feelings? Speak, Alyosha!"

"To be shot," murmured Alyosha, lifting his eyes to Ivan with a pale, twisted smile.

"Bravo!" cried Ivan delighted. "If even you say so. . . You're a pretty monk! So there is a little devil sitting in your heart, Alyosha Karamazov!"

"What I said was absurd, but——"

"That's just the point that 'but'!" cried Ivan. "Let me tell you, novice, that the absurd is only too necessary on earth. The world stands on absurdities, and perhaps nothing would have come to pass in it without them. We know what we know!"

"What do you know?"

"I understand nothing," Ivan went on, as though in delirium. "I don't want to understand anything now. I want to stick to the fact. I made up my mind long ago not to understand. If I try to understand anything, I shall be false to the fact and I have determined to stick to the fact."

"Why are you trying me?" Alyosha cried, with sudden distress. "Will you say what you mean at last?"

"Of course, I will; that's what I've been leading up to. You are dear to me, I don't want to let you go, and I won't give you up to your Zossima."

Ivan for a minute was silent, his face became all at once very sad.

"Listen! I took the case of children only to make my case clearer. Of the other tears of humanity with which the earth is soaked from its crust to its centre, I will say nothing. I have narrowed my subject on purpose. I am a bug, and I recognise in all humility that I cannot understand why the world is arranged as it is. Men are themselves to blame, I suppose; they were given paradise, they wanted freedom, and stole fire from heaven, though they knew they would become unhappy, so there is no need to pity them. With my pitiful, earthly, Euclidian understanding, all I know is that there is suffering and that there are none guilty; that cause follows effect, simply and directly; that everything flows and finds its level—but that's only Euclidian nonsense, I know that, and I can't consent to live by it! What comfort is it to me that there are none guilty and that cause follows effect simply and directly, and that I know it—I must have justice, or I will destroy myself. And not justice in some remote infinite time and space, but here on earth, and that I could see myself. I have believed in it. I want to see it, and if I am dead by then, let me rise again, for if it all happens without me, it will be too unfair. Surely I haven't suffered, simply that I, my crimes and my sufferings, may manure the soil of the future harmony for somebody else. I want to see with my own eyes the hind lie down with the lion and the victim rise up and embrace his murderer. I want to be there when every one suddenly understands what it has all been for. All the religions of the world are built on this longing, and I am a believer. But then there are the children, and what am I to do about them? That's a question I can't answer. For the hundredth time I repeat, there are numbers of questions, but I've only taken the children, because in their case what I mean is so unanswerably clear. Listen! If all must suffer to pay for the eternal harmony, what have children to do with it, tell me, please? It's beyond all comprehension why they should suffer, and why they should pay for the harmony. Why should they, too, furnish material to enrich the soil for the harmony of the future? I understand solidarity in sin among men. I understand solidarity in retribution, too; but there can be no such solidarity with children. And if it is really true that they must share responsibility for all their fathers' crimes, such a truth is not of this world and is beyond my comprehension. Some jester will say, perhaps, that the child would have grown up and have sinned, but you see he didn't grow up, he was torn to pieces by the dogs, at eight years old. Oh, Alyosha, I am not blaspheming! I understand, of course, what an upheaval of the universe it will be, when everything in heaven and earth blends in one hymn of praise and everything that lives and has lived cries aloud: 'Thou art just, O Lord, for Thy ways are revealed.' When the mother embraces the fiend who threw her child to the dogs, and all three cry aloud with tears, 'Thou art just, O Lord!' then, of course, the crown of knowledge will be reached and all will be made clear. But what pulls me up here is that I can't accept that harmony. And while I am on earth, I make haste to take my own measures. You see, Alyosha, perhaps it really may happen that if I live to that moment, or rise again to see it, I, too, perhaps, may cry aloud with the rest, looking at the mother embracing the child's torturer, 'Thou art just, O Lord!' but I don't want to cry aloud then. While there is still time, I hasten to protect myself and so I renounce the higher harmony altogether. It's not worth the tears of that one tortured child who beat itself on the breast with its little fist and prayed in its stinking outhouse, with its unexpiated tears to 'dear, kind God'! It's not worth it, because those tears are unatoned for. They must be atoned for, or there can be no harmony. But how? How are you going to atone for them? Is it possible? By their being avenged? But what do I care for avenging them? What do I care for a hell for oppressors? What good can hell do, since those children have already been tortured? And what becomes of harmony, if there is hell? I want to forgive. I want to embrace. I don't want more suffering. And if the sufferings of children go to swell the sum of sufferings which was necessary to pay for truth, then I protest that the truth is not worth such a price. I don't want the mother to embrace the oppressor who threw her son to the dogs! She dare not forgive him! Let her forgive him for herself, if she will, let her forgive the torturer for the immeasurable suffering of her mother's heart. But the sufferings of her tortured child she has no right to forgive; she dare not forgive the torturer, even if the child were to forgive him! And if that is so, if they dare not forgive, what becomes of harmony? Is there in the whole world a being who would have the right to forgive and could forgive? I don't want harmony. From love for humanity I don't want it. I would rather be left with the unavenged suffering. I would rather remain with my unavenged suffering and unsatisfied indignation, *even if I were wrong*. Besides, too high a price is asked for harmony; it's beyond our means to pay so much to enter on it. And so I hasten to give back my entrance ticket, and if I am an honest man I am bound to give it back as soon as possible. And that I am doing. It's not God that I don't accept, Alyosha, only I most respectfully return Him the ticket."

"That's rebellion," murmured Alyosha, looking down.

"Rebellion? I am sorry you call it that," said Ivan earnestly. "One can hardly live in rebellion, and I want to live. Tell me yourself, I challenge you —answer. Imagine that you are creating a fabric of human destiny with the object of making men happy in the end, giving them peace and rest at last, but that it was essential and inevitable to torture to death only one tiny creature—that baby beating its breast with its fist, for instance—and to found that edifice on its unavenged tears, would you consent to be the architect on those conditions? Tell me, and tell the truth."

"No, I wouldn't consent," said Alyosha softly.

"And can you admit the idea that men for whom you are building it would agree to accept their happiness on the foundation of the unexpiated blood of a little victim? And accepting it would remain happy for ever?"

"No, I can't admit it. Brother," said Alyosha suddenly, with flashing eyes, "you said just now, is there a being in the whole world who would have the right to forgive and could forgive? But there is a Being and He can forgive everything, all and for all, because He gave His innocent blood for all and everything. You have forgotten Him, and on Him is built the edifice, and it is to Him they cry aloud, 'Thou art just, O Lord, for Thy ways are revealed!' "

"Ah! the One without sin and His blood! No, I have not forgotten Him; on the contrary I've been wondering all the time how it was you did not bring Him in before, for usually all arguments on your side put Him in the foreground. . . .

J. L. MACKIE
Evil and Omnipotence

The traditional arguments for the existence of God have been fairly thoroughly criticised by philosophers. But the theologian can, if he wishes, accept this criticism. He can admit that no rational proof of God's existence is possible. And he can still retain all that is essential to his position, by holding that God's existence is known in some other, non-rational way. I think, however, that a more telling criticism can be made by way of the traditional problem of evil. Here it can be shown, not that religious beliefs lack rational support, but that they are positively irrational, that the several parts of the essential theological doctrine are inconsistent with one another, so that the theologian can maintain his position as a whole only by a much more extreme rejection of reason than in the former case. He must now be prepared to believe, not merely what cannot be proved, but what can be *disproved* from other beliefs that he also holds.

The problem of evil, in the sense in which I shall be using the phrase, is a problem only for someone who believes that there is a God who is both omnipotent and wholly good. And it is a logical problem, the problem of clarifying and reconciling a number of beliefs: it is not a scientific problem that might be solved by further observations, or a practical problem that might be solved by a decision or an action. These points are obvious; I mention them only because they are sometimes ignored by theologians, who sometimes parry a statement of the problem with such remarks as "Well, can you solve the problem yourself?" or "This is a mystery which may be revealed to us later" or "Evil is something to be faced and overcome, not to be merely discussed".

In its simplest form the problem is this: God is omnipotent; God is wholly good; and yet evil exists. There seems to be some contradiction between these three propositions, so that if any two of them were true the third would be false. But at the same time all three are essential parts of most theological positions: the theologian, it seems, at once *must* adhere and *cannot consistently* adhere to all three. (The problem does not arise only for theists, but I shall discuss it in the form in which it presents itself for ordinary theism.)

However, the contradiction does not arise immediately; to show it we need some additional premises, or perhaps some quasi-logical rules connect-

J. L. Mackie (1917–   ), born in Australia, has taught at colleges in New Zealand, Australia, and England. He is currently praelector in philosophy at University College, Oxford, and has published articles on a variety of philosophical subjects.

EVIL AND OMNIPOTENCE   From *Mind*, Vol. LXIV, No. 254, April 1955. Reprinted by permission of *Mind* and the author.

ing the terms 'good', 'evil', and 'omnipotent'. These additional principles are that good is opposed to evil, in such a way that a good thing always eliminates evil as far as it can, and that there are no limits to what an omnipotent thing can do. From these it follows that a good omnipotent thing eliminates evil completely, and then the propositions that a good omnipotent thing exists, and that evil exists, are incompatible.

A.   ADEQUATE SOLUTIONS

Now once the problem is fully stated it is clear that it can be solved, in the sense that the problem will not arise if one gives up at least one of the propositions that constitute it. If you are prepared to say that God is not wholly good, or not quite omnipotent, or that evil does not exist, or that good is not opposed to the kind of evil that exists, or that there are limits to what an omnipotent thing can do, then the problem of evil will not arise for you.

There are, then, quite a number of adequate solutions of the problem of evil, and some of these have been adopted, or almost adopted, by various thinkers. For example, a few have been prepared to deny God's omnipotence, and rather more have been prepared to keep the term 'omnipotence' but severely to restrict its meaning, recording quite a number of things that an omnipotent being cannot do. Some have said that evil is an illusion, perhaps because they held that the whole world of temporal, changing things is an illusion, and that what we call evil belongs only to this world, or perhaps because they held that although temporal things *are* much as we see them, those that we call evil are not really evil. Some have said that what we call evil is merely the privation of good, that evil in a positive sense, evil that would really be opposed to good, does not exist. Many have agreed with Pope that disorder is harmony not understood, and that partial evil is universal good. Whether any of these views is *true* is, of course, another question. But each of them gives an adequate solution of the problem of evil in the sense that if you accept it this problem does not arise for you, though you may, of course, have *other* problems to face.

But often enough these adequate solutions are only *almost* adopted. The thinkers who restrict God's power, but keep the term 'omnipotence', may reasonably be suspected of thinking, in other contexts, that his power is really unlimited. Those who say that evil is an illusion may also be thinking, inconsistently, that this illusion is itself an evil. Those who say that "evil" is merely privation of good may also be thinking, inconsistently, that privation of good is an evil. (The fallacy here is akin to some forms of the "naturalistic fallacy" in ethics, where some think, for example, that "good" is just what contributes to evolutionary progress, and that evolutionary progress is itself good.) If Pope meant what he said in the first line of his couplet, that "disorder" is only harmony not understood, the "partial evil" of the second line must, for consistency, mean "that which, taken in isolation, falsely appears to be evil", but it would more naturally mean "that which, in isolation, really is evil". The second line, in fact, hesitates between two views, that "partial evil" isn't really evil, since only the universal quality is real, and that "partial evil" is really an evil, but only a little one.

In addition, therefore, to adequate solutions, we must recognise unsatisfactory inconsistent solutions, in which there is only a half-hearted or temporary rejection of one of the propositions which together constitute the problem. In these, one of the constituent propositions is explicitly rejected, but it is covertly re-asserted or assumed elsewhere in the system.

B.   FALLACIOUS SOLUTIONS

Besides these half-hearted solutions, which explicitly reject but implicitly assert one of the constituent propositions, there are definitely fallacious solutions which explicitly maintain all the constituent propositions, but implicitly reject at least one of them in the course of the argument that explains away the problem of evil.

There are, in fact, many so-called solutions which purport to remove the contradiction without abandoning any of its constituent propositions. These must be fallacious, as we can see from the very statement of the problem, but it is not so easy to see in each case precisely where the fallacy lies. I suggest that in all cases the fallacy has the general form suggested above in order to solve the problem one (or perhaps more) of its constituent propositions is given up, but in such a way that it appears to have been retained, and can therefore be asserted without qualification in other contexts. Sometimes there is a further complication: the supposed solution moves to and fro between, say, two of the constituent propositions, at one point asserting the first of these but covertly abandoning the second, at another point asserting the second but covertly abandoning the first. These fallacious solutions often turn upon some equivocation with the words 'good' and 'evil', or upon some vagueness about the way in which good and evil are opposed to one another, or about how much is meant by 'omnipotence'. I propose to examine some of these so-called solutions, and to exhibit their fallacies in detail. Incidentally, I shall also be considering whether an adequate solution could be reached by a minor modification of one or more of the constituent propositions, which would, however, still satisfy all the essential requirements of ordinary theism.

(1) "Good cannot exist without evil" or "Evil is necessary as a counterpart to good."

It is sometimes suggested that evil is necessary as a counterpart to good, that if there were no evil there could be no good either, and that this solves the problem of evil. It is true that it points to an answer to the question

"Why should there be evil?" But it does so only by qualifying some of the propositions that constitute the problem.

First, it sets a limit to what God can do, saying that God *cannot* create good without simultaneously creating evil, and this means either that God is not omnipotent or that there are *some* limits to what an omnipotent thing can do. It may be replied that these limits are always presupposed, that omnipotence has never meant the power to do what is logically impossible, and on the present view the existence of good without evil would be a logical impossibility. This interpretation of omnipotence may, indeed, be accepted as a modification of our original account which does not reject anything that is essential to theism, and I shall in general assume it in the subsequent discussion. It is, perhaps, the most common theistic view, but I think that some theists at least have maintained that God can do what is logically impossible. Many theists, at any rate, have held that logic itself is created or laid down by God, that logic is the way in which God arbitrarily chooses to think. (This is, of course, parallel to the ethical view that morally right actions are those which God arbitrarily chooses to command, and the two views encounter similar difficulties.) And *this* account of logic is clearly inconsistent with the view that God is bound by logical necessities—unless it is possible for an omnipotent being to bind himself, an issue which we shall consider later, when we come to the Paradox of Omnipotence. This solution of the problem of evil cannot, therefore, be consistently adopted along with the view that logic is itself created by God.

But, secondly, this solution denies that evil is opposed to good in our original sense. If good and evil are counterparts, a good thing will not "eliminate evil as far as it can". Indeed, this view suggests that good and evil are not strictly qualities of things at all. Perhaps the suggestion is that good and evil are related in much the same way as great and small. Certainly, when the term 'great' is used relatively as a condensation of 'greater than so-and-so', and 'small' is used correspondingly, greatness and smallness are counterparts and cannot exist without each other. But in this sense greatness is not a quality, not an intrinsic feature of anything; and it would be absurd to think of a movement in favour of greatness and against smallness in this sense. Such a movement would be self-defeating, since relative greatness can be promoted only by a simultaneous promotion of relative smallness. I feel sure that no theists would be content to regard God's goodness as analogous to this—as if what he supports were not the *good* but the *better*, and as if he had the paradoxical aim that all things should be better than other things.

This point is obscured by the fact that 'great' and 'small' seem to have an absolute as well as a relative sense. I cannot discuss here whether there is absolute magnitude or not, but if there is, there could be an absolute sense for 'great', it could mean of at least a certain size, and it would make sense to speak of all things getting bigger, of a universe that was expanding all over, and therefore it would make sense to speak of promoting greatness.

But in *this* sense great and small are not logically necessary counterparts: either quality could exist without the other. There would be no logical impossibility in everything's being small or in everything's being great.

Neither in the absolute nor in the relative sense, then, of 'great' and 'small' do these terms provide an analogy of the sort that would be needed to support this solution of the problem of evil. In neither case are greatness and smallness *both* necessary counterparts *and* mutually opposed forces or possible objects for support and attack.

It may be replied that good and evil are necessary counterparts in the same way as any quality and its logical opposite redness can occur, it is suggested, only if non-redness also occurs. But unless evil is merely the privation of good, they are not logical opposites, and some further argument would be needed to show that they are counterparts in the same way as genuine logical opposites. Let us assume that this could be given. There is still doubt of the correctness of the metaphysical principle that a quality must have a real opposite: I suggest that it is not really impossible that everything should be, say, red, that the truth is merely that if everything were red we should not notice redness, and so we should have no word 'red'; we observe and give names to qualities only if they have real opposites. If so, the principle that a term must have an opposite would belong only to our language or to our thought, and would not be an ontological principle, and, correspondingly, the rule that good cannot exist without evil would not state a logical necessity of a sort that God would just have to put up with. God might have made everything good, though *we* should not have noticed it if he had.

But, finally, even if we concede that this *is* an ontological principle, it will provide a solution for the problem of evil only if one is prepared to say, "Evil exists, but only just enough evil to serve as the counterpart of good". I doubt whether any theist will accept this. After all, the *ontological* requirement that non-redness should occur would be satisfied even if all the universe, except for a minute speck, were red, and, if there were a corresponding requirement for evil as a counterpart to good, a minute dose of evil would presumably do. But theists are not usually willing to say, in all contexts, that all the evil that occurs is a minute and necessary dose.

(2) "Evil is necessary as a means to good."

It is sometimes suggested that evil is necessary for good not as a counterpart but as a means. In its simple form this has little plausibility as a solution of the problem of evil, since it obviously implies a severe restriction of God's power. It would be a *causal* law that you cannot have a certain end without a certain means, so that if God has to introduce evil as a means to good, he must be subject to at least some causal laws. This certainly conflicts with what a theist normally means by omnipotence. This view of God as limited by causal laws also conflicts with the view that causal laws are themselves made by God, which is more widely held than the corresponding view about the laws of logic. This conflict would, indeed, be resolved if it were possible for an omnipotent being to bind himself, and this possibility has still to be considered. Unless a favourable answer can be given to this question, the suggestion that evil is necessary as a means to good solves the problem of evil only by denying one of its constituent propositions, either that God is omnipotent or that 'omnipotent' means what it says.

(3) "The universe is better with some evil in it than it could be if there were no evil."

Much more important is a solution which at first seems to be a mere variant of the previous one, that evil may contribute to the goodness of a whole in which it is found, so that the universe as a whole is better as it is, with some evil in it, than it would be if there were no evil. This solution may be developed in either of two ways. It may be supported by an aesthetic analogy, by the fact that contrasts heighten beauty, that in a musical work, for example, there may occur discords which somehow add to the beauty of the work as a whole. Alternatively, it may be worked out in connexion with the notion of progress, that the best possible organisation of the universe will not be static, but progressive, that the gradual overcoming of evil by good is really a finer thing than would be the eternal unchallenged supremacy of good.

In either case, this solution usually starts from the assumption that the evil whose existence gives rise to the problem of evil is primarily what is called physical evil, that is to say, pain. In Hume's rather half-hearted presentation of the problem of evil, the evils that he stresses are pain and disease, and those who reply to him argue that the existence of pain and disease makes possible the existence of sympathy, benevolence, heroism, and the gradually successful struggle of doctors and reformers to overcome these evils. In fact, theists often seize the opportunity to accuse those who stress the problem of evil of taking a low, materialistic view of good and evil, equating these with pleasure and pain, and of ignoring the more spiritual goods which can arise in the struggle against evils.

But let us see exactly what is being done here. Let us call pain and misery 'first order evil' or 'evil (1)'. What contrasts with this, namely, pleasure and happiness, will be called 'first order good' or 'good (1)'. Distinct from this is 'second order good' or 'good (2)' which somehow emerges in a complex situation in which evil (1) is a necessary component—logically not merely causally, necessary. (Exactly *how* it emerges does not matter: in the crudest version of this solution good [2] is simply the heightening of happiness by the contrast with misery, in other versions it includes sympathy with suffering, heroism in facing danger, and the gradual decrease of first order evil and increase of first order good.) It is also being assumed that second order good is more important than first order good or evil, in particular that it more than outweighs the first order evil it involves.

Now this is a particularly subtle attempt to solve the problem of evil. It defends God's goodness and omnipotence on the ground that (on a sufficiently long view) this is the best of all logically possible worlds, because it includes the important second order goods, and yet it admits that real evils, namely first order evils, exist. But does it still hold that good and evil are opposed? Not, clearly, in the sense that we set out originally: good does not tend to eliminate evil in general. Instead, we have a modified, a more complex pattern. First order good (*e.g.* happiness) *contrasts with* first order evil (*e.g.* misery): these two are opposed in a fairly mechanical way; some second order goods (*e.g.* benevolence) try to maximise first order good and minimise first order evil; but God's goodness is not this, it is rather the will to maximise *second* order good. We might, therefore, call God's goodness an example of a third order goodness, or good (3). While this account is different from our original one, it might well be held to be an improvement on it, to give a more accurate description of the way in which good is opposed to evil, and to be consistent with the essential theist position.

There might, however, be several objections to this solution.

First, some might argue that such qualities as benevolence—and *a fortiori* the third order goodness which promotes benevolence—have a merely derivative value, that they are not higher sorts of good, but merely means to good (1), that is, to happiness, so that it would be absurd for God to keep misery in existence in order to make possible the virtues of benevolence, heroism, etc. The theist who adopts the present solution must, of course, deny this, but he can do so with some plausibility, so I should not press this objection.

Secondly, it follows from this solution that God is not in our sense benevolent or sympathetic: he is not concerned to minimise evil (1), but only to promote good (2); and this might be a disturbing conclusion for some theists.

But, thirdly, the fatal objection is this. Our analysis shows clearly the possibility of the existence of a *second* order evil, an evil (2) contrasting with good (2) as evil (1) contrasts with good (1). This would include malevolence, cruelty, callousness, cowardice, and states in which good (1) is decreasing and evil (1) increasing. And just as good (2) is held to be the important kind of good, the kind that God is concerned to promote, so evil (2) will, by analogy, be the important kind of evil, the kind which God, if he were wholly good and omnipotent, would eliminate. And yet evil (2) plainly exists, and indeed most theists (in other contexts) stress its existence more than that of evil (1). We should, therefore, state the problem of evil in terms of second order evil, and against this form of the problem the present solution is useless.

An attempt might be made to use this solution again, at a higher level, to explain the occurrence of evil (2); indeed the next main solution that we shall examine does just this, with the help of some new notions. Without any fresh notions, such a solution would have little plausibility: for example, we could hardly say that the really important good was a good (3), such as the increase of benevolence in proportion to cruelty, which logically required for its occurrence the occurrence of some second order evil. But even if evil (2) could be explained in this way, it is fairly clear that there would be third order evils contrasting with this third order good: and we should be well on the way to an infinite regress, where the solution of a problem of evil, stated in terms of evil (n), indicated the existence of an evil ($n + 1$), and a further problem to be solved.

(4) "Evil is due to human freewill."

Perhaps the most important proposed solution of the problem of evil is that evil is not to be ascribed to God at all, but to the independent actions of human beings, supposed to have been endowed by God with freedom of the will. This solution may be combined with the preceding one: first order evil (e.g. pain) may be justified as a logically necessary component in second order good (e.g. sympathy) while second order evil (e.g. cruelty) is not justified, but is so ascribed to human beings that God cannot be held responsible for it. This combination evades my third criticism of the preceding solution.

The freewill solution also involves the preceding solution at a higher level. To explain why a wholly good God gave men freewill although it would lead to some important evils, it must be argued that it is better on the whole that men should act freely, and sometimes err, than that they should be innocent automata, acting rightly in a wholly determined way. Freedom that is to say, is now treated as a third order good, and as being more valuable than second order goods (such as sympathy and heroism) would be if they were deterministically produced, and it is being assumed that second order evils, such as cruelty, are logically necessary accompaniments of freedom, just as pain is a logically necessary pre-condition of sympathy.

I think that this solution is unsatisfactory primarily because of the incoherence of the notion of freedom of the will: but I cannot discuss this topic adequately here, although some of my criticisms will touch upon it.

First I should query the assumption that second order evils are logically necessary accompaniments of freedom. I should ask this: if God has made men such that in their free choices they sometimes prefer what is good and sometimes what is evil, why could he not have made men such that they always freely choose the good? If there is no logical impossibility in a man's freely choosing the good on one, or on several, occasions, there cannot be a logical impossibility in his freely choosing the good on every occasion. God was not, then, faced with a choice between making innocent automata and making beings who, in acting freely, would sometimes go wrong: there was open to him the obviously better possibility of making beings who would act freely but always go right. Clearly, his failure to avail himself of this possibility is inconsistent with his being both omnipotent and wholly good.

If it is replied that this objection is absurd, that the making of some wrong choices is logically necessary for freedom, it would seem that 'freedom' must here mean complete randomness or indeterminacy, including randomness with regard to the alternatives good and evil, in other words that men's choices and consequent actions can be "free" only if they are not determined by their characters. Only on this assumption can God escape the responsibility for men's actions; for if he made them as they are, but did not determine their wrong choices, this can only be because the wrong choices are not determined by men as they are. But then if freedom is randomness, how can it be a characteristic of *will*? And, still more, how can it be the most important good? What value or merit would there be in free choices if these were random actions which were not determined by the nature of the agent?

I conclude that to make this solution plausible two different senses of 'freedom' must be confused, one sense which will justify the view that freedom is a third order good, more valuable than other goods would be without it, and another sense, sheer randomness, to prevent us from ascribing to God a decision to make men such that they sometimes go wrong when he might have made them such that they would always freely go right.

This criticism is sufficient to dispose of this solution. But besides this there is a fundamental difficulty in the notion of an omnipotent God creating men with free will, for if men's wills are really free this must mean that even God cannot control them, that is, that God is no longer omnipotent. It may be objected that God's gift of freedom to men does not mean that he *cannot* control their wills, but that he always *refrains* from controlling their wills. But why, we may ask, should God refrain from controlling evil wills? Why should he not leave men free to will rightly, but intervene when he sees them beginning to will wrongly? If God could do this, but does not, and if he is wholly good, the only explanation could be that even a wrong free act of will is not really evil, that its freedom is a value which outweighs its wrongness, so that there would be a loss of value if God took away the wrongness and the freedom together. But this is utterly opposed to what theists say about sin in other contexts. The present solution of the problem of evil, then, can be maintained only in the form that God has made men so free that he *cannot* control their wills.

This leads us to what I call the Paradox of Omnipotence: can an omnipotent being make things which he cannot subsequently control? Or, what is practically equivalent to this, can an omnipotent being make rules which then bind himself? (These are practically equivalent because any such rules could be regarded as setting certain things beyond his control, and *vice versa*.) The second of these formulations is relevant to the suggestions that we have already met, that an omnipotent God creates the rules of logic or causal laws, and is then bound by them.

It is clear that this is a paradox: the questions cannot be answered satisfactorily either in the affirmative or in the negative. If we answer "Yes", it follows that if God actually makes things which he cannot control, or makes rules which bind himself, he is not omnipotent once he has made them: there are *then* things which he cannot do. But if we answer "No", we are immediately asserting that there are things which he cannot do, that is to say that he is already not omnipotent.

It cannot be replied that the question which sets this paradox is not a proper question. It would make perfectly good sense to say that a human mechanic has made a machine which he cannot control: if there is any difficulty about the question it lies in the notion of omnipotence itself.

This, incidentally, shows that although we have approached this paradox from the free will theory, it is equally a problem for a theological determinist. No one thinks that machines have free will, yet they may well be beyond the control of their makers. The determinist might reply that anyone who makes anything determines its ways of acting, and so determines its subsequent behaviour: even the human mechanic does this by his *choice* of materials and structure for his machine, though he does not know all about either of these: the mechanic thus determines, though he may not foresee, his machine's actions. And since God is omniscient, and since his creation of things is total, he both determines and foresees the ways in which his creatures will act. We may grant this, but it is beside the point. The question is not whether God *originally* determined the future actions of his creatures, but whether he can *subsequently* control their actions, or whether he was able in his original creation to put things beyond his subsequent control. Even on determinist principles the answers "Yes" and "No" are equally irreconcilable with God's omnipotence.

Before suggesting a solution of this paradox, I would point out that there is a parallel Paradox of Sovereignty. Can a legal sovereign make a law restricting its own future legislative power? For example, could the British parliament make a law forbidding any future parliament to socialise banking, and also forbidding the future repeal of this law itself? Or could the British parliament, which was legally sovereign in Australia in, say, 1899, pass a valid law, or series of laws, which made it no longer sovereign in 1933? Again, neither the affirmative nor the negative answer is really satisfactory. If we were to answer "Yes", we should be admitting the validity of a law which, if it were actually made, would mean that parliament was no longer sovereign. If we were to answer "No", we should be admitting that there is a law, not logically absurd, which parliament cannot validly make, that is, that parliament is not now a legal sovereign. This paradox can be solved in the following way. We should distinguish between first order laws, that is laws governing the actions of individuals and bodies other than the legislature, and second order laws, that is laws about laws, laws governing the actions of the legislature itself. Correspondingly, we should distinguish two orders of sovereignty, first order sovereignty (sovereignty (1)) which is unlimited authority to make first order laws, and second order sovereignty (sovereignty (2)) which is unlimited authority to make second order laws. If we say that parliament is sovereign we might mean that any parliament at any time has sovereignty (1), or we might mean that parliament has both sovereignty (1) and sovereignty (2) at present, but we cannot without contradiction mean both that the present parliament has sovereignty (2) and that every parliament at every time has sovereignty (1), for if the present parliament has sovereignty (2) it may use it to take away the sovereignty (1) of later parliaments. What the paradox shows is that we cannot ascribe to any continuing institution legal sovereignty in an inclusive sense.

The analogy between omnipotence and sovereignty shows that the paradox of omnipotence can be solved in a similar way. We must distinguish between first order omnipotence (omnipotence (1)), that is unlimited power to act, and second order omnipotence (omnipotence (2)), that is unlimited power to determine what powers to act things shall have. Then we could consistently say that God all the time has omnipotence (1), but if so no beings at any time have powers to act independently of God. Or we could say that God at one time had omnipotence (2), and used it to assign independent powers to act to certain things, so that God thereafter did not have omnipotence (1). But what the paradox shows is that we cannot consistently ascribe to any continuing being omnipotence in an inclusive sense.

An alternative solution of this paradox would be simply to deny that God is a continuing being, that any times can be assigned to his actions at all. But on this assumption (which also has difficulties of its own) no meaning can be given to the assertion that God made men with wills so free that he could not control them. The paradox of omnipotence can be avoided by putting God outside time, but the freewill solution of the problem of evil cannot be saved in this way, and equally it remains impossible to hold that an omnipotent God *binds himself* by causal or logical laws.

CONCLUSION

Of the proposed solutions of the problem of evil which we have examined, none has stood up to criticism. There may be other solutions which require examination, but this study strongly suggests that there is no valid solution of the problem which does not modify at least one of the constituent propositions in a way which would seriously affect the essential core of the theistic position.

Quite apart from the problem of evil, the paradox of omnipotence has shown that God's omnipotence must in any case be restricted in one way or another, that unqualified omnipotence cannot be ascribed to any being that continues through time. And if God and his actions are not in time, can omnipotence, or power of any sort, be meaningfully ascribed to him?

ALVIN PLANTINGA
The Free Will Defence

Since the days of Epicurus many philosophers have suggested that the existence of evil constitutes a problem for those who accept theistic belief.[1] Those contemporaries who follow Epicurus here claim, for the most part, to detect logical inconsistency in such belief. So McCloskey:

> Evil is a problem for the theist in that a *contradiction* is involved in the fact of evil, on the one hand, and the belief in the omnipotence and perfection of God on the other.[2]

and Mackie:

> I think, however, that a more telling criticism can be made by way of the traditional problem of evil. Here it can be shown, not that religious beliefs lack rational support, but that they are positively irrational, that the several parts of the essential theological doctrine are *inconsistent* with one another . . .[3]

and essentially the same charge is made by Professor Aiken in an article entitled 'God and Evil'.[4]

These philosophers, then, and many others besides, hold that traditional theistic belief is self-contradictory and that the problem of evil, for the theist, is that of deciding which of the relevant propositions he is to abandon. But just which propositions are involved? What is the set of theistic beliefs whose conjunction yields a contradiction? The authors referred to above take the following five propositions to be essential to traditional theism: (*a*) that God exists, (*b*) that God is omnipotent, (*c*) that God is omniscient, (*d*) that God is wholly good, and (*e*) that evil exists. Here they are certainly right: each of these propositions is indeed an essential feature of orthodox theism. And it is just these five propositions whose conjunction is said, by our atheologians,[5] to be self-contradictory.

Alvin Plantinga (1932–   ) is a professor of philosophy at Calvin College. His book *God and Other Minds* is one of the best works on philosophical theology to appear in recent years.

THE FREE WILL DEFENCE   Reprinted from *Philosophy in America*, edited by Max Black. Copyright under the Berne Convention by George Allen & Unwin Ltd. Used by permission of Cornell University Press and George Allen & Unwin Ltd.

[1] David Hume and some of the French encyclopedists, for example, as well as F. H. Bradley, J. McTaggart, and J. S. Mill.

[2] H. J. McCloskey, 'God and Evil'. *The Philosophical Quarterly*, Vol. 10 (April 1960), p. 97.

[3] 'Evil and Omnipotence'. J. L. Mackie, *Mind*, Vol. 64, No. 254 (April 1955), p. 200 [in *Philosophy of Religion: Selected Readings*, p. 206].

[4] *Ethics*, Vol. 48 (1957–58), p. 79.

[5] *Natural theology* is the attempt to infer central religious beliefs from premises that are either obvious to common sense (e.g., *that some things are in motion*) or logically necessary. *Natural atheology* is the attempt to infer the falsity of such religious beliefs from premises of the same sort.

Apologists for theism, of course, have been quick to repel the charge. A line of resistance they have often employed is called *The Free Will Defence;* in this paper I shall discuss and develop that idea.

First of all, a distinction must be made between *moral evil* and *physical evil*. The former, roughly, is the evil which results from human choice or volition; the latter is that which does not. Suffering due to an earthquake, for example, would be a case of physical evil; suffering resulting from human cruelty would be a case of moral evil. This distinction, of course, is not very clear and many questions could be raised about it; but perhaps it is not necessary to deal with these questions here. Given this distinction, the Free Will Defence is usually stated in something like the following way. A world containing creatures who freely perform both good and evil actions—and do more good than evil—is more valuable than a world containing quasi-automata who always do what is right because they are unable to do otherwise. Now God can create free creatures, but He cannot causally or otherwise determine them to do only what is right; for if he does so then they do not do what is right *freely*. To create creatures capable of moral good, therefore, he must create creatures capable of moral evil; but he cannot create the possibility of moral evil and at the same time prohibit its actuality. And as it turned out, some of the free creatures God created exercised their freedom to do what is wrong: hence moral evil. The fact that free creatures sometimes err, however, in no way tells against God's omnipotence or against his goodness; for he could forestall the occurrence of moral evil only by removing the possibility of moral good.

In this way some traditional theists have tried to explain or justify part of the evil that occurs by ascribing it to the will of man rather than to the will of God. At least three kinds of objections to this idea are to be found both in the tradition and in the current literature. I shall try to develop and clarify the Free Will Defence by restating it in the face of these objections.

I

The first objection challenges the assumption, implicit in the above statement of the Free Will Defence, that free will and causal determinism are logically incompatible. So Flew:

> . . . to say that a person could have helped doing something is not to say that what he did was in principle unpredictable nor that there were no causes anywhere which determined that he would as a matter of fact act in this way. It is to say that if he had chosen to do otherwise he would have been able to do so; that there were alternatives, within the capacities of one of his physical strength, of his I.Q., of his knowledge, open to a person in his situation.
>
> . . . There is no contradiction involved in saying that a particular action or choice was: *both* free, and could have been helped, and so on; *and* predictable, or even foreknown, and explicable in terms of caused causes.

. . . if it is really logically possible for an action to be both freely chosen and yet fully determined by caused causes, then the keystone argument of the Free Will Defence, that there is contradiction in speaking of God so arranging the laws of nature that all men always as a matter of fact freely choose to do the right, cannot hold.[6]

Flew's objection, I think, can be dealt with in a fairly summary fashion. He does not, in the paper in question, explain what he means by 'causal determination' (and of course in that paper this omission is quite proper and justifiable). But presumably he means to use the locution in question in such a way that to say of Jones' action A that it is *causally determined* is to say that the action in question has causes and that given these causes, Jones could not have refrained from doing A. That is to say, Flew's use of 'causally determined', presumably, is such that one or both of the following sentences, or some sentences very much like them, express necessarily true propositions:

(a) If Jones' action A is causally determined, then a set S of events has occurred prior to Jones' doing A such that, given S, it is causally impossible for Jones to refrain from doing A.

(b) If Jones' action A is causally determined, then there is a set S of propositions describing events occurring before A and a set L of propositions expressing natural laws such that
(1) the conjunction of S's members does not entail that Jones does A, and
(2) the conjunction of the members of S with the members of L does entail that Jones does A.

And Flew's thesis, then, is that there is no contradiction in saying of a man, both that all of his actions are causally determined (in the sense just explained) and that some of them are free.

Now it seems to me altogether paradoxical to say of anyone all of whose actions are causally determined, that on some occasions he acts freely. When we say that Jones acts freely on a given occasion, what we say entails, I should think, that either his action on that occasion is not causally determined, or else he has previously performed an undetermined action which is a causal ancestor of the one in question. But this is a difficult and debatable issue; fortunately we need not settle it in order to assess the force of Flew's objection to the Free Will Defence. The Free Will Defender claims that the sentence 'Not all free actions are causally determined' expresses a necessary truth; Flew denies this claim. This strongly suggests that Flew and the Free Will Defender are not using the words 'free' and 'freedom' in the same way. The Free Will Defender, apparently, uses the words in question in such a way that sentences 'Some of Jones' actions are free' and 'Jones did action A freely' express propositions which are inconsistent with the proposition that

6 'Divine Omnipotence and Human Freedom', in *New Essays in Philosophical Theology*, ed. A. Flew and A. MacIntyre, London 1955, pp. 150, 151, 153. [Reprinted here by permission of The Macmillan Company.]

all of Jones' actions are causally determined. Flew, on the other hand, claims that with respect to the ordinary use of these words, there is no such inconsistency. It is my opinion that Flew is mistaken here; I think it is he who is using these words in a non-standard, unordinary way. But we need not try to resolve that issue; for the Free Will Defender can simply make Flew a present of the word 'freedom' and state his case using other locutions. He might now hold, for example, not that God made men free and that a world in which men freely do both good and evil is more valuable than a world in which they unfreely do only what is good; but rather that God made men such that some of their actions are *unfettered* (both free in Flew's sense and also causally undetermined) and that a world in which men perform both good and evil unfettered actions is superior to one in which they perform only good, but fettered, actions. By substituting 'unfettered' for 'free' throughout this account, the Free Will Defender can elude Flew's objection altogether.[7] So whether Flew is right or wrong about the ordinary sense of 'freedom' is of no consequence; his objection is in an important sense merely verbal and thus altogether fails to damage the Free Will Defence.

II

Flew's objection, in essence, is the claim that an omnipotent being could have created men in such a way that although free they would be *causally determined* to perform only right actions. According to a closely allied objection, an omnipotent being could have made men in such a way that although free, and free from any such causal determination, they would nonetheless *freely refrain* from performing any evil actions. Here the contemporary spokesman is Mackie:

> . . . if God has made men such that in their free choices they sometimes prefer what is good and sometimes what is evil, why could he not have made men such that they always freely choose the good? If there is no logical impossibility in a man's freely choosing the good on one, or on several occasions, there cannot be a logical impossibility in his freely choosing the good on every occasion. God was not, then, faced with a choice between making innocent automata and making beings who, in acting freely, would sometimes go wrong; there was open to him the obviously better possibility of making beings who would act freely but always go right. Clearly, his failure to avail himself of this possibility is inconsistent with his being both omnipotent and wholly good.[8]

This objection is more serious than Flew's and must be dealt with more fully. Now the Free Will Defence is an argument for the conclusion that (*a*) is not contradictory or necessarily false: [9]

---

[7] And since this is so in what follows I shall continue to use the words 'free' and 'freedom' in the way the Free Will Defender uses them.

[8] *Op. cit.,* p. 209 [in *Philosophy of Religion: Selected Readings,* p. 213].

[9] And of course if (*a*) is consistent, so is the set (*a*)–(*e*) mentioned on page 217, for (*a*) entails each member of that set.

(*a*) God is omnipotent, omniscient, and all-good and God creates free men who sometimes perform morally evil actions.

What Mackie says, I think, may best be construed as an argument for the conclusion that (*a*) *is* necessarily false; in other words, that *God is omnipotent, omniscient and all good* entails *no free men He creates ever perform morally evil actions*. Mackie's argument seems to have the following structure:

(1) God is omnipotent and omniscient and all-good.
(2) If God is omnipotent, He can create any logically possible state of affairs.
∴(3) God can create any logically possible state of affairs. (1, 2)
(4) That all free men do what is right on every occasion is a logically possible state of affairs.
∴(5) God can create free men such that they always do what is right. (3, 4)
(6) If God can create free men such that they always do what is right and God is all-good, then any free men created by God always do what is right.
∴(7) Any free men created by God always do what is right. (1, 5, 6)
∴(8) No free men created by God ever perform morally evil actions. (7)

Doubtless the Free Will Defender will concede the truth of (4); there is a difficulty with (2), however; for

(*a*) that there are men who are not created by God is a logically possible state of affairs

is clearly true. But (2) and (*a*) entail

(*b*) If God is omnipotent, God can create men who are not created by God.

And (*b*), of course, is false; (2) must be revised. The obvious way to repair it seems to be something like the following:

(2') If God is omnipotent, then God can create any state of affairs S such that *God creates S* is consistent.

Similarly, (3) must be revised:

(3') God can create any state of affairs S such that *God creates S* is consistent.

(2') and (3') do not seem to suffer from the faults besetting (2) and (3); but now it is not at all evident that (3') and (4) entail

(5) God can create free men such that they always do what is right

as the original argument claims. To see this, we must note that (5) is true only if

(5*a*) God creates free men such that they always do what is right

is consistent. But (5*a*), one might think, is equivalent to:

(5*b*) God creates free men and brings it about that they always freely do what is right.

And (5*b*), of course, is *not* consistent; for if God *brings it about* that the men He creates always do what is right, then they do not do what is right *freely*. So if (5*a*) is taken to express (5*b*), then (5) is clearly false and clearly not entailed by (3′) and (4).

On the other hand, (5*a*) could conceivably be used to express:

(5*c*) God creates free men and these free men always do what is right.

(5*c*) is surely consistent; it is indeed logically possible that God creates free men and that the free men created by Him always do what is right. And conceivably the objector is using (5) to express this possibility—i.e., it may be that (5) is meant to express:

(5*d*) the proposition God creates free men and the free men created by God *always do what is right* is consistent.

If (5) is equivalent to (5*d*), then (5) is true—in fact necessarily true (and hence trivially entailed by (3′) and (4)). But now the difficulty crops up with respect to (6) which, given the equivalence of (5) and (5*d*) is equivalent to

(6′) If God is all-good and the proposition God creates free men and the free men He creates always do what is right is consistent, then any free men created by God always do what is right.

Now Mackie's aim is to show that the proposition God is omnipotent, omniscient and all-good entails the proposition no free men created by God ever perform morally evil actions. His attempt, as I outlined it, is to show this by constructing a valid argument whose premise is the former and whose conclusion is the latter. But then any additional premise appealed to in the deduction must be necessarily true if Mackie's argument is to succeed. (6′) is one such additional premise; but there seems to be no reason for supposing that (6′) is true at all, let alone necessarily true. Whether the free men created by God would always do what is right would presumably be up to them; for all we know they might sometimes exercise their freedom to do what is wrong. Put in a nutshell the difficulty with the argument is the following. (5*a*) (God creates free men such that they always freely do what is right) is susceptible of two interpretations ((5*b*) and (5*c*)). Under one of these interpretations (5) turns out to be false and the argument therefore fails. Under the other interpretation (6) turns out to be utterly groundless and question begging, and again the argument fails.

So far, then, the Free Will Defence has emerged unscathed from Mackie's objection. One has the feeling, however, that more can be said here; that there is something to Mackie's argument. What more? Well, perhaps something along the following lines. It is agreed that it is logically possible that all men always do only what is right. Now God is said to be omniscient and hence knows, with respect to any person he proposes to create, whether that person would or would not commit morally evil acts. For every person P who in fact performs morally evil actions, there is, evidently, a possible person P' who is exactly like P in every respect except that P' never performs any evil actions. If God is omnipotent, He could have created these possible persons instead of the persons He in fact did create. And if He is also all-good, He *would*, presumably, have created them, since they differ from the persons He did create only in being morally better than they are.

Can we make coherent sense out of this revised version of Mackie's objection? What, in particular, could the objector mean by 'possible person'? and what are we to make of the suggestion that God could have created possible persons? I think these questions can be answered. Let us consider first the set of all those properties it is logically possible for human beings to have. Examples of properties *not* in this set are the properties of *being over a mile long; being a hippopotamus; being a prime number; being divisible by four;* and the like. Included in the set are such properties as *having red hair; being present at the Battle of Waterloo; being the President of the United States; being born in 1889;* and *being a pipe-smoker.* Also included are such moral properties as *being kind to one's maiden aunt, being a scoundrel, performing at least one morally wrong action,* and so on. Let us call the properties in this set H properties. The complement $\bar{P}$ of an H property P is the property a thing has just in case it does not have P. And a *consistent set of H* properties is a set of H properties such that it is logically possible that there be a human being having every property in the set. Now we can define 'possible person' in the following way:

x is a possible person = x is a consistent set of H properties such that for every H property P, either P or $\bar{P}$ is a member of x.

To *instantiate* a possible person P is to create a human being having every property in P. And a set S of possible persons is a *co-possible set of possible persons* just in case it is logically possible that every member of S is instantiated.[10]

Given this technical terminology, Mackie's objection can be summarily restated. It is granted by everyone that there is no absurdity in the claim that some man who is free to do what is wrong never, in fact, performs any wrong action. It follows that there are many possible persons containing the property *is free to do wrong but always does right.* And since it is logically possible that all men always freely do what is right, there are presumably several co-possible sets of possible persons such that each member of each set contains the property in question. Now God, if he is omnipotent, can instantiate

---

[10] The definiens must not be confused with: For every member M of S, it is logically possible that M is instantiated.

any possible person and any co-possible set of possible persons he chooses. Hence, if He were all-good, He would have instantiated one of the sets of co-possible persons all of whose members freely do only what is right.

In spite of its imposing paraphernalia the argument, thus restated, suffers from substantially the same defect that afflicts Mackie's original version. There are *some* possible persons God obviously cannot instantiate—those, for example, containing the property *is not created by God*. Accordingly it is *false* that God can instantiate just any possible person He chooses. But of course the interesting question is whether

(1) God can instantiate possible persons containing the property of always freely doing what is right

is true; for perhaps Mackie could substitute (1) for the premise just shown to be false.

Is (1) true? Perhaps we can approach this question in the following way. Let P be any possible person containing the property *always freely does what is right*. Then there must be some action A such that P contains the property of being free with respect to A (i.e., the property of being free to perform A and free to refrain from performing A). The *instantiation* of a possible person S, I shall say, is a person having every property in S; and let us suppose that if P were instantiated, its instantiation would be doing something morally wrong in performing A. And finally, let us suppose that God wishes to instantiate P. Now P contains many properties in addition to the ones already mentioned. Among them, for example, we might find the following: *is born in 1910, has red hair, is born in Stuttgart, has feeble-minded ancestors, is six feet tall at the age of fourteen*, and the like. And there is no difficulty in God's creating a person with these properties. Further, there is no difficulty in God's bringing it about that this person (let's call him Smith) is free with respect to A. But if God *also* brings it about that Smith refrains from performing A (as he must to be the instantiation of P) then Smith is no longer free with respect to A and is hence not the instantiation of P after all. God cannot cause Smith to refrain from performing A, while allowing him to be free with respect to A; and therefore whether or not Smith does A will be entirely up to Smith; it will be a matter of free choice for him. Accordingly, whether God can instantiate P depends upon what Smith would freely decide to do.

This point may be put more accurately as follows: First, we shall say that an H property Q is *indeterminate* if *God creates a person and causes him to have Q* is necessarily false; an H property is *determinate* if it is not indeterminate. Of the properties we ascribed to P, all are determinate except *freely refrains from doing A* and *always freely does what is right*. Now consider P_1, the subset of P containing just the determinate members of P. In order to instantiate P God must instantiate P_1. It is evident that there is at most one instantiation of P_1, for among the members of P_1 will be some such individuating properties as for example, *is the third son of Richard and Lena Dykstra*. P_1 also contains the property of being free with respect to A; and if P_1 is instantiated, its instantiation will either perform A or refrain from performing A. It is, of course, possible that P_1 is such that if it is instantiated its instantiation I will perform A. If so, then if God allows I to remain free with respect to A, I will do A; and if God prevents I from doing A, then I is not free with respect to A and hence not the instantiation of P after all. Hence in neither case does God succeed in instantiating P. And accordingly God can instantiate P only if P_1 is *not* such that if it is instantiated, its instantiation will perform A. Hence it is possible that God cannot instantiate P. And evidently it is also possible, further, that *every* possible person containing the property *always freely does what is right* is such that neither God nor anyone else can instantiate it.

Now we merely supposed that P_1 is such that if it is instantiated, its instantiation will perform A. And this supposition, if true at all, is merely contingently true. It might be suggested, therefore, that God could instantiate P by instantiating P_1 and bringing it about that P_1 is *not* such that if it is instantiated, its instantiation will perform A. But to do this God must instantiate P_1 and bring it about that P_1 is such that if it is instantiated, its instantiation I will *refrain* from performing A. And if God does this then God brings it about that I will not perform A. But then I is not free to perform A and hence once more is not the instantiation of P.

It is possible, then, that God cannot instantiate any possible person containing the property *always freely does what is right*. It is also possible, of course, that He *can* instantiate some such possible persons. But *that* He can, if indeed He can, is a contingent truth. And since Mackie's project is to prove an entailment, he cannot employ any contingent propositions as added premises. Hence the reconstructed argument fails.

Now the difficulty with the reconstructed argument is the fact that God cannot instantiate just any possible person he chooses, and the possibility that God cannot instantiate any possible persons containing the property of always freely doing what is right. But perhaps the objector can circumvent this difficulty.

The H properties that make trouble for the objector are the indeterminate properties—those which God cannot cause anyone to have. It is because possible persons contain indeterminate properties that God cannot instantiate just any possible person He wishes. And so perhaps the objector can reformulate his definition of 'possible person' in such a way that a possible person is a consistent set S of *determinate* properties such that for any determinate H property P, either P or $\bar{P}$ is a member of S. Unfortunately the following difficulty arises. Where I is any indeterminate H property and D a determinate H property, D or I (the property a person has if he has either D or I) is determinate. And so, of course, is $\bar{D}$. The same difficulty, accordingly, arises all over again—there will be some possible persons God can't instantiate (those containing the properties *is not created by God or has red hair* and *does not have red hair,* for example). We must add, therefore, that no possible person *entails* an indeterminate property.[11]

Even so our difficulties are not at an end. For the definition as now stated entails that there are no *possible free persons,* i.e., possible persons containing the property *on some occasions free to do what is right and free to do what is wrong.*[12] We may see this as follows: Let P be any possible free person. P then contains the property of being free with respect to some action A. Furthermore, P would contain either the property of performing A (since that is a determinate property) or the property of refraining fom performing A. But if P contains the property of performing A and the property of being free with respect to A, then P entails the property of freely performing A— which is an indeterminate property. And the same holds in case P contains the property of refraining from performing A. Hence in either case P entails an indeterminate property and accordingly is not a possible person.

Clearly the objector must revise the definition of 'possible person' in such a way that for any action with respect to which a given possible person P is free, P contains neither the property of performing that action nor the property of refraining from performing it. This may be accomplished in the following way. Let us say that a person S is *free with respect to a property P* just in case there is some action A with respect to which S is free and which is such that S has P if and only if he performs A. So, for example, if a person is free to leave town and free to stay, then he is free with respect to the property *leaves town.* And let us say that a set of properties is free with respect to a given property P just in case it contains the property is *free with respect to P.* Now we can restate the definition of 'possible person' as follows:

x is a possible person = x is a consistent set of determinate H properties such that (1) for every determinate H property P with respect to which x is not free, either P or $\bar{P}$ is a member of x, and (2) x does not entail any indeterminate property.

Now let us add the following new definition:

Possible person P has indeterminate property I = if P were instantiated, P's instantiation would have I.

Under the revised definition of 'possible person' it seems apparent that God, if he is omnipotent, can instantiate any possible person, and any co-possible set of possible persons, he chooses. But, the objector continues, if God is also all-good, He will, presumably, instantiate only those possible persons

---

[11] Where a set S of properties entails a property P if and only if it is necessarily true that anything having every property in S also has P.

[12] This was pointed out to me by Mr. Lewis Creary.

who have some such indeterminate H property as that of *always freely doing what is right*. And here the Free Will Defender can no longer make the objection which held against the previous versions of Mackie's argument. For if God can instantiate any possible person he chooses, he can instantiate any possible free person he chooses.

The Free Will Defender can, however, raise what is essentially the same difficulty in a new guise: what reason is there for supposing that there are *any* possible persons, in the present sense of 'possible person', having the indeterminate property in question? For it is clear that, given any indeterminate H property I, the proposition *no possible person has I* is a contingent proposition. Further, the proposition *every possible free person freely performs at least one morally wrong action* is possibly true. But if every *possible* free person performs at least one wrong action, then every *actual* free person also freely performs at least one wrong action; hence if every possible free person performs at least one wrong action, God could create a universe without moral evil only by refusing to create any free persons at all. And, the Free Will Defender adds, a world containing free persons and moral evil (provided that it contained more moral good than moral evil) would be superior to one lacking both free persons and moral good and evil. Once again, then, the objection seems to fail.

The definitions offered during the discussion of Mackie's objection afford the opportunity of stating the Free Will Defence more formally. I said above [p. 220] that the Free Will Defence is in essence an argument for the conclusion that (*a*) is consistent:

(*a*) God is omnipotent, omniscient, and all-good and God creates persons who sometimes perform morally evil actions.

One way of showing (*a*) to be consistent is to show that its first conjunct does not entail the negation of its second conjunct, i.e., that

(*b*) God is omnipotent, omniscient and all-good

does not entail

(*c*) God does not create persons who perform morally evil actions.

Now one can show that a given proposition *p* does not entail another proposition *q* by producing a third proposition *r* which is such that (1) the conjunction of *p* and *r* is consistent and (2) the conjunction of *p* and *r* entails the negation of *q*. What we need here, then, is a proposition whose conjunction with (*b*) is both logically consistent and a logically sufficient condition of the denial of (*c*).

Consider the following argument:

(*b*) God is omnipotent, omniscient and all-good.
(*r*1) God creates some free persons.

(r2) Every possible free person performs at least one wrong action.
∴ (d) Every actual free person performs at least one wrong action. (r2)
∴ (e) God creates persons who perform morally evil actions. ((r1), (d))

This argument is valid (and can easily be expanded so that it is *formally* valid). Furthermore, the conjunction of (b), (r1) and (r2) is evidently consistent. And as the argument shows, (b), (r1) and (r2) jointly entail (e). But (e) is the denial of (c); hence (b) and (r) jointly entail the denial of (c). Accordingly (b) does not entail (c), and (a) (God is omnipotent, omniscient and all-good and God creates persons who perform morally evil acts) is shown to be consistent. So stated, therefore, the Free Will Defence appears to be successful.

At this juncture it might be objected that even if the Free Will Defence, as explained above, shows that there is no contradiction in the supposition that God, who is all-good, omnipotent and omniscient, creates persons who engage in moral evil, it does nothing to show that an all-good, omnipotent and omniscient Being could create a universe containing as *much* moral evil as this one seems to contain. The objection has a point, although the fact that there seems to be no way of measuring or specifying amounts of moral evil makes it exceedingly hard to state the objection in any way which does not leave it vague and merely suggestive. But let us suppose, for purposes of argument, that there is a way of measuring moral evil (and moral good) and that the moral evil present in the universe amounts to ϕ. The problem then is to show that

(b) God is omnipotent, omniscient and all-good

is consistent with

(f) God creates a set of free persons who produce ϕ moral evil.

Here the Free Will Defender can produce an argument to show that (b) is consistent with (f) which exactly parallels the argument for the consistency of (b) with (c):

(b) God is omnipotent, omniscient and all-good.
(r3) God creates a set S of free persons such that there is a balance of moral good over moral evil with respect to the members of S.
(r4) There is exactly one co-possible set S' of free possible persons such that there is a balance of moral good over moral evil with respect to its members; and the members of S' produce ϕ moral evil.

Set S is evidently the instantiation of S' (i.e. every member of S is an instantiation of some member of S' and every member of S' is instantiated by some member of S); hence the members of S produce ϕ moral evil. Accordingly, (b), (r3) and (r4) jointly entail (f); but the conjunction of (b), (r3) and (r4) is consistent; hence (b) is consistent with (f).

The preceding discussion enables us to conclude, I believe, that the Free Will Defence succeeds in showing that there is no inconsistency in the assertion that God creates a universe containing as much moral evil as the universe in fact contains. There remains but one objection to be considered. McCloskey, Flew and others charge that the Free Will Defence, even if it is successful, accounts for only *part* of the evil we find; it accounts only for moral evil, leaving physical evil as intractable as before. The atheologian can therefore restate his position, maintaining that the existence of *physical evil*, evil which cannot be ascribed to the free actions of human beings, is inconsistent with the existence of an omniscient, omnipotent and all-good Deity.

To make this claim, however, is to overlook an important part of traditional theistic belief; it is part of much traditional belief to attribute a good deal of the evil we find to Satan, or to Satan and his cohorts. Satan, so the traditional doctrine goes, is a mighty non-human spirit, who, along with many other angels, was created long before God created men. Unlike most of his colleagues, Satan rebelled against God and has since been creating whatever havoc he could; the result, of course, is physical evil. But now we see that the moves available to the Free Will Defender in the case of moral evil are equally available to him in the case of physical evil. First he provides definitions of 'possible non-human spirit', 'free non-human spirit', etc., which exactly parallel their counterparts where it was moral evil that was at stake. Then he points out that it is logically possible that

(r5) God creates a set S of free non-human spirits such that the members of S do more good than evil,

and

(r6) there is exactly one co-possible set S' of possible free non-human spirits such that the members of S' do more good than evil,

and

(r7) all of the physical evil in the world is due to the actions of the members of S.

He points out further that (r5), (r6,), and (r7) are jointly consistent and that their conjunction is consistent with the proposition that God is omnipotent, omniscient and all-good. But (r5) through (r7) jointly entail that God creates a universe containing as much physical evil as the universe in fact contains; it follows then, that the existence of physical evil is not inconsistent with the existence of an omniscient, omnipotent, all-good Deity.

Now it must be conceded that views involving devils and other non-human spirits do not at present enjoy either the extensive popularity or the high esteem of (say) the Theory of Relativity. Flew, for example, has this to say about the view in question.

> To make this more than just another desperate *ad hoc* expedient of apologetic it is necessary to produce independent evidence for launching such an hypothesis (if 'hypothesis' is not too flattering a term for it).[13]

But in the present context this claim is surely incorrect; to rebut the charge of contradiction the theist need not hold that the hypothesis in question is probable or even true. He need hold only that it is not inconsistent with the proposition that God exists. Flew suspects that 'hypothesis' may be too flattering a term for the sort of view in question. Perhaps this suspicion reflects his doubts as to the meaningfulness of the proposed view. But it is hard to see how one could plausibly argue that the views in question are nonsensical (in the requisite sense) without invoking some version of the Verifiability Criterion, a doctrine whose harrowing vicissitudes are well known. Furthermore, it is likely that any premises worth considering which yield the conclusion that hypotheses about devils are nonsensical will yield the same conclusion about the hypothesis that God exists. And if *God exists* is nonsensical, then presumably theism is not self-contradictory after all.

We may therefore conclude that the Free Will Defence successfully rebuts the charge of contradiction brought against the theist. The Problem of Evil (if indeed evil constitutes a problem for the theist) does not lie in any inconsistency in the belief that God, who is omniscient, omnipotent and all-good, has created a world containing moral and physical evil.

[13] *Op. cit.*, p. 17.

RELIGIOUS OBJECTIONS
TO THEISM

JOHN ROBINSON
The Religious Inadequacies of Traditional Theism

The Bible speaks of a God 'up there'. No doubt its picture of a three-decker universe, of 'the heaven above, the earth beneath and the waters under the earth', was once taken quite literally. No doubt also its more sophisticated writers, if pressed, would have been the first to regard this as symbolic language to represent and convey spiritual realities. Yet clearly they were not pressed. Or at any rate they were not oppressed by it. Even such an educated man of the world as St Luke can express the conviction of Christ's ascension —the conviction that he is not merely alive but reigns in the might and right of God—in the crudest terms of being 'lifted up' into heaven, there to sit down at the right hand of the Most High.[1] He feels no need to offer any apology for this language, even though he of all New Testament writers was commending Christianity to what Schleiermacher called its 'cultured de-

John Robinson (1919–   ), formerly the suffragan Bishop of Woolwich (Anglican), is a lecturer in theology at Trinity College, Cambridge, and Assistant Bishop of Southwark. A New Testament scholar, he is also the author of many works on various theological questions.

THE RELIGIOUS INADEQUACIES OF TRADITIONAL THEISM   From *Honest to God,* by John A. T. Robinson. Published in the U.S.A., 1963, by The Westminster Press, Philadelphia. © SCM Press, Ltd., London, 1963. Used by permission of The Westminster Press and SCM Press, Ltd.

[1] Acts 1.9–11.

spisers'. This is the more remarkable because, in contrast, he leaves his readers in no doubt that what we might regard as the scarcely more primitive notions of God entertained by the Athenians,[2] that the deity lives in temples made by man and needs to be served by human hands, were utterly superseded by Christianity.

Moreover, it is the two most mature theologians of the New Testament, St John and the later Paul, who write most uninhibitedly of this 'going up' and 'coming down'.

> No one has ascended into heaven but he who descended from heaven, the Son of man.[3]
>
> Do you take offence at this? Then what if you were to see the Son of man ascending where he was before? [4]
>
> In saying, 'He ascended', what does it mean but that he had also descended into the lower parts of the earth? He who descended is he who also ascended far above all the heavens, that he might fill all things.[5]

They are able to use this language without any sense of constraint because it had not become an embarrassment to them. Everybody accepted what it meant to speak of a God up there, even though the groundlings might understand it more grossly than the gnostics. For St Paul, no doubt, to be 'caught up to the third heaven'[6] was as much a metaphor as it is to us (though for him a considerably more precise metaphor). But he could use it to the spiritually sophisticated at Corinth with no consciousness that he must 'demythologize' if he were to make it acceptable.

For the New Testament writers the idea of a God 'up there' created no embarrassment—because it had not yet become a difficulty. For us too it creates little embarrassment—because, for the most part, it has ceased to be a difficulty. We are scarcely even conscious that the majority of the words for what we value most are still in terms of height, though as Edwyn Bevan observed in his Gifford Lectures,[7] 'The proposition: Moral and spiritual worth is greater or less in ratio to the distance outwards from the earth's surface, would certainly seem to be, if stated nakedly like that, an odd proposition.' Yet it is one that we have long ago found unnecessary to explain away. We may indeed continue to have to tell our children that heaven is not in fact over their heads nor God literally 'above the bright blue sky'. Moreover, whatever we may accept with the top of our minds, most of us still retain deep down the mental image of 'an old man in the sky'. Nevertheless, for most of us most of the time the traditional language of a three-storeyed universe is not a serious obstacle. It does not worry us intellectually, it is not an 'offence' to faith, because we have long since made a remarkable

---

[2] Acts 17.22–31.   [3] John 3.13.   [4] John 6.61 f.   [5] Eph. 4.9 f.   [6] II Cor. 12.2.
[7] *Symbolism and Belief* (1938), p. 30. Chs. II and III on 'Height' are a *locus classicus* for the conception of God 'up there'.

transposition, of which we are hardly aware. In fact, we do not realize how crudely spatial much of the Biblical terminology is, for we have ceased to perceive it that way. It is as though when reading a musical score what we actually saw was not the notes printed but the notes of the key into which mentally we were transposing it. There are some notes, as it were, in the Biblical score which still strike us in the old way (the Ascension story, for instance) and which we have to make a conscious effort to transpose, but in general we assimilate the language without trouble.

For in place of a God who is literally or physically 'up there' we have accepted, as part of our mental furniture, a God who is spiritually or metaphysically 'out there'. There are, of course, those for whom he is almost literally 'out there'. They may have accepted the Copernican revolution in science, but until recently at any rate they have still been able to think of God as in some way 'beyond' outer space. In fact the number of people who instinctively seem to feel that it is no longer possible to believe in God in the space-age shows how crudely physical much of this thinking about a God 'out there' has been. Until the last recesses of the cosmos had been explored or were capable of being explored (by radio-telescope if not by rocketry), it was still possible to locate God mentally in some *terra incognita*. But now it seems there is no room for him, not merely in the inn, but in the entire universe: for there are no vacant places left. In reality, of course, our new view of the universe has made not the slightest difference. Indeed, the limit set to 'space' by the speed of light (so that beyond a certain point— not all that much further than our present range—everything recedes over the horizon of visibility) is even more severe. And there is nothing to stop us, if we wish to, locating God 'beyond' it. And there he would be quite invulnerable—in a 'gap' science could never fill. But in fact the coming of the space-age has destroyed this crude projection of God—and for that we should be grateful. For if God is 'beyond', he is not *literally* beyond anything.

But the idea of a God spiritually or metaphysically 'out there' dies very much harder. Indeed, most people would be seriously disturbed by the thought that it should need to die at all. For it *is* their God, and they have nothing to put in its place. And for the words 'they' and 'their' it would be more honest to substitute 'we' and 'our'. For it is the God of our own upbringing and conversation, the God of our fathers and of our religion, who is under attack. Every one of us lives with some mental picture of a God 'out there', a God who 'exists' above and beyond the world he made, a God 'to' whom we pray and to whom we 'go' when we die. In traditional Christian theology, the doctrine of the Trinity witnesses to the self-subsistence of this divine Being outside us and apart from us. The doctrine of creation asserts that at a moment of time this God called 'the world' into existence over against himself. The Biblical record describes how he proceeds to enter into contact with those whom he has made, how he establishes a 'covenant' with them, how he 'sends' to them his prophets, and how in the fullness of time he 'visits' them in the person of his Son, who must one day 'come again' to gather the faithful to himself.

This picture of a God 'out there' coming to earth like some visitor from outer space underlies every popular presentation of the Christian drama of salvation, whether from the pulpit or the presses. Indeed, it is noticeable that those who have been most successful in communicating it in our day—Dorothy Sayers, C. S. Lewis, J. B. Phillips—have hesitated least in being boldly anthropomorphic in the use of this language. They have not, of course, taken it literally, any more than the New Testament writers take literally the God 'up there', but they have not apparently felt it any embarrassment to the setting forth of the Gospel. This is sufficient testimony to the fact that there is a ready-made public for whom this whole frame of reference still presents no difficulties, and their very achievement should make us hesitate to pull it down or call it in question.

Indeed, the last thing I want to do is to appear to criticize from a superior position. I should like to think that it were possible to use this mythological language of the God 'out there' and make the same utterly natural and unself-conscious transposition as I have suggested we already do with the language of the God 'up there'. Indeed, unless we become used to doing this and are able to take this theological notation, as it were, in our stride, we shall cut ourselves off from the classics of the Christian faith, just as we should be unable to read the Bible were we to stumble at *its* way of describing God. I believe, however, that we may have to pass through a century or more of reappraisal before this becomes possible and before this language ceases to be an offence to faith for a great many people. No one wants to live in such a period, and one could heartily wish it were not necessary. But the signs are that we are reaching the point at which the whole conception of a God 'out there', which has served us so well since the collapse of the three-decker universe, is itself becoming more of a hindrance than a help.

In a previous age there came a moment when the three-decker likewise proved an embarrassment, even as a piece of mental furniture. But in this case there was a considerable interval between the time when it ceased to be taken literally as a model of the universe and the time when it ceased to perform a useful function as a metaphor. An illustration of this is to be seen in the doctrine of hell. In the old scheme, hell was 'down there'. By Shakespeare's time no one thought of it as literally under the earth, but still in *Hamlet* it is lively and credible enough as a metaphor. But a localized hell gradually lost more and more of its purchase over the imagination, and revivalist attempts to stoke its flames did not succeed in restoring its power. The tragedy in this instance is that no effective translation into terms of the God 'out there' was found for the Devil and his angels, the pit and the lake of fire. This element therefore tended to drop out of popular Christianity altogether—much to the detriment of the depth of the Gospel.

But the point I wish to make here is that the supersession of the old scheme was a gradual one. After it had been discredited scientifically, it continued to serve theologically as an acceptable frame of reference. The image of a God 'up there' survived its validity as a literal description of reality by many centuries. But today I believe we may be confronted by a double crisis. The final psychological, if not logical, blow delivered by modern science and technology to the idea that there might *literally* be a God 'out there' has *coincided* with an awareness that the *mental* picture of such a God may be more of a stumbling-block than an aid to belief in the Gospel. There is a double pressure to discard this entire construction, and with it any belief in God at all.

Moreover, it is not merely a question of the speed of adjustment required. The abandonment of a God 'out there' represents a much more radical break than the transition to this concept from that of a God 'up there'. For this earlier transposition was largely a matter of verbal notation, of a change in spatial metaphor, important as this undoubtedly was in liberating Christianity from a flat-earth cosmology. But to be asked to give up any idea of a Being 'out there' at all will appear to be an outright denial of God. For, to the ordinary way of thinking, to believe in God means to be convinced of the existence of such a supreme and separate Being. 'Theists' are those who believe that such a Being exists, 'atheists' those who deny that he does.

But suppose such a super-Being 'out there' is really only a sophisticated version of the Old Man in the sky? Suppose belief in God does not, indeed cannot, mean being persuaded of the 'existence' of some entity, even a supreme entity, which might or might not be there, like life on Mars? Suppose the atheists are right—but that this is no more the end or denial of Christianity than the discrediting of the God 'up there', which must in its time have seemed the contradiction of all that the Bible said? Suppose that all such atheism does is to destroy an idol, and that we can and must get on without a God 'out there' at all? Have we seriously faced the possibility that to abandon such an idol may in the future be the only way of making Christianity meaningful, except to the few remaining equivalents of flat-earthers (just as to have clung earlier to the God 'up there' would have made it impossible in the modern world for any but primitive peoples to believe the Gospel)? Perhaps after all the Freudians are right, that such a God— the God of traditional popular theology—*is* a projection, and perhaps we are being called to live without that projection in any form.

That is not an attractive proposition: inevitably it feels like being orphaned. And it is bound to be misunderstood and resisted as a denial of the Gospel, as a betrayal of what the Bible says (though actually the Bible speaks in literal terms of a God whom we have already abandoned). And it will encounter the opposition not only of the fundamentalists but of 90 per cent of Church people. Equally it will be resented by most unthinking non-churchgoers, who tend to be more jealous of the beliefs they have rejected and deeply shocked that they should be betrayed. Above all, there is the large percentage of oneself that finds this revolution unacceptable and wishes it were unnecessary.

This raises again the insistent question, Why? Is it really necessary to pass through this Copernican revolution? Must we upset what most people happily believe—or happily choose not to believe? And have we anything to put in its place?

SOME CHRISTIAN QUESTIONERS

In some moods, indeed, I wonder. But I know in my own mind that these are questions that must be explored. Or rather, they are questions that are already being explored on many sides. The only issue is whether they remain on the fringe of the intellectual debate or are dragged into the middle and placed squarely under men's noses. I know that as a bishop I could happily get on with most of my work without ever being forced to discuss such questions. I could keep the ecclesiastical machine going quite smoothly, in fact much more smoothly, without raising them. The kind of sermons I normally have to preach do not require one to get within remote range of them. Indeed, such is the pressure of regular priorities that I should not have been able, let alone obliged, to let them occupy my mind for long enough to write this, were it not that I was forcibly laid up for three months. But they were questions that had long been dogging me, and I felt from the beginning the spiritual necessity laid upon me to use this period to allow them their head.

The only way I can put it is to say that over the years a number of things have unaccountably 'rung a bell'; various unco-ordinated aspects of one's reading and experience have come to 'add up'. The inarticulate conviction forms within one that certain things are true or important. One may not grasp them fully or understand why they matter. One may not even welcome them. One simply knows that if one is to retain one's integrity one must come to terms with them. For if their priority is sensed and they are not attended to, then subtly other convictions begin to lose their power: one continues to trot these convictions out, one says one believes in them (and one does), but somehow they seem emptier. One is aware that insights that carry their own authentication, however subjective, are not being allowed to modify them.

And then, equally, there are certain other things which have *not* rung a bell, certain areas of traditional Christian expression—devotional and practical—which have evidently meant a great deal for most people but which have simply left one cold. The obvious conclusion is that this is due to one's own spiritual inadequacy. And there is clearly a very large amount of truth in this. But I have not forgotten the relief with which twenty years ago, back at my theological college, I discovered in a conversation of the small hours a kindred spirit, to whom also the whole of the teaching we received on prayer (as it happened to be in this case) meant equally little. There was nothing about it one could say was wrong. Indeed, it was an impressive roundabout: but one was simply not on it—and, what was worse, had no particular urge to be. To realize that after all one might not be the chief of sinners, or the only man out of step, lifted a load of secret, yet basically unadmitted, guilt. And since then I have found others—and in each situation a surprisingly large minority—who confess to the same blind spot. The traditional material is all true, no doubt, and one recognizes it as something one ought to be able to respond to, but somehow it seems to be going on around one rather than within. Yet to question it openly is to appear to let down the side, to be branded as hopelessly unspiritual, and to cause others to stumble.

And this is only one particular instance. Indeed, as one goes on, it is the things one doesn't believe and finds one doesn't have to believe which are as liberating as the things one does. James Pike, the Bishop of California, is one who has admitted to finding the same. In a stimulating—and thoroughly constructive—article,[8] which rocked the American Church and even drew the charge of heresy from the clergy of one diocese, he wrote: 'I stand in a religious tradition . . . which really does not know very much about religion. The Roman Catholics and the Southern Baptists know a great deal more about religion than we do. And . . . I feel that many people within my own church—and some of them write tracts for the book-stalls of churches—know too many answers. I do not deny the truth of these answers; I simply don't know as much as the authors of the pamphlets.'

But the point I want to make is that I gradually came to realize that some of the things that rang bells and some of the things that didn't seemed to be connected. I began to find that I was questioning one whole set of presuppositions and feeling towards another in its place. All I am doing in this book is to try to think this process aloud and help to articulate it for others. For I believe it is a process common in some form or other to many in our age. Indeed, it is the number of straws apparently blowing in the same direction that strikes me as significant. I have done little more than pick a few of them up and I am conscious that in this book, more than in any other I have written, I am struggling to think other people's thoughts after them. I cannot claim to have understood all I am trying to transmit. And it is for this reason partly that I have chosen to let them speak, through extended quotations, in their own words. But it is also because I see this as an attempt at communication, at mediation between a realm of discourse in which anything I have to say is very familiar and unoriginal and another, popular world, both within and without the Church, in which it is totally unfamiliar and almost heretical.

At this stage, to indicate what I am talking about, let me instance three

---

[8] 'Three-pronged Synthesis', *The Christian Century*, December 21, 1960.

pieces of writing, all brief, which contain ideas that immediately found lodgement when I first read them and which have since proved seminal not only for me but for many of this generation.

The first of these in date for me (though not in composition) was a sermon by Paul Tillich, which appeared in his collection *The Shaking of the Foundations*, published in England in 1949.[9] It was called 'The Depth of Existence' and it opened my eyes to the transformation that seemed to come over so much of the traditional religious symbolism when it was transposed from the heights to the depths. God, Tillich was saying, is not a projection 'out there', an Other beyond the skies, of whose existence we have to convince ourselves, but the Ground of our very being.

> The name of this infinite and inexhaustible depth and ground of all being is *God*. That depth is what the word *God* means. And if that word has not much meaning for you, translate it, and speak of the depths of your life, of the source of your being, of your ultimate concern, of what you take seriously without any reservation. Perhaps, in order to do so, you must forget everything traditional that you have learned about God, perhaps even that word itself. For if you know that God means depth, you know much about him. You cannot then call yourself an atheist or unbeliever. For you cannot think or say: Life has no depth! Life is shallow. Being itself is surface only. If you could say this in complete seriousness, you would be an atheist; but otherwise you are not. He who knows about depth knows about God.[10]

I remember at the time how these words lit up for me. I did what I have never done before or since: I simply read Tillich's sermon, in place of an address of my own, to the students I was then teaching. I do not remember looking at the words again till I came to write this, but they formed one of the streams below the surface that were to collect into the underground river of which I have since become conscious. I shall return to them, as to the other influences I mention in this chapter, subsequently. Here it is enough to say they seemed to speak of God with a new and indestructible relevance and made the traditional language of a God that came in from outside both remote and artificial.

Next, I must register the impact of the now famous passages about 'Christianity without religion' in Dietrich Bonhoeffer's *Letters and Papers from Prison*.[11] I first encountered extracts from these in *The Ecumenical Review* for January 1952, shortly after their first publication in German. One felt at once that the Church was not yet ready for what Bonhoeffer was giving us as his last will and testament before he was hanged by the S.S.: indeed, it might be understood properly only a hundred years hence. But it seemed one of those trickles that must one day split rocks. Hitherto, Bonhoeffer was

---

[9] Now available in a Pelican edition (1962), to which the page references are given.

[10] *Op. cit.*, pp. 63 f. [Reprinted here by permission of Charles Scribner's Sons.]

[11] Ed. E. Bethge (1953; 2nd ed.—to which all references are made—1956). The American edition is entitled *Prisoner for God*.

saying, the Church has based its preaching of the Gospel on the appeal to religious experience, to the fact that deep down every man feels the need for religion in some form, the need for a God to whom to give himself, a God in terms of whom to explain the world. But suppose men come to feel that they can get along perfectly well without 'religion', without any desire for personal salvation, without any sense of sin, without any need of 'that hypothesis'? Is Christianity to be confined to those who still have this sense of insufficiency, this 'God-shaped blank', or who can be induced to have it? Bonhoeffer's answer was to say that God is deliberately calling us in this twentieth century to a form of Christianity that does not depend on the premise of religion, just as St Paul was calling men in the first century to a form of Christianity that did not depend on the premise of circumcision.

What that meant I hardly began to understand. But I knew that this was something we must learn to assimilate: the system could not simply eject it. And now after a bare decade it feels as if we have been living with it for very much longer.

Then, thirdly, there was an essay which created an almost immediate explosion when it appeared in 1941, though I did not read it in detail till it was translated into English in 1953. This was the manifesto by Rudolf Bultmann entitled, 'New Testament and Mythology'.[12]

Once more Bultmann seemed to be putting a finger on something very near the quick of the Gospel message. For when he spoke of the 'mythological' element in the New Testament he was really referring to all the language which seeks to characterize the Gospel history as *more* than bare history like any other history. The importance of this 'plus' is that it is precisely what makes events of two thousand years ago a preaching or gospel for today at all. And his contention was that this whole element is unintelligible jargon to the modern man. In order to express the 'trans-historical' character of the historical event of Jesus of Nazareth, the New Testament writers used the 'mythological' language of pre-existence, incarnation, ascent and descent, miraculous intervention, cosmic catastrophe, and so on, which according to Bultmann, makes sense only on a now completely antiquated world-view. Thus, modern man, instead of stumbling on the real rock of offence (the scandal of the Cross), is put off by the very things which *should* be translating that historical occurrence into an act of God for him, but which in fact merely make it incredible. The relevance of Bultmann's analysis and of his programme of 'demythologizing' to the whole question of God 'out there' from which we started is obvious enough. If he is right, the entire conception of a supernatural order which invades and 'perforates' [13] this one must be abandoned. But if so, what do we mean by God, by revelation, and what becomes of Christianity?

---

[12] *Kerygma and Myth* (ed. H. W. Bartsch), Vol. i, pp. 1–44.
[13] The phrase is used by Bultmann in a subsequent and more popular presentation of his thesis, *Jesus Christ and Mythology* (1960), p. 15.

Now all these three writers might appear to have been raising theological issues fairly far removed from the everyday concerns of ordinary men. But what convinced me of their importance was not simply the spark they struck in myself. It was that for all their apparent difficulty and Teutonic origin they so evidently spoke not only to intelligent non-theologians but to those in closest touch with the unchurched masses of our modern urban and industrial civilization. Tillich is one of the few theologians to have broken through what he himself calls, in another connection, 'the theological circle'. Bonhoeffer is talked of where 'religion' does not penetrate, and the kind of ideas he threw out have been taken up by two men, the Bishop of Middleton [14] and Dr George Macleod,[15] who are as exercised as any in our generation by the relation of theology to the real world. Again, I was astonished to discover how Bultmann's ideas, for all their forbidding jargon, seemed to come like a breath of fresh air to entirely untheological students. Indeed, he had in the first instance been driven to them by the practical impossibility of communicating the Gospel to soldiers at the front. And one of my valued possessions is a copy of a letter written by Bultmann to the Sheffield Industrial Mission, setting out with a profound simplicity the Gospel as he would present it to steel-workers in a demythologized form.

Moreover, though I said earlier that such thinking would be rejected and resented by those who had turned their backs on Christianity, I find that it comes with refreshing relevance to many who have nothing to undo. It seems to speak far more directly to their entirely non-religious experience than the traditional 'popular' apologetic. . . .

[14] E. R. Wickham, *Church and People in an Industrial City* (1957), pp. 232–8.
[15] *Only One Way Left* (1956; 2nd ed. 1958).

Religion as a Dimension in Man's Spiritual Life

The title of my talk is in itself a problem. Even before one has said anything about it, one is questioned from two sides. Some Christian theologians will ask whether religion is here considered as a creative element of the human spirit rather than as a gift of divine revelation. And if one replies that religion is an aspect of man's spiritual life, they will turn away. And some secular scientists will ask whether religion is to be considered a lasting quality of the human spirit instead of an effect of changing psychological and sociological conditions. And if one answers that religion is a necessary aspect of man's spiritual life, they turn away like the theologians, but in an opposite direction.

This situation shows an almost schizophrenic split in our collective consciousness, a split which threatens our spiritual freedom by driving the contemporary mind into irrational and compulsive affirmations or negations of religion. And there is as much compulsive reaction to religion on the scientific side as there is on the religious side. Therefore, it is very fitting that a symposium which is guided by the idea of human freedom deals with the religious aspect of the human spirit.

Those theologians who deny that religion is an element of man's spiritual life have a real point. According to them, the meaning of religion is that man received something which does not come *from* him, but which is given *to* him and may stand against him. They insist that the relation to God is not a human possibility and that God must first relate Himself to man. One could summarize the intention of these theologians in the sentence that religion is not a creation of the human spirit (spirit with a small s) but a gift of the divine Spirit (Spirit with a capital S). Man's spirit, they would continue, is creative with respect to itself and its world, but not with respect to God. With respect to God, man is receptive and only receptive. He has no freedom to relate himself to God. This, they would add, is the meaning of the classical doctrine of the Bondage of the Will as developed by Paul, Augustine, Thomas, Luther, and Calvin. In the face of these witnesses, we must certainly ask: Is it then justified to speak of religion as an aspect of the human spirit?

Paul Tillich (1886–1965) was born and educated in Germany, where he pursued a successful academic career until 1933. Dismissed by Hitler, he came to the United States, taught for many years at the Union Theological Seminary in New York, and later at Harvard and the University of Chicago. Tillich has perhaps had more influence on the development of theology in the United States over the past thirty years than any other single figure. Among his most important works are *Systematic Theology*, *Dynamics of Faith*, and *The Courage to Be*.

RELIGION AS A DIMENSION IN MAN'S SPIRITUAL LIFE   Reproduced from *Man's Right to Knowledge* (2nd series), New York: Herbert Muschel, 1954, by permission of the Trustees of Columbia University in the City of New York.

241

The opposite criticism of the title of this talk also has its valid point. It comes from the side of the sciences of man, psychology, sociology, anthropology, and history. They emphasize the infinite diversity of religious ideas and practices, the mythological character of all religious concepts, the existence of many forms of non-religion in individuals and groups. Religion, they say (with the philosopher Comte), is characteristic for a special stage of human development (the mythological stage), but it has no place in the scientific stage in which we are living. Religion, according to this attitude, is a transitory creation of the human spirit but certainly not an essential quality of it.

If we analyze carefully these two groups of arguments, we discover the surprising fact that although they come from opposite directions, they have something definite in common. Both the theological and the scientific critics of the belief that religion is an aspect of the human spirit define religion as man's relation to divine beings, whose existence the theological critics assert and the scientific critics deny. But it is just this idea of religion which makes any understanding of religion impossible. If you start with the question whether God does or does not exist, you can never reach Him; and if you assert that He does exist, you can reach Him even less than if you assert that He does not exist. A God about whose existence or non-existence you can argue is a thing beside others within the universe of existing things. And the question is quite justified whether such a thing does exist, and the answer is equally justified that it does not exist. It is regrettable that scientists believe that they have refuted religion when they rightly have shown that there is no evidence whatsoever for the assumption that such a being exists. Actually, they have not only not refuted religion, but they have done it a considerable service. They have forced it to reconsider and to restate the meaning of the tremendous word *God*. Unfortunately, many theologians make the same mistake. They begin their message with the assertion that there is a highest being called God, whose authoritative revelations they have received. They are more dangerous for religion than the so-called atheistic scientists. They take the first step on the road which inescapably leads to what is called atheism. Theologians who make of God a highest being who has given some people information about Himself, provoke inescapably the resistance of those who are told they must subject themselves to the authority of this information.

Against both groups of critics we affirm the validity of our subject: religion as an aspect of the human spirit. But, in doing so, we take into consideration the criticisms from both sides and the elements of truth in each of them.

When we say that religion is an aspect of the human spirit, we are saying that if we look at the human spirit from a special point of view, it presents itself to us as religious. What is this view? It is the point of view from which we can look into the depth of man's spiritual life. Religion is not a special function of man's spiritual life, but it is the dimension of depth in all of its functions. The assertion has far-reaching consequences for the interpretation of religion, and it needs comment on each of the terms used in it. Religion is not a special function of the human spirit! History tells us the story of how religion goes from one spiritual function to the other to find a home, and is either rejected or swallowed by them. Religion comes to the moral function and knocks at its door, certain that it will be received. Is not the ethical the nearest relative of the religious? How could it be rejected? Indeed, it is not rejected; it is taken in. But it is taken in as a "poor relation" and asked to earn its place in the moral realm by serving morality. It is admitted as long as it helps to create good citizens, good husbands and children, good employees, officials, and soldiers. But the moment in which religion makes claims of its own, it is either silenced or thrown out as superfluous or dangerous for morals. So religion must look around for another function of man's spiritual life, and it is attracted by the cognitive function. Religion as a special way of knowledge, as mythological imagination or as mystical intuition, this seems to give a home to religion. Again religion is admitted, but as subordinate to pure knowledge, and only for a brief time. Pure knowledge, strengthened by the tremendous success of its scientific work, soon recants its half-hearted acceptance of religion and declares that religion has nothing whatsoever to do with knowledge. Once more religion is without a home within man's spiritual life. It looks around for another spiritual function to join. And it finds one, namely, the esthetic function. Why not try to find a place within the artistic creativity of man? religion asks itself, through the mouths of the philosophers of religion. And the artistic realm answers, through the mouths of many artists, past and present, with an enthusiastic affirmative, and invites religion not only to join with it but also to acknowledge that art *is* religion. But now religion hesitates. Does not art express reality, while religion transforms reality? Is there not an element of unreality even in the greatest work of art? Religion remembers that it has old relations to the moral and the cognitive realms, to the good and to the true, and it resists the temptation to dissolve itself into art. But now where shall religion turn? The whole field of man's spiritual life is taken, and no section of it is ready to give religion an adequate place. So religion turns to something that accompanies every activity of man and every function of man's spiritual life. We call it feeling. Religion a feeling: this seems to be the end of the wanderings of religion. And this end is strongly acclaimed by all those who want to have the realms of knowledge and morals free from any religious interference. Religion, if banned to the realm of mere feeling, has ceased to be dangerous for any rational and practical human enterprise. But, we must add, it also has lost its seriousness, its truth, and its ultimate meaning. In the atmosphere of mere subjectivity of feeling without a definite object of emotion, without an ultimate content, religion dies. This also is not the answer to the question of religion as an aspect of the human spirit.

In this situation, without a home, without a place to dwell in, religion suddenly realizes that it does not need such a place, that it does not need to seek for a home. It is at home everywhere, namely, in the depth of all functions of man's spiritual life. Religion is the dimension of depth in all of them. Religion is the aspect of depth in the totality of the human spirit.

What does the metaphor *depth* mean? It means that the religious aspect points to that which is ultimate, infinite, unconditional in man's spiritual life. Religion, in the largest and most basic sense of the word, is ultimate concern. And ultimate concern is manifest in all creative functions of the human spirit. It is manifest in the moral sphere as the unconditional seriousness of the moral demand. Therefore, if someone rejects religion in the name of the moral function of the human spirit, he rejects religion in the name of religion. Ultimate concern is manifest in the realm of knowledge as the passionate longing for ultimate reality. Therefore, if anyone rejects religion in the name of the cognitive function of the human spirit, he rejects religion in the name of religion. Ultimate concern is manifest in the esthetic function of the human spirit as the infinite desire to express ultimate meaning. Therefore, if anyone rejects religion in the name of the esthetic function of the human spirit, he rejects religion in the name of religion. You cannot reject religion with ultimate seriousness, because ultimate seriousness, or the state of being ultimately concerned, is itself religion. Religion is the substance, the ground, and the depth of man's spiritual life. This is the religious aspect of the human spirit.

But now the question arises, what about religion in the narrower and customary sense of the word, be it institutional religion or the religion of personal piety? If religion is present in all functions of the spiritual life, why has mankind developed religion as a special sphere among others, in myth, cult, devotion, and ecclesiastical institutions? The answer is, because of the tragic estrangement of man's spiritual life from its own ground and depth. According to the visionary who has written the last book of the Bible, there will be no temple in the heavenly Jerusalem, for God will be all in all. There will be no secular realm, and for this very reason there will be no religious realm. Religion will be again what it is essentially, the all-determining ground and substance of man's spiritual life. But this is vision, not reality. In the real world, which is our destiny, religion has received a narrower meaning. It has become a function of the human spirit among others and often in conflict with them. This situation is unavoidable; it is an element in man's tragic predicament. Religion is, like everything human, great and tragic at the same time. And since it expresses our *ultimate* concern, it is greater and more tragic than anything else.

It opens up the depth of man's spiritual life which is mostly covered by the dust of our daily life and the noise of our secular work. Religion gives us the experience of the Holy, of something which is untouchable, awe-inspiring, an ultimate meaning, the source of ultimate courage. This is the glory of what we call religion. But beside its glory lies its shame. It makes itself the ultimate and despises the secular realm. It makes its myths and doctrines, its rites and laws into ultimates and persecutes those who do not subject themselves to it. It forgets that its own existence is a result of man's tragic estrangement from his true being. It forgets its own emergency character.

This is the reason for the passionate reaction of the secular world against religion, a reaction which has tragic consequences for the secular realm itself. For the religious and the secular realm are in the same predicament. Neither of them should be in separation from the other, and both should realize that their very existence as separated is an emergency, that both of them are rooted in religion in the larger sense of the word, in the experience of ultimate concern. To the degree in which this is realized the conflicts between the religious and the secular are overcome, and religion has rediscovered its true place in man's spiritual life, namely, in its depth, out of which it gives substance, ultimate meaning, judgment, and creative courage to all functions of the human spirit.

PAUL TILLICH
Theism Transcended

The courage to take meaninglessness into itself presupposes a relation to the ground of being which we have called "absolute faith." It is without a *special* content, yet it is not without content. The content of absolute faith is the "God above God." Absolute faith and its consequence, the courage that takes the radical doubt, the doubt about God, into itself, transcends the theistic idea of God.

Theism can mean the unspecified affirmation of God. Theism in this sense does not say what it means if it uses the name of God. Because of the traditional and psychological connotations of the word God such an empty theism can produce a reverent mood if it speaks of God. Politicians, dictators, and other people who wish to use rhetoric to make an impression on their audience like to use the word God in this sense. It produces the feeling in their listeners that the speaker is serious and morally trustworthy. This is especially successful if they can brand their foes as atheistic. On a higher level people without a definite religious commitment like to call themselves theistic, not for special purposes but because they cannot stand a world without God, whatever this God may be. They need some of the connotations of the word God and they are afraid of what they call atheism. On the highest level of this kind of theism the name of God is used as a poetic or practical symbol, expressing a profound emotional state or the highest ethical idea. It is a theism which stands on the boundary line between the second type of theism and what we call "theism transcended." But it is still too indefinite to cross this boundary line. The atheistic negation of this whole type of theism is as vague as the theism itself. It may produce an irreverent mood and angry reaction of those who take their theistic affirmation seriously. It may even be felt as justified against the rhetorical-political abuse of the name God, but it is ultimately as irrelevant as the theism which it negates. It cannot reach the state of despair any more than the theism against which it fights can reach the state of faith.

Theism can have another meaning, quite contrary to the first one: it can be the name of what we have called the divine-human encounter. In this case it points to those elements in the Jewish-Christian tradition which emphasize the person-to-person relationship with God. Theism in this sense emphasizes the personalistic passages in the Bible and the Protestant creeds, the personalistic image of God, the word as the tool of creation and revelation, the ethical and social character of the kingdom of God, the personal nature of human faith and divine forgiveness, the historical vision of the universe, the idea of a divine purpose, the infinite distance between creator and creature, the absolute separation between God and the world, the conflict between holy God and sinful man, the person-to-person character of prayer and practical devotion. Theism in this sense is the nonmystical side of biblical religion and historical Christianity. Atheism from the point of view of this theism is the human attempt to escape the divine-human encounter. It is an existential—not a theoretical—problem.

Theism has a third meaning, a strictly theological one. Theological theism is, like every theology, dependent on the religious substance which it conceptualizes. It is dependent on theism in the first sense insofar as it tries to prove the necessity of affirming God in some way; it usually develops the so-called arguments for the "existence" of God. But it is more dependent on theism in the second sense insofar as it tries to establish a doctrine of God which transforms the person-to-person encounter with God into a doctrine about two persons who may or may not meet but who have a reality independent of each other.

Now theism in the first sense must be transcended because it is irrelevant, and theism in the second sense must be transcended because it is one-sided. But theism in the third sense must be transcended because it is wrong. It is bad theology. This can be shown by a more penetrating analysis. The God of theological theism is a being beside others and as such a part of the whole of reality. He certainly is considered its most important part, but as a part and therefore as subjected to the structure of the whole. He is supposed to be beyond the ontological elements and categories which constitute reality. But every statement subjects him to them. He is seen as a self which has a world, as an ego which is related to a thou, as a cause which is separated from its effect, as having a definite space and an endless time. He is a being, not being-itself. As such he is bound to the subject-object structure of reality, he is an object for us as subjects. At the same time we are objects for him as a subject. And this is decisive for the necessity of transcending theological theism. For God as a subject makes me into an object which is nothing more than an object. He deprives me of my subjectivity because he is all-powerful and all-knowing. I revolt and try to make *him* into an object, but the revolt fails and becomes desperate. God appears as the invincible tyrant, the being in contrast with whom all other beings are without freedom and subjectivity. He is equated with the recent tyrants who with the help of terror try to transform everything into a mere object, a thing among things, a cog in the machine they control. He becomes the model of everything against which Existentialism revolted. This is the God Nietzsche said had to be killed because nobody can tolerate being made into a mere object of absolute knowledge and absolute control. This is the deepest root of atheism. It is an atheism which is justified as the reaction against theological theism and its disturbing implications. It is also the deepest root of the Existential-ist despair and the widespread anxiety of meaninglessness in our period.

Theism in all its forms is transcended in the experience we have called absolute faith. It is the accepting of the acceptance without somebody or something that accepts. It is the power of being-itself that accepts and gives the courage to be. This is the highest point to which our analysis has brought us. It cannot be described in the way the God of all forms of theism can be described. It cannot be described in mystical terms either. It transcends both mysticism and personal encounter, as it transcends both the courage to be as a part and the courage to be as oneself.

THE GOD ABOVE GOD AND THE COURAGE TO BE

The ultimate source of the courage to be is the "God above God"; this is the result of our demand to transcend theism. Only if the God of theism is transcended can the anxiety of doubt and meaninglessness be taken into the courage to be. The God above God is the object of all mystical longing, but mysticism also must be transcended in order to reach him. Mysticism does not take seriously the concrete and the doubt concerning the concrete. It plunges directly into the ground of being and meaning, and leaves the concrete, the world of finite values and meanings, behind. Therefore it does not solve the problem of meaninglessness. In terms of the present religious situation this means that Eastern mysticism is not the solution of the prob-lems of Western Existentialism, although many people attempt this solution. The God above the God of theism is not the devaluation of the meanings which doubt has thrown into the abyss of meaninglessness; he is their potential restitution. Nevertheless absolute faith agrees with the faith implied in mysticism in that both transcend the theistic objectivation of a God who is a being. For mysticism such a God is not more real than any finite being, for the courage to be such a God has disappeared in the abyss of meaninglessness with every other value and meaning.

The God above the God of theism is present, although hidden, in every divine-human encounter. Biblical religion as well as Protestant theology are aware of the paradoxical character of this encounter. They are aware that if God encounters man God is neither object nor subject and is therefore above the scheme into which theism has forced him. They are aware that personalism with respect to God is balanced by a transpersonal presence of the divine. They are aware that forgiveness can be accepted only if the power of acceptance is effective in man—biblically speaking, if the power of grace is effective in man. They are aware of the paradoxical character of every prayer, of speaking to somebody to whom you cannot speak because he is not "somebody," of asking somebody of whom you cannot ask anything because he gives or gives not before you ask, of saying "thou" to somebody who is nearer to the I than the I is to itself. Each of these paradoxes drives the religious consciousness toward a God above the God of theism.

The courage to be which is rooted in the experience of the God above the God of theism unites and transcends the courage to be as a part and the courage to be as oneself. It avoids both the loss of oneself by participation and the loss of one's world by individualization. The acceptance of the God above the God of theism makes us a part of that which is not also a part but is the ground of the whole. Therefore our self is not lost in a larger whole, which submerges it in the life of a limited group. If the self participates in the power of being-itself it receives itself back. For the power of being acts through the power of the individual selves. It does not swallow them as every limited whole, every collectivism, and every conformism does. This is why the Church, which stands for the power of being-itself or for the God who transcends the God of the religions, claims to be the mediator of the courage to be. A church which is based on the authority of the God of theism cannot make such a claim. It inescapably develops into a collectivist or semicollectivist system itself.

But a church which raises itself in its message and its devotion to the God above the God of theism without sacrificing its concrete symbols can mediate a courage which takes doubt and meaninglessness into itself. It is the Church under the Cross which alone can do this, the Church which preaches the Crucified who cried to God who remained his God after the God of confidence had left him in the darkness of doubt and meaninglessness. To be as a part in such a church is to receive a courage to be in which one cannot lose one's self and in which one receives one's world.

Absolute faith, or the state of being grasped by the God beyond God, is not a state which appears beside other states of the mind. It never is something separated and definite, an event which could be isolated and described. It is always a movement in, with, and under other states of the mind. It is the situation on the boundary of man's possibilities. It *is* this boundary. Therefore it is both the courage of despair and the courage in and above every courage. It is not a place where one can live, it is without the safety of words and concepts, it is without a name, a church, a cult, a theology. But it is moving in the depth of all of them. It is the power of being, in which they participate and of which they are fragmentary expressions.

One can become aware of it in the anxiety of fate and death when the traditional symbols, which enable men to stand the vicissitudes of fate and the horror of death have lost their power. When "providence" has become a superstition and "immortality" something imaginary that which once was the power in these symbols can still be present and create the courage to be in spite of the experience of a chaotic world and a finite existence. The Stoic courage returns but not as the faith in universal reason. It returns as the absolute faith which says Yes to being without seeing anything concrete which could conquer the nonbeing in fate and death.

And one can become aware of the God above the God of theism in the anxiety of guilt and condemnation when the traditional symbols that enable men to withstand the anxiety of guilt and condemnation have lost their power. When "divine judgment" is interpreted as a psychological complex and forgiveness as a remnant of the "father-image," what once was the power in those symbols can still be present and create the courage to be in spite of the experience of an infinite gap between what we are and what we ought to be. The Lutheran courage returns but not supported by the faith in a judging and forgiving God. It returns in terms of the absolute faith which says Yes although there is no special power that conquers guilt. The courage to take the anxiety of meaninglessness upon oneself is the boundary line up to which the courage to be can go. Beyond it is mere non-being. Within it all forms of courage are re-established in the power of the God above the God of theism. *The courage to be is rooted in the God who appears when God has disappeared in the anxiety of doubt.*

Clear and comparatively simple examinations of the consistency of *God exists* and *evil exists* can be found in M. B. Ahern, *The Problem of Evil* (Schocken, 1971) and in Keith Yandell, "Ethics, Evils and Theism," *Sophia*, 8 (1969). The view that evil is a necessary condition of certain moral goods is explored in Clement Dore, "An Examination of the Soul Making Theodicy," *American Philosophical Quarterly*, 7 (1970) and in John Hick, *Evil and the God of Love* (Harper, 1966). Antony Flew's essay, "Divine Omnipotence and Human Freedom," included in A. Flew and A. MacIntyre, eds., *New Essays in Philosophical Theology* * (Macmillan, 1964), presents a standard objection to the free will defense. A classical Christian discussion of the existence of evil may be found in St. Thomas Aquinas, *Summa Theologica*, Part 1, Questions 48 and 49, and the first part of Part 2, Question 79. For a rather different but interesting attempt to solve the problem of evil, see George Schlesinger, "The Problem of Evil and the Problem of Suffering," *American Philosophical Quarterly*, 1 (1964). Diogenes Allen discusses the requirements for a theodicy in "Motives, Rationales and Religious Beliefs," *American Philosophical Quarterly*, 3 (1966). In addition to the book by Hick that is mentioned above, good general discussions of the problem of evil are provided by C. S. Lewis, *The Problem of Pain* * (Macmillan, 1943) and H. J. McCloskey, "God and Evil," *Philosophical Quarterly*, 10 (1960).

As their name implies, naturalists reject all varieties of supernaturalism. Nevertheless, some naturalists retain a sympathy for various elements of religion. See, for example, John Dewey, *A Common Faith* * (Yale University Press, 1934) and George Santayana, *Reason in Religion* * (Macmillan, 1962). Representative writings by the Death of God theologians, who reject theism in the name of a kind of Christian atheism, can be found in Thomas Altizer, *The Gospel of Christian Atheism* * (Westminster Press, 1966) and in Thomas Altizer and William Hamilton, *Radical Theology and the Death of God* (Bobbs-Merrill, 1966). For a good introduction to some of the nontheistic religions, see Edward Conze, *Buddhism, Its Essence and Development* * (Harper, 1959) and *Buddhist Thought in India* * (University of Michigan Press, 1967); D. T. Suzuki, *Zen Buddhism: Selected Writings of D. T. Suzuki,** edited by William Barrett (Doubleday, 1956); and Heinrich Zimmer, *Philosophies of India* * (Princeton University Press, 1969). The comparative adequacy of theism and some nontheistic religions is discussed in Ninian Smart, *A Dialogue of Religions* (SCM Press, 1960).

* Available in paperback.

MYSTICISM
AND RELIGIOUS
EXPERIENCE

IV

t is generally agreed that there is more than one type of religious experience. Rudolf Otto coined the expression "numinous feeling" to refer to a complex experience that involves (1) awe or dread, "the feeling of 'something uncanny,' 'eerie,' or 'weird,' "[1] (2) a sense of "impotence and general nothingness as against overpowering might,"[2] (3) the conviction that one is confronted with something overwhelmingly alive, vital, and active, (4) a sense of mystery, of wonder over something which is, in at least some respects, radically other than the objects of ordinary experience, and finally (5) fascination or attraction. One wishes to possess, or be possessed by, the object of the experience. In some cases the experience is focused on an ordinary object—a place, a peculiar stone, or a human being. In other cases the apparent object of the experience is something that altogether transcends ordinary objects.

Although numinous experiences and mystical experiences resemble each other in some respects, they should be distinguished. For one thing, a sense of distance or otherness is a characteristic feature of numinous experience. Mystical consciousness, on the other hand, typically involves a sense of union with, or merging into, the object of the experience. Again, those who enjoy numinous experiences tend to speak as if the object of those experiences is personal, whereas even those mystics who are theists tend to describe the object of their experience impersonally. (For example, Christian mystics often distinguish between an experience of God as a person and a deeper experience in which the mystic passes beyond the personality of God to what is referred to as "the desert," "the dazzling darkness," "the abyss.")

Two types of mysticism must be distinguished. The object of extrovertive, or nature, mysticism is the world of which we are a part and the objects it comprises.[3] Rather than being seen in the usual way, however, all things are found to be transfigured and one. The mind of the introvertive mystic, on the other hand, is devoid of images and clear concepts. Awareness of the external world becomes peripheral or vanishes altogether, and the mystic experiences a blissful union with "an undifferentiated One." Mystics who have enjoyed both experiences almost always regard the introvertive experience as superior.

R. C. Zaehner and others have suggested that there are two kinds of introvertive experience—soul mysticism, or monistic mysticism, and theistic mysticism. Monistic mysticism is an experience of a soul stripped of all its ordinary contents. "It is the soul contemplating itself in its essence."[4] Theistic

[1] Rudolf Otto, *The Idea of the Holy* (Oxford University Press, 1950), p. 14.

[2] Ibid., p. 21.

[3] Both Stace (*Mysticism and Philosophy,* pp. 80–81) and Otto (*Mysticism East and West,* pp. 73ff.) attach slightly different meanings to the term "nature mysticism." Roughly speaking, we may equate Stace's "extrovertive mysticism," Zaehner's "nature mysticism," and the first two stages of Otto's mysticism of unifying vision. (The third stage of unifying vision is perhaps best thought of as a form of introvertive vision.)

[4] R. C. Zaehner, *Mysticism: Sacred and Profane* (Oxford University Press, 1961), p. 128.

mysticism involves an experience of differentiation in unity. The mystic is united by love with a One which transcends him.

Zaehner's distinction may be a spurious one. It is true that some introvertive mystics assert that their experience is an experience of the depth of their souls, while other introvertive mystics tell us that at the height of their experience they are united with God by love. It is nevertheless possible that we are dealing with different interpretations of what is one and the same experience rather than with two different sorts of experience. This is the position adopted by Walter Stace. However, in the absence of clear criteria for distinguishing between claims which are inherent in the experience itself and claims which are part of an interpretation of that experience, it is difficult to determine which of these two positions is correct.

Before concluding this discussion, it should be pointed out that there are types of religious experience which are neither numinous nor mystical. Both numinous and mystical experiences are noetic in character; that is, they involve a conviction that the object of the experience exists and that one is immediately present to it. In this respect, they resemble sense experiences. Intense experiences bound up with prayer, worship, and other devotional acts are religious in character, but they are not usually noetic. Adoration, for example, does not normally involve a feeling of presence.

There is mounting evidence that some drugs can, under certain conditions, induce religious experience. It is true that one must be careful in evaluating this evidence. By itself, the fact that a researcher or his subject claims that a drug-induced experience was religious has little or no significance. Unless they are familiar with the nature of man's religious experience, we have no assurance that the experiences which they call religious are indeed religious. Again, if we are only told that a drug-induced experience exhibits many of the characteristics of mystical experience, we are in no position to determine whether the experience is introvertive or extrovertive. In spite of these problems, however, it is generally agreed not only that some drug-induced experiences are religious but also that some drug-induced experiences are phenomenologically indistinguishable from those of the nature mystic. Introvertive experiences, on the other hand, are comparatively rare, if they occur at all. Houston and Masters report that only 6 of their 206 subjects enjoyed an introvertive experience. It is perhaps significant that all of these subjects were persons who had "in the course of their lives either actively sought the mystical experience in meditation or other spiritual disciplines or who [had] for many years demonstrated a considerable interest in [it]" and that all "were over forty years of age, were of superior intelligence, and were well adjusted and creative personalities." [5] Finally, the evidence that drugs can

5 R. E. Masters and J. Houston, *Varieties of Psychedelic Experience* (Holt, Rinehart, and Winston, 1966), p. 307.

induce theistic mysticism is very inconclusive. (Huston Smith's few remarks on this point are inadequate. It is not clear that the experiences reported by Slotkin and Carstairs are mystical experiences in any sense, let alone experiences which are peculiar to theistic mystics.)

The value of these experiences is subject to dispute. One of the most important things to consider is the consequences of the experience both for the chemical mystic and for those around him. There is some evidence that drug-induced religious experiences have had beneficial effects on alcoholics and convicts. It is clear that they sometimes lead to a heightened sense of benevolence and sympathy. On the other hand, it is also clear that the effect is not always beneficial, and it is perhaps significant that there is a tendency for chemical mystics to abandon the use of drugs and adopt "other methods of pursuing the religious quest." [6]

There is another philosophically significant issue. It will inevitably occur to someone who considers these findings that science may someday discover a completely adequate natural explanation of religious experience. (No such explanation exists at present. It is not claimed, for example, that the physiological changes induced by the drug completely explain the experiences.) If this were to occur, would we be forced to conclude that religious experience has no cognitive value? It is sometimes argued that we would on the grounds that an apparent experience of x is a genuine experience of x only if x is a cause of the experience of x. Hence (it is argued) if religious experience can be completely explained by natural causes, then God (or some other transcendent object) cannot be a cause of it and so the experience cannot be a real experience of God (or that transcendent object). One should notice that the argument makes two crucial assumptions: that an apparent experience of x is a real experience of x only if x is a cause of that experience, and that if there are natural causes which are sufficient to explain something, then God cannot be a cause of that thing. Neither of these assumptions is entirely implausible, but both can be, and have been, denied.

Are these experiences cognitive? Do they involve a perception of some aspect of reality which is normally hidden from us? William Alston distinguishes two arguments for the claim that religious experience has cognitive value.

The argument from analogy: If the analogy between religious experience and the paradigmatic case of genuine perceptual experience (= veridical sense experience) is very close, then we are justified in ascribing cognitive value to religious experience. The analogy is very close. Therefore, we are justified in ascribing cognitive value to religious experience.

Cognitivity as the best explanation of the facts: The facts to be explained include such things as the sanity, sanctity, and goodness of many of the great

[6] Walter Clark, *Chemical Ecstasy: Psychedelic Drugs and Religion* (Sheed & Ward, 1969), p. 159.

mystics, the fact that mysticism is a cross-cultural phenomenon which occurs in many different places and at many different times, and the fact that mystics tend to agree both that their experience involves a glimpse of some aspect of reality which is usually hidden from us and that what is beheld is one, timeless, and supremely valuable. It is argued that since the hypothesis that the experiences are essentially what they purport to be (namely, glimpses of a divine order) does more justice to these facts than alternative hypotheses, it should be provisionally accepted.

There is another argument for the cognitive value of these experiences. If God exists and is what He has been thought to be (all-good and all-powerful, willing to allow others to share in His own vision of Himself, etc.), then a direct experience of God is possible and would, if it occurred, involve a conviction of divine presence, reinforce both the individual who enjoys the experience and the community of which he is a member, not lead to silly or false claims, and so on. Now (it may be argued), there are experiences which exhibit these characteristics (for example, those of St. Teresa or St. John of the Cross). Given, then, that God exists and is what He has been thought to be, it is not implausible to conclude that the experiences in question did in fact involve a direct awareness of God.

Three comments on these arguments seem in order. First, the crucial premise of the first argument is *the analogy is very close*. The hypothesis *that the experiences are what they purport to be is the best explanation of the facts* is the crucial premise of the second argument. There is no mechanical decision procedure which can be employed to determine the truth of these premises. On the contrary, when we ask whether these premises are true, we are asking what judgment should be made in view of all the facts; two intelligent and informed people may make conflicting judgments without either of them being obviously irrational or demonstrably wrong (from which it does not follow that both of their positions are equally reasonable). Consider for a moment the second premise of the first argument. Sense experience and religious experience (or at least mystical experience) are alike in that in both cases the subject of the experience believes himself to have been in contact with something other than himself and would, on the basis of his experience, be prepared to make an objective claim to that effect. Further, it is fairly clear that religious experiences, unlike sense experiences, cannot be used as a basis for predicting the course of future events. (This is perhaps not surprising if the object of the mystic's experience is, as he believes, either something which transcends the world altogether or an all-pervasive feature of it. We should not, I think, expect an apprehension of such an object to furnish a basis for the prediction of the course of events.) But in other respects there is considerable disagreement. There are "tests and check up procedures" (C. B. Martin) which are relevant to an evaluation of the claims based upon sense experiences. Again, agreement and disagreement among those who are similarly placed must be taken into account when evaluating cognitive claims which purport to be based upon sense experience. The fact that others fail to see the pink elephant which the alcoholic says he sees is taken as counting rather decisively against his claim. Martin argues that religious experience is unlike sense experience in these respects. (If he is right, the analogy is considerably weakened.) Others would deny this, pointing to the fact that there are tests which are used in the religious community to distinguish genuine religious experiences from those which are not genuine. (The community attempts to determine such things as the sanity and sanctity of the mystic, the effects of his experience upon himself and others, and whether or not he makes false or silly claims on the basis of his experience.) They would also suggest that agreement or disagreement among those who have attempted to employ the procedures which are recommended to would-be contemplatives (for example, moral discipline, mortification of the body, meditation, and so on) would not be considered totally irrelevant by the mystics themselves. There is, then, considerable disagreement as to the respects in which religious experience is like and unlike sense experience. However, even if the disputants were to agree on the points of likeness and unlikeness, they might still disagree as to their relative importance. When we reflect upon the situation, it becomes obvious that while there are, for example, mechanical procedures which can be used to conclusively determine whether someone has correctly solved an arithmetical problem, no similar procedures are available to us in the present instance. The most that can be done is to make as careful an assessment as possible in view of all the evidence. This calls for knowledge and judgment, and it is not surprising that intelligent and reasonable men sometimes disagree.

Second, the three arguments for the cognitive value of religious experience are not entirely independent. In particular, material that is used in the first and third arguments might be introduced into the second argument in order to strengthen it. Thus, the analogy between veridical sense experience and religious experience, and the probability that if God exists, we should expect to find something like the sort of experience which we do find (experiences like those of St. Teresa and St. John of the Cross) might be added to the facts to be explained.

Finally, the first two arguments do not depend upon already having established the truth of theism. The third argument obviously does depend upon having done so. One should consider the possibility that if theism can be shown to be true on other grounds, then the case for the cognitive value of religious experience is a fairly good one. On the other hand, if theism cannot be shown to be true on other grounds, then the case is weaker than it would otherwise be, though it may not be altogether destroyed.

w. j. w.

THE NATURE
AND TYPES OF RELIGIOUS
AND MYSTICAL EXPERIENCE

RUDOLF OTTO
The Mysticism of Unifying Vision

THE LOWEST STAGE

(a) Things and events in so far as they are conceived by this "intuitive" vision, are no longer multiple, separate, divided, but are, in an inexpressible way an All, a Sarvam, a whole, one whole and therefore One. I repeat "in an inexpressible way," for if we add that they now form an "organic whole," "a universal life," or suchlike phrases, these are all rational explanations of the matter, derived from current scientific terminology, which are at most only analogous and not in the least adequate.

Thus Eckhart says:

> In the eternal goodness of the divine nature (as in a miraculous mirror) the essence of all creatures is seen as one.

(b) Further, within this One all otherness as opposition immediately disappears—things are no longer distinguished as this and the other. But, rather,

Rudolf Otto (1869–1937) was a philosopher, theologian, New Testament scholar, and student of the religions of India. He is best known for *The Idea of the Holy* in which he introduces the notion of numinous feelings. (See the selection by Ninian Smart.) Most recent discussions of religious experience derive, at least in part, from Otto's work in this area.

THE MYSTICISM OF UNIFYING VISION   Reprinted with permission of The Macmillan Company from *Mysticism East and West* by Rudolf Otto, translated by Bertha L. Bracey and Richenda C. Payne. Copyright 1932 by The Macmillan Company, renewed 1960 by Margarete Ottmer.

this is that, and that is this; here is there and there, here.[1] This does not mean that all things in the fullness and richness of their individual being disappear, but rather that each with each and all with all is identical—one and the same. The Indian expression for such intuition is: "nānātvam na paśyati," or expressed positively: "samam paśyati," or "dharmān samatām gatān paśyati," he sees objects as coalescing in identity.[2]

This results in the peculiar logic of mysticism, which discounts the two fundamental laws of natural logic: the law of Contradiction and of the Excluded Third. As non-Euclidian geometry sets aside the axiom of parallels so mystical logic disregards these two axioms; and thence the "coincidentia oppositorum," the "identity of opposites" and the "dialectic conceptions" arise.

Eckhart says:

> There all is one, and one all in all. There to her (the perceiving soul) all is one, and one is in all. It (i.e. the empirical world) carries contradiction in itself. What is contradiction? Love and suffering, white and black, these are contradictions, and as such these cannot remain in essential Being itself.
>
> Herein lies the soul's purity, that it is purified from a life that is divided and that it enters into a life that is unified. All that is divided in lower things, will be unified so soon as the (perceptive) soul climbs up into a life where there is no contrast. When the soul comes into the light of reasonableness (the true insight) it knows no contrasts. Say, Lord, when is a man in mere "understanding" (in discursive intellectual understanding). I say to you: "When a man sees one thing separated from another." And when is a man above mere understanding? That I can tell you: "When he sees all in all, then a man stands beyond mere understanding."

(c) Together with (a) and (b) we must take into account what is called "visio sub specie aeterni": that is, not only the negation of the usual association of things together in space and time, but a positive ordering of their

---

[1] Thus Plotinus says of the locus intelligibilis:

There . . . they see all, not in process of becoming but in Being. Each Being contains within itself the whole intelligible world and also beholds it complete in each particular Being. Therefore All is everywhere. Each is there All and All is each. (*Ennead*, 5:8)

[2] This is also the chief meaning of the term advitīyam, advaitam, without a second.

In the principal text of the Advaita doctrine, the Chhāndogyaupanishad 6.2.1, the word means that the "idam," the "prapañcha," i.e. the world apparently extended in name and form, is "one only," without a second—is in itself without multiplicity. That it is "without a second" does not mean here as yet the identity of Brahman and the inner ātman, but the identity of the multiplicity of the world as the "One only." The same thought often occurs later, cf. Māndūkya Kār. 1. 17:

Māyāmātram idam dvaitam, advaitam paramārthataḥ.

The "idam" here is also the "prapañcha" as in the Chhāndogya, for as Sankara expressly states in his commentary: "Idam prapañchâkhyam," cf. also 3.19: "Māyayā bhidyate hi etat, na anyatha 'jam kathamchana": "Only by delusion is the (One) divided." In truth it is "samatām gatam" (3.2), and 4.91:

. . . sarve dharmāḥ.
Vidyate na hi nanatvam tesham kvachana kimchana.
For there is in them (viz. in all objects) absolutely no multiplicity.

existence in and with one another in a higher but inexpressible way in the eternal "Now."

(d) Closely connected with this as the accompaniment of the "unification" of things is what we may call their "transfiguration." They become transparent, luminous, visionary. They are seen—and this relates to their perception sub specie aeterni—"in ratione ydeali" as Eckhart puts it, that is, not in their "obviousness" but in their eternal idea.[3] "So I see in all the eternal glory," sings Lynkeus. And Plotinus says: "There is the perfected beauty." Eckhart has expressed it thus:

> The man who has let things pass away in their lower forms where they are mortal, receives them again in God (that means first in their ideal "unity"), where alone they are real. All that is dead here, is life there. And all that is here gross and tangible is there (sub specie ydeali) spirit. It is as when a man pours water into a clean vessel and lets it stand, and then, if he holds his face over it he sees his face at the bottom (resplendent) as it is in itself.

Eckhart here clearly refers to the peculiar transfiguration of the features seen in water, filled with the light and transparency of the medium in which they are reflected.[4]

The chief points included in the paragraphs (a)–(d) are embraced by the Indian formula: nānātvam na paśyati—"he no longer sees multiplicity." Such nānātvam we maintain has not yet in itself any bearing upon the distinction between Brahman and ātman, but denotes the manifoldness of the nāmā-rūpādi, the multiplicity of "names and forms," which are at the same time "kāla-deśa-nimitta," determined by space and time. Positively expressed it is: samam paśyati—"he sees all in its identity." The perception of the samam is, however, the same as perception freed from space and time, in principio, sub specie aeterni, and in ratione ydeali.

(e) Together with this there now appears not only the identification of all things with all, but also of the perceiver with the perceived, an identification which is clearly different from that of the mystical experience of the first way, the subjective, inward way, and of a different origin. There is here no mention of the soul as an inner reality, and of the soul's unification with the Highest. No consideration is given to the soul of the perceiver, but simply to the perceiver himself. He is what everything is, and everything is what he is. So unified with the All and the One, he then sees all things "in himself," or, more precisely, "as himself"—as not differentiated from himself.

---

[3] To see creatures intuitively in their "uncreated" nature.

[4] This symbol of Eckhart's curiously plastic speech, so entirely free from the ornateness of the schools, shows us much more clearly what he means by his "sub ratione ydeali" than his whole, scholarly, Platonized system of ideas. At the same time it is an illustration of the fact mentioned in the previous chapter, viz. that Eckhart would have expressed his opinions, and perhaps expressed them better if he had not been a scholar but only a preacher in his poetic German mother-tongue.

Plotinus, with paradigmatical acuteness summarizes the points (a)–(e) in the *First Ennead*, 8, 1:

ἔχει πάντα καὶ ἔστι πάντα καὶ σύνεστιν αὐτῷ συνὼν καὶ ἔχει πάντα οὐκ ἔχων. Οὐ γὰρ ἄλλα, ὁ δε ἄλλος· οὐδὲ χωρὶς ἕκαστον τῶν ἐν αὐτῷ· ὅλον τε γάρ ἐστιν ἕκαστον καὶ πανταχῇ πᾶν· καὶ οὐ συγκέχυται, ἀλλὰ αὖ χωρίς. But he is not spirit in the sense in which we conceive spirit, which gains its content from logical propositions and its understanding by processes of thought and reflection on cause and effect, and which recognizes being by the principle of sufficient reason. Rather, every spirit has all and is all and is with all because he is with it, and possesses all things, without possessing them in the usual sense (as individual objects external to himself). For he does not possess it as something different from himself. That which is possessed is not one thing and he himself another. What there is (of that which is possessed) in him is not each thing separate for itself. For each is the whole, and is wholly all. Yet still it is not mingled but is again itself separate. (Cf. above: "Black does not cease to be black nor white, white. But black is white and white is black. The opposites coincide without ceasing to be what they are in themselves.")

The spirit which here perceives is opposed to the process of "ordinary" thinking—to discursive thought activity. In contrast to the latter it perceives by means of mystical intuition.[5]

Mystical intuition can stop short at this stage, and mystical experience can be indicated and described without going further. There are plenty of examples where such experience has been content to find its expression in the phrases of this first halting place: "To see no other, to perceive in Unity, beyond space and time—to see yourself and all else in one, and all as in yourself," without using the higher affirmations of the later stages. Mystical intuition is indeed present here, though there is no mention of beholding God or Brahman. For it, all is in unity, is indeed in a fully mystical unity. When he sees things in such unity, the perceiver himself becomes one with the objects perceived, and sees them now within himself:

> He who has allowed the beauty of that world (seen in ideal unity) to penetrate his soul goes away no longer a mere observer. For the object perceived and the perceiving soul are no longer two things separated from one another, but the perceiving soul has (now) within itself the perceived object.[6] (Plotinus)

The union which here occurs is not yet union with God, but that of the self with the object perceived in the unity of the ideal world.

---

[5] This spirit is here the divine. But the divine spirit is for the mystic the original type of the mystical spirit itself, the subject of mysticism, and what has place in the divine has place also in man when he perceives aright. This is a fundamental conception of the mystical attitude. This analogous relationship which then passes into a relationship of identity is indicated in Indian writings even as early as the Upanishads by the regular parallels between "iti adhidaivatam. Atha adhyātman": "So with regard to the divine, and now with regard to the soul" (cf. Kena 4, 29). The same distinction of analogy and identity is found also in Eckhart.

[6] N.B. The "perceiving soul" is here simply the perceiver himself.

The Indian expression for the points contained in sections (a)–(e) is "anyad na paśyati"; "he perceives no other." That means both that he sees no variety in the object, and that he no longer sees distinction between subject and object.

THE SECOND STAGE

But to go further, we said in the first place that "the many is seen as one," thereby the One is now beheld. This means that the One is no longer a mere interrelation but a peculiar correlate of the many. Unity now becomes "One." "The One" is no longer a predicate of the many but becomes an equation of the One and the many: Many is one, and the One is many. Still further, these pronouncements do not remain of equal value. The One comes to the fore. Oneness is not a result of the many, nor is the relationship such that Oneness and multiplicity are mutual results of each other. The One soon receives the emphasis and takes precedence over the many. As Eckhart says: What in many things is one, must of necessity be above things (and that in the following four intermediate stages):

> Many is seen as one (and only thus rightly seen).
> Many is seen in the One (where the One is still a form of the many).
> The One is seen in the many (as supporting and conditioning reality).
> The One is seen.

The One itself becomes the object of intuition as that which is superior and prior to the many. It is the many, not as the many is one but as the principle in which the many is grounded. In relation to the many it becomes the subject in so far as it unifies, comprehends and bears the many. It is in fact its essence, being, existence. Already at this point the One concentrates attention upon itself, draws the value of the many to itself, silently becoming that which is and remains the real value behind the many. The many is now only the changing modes of the One. It is itself the constant behind these modes, which remains and is identical with itself, the unchangeable foundation as opposed to the changing and fleeting. Thus al Hallâj says: [7]

> Nul ne peut fouler le tapis étendu de la Vérité, tant qu'il demeure au seuil de la séparation, tant qu'il ne voit en toutes les essences une seule Essence, tant qu'il ne voit ce qui passe comme périssant, et celui qui demeure comme subsistant.

It will at once be clear that we have here the beginning of the two elements usually contained in this type of mysticism:

(a) That on the one hand it is necessarily systematized by speculation on the Absolute; the One is the unconditioned, the absolute which conditions all things.

(b) On the other, that it attracts or originates an ontology, or a particular

---

[7] L. Massignon: *La Passion d'al Hussayn ibn Mansour al Hallâj*, Paris, 1922, Vol. 2, 517.

speculation about Being. The One is the only true and complete Being be-hind the many; the many sinks down into the half-being of changing, becom-ing, perishing, and of fleeting modes, which compared with the One is anrita, the untrue, and "cannot be defined either as Being or as Not-Being," etc. At the same time it is obvious that the conditioning relation of the One to that which it determines is beyond our rational categories of determination.

In theism the conditioning relation is that of the rational category of cause and effect. But it is not so with the mystical One. It has the power of conditioning but not in the category of causation; it is a mystical and non-rational relation, not to be grasped by rational thought. One can only use an ideogram, and I am accustomed in my lectures to use the expression: "The verb 'to condition,' here means to lie at the basis of a thing as its principle, and to comprise it."

Where mystical intuition is grafted upon Theism (which, as the oldest Upanishads prove, is not always the case) this non-rational One lying at the basis of all things is called God. The name, God, then takes on that opales-cence which is so characteristic where belief in God becomes mysticism, or where mysticism includes belief in God. The personal form of address applies without further ado to the mystic One, and mystical and personal attitudes slip into one another.

An example of all these relationships is furnished by the following quota-tion from al Hallâj, in which the first and the second types of approach are mingled:

> O Conscience de ma conscience, qui te fais si tenue
> Que Tu échappes á l'imagination de toute créature vivante!
> Et qui, en même temps, et patente et cachée, transfigures
> Toute chose, par devers toute chose. . . .
> O Toi, qui es la Réunion du tout, Tu ne m'es plus "un autre" mais moi-même.[8]

Or compare what the Īśā says, in verse 6:

> But he who beholds all Beings in himself and himself in all Beings . . .

and in verse 7:

> In whom the self of the perceiver became all Beings—
> What disturbance, what care could be in him who beholds Oneness?

In the first place this is simply the "anyad na paśyati," the intuition of unity, but soon this peculiar Oneness as mere form rises to the higher stage of vision of "The One" above the many, till in verse 8 it becomes "He":

> He comprises all things, in a luminous incorporeal, faultless, sinewless, pure, sinless way. He the seer, the sage, the encompassing one, who *is* through himself.

[8] Massignon, p. 520.

This "He" is "Iś," the Lord, of whom the introductory verse says:

The Lord is immanent in all that moves in this world.

Thus, what first began as a mere form of the many appears now as the *real* above the many. Only a step further is necessary for it to appear in contrast and opposition to the many. If it is One it can no longer be many. The many, at first identical with the One, comes into conflict with it, and disappears. It disappears either by sinking down into the indivisible One, as with Eckhart, or by becoming the obscuring veil of the One, the illusion of māyā in Avidyā, as with Śankara.

Thereby the meaning of unity and of oneness changes. At first, Unity, being one, was a fact in the sense of a (mystical) synthesis of multiplicity, which though not reproducible by any of our rational categories was nevertheless a synthesis. But out of this synthetic unity, out of this one in the sense of united, grows a unity as One and Aloneness. That is, in other words, out of the united comes the One only, out of the All-One the Alone. Immediately, as with Śankara, the relationship of original immanence—the immanence of the unity in and of things and the immanence of things in the One—passes, and is transformed into complete transcendence. The realm of the many is now the wholly evil in contrast to the realm of the One—it is mithya-jñāna and bhrama (error).

In Eckhart's teaching the vital immanence of the One which mediates itself is always present and is peculiar to his speculation, but at the same time, above this rises the One in absolute transcendence—the "silent void of the Godhead" into which difference or multiplicity never entered. For him, the second stage remains bound up with the third.

WALTER STACE
Subjectivity, Objectivity and the Self

In these pages I shall often use the expressions "mysticism," "mystic," "mystical experience," "mystical consciousness," "mystical idea." "Mysticism," of course, is the general name of our entire subject, and its meaning will be gradually developed. By the word "mystic" I shall always mean a person who himself has had mystical experience. Often the word is used in a much wider and looser way. Anyone who is sympathetic to mysticism is apt to be labeled a mystic. But I shall use the word always in a stricter sense. However sympathetic toward mysticism a man may be, however deeply interested, involved, enthusiastic, or learned in the subject, he will not be called a mystic unless he has, or has had, mystical experience. The phrases "mystical experience" and "mystical consciousness" will be used as synonymous with each other. But "mystical consciousness" is the better term, the word "experience" being misleading in certain respects. It will be seen that both "mysticism" and "mystic" are defined in terms of mystical experience or consciousness. This is therefore the basic thing on which we have to fasten attention and in terms of which we have to understand the whole subject. Our question "What is mysticism?" really means "What is mystical experience?"

The phrase "mystical idea" has also to be defined in terms of mystical experience. It means an idea, belief, opinion, or proposition which was originally based on mystical experience, although the connection between the experience and the opinion may have been quite forgotten. The point is that a mystical idea is a product of the conceptual intellect, whereas a mystical experience is a nonintellectual mode of consciousness. The proposition that "time is unreal" is an example of a mystical idea. It must have arisen because mystics usually feel (a) that their experience is timeless and (b) it is more "real" (in some sense) than any other experience. But many philosophers who have never had any mystical experience, nor any knowledge of how the idea originated, yet come to adopt it in their philosophies and treat it as if it were a product of a process of reasoning. A mystical idea may be

Walter Stace (1886–1967) served for twenty-two years in the British Civil Service, occupying various government posts in Ceylon. During this period he produced several books, including a study of the German philosopher Hegel. He became a member of the Department of Philosophy at Princeton in 1932 and remained at that university until his retirement in 1955. An empiricist in the tradition of Hume, he was nonetheless deeply sympathetic to mysticism. Among his many works are *Religion and the Modern Mind*, *Time and Eternity*, and *Mysticism and Philosophy*.

SUBJECTIVITY, OBJECTIVITY AND THE SELF   From *The Teachings of the Mystics* by Walter T. Stace. Reprinted by permission of Mrs. Walter T. Stace.

either true or false, though it must have originated in a genuine mystical experience.

On a dark night out of doors one may see something glimmering white. One person may think it is a ghost. A second person may take it for a sheet hung out on a clothesline. A third person may suppose that it is a white-painted rock. Here we have a single experience with three different interpretations. The experience is genuine, but the interpretations may be either true or false. If we are to understand anything at all about mysticism, it is essential that we should make a similar distinction between a mystical experience and the interpretations which may be put upon it either by mystics themselves or by nonmystics. For instance, the same mystical experience may be interpreted by a Christian in terms of Christian beliefs and by a Buddhist in terms of Buddhistic beliefs.

III.   SOME THINGS WHICH MYSTICISM IS NOT

The word "mysticism" is popularly used in a variety of loose and inaccurate ways. Sometimes anything is called "mystical" which is misty, foggy, vague, or sloppy. It is absurd that "mysticism" should be associated with what is "misty" because of the similar sound of the words. And there is nothing misty, foggy, vague, or sloppy about mysticism.

A second absurd association is to suppose that mysticism is sort of mystery-mongering. There is, of course, an etymological connection between "mysticism" and "mystery." But mysticism is not any sort of hocus-pocus such as we commonly associate with claims to the elucidation of sensational mysteries. Mysticism is not the same as what is commonly called the "occult"— whatever that may mean. Nor has it anything to do with spiritualism, or ghosts, or table-turning. Nor does it include what are commonly called para-psychological phenomena such as telepathy, telekinesis, clairvoyance, pre-cognition. These are not mystical phenomena. It is perhaps true that mystics may sometimes claim to possess such special powers, but even when they do so they are well aware that such powers are not part of, and are to be clearly distinguished from, their mystical experience. Such powers, if they exist—as to which I express no opinion—may be possessed by persons who are not mystics. And conversely, even the greatest mystics may be devoid of them and know nothing about them. The closest connection one can admit will be to say that it may be the case that the sort of persons who are mystics also tend to be the sort of persons who have parapsychological powers.

Finally, it is most important to realize that visions and voices are not mystical phenomena, though here again it seems to be the case that the sort of persons who are mystics may often be the sort of persons who see visions and hear voices. A few years ago it was reported that certain persons in Italy saw a vision of the Virgin Mary in the clouds. Even if we suppose that these persons really did have this vision, it must be emphatically asserted that this was not a mystical experience and had nothing to do with mysticism. Nor are the voices which certain persons in history, such as Socrates, Mohammed, and Joan of Arc, are supposed to have heard to be classed as mystical experiences. Socrates, Mohammed, and Joan of Arc may have been mystics for all I know, but they are not to be classed as such because of these voices. Returning for a moment to the subject of visions, it is well known that certain mystics saw visions but that they did not themselves regard these visions as mystical experiences. A case in point is St. Teresa of Avila. She had frequent visions, but she knew that they were not the experiences she desired. Some of them, she thought, may have been sent to her by God to comfort and encourage her in trying to attain the mystical consciousness. Others, she supposed, might have been sent by the devil in order to confuse her and distract her from the true mystic quest.

The reader may perhaps suppose that the exclusion of visions and voices from the class of mystical phenomena is a matter of arbitrary choice on the part of the present writer. Of course, one is logically entitled to define his terms as he pleases. Therefore if anyone says that he intends to use the phrase "mystical experience" so as to include visions and voices, spiritualism, telepathy, and the like, we do not say that he is wrong. But we say that his usage does not conform to that which has been usual with those who have been recognized as the great mystics of the world. The case of St. Teresa has just been mentioned. St. John of the Cross specifically warns his readers not to seek visions, not to be misled by them, and not to mistake them for the true mystical union. And there are, one must add, good reasons for this. What mystics say is that a genuine mystical experience is nonsensuous. It is formless, shapeless, colorless, odorless, soundless. But a vision is a piece of visual imagery having color and shape. A voice is an auditory image. Visions and voices are sensuous experiences.

IV.   A NEW KIND OF CONSCIOUSNESS

In his book *The Varieties of Religious Experience* William James suggests, as a result of his psychological researches, that "our normal consciousness, rational consciousness as we call it, is but one special type of consciousness, whilst all about it, parted from it by the filmiest of screens, there lie potential forms of consciousness entirely different." This statement exactly fits mystical consciousness. It is entirely unlike our everyday consciousness and is wholly incommensurable with it. What are the fundamental characteristics or elements of our ordinary consciousness? We may think of it as being like a building with three floors. The ground floor consists of physical sensations—sights, sounds, smells, tastes, touch sensations, and organic sensations. The second floor consists of images, which we tend to think of as mental copies of sensations. The third floor is the level of the intellect, which is the faculty of concepts. On this floor we find abstract thinking and reasoning processes. This account of the mind may be open to cavil. Some philosophers think that colors, sounds, and so on, are not properly called "sensations"; others that images are not "copies" of sensations. These fine points, however, need not seriously concern us. Our account is sufficiently clear to indicate what we are referring to when we speak of sensations, images, and concepts as being the fundamental elements of the cognitive aspects of our ordinary consciousness. Arising out of these basic cognitive elements and dependent upon them are emotions, desires, and volitions. In order to have a name for it we may call this whole structure—including sensations, images, concepts, and their attendant desires, emotions, and volitions—our *sensory-intellectual consciousness.*

Now the mystical consciousness is quite different from this. It is not merely that it involves different kinds of sensation, thought, or feeling. We are told that some insects or animals can perceive ultraviolet color and infrared color; and that some animals can hear sounds which are inaudible to us; even that some creatures may have a sixth sense quite different from any of our five senses. These are all, no doubt, kinds of sensations different from any we have. But they are still sensations. And the mystical consciousness is destitute of any sensations at all. Nor does it contain any concepts or thoughts. It is not a sensory-intellectual consciousness at all. Accordingly, it cannot be described or analyzed in terms of any of the elements of the sensory-intellectual consciousness, with which it is wholly incommensurable.

This is the reason why mystics always say that their experiences are "ineffable." All words in all languages are the products of our sensory-intellectual consciousness and express or describe its elements or some combination of them. But as these elements (with the doubtful exception of emotions) are not found in the mystical consciousness, it is felt to be impossible to describe it in any words whatever. In spite of this the mystics do describe their experiences in roundabout ways, at the same time telling us that the words they use are inadequate. This raises a serious problem for the philosophy of mysticism, but it is not possible for us to dwell on it here.

The incommensurability of the mystical with the sensory-intellectual consciousness is also the ultimate reason why we have to exclude visions and voices, telepathy, precognition, and clairvoyance from the category of the mystical. Suppose someone sees a vision of the Virgin Mary. What he sees has shape, the shape of a woman, and color—white skin, blue raiment, a golden halo, and so on. But these are all images or sensations. They are therefore composed of elements of our sensory-intellectual consciousness. The same is true of voices. Or suppose one has a precognition of a neighbor's death. The components one is aware of—a dead man, a coffin, etc.—are composed of elements of our sensory-intellectual consciousness. The only difference is that these ordinary elements are arranged in unfamiliar patterns which we have come to think cannot occur, so that if they do occur they seem supernormal. Or the fact that such elements are combined in an unusual way so as to constitute the figure of a woman up in the clouds, perhaps surrounded by other humanlike figures with wings added to them—all this does not constitute a different *kind* of consciousness at all. And just as sensory elements of any sort are excluded from the mystical consciousness, so are conceptual elements. It is not that the thoughts in the mystical consciousness are different from those we are accustomed to. It does not include any thoughts at all. The mystic, of course, expresses thoughts about his experience after that experience is over, and he remembers it when he is back again in his sensory-intellectual consciousness. But there are no thoughts *in* the experience itself.

If anyone thinks that a kind of consciousness without either sensations, images, or thoughts, because it is totally unimaginable and inconceivable to most of us, cannot exist, he is surely being very stupid. He supposes that the possibilities of this vast universe are confined to what can be imagined and understood by the brains of average human insects who crawl on a minute speck of dust floating in illimitable space.

On the other hand, there is not the least reason to suppose that the mystical consciousness is miraculous or supernatural. No doubt it has, like our ordinary consciousness, been produced by the natural processes of evolution. Its existence in a few rare men is a psychological fact of which there is abundant evidence. To deny or doubt that it exists as a psychological fact is not a reputable opinion. It is ignorance. Whether it has any value or significance beyond itself, and if so what—these, of course, are matters regarding which there can be legitimate differences of opinion. Owing to the comparative rarity of this kind of consciousness, it should no doubt be assigned to the sphere of abnormal psychology.

V.   THE CORE OF MYSTICISM

I shall, for the present, treat it as an hypothesis that although mystical experiences may in certain respects have different characteristics in different parts of the world, in different ages, and in different cultures, there are nevertheless a number of fundamental common characteristics. I shall also assume that the agreements are more basic and important, the differences more superficial and relatively less important. This hypothesis can only be fully justified by an elaborate empirical survey of the descriptions of their experiences given by mystics and collected from all over the world. But I believe that enough of the evidence for it will appear in the following pages to convince any reasonable person.

The most important, the central characteristic in which all *fully developed* mystical experiences agree, and which in the last analysis is definitive of them and serves to mark them off from other kinds of experiences, is that they involve the apprehension of *an ultimate nonsensuous unity in all things,* a oneness or a One to which neither the senses nor the reason can penetrate. In other words, it entirely transcends our sensory-intellectual consciousness.

It should be carefully noted that only fully developed mystical experiences are necessarily apprehensive of the One. Many experiences have been recorded which lack this central feature but yet possess other mystical characteristics. These are borderline cases, which may be said to shade off from the central core of cases. They have to the central core the relation which some philosophers like to call "family resemblance."

We should also note that although at this stage of our exposition we speak of mystical experience as an apprehension *of* the Unity, the mystics of the Hindu and Buddhist cultures, as well as Plotinus and many others, generally insist that this is incorrect since it supposes a division between subject and object. We should rather say that the experience *is* the One. Thus Plotinus writes: "We should not speak of seeing, but instead of seen and seer, speak boldly of a simple Unity for in this seeing we neither distinguish nor are there two." But we will leave the development of this point till later. And often for convenience' sake we shall speak of the experience *of* the unity.

VI.   EXTROVERTIVE MYSTICISM

There appear to be two main distinguishable types of mystical experience, both of which may be found in all the higher cultures. One may be called extrovertive mystical experience, the other introvertive mystical experience. Both are apprehensions of the One, but they reach it in different ways. The extrovertive way looks outward and through the physical senses into the external world and finds the One there. The introvertive way turns inward, introspectively, and finds the One at the bottom of the self, at the bottom of the human personality. The latter far outweighs the former in importance both in the history of mysticism and in the history of human thought generally. The introvertive way is the major strand in the history of mysticism, the extrovertive way a minor strand. I shall only briefly refer to extrovertive mysticism and then pass on, and shall take introvertive mysticism as the main subject of this book.

The extrovertive mystic with his physical senses continues to perceive the same world of trees and hills and tables and chairs as the rest of us. But he sees these objects transfigured in such manner that the Unity shines through them. Because it includes ordinary sense perceptions, it only partially realizes the description given in section (4). For the full realization of this we have to wait for the introvertive experience. I will give two brief historical instances of extrovertive experience. The great Catholic mystic Meister Eckhart (circa 1260–1329) wrote as follows: "Here [i.e., in this experience] all blades of grass, wood, and stone, all things are One. . . . When is a man in mere understanding? When he sees one thing separated from another. And when is he above mere understanding? When he sees all in all, then a man stands above mere understanding."

In this quotation we note that according to Eckhart seeing a number of things as separate and distinct, seeing the grass and the wood and the stone as three different things, is the mark of the sensory-intellectual consciousness. For Eckhart's word "understanding" means the conceptual intellect. But if one passes beyond the sensory-intellectual consciousness into the mystical consciousness, then one sees these three things as being "all one." However, it is evident that in this extrovertive experience the distinctions between things have not wholly disappeared. There is no doubt that what Eckhart means is that he sees the three things as distinct and separate and yet at the same time as not distinct but identical. The grass is identical with the stone, and the stone with the wood, although they are all different. Rudolph Otto, commenting on this, observes that it is as if one said that black is the same as white, white the same as black, although at the same time white remains white and black remains black. Of course this is a complete paradox. It is in fact contradictory. But we shall find that paradoxicality is one of the common characteristics of all mysticism. And it is no use saying that this is all logically impossible, and that no consciousness of this kind can exist, unless we wish, on these a priori grounds, to refuse to study the evidence—which is overwhelming.

What some mystics simply call the One other mystics often identify with God. Hence we find Jakob Böhme (1575–1624) saying much the same thing about the grass and the trees and the stones as Eckhart does, but saying that they are all God instead of just all One. The following is a statement of one of his experiences: "In this light my spirit saw through all things and into all creatures and I recognized God in grass and plants."

It is suggested that the extrovertive type of experience is a kind of halfway house to the introvertive. For the introvertive experience is wholly nonsensuous and nonintellectual. But the extrovertive experience is sensory-intellectual in so far as it still perceives physical objects but is nonsensuous and nonintellectual in so far as it perceives them as "all one."

We may sum up this short account of the extrovertive consciousness by saying that it is a perception of the world as transfigured and unified in one ultimate being. In some cultures the one being is identified with God; and since God is then perceived as the inner essence of all objects, this type of experience tends toward pantheism. But in some cultures—for example, Buddhism—the unity is not interpreted as God at all.

VII.   INTROVERTIVE MYSTICISM

Suppose that one could shut all physical sensations out of one's consciousness. It may be thought that this would be easy as regards some of the senses, namely sight, hearing, taste, and smell. One can shut one's eyes, stop up one's ears, and hold one's nose. One can avoid taste sensations by keeping one's mouth empty. But one cannot shut off tactual sensations in any simple way of this kind. And it would be even more difficult to get rid of organic sensations. However, one can perhaps suppose it possible somehow to thrust tactual and organic sensations out of conscious awareness—perhaps into the unconscious. Mystics do not, as far as I know, descend to the ignominious level of holding their noses and stopping their ears. My only point is that it is possible to conceive of getting rid of all sensations, and in one way or other mystics claim that they do this.

Suppose now, after this has been done, we next try to get rid of all sensuous *images* from our minds. This is very difficult. Most people, try as they will not to picture anything at all, will find vague images floating about in consciousness. Suppose, however, that it is possible to suppress all images. And suppose finally that we manage to stop all thinking and reasoning. Having got rid of the whole empirical content of sensations, images, and thoughts, presumably all emotions and desires and volitions would also disappear, since they normally exist only as attachments to the cognitive content. What, then, would be left of consciousness? What would happen? It is natural to suppose that with all the elements of consciousness gone consciousness itself would lapse and the subject would fall asleep or become *un*conscious.

Now it happens to be the case that this total suppression of the whole empirical content of consciousness is precisely what the introvertive mystic claims to achieve. And he claims that what happens is not that all consciousness disappears but that only the ordinary sensory-intellectual consciousness disappears and is replaced by an entirely new kind of consciousness, the mystical consciousness. Naturally we now ask whether any description of this new consciousness can be given. But before trying to answer that difficult question, I propose to turn aside for a brief space to speak about the methods which mystics use to suppress sensuous images, and thinking, so as to get rid of their sensory-intellectual consciousness. There are the Yoga techniques of India; and Christian mystics in Catholic monasteries also evolved their own methods. The latter usually call their techniques "prayers," but they are not prayers in the vulgar sense of asking God for things; they are much more like the "meditation" and "concentration" of Yogis than may be commonly supposed. This is too vast a subject to be discussed in detail here. But I will give two elementary illustrations.

Everyone has heard of the breathing exercises undertaken by the yogins of India seeking samadhi—samadhi being the Indian name for mystical consciousness. What is this special method of breathing, and what is it supposed to accomplish? The theory of the matter is, I understand, something like this: It is practically impossible, or at least very difficult, to stop all sensing, imaging, and thinking by a forcible act of the will. What comes very near to it, however, is to concentrate one's attention on some single point or object so that all other mental content falls away and there is left nothing but the single point of consciousness. If this can be done, then ultimately that single point will itself disappear because contrast is necessary for our ordinary consciousness, and if there is only one point of consciousness left, there is nothing to form a contrast to it.

The question then is: On what single thing should one concentrate? A simple way is to concentrate on the stream of one's own breath. Simple instructions which I have heard given are these. One first adopts a suitable physical position with spine and neck perfectly erect. Then breathe in and out slowly, evenly, and smoothly. Concentrate your attention on this and nothing else. Some aspirants, I believe, count their breaths, 1, 2, 3, . . . up to 10, and then begin the count again. Continue this procedure till you attain the desired results.

A second method is to keep repeating in one's mind some short formula of words over and over again till the words lose all meaning. So long as they carry meaning, of course, the mind is still occupied with the thought of this meaning. But when the words become meaningless there is nothing left of consciousness except the monotonous sound image, and that too, like the consciousness of one's breath, will in the end disappear. There is an interesting connection between this method and a remark made by the poet Tennyson. From childhood up Tennyson had frequent mystical experiences. They came to him spontaneously, without effort, and unsought. But he mentions the curious fact that he could induce them at will by the odd procedure of repeating his own name over and over again to himself. I know of no evidence that he studied mysticism enough to understand the theory of his own procedure, which would presumably be that the constantly repeated sound image served as the focus of the required one-pointed attention.

This leads to another curious reflection. Mystics who follow the procedure of constantly repeating a verbal formula often, I believe, tend to choose some religious set of words, for instance a part of the Lord's Prayer or a psalm. They probably imagine that these uplifting and inspirational words will carry them upwards toward the divine. But Tennyson's procedure suggests that any nonsense words would probably do as well. And this seems to agree with the general theory of concentration. It doesn't seem to matter what is chosen as the single point of concentration, whether it be one's breathing, or the sound of one's own name, or one's navel, or anything else, provided only it serves to shut off all other mental content.

Another point on which mystics usually insist in regard to spiritual training is what they call "detachment." Emphasis on this is found just as much in Hinduism and Buddhism as in Christianity. What is sought is detachment from desire, the uprooting of desire, or at any rate of all self-centered desires. The exact psychology of the matter presents great difficulties. In Christian mysticism the idea of detachment is usually given a religious and moral twist by insisting that it means the destruction of self-will or any kind of self-assertiveness, especially the rooting out of pride and the attainment of absolute humility. In non-Christian mysticism detachment does not usually get this special slant. But in the mysticism of all cultures detachment from desires for sensations and sensory images is emphasized.

We will now return to the main question. Supposing that the sensory-intellectual consciousness has been successfully supplanted by the mystical consciousness, can we find in the literatures of the subject any descriptions of this consciousness that will give us any idea of what it is like? The answer is that although mystics frequently say that their experiences are ineffable and indescribable, they nevertheless do often in fact describe them, and one can find plenty of such descriptive statements in the literature. They are usually extremely short—perhaps only three or four lines. And frequently they are indirect and not in the first person singular. Mystics more often than not avoid direct references to themselves.

I will give here a famous description which occurs in the Mandukya Upanishad. The Upanishads are supposed to have been the work of anonymous forest seers in India who lived between three thousand and twenty-five hundred years ago. They are among the oldest records of mysticism in the world. But they are of an unsurpassable depth of spirituality. For long ages and for countless millions of men in the East they have been, and they remain, the supreme source of the spiritual life. Of the introvertive mystical consciousness the Mandukya says that it is "beyond the senses, beyond the understanding, beyond all expression. . . . It is the pure unitary consciousness, wherein awareness of the world and of multiplicity is completely obliterated. It is ineffable peace. It is the Supreme Good. It is One without a second. It is the Self."

It will repay us, not to just slur over this passage, but to examine it carefully clause by clause. The first sentence is negative, telling us only what the experience is *not*. It is "beyond the senses, beyond the understanding." That is to say, it is beyond the sensory-intellectual consciousness; and there are in it no elements of sensation or sensuous imagery and no elements of conceptual thought. After these negatives there comes the statement that "it is the unitary consciousness, wherein all awareness of multiplicity has been obliterated." The core of the experience is thus described as an undifferentiated unity—a oneness or unity in which there is no internal division, no multiplicity.

I happen to have quoted a Hindu source. But one can find exactly the same thing in Christian mysticism. For instance the great Flemish mystic Jan van Ruysbroeck (1293–1381) says of what he calls "the God-seeing man" that "his spirit is undifferentiated and without distinction, and therefore it feels nothing but the unity." We see that the very words of the faithful Catholic are almost identical with those of the ancient Hindu, and I do not see how it can be doubted that they are describing the same experience. Not only in Christianity and Hinduism but everywhere else we find that the essence of the experience is that it is an *undifferentiated unity*, though each culture and each religion interprets this undifferentiated unity in terms of its own creeds or dogmas.

It may be objected that "undifferentiated unity" is a conceptual thought, and this is inconsistent with our statement that the experience is wholly nonintellectual. The answer is that concepts such as "one," "unity," "undifferentiated," "God," "Nirvana," etc., are only applied to the experience *after* it has passed and when it is being *remembered*. None can be applied during the experience itself.

The passage of the Upanishad goes on to say that the undifferentiated unity "is the Self." Why is this? Why is the unity now identified with the Self? The answer is plain. We started with the full self or mind of our ordinary everyday consciousness. What was it full of? It was full of the multiplicity of sensations, thoughts, desires, and the rest. But the mind was not merely this multiplicity. These disparate elements were held together in a unity, the unity of the single mind or self. A multiplicity without a unity in which the multiple elements are together is inconceivable—e.g., many objects in one space. Now when we emptied all the multiple contents out of this unity of the self what is left, according to the Upanishad, is the unity of the self, the original unity minus its contents. And this is the self. The Upanishads go further than this. They always identify this individual self with the Universal Self, the soul of the world. We will consider this in Chapter 2. For the moment we may continue to think in terms of the individual self, the pure ego of you or me. The undifferentiated unity is thought to be the pure ego.

I must draw the reader's attention to several facts about this situation. In the first place it flatly contradicts what David Hume said in a famous passage about the self. He said that when he looked introspectively into himself and searched for the I, the self, the ego, all he could ever introspect was the multiplicity of the sensations, images, thoughts, and feelings. He could never observe any I, any pure self apart from its contents, and he inferred that the I is a fiction and does not really exist. But now a vast body of empirical evidence, that of the mystics from all over the world, affirms that Hume was simply mistaken on a question of psychological fact, and that it is possible to get rid of all the mental contents and find the pure self left over and to experience this. This evidence need not mean that the self is a thing or a "substance," but can be taken as implying that it is a pure unity, the sort of being which Kant called the "transcendental unity" of the self.

The next thing to note is that the assertion of this new kind of consciousness is completely paradoxical. One way of bringing out the paradox is to point out that what we are left with here, when the contents of consciousness are gone, is a kind of consciousness which has no objects. It is not a consciousness *of* anything, but yet it is still consciousness. For the contents of our ordinary daily consciousness, the colors, sounds, wishes, thoughts are the same as the objects of consciousness, so that when the contents are gone the objects are gone. This consciousness of the mystics is not even a consciousness of consciousness, for then there would be a duality which is incompatible with the idea of an undifferentiated unity. In India it is called *pure* consciousness. The word "pure" is used in somewhat the same sense as Kant used it—meaning "without any empirical contents."

Another aspect of the paradox is that this pure consciousness is simultaneously both positive and negative, something and nothing, a fullness and an emptiness. The positive side is that it is an actual and positive consciousness. Moreover, all mystics affirm that it is pure peace, beatitude, joy, bliss, so that it has a positive affective tone. The Christians call it "the peace of God which passeth all understanding." The Buddhists call it Nirvana. But although it has this positive character, it is quite correct to say also that when we empty out all objects and contents of the mind *there is nothing whatever left*. That is the negative side of the paradox. What is left is sheer Emptiness. This is fully recognized in all mystical literature. In Mahayana Buddhism this total emptiness of the mystical consciousness is called the Void. In Christian mysticism the experience is identified with God. And this causes Eckhart and others to say that God, or the Godhead, is pure Nothingness, is a "desert," or "wilderness," and so on. Usually the two sides of the paradox are expressed in metaphors. The commonest metaphor for the positive side is light and for the negative side darkness. This is the darkness of God. It is called darkness because all distinctions disappear in it just as all distinctions disappear in a physical darkness.

We must not say that what we have here is a light *in* the darkness. For that would be no paradox. The paradox is that the light *is* the darkness, and the darkness *is* the light. This statement can be well documented from the literature of different cultures. I will give two examples, one from Christianity, one from Buddhism—and from the Buddhism of Tibet of all places in the world. Dionysius the Areopagite, a Christian, speaks of God as "the dazzling obscurity which outshines all brilliance with the intensity of its darkness." And the Tibetan Book of the Dead puts the same paradox in the words, "the clear light of the Void." In Dionysius we see that the obscurity, or the darkness, *is* the brilliance, and in the Tibetan book we see that the Void itself *is* a clear light.

VIII.   MYSTICISM AND RELIGION

Most writers on mysticism seem to take it for granted that mystical experience is a religious experience, and that mysticism is necessarily a religious phenomenon. They seem to think that mysticism and religious mysticism are one and the same thing. But this is far from being correct. It is true that there is an important connection between mysticism and religion, but it is not nearly so direct and immediate as most writers have seemed to think, nor can it be simply taken for granted as an obvious fact.

There are several grounds for insisting that intrinsically and in itself mystical experience is not a religious phenomenon at all and that its connection with religions is subsequent and even adventitious. In the first place, it seems to be clear that if we strip the mystical experience of all intellectual interpretation such as that which identifies it with God, or with the Absolute, or with the soul of the world, what is left is simply the undifferentiated unity. Now what is there that is religious about an undifferentiated unity? The answer seems to be, in the first instance, "Nothing at all." There seems to be nothing religious about an undifferentiated unity as such.

In the theistic religions of the West, in Christianity, Judaism, and Islam, the experience of the undifferentiated unity is interpreted as "union with God." But this is an interpretation and is not the experience itself. It is true that some Christian mystics, such as St. Teresa of Avila, invariably speak simply of having experienced "union with God," and do not talk about an undifferentiated unity. St. Teresa did not have a sufficiently analytical mind to distinguish between the experience and its interpretation. But other Christian mystics who are more analytically minded, such as Eckhart and Ruysbroeck, do speak of the undifferentiated unity.

These considerations are further underlined by the fact that quite different interpretations of the same experience are given in different cultures. The undifferentiated unity is interpreted by Eckhart and Ruysbroeck in terms of the Trinitarian conception of God, but by Islamic mystics as the unitarian God of Islam, and by the leading school of the Vedantists as a more impersonal Absolute. And when we come to Buddhism we find that the experience is not interpreted as any kind of God at all. For the Buddhist it becomes the Void or Nirvana. Buddha denied the existence of a Supreme Being altogether. It is often said that Buddhism is atheistic. And whether this description of Buddhism is true or not, it is certainly the case that there can exist an atheistic mysticism, a mystical experience naked and not clothed in any religious garb.

In view of these facts, we have a problem on our hands. Why is it that, in spite of exceptions, mysticism *usually* takes on some religious form and is usually found in connection with a definitely religious culture and as being a part of some definite religion? The following are, I think, the main reasons.

First, there is a very important feature of the introvertive mystical experience which I have not mentioned yet. I refer to the experience of the "melting away" into the Infinite of one's own individuality. Such phrases as "melting away," "fading away," "passing away" are found in the mystical literature of Christianity, Islam, Hinduism, and Buddhism. Among the Sufis of Islam there is a special technical term for it. It is called fanā. It must be insisted that this is not an inference or an interpretation or a theory or a speculation. It is an actual experience. The individual, as it were, directly experiences the disappearance of his own individuality, its fading away into the Infinite. To document this, one could quote from Eckhart, or from the Upanishads or the Sufis. But I believe I can bring home the point to a modern reader better by quoting a modern author. I referred earlier to the fact that Tennyson had frequent mystical experiences. His account of them is quoted by William James in his *The Varieties of Religious Experience*. Tennyson wrote, "All at once, as it were out of the intensity of the consciousness of individuality, individuality itself seemed to dissolve and fade away into boundless being. . . . the loss of personality, if such it were, seeming no extinction but the only true life." "Boundless being" seems to have the same meaning as "the Infinite." The Infinite is in most minds identified with the idea of God. We are finite beings, God is the only Infinite Being. One can see at once, therefore, how this experience of the dissolution of one's own individuality, its being merged into the Infinite, takes on a religious meaning. In theistic cultures the experience of melting away into boundless being is interpreted as union with God.

A second reason for the connection between mysticism and religion is that the undifferentiated unity is necessarily thought of by the mystics as being *beyond space and beyond time.* For it is without any internal division or multiplicity of parts, whereas the essence of time is its division into an endless multitude of successive parts, and the essence of space is its division into a multitude of parts lying side by side. Therefore the undifferentiated unity, being without any multiplicity of parts, is necessarily spaceless and timeless. Being timeless is the same as being eternal. Hence Eckart is constantly telling us that the mystical experience transcends time and is an experience of "the Eternal Now." But in religious minds the Eternal, like the Infinite, is another name for God. Hence the mystical experience is thought of as an experience of God.

A third reason for this identification of the undifferentiated unity with God lies in the emotional side of the experience. It is the universal testimony of the mystics that their kind of consciousness brings feelings of an exalted peace, blessedness, and joy. It becomes identified with the peace of God, the gateway of the Divine, the gateway of salvation. This is also why in Buddhism, though the experience is not personified or called God, it nevertheless becomes Nirvana which is the supreme goal of the Buddhist religious life.

Thus we see that mysticism naturally, though not necessarily, becomes intimately associated with whatever is the religion of the culture in which it appears. It is, however, important to realize that it does not favor any particular religion. Mystical experience in itself does not have any tendency to make a man a Christian or a Buddhist. Into the framework of what creed he will fit his experience will tend to depend mostly on the culture in which he lives. In a Buddhist country the mystic interprets his experience as a glimpse of Nirvana, in a Christian country he may interpret it as union with God or even (as in Eckhart) as penetrating into the Godhead which is beyond God. Or if he is a highly sophisticated modern individual, who has been turned by his education into a religious skeptic, he may remain a skeptic as regards the dogmas of the different religions; he may allow his mystical experience to remain naked without any clothing of creeds or dogmas; but he is likely at the same time to feel that in that experience he has found something *sacred*. And this feeling of the sacred may quite properly be called "religious" feeling though it does not clothe itself in any dogmas. And this alone may be enough to uplift his ideals and to revolutionize his life and to give it meaning and purpose.

IX.   THE ETHICAL ASPECTS OF MYSTICISM

It is sometimes asserted that mysticism is merely an escape from life and from its duties and responsibilities. The mystic, it is said, retreats into a private ecstasy of bliss, turns his back on the world, and forgets not only his own sorrows but the needs and sorrows of his fellow-men. In short, his life is essentially selfish.

It is possible that there have been mystics who deserved this kind of condemnation. To treat the bliss of the mystical consciousness as an end in itself is certainly a psychological possibility. And no doubt there have been men who have succumbed to this temptation. But this attitude is not the mystic ideal, and it is severely condemned by those who are most representative of the mystics themselves. For instance, St. John of the Cross condemns it as "spiritual gluttony." Eckhart tells us that if a man were in mystical ecstasy and knew of a poor man who needed his help, he should leave his ecstasy in order to go and serve the poor man. The Christian mystics especially have always emphasized that mystical union with God brings with it an intense and burning love of God which must needs overflow into the world in the form of love for our fellow-men; and that this must show itself in deeds of charity, mercy, and self-sacrifice, and not merely in words.

Some mystics have gone beyond this and have insisted that the mystical consciousness is the secret fountain of all love, human as well as divine; and that since love in the end is the only source of true moral activity, therefore mysticism is the source from which ethical values ultimately flow. For all selfishness and cruelty and evil result from the separateness of one human being from another. This separateness of individuals breeds egoism and the war of all against all. But in the mystical consciousness all distinctions disappear and therefore the distinction between "I" and "you" and "he" and "she." This is the mystical and metaphysical basis of love, namely the realization that my brother and I are one, and that therefore his sufferings are my sufferings and his happiness is my happiness. This reveals itself dimly in the psychological phenomena of sympathy and more positively in actual love.

For one who had no touch of the mystical vision all men would be islands. And in the end it is because of mysticism that it is possible to say that "no man is an island" and that on the contrary every man is "a part of the main."

X.   ALTERNATIVE INTERPRETATIONS OF MYSTICISM

We have seen that the same experience may be interpreted in terms of different religious creeds. There is also another set of alternative interpretations which we ought to mention. We may believe that the mystic really is in touch, as he usually claims, with some being greater than himself, some spiritual Infinite which transcends the temporal flux of things. Or we may, on the other hand, adopt the alternative solution of the skeptic who will think that the mystical consciousness is entirely subjective and imports nothing outside itself. My own vote would be cast for the former solution. I would agree with the words of Arthur Koestler which are quoted in the final selection printed in this book. He speaks of a higher order of reality which for us is like a text written in invisible ink. "I also liked to think," he says, "that the founders of religions, prophets, saints and seers had at moments been able to read a fragment of the invisible text; after which they had so much padded, dramatised and ornamented it, that they themselves could no longer tell what parts of it were authentic." [1]

But I wish to point out that even if one should choose the skeptical alternative and suppose that the mystical consciousness reveals no reality outside its owner's brain, one is far from having disposed of mysticism as some worthless delusion which ought to be got rid of. Even if it is wholly subjective, it still reveals something which is supremely great in human life. It is still the peace which passeth all understanding. It is still the gateway to salvation —not, I mean, in a future life, but as the highest beatitude that a man can reach in this life, and out of which the greatest deeds of love can flow. But it must be added, of course, that it belongs among those things of which Spinoza wrote in those famous words: "If the road which I have shown is very difficult, it yet can be discovered. And clearly it must be very hard if it is so rarely found. For how could it be that it is neglected by practically all, if salvation . . . could be found without difficulty. But all excellent things are as difficult as they are rare."

---

[1] See p. 235 [in *Teachings of the Mystics*. The quotation from Arthur Koestler's *The Invisible Writing*, copyright 1954 by Arthur Koestler, is reproduced by permission of The Macmillan Company and A. D. Peters and Co.].

R. C. ZAEHNER
Nature Mysticism, Soul Mysticism and Theistic Mysticism

Thus Śankara maintains that the highest Brahman, the One without a second, can only be attained by *sannyāsins*, men who renounce everything but their Selves, refuse to take part in religious ceremonies or to accept the grace of any God, and who abandon all works, whether good or evil.[1] 'By ceasing to do good to one's friends or evil to one's enemies (the *sannyāsin*) attains to the eternal Brahman by the *yoga* of meditation.'[2]

Now just as Rāmānuja and the other theistic philosophers in India attack Śankara and his followers for their extreme monism and for precisely this type of conduct which is its logical sequel, so did Ruysbroeck and Suso attack the Beghards in the European Middle Ages, for the latter held similar views and indulged in a similar quietism, believing themselves to be perfect and incapable of sin. In his *Spiritual Espousals* Ruysbroeck attacks those who seek to find perfect tranquillity in themselves. This passage is extraordinarily relevant to our theme and must be extensively quoted.

'Now observe', Ruysbroeck writes, 'that whenever man is empty and undistracted in his senses by images, and free and unoccupied in his highest powers, he attains rest by purely natural means. And all men can find and possess this rest in themselves by their mere nature, without the grace of God, if they are able to empty themselves of sensual images and of all action.'[3] Though he had obviously never heard of Vedāntin monism and could never have done so, Ruysbroeck seems not only to know exactly what this state of 'oneness without a second' is, but he describes it so accurately that one cannot but conclude that he is writing from actual experience. 'Whenever man is empty and undistracted in his senses by images, and free and unoccupied in his highest powers', such a man, we might continue, achieves the highest Brahman: for herein, precisely, lies the essence of the non-dualist Vedānta.

However, as Ruysbroeck rightly saw, such an emptying of the human person can only be the beginning of the mystical life for those who have experienced the grace of a personal God; for according to Christianity God

R. C. Zaehner (1913–   ) is a professor of eastern religions and ethics at Oxford University and a fellow of All Souls College. His many works include *The Comparison of Religion, Hindu and Muslim Mysticism*, and *Concordant Discord: the Interdependence of Faiths.*

NATURE MYSTICISM, SOUL MYSTICISM AND THEISTIC MYSTICISM   From *Mysticism: Sacred and Profane* by R. C. Zaehner. Reprinted by permission of the Clarendon Press, Oxford.

[1] See *Māndūkya Up., Kārikā,* 2. 35.

[2] *Nārada Upaniṣad*, Schrader, p. 145: 'priyeṣu sveṣu sukṛtam apriyeṣu ca duṣkṛtam visṛjya dhyāna-yogena brahmāpyeti sanātanam.'

[3] Blessed Jan van Ruysbroeck, *The Spiritual Espousals,* tr. Eric Colledge, London, Faber and Faber, 1952, pp. 166–7.

is Love, and the Muslim mystics, particularly in Persia, were later to make this idea their own. It is present too in the tenth and thirteenth chapters of the Bhagavad-Gītā and in all the devotional, as opposed to the philosophical, writing of the Hindus. Just as Śankara despises his fellow countrymen who continue to worship 'illusory' gods for being on a lower level than himself, so does Ruysbroeck fulminate against contemporary European quietists. There are two states of tranquillity, Ruysbroeck maintains, two types of *śānti*,—the rest one takes in one's self, purged as it has been of all affections and desires, and the rest in God when the living flame kindled by the fire of God is reunited with the divine fire. Thus Ruysbroeck has no patience with those who are content to rest in the self or Self,—and it can make no difference whether we spell this word with a capital letter or not since, in Sanskrit, there are no capital letters,—for this state, blissful though it undoubtedly is, is not union with God. It is the eternal spirit of the individual man contemplating itself in itself, as it issued from the mind of God but, because of original sin, separated from God, though otherwise sinless.

These men, says Ruysbroeck, 'are, as it seems to them, occupied in the contemplation of God, and they believe themselves to be the holiest men alive. Yet they live in opposition and dissimilarity to God and all saints and all good men. . . .

'Through the natural rest which they feel and have in themselves in emptiness, they maintain that they are free, and united with God without mean, and that they are advanced beyond all the exercises of Holy Church, and beyond the commandments of God, and beyond the law, and beyond all the virtuous works which one can in any way practise.' Here one calls to mind Śankara's contempt for those who perform the duties laid down by their religion and his preference for the perfect Yogin's withdrawal from all works. 'For', Ruysbroeck goes on to say, 'this emptiness seems to them to be so great that no-one ought to hinder them with the performance of any work, however good it be, for their emptiness is of greater excellence than are all virtues. And therefore they remain in mere passivity without the performance of any work directed up towards God or down towards man, just like the instrument which is itself passive and awaits the time when its owner wishes to work.' [4] Such men are indeed suspended between heaven and earth, isolated from man and Nature because they have severed all attachments, and isolated from God because the oneness of isolation is their end and goal, and because a conviction that they are the Absolute constitutes the toughest possible barrier between them and a possible irruption of grace: they 'maintain that they cannot advance, for they have achieved a life of unity and emptiness beyond which one cannot advance and in which there is no exercise'.[5]

It will be remembered that Christ said, 'No man cometh to the Father,

[4] Ibid., pp. 170–1.   [5] Ibid., p. 173.

but by me'.[6] It is, of course, possible to take this saying in an absolutely literal sense and thereby to dismiss all non-Christian religions as being merely false. It is, however, legitimate and certainly more charitable to interpret this saying, so far as it applies to mysticism, to mean that unless one approaches the Father through the Son and as a son with the trust and helplessness of a child, there is very little chance of finding Him,—none at all, it would appear, if you insist either that you are identical with the Father or that the Father is an illusion. Hence a sharp distinction must be drawn between those forms of religion in which love or charity plays a predominant part and those in which it does not. In Christian mysticism love is all-important, and it must be so, since God Himself is defined as Love. In Islam too, because the Muslims inherited more than they knew from the Christians, it assumes ever-increasing importance despite the predominantly terrifying picture of God we find in the Qur'ān. In Hinduism this religion of love breaks through in the Gītā and in the cults of both Viṣṇu and Śiva, and, of course, in the worship of Rāma and Krishna as incarnations of Viṣṇu. 'I am the origin of all,' says Krishna in the Bhagavad-Gītā, 'from me all things evolve. Thinking thus do wisemen, immersed in love (bhāva), worship Me. Thinking of Me, devoting their lives to Me, enlightening each other, and speaking of Me always, they are contented and rejoice. To these worshippers of Mine, always controlled, I give a steady mind by which they may approach Me, for I loved them first.'[7] This and very much else that is similar will be found in Hindu literature, yet always the shadow of a self-satisfied monism stalks behind it.

And in monism there can be no love,—there is ecstasy and trance and deep peace, what Ruysbroeck calls 'rest', but there cannot be the ecstasy of union nor the loss of self in God which is the goal of Christian, Muslim, and all theistic mysticism.

> 'And therefore', says Ruysbroeck, 'all those men are deceived whose intention it is to sink themselves in natural rest, and who do not seek God with desire nor find Him in delectable love. For the rest which they possess consists in an emptying of themselves, to which they are inclined by nature and by habit. And in this natural rest men cannot find God. But it brings man indeed into an emptiness which heathens and Jews are able to find, and all men, however evil they may be, if they live in their sins with untroubled conscience, and are able to empty themselves of all images and all action. In this emptiness rest is sufficient and great, and it is in itself no sin, for it is in all men by nature, if they knew how to make themselves empty.'[8]

All mystics, including Ruysbroeck, agree that no progress in the inner life is possible without detachment from all things worldly, from all that comes

[6] John xiv. 6.
[7] *BhagG.* 10. 8–10: 'ahaṁ sarvasya prabhavo, mattaḥ sarvaṁ pravartate; / iti matvā bhajante māṁ budhā bhāvasamanvitāḥ. / mac-cittā mad-gata-prāṇā bodhayantaḥ parasparam, / kathayantaśca māṁ nityaṁ tuṣyantica ramantica. / teṣāṁ satata-yuktānāṁ bhajatāṁ prīti-pūrvakam / dadāmi buddhi-yogaṁ taṁ yena mām upayānti te.'
[8] Op. cit., p. 167.

to be and passes away, and above all from the individual ego or self. They are agreed that the 'second self', as Proust calls it, must be discovered and brought out into the open. The temptation is that with the finding of this second self the aspirant after spiritual perfection should think that he has reached his goal and that the 'second self', the *ātman* of the Vedānta, is God. . . .

In this book our investigations have led to the tentative conclusion that what goes by the name of mysticism, so far from being an identical expression of the selfsame Universal Spirit, falls into three distinct categories. Under the general heading of mysticism we have not included those experiences that are sometimes associated with it,—clairvoyance, clair-audition, telepathy, thought-reading, levitation, bi-location, and the rest: we have confined ourselves to praeternatural experiences in which sense perception and discursive thought are transcended in an immediate apperception of a unity or union which is apprehended as lying beyond and transcending the multiplicity of the world as we know it. Because these experiences are recorded at all times and from all parts of the world, it is fatally easy to assume that because they are, one and all, praeternatural, that is, not explicable in the present state of our knowledge, and because the keynote of all of them is 'union', they must necessarily be the same. It is not realized often enough that once these experiences are assumed to be identical and of identical provenance, the conclusion that the transports of the saint and the ecstasies of the manic are identical cannot be escaped. If this were really so, and if these praeternatural experiences were what religion is principally concerned with, then the only sensible course to adopt would be that which Rimbaud followed: we should all attempt to induce in ourselves an attack of acute mania; and this is in fact the solution that Mr. Huxley seems to propound in *The Doors of Perception*.

That 'nature mysticism' exists and is widely attested is not open to serious doubt. How the experience is to be explained is quite another matter. To identify it with the experience of Christian or Muslim saints, however, is hardly admissible, as I hope to have shown, however inadequately, in the course of this work. In this connexion it is significant that though Mr. Custance christened his familiar spirit Tyche-Teresa in recognition of the supposed fact that the Saint of Avila's experiences were comparable to, or even identical with, his own, he never quotes from her works though the words of Plotinus come readily enough to his lips.

Though it is easy enough to dismiss the experiences of the nature mystic as mere hallucination, this is really begging the question; for, in all cases of this experience, the impression of *reality* they leave behind is quite overwhelming. In every case,—whether the experience comes unheralded or whether it is produced by drugs or Yoga techniques,—the result is the same;—the person who has had the experience feels that he has gone through something of tremendous significance beside which the ordinary world of sense perception and discursive thought is almost the shadow of a shade. Huxley expresses this with the German word *Istigkeit,* and he has thereby fully caught the mood. The experience seems overpoweringly *real;* its authority obtrudes itself and will not be denied. It is this quality in it, I believe, which makes those who have been the subject of such a visitation assume that this must be identical with what the mystical saints have experienced. The Ṣūfīs reply to their critics by saying that their criticism is about as valid as that of a teetotaller who vainly tries to understand the pleasures of drunkenness without ever having tasted wine. It will not help him to know that wine is the fermented juice of the grape or what its chemical constituents are: until he has actually drunk deeply, he will never understand the exhilaration of the drinker. Similarly no child who has not reached the age of adolescence can understand what pleasure there can possibly be in the sexual act which seems to him revolting. So with the nature mystics,—it is extremely difficult for the purely rational man to understand in what the excitement and the joy consist, or why it should be that the sensation of losing one's individuality should be so intensely prized. No comparison is adequate: the nearest, perhaps, as Huxley saw, is an intense absorption in music or painting, or in dancing, for all these can be used as aids to produce such a condition, and the Ṣūfīs introduced song and dance, and the contemplation of beautiful boys, very early as aids to the attainment of praeternatural states. Yet even so, they can serve only as the faintest adumbrations, they can scarcely claim even to approximate to the real thing.

Ṣūfism is, in this respect, perhaps more instructive than either Christian or Indian mysticism. The distinction that Qushayrī drew between *basṭ,* or the sense of one's personality expanding indefinitely, and actual communion with God, is rarely met with again, and the opposition of the conservatives to the use of song and dance as stimulants broke down all too soon, because, as Ṣūfism degenerated, the achievement of ecstasy as such became the Ṣūfī's goal regardless of whether such ecstasies proceeded from the hand of God or not. The later Ṣūfīs came to assume that all ecstasy was divine, and thereby put a ready weapon into the hands of the orthodox: for whereas sanctity is its own argument, mania is not, and no genuinely religious person is likely to be impressed by one who claims either to be in direct communion with God or actually to be identical with Him, if his conduct is, in fact, sub-human. Thus the confusion that is popularly made between nature mysticism and the mysticism of the Christian saints can only discredit the latter. By making the confusion one is forced into the position that God is simply another term for Nature; and it is an observable fact that in Nature there is neither morality nor charity nor even common decency. God, then, is reduced to the sum-total of natural impulses in which the terms 'good' and 'evil' have no meaning. Such a god is subhuman, a god fit for animals, not for rational creatures; and to experience such a god has rightly been termed 'downward transcendence' by Mr. Huxley.

However, if there is a God, and if it is true that our relations with Him will be very much more intimate after death, then 'it is not enough to know only that He exists, but one must know His nature and His will'.[9] This is even more important for the mystic than it is for the ordinary man, for the mystic is in fact the man who has a foretaste in this life of life after death; and just as the experiences of those who have taken mescalin have, to a certain extent, varied according to their beliefs, so will the experiences of persons who tame their senses and discipline their minds with a view to reaching a higher reality.

Indian religion is right in describing the object of religious disciplines as being *mokṣa* or liberation. By this they mean liberation from what St. Paul calls 'the flesh', that is, the life of blind instinct, the animal in man. Beyond this they also seek liberation from the third of Avicenna's three components of the lower soul, 'imagination' or distracting thought. As their final goal the Sāṃkhya-Yogins seek their own immortal soul in its nakedness and isolation. Having no clear idea of God, they cannot seek union with Him, nor do they claim to.

The Vedāntins are in a different case. The Upaniṣads teach that Brahman is both the source of all things and that he includes all things. Greater than all the universe, he is yet the fine point without magnitude which is the deep centre of the human heart. In so far as they teach this, they are fully at one with the mystical teaching of the Catholic Church. However, they also teach that Brahman *is* the universe and that he *is* the human soul. Rāmānuja and his followers interpret this as being a metaphor and as meaning that the universe and human souls are what he calls the 'body' of God whereas God or Brahman remains distinct from them though they are wholly dependent on him. Here again there is full agreement between Rāmānuja and Catholic mystical tradition. Whether Rāmānuja or Śankara more accurately represents the general trend of Upaniṣadic teaching must be left to the Hindus to decide. It is, however, fair to point out that the concept of *māyā*, the cosmic illusion, is only adumbrated and never formulated in the classical Upaniṣads themselves. Śankara and his followers, by establishing complete identity between the human soul and the Absolute, do in fact accept the Sāṃkhya-Yoga view *in practice*, for self-realization means for them, no less than for the Sāṃkhya-Yogin, the isolation of the immortal soul from all that is not itself. As we have tried to point out in another chapter there is much in the Vedānta philosophy which fits in with what Mr. Custance says when in a manic state, particularly the claim that the 'released' individual must make to be identical with the creator (of an imaginary universe). Precisely these views were attacked by Ruysbroeck who rightly saw that all people who firmly held them, must think that they had reached the highest possible mystical state, what the Hindus call the *paramā gatiḥ*, whereas they had only reached the stage of self-isolation, of rest and 'emptiness' within themselves. Believing this to be union with God, they were prevented from taking any further step because they believed there was no

---

[9] *Škand-Gumānīk Vičār*, ed. Menasce, Fribourg, 1945, p. 117 (ch. 10, § 37).

further step to take. This, for Ruysbroeck, as for any Christian, was manifestly absurd, for how, as Abū Yazīd once said,[10] could one ever come to the
end of the Godhead?

Here, then, are two distinct and mutually opposed types of mysticism,—the
monist and the theistic. This is not a question of Christianity and Islam
versus Hinduism and Buddhism: it is an unbridgeable gulf between all those
who see God as incomparably greater than oneself, though He is, at the same
time, the root and ground of one's being, and those who maintain that soul
and God are one and the same and that all else is pure illusion. For them
Christian mysticism is simply *bhakti* or devotion to a personal god carried to
ludicrous extremes, whereas for the theist the monist's idea of 'liberation' is
simply the realization of his immortal soul in separation from God, and is
only, as Junayd pointed out, a stage in the path of the beginner. He is still
in the bondage of original sin.

Hinduism has its theists as well as its monists; and the Bhagavad-Gītā as
well as Rāmānuja stand nearer to St. John of the Cross than they do to
Śankara. This is a quarrel that cuts clean across the conventional distinctions
of creeds. In each of the great religions there have been upholders of both
doctrines. Even Christianity has not completely avoided the monistic extreme
even though it makes nonsense of its basic doctrine that God is Love. Meister
Eckhart, for instance, at times adopted a fully monistic position, and Angelus
Silesius could well be interpreted monistically though a literal interpretation
of the *Cherubinischer Wandersmann*, taken out of the context of his other
work, is scarcely permissible since mystics, when writing in verse, allow themselves, like all poets, the boldest figures of speech. . . .

NINIAN SMART
Numinous Experience and Mystical Experience

. . . It's primarily in the *numinous* experience—the experience which grows
out of worship and the submission of oneself to God—that the notion of His
Otherness arises. It's the contrast between the unholy, unclean, puny sinner
and the terrible, holy, pure, majestic Godhead that gives us an inkling of His

Ninian Smart (1927–   ) is a professor of religious studies at the University of Lancaster. His works
include *Reasons and Faiths, Doctrine and Argument in Indian Philosophy,* and *Philosophers and
Religious Truth.*

NUMINOUS EXPERIENCE AND MYSTICAL EXPERIENCE   From *A Dialogue of Religions* by Ninian
Smart. Copyright 1960 by SCM Press Ltd. Reprinted by their permission.

[10] See p. 165 [in *Mysticism: Sacred and Profane*].

transcendence. Now if this Being whom we encounter in worship and prostration appears to have personal characteristics (and don't the great prophets and teachers speak thus?), it's not surprising that theists ascribe to Him such personal attributes! But my main point is that the notion of Otherness is yielded by this kind of experience—the sort that Job had when he wished to clothe himself in dust and ashes and which one of your Hindu saints had when he cried that he was a cur and that it was sinful to think of any creature as Viṣṇu. . . .

. . . It's indeed typical of the mystical experience that there should be difficulty in distinguishing between subject and object (as the matter is often put), and so there arises a sense of merging with God or the Absolute. This is a special kind of religious experience which is different, I think, from the numinous experience of the worshipper. I know this is a very crude way of describing the situation, but perhaps you understand what I'm getting at. I'd like to propose the working hypothesis, which we can discuss later if you like, that the mystical experience has a distinctive connection with the more 'impersonalist' doctrines, such as those of Advaita Vedānta and of certain forms of Buddhism. . . .

. . . I suppose that the Brahman-Ātman doctrine is a way of bringing together the religion of sacrifice on the one hand with the inner contemplative quest towards insight and knowledge on the other. And certainly the identification of the Self with Brahman, the Power pervading and sustaining the cosmos, presents its difficulties, as also the Ṣūfī teachings created tensions within Islam. Assuredly it is a little surprising that the great God who rules the cosmos can be found within the heart 'tinier than a mustard-seed', as the *Upaniṣad* says. And it's difficult sometimes to resist the impression that the mystics' tendency to speak of deification is unorthodox and even perhaps blasphemous. All this I grant. But if one believes in a personal God it is hard not to allow that there is a way to Him through mysticism, through contemplation. This may lead to complications of doctrine, absurdities, difficulties; but the result is a marvellous welding together of the insights of different types of religious practice. And history may be on my side in these remarks. For, on my reading of the situation, early Islam was understood in its early days simply as a religion of worship of and obedience to Allah, and yet it flowered also, through the Ṣūfīs, into a faith where the profound and beautiful interior visions were also seen as a kind of contact with God. Then, conversely, isn't it significant that Buddhism itself became proliferated, in the Mahāyāna, in such a way that the intuitions of the numinous were given a central place? . . .

THE COGNITIVE STATUS
OF RELIGIOUS
AND MYSTICAL EXPERIENCE

C. B. MARTIN
"Seeing" God

Religious people may feel impatient with the harshness of argument in the last chapter. They may feel confident that they have something that non-religious people lack, namely, a direct experience or apprehension of God. They may claim that such religious experience is a way of knowing God's existence. This claim must now be examined.

We shall first consider accounts of religious experience that seem to sacrifice an existential claim for the security of the feeling of the moment. There is an influential and subtle group of religious thinkers who would not insist upon any existential claim. My remarks are largely irrelevant to this group. It would be hasty to describe their religious belief as "subjective" or to employ any other such general descriptive term. For example, the "call," in even the most liberal and "subjective" Quaker sects, could not be reduced to statements about feelings. The "call," among other things, implies a mission or intricate pattern of behavior. The nonsubjective element of the "call" is evident, because insofar as one failed to live in accordance with a mission just so far would the genuineness of the "call" be questioned. It will be seen

C. B. Martin (1924–) has taught for many years in Australia, where he is currently a professor of philosophy at the University of Sydney. His philosophical writings are in the analytic tradition.

SEEING GOD   Reprinted from C. B. Martin: *Religious Belief.* © 1959 by Cornell University. Used by permission of Cornell University Press.

that this verification procedure is necessarily not available in the religious way of knowing to be examined.

In the second part of the chapter we shall consider accounts of religious experience that are not so easily reduced to mere subjectivity.

I

> We are rejecting logical argument of any kind as the first chapter of our theology or as representing the process by which God comes to be known. We are holding that our knowledge of God rests rather on the revelation of His personal Presence as Father, Son, and Holy Spirit. . . . Of such a Presence it must be true that to those who have never been confronted with it argument is useless, while to those who have it is superfluous.[1]

> It is not as the result of an inference of any kind, whether explicit or implicit, whether laboriously excogitated or swiftly intuited, that the knowledge of God's reality comes to us. It comes rather through our direct, personal encounter with Him in the Person of Jesus Christ His Son our Lord.[2]

> It will not be possible to describe the compelling touch of God otherwise than as the compelling touch of God. To anyone who has no such awareness of God, leading as it does to the typically religious attitudes of obeisance and worship, it will be quite impossible to indicate what is meant; one can only hope to evoke it, on the assumption that the capacity to become aware of God is part of normal human nature like the capacity to see light or to hear sound.[3]

The arguments of the theologians quoted have been taken out of context. The quotations by themselves do not give a faithful or complete impression of their total argument. The following quotations from Professor Farmer indicate two further lines of argument which cannot be discussed here.

> For what we have now in mind is no demonstrative proofs *from* the world, but rather confirmatory considerations which present themselves to us when we bring belief in God with us *to* the world. It is a matter of the coherence of the belief with other facts. If we find that the religious intuition which has arisen from other sources provides the mind with a thought in terms of which much else can without forcing be construed, then that is an intellectual satisfaction, and a legitimate confirmation of belief, which it would be absurd to despise.[4]

> We shall first speak in general terms of what may be called the human situation and need, and thereafter we shall try to show how belief in God, as particularized in its Christian form (though still broadly set forth), fits on to this situation and need.[5]

The alleged theological way of knowing may be described as follows: I have direct experience (knowledge, acquaintance, apprehension) of God; therefore

---

[1] John Baillie, *Our Knowledge of God* (London: Oxford University Press, 1949), p. 132.
[2] *Ibid.*, p. 143.
[3] H. H. Farmer, *Towards Belief in God* (London: S. C. M. Press, 1942), Pt. II, p. 40.
[4] *Ibid.*, p. 113.   [5] *Ibid.*, p. 62.

I have valid reason to believe that God exists. By this it may be meant that the statement "I have had direct experience of God, but God does not exist" is contradictory. If so, the assertion that "I have had direct experience of God" commits one to the assertion that God exists. From this it follows that "I have had direct experience of God" is more than a psychological statement, because it claims more than the fact that I have certain experiences— it claims that God exists. On this interpretation the argument is deductively valid. The assertion "I have direct experience of God" includes the assertion "God exists." Thus, the conclusion "Therefore, God exists" follows tautologically.

Unfortunately, this deduction is useless. If the deduction were to be useful, the addition of the existential claim "God exists" to the psychological claim of having religious experiences would have to be shown to be warrantable, and this cannot be done.

Consider the following propositions: (1) I feel as if an unseen person were interested in (willed) my welfare. (2) I feel an elation quite unlike any I have ever felt before. (3) I have feelings of guilt and shame at my sinfulness. (4) I feel as if I were committed to bending all my efforts to living in a certain way. These propositions state only that I have certain complex feelings and experiences. Nothing else follows deductively. The only thing that I can establish beyond possible correction on the basis of having certain feelings and experiences is that I have these feelings and sensations. No matter how unique people may think their experience to be, it cannot do the impossible.

Neither is the addition of the existential claim "God exists" to the psychological claim made good by any inductive argument. There are no tests agreed upon to establish genuine experience of God and distinguish it decisively from the nongenuine.[6] Indeed, many theologians deny the possibility of any such test or set of tests.

The believer may persuade us that something extraordinary has happened by saying, "I am a changed man since 6:37 P.M., May 6, 1939." This is a straightforward empirical statement. We can test it by noticing whether or not he has given up his bad habits. We may allow the truth of the statement even if he has not given up his bad habits, because we may find evidence of bad conscience, self-searchings and remorse that had not been present before that date.

However, if the believer says, "I had a direct experience of God at 6:37 P.M., May 6, 1939," this is not an empirical statement in the way that the other statement is. How could we check its truth? No matter how much or how little his subsequent behavior, such as giving up bad habits and so on, is affected, it could never prove or disprove his statement.

An important point to note is that theologians tend to discourage any detailed description of the required experience ("apprehension of God").[7] The

---

[6] This will be qualified in the second part of this chapter.
[7] The detailed descriptions of the Catholic mystics will be discussed later.

more naturalistic and detailed the description of the required experience be-comes, the easier would it become to deny the existential claim. One could say, "Yes, I had those very experiences, but they certainly did not convince me of God's existence." The only sure defense here would be for the theo-logian to make the claim analytic: "You couldn't have those experiences and at the same time sincerely deny God's existence."

The way in which many theologians talk would seem to show that they think of knowing God as something requiring a kind of sixth sense. The Divine Light is not of a color usually visible only to eagles, and the Voice of God is not of a pitch usually audible only to dogs. No matter how much more keen our senses became, we should be no better off than before. The sixth sense, therefore, must be very different from the other five.

This supposed religious sense has no vocabulary of its own but depends upon metaphors drawn from the other senses. There are no terms which apply to it and it alone. There is a vocabulary for what is sensed but not for the sense. We "see" the Holy, the Numinous, the Divine. In a similar way we often speak of "hearing" the voice of conscience and "seeing" logical connections. By using this metaphor we emphasize the fact that often we come to understand the point of an argument or problem in logic suddenly. We mark this occurrence by such phrases as "the light dawned," "understood it in a flash." Such events are usually described in terms of a complete assur-ance that one's interpretation is correct and a confidence that one will tend to be able to reproduce or recognize the argument or problem in various con-texts in the future. But a vitally important distinction between this "seeing" and the religious "seeing" is that there is a checking procedure for the former but not for the latter. If, while doing a problem in geometry you "see" that one angle is equal to another and then on checking over your proof find that they are not equal after all, you say "I didn't really 'see,' I only thought I did."

The religious way of knowing is described as being unique. No one can deny the existence of feelings and experiences which the believer calls "re-ligious," and no one can deny their power. Because of this and because the way of knowing by direct experience is neither inductive nor deductive, theologians have tried to give this way of knowing a special status. One way of doing this is to claim that religious experience is unique and incommuni-cable.

Professor Baillie, in likening our knowledge of God to our knowledge of other minds, says that it is "like our knowledge of tridimensional space and all other primary modes of knowledge, something that cannot be imagined by one who does not already possess it, since it cannot be described to him in terms of anything else than itself." [8] This kind of comparison is stated in the two sentences following, and we shall now examine the similarities and dis-

---

[8] Baillie, *Our Knowledge of God*, p. 217.

similarities between them. (1) You don't know what the experience of God is until you have had it. (2) You don't know what the color blue is until you have seen it. Farmer says, "All the basic elements in our experience are incommunicable. Who could describe light and colour to one who has known nothing but darkness?" [9] All that Farmer proves is that a description of one group of sensations A in terms of another set of sensations B is never sufficient for knowing group A. According to this definition of "know," in order to know one must have those sensations. Thus, all that is proved is that, in order to know what religious experience is, one must have a religious experience. This helps in no way at all to prove that such experience is direct apprehension of God and helps in no way to support the existential claim "God exists."

Farmer makes the point that describing the experience of God to an unbeliever is like describing color to a man blind from birth. So it is, in the sense that the believer has usually had experiences which the unbeliever has not. However, it is also very much unlike. The analogy breaks down at some vital points.

The blind man may have genuine, though incomplete knowledge of color. He may have an instrument for detecting wave lengths, and the like. Indeed, he may even increase our knowledge of color. More important still, the blind man may realize the differences in powers of prediction between himself and the man of normal eyesight. He is well aware of the fact that, unlike himself, the man of normal eyesight does not have to wait to hear the rush of the bull in order to be warned.

This point concerning differences in powers of prediction is connected with the problem of how we are to know when someone has the direct experience of God or even when we ourselves have the direct experience of God. It was shown above how the situation is easier in the case of the blind man knowing about color. It is only when one comes to such a case as knowing God that the society of tests and checkup procedures, which surround other instances of knowing, completely vanishes. What is put in the place of these tests and checking procedures is an immediacy of knowledge that is supposed to carry its own guarantee. This feature will be examined later.

It is true that the man of normal vision has a way of knowing color which the blind man does not have, that is, he can see colored objects. However, as we have seen, it would be wrong to insist that this is the only way of knowing color and that the blind man has *no* way of knowing color. Perhaps Farmer has this in mind when he tries to make an analogy between the incommunicability of the believer's direct knowledge of God to the unbeliever and the incommunicability of the normal man's knowledge of color to the blind man. The analogy is justified if "knowing color" is made synonymous with "having color sensations." On this account, no matter how good

___

[9] Farmer, *Towards Belief in God*, p. 41.

his hearing, reliable his color-detecting instruments, and so on, the blind man could not know color, and the man of normal vision could not communicate to him just what this knowledge would be like.

The believer has had certain unusual experiences, which, presumably, the unbeliever has not had. If "having direct experience of God" is made synonymous with "having certain religious experiences," and the believer has had these and the unbeliever has not, then we may say that the believer's knowledge is incommunicable to the unbeliever in that it has already been legislated that in order to know what the direct experience of God is one must have had certain religious experiences. "To anyone who has no such awareness of God, leading as it does to the typically religious attitudes of obeisance and worship, it will be quite impossible to indicate what is meant; one can only hope to evoke it." [10] Reading theological textbooks and watching the behavior of believers is not sufficient.

The theologian has made the analogy above hold at the cost of endangering the existential claim about God which he hoped to establish. If "knowing color" is made synonymous with "having color sensations" and "having direct experience of God" is made synonymous with "having certain religious experiences," then it is certainly true that a blind man cannot "know color" and that a nonreligious man cannot "have direct experience of God." By definition, also, it is true that the blind man and the nonreligious man cannot know the meaning of the phrases "knowing color" and "having direct experience of God," because it has been previously legislated that one cannot know their meaning without having the relevant experiences.

If this analogy is kept, the phrases "knowing color" and "having direct experience of God" seem to make no claim beyond the psychological claims about one's color sensations and religious feelings.

If this analogy is not kept, there is no sense in the comparison of the incommunicability between the man of normal vision and the blind man with the incommunicability between the believer and the unbeliever.

If "knowing color" is to be shaken loose from its purely psychological implications and made to have an existential reference concerning features of the world, then a whole society of tests and checkup procedures, which would be wholly irrelevant to the support of the psychological claim about one's own color sensations, become relevant. For example, what other people see, the existence of light waves, and the description of their characteristics, which needs the testimony of research workers and scientific instruments, all must be taken into account.

Because "having direct experience of God" does not admit the relevance of a society of tests and checking procedures, it tends to place itself in the company of the other ways of knowing which preserve their self-sufficiency, "uniqueness," and "incommunicability" by making a psychological and not

[10] *Ibid.*, p. 40.

an existential claim. For example, "I seem to see a piece of blue paper," [11] requires no further test or checking procedure in order to be considered true. Indeed, if Jones says, "I seem to see a piece of blue paper," he not only needs no further corroboration but cannot be shown to have been mistaken. If Smith says to Jones, "It does not seem to me as if I were seeing a piece of blue paper," this cannot rightly raise any doubts in Jones's mind, though it may express Smith's doubts. That is, Smith may feel that Jones is lying. However, if Jones had said, "I see a piece of blue paper," and Smith, in the same place and at the same time, had replied, "I do not see a piece of blue paper," or, "It does not seem to me as if I were now seeing a piece of blue paper," then Smith's remarks can rightly raise doubts in Jones's mind. Further investigation will then be proper, and if no piece of paper can be felt and other investigators cannot see or feel the paper and photographs reveal nothing, then Jones's statement will be shown to have been false. Jones's only refuge will be to say, "Well, I certainly seem to see a piece of blue paper." This is a perfect refuge, because no one can prove him wrong, but its unassailability has been bought at the price of making no claim about the world beyond the claim about his own experience of the moment.

The closeness of the religious statement to the psychological statement can be brought out in another way, as follows. When one wishes to support the assertion that a certain physical object exists, the tests and checking procedures made by Jones himself are not the only things relevant to the truth of his assertion. Testimony of what others see, hear, and so on is also relevant. That is, if Jones wanted to know whether it was really a star that he saw, he could not only take photographs, look through a telescope, and the like but also ask others if they saw the star. If a large proportion of a large number of people denied seeing the star, Jones's claim about the star's existence would be weakened. Of course, he might still trust his telescope. However, let us now imagine that Jones does not make use of the tests and checking procedures (photographs and telescopes) but is left with the testimony of what he sees and the testimony of others concerning what they see. In this case, it is so much to the point if a large number of people deny seeing the star that Jones will be considered irrational or mad if he goes on asserting its existence. His only irrefutable position is to reduce his physical object claim to an announcement concerning his own sensations. Then the testimony of men and angels cannot disturb his certitude. These sensations of the moment he knows directly and immediately, and the indirect and nonimmediate testimony of men and angels is irrelevant. Absolute confidence and absolute indifference to the majority judgment is bought at the price of reducing the existential to the nonexistential.

The religious claim is similar to, though not identical with, the case above in certain important features. We have seen that there are no tests or check-

---

[11] I shall call such statements "low-claim assertions."

ing procedures open to the believer to support his existential claim about God. Thus, he is left with the testimony of his own experience and the similar testimony of the experience of others. And, of course, he is not left wanting for such testimony, for religious communities seem to serve just this sort of function.

Let us imagine a case comparable to the one concerning the existence of a physical object. In this case Brown is a professor of divinity, and he believes that he has come to know of the existence of God through direct experience of God. In order to understand the intricate character of what Professor Brown is asserting we must imagine a highly unusual situation. The other members of the faculty and the members of Professor Brown's religious community suddenly begin sincerely to deny his, and what has been their own, assertion. Perhaps they still attend church services and pray as often as they used to do, and perhaps they claim to have the same sort of experiences as they had when they were believers, but they refuse to accept the conclusion that God exists. Whether they give a Freudian explanation or some other explanation or no explanation of their experiences, they are agreed in refusing to accept the existential claim (about God) made by Professor Brown. How does this affect Professor Brown and his claim? It may affect Professor Brown very deeply—indeed, he may die of broken-hearted disappointment at the loss of his fellow believers. However, the loss of fellow believers may not weaken his confidence in the truth of his assertion or in the testimony of his experience. In this matter his experience may be all that ultimately counts for him in establishing his confidence in the truth of his claim about the existence of God. It has been said that religious experience carries its own guarantee, and perhaps the account above describes what is meant by this.

It is quite obvious from these examples that the religious statement "I have direct experience of God" is of a different status from the physical-object statement "I see a star" and shows a distressing similarity to the low-claim assertion "I seem to see a star." The bulk of this chapter has so far been devoted to showing some of the many forms this similarity takes. Does this mean then that the religious statement and its existential claim concerning God amount to no more than a reference to the complex feelings and experiences of the believer?

Perhaps the best way to answer this question is to take a typical low-claim assertion and see if there is anything which must be said of it and all other low-claim assertions which cannot be said of the religious statement. One way of differentiating a physical object statement from a low-claim assertion is by means of prefixing the phrase "I seem." [12] For instance, the statement "I see a star" may be transformed into a statement concerning my sensations by translating it into the form "I seem to see a star." The first statement in-

---

[12] This, clearly, is a superficial and mechanical move, for the prefixing of this phrase ordinarily would result in a qualified and hedging physical object statement. I shall just have to plead that the possibility that such a prefixing should result in a low-claim assertion is here realized.

volves a claim about the existence of an object as well as an announcement concerning my sensations and therefore subjects itself to the risk of being wrong concerning that further claim. Whether one is wrong in this case is determined by a society of tests and checking procedures such as taking photographs and looking through telescopes and by the testimony of others that they see or do not see a star. The second statement involves no claim about the existence of an object and so requires no such tests and no testimony of others; indeed, the final judge of the truth of the statement is the person making it. If no existential claim is lost by the addition of this phrase to a statement then the assertion is low-claim. For instance, the statement "I feel pain" loses nothing by the addition "I seem to feel pain."

In the case of the religious statement "I have direct experience of God" the addition of the phrase is fatal to all that the believer wants to assert. "I seem to be having direct experience of God" is a statement concerning my feelings and sensations of the moment, and as such it makes no claim about the existence of God. Thus, the original statement "I have direct experience of God" is not a low-claim assertion. This should not surprise us. We should have known it all along, for is it not an assertion that one comes to know something, namely God, by means of one's feelings and sensations and this something is not reducible to them? The statement is not a low-claim one just because it is used to assert the existence of something. Whether this assertion is warranted and what exactly it amounts to is quite another question.

We are tempted to think that the religious statement must be of one sort or another. The truth is that *per impossible* it is both at once. The theologian must use it in both ways, and which way he is to emphasize at a particular time depends upon the circumstances of its use and most particularly the direction of our probings.

The statement "I seem to be having direct experience of God" is an eccentric one. It is eccentric not only because introspective announcements are unusual and because statements about God have a peculiar obscurity but for a further and more important reason. This eccentricity may be brought out by comparing this statement with others having the same form. A first formulation of this may be put in the following way. In reference to things other than our sensations of the moment knowledge is prior to seeming as if.

The statement "I seem to be looking directly at a chair" has a meaning only insofar as I already *know* what it is like to look directly at a chair. The statement "I seem to be listening to a choir," has a meaning only insofar as I already *know* what it is like to be listening to a choir. The assumption of knowledge in both these cases is one which all normal people are expected to be able to make and do in fact make.

The statement "I seem to be having direct experience of God" does not lend itself so easily to the criterion for meaning exemplified above, because if this statement has meaning only insofar as one already *knows* what it is like to have direct experience of God, the assumption of such knowledge is certainly not one which all normal people may be expected to be able to make or do in fact make. However, it may be said that the assumption of such knowledge as knowledge of what it is like to see a gorgon may not be made of all normal people and, therefore, the case of religious knowledge is in no peculiar position. This objection can be answered when we ask the question "How do we come to learn what it would be like to look directly at a chair, hear a choir, see a gorgon, have direct experience of God?"

It is not that there are no answers to the question concerning how we come to learn what it would be like to have direct experience of God. We are not left completely in the dark. Instead, the point is that the answers to this question are quite different from the answers to the questions concerning how we come to learn what it would be like to look directly at a chair, hear a choir, and see a gorgon. No one in our society has seen a gorgon, yet there are people who, by means of their specialized knowledge of mythical literature, may claim in a perfectly meaningful way that it now seems to them as if they were seeing a gorgon.

Let us imagine a society in which there are no chairs and no one knows anything at all about chairs. If we were to try to teach one of the members of this society what it would be like to see a chair and if we were not allowed to construct a chair, what might we do? We might look around at the furniture and say, "A chair is a kind of narrow settee. It is used to sit on." This would be a beginning. Then we might compare different settees as to which are more chairlike. We might draw pictures of chairs, make gestures with our hands showing the general shape and size of different sorts of chairs. If, on the following day, the person being instructed said, "I had a most unusual dream last night—I seemed to be looking directly at a chair," we should admit that his statement was closer in meaning to a similar one which we who have seen chairs might make than it would be to a similar one which another member might make who had no information or instruction or experience of chairs. We would insist that we had better knowledge of what it is to see a chair than has the instructed member of society who has still actually to see a chair. However, to know pictures of chairs is to know about chairs in a legitimate sense.

But let us now imagine a utopian society in which none of the members has ever been in the least sad or unhappy. If we were to try to teach one of the members of this society what it would be like to feel sad, how would we go about it? It can be said that giving definitions, no matter how ingenious, would be no help; drawing pictures of unhappy faces, no matter how well drawn, would be no help, so long as these measures failed to evoke a feeling of sadness in this person. Comparing the emotion of sadness with other emotions would be no help, because no matter how like other emotions (weariness and the like) are to sadness they fail just because they are not sadness. No, sadness is unique and incomparable.

To anyone who has no such awareness of sadness, leading, as it does, to the typically unhappy behavior of tears and drawn faces, it will be quite impossible to indicate what is meant. One can only hope to evoke it on the assumption that the capacity to become aware of sadness is part of normal human nature like the capacity to see light or to hear sound.

This last paragraph is a play upon a quotation given at the very beginning of this chapter. The following is the original version.

> To anyone who has no such awareness of God, leading as it does to the typically religious attitudes of obeisance and worship, it will be quite impossible to indicate what is meant; one can only hope to evoke it, on the assumption that the capacity to become aware of God is part of normal human nature like the capacity to see light or to hear sound.[13]

Consider the following statements:

(1) We are rejecting logical argument of any kind as the first chapter of our epistemology of aesthetics, or as representing the process by which beauty comes to be known.

(2) It is not as the result of an inference of any kind, whether explicit or implicit, whether laboriously excogitated or swiftly intuited, that the knowledge of beauty comes to us.

(3) To those who have never been confronted with the experience of seeing the beauty of something, argument is useless.

As these statements stand, they are plainly false. Professors of aesthetics and professional art critics often do help us to come to "knowledge of beauty" by all kinds of inference and arguments. They may, and often do, help us to come to a finer appreciation of beautiful things. Knowledge of the rules of perspective and understanding of an artist's departure from them is relevant to an aesthetic appreciation of his work.

However, it is possible to interpret these statements as true, and this is more important for our purpose. There is sense in saying that an art critic, who has vastly increased our aesthetic sensitivity and whose books of art criticism are the very best, may never have known beauty. If there are no signs of this critic ever having been stirred by any work of art, then no matter how subtle his analyses, there is sense in claiming that he has never been confronted with the experience of seeing the beauty of something. This sense just is that we may be determined not to say that a person has seen the beauty of something or has knowledge of beauty if he does not at some time have certain complex emotions and feelings which are typically associated with looking at paintings, hearing music, and reading poetry. To "know beauty" or to "see the beauty of something" here means, among other things, to have certain sorts of emotions and feelings.

The statements on aesthetics given above are a play on a quotation given

[13] Farmer, *Towards Belief in God*, p. 40.

at the beginning of this chapter. The following is the original version with the appropriate omissions and transpositions.

> We are rejecting logical argument of any kind as the first chapter of our theology or as representing the process by which God comes to be known. . . .
> It is not as the result of an inference of any kind, whether explicit or implicit, whether laboriously excogitated or swiftly intuited, that the knowledge of God's reality comes to us.
> . . . To those who have never been confronted with it [direct, personal encounter with God] argument is useless.[14]

As these statements stand they are plainly false. Professors of divinity and clergymen are expected to do what Baillie claims cannot be done.

However, it is possible to interpret these statements as true, and this is more important for our purpose. There is sense in saying that a theologian (who has vastly increased our religious sensitivity and whose books of theology are the very best) may never have known God. If there are no signs of this theologian's ever having been stirred by a religious ritual or act of worship, then, no matter how subtle his analyses, there is sense in claiming that he has never been confronted with God's personal Presence. This sense just is that we are determined not to say that a person has knowledge of God if he does not at some time have certain complex emotions and feelings which are associated with attending religious services, praying, and reading the Bible. To "know God" or to be confronted with God's "personal Presence" means, of necessity, having certain sorts of emotions and feelings.

In this section the analogy between seeing blue and experiencing God has been examined and found to be misleading. I shall not deal in this chapter with the connexion between what the believer expects from immortality and his religious belief. This peculiar kind of test or verification has special difficulties which will be treated in another chapter.

So far I have tried to indicate how statements concerning a certain alleged religious way of knowing betray a logic extraordinarily like that of statements concerning introspective and subjective ways of knowing. It is not my wish to go from a correct suggestion that the logic is *very, very* like to an incorrect suggestion that their logic is *just* like that of introspective and subjective statements, for, after all, such statements are logically in order.

I have argued that one cannot read off the existence of God from the existence of religious experience. Now, I must insist, in all charity, that *neither* can one read off the *non*-existence of God from the existence of religious experience.

In criticizing some of the foregoing argument, Mr. W. D. Glasgow claims,

> It is essential here for the defender of the religious way of knowing to assert that there are cases where a man *knows* himself to be experiencing an objec-

[14] Baillie, *Our Knowledge of God,* pp. 132, 143.

tive Deity, just as there are cases where he knows himself to be experiencing a subjective pain. Unless it is insisted that there is such a thing as *cognitive experience* in religion, Martin's assimilation of all religious existential statements to psychological statements (or what ought to be called psychological statements) becomes highly plausible. Indeed, even the phrase "*may* be objective" has no meaning, probably, for Martin, unless theoretically at least it is possible to find out or test whether religious experience *is* objective. The position is only saved, again, if we say that in some cases the agent himself anyhow *does* know.[15]

Glasgow cannot mean "a man *knows* himself to be experiencing an objective Deity" *in just the same way as* "he knows himself to be experiencing a subjective pain." One's pain is not a thing that exists independently of one's experience. I do not establish the existence of my pain on the basis of experience. There is nothing to establish beyond the experience. Presumably there is something to establish on the basis of religious experience, namely, the presence of God. When Glasgow says "there is such a thing as *cognitive experience* in religion" and "in some cases the agent himself anyhow *does* know," he must be read as saying that the presence of God is known on the basis of religious experience. That is, the presence of God is something over and above the experience itself. The model that Glasgow implies is that a cognitive experience is rather like a photograph of a friend: one can read off from the photograph that it is of that friend: and though this is a misleading model, there is something in it. If I am sitting at my desk and someone asks me if there is an ash tray on my desk, *all* that I have to do is have a look and say "Yes" or "No." But whether or not I know there is an ash tray on my desk is not to be read off simply from what my eyes at that moment told me. For if my eyes can tell me the truth they can tell me a lie, and the difference here would not be decided by what they tell. For me really to have seen and known there was an ash tray, other people must have been able to have seen it if they had looked. If I have only the testimony of my eyes and discount all else, then that testimony is mute concerning the existence of what is external. My eyes can tell me (in an hallucination) of the presence of an ash tray when there is no ash tray.

When someone uses the sentence "I see an ash tray" in such a way that he counts as relevant to its truth *only* his visual experience at the time, he is talking *only* about that experience, though the sentence has the form of making a statement about an ash tray. It does not help if he calls it a "cognitive experience" or if he says that he "anyhow *does* know" or if he says that his experience is "self-authenticating" or is a "direct encounter." We cannot allow a speaker any final authority in the account of how he is using his sentences. If such special dispensation were allowable, conceptual confusion would be rare indeed.

[15] W. D. Glasgow, "Knowledge of God," *Philosophy*, XXXII (1957), 236. This article is a criticism of my article "A Religious Way of Knowing," printed in Flew and MacIntyre, *New Essays in Philosophical Theology* (London: S. C. M. Press, 1955), pp. 76–95.

Similarly, I have argued, when someone uses the sentence "I have or have had direct experience of God" in such a way that he counts as relevant to its truth *only* his experience at the time, he is talking *only* about that experience, though the sentence has the form of making a statement about the presence of God, and neither does it help if he calls it a "cognitive experience."

From the fact that someone uses the sentence "I see an ash tray" so that he is talking *only* about his visual experience, nothing at all follows about whether or not he is actually seeing an ash tray in front of him. His *statement* may be only about his visual experience itself, and his actual *situation* may be that of seeing the ash tray. Also, from the fact that someone uses the sentence "I have or have had direct experience of God" in such a way that he is talking *only* about his experience at the time, nothing at all follows about whether or not he is actually experiencing the presence of a supernatural being. His *statement* may be only about his experience itself, and his actual *situation* may be that of experiencing the presence of a supernatural being.

The religious person will want, in what he says, to be able to distinguish between a "delusive" and a "veridical" experience of God. The experience should be due to the actual presence of God and not due only to a drug or to self-deception or to the action of Satan. Therefore he must use his sentence to refer to more than an experience that is, in principle, compatible with these and other similar causes.

What makes a form of experience a way of knowing? It is often suggested that the mystic who "sees" God is like a man (in a society of blind men) who sees colors. It is claimed that each has a form of experience and a way of knowing that others lack. Let us now work out this analogy. A society of blind men is told by one of its members that he has come to have a form of experience and a way of knowing by means of which he has been able to discover the existence of things not discoverable by ordinary experience. He says that these things have a *kind* of size (not just like size as it is felt by the blind) and a *kind* of shape (not just like shape as it is felt by the blind); he further says that these things are somehow "everywhere" and that they cannot expect to understand what these things are like and what he means by experiencing them unless they themselves have these experiences. He then tells them of a procedure by which they will be able to discover for themselves the existence of these things. He warns them that these things do not always reveal themselves when the procedure is carried out, but, if a person is sufficiently diligent and believes strongly enough in their existence, he will probably come to know by means of unique and incomparable experiences of the existence of these things.

Some people, with faith and diligence, submit themselves to the required procedure, and some of these are rewarded by a kind of experience they have not known before. Color shapes float before them—things that they cannot touch or feel and that are beyond the reach of their senses, and things that may be present to one of their group and not experienced by the others, things that may as well be everywhere as anywhere, since they are locatable only in the sense of being "before" each observer to whom they appear. These people cannot correlate this new form of experience with the rest of experience, they cannot touch or smell these "things." Indeed, they "see" visions, not things. Or rather these people have no way of *knowing* the existence of the things that may or may not exist over and above the momentary experiences. May these experiences all the same be "cognitive"? Yes and no. Yes, there may be something, they know not what, responsible for their having these experiences. No, their experiences are not a way of *knowing* about this something. For the experience of a colored shape that needs no corroboration by the experience of others similarly placed, and that is not related to one's other senses, is not in itself a way of knowing what in the world is responsible for this experience even if there is something beyond the condition of the "observer" that is so responsible. So far, even the people concerned have no *way of knowing* what more is involved than the fact of their experiencing momentary "visions."

I have not denied that the religious mystic may have experiences that others do not. Neither have I denied that there might be some external agency responsible for these experiences. What I have denied is that the mystic's possession of these experiences is in itself a way of knowing the existence or nature of such an agency.

The argument of this chapter lies in an area in which confusion is common. I shall consider two cases of such confusion especially relevant to what I have been saying.

> You are acquainted with the distinction between feeling and emotion. Feeling, such as pleasure or pain, is in itself a purely subjective experience; emotion implies an objective situation within which there is something which arouses the emotion, and towards which the emotion is directed. The Divine is, it would seem, first experienced in such a situation; and is initially apprehended solely and exclusively as that which arouses certain types of emotion. If the emotion be awe, then the Divine is so far apprehended as the awesome, what Otto has so helpfully entitled the numinous.[16]

There are two questionable assumptions here: first, that whether or not an experience refers to an objective state of affairs can be read off from the experience itself; second, that emotions *must* do so.

The second claim that an emotion as such implies an objective situation can be refuted very simply. My feeling of pleasure while watching a game of football is related to something in my environment, but my feeling of pleasure at a tune running through my head is not. My emotion of awe in the presence of a particularly magnificent race horse is related to something

---

[16] N. Kemp Smith, *Is Divine Existence Credible?*, British Academy Lecture (London: British Academy, 1931), p. 23.

in my environment, but my emotion of awe during a dream of a coronation service is not. Some people have aesthetic emotions aroused by the contemplation of mathematical proofs and theorems, and others have the emotion of fear toward ghosts and goblins.

In a criticism of the argument of the first part of this chapter (as originally published in "A Religious Way of Knowing," in *Mind*, October, 1952) Professor H. D. Lewis seems to be making the first claim, that a reference to an objective state of affairs can be read off from the experience itself.

> He [Martin] seems to think that the only claim to objectivity which an experience may have is that which is established by tests and checking procedures. A man's statement that he "seems to see a blue piece of paper" is thus said to be unassailable only because it is a "claim about his own state of mind." This I would doubt, for the colour expanse which we only seem to see is neither a mere appearance nor a state of mind. It is "out there before me" and real enough while I seem to see it, however many problems may be involved in distinguishing between it and physical entities. . . . "Having been stirred" by a religious ritual or act of worship, or having "certain sorts of emotions and feelings," is not the essential thing in religious experience; it is what we apprehend that comes first.[17]

However, "what we apprehend," if anything, is the whole problem and cannot "come first." Certainly, people have had special sorts of experience which incline them to claim with the greatest confidence that their experiences are of God. But whether the experiences are or are not of God is not to be decided by describing or having those experiences. For whether anything or nothing is apprehended by experiences is not to be read off from the experiences themselves. The presence of a piece of blue paper is not to be read off from my experience as of a piece of blue paper. Other things are relevant: What would a photograph reveal? Can I touch it? What do others see? It is only when I admit the relevance of such checking procedures that I can lay claim to apprehending the paper, and, indeed, the admission of the relevance of such procedures is what gives meaning to the assertion that I am apprehending the paper. *What I apprehend is the sort of thing that can be photographed, touched, and seen by others.*

It does not help when Lewis says,

> The colour expanse which we only seem to see is neither a mere appearance nor a state of mind. It is "out there before me" and real enough while I seem to see it, however many problems may be involved in distinguishing between it and physical entities.

Think now of a man who claims to see a blue piece of paper, and when we complain that we cannot, he replies, "Oh, it isn't the sort of thing that can be photographed, touched, or seen by others, but all the same, it is out there before me." Are we to think that he has come upon a special sort of object

[17] H. D. Lewis, "Philosophical Surveys X, The Philosophy of Religion, 1945–1952," *Philosophical Quarterly,* IV (July, 1954), p. 263.

that is nevertheless "out there" as are desks and tables and the rest of the furniture of the world? No, ontological reference is something to be earned. We earn the designation "out there" of a thing by allowing its presence to be determined by the procedures we all know. We cannot just *say* "out there" of it, and we cannot just *say* "apprehended" of God.

It can be objected, "But God is different, and we never meant that our experiences of God should be checked by procedures relevant to physical objects." Of course not, but what *sort* of checks are there then, so that we are left with more than the mere experiences whose existence even the atheist need not deny?

II

Yet checking procedures are not on all accounts in all ways irrelevant. As in all theological discourse concerning the status of religious experience there are many, many voices, and so far we have listened to too few.

A religious experience is not just an ineffable, indescribable something that comes and goes unbidden and amenable to no criteria of identity. At least, the mystics seldom describe it in this way. There are certain steps one can take to bring about such experiences, and the experiences are describable within limits, and they leave certain kinds of identifiable aftereffects.

Alvarez de Paz and other mystics have emphasized the importance of practicing austerities, conquering the flesh, and mortifying the body.

Of course, this training of the body is not sufficient. The mind must be trained as well. To have a vision of the Holy Virgin one must be acquainted with the basic facts of "Christ's birth and life and death." To have the highest mystical apprehension of the Trinity, as did St. Teresa, one must have some elementary theological training.

Nor is bodily and intellectual training enough, for there must be moral and emotional training as well. The commandment to love one another was given not only to lead us to peace and brotherhood on earth but also to change our hearts so that we might see God.

Yet all of these may not be enough, for it is possible one should train oneself most assiduously in all of these ways and still not have truly religious experience. This possibility is characterized by saying that finally the favor and grace of God are required.

The paradoxical and negative ways in which mystics most often describe their experiences may seem, at first, unsatisfactory. But it helps to consider how similar sorts of descriptions are employed outside the religious context. One might say of one's emotion at a particular time that one felt both love and hate toward someone. This would be understood as a description of a complex emotion that most of us have experienced. And the paradoxical expression is not reducible to "in some ways love, in other ways hate," because it refers not only to different patterns of behaving and feeling but also to a particular feeling at a particular moment.

Alvarez de Paz gives a particularly sharp description that must strike even the most sceptical reader as in no way obscure or evasive.

> One perceives no representation of the face or the body, yet one knows with greater certainty than if one saw it with one's eyes that the person (Jesus Christ or the Blessed Virgin) is present on one's right hand or in one's heart. . . . It is as if, in darkness, one should feel at once that someone is at one's side, knowing that he has goodwill and not enmity towards you; while one remains absolutely ignorant whether it is a man or a woman, young or old, handsome or ugly, standing or seated.[18]

It would be wrong for us to legislate against the mystic's claim that his experience is not sensory. For in a nonreligious context there may be a parallel. Many of us have felt or experienced the presence of some loved one dead or living but distant. (Of course, we do not tend to think that the person is in any way *actually* present unless the person is dead.) Certainly in such cases we do not see or hear the person. It is not even *as if* we heard or saw the person. Making the parallel even closer to the mystical, we do not even have to have any kind of mental image of the loved one. Neither is the presence felt as being in any specific place. The very subtle feelings and emotions typically directed to this one person and no other are now aroused as once they were by this person alone. The unique love and regard this person showed us, we, as it were, receive again. And we can feel ashamed at having done things of which the loved one would disapprove. And so we can feel guided where there is no guide and loved where the lover is dead. The emotion is in shadow felt but is no less real for that.

A child may read of a fairy-story giant who eats the children who do not think he is real and even some who do. He is described in detail (perhaps there is even a picture), and his hatred of children is made too clear. The child may have a bad dream about the giant. Or he may, as in the case above, just feel the giant's presence in no very localized place yet somewhere near. That is, the child reads the story, comes to feel a kind of fear toward the giant, and hates him in a way that others do not. Then the child, hearing and seeing nothing, may, in the dark, feel that fear and sense that hate so strongly that he will claim, even when the light is turned on and in spite of the most tender parental reassurance, that the giant had been in the room. That is, the experience of the child is such that he is left with a certitude which he considers the giant alone could give.

In order to have such an experience, then, with all of the sense of reality and conviction that it carries, it is not necessary that the being whose presence is so felt should ever have existed.

As children we are taught to love Christ in a very special way, and we are taught of Christ's very special love for us. Christ, as a person, is made extremely real to us. That we cannot see or hear him takes very little from his

---

[18] Quoted in Joseph Marechal, *Studies in the Psychology of the Mystics* (London: Burns Oates & Washbourne, 1927), p. 110.

reality. He was once seen and heard, and we are told so much of his life and actions and visible love that we are apt to feel that we know him more clearly than we do any other historical person. As children (or, indeed, as adults) we are encouraged in this feeling by being told that he is somehow, if not actually somewhere, alive. We are told that God loves us as Christ loves us, and we learn that Christ and God are somehow One. So we know roughly how we *should* feel in God's presence. We have as reference countless stories of how others have felt. These experiences are very different, but they form a kind of family. At one extreme there is a visible vision, and at the other extreme there is almost a kind of unconscious trance.

> Let us now speak of the sign which proves the prayer of union to have been genuine. As you have seen, God then deprives the soul of all its senses that he may the better imprint in it true wisdom; it neither sees, hears, nor understands anything while this state lasts. . . . God visits the soul in a manner which prevents its doubting, on returning to itself, that it dwelt in him and that he was within it. . . . But, you may ask, how can a person who is incapable of sight and hearing see or know these things? I do not say that she saw it at the time, but that she perceives it clearly afterwards, not by any vision but by a certitude which remains in the heart which God alone could give. . . . If we did not see it, how can we feel so sure of it? That I do not know: it is the work of the Almighty and I am certain that what I say is the fact. I maintain that a soul which does not feel this assurance has not been united to God entirely, but only by one of its powers, or has received one of the many other favours God is accustomed to bestow on men.[19]

Yet, with all of this, it could be argued that all that has been accomplished is a description of a class of experiences and of methods of obtaining and recognizing them. Their ontological reference has still to be established. It could be dogmatically asserted that these experiences by definition come only through the grace of God, but this would be no more than a way of stamping one's foot and insisting on, rather than arguing for, that reference. St. Teresa once again is of help. She was plagued during her lifetime not by doubts about the character of her experiences but about their source. Was she perhaps being subtly deceived by Satan? She was not at a loss to provide a kind of settlement procedure.

> I could not believe that Satan, if he wished to deceive me, could have recourse to means so adverse to his purpose as this, of rooting out my faults and implanting virtues and spiritual strength: for I saw clearly that I had become another person by means of these visions. . . . Neither the imagination nor the evil one could represent what leaves such peace, calm, and good fruits in the soul, and particularly the following three graces of a very high order. The first of these is a perception of the greatness of God, which becomes clearer to us as we witness more of it. Secondly, we gain self-knowledge and humility as we see how creatures so base as ourselves in

---

[19] St. Teresa, *Interior Castle* (London: Thomas Baker, 1930), pp. 91–93.

comparison with the Creator of such wonders, have dared to offend Him in the past or venture to gaze on Him now. The third grace is a contempt of all earthly things unless they are consecrated to the service of so great a God.[20]

But now, what more has really been accomplished by this? To say that the source of these experiences is God and not Satan in the absence of further criteria reduces to saying that these experiences have certain sorts of profound effects upon one's character, attitudes, and behavior. And why should an atheist deny any of this? If there is more that cannot be so reduced and if it is inconsistent with the claims of an atheist, it still remains to be said.

Unlike the first section of this chapter, this section has been concerned with views (those of the great Catholic mystics) in which statements about religious experience are not employed as in any way arguments for, or evidence of, the existence of God. The mystics are convinced on other grounds of the existence of God. Religious experience, then, is conceived by them as a way of coming to know better the object of their worship, whose existence is proved or assumed independent of that experience.

This conservative estimate of the status of religious experience in theology is not, however, necessarily safe from censure. The conceptual weight is shifted from the experience to the previously established or assumed notion of the object of the experience. In the previous chapter difficulties were found in typical notions of the qualities of God. No Catholic theologian and few Protestant theologians would claim that religious experience could resolve problems of this conceptual sort.

C. D. BROAD
The Appeal to Religious Experience

. . . Founders of religions and saints, e.g., often claim to have been in direct contact with God, to have seen and spoken with Him, and so on. An ordinary religious man would certainly not make any such claim, though he might say that he had had experiences which assured him of the existence and presence of God. So the first thing that we have to notice is that capacity for religious experience is in certain respects like an ear for music.

THE APPEAL TO RELIGIOUS EXPERIENCE   From *Religion, Philosophy and Psychical Research* by C. D. Broad. Reprinted by permission of Routledge & Kegan Paul Ltd.

[20] *Ibid.*, p. 171.

There are a few people who are unable to recognize and distinguish the simplest tune. But they are in a minority, like the people who have absolutely no kind of religious experience. Most people have some slight appreciation of music. But the differences of degree in this respect are enormous, and those who have not much gift for music have to take the statements of accomplished musicians very largely on trust. Let us, then, compare tone-deaf persons to those who have no recognizable religious experience at all; the ordinary followers of a religion to men who have some taste for music but can neither appreciate the more difficult kinds nor compose; highly religious men and saints to persons with an exceptionally fine ear for music who may yet be unable to compose it; and the founders of religions to great musical composers, such as Bach and Beethoven.

This analogy is, of course, incomplete in certain important respects. Religious experience raises three problems, which are different though closely interconnected. (i) What is the *psychological analysis* of religious experience? Does it contain factors which are present also in certain experiences which are not religious? Does it contain any factor which never occurs in any other kind of experience? If it contains no such factor, but is a blend of elements each of which can occur separately or in non-religious experiences, its psychological peculiarity must consist in the characteristic way in which these elements are blended in it. Can this peculiar structural feature of religious experience be indicated and described? (ii) What are the *genetic and causal conditions* of the existence of religious experience? Can we trace the origin and development of the disposition to have religious experiences (*a*) in the human race, and (*b*) in each individual? Granted that the disposition is present in nearly all individuals at the present time, can we discover and state the variable conditions which call it into activity on certain occasions and leave it in abeyance on others? (iii) Part of the content of religious experience is alleged knowledge or well-founded belief about the nature of reality, e.g., that we are dependent on a being who loves us and whom we ought to worship, that values are somehow conserved in spite of the chances and changes of the material world at the mercy of which they seem *prima facie* to be, and so on. Therefore there is a third problem. Granted that religious experience exists, that it has such-and-such a history and conditions, that it seems vitally important to those who have it, and that it produces all kinds of effects which would not otherwise happen, is it *veridical*? Are the claims to knowledge or well-founded belief about the nature of reality, which are an integral part of the experience, *true or probable*? Now, in the case of musical experience, there are analogies to the psychological problem and to the genetic or causal problem, but there is no analogy to the epistemological problem of validity. For, so far as I am aware, no part of the content of musical experience is alleged knowledge about the nature of reality; and therefore no question of its being veridical or delusive can arise.

Since both musical experience and religious experience certainly exist, any theory of the universe which was incompatible with their existence would be false, and any theory which failed to show the connexion between their existence and the other facts about reality would be inadequate. So far the two kinds of experience are in exactly the same position. But a theory which answers to the condition that it allows of the *existence* of religious experience and indicates the *connexion* between its existence and other facts about reality may leave the question as to its *validity* quite unanswered. Or, alternatively, it may throw grave doubt on its cognitive claims, or else it may tend to support them. Suppose, e.g., that it could be shown that religious experience contains no elements which are not factors in other kinds of experience. Suppose further it could be shown that this particular combination of factors tends to originate and to be activated only under certain conditions which are known to be very commonly productive of false beliefs held with strong conviction. Then a satisfactory answer to the questions of psychological analysis and causal antecedents would have tended to answer the epistemological question of validity in the negative. On the other hand, it might be that the only theory which would satisfactorily account for the origin of the religious disposition and for the occurrence of actual religious experiences under certain conditions was a theory which allowed some of the cognitive claims made by religious experience to be true or probable. Thus the three problems, though entirely distinct from each other, may be very closely connected; and it is the existence of the third problem in connexion with religious experience which puts it, for the present purpose, in a different category from musical experience.

In spite of this essential difference the analogy is not to be despised, for it brings out at least one important point. If a man who had no ear for music were to give himself airs on that account, and were to talk *de haut en bas* about those who can appreciate music and think it highly important, we should regard him, not as an advanced thinker, but as a self-satisfied Philistine. And, even if he did not do this but only propounded theories about the nature and causation of musical experience, we might think it reasonable to feel very doubtful whether his theories would be adequate or correct. In the same way, when persons without religious experience regard themselves as being *on that ground* superior to those who have it, their attitude must be treated as merely silly and offensive. Similarly, any theories about religious experience constructed by persons who have little or none of their own should be regarded with grave suspicion. (For that reason it would be unwise to attach very much weight to anything that the present writer may say on this subject.)

On the other hand, we must remember that the possession of a great capacity for religious experience, like the possession of a great capacity for musical appreciation and composition, is no guarantee of high general intelligence. A man may be a saint or a magnificent musician and yet have very little common sense, very little power of accurate introspection or of seeing causal connexions, and scarcely any capacity for logical criticism. He may also be almost as ignorant about other aspects of reality as the non-musical or non-religious man is about musical or religious experience. If such a man starts to theorize about music or religion, his theories may be quite as absurd, though in a different way, as those made by persons who are devoid of musical or religious experience. Fortunately it happens that some religious mystics of a high order have been extremely good at introspecting and describing their own experiences. And some highly religious persons have had very great critical and philosophical abilities. St. Teresa is an example of the first, and St. Thomas Aquinas of the second.

Now I think it must be admitted that, if we compare and contrast the statements made by religious mystics of various times, races, and religions, we find a common nucleus combined with very great differences of detail. Of course the interpretations which they have put on their experiences are much more varied than the experiences themselves. It is obvious that the interpretations will depend in a large measure on the traditional religious beliefs in which various mystics have been brought up. I think that such traditions probably act in two different ways.

(i) The tradition no doubt affects the theoretical interpretation of experiences which would have taken place even if the mystic had been brought up in a different tradition. A feeling of unity with the rest of the universe will be interpreted very differently by a Christian who has been brought up to believe in a personal God and by a Hindu mystic who has been trained in a quite different metaphysical tradition.

(ii) The traditional beliefs, on the other hand, probably determine many of the details of the experience itself. A Roman Catholic mystic may have visions of the Virgin and the saints, whilst a Protestant mystic pretty certainly will not.

Thus the relations between the experiences and the traditional beliefs are highly complex. Presumably the outlines of the belief are determined by the experience. Then the details of the belief are fixed for a certain place and period by the special peculiarities of the experiences had by the founder of a certain religion. These beliefs then become traditional in that religion. Thenceforth they in part determine the details of the experiences had by subsequent mystics of that religion, and still more do they determine the interpretations which these mystics will put upon their experiences. Therefore, when a set of religious beliefs has once been established, it no doubt tends to produce experiences which can plausibly be taken as evidence for it. If it is a tradition in a certain religion that one can communicate with saints, mystics of that religion will seem to see and to talk with saints in their mystical visions; and this fact will be taken as further evidence for the belief that one can communicate with saints.

Much the same double process of causation takes place in sense-perception. On the one hand, the beliefs and expectations which we have at any moment largely determine what *interpretation* we shall put on a certain sensation which we should in any case have had then. On the other hand, our beliefs and expectations do to some extent determine and modify some of the sensible characteristics of the *sensa themselves*. When I am thinking only of diagrams a certain visual stimulus may produce a sensation of a sensibly flat sensum; but a precisely similar stimulus may produce a sensation of a sensibly solid sensum when I am thinking of solid objects.

Such explanations, however, plainly do not account for the first origin of religious beliefs, or for the features which are common to the religious experiences of persons of widely different times, races, and traditions.

Now, when we find that there are certain experiences which, though never very frequent in a high degree of intensity, have happened in a high degree among a few men at all times and places; and when we find that, in spite of differences in detail which we can explain, they involve certain fundamental conditions which are common and peculiar to them; two alternatives are open to us. (i) We may suppose that these men are in contact with an aspect of reality which is not revealed to ordinary persons in their everyday experience. And we may suppose that the characteristics which they agree in ascribing to reality on the basis of these experiences probably do belong to it. Or (ii) we may suppose that they are all subject to a delusion from which other men are free. In order to illustrate these alternatives it will be useful to consider three partly analogous cases, two of which are real and the third imaginary.

(*a*) Most of the detailed facts which biologists tell us about the minute structure and changes in cells can be perceived only by persons who have had a long training in the use of the microscope. In this case we believe that the agreement among trained microscopists really does correspond to facts which untrained persons cannot perceive. (*b*) Persons of all races who habitually drink alcohol to excess eventually have perceptual experiences in which they seem to themselves to see snakes or rats crawling about their rooms or beds. In this case we believe that this agreement among drunkards is merely a uniform hallucination. (*c*) Let us now imagine a race of beings who can walk about and touch things but cannot see. Suppose that eventually a few of them developed the power of sight. All that they might tell their still blind friends about colour would be wholly unintelligible to and unverifiable by the latter. But they would also be able to tell their blind friends a great deal about what the latter would feel if they were to walk in certain directions. These statements would be verified. This would not, of course, *prove* to the blind ones that the unintelligible statements about colour correspond to certain aspects of the world which they cannot perceive. But it would show that the seeing persons had a source of additional information about matters which the blind ones could understand and test for themselves. It would not be unreasonable then for the blind ones to believe that probably the seeing ones are also able to perceive other aspects of reality which they are describing correctly when they make their unintelligible statements containing colour-names. The question then is whether it is reasonable to regard the agreement between the experiences of religious mystics as more like the agreement among trained microscopists about the minute structure of cells, or as more like the agreement among habitual drunkards about the infestation of their rooms by pink rats or snakes, or as more like the agreement about colours which the seeing men would express in their statements to the blind men.

Why do we commonly believe that habitual excess of alcohol is a cause of a uniform delusion and not a source of additional information? The main reason is as follows. The things which drunkards claim to perceive are not fundamentally different in kind from the things that other people perceive. We have all seen rats and snakes, though the rats have generally been grey or brown and not pink. Moreover the drunkard claims that the rats and snakes which he sees are literally present in his room and on his bed, in the same sense in which his bed is in his room and his quilt is on his bed. Now we may fairly argue as follows. Since these are the sort of things which we could see if they were there, the fact that we cannot see them makes it highly probable that they are not there. Again, we know what kinds of perceptible effect would generally follow from the presence in a room of such things as rats or snakes. We should expect fox-terriers or mongooses to show traces of excitement, cheese to be nibbled, corn to disappear from bins, and so on. We find that no such effects are observed in the bedrooms of persons suffering from *delirium tremens*. It therefore seems reasonable to conclude that the agreement among drunkards is a sign, not of a revelation, but of a delusion.

Now the assertions in which religious mystics agree are not such that they conflict with what we can perceive with our senses. They are about the structure and organization of the world as a whole and about the relations of men to the rest of it. And they have so little in common with the facts of daily life that there is not much chance of direct collision. I think that there is only one important point on which there is conflict. Nearly all mystics seem to be agreed that time and change and unchanging duration are unreal or extremely superficial, whilst these seem to plain men to be the most fundamental features of the world. But we must admit, on the one hand, that these temporal characteristics present very great philosophical difficulties and puzzles when we reflect upon them. On the other hand, we may well suppose that the mystic finds it impossible to state clearly in ordinary language what it is that he experiences about the facts which underlie the appearance of time and change and duration. Therefore it is not difficult to allow that what we experience as the temporal aspect of reality corresponds in some sense to certain facts, and yet that these facts appear to us in so distorted a form in our ordinary experience that a person who sees them more accurately and directly might refuse to apply temporal names to them.

Let us next consider why we feel fairly certain that the agreement among trained microscopists about the minute structure of cells expresses an objective fact, although we cannot get similar experiences. One reason is that we have learned enough, from simpler cases of visual perception, about the laws of optics to know that the arrangement of lenses in a microscope is such that it will reveal minute structure, which is otherwise invisible, and will not simply create optical delusions. Another reason is that we know of other cases in which trained persons can detect things which untrained people will overlook, and that in many cases the existence of these things can be verified by indirect methods. Probably most of us have experienced such results of training in our own lives.

Now religious experience is not in nearly such a strong position as this. We do not know much about the laws which govern its occurrence and determine its variations. No doubt there are certain standard methods of training and meditation which tend to produce mystical experiences. These have been elaborated to some extent by certain Western mystics and to a very much greater extent by Eastern Yogis. But I do not think that we can see here, as we can in the case of microscopes and the training which is required to make the best use of them, any conclusive reason why these methods should produce veridical rather than delusive experiences. Uniform methods of training and meditation would be likely to produce more or less similar experiences, whether these experiences were largely veridical or wholly delusive.

Is there any analogy between the facts about religious experience and the fable about the blind men some of whom gained the power of sight? It might be said that many ideals of conduct and ways of life, which we can all recognize now to be good and useful, have been introduced into human history by the founders of religions. These persons have made actual ethical discoveries which others can afterwards recognize to be true. It might be said that this is at least roughly analogous to the case of the seeing men telling the still blind men of facts which the latter could and did verify for themselves. And it might be said that this makes it reasonable for us to attach some weight to what founders of religions tell us about things which we cannot understand or verify for ourselves; just as it would have been reasonable for the blind men to attach some weight to the unintelligible statements which the seeing men made to them about colours.

I think that this argument deserves a certain amount of respect, though I should find it hard to estimate how much weight to attach to it. I should be inclined to sum up as follows. When there is a nucleus of agreement between the experiences of men in different places, times, and traditions, and when they all tend to put much the same kind of interpretation on the cognitive content of these experiences, it is reasonable to ascribe this agreement to their all being in contact with a certain objective aspect of reality *unless* there be some positive reason to think otherwise. The practical postulate which we go upon everywhere else is to treat cognitive claims as veridical unless there be some positive reason to think them delusive. This, after all, is our only guarantee for believing that ordinary sense-perception is veridical. We cannot *prove* that what people agree in perceiving really exists independently of them; but we do always assume that ordinary waking sense-perception is veridical unless we can produce some positive ground for thinking that it is delusive in any given case. I think it would be inconsistent to treat the experiences of religious mystics on different principles. So far as they agree they should be provisionally accepted as veridical unless there be some positive ground for thinking that they are not. So the next question is whether there is any positive ground for holding that they are delusive.

There are two circumstances which have been commonly held to cast doubt on the cognitive claims of religious and mystical experience. (i) It is alleged that founders of religions and saints have nearly always had certain neuropathic symptoms or certain bodily weaknesses, and that these would be likely to produce delusions. Even if we accept the premises, I do not think that this is a very strong argument. (*a*) It is equally true that many founders of religions and saints have exhibited great endurance and great power of organization and business capacity which would have made them extremely successful and competent in secular affairs. There are very few offices in the cabinet or in the highest branches of the civil service which St. Thomas Aquinas could not have held with conspicuous success. I do not, of course, regard this as a positive reason *for* accepting the metaphysical doctrines which saints and founders of religions have based on their experiences; but it is relevant as a *rebuttal* of the argument which we are considering. (*b*) Probably very few people of extreme genius in science or art are perfectly normal mentally or physically, and some of them are very crazy and eccentric indeed. Therefore it would be rather surprising if persons of religious genius were completely normal, whether their experiences be veridical or delusive. (*c*) Suppose, for the sake of argument, that there is an aspect of the world which remains altogether outside the ken of ordinary persons in their daily life. Then it seems very likely that some degree of mental and physical abnormality would be a necessary condition for getting sufficiently loosened from the objects of ordinary sense-perception to come into cognitive contact with this aspect of reality. Therefore the fact that those persons who claim to have this peculiar kind of cognition generally exhibit certain mental and physical abnormalities is rather what might be anticipated if their claims were true. One might need to be slightly 'cracked' in order to have some peep-holes into the super-sensible world. (*d*) If mystical experience were veridical, it seems quite likely that it would *produce* abnormalities of behaviour in those who had it strongly. Let us suppose, for the sake of argument, that those who have religious experience are in frequent contact with an aspect of reality of which most men get only rare and faint glimpses. Then such persons are, as it were, living in two worlds, while the ordinary man is living in only one of them. Or, again, they might be compared to a man who has to conduct his life with one ordinary eye and another of a telescopic kind. Their behaviour may be appropriate to the aspect of reality which they alone perceive and think all-important; but, for that very reason, it may be inappropriate to those other aspects of reality which are all that most men perceive or judge to be important and on which all our social institutions and conventions are built.

(ii) A second reason which is commonly alleged for doubt about the claims of religious experience is the following. It is said that such experience always originates from and remains mixed with certain other factors, e.g., sexual emotion, which are such that experiences and beliefs that arise from them are very likely to be delusive. I think that there are a good many confusions on this point, and it will be worth while to begin by indicating some of them.

When people say that B 'originated from' A, they are liable to confuse at least three different kinds of connexion between A and B. (i) It might be that A is a necessary but insufficient condition of the existence of B. (ii) It might be that A is a necessary and sufficient condition of the existence of B. Or (iii) it might be that B simply *is* A in a more complex and disguised form. Now, when there is in fact evidence only for the first kind of connexion, people are very liable to jump to the conclusion that there is the third kind of connexion. It may well be the case, e.g., that no one who was incapable of strong sexual desires and emotions could have anything worth calling religious experience. But it is plain that the possession of a strong capacity for sexual experience is not a *sufficient* condition of having religious experience; for we know that the former quite often exists in persons who show hardly any trace of the latter. But, even if it could be shown that a strong capacity for sexual desire and emotion is *both* necessary and sufficient to produce religious experience, it would not follow that the latter is just the former in disguise. In the first place, it is not at all easy to discover the exact meaning of this metaphorical phrase when it is applied to psychological topics. And, if we make use of physical analogies, we are not much helped. A mixture of oxygen and hydrogen in the presence of a spark is necessary and sufficient to produce water accompanied by an explosion. But water accompanied by an explosion is not a mixture of oxygen and hydrogen and a spark 'in a disguised form', whatever that may mean.

Now I think that the present rather vaguely formulated objection to the validity of the claims of religious experience might be stated somewhat as follows. 'In the individual religious experience originates from, and always remains mixed with, sexual desires and emotions. The other generative factor of it is the religious tradition of the society in which he lives, the teachings of his parents, nurses, schoolmasters, etc. In the race religious experience originated from a mixture of false beliefs about nature and man, irrational fears, sexual and other impulses, and so on. Thus the religious tradition arose from beliefs which we now recognize to have been false and from emotions which we now recognize to have been irrelevant and misleading. It is now drilled into children by those who are in authority over them at a time of life when they are intellectually and emotionally at much the same stage as the primitive savages among whom it originated. It is, therefore, readily accepted, and it determines beliefs and emotional dispositions which persist long after the child has grown up and acquired more adequate knowledge of nature and of himself.'

Persons who use this argument might admit that it does not definitely *prove* that religious beliefs are false and groundless. False beliefs and irrational fears in our remote ancestors *might* conceivably be the origin of true beliefs and of an appropriate feeling of awe and reverence in ourselves. And, if sexual desires and emotions be an essential condition and constituent of religious experience, the experience *may* nevertheless be veridical in important respects. We might merely have to rewrite one of the beatitudes and say 'Blessed are the *im*pure in heart, for they shall see God'. But, although it is logically possible that such causes should produce such effects, it would be said that they are most unlikely to do so. They seem much more likely to produce false beliefs and misplaced emotions.

It is plain that this argument has considerable plausibility. But it is worth while to remember that modern science has almost as humble an ancestry as contemporary religion. If the primitive witch-smeller is the spiritual progenitor of the Archbishop of Canterbury, the primitive rain-maker is equally the spiritual progenitor of the Cavendish Professor of Physics. There has obviously been a gradual refinement and purification of religious beliefs and concepts in the course of history, just as there has been in the beliefs and concepts of science. Certain persons of religious genius, such as some of the Hebrew prophets and the founders of Christianity and of Buddhism, do seem to have introduced new ethico-religious concepts and beliefs which have won wide acceptance, just as certain men of scientific genius, such as Galileo, Newton, and Einstein, have done in the sphere of science. It seems somewhat arbitrary to count this process as a continual approximation to true knowledge of the material aspect of the world in the case of science, and to refuse to regard it as at all similar in the case of religion. Lastly, we must remember that all of us have accepted the current common-sense and scientific view of the material world on the authority of our parents, nurses, masters, and companions at a time when we had neither the power nor the inclination to criticize it. And most of us accept, without even understanding, the more recondite doctrines of contemporary physics simply on the authority of those whom we have been taught to regard as experts.

On the whole, then, I do not think that what we know of the conditions under which religious beliefs and emotions have arisen in the life of the individual and the race makes it reasonable to think that they are *specially* likely to be delusive or misdirected. At any rate any argument which starts from that basis and claims to reach such a conclusion will need to be very carefully handled if its destructive effects are to be confined within the range contemplated by its users. It is reasonable to think that the concepts and beliefs of even the most perfect religions known to us are extremely inadequate to the facts which they express; that they are highly confused and are mixed up with a great deal of positive error and sheer nonsense; and that, if the human race goes on and continues to have religious experiences and to reflect on them, they will be altered and improved almost out of recognition. But all this could be said, *mutatis mutandis,* of scientific concepts and theories. The claim of any particular religion or sect to have complete or final truth on these subjects seems to me to be too ridiculous to be worth a moment's consideration. But the opposite extreme of holding that the whole religious experience of mankind is a gigantic system of pure delusion seems to me to be almost (though not quite) as far-fetched.

WALTER STACE
The Nature of Mysticism

. . . It is quite certain that mere agreement or unanimity as regards experiences is not enough to establish objectivity since many illusions, such as double vision or the yellow appearance of objects to one who has swallowed santonin, are quite universal. This was the argument by which the sceptic sought to defeat the case for mystical objectivity. And it is plainly a valid objection. But the sceptic in pointing it out seems also to have defeated himself if it is a part of his claim that universal verifiability is sufficient to prove the objectivity of a sense experience. For he has shown that there are many illusions which are universally verifiable.

But the conclusion which we ought to draw is not difficult to see. It is that unanimity, even universal agreement of experiences, though it may be a *part* of what constitutes objectivity, is not the *whole* of what constitutes it, either in the case of mystical experience or in that of sense experience. There must be some other condition, some x, which is required, as well as universality, to make an experience objective. Therefore if we wish to enquire whether the claim to mystical objectivity is valid there are two steps which we must take.

THE NATURE OF MYSTICISM   From the book, *Mysticism and Philosophy,* by Walter T. Stace. Copyright, ©, 1960, by W. T. Stace. Reprinted by permission of J. B. Lippincott Company and The Macmillan Company, London and Basingstoke.

We must first discover what x is. And then we must enquire whether x is possessed by mystical experience. For the argument of the last few paragraphs, in which we expounded the reply which the proponent of mystical objectivity could give to the criticism of the sceptic, has shown satisfactorily, I think, that mystical experience does possess the requisite kind and degree of universality. The case for mystical objectivity therefore now wholly depends on whether x is a characteristic of it or not.

The view which I advocate is that x is *order*. An experience is objective when it is orderly both in its internal and its external relations. An experience is subjective when it is disorderly either in its internal or its external relations.[1] Being public is *one* of the characteristics of being orderly, whereas being private is *one* of the marks of the disorderly. Publicity is therefore *part* of the definition of objectivity. But objectivity can only be completely and satisfactorily defined in terms of the much wider concept of order.

By order I mean law, that is to say, regularity of succession, repetition of pattern, "constant conjunction" of specifiable items. Order is thus a quite general concept of which what we call nature or the natural order of our daily world is a particular instance. Strictly speaking, objectivity is to be defined in terms of the general concept of order and not in terms of our particular world order. It is possible to conceive that there is somewhere a systematic order of events of which the laws would be quite different from those with which we are familiar. There might be a universe in which universal gravitation would be replaced by universal mutual repulsion of objects, in which heat invariably produced the solidification of water and cold invariably produced boiling. This could be an instance of order. An experience in such a universe which was orderly in terms of that kind of order would be objective in that order.

But, if we confine ourselves to speaking here only of the world of our daily experience, we may observe that the objectively real world is what we call the order of nature, i.e., the system of orderly events stretching in a time series into a past to which there is no discernible beginning and which, it is presumed, will extend indefinitely into the future. Those of our experiences which are orderly in terms of this world order are called objective. Those which are disorderly in the sense that, either internally or externally, they infringe the laws of this world order are called subjective and are labeled dreams or hallucinations. (There is of course a distinction between dreams

---

[1] This view is also at least implicit in what Professor Broad says about the snakes and rats seen by the drunkard. For he points out that we brand these creatures as hallucinatory because they do not produce the effects which are always produced by such animals if they are real. If they were real, we should expect fox terriers or mongooses to show traces of excitement, cheese to be nibbled, corn to disappear from bins, and so on. We find that no such effects are observed in the bedrooms of persons suffering from delirium tremens. (Broad, *op. cit.,* p. 195.) In short, the rat and snake experience is disorderly in its external relations. [Broad's discussion is found on p. 307-17 in *Philosophy of Religion: Selected Readings.*]

and hallucinations, but the nature of this distinction does not concern us because both are in the same sense subjective, i.e., in the sense just explained.) It must be recognized that the concept of a world order is not and could not be the product of a single mind and could not be erected on the basis of a single individual's experience. It is a product of all human experiences stretching back into a remote past. That is why publicity, the capacity to be shared by all persons, the possibility of being publicly verified, is a part, but only a part, of the criterion of objectivity. This will have to be more fully explained.

Hallucinations and dreams are always disorderly; that is, they infringe the laws of nature, in one or both of two ways. What happens in a dream may *in itself* be a breach of natural law. Thus a real, objective kettle put on the fire always boils. But a dream-kettle put on the fire might freeze. We say "anything might happen in a dream," meaning that a dream does not have to obey natural laws while an objective experience does. If someone asserted he had seen a kettle of water freeze when it was put on the fire, we might say "you must have been dreaming." This is an example of an experience which is condemned as subjective because it is disorderly in its internal relations or within its own borders.

But sometimes a dream may be perfectly orderly within itself and commit no breaches of natural law. But in that case it will be found that a breach of natural law occurs in the external relations of the dream experience with the other areas of experience which immediately surround it and in the matrix of which it is embedded. The breach occurs at the edges of the dream, so to speak, at the boundaries between dreaming and waking. For instance, I go to bed in my house in the United States. I dream that I am walking down a familiar London street and that I meet my brother and converse with him. Then I wake up and find myself once more in my bed in America. Nothing within the dream was in any way disorderly. The street, the walking, the conversation with my brother—all could have happened and were perfectly natural. But what could *not* have happened, and would if it did happen involve breaches of natural law, is that I should pass from my bed in America to a London street without crossing the intervening distance and then come back again in the same supernatural way. Of course it might be possible to explain otherwise than by the hypothesis of dream some experience—though hardly the whole dream experience just mentioned—in which I seemed to myself to pass suddenly from my bed in America to London. I might have fallen alseep in America, gone into a cataleptic trance, been transported unconscious across the Atlantic, and awakened in London, and then in another cataleptic trance have been brought back to America! But when we say that this did not happen, but that I had a dream, part of our *meaning* is that what seemed to happen was not actually explained by any such series of natural and orderly events.

To complete the theory it is necessary only to show the role which publicity, or universal agreement of experiences, plays in it and why such agreement, though it is a part of the criterion of objectivity, is not by itself sufficient to ensure it. According to our view, to say that an experience is objective means that it is orderly, and it can only be this if it is part of the systematic order of the world. Any other experience will be found to be disorderly either internally or in its external relations or both. Now the world order, since it is a series of events extending from the indefinite past into the indefinite future, transcends the experiences of any single mind. The evidence of it is the evidence of the whole human race. There is only one world order (so far as we know), namely, that in the experiencing of which all normal human beings participate—that on which, so to speak, all windows open. There are not a multitude of orderly systems of events, one for each individual. Therefore an experience which is merely private is not objective, not because it is private, but because, being private, it will always be found to be disorderly.

What we have, however, especially to explain is why the mere fact that all men agree in their accounts of an experience is insufficient to establish its objectivity. This was the defect which we found in the argument from unanimity in its application to mystical experience. We pointed out that an experience might be universal and publicly accessible and yet subjective. And we gave the examples of mirages, santonin experiences, and double vision. What our theory has to show is that these experiences are subjective not because they are private—since in fact they are not private—but because they are disorderly. Let us take the case of double vision. It is not disorderly that a man whose eyes are crossed should *see* things double. But it is disorderly that the crossing of the eyes should produce the actual objective duplication of objects. For there is no law of nature under which this could be subsumed and explained. On the contrary, according to all known causal laws, the crossing of a man's eyes produces no effect on the objects which he is seeing. Therefore what he is experiencing, viz., the appearance of duplication, is in conflict with natural law, is disorderly, and is for that reason subjective.

Since orderliness is the criterion of objectivity, we have now to apply it to mystical states of consciousness to ascertain whether they are objective. Are mystical experiences orderly in the sense required? The definition of order is the constant conjunction of repeatable items of experience. The definition makes no mention of sense experience and is quite independent of it. It will apply to any kind of experience. The orderliness and objectivity of sense contents will mean the constant conjunction of specifiable items of sense experience. The orderliness and objectivity of nonsensuous contents will mean the constant conjunction of specifiable items of nonsensuous experience. We have simply to ask therefore whether mystical experiences are orderly in this sense.

We will take first the introvertive type of mystical experience. It is non-sensuous, since all sensations and images are specifically excluded from it. Does it consist of constant conjunctions of items of nonsensuous experiences? The answer is obviously that it does not. For this would require that there should be within the introvertive experience a multiplicity of particular items of experience. But the very essence of the experience is that it is undifferentiated, distinctionless, and destitute of all multiplicity. There are no distinguishable items or events among which repeatable patterns or regular sequences could be traced. With this the claim of introvertive experience to objectivity collapses. It cannot be objective. But the sceptic should not at this point prematurely claim a victory. For we shall find that, although the experience is not objective, neither is it subjective. We have indeed a long way still to go before we can determine its status.

To see this we must now apply to the experience the criterion of subjectivity as we previously applied the criterion of objectivity. To be subjective in the sense in which an hallucination or a dream is subjective an experience must exhibit positive infringements of natural law, either internally or externally. It must be *dis*orderly. It is not enough to establish the merely negative conclusion that it lacks order—which is all we have shown so far. Mystical experiences are of course parts of the natural order in the same sense in which dreams and hallucinations are so. They have their causes and effects, and it is an objective fact that this man at this time and at this place has a dream or an hallucination or a mystical experience. But to discover whether an experience of any kind is subjective in the sense in which a dream is subjective, or objective in the sense in which a veridical sense perception is objective, we have to look at the internal content of the experience to see whether, either in itself or in its relations to what lies outside its boundaries, it is orderly or disorderly. Now if we apply this test to the introvertive mystical experience we find that it cannot be subjective for precisely the same reason which shows that it cannot be objective. It cannot be disorderly within its own boundaries as would be a dream of a kettle of water freezing when put on the fire. For there are no distinguishable items within it to constitute sequences which are contrary to the constant conjunctions in the world order. For the same reason it cannot conflict with the natural order in its external relations, for this too requires that specifiable items within the experience should conflict with items outside it—as for instance being in London in my dream conflicts with being in bed in America without traversing the intervening distance. But there are no items within the introvertive experience which could conflict with anything outside it. It follows from these considerations that it is not subjective.

There is really nothing new in the conclusion which we have reached. We shall find that the proposition that mystical experience is neither subjective nor objective is itself a mystical doctrine which is explicitly put forward by all the more philosophical mystics. They have not reached it by a process of reasoning as we have done in this section. They have simply felt intuitively that it is the natural and proper interpretation of their experience. It is true that this seems to conflict with our finding in the last chapter that a sense of objectivity is one of the common characteristics of all mystical experience. But "sense of objectivity" is in reality a very unsophisticated phrase, though it was a convenient one to use at a certain stage of thinking. The fact is that the mystic feels an intense and burning conviction that his experience is not a mere dream—a something which is shut up entirely inside his own consciousness. He feels that it transcends his own petty personality, that it is vastly greater than himself, that it in some sense passes out beyond his individuality into the infinite. This he expresses—for lack of better words—by saying that it is "real," that it is the "true and only reality," and so on. It is natural to pass on from this to saying that it "exists" outside himself, that it is objective, etc. We shall have to do our best to illuminate all this in the sequel. Our immediate concern is only to show that there is no real contradiction between the earlier expression "sense of objectivity" and the more accurate statement that mystical experience is neither subjective nor objective.

Do the same arguments and conclusions apply to the extrovertive type of experience? At first sight it would seem that the case is quite different here because in this experience there does exist a multiplicity of distinguishable items, and these items are in space even if they do not exhibit any temporal flux. The extrovertive mystic perceives with his physical senses the blades of grass, the wood, the stone, but he perceives them as "all one." He perceives them as both distinct and identical. In so far as he perceives them as distinct, they are of course the sort of distinguishable items which exhibit orderliness. The grass, the wood, and the stone are simply objective parts of the natural order.

But it seems to me that although the grass, the wood, and the stone are thus objective, their oneness is not. The multiplicity in the experience is not as such a mystical perception. Only the oneness is. But the oneness as such has no multiplicity and no distinguishable items in it. Indeed it is, in the mystic's view, the very same oneness as is perceived in the introvertive experience. There is the unity outside and the unity inside. But these are not two unities, but one and the same. This is certainly the mystical claim. At any rate the exterior oneness, like the interior oneness, has in it no multiplicity of items or events. Hence the same arguments apply to it as to the introvertive experience, and the same conclusion must be drawn. It is neither objective nor subjective.

. . . There is a line of reasoning which, so far as I know, no mystic or anyone else has ever urged or even been conscious of, but which, on the condition that we accept its premiss, decisively supports the view of the mystic against that of the sceptic. The premiss of the argument is that the mystic has in fact eliminated all the empirical contents of his consciousness and is left with the pure consciousness which is his own individual pure ego. This premiss does not go beyond his own subjectivity. But once this is admitted, we shall find that it is logically impossible to stop there and that we are compelled to postulate that the pure individual ego is in reality not merely individual but is universal and cosmic. The reasoning is as follows:

Suppose that two persons A and B each suppresses in himself all specific mental content, and that therefore each attains the mystical consciousness of his own pure ego. Would it then be the case that A has reached A's private pure ego, and that B has reached B's private pure ego, so that what we have here in this situation is two distinct and separate pure egos? The natural answer to expect would of course be, Yes. But if so, then there must be something which separates A's ego from B's ego, some principle of division or individuation which makes them two distinct entities. What is the principle of individuation?

Let us first ask what is the principle of individuation which separates two minds in ordinary life, two minds which have not sought or attained any mystical consciousness but are operating at the level of everyday experience. What, for example, makes the mind of the writer of this book a different psychical entity from the mind of the reader? If this question were asked, not about the minds, but about the physical bodies of the writer and the reader, the answer would be very simple. The basic principle of individuation here would be space. An interval of space separates our two bodies and makes them two distinct entities. This is no doubt oversimple. Where two persons live at different periods, time will separate them as well as space. Also different physical qualities may enter into the differentiation. The writer's hair may be white, the reader's brown. But we can ignore these complications and concentrate only on the basic principle of differentiation which in this case is space.

But we are here asking what the principle of division is as between two minds, not two bodies. Perhaps the preliminary objection will be raised that we cannot ask such a question without assuming a mind-body dualism, and that to make such an assumption is objectionable. This is a misunderstanding. The question assumes no theory at all, either dualistic or monistic, as to the relation between mind and body. It only assumes that it is possible to speak and think intelligibly in "mentalistic" or introspective terms as well as in physical terms. It assumes that it is not meaningless to talk of one's inner thoughts and feelings and that statements about them are not simply statements about the body, although there is no doubt some very intimate connection between them. Our question does not involve any theory at all, or the denial of any theory. It does not move on the level of theory but on the level of experience. It is a plain statement of experienced fact that a man can talk sensibly about his ideas, feelings, intentions, wishes, etc., and that when he does so he is not talking about his stomach, legs, or brain. We may now therefore return to our question and ask what is the principle of individuation which distinguishes two minds which are both operating at the level of every-day experience.

If we thus abstract from bodily differences, it seems clear to me that there is only one circumstance which distinguishes one mind from another, namely that each has a different stream of consciousness or, what amounts to the same thing, a different stream of experiences. Over any given period of time the sensations, images, emotions, and thoughts which constitute A's inner biography will be different from those which constitute B's inner biography. We need not trouble ourselves about the puzzle whether, when A and B are said in common speech to be looking at the "same" material object, they are actually having one identical sensation or two private but similar sensations. For whether there is at such a point of time an actual intersection of the two streams of consciousness or only a similarity, the fact remains that by and large A's stream of mental contents is during most of its duration entirely distinct from B's. And this, so far as I can see, is the *only* thing which distinguishes any one mind from any other. In other words, minds are distinguished from one another by their empirical contents and by nothing else. It follows that if A and B have suppressed within themselves all empirical contents then there is left nothing whatever which can distinguish them and make them two; and if A and B have thereby reached the mystical consciousness of their pure egos, then there is nothing to distinguish them or make them two pure egos.

If we make use of the philosopher's distinction between the pure ego and the empirical ego, then what follows from this argument is that there exists a multiplicity of empirical egos in the universe, but that there can be only one pure ego. Hence the mystic who has reached what seems at first to be his own private pure ego has in fact reached the pure ego of the universe, the pure cosmic ego.

This explains and agrees with the experience of self-transcendence which the mystic always reports. Both the experience of the mystic and the wholly independent speculative reasoning of the philosopher just outlined converge on the same conclusion and support each other. If it were not for the speculative reasoning, the sceptic might well explain away the experienced feeling of self-transcendence, the fading away of personal identity into "boundless being" reported by Tennyson, the disappearance of the "I" and its dissolution in the "universal pool" reported by Koestler, the same experiences reported by Christian mystics and Sufis in their own theological language, and by Hindus and Buddhists in terms appropriate to their special cultures and theories—the sceptic might explain all this away by an appeal to the self-forgetfulness of a person absorbed in some all-engrossing object of attention. Such an obvious commonplace of everyday psychological fact would in any case seem—at least to the present writer—utterly insufficient to bear the weight of explaining the entirely unusual and uncommonplace and indeed extraordinary experiences of the mystics. But it is better to rely on the reasoned argument which has been discovered and set forth in this section.

There *is* therefore a universal cosmic self with which the mystic makes contact and with which he becomes identified. . . .

HUSTON SMITH
Do Drugs Have Religious Import? [1]

Until six months ago, if I picked up my phone in the Cambridge area and dialed KISS-BIG, a voice would answer, "If-if." These were coincidences: KISS-BIG happened to be the letter equivalents of an arbitrarily assigned telephone number, and I.F.I.F. represented the initials of an organization with the improbable name of the International Federation for Internal Freedom. But the coincidences were apposite to the point of being poetic. "Kiss big" caught the euphoric, manic, life-embracing attitude that characterized this most publicized of the organizations formed to explore the newly synthesized consciousness-changing substances; the organization itself was surely one of the "iffy-est" phenomena to appear on our social and intellectual scene in some time. It produced the first firings in Harvard's history, an ultimatum to get out of Mexico in five days, and "the miracle of Marsh Chapel," in which, during a two-and-one-half-hour Good Friday service, ten theological students and professors ingested psilocybin and were visited by what they generally reported to be the deepest religious experiences of their lives.

Despite the last of these phenomena and its numerous if less dramatic parallels, students of religion appear by and large to be dismissing the psychedelic drugs that have sprung to our attention in the '60s as having little religious relevance. The position taken in one of the most forward-looking volumes of theological essays to have appeared in recent years—*Soundings,*

Huston Smith (1919–   ) was born in China and lived there for the first seventeen years of his life. He received his higher education in the United States and is currently a professor of philosophy at the Massachusetts Institute of Technology. His many publications include *The Religions of Man.*

DO DRUGS HAVE RELIGIOUS IMPORT?   From *The Journal of Philosophy,* Volume LXI, No. 18, October 1, 1964. Copyright 1964 by The Journal of Philosophy, Inc. Reprinted by permission of *The Journal of Philosophy* and the author.

[1] The emended version of a paper presented to The Woodrow Wilson Society, Princeton University, on May 16, 1964.

edited by A. R. Vidler [2]—accepts R. C. Zaehner's *Mysticism: Sacred and Profane* as having "fully examined and refuted" the religious claims for mescalin which Aldous Huxley sketched in *The Doors of Perception*. This closing of the case strikes me as premature, for it looks as if the drugs have light to throw on the history of religion, the phenomenology of religion, the philosophy of religion, and the practice of the religious life itself.

I.   DRUGS AND RELIGION VIEWED
HISTORICALLY

In his trial-and-error life explorations man almost everywhere has stumbled upon connections between vegetables (eaten or brewed) and actions (yogi breathing exercises, whirling-dervish dances, flagellations) that alter states of consciousness. From the psychopharmacological standpoint we now understand these states to be the products of changes in brain chemistry. From the sociological perspective we see that they tend to be connected in some way with religion. If we discount the wine used in Christian communion services, the instances closest to us in time and space are the peyote of The Native American [Indian] Church and Mexico's 2000-year-old "sacred mushrooms," the latter rendered in Aztec as "God's Flesh"—striking parallel to "the body of our Lord" in the Christian eucharist. Beyond these neighboring instances lie the *soma* of the Hindus, the *haoma* and hemp of the Zoroastrians, the Dionysus of the Greeks who "everywhere . . . taught men the culture of the vine and the mysteries of his worship and everywhere [was] accepted as a god," [3] the *benzoin* of Southeast Asia, Zen's tea whose fifth cup purifies and whose sixth "calls to the realm of the immortals," [4] the *pituri* of the Australian aborigines, and probably the mystic *kykeon* that was eaten and drunk at the climactic close of the sixth day of the Eleusinian mysteries.[5] There is no need to extend the list, as a reasonably complete account is available in Philippe de Félice's comprehensive study of the subject, *Poisons sacrés, ivresses divines*.

More interesting than the fact that consciousness-changing devices have been linked with religion is the possibility that they actually initiated many of the religious perspectives which, taking root in history, continued after their psychedelic origins were forgotten. Bergson saw the first movement of Hindus and Greeks toward "dynamic religion" as associated with the "divine rapture" found in intoxicating beverages; [6] more recently Robert Graves, Gor-

---

[2] *Soundings: Essays concerning Christian Understandings,* A. R. Vidler, ed. (Cambridge: University Press, 1962). The statement cited appears on page 72, in H. A. Williams's essay on "Theology and Self-awareness."

[3] Edith Hamilton, *Mythology* (New York: Mentor, 1953), p. 55.

[4] Quoted in Alan Watts, *The Spirit of Zen* (New York: Grove Press, 1958), p. 110.

[5] George Mylonas, *Eleusis and the Eleusinian Mysteries* (Princeton, N.J.: Princeton Univ. Press, 1961), p. 284.

[6] *Two Sources of Morality and Religion* (New York: Holt, 1935), pp. 206–212.

don Wasson, and Alan Watts have suggested that most religions arose from such chemically induced theophanies. Mary Barnard is the most explicit proponent of this thesis. "Which . . . was more likely to happen first," she asks,[7] "the spontaneously generated idea of an afterlife in which the disembodied soul, liberated from the restrictions of time and space, experiences eternal bliss, or the accidental discovery of hallucinogenic plants that give a sense of euphoria, dislocate the center of consciousness, and distort time and space, making them balloon outward in greatly expanded vistas?" Her own answer is that "the [latter] experience might have had . . . an almost explosive effect on the largely dormant minds of men, causing them to think of things they had never thought of before. This, if you like, is direct revelation." Her use of the subjunctive "might" renders this formulation of her answer equivocal, but she concludes her essay on a note that is completely unequivocal: "Looking at the matter coldly, unintoxicated and unentranced, I am willing to prophesy that fifty theobotanists working for fifty years would make the current theories concerning the origins of much mythology and theology as out-of-date as pre-Copernican astronomy."

This is an important hypothesis—one which must surely engage the attention of historians of religion for some time to come. But as I am concerned here only to spot the points at which the drugs erupt onto the field of serious religious study, not to ride the geysers to whatever heights, I shall not pursue Miss Barnard's thesis. Having located what appears to be the crux of the historical question, namely the extent to which drugs not merely duplicate or simulate theologically sponsored experiences but generate or shape theologies themselves, I turn to phenomenology.

II.   DRUGS AND RELIGION VIEWED
PHENOMENOLOGICALLY

Phenomenology attempts a careful description of human experience. The question the drugs pose for the phenomenology of religion, therefore, is whether the experiences they induce differ from religious experiences reached naturally, and if so how.

Even the Bible notes that chemically induced psychic states bear *some* resemblance to religious ones. Peter had to appeal to a circumstantial criterion —the early hour of the day—to defend those who were caught up in the Pentecostal experience against the charge that they were merely drunk: "These men are not drunk, as you suppose, since it is only the third hour of the day" (Acts 2:15); and Paul initiates the comparison when he admonishes the Ephesians not to "get drunk with wine . . . but [to] be filled with the spirit" (Ephesians 5:18). Are such comparisons, paralleled in the accounts of virtually every religion, superficial? How far can they be pushed?

[7] "The God in the Flowerpot," *The American Scholar* 32, 4 (Autumn, 1963): 584, 586.

Not all the way, students of religion have thus far insisted. With respect to the new drugs, Prof. R. C. Zaehner has drawn the line emphatically. "The importance of Huxley's *Doors of Perception*," he writes, "is that in it the author clearly makes the claim that what he experienced under the influence of mescalin is closely comparable to a genuine mystical experience. If he is right, . . . the conclusions . . . are alarming." [8] Zaehner thinks that Huxley is not right, but I fear that it is Zaehner who is mistaken.

There are, of course, innumerable drug experiences that have no religious feature; they can be sensual as readily as spiritual, trivial as readily as transforming, capricious as readily as sacramental. If there is one point about which every student of the drugs agrees, it is that there is no such thing as the drug experience *per se*—no experience that the drugs, as it were, merely secrete. Every experience is a mix of three ingredients: drug, set (the psychological make-up of the individual), and setting (the social and physical environment in which it is taken). But given the right set and setting, the drugs can induce religious experiences indistinguishable from experiences that occur spontaneously. Nor need set and setting be exceptional. The way the statistics are currently running, it looks as if from one-fourth to one-third of the general population will have religious experiences if they take the drugs under naturalistic conditions, meaning by this conditions in which the researcher supports the subject but does not try to influence the direction his experience will take. Among subjects who have strong religious inclinations to begin with, the proportion of those having religious experiences jumps to three-fourths. If they take the drugs in settings that are religious too, the ratio soars to nine in ten.

How do we know that the experiences these people have really are religious? We can begin with the fact that they say they are. The "one-fourth to one-third of the general population" figure is drawn from two sources. Ten months after they had had their experiences, 24 per cent of the 194 subjects in a study by the California psychiatrist Oscar Janiger characterized their experiences as having been religious.[9] Thirty-two per cent of the 74 subjects in Ditman and Hayman's study reported, looking back on their LSD experience, that it looked as if it had been "very much" or "quite a bit" a religious experience; 42 per cent checked as true the statement that they "were left with a greater awareness of God, or a higher power, or ultimate reality." [10] The statement that three-fourths of subjects having religious "sets" will have religious experiences comes from the reports of sixty-nine religious professionals who took the drugs while the Harvard project was in progress.[11]

---

[8] *Mysticism: Sacred and Profane* (New York: Oxford, 1961), p. 12.

[9] Quoted in William H. McGlothlin, "Long-lasting Effects of LSD on Certain Attitudes in Normals," printed for private distribution by the RAND Corporation, May, 1962, p. 16.

[10] *Ibid.*, pp. 45, 46.

[11] Timothy Leary, "The Religious Experience: Its Production and Interpretation," *The Psychedelic Review*, 1, 3 (1964): 325.

In the absence of (a) a single definition of religious experience acceptable to psychologists of religion generally and (b) foolproof ways of ascertaining whether actual experiences exemplify any definition, I am not sure there is any better way of telling whether the experiences of the 333 men and women involved in the above studies were religious than by noting whether they seemed so to them. But if more rigorous methods are preferred, they exist; they have been utilized, and they confirm the conviction of the man in the street that drug experiences can indeed be religious. In his doctoral study at Harvard University, Walter Pahnke worked out a typology of religious experience (in this instance of the mystical variety) based on the classic cases of mystical experiences as summarized in Walter Stace's *Mysticism and Philosophy*. He then administered psilocybin to ten theology students and professors in the setting of a Good Friday service. The drug was given "double-blind," meaning that neither Dr. Pahnke nor his subjects knew which ten were getting psilocybin and which ten placebos to constitute a control group. Subsequently the reports the subjects wrote of their experiences were laid successively before three college-graduate housewives who, without being informed about the nature of the study, were asked to rate each statement as to the degree (strong, moderate, slight, or none) to which it exemplified each of the nine traits of mystical experience enumerated in the typology of mysticism worked out in advance. When the test of significance was applied to their statistics, it showed that "those subjects who received psilocybin experienced phenomena which were indistinguishable from, if not identical with . . . the categories defined by our typology of mysticism." [12]

With the thought that the reader might like to test his own powers of discernment on the question being considered, I insert here a simple test I gave to a group of Princeton students following a recent discussion sponsored by the Woodrow Wilson Society:

> Below are accounts of two religious experiences. One occurred under the influence of drugs, one without their influence. Check the one you think *was* drug-induced.
>
> I
>
> Suddenly I burst into a vast, new, indescribably wonderful universe. Although I am writing this over a year later, the thrill of the surprise and amazement, the awesomeness of the revelation, the engulfment in an overwhelming feeling-wave of gratitude and blessed wonderment, are as fresh, and the memory of the experience is as vivid, as if it had happened five minutes ago. And yet to concoct anything by way of description that would even hint at the magnitude, the sense of ultimate reality . . . this seems such an impossible task. The knowledge which has infused and affected every aspect of my life came instantaneously and with such complete force of certainty that it was impossible, then or since, to doubt its validity.

---

[12] "Drugs and Mysticism: An Analysis of the Relationship between Psychedelic Drugs and the Mystical Consciousness," a thesis presented to the Committee on Higher Degrees in History and Philosophy of Religion, Harvard University, June 1963.

II

All at once, without warning of any kind, I found myself wrapped in a flame-colored cloud. For an instant I thought of fire . . . the next, I knew that the fire was within myself. Directly afterward there came upon me a sense of exultation, of immense joyousness accompanied or immediately followed by an intellectual illumination impossible to describe. Among other things, I did not merely come to believe, but I saw that the universe is not composed of dead matter, but is, on the contrary, a living Presence; I became conscious in myself of eternal life. . . . I saw that all men are immortal: that the cosmic order is such that without any preadventure all things work together for the good of each and all; that the foundation principle of the world . . . is what we call love, and that the happiness of each and all is in the long run absolutely certain.

On the occasion referred to, twice as many students (46) answered incorrectly as answered correctly (23). I bury the correct answer in a footnote to preserve the reader's opportunity to test himself.[13]

Why, in the face of this considerable evidence, does Zaehner hold that drug experiences cannot be authentically religious? There appear to be three reasons:

1. His own experience was "utterly trivial." This of course proves that not all drug experiences are religious; it does not prove that no drug experiences are religious.

2. He thinks the experiences of others that appear religious to them are not truly so. Zaehner distinguishes three kinds of mysticism: nature mysticism, in which the soul is united with the natural world; monistic mysticism, in which the soul merges with an impersonal absolute; and theism, in which the soul confronts the living, personal God. He concedes that drugs can induce the first two species of mysticism, but not its supreme instance, the theistic. As proof, he analyzes Huxley's experience as recounted in *The Doors of Perception* to show that it produced at best a blend of nature and monistic mysticism. Even if we were to accept Zaehner's evaluation of the three forms of mysticism, Huxley's case, and indeed Zaehner's entire book, would prove only that not every mystical experience induced by the drugs is theistic. Insofar as Zaehner goes beyond this to imply that drugs do not and cannot induce theistic mysticism, he not only goes beyond the evidence but proceeds in the face of it. James Slotkin reports that the peyote Indians "see visions, which may be of Christ Himself. Sometimes they hear the voice of the Great Spirit. Sometimes they become aware of the presence of God and of those personal shortcomings which must be corrected if they are to do His will." [14] And G. M. Carstairs, reporting on the use of psychedelic *bhang* in India, quotes

---

[13] The first account is quoted anonymously in "The Issue of the Consciousness-expanding Drugs," *Main Currents in Modern Thought*, **20**, 1 (September–October, 1963): 10–11. The second experience was that of Dr. R. M. Bucke, the author of *Cosmic Consciousness,* as quoted in William James, *The Varieties of Religious Experience* (New York: Modern Library, 1902), pp. 390–391. The former experience occurred under the influence of drugs; the latter did not.

[14] James S. Slotkin, *Peyote Religion* (New York: Free Press of Glencoe, 1956)

a Brahmin as saying, "It gives good bhakti. . . . You get a very good bhakti with bhang," *bhakti* being precisely Hinduism's theistic variant.[15]

3. There is a third reason why Zaehner might doubt that drugs can induce genuinely mystical experiences. Zaehner is a Roman Catholic, and Roman Catholic doctrine teaches that mystical rapture is a gift of grace and as such can never be reduced to man's control. This may be true; certainly the empirical evidence cited does not preclude the possibility of a genuine ontological or theological difference between natural and drug-induced religious experiences. At this point, however, we are considering phenomenology rather than ontology, description rather than interpretation, and on this level there is no difference. Descriptively, drug experiences cannot be distinguished from their natural religious counterpart. When the current philosophical authority on mysticism, W. T. Stace, was asked whether the drug experience is similar to the mystical experience, he answered, "It's not a matter of its being *similar* to mystical experience; it *is* mystical experience."

What we seem to be witnessing in Zaehner's *Mysticism: Sacred and Profane* is a reenactment of the age-old pattern in the conflict between science and religion. Whenever a new controversy arises, religion's first impulse is to deny the disturbing evidence science has produced. Seen in perspective, Zaehner's refusal to admit that drugs can induce experiences descriptively indistinguishable from those which are spontaneously religious is the current counterpart of the seventeenth-century theologians' refusal to look through Galileo's telescope or, when they did, their persistence in dismissing what they saw as machinations of the devil. When the fact that drugs can trigger religious experiences becomes incontrovertible, discussion will move to the more difficult question of how this new fact is to be interpreted. The latter question leads beyond phenomenology into philosophy.

III.   DRUGS AND RELIGION VIEWED
PHILOSOPHICALLY

Why do people reject evidence? Because they find it threatening, we may suppose. Theologians are not the only professionals to utilize this mode of defense. In his *Personal Knowledge*,[16] Michael Polanyi recounts the way the medical profession ignored such palpable facts as the painless amputation of human limbs, performed before their own eyes in hundreds of successive cases, concluding that the subjects were imposters who were either deluding their physicians or colluding with them. One physician, Esdaile, carried out about 300 major operations painlessly under mesmeric trance in India, but neither in India nor in Great Britain could he get medical journals to print accounts of his work. Polanyi attributes this closed-mindedness to "lack of a

[15] "Daru and Bhang," *Quarterly Journal of the Study of Alcohol,* **15** (1954): 229.
[16] Chicago: Univ. of Chicago Press, 1958.

conceptual framework in which their discoveries could be separated from specious and untenable admixtures."

The "untenable admixture" in the fact that psychotomimetic drugs can induce religious experience is its apparent implicate: that religious disclosures are no more veridical than psychotic ones. For religious skeptics, this conclusion is obviously not untenable at all; it fits in beautifully with their thesis that *all* religion is at heart an escape from reality. Psychotics avoid reality by retiring into dream worlds of make-believe; what better evidence that religious visionaries do the same than the fact that identical changes in brain chemistry produce both states of mind? Had not Marx already warned us that religion is the "opiate" of the people?—apparently he was more literally accurate than he supposed. Freud was likewise too mild. He "never doubted that religious phenomena are to be understood only on the model of the neurotic symptoms of the individual." [17] He should have said "psychotic symptoms."

So the religious skeptic is likely to reason. What about the religious believer? Convinced that religious experiences are not fundamentally delusory, can he admit that psychotomimetic drugs can occasion them? To do so he needs (to return to Polanyi's words) "a conceptual framework in which [the discoveries can] be separated from specious and untenable admixtures," the "untenable admixture" being in this case the conclusion that religious experiences are in general delusory.

One way to effect the separation would be to argue that, despite phenomenonlogical similarities between natural and drug-induced religious experiences, they are separated by a crucial *ontological* difference. Such an argument would follow the pattern of theologians who argue for the "real presence" of Christ's body and blood in the bread and wine of the Eucharist despite their admission that chemical analysis, confined as it is to the level of "accidents" rather than "essences," would not disclose this presence. But this distinction will not appeal to many today, for it turns on an essence-accident metaphysics which is not widely accepted. Instead of fighting a rear-guard action by insisting that if drug and non-drug religious experiences cannot be distinguished empirically there must be some transempirical factor that distinguishes them and renders the drug experience profane, I wish to explore the possibility of accepting drug-induced experiences as religious without relinquishing confidence in the truth-claims of religious experience generally.

To begin with the weakest of all arguments, the argument from authority: William James did not discount *his* insights that occurred while his brain chemistry was altered. The paragraph in which he retrospectively evaluates his nitrous oxide experiences has become classic, but it is so pertinent to the present discussion that it merits quoting once again.

> One conclusion was forced upon my mind at that time, and my impression of its truth has ever since remained unshaken. It is that our normal waking

---

[17] *Totem and Taboo* (New York: Modern Library, 1938).

consciousness, rational consciousness as we call it, is but one special type of consciousness, whilst all about it, parted from it by the filmiest of screens, there lie potential forms of consciousness entirely different. We may go through life without suspecting their existence; but apply the requisite stimulus, and at a touch they are there in all their completeness, definite types of mentality which probably somewhere have their field of application and adaptation. No account of the universe in its totality can be final which leaves these other forms of consciousness quite disregarded. How to regard them is the question—for they are so discontinuous with ordinary consciousness. Yet they may determine attitudes though they cannot furnish formulas, and open a region though they fail to give a map. At any rate, they forbid a premature closing of our accounts with reality. Looking back on my own experiences, they all converge toward a kind of insight to which I cannot help ascribing some metaphysical significance (*op. cit.*, 378–379).

To this argument from authority, I add two arguments that try to provide something by ways of reasons. Drug experiences that assume a religious cast tend to have fearful and/or beatific features, and each of my hypotheses relates to one of these aspects of the experience.

Beginning with the ominous, "fear of the Lord," awe-ful features, Gordon Wasson, the New York banker-turned-mycologist, describes these as he encountered them in his psilocybin experience as follows: "Ecstasy! In common parlance . . . ecstasy is fun. . . . But ecstasy is not fun. Your very soul is seized and shaken until it tingles. After all, who will choose to feel undiluted awe? . . . The unknowing vulgar abuse the word; we must recapture its full and terrifying sense." [18] Emotionally the drug experience can be like having forty-foot waves crash over you for several hours while you cling desperately to a life-raft which may be swept from under you at any minute. It seems quite possible that such an ordeal, like any experience of a close call, could awaken rather fundamental sentiments respecting life and death and destiny and trigger the "no atheists in foxholes" effect. Similarly, as the subject emerges from the trauma and realizes that he is not going to be insane as he had feared, there may come over him an intensified appreciation like that frequently reported by patients recovering from critical illness. "It happened on the day when my bed was pushed out of doors to the open gallery of the hospital," reads one such report:

> I cannot now recall whether the revelation came suddenly or gradually; I only remember finding myself in the very midst of those wonderful moments, beholding life for the first time in all its young intoxication of loveliness, in its unspeakable joy, beauty, and importance. I cannot say exactly what the mysterious change was. I saw no new thing, but I saw all the usual things in a miraculous new light—in what I believe is their true light. I saw for the first time how wildly beautiful and joyous, beyond any words of mine to describe, is the whole of life. Every human being moving across that porch, every sparrow that flew, every branch tossing in the wind, was

---

[18] "The Hallucinogenic Fungi of Mexico: An Inquiry into the Origins of the Religious Idea among Primitive Peoples," *Harvard Botanical Museum Leaflets,* **19,** 7 (1961).

caught in and was a part of the whole mad ecstasy of loveliness, of joy, of importance, of intoxication of life.[19]

If we do not discount religious intuitions because they are prompted by battlefields and *physical* crises; if we regard the latter as "calling us to our senses" more often than they seduce us into delusions, need comparable intuitions be discounted simply because the crises that trigger them are of an inner, *psychic* variety?

Turning from the hellish to the heavenly aspects of the drug experience, *some* of the latter may be explainable by the hypothesis just stated; that is, they may be occasioned by the relief that attends the sense of escape from high danger. But this hypothesis cannot possibly account for *all* the beatific episodes, for the simple reason that the positive episodes often come first, or to persons who experience no negative episodes whatever. Dr. Sanford Unger of the National Institute of Mental Health reports that among his subjects "50 to 60% will not manifest any real disturbance worthy of discussion," yet "around 75% will have at least one episode in which exaltation, rapture, and joy are the key descriptions." [20] How are we to account for the drug's capacity to induce peak experiences, such as the following, which are *not* preceded by fear?

> A feeling of great peace and contentment seemed to flow through my entire body. All sound ceased and I seemed to be floating in a great, very very still void or hemisphere. It is impossible to describe the overpowering feeling of peace, contentment, and being a part of goodness itself that I felt. I could feel my body dissolving and actually becoming a part of the goodness and peace that was all around me. Words can't describe this. I feel an awe and wonder that such a feeling could have occurred to me.[21]

Consider the following line of argument. Like every other form of life, man's nature has become distinctive through specialization. Man has specialized in developing a cerebral cortex. The analytic powers of this instrument are a standing wonder, but the instrument seems less able to provide man with the sense that he is meaningfully related to his environment: to life, the world, and history in their wholeness. As Albert Camus describes the situation, "If I were . . . a cat among animals, this life would have a meaning, or rather this problem would not arise, for I should belong to this world. I would *be* this world to which I am now opposed by my whole consciousness." [22] Note that it is Camus' consciousness that opposes him to his world. The drugs do not knock this consciousness out, but while they leave it opera-

---

[19] Margaret Prescott Montague, *Twenty Minutes of Reality* (St. Paul, Minn.: Macalester Park, 1947), pp. 15, 17.

[20] "The Current Scientific Status of Psychedelic Drug Research," read at the Conference on Methods in Philosophy and the Sciences, New School for Social Research, May 3, 1964, and scheduled for publication in David Solomon, ed., *The Conscious Expanders* (New York: Putnam, fall of 1964).

[21] Quoted by Dr. Unger in the paper just mentioned.

[22] *The Myth of Sisyphus* (New York: Vintage, 1955), p. 38.

SMITH: DO DRUGS HAVE RELIGIOUS IMPORT? 335

tive they also activate areas of the brain that normally lie below its threshold of awareness. One of the clearest objective signs that the drugs are taking effect is the dilation they produce in the pupils of the eyes, and one of the most predictable subjective signs is the intensification of visual perception. Both of these responses are controlled by portions of the brain that lie deep, further to the rear than the mechanisms that govern consciousness. Meanwhile we know that the human organism is interlaced with its world in innumerable ways it normally cannot sense—through gravitational fields, body respiration, and the like: the list could be multiplied until man's skin began to seem more like a thoroughfare than a boundary. Perhaps the deeper regions of the brain which evolved earlier and are more like those of the lower animals—"If I were . . . a cat . . . I should belong to this world"— can sense this relatedness better than can the cerebral cortex which now dominates our awareness. If so, when the drugs rearrange the neurohumors that chemically transmit impulses across synapses between neurons, man's consciousness and his submerged, intuitive, ecological awareness might for a spell become interlaced. This is, of course, no more than a hypothesis, but how else are we to account for the extraordinary incidence under the drugs of that kind of insight the keynote of which James described as "invariably a reconciliation"? "It is as if the opposites of the world, whose contradictoriness and conflict make all our difficulties and troubles, were melted into one and the same genus, but *one of the species,* the nobler and better one, *is itself the genus, and so soaks up and absorbs its opposites into itself*" (*op. cit.,* 379).

IV.   THE DRUGS AND RELIGION VIEWED
"RELIGIOUSLY"

Suppose that drugs can induce experiences indistinguishable from religious experiences and that we can respect their reports. Do they shed any light, not (we now ask) on life, but on the nature of the religious life?

One thing they may do is throw religious experience itself into perspective by clarifying its relation to the religious life as a whole. Drugs appear able to induce religious experiences; it is less evident that they can produce religious lives. It follows that religion is more than religious experiences. This is hardly news, but it may be a useful reminder, especially to those who incline toward "the religion of religious experience"; which is to say toward lives bent on the acquisition of desired states of experience irrespective of their relation to life's other demands and components.

Despite the dangers of faculty psychology, it remains useful to regard man as having a mind, a will, and feelings. One of the lessons of religious history is that, to be adequate, a faith must rouse and involve all three components of man's nature. Religions of reason grow arid; religions of duty, leaden. Religions of experience have their comparable pitfalls, as evidenced by Taoism's struggle (not always successful) to keep from degenerating into quietism, and the vehemence with which Zen Buddhism has insisted that once students have attained *satori*, they must be driven out of it, back into the world. The case of Zen is especially pertinent here, for it pivots on an enlightenment experience—*satori*, or *kensho*—which some (but not all) Zennists say resembles LSD. Alike or different, the point is that Zen recognizes that unless the experience is joined to discipline, it will come to naught:

> Even the Buddha . . . had to sit. . . . Without *joriki*, the particular power developed through *zazen* [seated meditation], the vision of oneness attained in enlightenment . . . in time becomes clouded and eventually fades into a pleasant memory instead of remaining an omnipresent reality shaping our daily life. . . . To be able to live in accordance with what the Mind's eye has revealed through *satori* requires, like the purification of character and the development of personality, a ripening period of *zazen*.[23]

If the religion of religious experience is a snare and a delusion, it follows that no religion that fixes its faith primarily in substances that induce religious experiences can be expected to come to a good end. What promised to be a short cut will prove to be a short circuit; what began as a religion will end as a religion surrogate. Whether chemical substances can be helpful *adjuncts* to faith is another question. The peyote-using Native American Church seems to indicate that they can be; anthropologists give this church a good report, noting among other things that members resist alcohol and alcoholism better than do nonmembers.[24] The conclusion to which evidence currently points would seem to be that chemicals *can* aid the religious life, but only where set within a context of faith (meaning by this the conviction that what they disclose is true) and discipline (meaning diligent exercise of the will in the attempt to work out the implications of the disclosures for the living of life in the everyday, common-sense world).

Nowhere today in Western civilization are these two conditions jointly fulfilled. Churches lack faith in the sense just mentioned; hipsters lack discipline. This might lead us to forget about the drugs, were it not for one fact: the distinctive religious emotion and the emotion that drugs unquestionably can occasion—Otto's *mysterium tremendum, majestas, mysterium fascinans*; in a phrase, the phenomenon of religious awe—seems to be declining sharply. As Paul Tillich said in an address to the Hillel Society at Harvard several years ago:

> The question our century puts before us [is]: Is it possible to regain the lost dimension, the encounter with the Holy, the dimension which cuts through the world of subjectivity and objectivity and goes down to that which is not world but is the mystery of the Ground of Being?

Tillich may be right; this may be the religious question of our century. For if (as we have insisted) religion cannot be equated with religious experiences, neither can it long survive their absence.

---

[23] Philip Kapleau, *Zen Practice and Attainment,* a manuscript in process of publication.
[24] Slotkin, *op. cit.*

The seminal discussion of numinous experience is to be found in Rudolf Otto, *The Idea of the Holy* * (Oxford University Press, 1958). Interesting discussions of mysticism can be found in William Johnston, *The Still Point: Reflections on Zen and Christian Mysticism* * (Fordham University Press, 1970) and in Evelyn Underhill, *Mysticism* * (World, 1955); both books include not only discussions of the nature of mysticism and religious experience but also discussions of its cognitive status—as does William James, *The Varieties of Religious Experience* * (Modern Library, 1936). Ninian Smart, "Interpretations of Mystical Experience," *Religious Studies*, 1 (1965) provides a critical study of Zaehner's distinction between soul mysticism and theistic mysticism.

Good discussions of "drug mysticism" may be found in Walter Huston Clark, *Chemical Ecstasy: Psychedelic Drugs and Religion* (Sheed & Ward, 1969), in R. E. L. Masters and Jean Houston, *Varieties of Psychedelic Experience* * (Holt, 1966), and in C. B. Osborn, "Artificial Paradises, Baudelaire and Psychedelic Experience," *The American Scholar*, 36 (1967). The claim that mystical experiences and their objects are ineffable is ably discussed in William Alston, "Ineffability," *Philosophical Review*, 65 (1956) and in Paul Henle, "Mysticism and Semantics," *Philosophy and Phenomenological Research*, 9 (1949). A critical examination of Walter Stace's arguments can be found in William J. Wainwright, "Stace and Mysticism," *Journal of Religion*, 50 (1970). For a somewhat different but interesting approach to the question of the cognitivity of mystical experience (which is broadly in the tradition that stems from St. Thomas Aquinas), see Etienne Gilson, *The Mystical Theology of St. Bernard* (Sheed & Ward, 1940, 1955) and Jacques Maritain, *The Degrees of Knowledge* (Scribner's, 1959).

* Available in paperback.

REVELATION, FAITH, AND MIRACLES

V

The concepts of faith and revelation can be construed in several ways. By revelation we may mean the communication, by God or some other supernatural agency, of true propositions which cannot be discovered, or at least not easily discovered, by natural means. Faith is the belief that these propositions have been divinely communicated and are, therefore, true. Revelation may also be understood as the self-manifestation of God. What is revealed is not propositions but God Himself. He unveils Himself, communicates Himself to man. Faith is a radical form of devotion, a belief in God—a complete trust in, an utter commitment to, the being who has so revealed Himself. Aquinas construes faith and revelation in the first sense. Paul Tillich interprets them in the second sense.

It is frequently asserted that although faith has often been understood in the first sense, it should be understood in the second sense. Whatever merits this view may have, we should not be misled into supposing that *believing in* is possible without *believing that*. Belief in a friend presupposes a belief that he exists, has such and such a character, and will respond in such and such a way. Similarly, a faithful response to the self-disclosure of God involves the belief that God is real, that He has disclosed Himself, that one is in relation to Him, and so on. It is also a mistake to suppose that classical theists like Aquinas thought that the object of faith was propositions about God rather than God Himself. In the first place, the propositions in question were accepted only because it was believed that they had been communicated by God. In the second place, the object of faith was not just these propositions but that reality which they were thought to express.

Faith may also be defined as a way of seeing the world religiously and/or as a decision to interpret the world in terms of religious categories and concepts. As it is usually developed, this position has affinities with the first notion of faith discussed above. To adopt a religious world view involves believing that certain propositions are true. The resemblance becomes even more obvious if (as is often the case) it is added that world views cannot be shown to be correct, that one must simply adopt them, and that such adoption always involves a certain amount of risk. If, on the other hand, the element of decision and risk is de-emphasized, and stress is placed upon the (supposed) fact that the believer sees things differently from the nonbeliever, we can connect this view of faith with such theological notions as that of the inner light (which is either bestowed by grace or is naturally present within the depths of man's soul), by means of which one discerns the presence of God in nature, history, and scripture.

It is frequently argued that faith is morally objectionable because it involves holding beliefs that are not adequately supported by evidence. At this point certain distinctions must be made. First, we must distinguish cases in which we have no reasons for believing a proposition p from cases in which we have no reasons for p itself, but do have good reasons for accepting the authority of some person, institution, or book which asserts p. Second, we must also distinguish cases in which we have no reasons for believing p from cases in which we have good reasons for p, but are unable to fully state them or to present them in a way that will or should convince others. (Thus, because of her intimate knowledge of him, a mother may be rightly convinced of her son's innocence even though she can present no reasons that will or should convince a jury of that innocence.)

It is sometimes asserted that while religious faith involves accepting on authority propositions that cannot themselves be supported by reason, good reasons can be provided for accepting that authority. Or it is asserted that, while the believer cannot provide reasons for his convictions which would convince the nonbeliever, his convictions are justified by an intimate acquaintance with the divine, which is the very heart of faith. It is not entirely clear that good reasons can be provided for accepting any religious authority or that intimate acquaintance with the divine is possible. (On this last point, see Section IV, Mysticism and Religious Experience.) But if such reasons can be provided, or if such an acquaintance is possible, then belief may well be rationally justified even though what is believed cannot itself be shown to be true and/or the believer cannot produce reasons for that belief which would satisfy nonbelievers.

The problematic cases are those in which one believes against the weight of the evidence or in the absence of any evidence, and those in which the strength of one's belief is greater than the evidence would appear to warrant. Theologians have rarely advocated believing against the evidence or in the absence of any evidence. (For one thing, they have not usually thought that the weight of evidence was against their beliefs or that there was no evidence for them.) They have, however, commonly supposed that faith involves a belief whose strength goes beyond that which the evidence would warrant. Is this morally legitimate?

It is illegitimate if (as John Locke and William Clifford maintained) the strength of our belief should be directly determined by, and should therefore never exceed, the strength of the evidence. Is this dictum true? Consider the following principles:

(1) We ought not to believe p if the weight of evidence is against p.
(2) We ought not to believe p if there is no evidence at all for p.

Neither of these principles implies that—

(3) One's belief in p should never exceed the strength of the evidence for p.

One must not, then, conclude that because 1 or 2 is plausible or true, 3 is also plausible or true.

However, it must be admitted that principle 3 is rather plausible. How, it may be asked, can a man be considered rational if he does not allow the strength of his belief to be directly determined by the strength of the evidence? Several responses are possible. It is sometimes asserted that principle 3 expresses a commitment that is itself unsupported by evidence and that, therefore, anyone who believes principle 3 violates it. As James points out, the acceptance of this principle involves as many risks as its rejection. If one rejects principle 3, one exposes oneself to the danger of believing something that is in fact false. On the other hand, if one embraces it, he may find himself in a position in which he is unable to accept and act upon propositions that are both true and important, and the consequences of this incapacity may well be disastrous. Thus, for example, if our well-being depends upon our embracing theism and the evidence for theism is inadequate, an acceptance of principle 3 would prevent us from securing our well-being. Or, if belief in theism (or some other view of the kind) is, as James suggests, a necessary condition of our acquiring conclusive evidence that it is true, an acceptance of principle 3 would place us in a position in which we would be unable to obtain that evidence.

Two important philosophical questions are connected with the topic of miracles: Are miracles possible? How is the evidence for them to be assessed?

We must first ask if miracles are logically possible or, more broadly, if the concept of a miracle is a coherent one. P. Nowell-Smith offers several reasons for thinking that it is not. He provisionally accepts the notion that a miracle is "an event above or contrary to or exceeding nature which is explicable only as a direct act of God" but argues that to say that an event is a miracle in this sense is really to say no more than that it has occurred and is (at present) scientifically inexplicable. In this respect "e is a miracle" (i.e., is "an event above . . . nature which is explicable only as a direct act of God") is related to "e occurred but is (at present) scientifically inexplicable" as "opium has dormative power" is related to "opium puts people to sleep," and as "certain events in the past were caused by boojums" is related to "certain events occurred in the past." In short, to speak of events as miracles is (contrary to the intention of those who assert that miracles have occurred) simply to redescribe those events in a misleading way. At first glance, Nowell-Smith's analysis appears to be inapt. *Boojums* either has no meaning or simply means "the cause of those events which occurred in the past." *God* has a meaning, and it is not "the cause of e." "Opium has dormative power" and "opium [is the sort of thing which] puts people to sleep" are logically equivalent; however, the statements "e is a miracle" and "e occurred but is (at present) scientifically inexplicable" are not logically equivalent. (It is possible for the second to be true and the first to be false.) What then is Nowell-Smith's point? It would appear to be this: the empirical meaning of "e is a miracle" is roughly the same as the empirical meaning of "e occurred but is (at present) scientifically inexplicable"; that is, the empirically testable consequences (or at least those which we can now test) are the same in both cases. If we assume that the informative or factual meaning of a statement can be equated with its empirical meaning, then it follows that Nowell-Smith is essentially correct in asserting that the first of our two propositions does not mean anything significantly different from the second and that therefore we cannot explain a scientifically inexplicable event by interpreting it as a miracle and thus ascribing it to divine intervention. The assumption that factual meaning and empirical meaning are equivalent is, however, a suspect one. (See Section VI A.)

It is sometimes argued that the very concept of a miracle is contradictory, for (it is said) "*e* is a miracle" entails "*e* violates natural law," and yet it is impossible for *e* or any other event to violate natural law. To say that *e* violates natural law is to say that it is a law of nature (and therefore true) that events of that type never occur under certain specified conditions and yet, though conditions of that type have occurred, *e* has occurred also. This conjunction of circumstances is, of course, impossible. It may, however, be objected that this argument rests on an incorrect analysis of "*e* violates natural law." Thus, it is sometimes asserted that "*e* violates natural law" means only that it is a law of nature that *other things being equal, or barring divine intervention or something of the sort*, events of that type will not occur if certain kinds of conditions occur and that conditions of that sort have occurred and *e* has occurred also. This conjunction of circumstances is not impossible since, for example, other things may not be equal.

Even if the concept of a miracle is a coherent one, the world may be constituted in such a way that miracles are not really possible. If, for example, miracles are defined as "a transgression of a law of nature by a particular volition of the Deity, or by the interposition of some invisible agent," (Hume) and there are no invisible agents of any kind, then, while miracles may be logically possible, they are not really possible. Or, if a miracle is defined as (among other things) an event for which there are no (sufficient) natural causes, and if everything has (sufficient) natural causes, then, again, miracles are not a real possibility. It is sometimes asserted that even if God exists, He would not perform miracles or allow other agents to perform them, and that therefore miracles cannot actually occur. Various reasons are given for this position. A miraculous intervention is sometimes thought to imply a lack of foresight on God's part or an inability to forestall evils which He foresaw. (For if He did foresee the evil to which the miracle provides the antidote and was able to forestall it, then why did He not do so?) Or it may be suggested that if miraculous intervention is required, then the world must be imperfect and incomplete. Or it is asserted that a miraculous intervention must be an irrational or arbitrary interference with the orderly processes of nature. None of these considerations is altogether compelling. In a standard theistic view, miracles are not added as an afterthought in order to mitigate evils which were unforeseen or unpreventable. That any given miracle will occur has been determined throughout eternity and is as much a part of the plan of creation as those events which transpire in accordance with natural law. The second objection appears to rest on the assumption that a world without miracles is, other things being equal, more perfect than one which includes them. This assumption is not obviously true. Finally, from the fact that there is no natural explanation for a miraculous event, it neither follows that there is no explanation for it nor that it is irrational or arbitrary. The miracle is explained by the fact that God (or some other agent) has freely produced it, and He (or they) may have a very good reason for doing so (to aid others, reveal God's glory). A miraculous intervention need be no more arbitrary or irrational than any other free or purposive act.

Even if miracles are possible, there may be no reason to believe that they occur. Reports of alleged miracles are quite common. How these reports should be evaluated is, however, rather unclear. Hume argues that human testimony must be weighed against the fact that the witnesses are usually few in number, uneducated, and gullible; the fact that since mankind loves prodigies and wonders, it is only too ready to believe stories about them; and so on. Most important, we must weigh this testimony against the fact that the whole experience of mankind points to the empirical impossibility of the occurrence of the alleged miracle. (If human experience didn't point to the empirical impossibility of resuscitated corpses, one would have no reason to believe the Resurrection to be a miracle.) The conclusion must be (says Hume) that not only is there insufficient evidence for the proposition that miracles have occurred, but that there *could* not (by the very nature of the case) be evidence which is strong enough to convince a reasonable man that miracles have occurred.

It is universally admitted that reports of alleged miracles must be cautiously examined. One wonders, however, whether Hume's requirements may not be too stringent, whether it is reasonable to insist on criteria the acceptance of which would spare us the trouble of actually examining the evidence for an alleged miracle. Whether his requirements are reasonable or not may partly depend upon whether or not theism is true. If (a certain kind of) theism is true, then it is not unreasonable to suppose that miracles occur, in which case the evidence for an alleged miracle need be no stronger than the evidence for any other unusual and extraordinary, but nonetheless (really) possible, event. However, if theism and other positions of this kind are mistaken, there is no general reason to suppose that miracles occur, and any evidence that events do occur which "violate" the laws of nature would have to be overwhelming to be convincing.

Because of these numerous difficulties, some theologians and philosophers have attempted to define *miracle* in such a way that an event can be called a miracle even though it is neither scientifically inexplicable nor due to the special intervention of some invisible agent. Paul Tillich advocates a view of this sort. Such a position allows us to continue to speak of miracles and to comfortably accommodate ourselves to science. On the other hand, it involves a radical alteration of the classical notion of a miracle, and one may wonder whether it succeeds in preserving all that is religiously significant in that notion.

w. j. w.

FAITH AND REVELATION

ST. THOMAS AQUINAS
Reason and Revelation

CHAPTER III.   ON THE WAY IN WHICH DIVINE TRUTH
IS TO BE MADE KNOWN

(1) The way of making truth known is not always the same, and, as the Philosopher has very well said, "it belongs to an educated man to seek such certitude in each thing as the nature of that thing allows." [1] The remark is also introduced by Boethius.[2] But, since such is the case, we must first show what way is open to us in order that we may make known the truth which is our object.

(2) There is a twofold mode of truth in what we profess about God. Some truths about God exceed all the ability of the human reason. Such is the truth that God is triune. But there are some truths which the natural reason also is able to reach. Such are that God exists, that He is one, and the like. In fact, such truths about God have been proved demonstratively by the philosophers, guided by the light of the natural reason.

(3) That there are certain truths about God that totally surpass man's abil-

REASON AND REVELATION   From *On the Truth of the Catholic Faith*, Volume I by St. Thomas Aquinas, translated by Anton C. Pegis. Copyright © 1955 by Doubleday & Company, Inc. Reprinted by permission of the publisher.

[1] Aristotle, *Nicomachean Ethics*, I, 3 (1094b 24).
[2] Boethius, *De Trinitate*, II (*PL*, 64, col. 1250).

ity appears with the greatest evidence. Since, indeed, the principle of all knowledge that the reason perceives about some thing is the understanding of the very substance of that being (for according to Aristotle "what a thing is" is the principle of demonstration),[3] it is necessary that the way in which we understand the substance of a thing determines the way in which we know what belongs to it. Hence, if the human intellect comprehends the substance of some thing, for example, that of a stone or of a triangle, no intelligible characteristic belonging to that thing surpasses the grasp of the human reason. But this does not happen to us in the case of God. For the human intellect is not able to reach a comprehension of the divine substance through its natural power. For, according to its manner of knowing in the present life, the intellect depends on the senses for the origin of knowledge; and so those things that do not fall under the senses cannot be grasped by the human intellect except in so far as the knowledge of them is gathered from sensible things. Now, sensible things cannot lead the human intellect to the point of seeing in them the nature of the divine substance; for sensible things are effects that fall short of the power of their cause. Yet, beginning with sensible things, our intellect is led to the point of knowing about God that He exists, and other such characteristics that must be attributed to the First Principle. There are, consequently, some intelligible truths about God that are open to the human reason; but there are others that absolutely surpass its power.

(4) We may easily see the same point from the gradation of intellects. Consider the case of two persons of whom one has a more penetrating grasp of a thing by his intellect than does the other. He who has the superior intellect understands many things that the other cannot grasp at all. Such is the case with a very simple person who cannot at all grasp the subtle speculations of philosophy. But the intellect of an angel surpasses the human intellect much more than the intellect of the greatest philosopher surpasses the intellect of the most uncultivated simple person; for the distance between the best philosopher and a simple person is contained within the limits of the human species, which the angelic intellect surpasses. For the angel knows God on the basis of a more noble effect than does man; and this by as much as the substance of an angel, through which the angel in his natural knowledge is led to the knowledge of God, is nobler than sensible things and even than the soul itself, through which the human intellect mounts to the knowledge of God. The divine intellect surpasses the angelic intellect much more than the angelic surpasses the human. For the divine intellect is in its capacity equal to its substance, and therefore it understands fully what it is, including all its intelligible attributes. But by his natural knowledge the angel does not know what God is, since the substance itself of the angel, through which he is led to the knowledge of God, is an effect that is not

---

[3] Aristotle, *Posterior Analytics*, II, 3 (90b 31).

equal to the power of its cause. Hence, the angel is not able, by means of his natural knowledge, to grasp all the things that God understands in Himself; nor is the human reason sufficient to grasp all the things that the angel understands through his own natural power. Just as, therefore, it would be the height of folly for a simple person to assert that what a philosopher proposes is false on the ground that he himself cannot understand it, so (and even more so) it is the acme of stupidity for a man to suspect as false what is divinely revealed through the ministry of the angels simply because it cannot be investigated by reason.

(5) The same thing, moreover, appears quite clearly from the defect that we experience every day in our knowledge of things. We do not know a great many of the properties of sensible things, and in most cases we are not able to discover fully the natures of those properties that we apprehend by the sense. Much more is it the case, therefore, that the human reason is not equal to the task of investigating all the intelligible characteristics of that most excellent substance.

(6) The remark of Aristotle likewise agrees with this conclusion. He says that "our intellect is related to the prime beings, which are most evident in their nature, as the eye of an owl is related to the sun." [4]

(7) Sacred Scripture also gives testimony to this truth. We read in Job: "Peradventure thou wilt comprehend the steps of God, and wilt find out the Almighty perfectly?" (11:7). And again: "Behold, God is great, exceeding our knowledge" (Job 36:26). And St. Paul: "We know in part" (I Cor. 13:9).

(8) We should not, therefore, immediately reject as false, following the opinion of the Manicheans and many unbelievers, everything that is said about God even though it cannot be investigated by reason.

CHAPTER IV.   THAT THE TRUTH ABOUT GOD
TO WHICH THE NATURAL REASON REACHES
IS FITTINGLY PROPOSED TO MEN FOR BELIEF

(1) Since, therefore, there exists a twofold truth concerning the divine being, one to which the inquiry of the reason can reach, the other which surpasses the whole ability of the human reason, it is fitting that both of these truths be proposed to man divinely for belief. This point must first be shown concerning the truth that is open to the inquiry of the reason; otherwise, it might perhaps seem to someone that, since such a truth can be known by the reason, it was uselessly given to men through a supernatural inspiration as an object of belief.

(2) Yet, if this truth were left solely as a matter of inquiry for the human reason, three awkward consequences would follow.

[4] Aristotle, *Metaphysics*, Ia, 1 (993b 9).

(3) The first is that few men would possess the knowledge of God. For there are three reasons why most men are cut off from the fruit of diligent inquiry which is the discovery of truth. Some do not have the physical disposition for such work. As a result, there are many who are naturally not fitted to pursue knowledge; and so, however much they tried, they would be unable to reach the highest level of human knowledge which consists in knowing God. Others are cut off from pursuing this truth by the necessities imposed upon them by their daily lives. For some men must devote themselves to taking care of temporal matters. Such men would not be able to give so much time to the leisure of contemplative inquiry as to reach the highest peak at which human investigation can arrive, namely, the knowledge of God. Finally, there are some who are cut off by indolence. In order to know the things that the reason can investigate concerning God, a knowledge of many things must already be possessed. For almost all of philosophy is directed towards the knowledge of God, and that is why metaphysics, which deals with divine things, is the last part of philosophy to be learned. This means that we are able to arrive at the inquiry concerning the aforementioned truth only on the basis of a great deal of labor spent in study. Now, those who wish to undergo such a labor for the mere love of knowledge are few, even though God has inserted into the minds of men a natural appetite for knowledge.

(4) The second awkward effect is that those who would come to discover the abovementioned truth would barely reach it after a great deal of time. The reasons are several. There is the profundity of this truth, which the human intellect is made capable of grasping by natural inquiry only after a long training. Then, there are many things that must be presupposed, as we have said. There is also the fact that, in youth, when the soul is swayed by the various movements of the passions, it is not in a suitable state for the knowledge of such lofty truth. On the contrary, "one becomes wise and knowing in repose," as it is said in the *Physics*.[5] The result is this. If the only way open to us for the knowledge of God were solely that of the reason, the human race would remain in the blackest shadows of ignorance. For then the knowledge of God, which especially renders men perfect and good, would come to be possessed only by a few, and these few would require a great deal of time in order to reach it.

(5) The third awkward effect is this. The investigation of the human reason for the most part has falsity present within it, and this is due partly to the weakness of our intellect in judgment, and partly to the admixture of images. The result is that many, remaining ignorant of the power of demonstration, would hold in doubt those things that have been most truly demonstrated. This would be particularly the case since they see that, among those who are reputed to be wise men, each one teaches his own brand of doctrine.

[5] Aristotle, *Physics*, VII, 3 (247b 9).

Furthermore, with the many truths that are demonstrated, there sometimes is mingled something that is false, which is not demonstrated but rather asserted on the basis of some probable or sophistical argument, which yet has the credit of being a demonstration. That is why it was necessary that the unshakeable certitude and pure truth concerning divine things should be presented to men by way of faith.[6]

(6) Beneficially, therefore, did the divine Mercy provide that it should instruct us to hold by faith even those truths that the human reason is able to investigate. In this way, all men would easily be able to have a share in the knowledge of God, and this without uncertainty and error.

(7) Hence it is written: "Henceforward you walk not as also the Gentiles walk in the vanity of their mind, having their understanding darkened" (Eph. 4:17–18). And again: "All thy children shall be taught of the Lord" (Isa. 54:13).

CHAPTER V.   THAT THE TRUTHS THE HUMAN REASON
IS NOT ABLE TO INVESTIGATE ARE FITTINGLY
PROPOSED TO MEN FOR BELIEF

(1) Now, perhaps some will think that men should not be asked to believe what the reason is not adequate to investigate, since the divine Wisdom provides in the case of each thing according to the mode of its nature. We must therefore prove that it is necessary for man to receive from God as objects of belief even those truths that are above the human reason.

(2) No one tends with desire and zeal towards something that is not already known to him. But, as we shall examine later on in this work, men are ordained by the divine Providence towards a higher good than human fragility can experience in the present life.[7] That is why it was necessary for the human mind to be called to something higher than the human reason here and now can reach, so that it would thus learn to desire something and with zeal tend towards something that surpasses the whole state of the present life. This belongs especially to the Christian religion, which in a unique way promises spiritual and eternal goods. And so there are many things proposed to men in it that transcend human sense. The Old Law, on the other hand, whose promises were of a temporal character, contained very few proposals that transcended the inquiry of the human reason. Following this same direction, the philosophers themselves, in order that they

---

[6] Although St. Thomas does not name Maimonides or his *Guide for the Perplexed* (*Dux neutrorum*), there are evident points of contact between the Catholic and the Jewish theologian. On the reasons for revelation given here, on our knowledge of God, on creation and the eternity of the world, and on Aristotelianism in general, St. Thomas has Maimonides in mind both to agree and to disagree with him. By way of background for *SCG*, I, the reader can usefully consult the references to Maimonides in E. Gilson, *History of Christian Philosophy in the Middle Ages* (New York, 1955), pp. 649–651.

[7] *SCG*, III, ch. 48.

might lead men from the pleasure of sensible things to virtue, were concerned to show that there were in existence other goods of a higher nature than these things of sense, and that those who gave themselves to the active or contemplative virtues would find much sweeter enjoyment in the taste of these higher goods.

(3) It is also necessary that such truth be proposed to men for belief so that they may have a truer knowledge of God. For then only do we know God truly when we believe Him to be above everything that it is possible for man to think about Him; for, as we have shown,[8] the divine substance surpasses the natural knowledge of which man is capable. Hence, by the fact that some things about God are proposed to man that surpass his reason, there is strengthened in man the view that God is something above what he can think.

(4) Another benefit that comes from the revelation to men of truths that exceed the reason is the curbing of presumption, which is the mother of error. For there are some who have such a presumptuous opinion of their own ability that they deem themselves able to measure the nature of everything; I mean to say that, in their estimation, everything is true that seems to them so, and everything is false that does not. So that the human mind, therefore, might be freed from this presumption and come to a humble inquiry after truth, it was necessary that some things should be proposed to man by God that would completely surpass his intellect.

(5) A still further benefit may also be seen in what Aristotle says in the *Ethics*.[9] There was a certain Simonides who exhorted people to put aside the knowledge of divine things and to apply their talents to human occupations. He said that "he who is a man should know human things, and he who is mortal, things that are mortal." Against Simonides Aristotle says that "man should draw himself towards what is immortal and divine as much as he can." And so he says in the *De animalibus* that, although what we know of the higher substances is very little, yet that little is loved and desired more than all the knowledge that we have about less noble substances.[10] He also says in the *De caelo et mundo* that when questions about the heavenly bodies can be given even a modest and merely plausible solution, he who hears this experiences intense joy.[11] From all these considerations it is clear that even the most imperfect knowledge about the most noble realities brings the greatest perfection to the soul. Therefore, although the human reason cannot grasp fully the truths that are above it, yet, if it somehow holds these truths at least by faith, it acquires great perfection for itself.

(6) Therefore it is written: "For many things are shown to thee above the understanding of men" (Ecclus. 3:25). Again: "So the things that are of

---

[8] See above, ch. 3.
[9] Aristotle, *Nicomachean Ethics*, X, 7 (1177b 31).
[10] Aristotle, *De partibus animalium*, I, 5 (644b 32).
[11] Aristotle, *De caelo et mundo*, II, 12 (291b 26).

God no man knoweth but the Spirit of God. But to us God hath revealed them by His Spirit" (I Cor. 2:11, 10).

CHAPTER VI.   THAT TO GIVE ASSENT TO THE TRUTHS
OF FAITH IS NOT FOOLISHNESS EVEN THOUGH
THEY ARE ABOVE REASON

(1) Those who place their faith in this truth, however, "for which the human reason offers no experimental evidence," [12] do not believe foolishly, as though "following artificial fables" (II Peter 1:16). For these "secrets of divine Wisdom" (Job 11:6) the divine Wisdom itself, which knows all things to the full, has deigned to reveal to men. It reveals its own presence, as well as the truth of its teaching and inspiration, by fitting arguments; and in order to confirm those truths that exceed natural knowledge, it gives visible manifestation to works that surpass the ability of all nature. Thus, there are the wonderful cures of illnesses, there is the raising of the dead, and the wonderful immutation in the heavenly bodies; and what is more wonderful, there is the inspiration given to human minds, so that simple and untutored persons, filled with the gift of the Holy Spirit, come to possess instantaneously the highest wisdom and the readiest eloquence. When these arguments were examined, through the efficacy of the above-mentioned proof, and not the violent assault of arms or the promise of pleasures, and (what is most wonderful of all) in the midst of the tyranny of the persecutors, an innumerable throng of people, both simple and most learned, flocked to the Christian faith. In this faith there are truths preached that surpass every human intellect; the pleasures of the flesh are curbed; it is taught that the things of the world should be spurned. Now, for the minds of mortal men to assent to these things is the greatest of miracles, just as it is a manifest work of divine inspiration that, spurning visible things, men should seek only what is invisible. Now, that this has happened neither without preparation nor by chance, but as a result of the disposition of God, is clear from the fact that through many pronouncements of the ancient prophets God had foretold that He would do this. The books of these prophets are held in veneration among us Christians, since they give witness to our faith.

(2) The manner of this confirmation is touched on by St. Paul: "Which," that is, human salvation, "having begun to be declared by the Lord, was confirmed unto us by them that hear Him: God also bearing them witness of signs, and wonders, and divers miracles, and distributions of the Holy Ghost" (Heb. 2:3–4).

(3) This wonderful conversion of the world to the Christian faith is the clearest witness of the signs given in the past; so that it is not necessary that they should be further repeated, since they appear most clearly in their effect.

[12] St. Gregory, *Homiliae in evangelia*, II, hom. 26, i (*PL*, 76, col. 1197).

For it would be truly more wonderful than all signs if the world had been led by simple and humble men to believe such lofty truths, to accomplish such difficult actions, and to have such high hopes. Yet it is also a fact that, even in our own time, God does not cease to work miracles through His saints for the confirmation of the faith.

(4) On the other hand, those who founded sects committed to erroneous doctrines proceeded in a way that is opposite to this. The point is clear in the case of Mohammed. He seduced the people by promises of carnal pleasure to which the concupiscence of the flesh goads us. His teaching also contained precepts that were in conformity with his promises, and he gave free rein to carnal pleasure. In all this, as is not unexpected, he was obeyed by carnal men. As for proofs of the truth of his doctrine, he brought forward only such as could be grasped by the natural ability of anyone with a very modest wisdom. Indeed, the truths that he taught he mingled with many fables and with doctrines of the greatest falsity. He did not bring forth any signs produced in a supernatural way, which alone fittingly gives witness to divine inspiration; for a visible action that can be only divine reveals an invisibly inspired teacher of truth. On the contrary, Mohammed said that he was sent in the power of his arms—which are signs not lacking even to robbers and tyrants. What is more, no wise men, men trained in things divine and human, believed in him from the beginning. Those who believed in him were brutal men and desert wanderers, utterly ignorant of all divine teaching, through whose numbers Mohammed forced others to become his followers by the violence of his arms. Nor do divine pronouncements on the part of preceding prophets offer him any witness. On the contrary, he perverts almost all the testimonies of the Old and New Testaments by making them into fabrications of his own, as can be seen by anyone who examines his law. It was, therefore, a shrewd decision on his part to forbid his followers to read the Old and New Testaments, lest these books convict him of falsity. It is thus clear that those who place any faith in his words believe foolishly.

CHAPTER VII.   THAT THE TRUTH OF REASON
IS NOT OPPOSED TO THE TRUTH
OF THE CHRISTIAN FAITH

(1) Now, although the truth of the Christian faith which we have discussed surpasses the capacity of the reason, nevertheless that truth that the human reason is naturally endowed to know cannot be opposed to the truth of the Christian faith. For that with which the human reason is naturally endowed is clearly most true; so much so, that it is impossible for us to think of such truths as false. Nor is it permissible to believe as false that which we hold by faith, since this is confirmed in a way that is so clearly divine. Since, therefore, only the false is opposed to the true, as is clearly evident from an examination of their definitions, it is impossible that the truth of faith should be opposed to those principles that the human reason knows naturally.

(2) Furthermore, that which is introduced into the soul of the student by the teacher is contained in the knowledge of the teacher—unless his teaching is fictitious, which it is improper to say of God. Now, the knowledge of the principles that are known to us naturally has been implanted in us by God; for God is the Author of our nature. These principles, therefore, are also contained by the divine Wisdom. Hence, whatever is opposed to them is opposed to the divine Wisdom, and, therefore, cannot come from God. That which we hold by faith as divinely revealed, therefore, cannot be contrary to our natural knowledge.

(3) Again. In the presence of contrary arguments our intellect is chained, so that it cannot proceed to the knowledge of the truth. If, therefore, contrary knowledges were implanted in us by God, our intellect would be hindered from knowing truth by this very fact. Now, such an effect cannot come from God.

(4) And again. What is natural cannot change as long as nature does not. Now, it is impossible that contrary opinions should exist in the same knowing subject at the same time. No opinion or belief, therefore, is implanted in man by God which is contrary to man's natural knowledge.

(5) Therefore, the Apostle says: "The word is nigh thee, even in thy mouth and in thy heart. This is the word of faith, which we preach" (Rom. 10:8). But because it overcomes reason, there are some who think that it is opposed to it: which is impossible.

(6) The authority of St. Augustine also agrees with this. He writes as follows: "That which truth will reveal cannot in any way be opposed to the sacred books of the Old and the New Testament." [13]

(7) From this we evidently gather the following conclusion: whatever arguments are brought forward against the doctrines of faith are conclusions incorrectly derived from the first and self-evident principles imbedded in nature. Such conclusions do not have the force of demonstration; they are arguments that are either probable or sophistical. And so, there exists the possibility to answer them.

CHAPTER VIII.   HOW THE HUMAN REASON IS RELATED
TO THE TRUTH OF FAITH

(1) There is also a further consideration. Sensible things, from which the human reason takes the origin of its knowledge, retain within themselves some sort of trace of a likeness to God. This is so imperfect, however, that it is absolutely inadequate to manifest the substance of God. For effects bear within themselves, in their own way, the likeness of their causes, since an agent produces its like; yet an effect does not always reach to the full likeness of its cause. Now, the human reason is related to the knowledge of the truth of faith (a truth which can be most evident only to those who see

[13] St. Augustine, *De genesi ad litteram*, II, c. 18 (*PL*, 34, col. 280).

the divine substance) in such a way that it can gather certain likenesses of it, which are yet not sufficient so that the truth of faith may be comprehended as being understood demonstratively or through itself. Yet it is useful for the human reason to exercise itself in such arguments, however weak they may be, provided only that there be present no presumption to comprehend or to demonstrate. For to be able to see something of the loftiest realities, however thin and weak the sight may be, is, as our previous remarks indicate, a cause of the greatest joy.

(2) The testimony of Hilary agrees with this. Speaking of this same truth, he writes as follows in his *De Trinitate:* "Enter these truths by believing, press forward, persevere. And though I may know that you will not arrive at an end, yet I will congratulate you in your progress. For, though he who pursues the infinite with reverence will never finally reach the end, yet he will always progress by pressing onward. But do not intrude yourself into the divine secret, do not, presuming to comprehend the sum total of intelligence, plunge yourself into the mystery of the unending nativity; rather, understand that these things are incomprehensible." [14]

WILLIAM JAMES
The Will to Believe [1]

I

Let us give the name of *hypothesis* to anything that may be proposed to our belief; and just as the electricians speak of live and dead wires, let us speak of any hypothesis as either *live* or *dead*. A live hypothesis is one which appeals as a real possibility to him to whom it is proposed. If I ask you to believe in the Mahdi, the notion makes no electric connection with your nature,—it refuses to scintillate with any credibility at all. As an hypothesis it is completely dead. To an Arab, however (even if he be not one of the

William James (1842–1910) was one of the outstanding figures in the philosophical movement known as Pragmatism; he was a notable psychologist as well. His major works include *Principles of Psychology, Pragmatism: A New Name for Some Old Ways of Thinking,* and *The Varieties of Religious Experience.*

THE WILL TO BELIEVE   From *The Will to Believe and Other Essays in Popular Philosophy* by William James. Copyright 1896 by William James.

[14] St. Hilary, *De Trinitate,* II, 10, ii (*PL,* 10, coll. 58–59).
[1] An Address to the Philosophical Clubs of Yale and Brown Universities. Published in the New World, June, 1896.

Mahdi's followers), the hypothesis is among the mind's possibilities: it is alive. This shows that deadness and liveness in an hypothesis are not intrinsic properties, but relations to the individual thinker. They are measured by his willingness to act. The maximum of liveness in an hypothesis means willingness to act irrevocably. Practically, that means belief; but there is some believing tendency wherever there is willingness to act at all.

Next, let us call the decision between two hypotheses an *option*. Options may be of several kinds. They may be—1, *living* or *dead*; 2, *forced* or *avoidable*; 3, *momentous* or *trivial*; and for our purposes we may call an option a *genuine* option when it is of the forced, living, and momentous kind.

(1) A living option is one in which both hypotheses are live ones. If I say to you: "Be a theosophist or be a Mohammedan," it is probably a dead option, because for you neither hypothesis is likely to be alive. But if I say: "Be an agnostic or be a Christian," it is otherwise: trained as you are, each hypothesis makes some appeal, however small, to your belief.

(2) Next, if I say to you: "Choose between going out with your umbrella or without it," I do not offer you a genuine option, for it is not forced. You can easily avoid it by not going out at all. Similarly, if I say, "Either love me or hate me," "Either call my theory true or call it false," your option is avoidable. You may remain indifferent to me, neither loving nor hating, and you may decline to offer any judgment as to my theory. But if I say, "Either accept this truth or go without it," I put on you a forced option, for there is no standing place outside of the alternative. Every dilemma based on a complete logical disjunction, with no possibility of not choosing, is an option of this forced kind.

(3) Finally, if I were Dr. Nansen and proposed to you to join my North Pole expedition, your option would be momentous; for this would probably be your only similar opportunity, and your choice now would either exclude you from the North Pole sort of immortality altogether or put at least the chance of it into your hands. He who refuses to embrace a unique opportunity loses the prize as surely as if he tried and failed. *Per contra*, the option is trivial when the opportunity is not unique, when the stake is insignificant, or when the decision is reversible if it later prove unwise. Such trivial options abound in the scientific life. A chemist finds an hypothesis live enough to spend a year in its verification: he believes in it to that extent. But if his experiments prove inconclusive either way, he is quit for his loss of time, no vital harm being done.

It will facilitate our discussion if we keep all these distinctions well in mind.

II

The next matter to consider is the actual psychology of human opinion. When we look at certain facts, it seems as if our passional and volitional nature lay at the root of all our convictions. When we look at others, it seems as if they could do nothing when the intellect had once said its say. Let us take the latter facts up first.

Does it not seem preposterous on the very face of it to talk of our opinions being modifiable at will? Can our will either help or hinder our intellect in its perceptions of truth? Can we, by just willing it, believe that Abraham Lincoln's existence is a myth, and that the portraits of him in *McClure's Magazine* are all of some one else? Can we, by any effort of our will, or by any strength of wish that it were true, believe ourselves well and about when we are roaring with rheumatism in bed, or feel certain that the sum of the two one-dollar bills in our pocket must be a hundred dollars? We can *say* any of these things, but we are absolutely impotent to believe them; and of just such things is the whole fabric of the truths that we do believe in made up,—matters of fact, immediate or remote, as Hume said, and relations between ideas, which are either there or not there for us if we see them so, and which if not there cannot be put there by any action of our own.

In Pascal's *Thoughts* there is a celebrated passage known in literature as Pascal's wager. In it he tries to force us into Christianity by reasoning as if our concern with truth resembled our concern with the stakes in a game of chance. Translated freely his words are these: You must either believe or not believe that God is—which will you do? Your human reason cannot say. A game is going on between you and the nature of things which at the day of judgment will bring out either heads or tails. Weigh what your gains and your losses would be if you should stake all you have on heads, or God's existence: if you win in such case, you gain eternal beatitude; if you lose, you lose nothing at all. If there were an infinity of chances, and only one for God in this wager, still you ought to stake your all on God; for though you surely risk a finite loss by this procedure, any finite loss is reasonable, even a certain one is reasonable, if there is but the possibility of infinite gain. Go, then, and take holy water, and have masses said; belief will come and stupefy your scruples,—*Cela vous fera croire et vous abêtira.* Why should you not? At bottom, what have you to lose?

You probably feel that when religious faith expresses itself thus, in the language of the gaming table, it is put to its last trumps. Surely Pascal's own personal belief in masses and holy water had far other springs; and this celebrated page of his is but an argument for others, a last desperate snatch at a weapon against the hardness of the unbelieving heart. We feel that a faith in masses and holy water adopted wilfully after such a mechanical calculation would lack the inner soul of faith's reality; and if we were ourselves in the place of the Deity, we should probably take particular pleasure in cutting off believers of this pattern from their infinite reward. It is evident that unless there be some pre-existing tendency to believe in masses and holy water, the option offered to the will by Pascal is not a living option.

Certainly no Turk ever took to masses and holy water on its account; and even to us Protestants these means of salvation seem such foregone impossibilities that Pascal's logic, invoked for them specifically, leaves us unmoved. As well might the Mahdi write to us, saying, "I am the Expected One whom God has created in his effulgence. You shall be infinitely happy if you confess me; otherwise you shall be cut off from the light of the sun. Weigh, then, your infinite gain if I am genuine against your finite sacrifice if I am not!" His logic would be that of Pascal; but he would vainly use it on us, for the hypothesis he offers us is dead. No tendency to act on it exists in us to any degree.

The talk of believing by our volition seems, then, from one point of view, simply silly. From another point of view it is worse than silly, it is vile. When one turns to the magnificent edifice of the physical sciences, and sees how it was reared; what thousands of disinterested moral lives of men lie buried in its mere foundations; what patience and postponement, what choking down of preference, what submission to the icy laws of outer fact are wrought into its very stones and mortar; how absolutely impersonal it stands in its vast augustness,—then how besotted and contemptible seems every little sentimentalist who comes blowing his voluntary smoke-wreaths, and pretending to decide things from out of his private dream! Can we wonder if those bred in the rugged and manly school of science should feel like spewing such subjectivism out of their mouths? The whole system of loyalties which grow up in the schools of science go dead against its toleration; so that it is only natural that those who have caught the scientific fever should pass over to the opposite extreme, and write sometimes as if the incorruptibly truthful intellect ought positively to prefer bitterness and unacceptableness to the heart in its cup.

> It fortifies my soul to know
> That, though I perish, Truth is so—

sings Clough, while Huxley exclaims: "My only consolation lies in the reflection that, however bad our posterity may become, so far as they hold by the plain rule of not pretending to believe what they have no reason to believe, because it may be to their advantage so to pretend [the word 'pretend' is surely here redundant], they will not have reached the lowest depth of immorality." And that delicious *enfant terrible* Clifford writes: "Belief is desecrated when given to unproved and unquestioned statements for the solace and private pleasure of the believer. . . . Whoso would deserve well of his fellows in this matter will guard the purity of his belief with a very fanaticism of jealous care, lest at any time it should rest on an unworthy object, and catch a stain which can never be wiped away. . . . If [a] belief has been accepted on insufficient evidence [even though the belief be true, as Clifford on the same page explains] the pleasure is a stolen one. . . . It is sinful because it is stolen in defiance of our duty to mankind. That duty is to guard ourselves from such beliefs as from a pestilence which may shortly master our own body and then spread to the rest of the town. . . . It is wrong always, everywhere, and for every one, to believe anything upon insufficient evidence.''

III

All this strikes one as healthy, even when expressed, as by Clifford, with somewhat too much of robustious pathos in the voice. Free-will and simple wishing do seem, in the matter of our credences, to be only fifth wheels to the coach. Yet if any one should thereupon assume that intellectual insight is what remains after wish and will and sentimental preference have taken wing, or that pure reason is what then settles our opinions, he would fly quite as directly in the teeth of the facts.

It is only our already dead hypotheses that our willing nature is unable to bring to life again. But what has made them dead for us is for the most part a previous action of our willing nature of an antagonistic kind. When I say 'willing nature,' I do not mean only such deliberate volitions as may have set up habits of belief that we cannot now escape from,—I mean all such factors of belief as fear and hope, prejudice and passion, imitation and partisanship, the circumpressure of our caste and set. As a matter of fact we find ourselves believing, we hardly know how or why. Mr. Balfour gives the name of 'authority' to all those influences, born of the intellectual climate, that make hypotheses possible or impossible for us, alive or dead. Here in this room, we all of us believe in molecules and the conservation of energy, in democracy and necessary progress, in Protestant Christianity and the duty of fighting for 'the doctrine of the immortal Monroe,' all for no reasons worthy of the name. We see into these matters with no more inner clearness, and probably with much less, than any disbeliever in them might possess. His unconventionality would probably have some grounds to show for its conclusions; but for us, not insight, but the *prestige* of the opinions, is what makes the spark shoot from them and light up our sleeping magazines of faith. Our reason is quite satisfied, in nine hundred and ninety-nine cases out of every thousand of us, if it can find a few arguments that will do to recite in case our credulity is criticised by some one else. Our faith is faith in some one else's faith, and in the greatest matters this is most the case. Our belief in truth itself, for instance, that there is a truth, and that our minds and it are made for each other,—what is it but a passionate affirmation of desire, in which our social system backs us up? We want to have a truth; we want to believe that our experiments and studies and discussions must put us in a continually better and better position towards it; and on this line we agree to fight out our thinking lives. But if a pyrrhonistic sceptic asks us *how we know* all this, can our logic find a reply? No! certainly it cannot. It is just one volition against another,—we willing to go in for life upon a trust or assumption which he, for his part, does not care to make.[2]

As a rule we disbelieve all facts and theories for which we have no use. Clifford's cosmic emotions find no use for Christian feelings. Huxley belabors the bishops because there is no use for sacerdotalism in his scheme of life. Newman, on the contrary, goes over to Romanism, and finds all sorts of reasons good for staying there, because a priestly system is for him an organic need and delight. Why do so few 'scientists' even look at the evidence for telepathy, so called? Because they think, as a leading biologist, now dead, once said to me, that even if such a thing were true, scientists ought to band together to keep it suppressed and concealed. It would undo the uniformity of Nature and all sorts of other things without which scientists cannot carry on their pursuits. But if this very man had been shown something which as a scientist he might *do* with telepathy, he might not only have examined the evidence, but even have found it good enough. This very law which the logicians would impose upon us—if I may give the name of logicians to those who would rule out our willing nature here—is based on nothing but their own natural wish to exclude all elements for which they, in their professional quality of logicians, can find no use.

Evidently, then, our non-intellectual nature does influence our convictions. There are passional tendencies and volitions which run before and others which come after belief, and it is only the latter that are too late for the fair; and they are not too late when the previous passional work has been already in their own direction. Pascal's argument, instead of being powerless, then seems a regular clincher, and is the last stroke needed to make our faith in masses and holy water complete. The state of things is evidently far from simple; and pure insight and logic, whatever they might do ideally, are not the only things that really do produce our creeds.

IV

Our next duty, having recognized this mixed-up state of affairs, is to ask whether it be simply reprehensible and pathological, or whether, on the contrary, we must treat it as a normal element in making up our minds. The thesis I defend is, briefly stated, this: *Our passional nature not only lawfully may, but must, decide an option between propositions, whenever it is a genuine option that cannot by its nature be decided on intellectual grounds; for to say, under such circumstances, "Do not decide, but leave the question open," is itself a passional decision,—just like deciding yes or no,— and is attended with the same risk of losing the truth. . . .*

[2] Compare the admirable page 310 in S. H. Hodgson's "Time and Space," London, 1865.

One more point, small but important, and our preliminaries are done. There are two ways of looking at our duty in the matter of opinion,—ways entirely different, and yet ways about whose difference the theory of knowledge seems hitherto to have shown very little concern. *We must know the truth*; and *we must avoid error*,—these are our first and great commandments as would-be knowers; but they are not two ways of stating an identical commandment, they are two separable laws. Although it may indeed happen that when we believe the truth A, we escape as an incidental consequence from believing the falsehood B, it hardly ever happens that by merely disbelieving B we necessarily believe A. We may in escaping B fall into believing other falsehoods, C or D, just as bad as B; or we may escape B by not believing anything at all, not even A.

Believe truth! Shun error!—these, we see, are two materially different laws; and by choosing between them we may end, coloring differently our whole intellectual life. We may regard the chase for truth as paramount, and the avoidance of error as secondary; or we may, on the other hand, treat the avoidance of error as more imperative, and let truth take its chance. Clifford, in the instructive passage which I have quoted, exhorts us to the latter course. Believe nothing, he tells us, keep your mind in suspense forever, rather than by closing it on insufficient evidence incur the awful risk of believing lies. You, on the other hand, may think that the risk of being in error is a very small matter when compared with the blessings of real knowledge, and be ready to be duped many times in your investigation rather than postpone indefinitely the chance of guessing true. I myself find it impossible to go with Clifford. We must remember that these feelings of our duty about either truth or error are in any case only expressions of our passional life. Biologically considered, our minds are as ready to grind out falsehood as veracity, and he who says, "Better go without belief forever than believe a lie!" merely shows his own preponderant private horror of becoming a dupe. He may be critical of many of his desires and fears, but this fear he slavishly obeys. He cannot imagine any one questioning its binding force. For my own part, I have also a horror of being duped; but I can believe that worse things than being duped may happen to a man in this world: so Clifford's exhortation has to my ears a thoroughly fantastic sound. It is like a general informing his soldiers that it is better to keep out of battle forever than to risk a single wound. Not so are victories either over enemies or over nature gained. Our errors are surely not such awfully solemn things. In a world where we are so certain to incur them in spite of all our caution, a certain lightness of heart seems healthier than this excessive nervousness on their behalf. At any rate, it seems the fittest thing for the empiricist philosopher.

And now, after all this introduction, let us go straight at our question. I have said, and now repeat it, that not only as a matter of fact do we find our passional nature influencing us in our opinions, but that there are some options between opinions in which this influence must be regarded both as an inevitable and as a lawful determinant of our choice.

I fear here that some of you my hearers will begin to scent danger, and lend an inhospitable ear. Two first steps of passion you have indeed had to admit as necessary,—we must think so as to avoid dupery, and we must think so as to gain truth; but the surest path to those ideal consummations, you will probably consider, is from now onwards to take no further passional step.

Well, of course, I agree as far as the facts will allow. Wherever the option between losing truth and gaining it is not momentous, we can throw the chance of *gaining truth* away, and at any rate save ourselves from any chance of *believing falsehood*, by not making up our minds at all till objective evidence has come. In scientific questions, this is almost always the case; and even in human affairs in general, the need of acting is seldom so urgent that a false belief to act on is better than no belief at all. Law courts, indeed, have to decide on the best evidence attainable for the moment, because a judge's duty is to make law as well as to ascertain it, and (as a learned judge once said to me) few cases are worth spending much time over: the great thing is to have them decided on *any* acceptable principle, and got out of the way. But in our dealings with objective nature we obviously are recorders, not makers, of the truth; and decisions for the mere sake of deciding promptly and getting on to the next business would be wholly out of place. Throughout the breadth of physical nature facts are what they are quite independently of us, and seldom is there any such hurry about them that the risks of being duped by believing a premature theory need be faced. The questions here are always trivial options, the hypotheses are hardly living (at any rate not living for us spectators), the choice between believing truth or falsehood is seldom forced. The attitude of sceptical balance is therefore the absolutely wise one if we would escape mistakes. What difference, indeed, does it make to most of us whether we have or have not a theory of the Röntgen rays, whether we believe or not in mind-stuff, or have a conviction about the causality of conscious states? It makes no difference. Such options are not forced on us. On every account it is better not to make them, but still keep weighing reasons *pro et contra* with an indifferent hand.

I speak, of course, here of the purely judging mind. For purposes of discovery such indifference is to be less highly recommended, and science would be far less advanced than she is if the passionate desires of individuals to get their own faiths confirmed had been kept out of the game. See for example the sagacity which Spencer and Weismann now display. On the other hand, if you want an absolute duffer in an investigation, you must, after all, take the man who has no interest whatever in its results: he is the warranted incapable, the positive fool. The most useful investigator, because the most sensitive observer, is always he whose eager interest in one side of the question is balanced by an equally keen nervousness lest he become deceived.[3] Science has organized this nervousness into a regular *technique*, her so-called method of verification; and she has fallen so deeply in love with the method that one may even say she has ceased to care for truth by itself at all. It is only truth as technically verified that interests her. The truth of truths might come in merely affirmative form, and she would decline to touch it. Such truth as that, she might repeat with Clifford, would be stolen in defiance of her duty to mankind. Human passions, however, are stronger than technical rules. "Le cœur a ses raisons," as Pascal says, "que la raison ne connaît pas;" and however indifferent to all but the bare rules of the game the umpire, the abstract intellect, may be, the concrete players who furnish him the materials to judge of are usually, each one of them, in love with some pet 'live hypothesis' of his own. Let us agree, however, that wherever there is no forced option, the dispassionately judicial intellect with no pet hypothesis, saving us, as it does, from dupery at any rate, ought to be our ideal.

The question next arises: Are there not somewhere forced options in our speculative questions, and can we (as men who may be interested at least as much in positively gaining truth as in merely escaping dupery) always wait with impunity till the coercive evidence shall have arrived? It seems *a priori* improbable that the truth should be so nicely adjusted to our needs and powers as that. In the great boarding-house of nature, the cakes and the butter and the syrup seldom come out so even and leave the plates so clean. Indeed, we should view them with scientific suspicion if they did.

IX

Moral questions immediately present themselves as questions whose solution cannot wait for sensible proof. A moral question is a question not of what sensibly exists, but of what is good, or would be good if it did exist. Science can tell us what exists; but to compare the *worths*, both of what exists and of what does not exist, we must consult not science, but what Pascal calls our heart. Science herself consults her heart when she lays it down that the infinite ascertainment of fact and correction of false belief are the supreme goods for man. Challenge the statement, and science can only repeat it oracularly, or else prove it by showing that such ascertainment and correction bring man all sorts of other goods which man's heart in turn declares. The question of having moral beliefs at all or not having them is decided by our

[3] Compare Wilfrid Ward's essay, "The Wish to Believe," in his *Witnesses to the Unseen*, Macmillan & Co., 1893.

will. Are our moral preferences true or false, or are they only odd biological phenomena, making things good or bad for *us*, but in themselves indifferent? How can your pure intellect decide? If your heart does not *want* a world of moral reality, your head will assuredly never make you believe in one. Mephistophelian scepticism, indeed, will satisfy the head's play-instincts much better than any rigorous idealism can. Some men (even at the student age) are so naturally cool-hearted that the moralistic hypothesis never has for them any pungent life, and in their supercilious presence the hot young moralist always feels strangely ill at ease. The appearance of knowingness is on their side, of *naïveté* and gullibility on his. Yet, in the inarticulate heart of him, he clings to it that he is not a dupe, and that there is a realm in which (as Emerson says) all their wit and intellectual superiority is no better than the cunning of a fox. Moral scepticism can no more be refuted or proved by logic than intellectual scepticism can. When we stick to it that there *is* truth (be it of either kind), we do so with our whole nature, and resolve to stand or fall by the results. The sceptic with his whole nature adopts the doubting attitude; but which of us is the wiser, Omniscience only knows.

Turn now from these wide questions of good to a certain class of questions of fact, questions concerning personal relations, states of mind between one man and another. *Do you like me or not?*—for example. Whether you do or not depends, in countless instances, on whether I meet you half-way, am willing to assume that you must like me, and show you trust and expectation. The previous faith on my part in your liking's existence is in such cases what makes your liking come. But if I stand aloof, and refuse to budge an inch until I have objective evidence, until you shall have done something apt, as the absolutists say, *ad extorquendum assensum meum*, ten to one your liking never comes. How many women's hearts are vanquished by the mere sanguine insistence of some man that they *must* love him! he will not consent to the hypothesis that they cannot. The desire for a certain kind of truth here brings about that special truth's existence; and so it is in innumerable cases of other sorts. Who gains promotions, boons, appointments, but the man in whose life they are seen to play the part of live hypotheses, who discounts them, sacrifices other things for their sake before they have come, and takes risks for them in advance? His faith acts on the powers above him as a claim, and creates its own verification.

A social organism of any sort whatever, large or small, is what it is because each member proceeds to his own duty with a trust that the other members will simultaneously do theirs. Wherever a desired result is achieved by the co-operation of many independent persons, its existence as a fact is a pure consequence of the precursive faith in one another of those immediately concerned. A government, an army, a commercial system, a ship, a college, an athletic team, all exist on this condition, without which not only is nothing achieved, but nothing is even attempted. A whole train of passengers (in-

dividually brave enough) will be looted by a few highwaymen, simply because the latter can count on one another, while each passenger fears that
if he makes a movement of resistance, he will be shot before any one else
backs him up. If we believed that the whole car-full would rise at once with
us, we should each severally rise, and train-robbing would never even be
attempted. There are, then, cases where a fact cannot come at all unless a
preliminary faith exists in its coming. *And where faith in a fact can help
create the fact,* that would be an insane logic which should say that faith
running ahead of scientific evidence is the 'lowest kind of immorality' into
which a thinking being can fall. Yet such is the logic by which our scientific
absolutists pretend to regulate our lives!

X

In truths dependent on our personal action, then, faith based on desire is
certainly a lawful and possibly an indispensable thing.

But now, it will be said, these are all childish human cases, and have
nothing to do with great cosmical matters, like the question of religious faith.
Let us then pass on to that. Religions differ so much in their accidents that
in discussing the religious question we must make it very generic and broad.
What then do we now mean by the religious hypothesis? Science says things
are; morality says some things are better than other things; and religion says
essentially two things.

First, she says that the best things are the more eternal things, the over-
lapping things, the things in the universe that throw the last stone, so to
speak, and say the final word. "Perfection is eternal,"—this phrase of Charles
Secrétan seems a good way of putting this first affirmation of religion, an
affirmation which obviously cannot yet be verified scientifically at all.

The second affirmation of religion is that we are better off even now if we
believe her first affirmation to be true.

Now, let us consider what the logical elements of this situation are *in case
the religious hypothesis in both its branches be really true.* (Of course, we
must admit that possibility at the outset. If we are to discuss the question at
all, it must involve a living option. If for any of you religion be a hypothesis
that cannot, by any living possibility be true, then you need go no farther. I
speak to the 'saving remnant' alone.) So proceeding, we see, first, that religion offers itself as a *momentous* option. We are supposed to gain, even
now, by our belief, and to lose by our nonbelief, a certain vital good. Secondly, religion is a *forced* option, so far as that good goes. We cannot escape
the issue by remaining sceptical and waiting for more light, because, although we do avoid error in that way *if religion be untrue,* we lose the good,
if it be true, just as certainly as if we positively chose to disbelieve. It is as if
a man should hesitate indefinitely to ask a certain woman to marry him because he was not perfectly sure that she would prove an angel after he

brought her home. Would he not cut himself off from that particular angel-possibility as decisively as if he went and married some one else? Scepticism, then, is not avoidance of option; it is option of a certain particular kind of risk. *Better risk loss of truth than chance of error,*—that is your faith-vetoer's exact position. He is actively playing his stake as much as the believer is; he is backing the field against the religious hypothesis, just as the believer is backing the religious hypothesis against the field. To preach scepticism to us as a duty until 'sufficient evidence' for religion be found, is tantamount therefore to telling us, when in presence of the religious hypothesis, that to yield to our fear of its being error is wiser and better than to yield to our hope that it may be true. It is not intellect against all passions, then; it is only intellect with one passion laying down its law. And by what, forsooth, is the supreme wisdom of this passion warranted? Dupery for dupery, what proof is there that dupery through hope is so much worse than dupery through fear? I, for one, can see no proof; and I simply refuse obedience to the scientist's command to imitate his kind of option, in a case where my own stake is important enough to give me the right to choose my own form of risk. If religion be true and the evidence for it be still insufficient, I do not wish, by putting your extinguisher upon my nature (which feels to me as if it had after all some business in this matter), to forfeit my sole chance in life of getting upon the winning side,—that chance depending, of course, on my willingness to run the risk of acting as if my passional need of taking the world religiously might be prophetic and right.

All this is on the supposition that it really may be prophetic and right, and that, even to us who are discussing the matter, religion is a live hypothesis which may be true. Now, to most of us religion comes in a still further way that makes a veto on our active faith even more illogical. The more perfect and more eternal aspect of the universe is represented in our religions as having personal form. The universe is no longer a mere *It* to us, but a *Thou*, if we are religious; and any relation that may be possible from person to person might be possible here. For instance, although in one sense we are passive portions of the universe, in another we show a curious autonomy, as if we were small active centres on our own account. We feel, too, as if the appeal of religion to us were made to our own active good-will, as if evidence might be forever withheld from us unless we met the hypothesis half-way. To take a trivial illustration: just as a man who in a company of gentlemen made no advances, asked a warrant for every concession, and believed no one's word without proof, would cut himself off by such churlishness from all the social rewards that a more trusting spirit would earn,—so here, one who should shut himself up in snarling logicality and try to make the gods extort his recognition willy-nilly, or not get it at all, might cut himself off forever from his only opportunity of making the gods' acquaintance. This feeling, forced on us we know not whence, that by obstinately believing that there are gods (although not to do so would be so easy both for our logic and our life) we are doing the universe the deepest service we can, seems part of the living essence of the religious hypothesis. If the hypothesis *were* true in all its parts, including this one, then pure intellectualism, with its veto on our making willing advances, would be an absurdity; and some participation of our sympathetic nature would be logically required. I, therefore, for one, cannot see my way to accepting the agnostic rules for truth-seeking, or wilfully agree to keep my willing nature out of the game. I cannot do so for this plain reason, that *a rule of thinking which would absolutely prevent me from acknowledging certain kinds of truth if those kinds of truth were really there, would be an irrational rule.* That for me is the long and short of the formal logic of the situation, no matter what the kinds of truth might materially be.

I confess I do not see how this logic can be escaped. But sad experience makes me fear that some of you may still shrink from radically saying with me, *in abstracto*, that we have the right to believe at our own risk any hypothesis that is live enough to tempt our will. I suspect, however, that if this is so, it is because you have got away from the abstract logical point of view altogether, and are thinking (perhaps without realizing it) of some particular religious hypothesis which for you is dead. The freedom to 'believe what we will' you apply to the case of some patent superstition; and the faith you think of is the faith defined by the schoolboy when he said, "Faith is when you believe something that you know ain't true." I can only repeat that this is misapprehension. *In concreto*, the freedom to believe can only cover living options which the intellect of the individual cannot by itself resolve; and living options never seem absurdities to him who has them to consider. When I look at the religious question as it really puts itself to concrete men, and when I think of all the possibilities which both practically and theoretically it involves, then this command that we shall put a stopper on our heart, instincts, and courage, and *wait*—acting of course meanwhile more or less as if religion were *not* true [4]—till doomsday, or till such time as our intellect and senses working together may have raked in evidence enough,—this command, I say, seems to me the queerest idol ever manufactured in the philosophic cave. Were we scholastic absolutists, there might be more excuse. If we had an infallible intellect with its objective certitudes, we might feel ourselves disloyal to such a perfect organ of knowledge in not trusting to it exclusively, in not waiting for its releasing word. But if we are empiricists, if we

---

[4] Since belief is measured by action, he who forbids us to believe religion to be true, necessarily also forbids us to act as we should if we did believe it to be true. The whole defence of religious faith hinges upon action. If the action required or inspired by the religious hypothesis is in no way different from that dictated by the naturalistic hypothesis, then religious faith is a pure superfluity, better pruned away, and controversy about its legitimacy is a piece of idle trifling, unworthy of serious minds. I myself believe, of course, that the religious hypothesis gives to the world an expression which specifically determines our reactions, and makes them in a large part unlike what they might be on a purely naturalistic scheme of belief.

believe that no bell in us tolls to let us know for certain when truth is in our grasp, then it seems a piece of idle fantasticality to preach so solemnly our duty of waiting for the bell. Indeed we *may* wait if we will,—I hope you do not think that I am denying that,—but if we do so, we do so at our peril as much as if we believed. In either case we *act*, taking our life in our hands.

PAUL TILLICH
The Nature of Faith

I.   FAITH AS ULTIMATE CONCERN

Faith is the state of being ultimately concerned: the dynamics of faith are the dynamics of man's ultimate concern. Man, like every living being, is concerned about many things, above all about those which condition his very existence, such as food and shelter. But man, in contrast to other living beings, has spiritual concerns—cognitive, aesthetic, social, political. Some of them are urgent, often extremely urgent, and each of them as well as the vital concerns can claim ultimacy for a human life or the life of a social group. If it claims ultimacy it demands the total surrender of him who accepts this claim, and it promises total fulfillment even if all other claims have to be subjected to it or rejected in its name. If a national group makes the life and growth of the nation its ultimate concern, it demands that all other concerns, economic well-being, health and life, family, aesthetic and cognitive truth, justice and humanity, be sacrificed. The extreme nationalisms of our century are laboratories for the study of what ultimate concern means in all aspects of human existence, including the smallest concern of one's daily life. Everything is centered in the only god, the nation—a god who certainly proves to be a demon, but who shows clearly the unconditional character of an ultimate concern.

But it is not only the unconditional demand made by that which is one's ultimate concern, it is also the promise of ultimate fulfillment which is accepted in the act of faith. The content of this promise is not necessarily defined. It can be expressed in indefinite symbols or in concrete symbols which cannot be taken literally, like the "greatness" of one's nation in which one participates even if one has died for it, or the conquest of mankind by

THE NATURE OF FAITH   From pp. 1–22, 30–40 from *Dynamics of Faith* by Paul Tillich. Copyright © 1957 by Paul Tillich. Reprinted by permission of Harper & Row, Publishers, Inc., and George Allen & Unwin Ltd.

the "saving race," etc. In each of these cases it is "ultimate fulfillment" that is promised, and it is exclusion from such fulfillment which is threatened if the unconditional demand is not obeyed.

An example—and more than an example—is the faith manifest in the religion of the Old Testament. It also has the character of ultimate concern in demand, threat and promise. The content of this concern is not the nation—although Jewish nationalism has sometimes tried to distort it into that —but the content is the God of justice, who, because he represents justice for everybody and every nation, is called the universal God, the God of the universe. He is the ultimate concern of every pious Jew, and therefore in his name the great commandment is given: "You shall love the Lord your God with all your heart, and with all your soul, and with all your might" (Deut. 6:5). This is what ultimate concern means and from these words the term "ultimate concern" is derived. They state unambiguously the character of genuine faith, the demand of total surrender to the subject of ultimate concern. The Old Testament is full of commands which make the nature of this surrender concrete, and it is full of promises and threats in relation to it. Here also are the promises of symbolic indefiniteness, although they center around fulfillment of the national and individual life, and the threat is the exclusion from such fulfillment through national extinction and individual catastrophe. Faith, for the men of the Old Testament, is the state of being ultimately and unconditionally concerned about Jahweh and about what he represents in demand, threat and promise.

Another example—almost a counter-example, yet nevertheless equally revealing—is the ultimate concern with "success" and with social standing and economic power. It is the god of many people in the highly competitive Western culture and it does what every ultimate concern must do: it demands unconditional surrender to its laws even if the price is the sacrifice of genuine human relations, personal conviction, and creative *eros*. Its threat is social and economic defeat, and its promise—indefinite as all such promises— the fulfillment of one's being. It is the breakdown of this kind of faith which characterizes and makes religiously important most contemporary literature. Not false calculations but a misplaced faith is revealed in novels like *Point of No Return*. When fulfilled, the promise of this faith proves to be empty.

Faith is the state of being ultimately concerned. The content matters infinitely for the life of the believer, but it does not matter for the formal definition of faith. And this is the first step we have to make in order to understand the dynamics of faith.

II.   FAITH AS A CENTERED ACT

Faith as ultimate concern is an act of the total personality. It happens in the center of the personal life and includes all its elements. Faith is the most centered act of the human mind. It is not a movement of a special section or a special function of man's total being. They all are united in the act of faith. But faith is not the sum total of their impacts. It transcends every special impact as well as the totality of them and it has itself a decisive impact on each of them.

Since faith is an act of the personality as a whole, it participates in the dynamics of personal life. These dynamics have been described in many ways, especially in the recent developments of analytic psychology. Thinking in polarities, their tensions and their possible conflicts, is a common characteristic of most of them. This makes the psychology of personality highly dynamic and requires a dynamic theory of faith as the most personal of all personal acts. The first and decisive polarity in analytic psychology is that between the so-called unconscious and the conscious. Faith as an act of the total personality is not imaginable without the participation of the unconscious elements in the personality structure. They are always present and decide largely about the content of faith. But, on the other hand, faith is a conscious act and the unconscious elements participate in the creation of faith only if they are taken into the personal center which transcends each of them. If this does not happen, if unconscious forces determine the mental status without a centered act, faith does not occur, and compulsions take its place. For faith is a matter of freedom. Freedom is nothing more than the possibility of centered personal acts. The frequent discussion in which faith and freedom are contrasted could be helped by the insight that faith is a free, namely, centered act of the personality. In this respect freedom and faith are identical.

Also important for the understanding of faith is the polarity between what Freud and his school call ego and superego. The concept of the superego is quite ambiguous. On the one hand, it is the basis of all cultural life because it restricts the uninhibited actualization of the always-driving libido; on the other hand, it cuts off man's vital forces, and produces disgust about the whole system of cultural restrictions, and brings about a neurotic state of mind. From this point of view, the symbols of faith are considered to be expressions of the superego or, more concretely, to be an expression of the father image which gives content to the superego. Responsible for this inadequate theory of the superego is Freud's naturalistic negation of norms and principles. If the superego is not established through valid principles, it becomes a suppressive tyrant. But real faith, even if it uses the father image for its expression, transforms this image into a principle of truth and justice to be defended even against the "father." Faith and culture can be affirmed only if the superego represents the norms and principles of reality.

This leads to the question of how faith as a personal, centered act is related to the rational structure of man's personality which is manifest in his meaningful language, in his ability to know the true and to do the good, in his sense of beauty and justice. All this, and not only his possibility to analyze, to calculate and to argue, makes him a rational being. But in spite of this larger concept of reason we must deny that man's essential nature is identical with the rational character of his mind. Man is able to decide for or against reason, he is able to create beyond reason or to destroy below reason. This power is the power of his self, the center of self-relatedness in which all elements of his being are united. Faith is not an act of any of his rational functions, as it is not an act of the unconscious, but it is an act in which both the rational and the nonrational elements of his being are transcended.

Faith as the embracing and centered act of the personality is "ecstatic." It transcends both the drives of the nonrational unconsicous and the structures of the rational conscious. It transcends them, but it does not destroy them. The ecstatic character of faith does not exclude its rational character although it is not identical with it, and it includes nonrational strivings without being identical with them. In the ecstasy of faith there is an awareness of truth and of ethical value; there are also past loves and hates, conflicts and reunions, individual and collective influences. "Ecstasy" means "standing outside of oneself"—without ceasing to be oneself—with all the elements which are united in the personal center.

A further polarity in these elements, relevant for the understanding of faith, is the tension between the cognitive function of man's personal life, on the one hand, and emotion and will, on the other hand. In a later discussion I will try to show that many distortions of the meaning of faith are rooted in the attempt to subsume faith to the one or the other of these functions. At this point it must be stated as sharply and insistently as possible that in every act of faith there is cognitive affirmation, not as the result of an independent process of inquiry but as an inseparable element in a total act of acceptance and surrender. This also excludes the idea that faith is the result of an independent act of "will to believe." There is certainly affirmation by the will of what concerns one ultimately, but faith is not a creation of the will. In the ecstasy of faith the will to accept and to surrender is an element, but not the cause. And this is true also of feeling. Faith is not an emotional outburst: this is not the meaning of ecstasy. Certainly, emotion is in it, as in every act of man's spiritual life. But emotion does not produce faith. Faith has a cognitive content and is an act of the will. It is the unity of every element in the centered self. Of course, the unity of all elements in the act of faith does not prevent one or the other element from dominating in a special form of faith. It dominates the character of faith but it does not create the act of faith.

This also answers the question of a possible psychology of faith. Everything that happens in man's personal being can become an object of psychology. And it is rather important for both the philosopher of religion and the practical minister to know how the act of faith is embedded in the totality of psychological processes. But in contrast to this justified and desirable form of a psychology of faith there is another one which tries to derive faith from something that is not faith but is most frequently fear. The presupposition of this method is that fear or something else from which faith is derived is more original and basic than faith. But this presupposition cannot be proved. On the contrary, one can prove that in the scientific method which leads to such consequences faith is already effective. Faith precedes all attempts to derive it from something else, because these attempts are themselves based on faith.

III.   THE SOURCE OF FAITH

We have described the act of faith and its relation to the dynamics of personality. Faith is a total and centered act of the personal self, the act of unconditional, infinite and ultimate concern. The question now arises: what is the source of this all-embracing and all-transcending concern? The word "concern" points to two sides of a relationship, the relation between the one who is concerned and his concern. In both respects we have to imagine man's situation in itself and in his world. The reality of man's ultimate concern reveals something about his being, namely, that he is able to transcend the flux of relative and transitory experiences of his ordinary life. Man's experiences, feelings, thoughts are conditioned and finite. They not only come and go, but their content is of finite and conditional concern—unless they are elevated to unconditional validity. But this presupposes the general possibility of doing so; it presupposes the element of infinity in man. Man is able to understand in an immediate personal and central act the meaning of the ultimate, the unconditional, the absolute, the infinite. This alone makes faith a human potentiality.

Human potentialities are powers that drive toward actualization. Man is driven toward faith by his awareness of the infinite to which he belongs, but which he does not own like a possession. This is in abstract terms what concretely appears as the "restlessness of the heart" within the flux of life.

The unconditional concern which is faith is the concern about the unconditional. The infinite passion, as faith has been described, is the passion for the infinite. Or, to use our first term, the ultimate concern is concern about what is experienced as ultimate. In this way we have turned from the subjective meaning of faith as a centered act of the personality to its objective meaning, to what is meant in the act of faith. It would not help at this point of our analysis to call that which is meant in the act of faith "God" or "a god." For at this step we ask: What in the idea of God constitutes divinity? The answer is: It is the element of the unconditional and of ultimacy. This carries the quality of divinity. If this is seen, one can understand why almost every thing "in heaven and on earth" has received ultimacy in the history of human religion. But we also can understand that a critical principle was and is at work in man's religious consciousness, namely, that which is really ultimate over against what claims to be ultimate but is only preliminary, transitory, finite.

The term "ultimate concern" unites the subjective and the objective side of the act of faith—the *fides qua creditur* (the faith through which one believes) and the *fides quae creditur* (the faith which is believed). The first is the classical term for the centered act of the personality, the ultimate concern. The second is the classical term for that toward which this act is directed, the ultimate itself, expressed in symbols of the divine. This distinction is very important, but not ultimately so, for the one side cannot be without the other. There is no faith without a content toward which it is directed. There is always something meant in the act of faith. And there is no way of having the content of faith except in the act of faith. All speaking about divine matters which is not done in the state of ultimate concern is meaningless. Because that which is meant in the act of faith cannot be approached in any other way than through an act of faith.

In terms like ultimate, unconditional, infinite, absolute, the difference between subjectivity and objectivity is overcome. The ultimate of the act of faith and the ultimate that is meant in the act of faith are one and the same. This is symbolically expressed by the mystics when they say that their knowledge of God is the knowledge God has of himself; and it is expressed by Paul when he says (I Cor. 13) that he will know as he is known, namely, by God. God never can be object without being at the same time subject. Even a successful prayer is, according to Paul (Rom. 8), not possible without God as Spirit praying within us. The same experience expressed in abstract language is the disappearance of the ordinary subject-object scheme in the experience of the ultimate, the unconditional. In the act of faith that which is the source of this act is present beyond the cleavage of subject and object. It is present as both and beyond both.

This character of faith gives an additional criterion for distinguishing true and false ultimacy. The finite which claims infinity without having it (as, e.g., a nation or success) is not able to transcend the subject-object scheme. It remains an object which the believer looks at as a subject. He can approach it with ordinary knowledge and subject it to ordinary handling. There are, of course, many degrees in the endless realm of false ultimacies. The nation is nearer to true ultimacy than is success. Nationalistic ecstasy can produce a state in which the subject is almost swallowed by the object. But after a period the subject emerges again, disappointed radically and totally, and by looking at the nation in a skeptical and calculating way does injustice even to its justified claims. The more idolatrous a faith the less it is able to overcome the cleavage between subject and object. For that is the difference between true and idolatrous faith. In true faith the ultimate concern is a concern about the truly ultimate; while in idolatrous faith preliminary, finite realities are elevated to the rank of ultimacy. The inescapable consequence of idolatrous faith is "existential disappointment," a disappointment which penetrates into the very existence of man! This is the dynamics of idolatrous faith: that it is faith, and as such, the centered act of a personality; that the centering point is something which is more or less on the periphery; and that, therefore, the act of faith leads to a loss of the center and to a disruption of the personality. The ecstatic character of even an idolatrous faith can hide this consequence only for a certain time. But finally it breaks into the open.

IV.   FAITH AND THE DYNAMICS OF THE HOLY

He who enters the sphere of faith enters the sanctuary of life. Where there is faith there is an awareness of holiness. This seems to contradict what has just been said about idolatrous faith. But it does not contradict our analysis of idolatry. It only contradicts the popular way in which the word "holy" is used. What concerns one ultimately becomes holy. The awareness of the holy is awareness of the presence of the divine, namely of the content of our ultimate concern. This awareness is expressed in a grand way in the Old Testament from the visions of the patriarchs and Moses to the shaking experiences of the great prophets and psalmists. It is a presence which remains mysterious in spite of its appearance, and it exercises both an attractive and a repulsive function on those who encounter it. In his classical book, *The Idea of the Holy*, Rudolph Otto has described these two functions as the fascinating and the shaking character of the holy. (In Otto's terminology: *mysterium fascinans et tremendum*.) They can be found in all religions because they are the way in which man always encounters the representations of his ultimate concern. The reason for these two effects of the holy is obvious if we see the relation of the experience of the holy to the experience of ultimate concern. The human heart seeks the infinite because that is where the finite wants to rest. In the infinite it sees its own fulfillment. This is the reason for the ecstatic attraction and fascination of everything in which ultimacy is manifest. On the other hand, if ultimacy is manifest and exercises its fascinating attraction, one realizes at the same time the infinite distance of the finite from the infinite and, consequently, the negative judgment over any finite attempts to reach the infinite. The feeling of being consumed in the presence of the divine is a profound expression of man's relation to the holy. It is implied in every genuine act of faith, in every state of ultimate concern.

This original and only justified meaning of holiness must replace the currently distorted use of the word. "Holy" has become identified with moral perfection, especially in some Protestant groups. The historical causes of this distortion give a new insight into the nature of holiness and of faith. Originally, the holy has meant what is apart from the ordinary realm of things and experiences. It is separated from the world of finite relations. This is the reason why all religious cults have separated holy places and activities from all other places and activities. Entering the sanctuary means encountering the holy. Here the infinitely removed makes itself near and present, without losing its remoteness. For this reason, the holy has been called the "entirely other," namely, other than the ordinary course of things or—to refer to a former statement—other than the world which is determined by the cleavage of subject and object. The holy transcends this realm; this is its mystery and its unapproachable character. There is no conditional way of reaching the unconditional; there is no finite way of reaching the infinite.

The mysterious character of the holy produces an ambiguity in man's ways of experiencing it. The holy can appear as creative and as destructive. Its fascinating element can be both creative and destructive (referring again to the fascinating character of the nationalistic idolatry), and the terrifying and consuming element can be destructive and creative (as in the double function of Siva or Kali in Indian thought). This ambiguity, of which we still find traces in the Old Testament, is reflected in the ritual or quasi-ritual activities of religions and quasi-religions (sacrifices of others or one's bodily or mental self) which are strongly ambiguous. One can call this ambiguity divine-demonic, whereby the divine is characterized by the victory of the creative over the destructive possibility of the holy, and the demonic is characterized by the victory of the destructive over the creative possibility of the holy. In this situation, which is most profoundly understood in the prophetic religion of the Old Testament, a fight has been waged against the demonic-destructive element in the holy. And this fight was so successful that the concept of the holy was changed. Holiness becomes justice and truth. It is creative and not destructive. The true sacrifice is obedience to the law. This is the line of thought which finally led to the identification of holiness with moral perfection. But when this point is reached, holiness loses its meaning as the "separated," the "transcending," the "fascinating and terrifying," the "entirely other." All this is gone, and the holy has become the morally good and the logically true. It has ceased to be the holy in the genuine sense of the word. Summing up this development, one could say that the holy originally lies below the alternative of the good and the evil; that it is both divine and demonic; that with the reduction of the demonic possibility the holy itself becomes transformed in its meaning; that it becomes rational and identical with the true and the good; and that its genuine meaning must be rediscovered.

These dynamics of the holy confirm what was said about the dynamics of faith. We have distinguished between true and idolatrous faith. The holy which is demonic, or ultimately destructive, is identical with the content of idolatrous faith. Idolatrous faith is still faith. The holy which is demonic is still holy. This is the point where the ambiguous character of religion is most visible and the dangers of faith are most obvious: the danger of faith is idolatry and the ambiguity of the holy is its demonic possibility. Our ultimate concern can destroy us as it can heal us. But we never can be without it.

V.   FAITH AND DOUBT

We now return to a fuller description of faith as an act of the human personality, as its centered and total act. An act of faith is an act of a finite being who is grasped by and turned to the infinite. It is a finite act with all the limitations of a finite act, and it is an act in which the infinite participates beyond the limitations of a finite act. Faith is certain in so far as it is an experience of the holy. But faith is uncertain in so far as the infinite to which it is related is received by a finite being. This element of uncertainty in faith cannot be removed, it must be accepted. And the element in faith which accepts this is courage. Faith includes an element of immediate awareness which gives certainty and an element of uncertainty. To accept this is courage. In the courageous standing of uncertainty, faith shows most visibly its dynamic character.

If we try to describe the relation of faith and courage, we must use a larger concept of courage than that which is ordinarily used.[1] Courage as an element of faith is the daring self-affirmation of one's own being in spite of the powers of "nonbeing" which are the heritage of everything finite. Where there is daring and courage there is the possibility of failure. And in every act of faith this possibility is present. The risk must be taken. Whoever makes his nation his ultimate concern needs courage in order to maintain this concern. Only certain is the ultimacy as ultimacy, the infinite passion as infinite passion. This is a reality given to the self with his own nature. It is as immediate and as much beyond doubt as the self is to the self. It *is* the self in its self-transcending quality. But there is not certainty of this kind about the content of our ultimate concern, be it nation, success, a god, or the God of the Bible: They all are contents without immediate awareness. Their acceptance as matters of ultimate concern is a risk and therefore an act of courage. There is a risk if what was considered as a matter of ultimate concern proves to be a matter of preliminary and transitory concern—as, for example, the nation. The risk to faith in one's ultimate concern is indeed the greatest risk man can run. For if it proves to be a failure, the meaning of one's life breaks down; one surrenders oneself, including truth and justice, to something which is not worth it. One has given away one's personal center without having a chance to regain it. The reaction of despair in people who have experienced the breakdown of their national claims is an irrefutable proof of the idolatrous character of their national concern. In the long run this is the inescapable result of an ultimate concern, the subject matter of which is not ultimate. And this is the risk faith must take; this is the risk which is unavoidable if a finite being affirms itself. Ultimate concern is ultimate risk and ultimate courage. It is not risk and needs no courage with respect to ultimacy itself. But it is risk and demands courage if it affirms a concrete con-

[1] Cf. Paul Tillich, *The Courage to Be.* Yale University Press.

cern. And every faith has a concrete element in itself. It is concerned about something or somebody. But this something or this somebody may prove to be not ultimate at all. Then faith is a failure in its concrete expression, although it is not a failure in the experience of the unconditional itself. A god disappears; divinity remains. Faith risks the vanishing of the concrete god in whom it believes. It may well be that with the vanishing of the god the believer breaks down without being able to re-establish his centered self by a new content of his ultimate concern. This risk cannot be taken away from any act of faith. There is only one point which is a matter not of risk but of immediate certainty and herein lies the greatness and the pain of being human; namely, one's standing between one's finitude and one's potential infinity.

All this is sharply expressed in the relation of faith and doubt. If faith is understood as belief that something is true, doubt is incompatible with the act of faith. If faith is understood as being ultimately concerned, doubt is a necessary element in it. It is a consequence of the risk of faith.

The doubt which is implicit in faith is not a doubt about facts or conclusions. It is not the same doubt which is the lifeblood of scientific research. Even the most orthodox theologian does not deny the right of methodological doubt in matters of empirical inquiry or logical deduction. A scientist who would say that a scientific theory is beyond doubt would at that moment cease to be scientific. He may believe that the theory can be trusted for all practical purposes. Without such belief no technical application of a theory would be possible. One could attribute to this kind of belief pragmatic certainty sufficient for action. Doubt in this case points to the preliminary character of the underlying theory.

There is another kind of doubt, which we could call skeptical in contrast to the scientific doubt which we could call methodological. The skeptical doubt is an attitude toward all the beliefs of man, from sense experiences to religious creeds. It is more an attitude than an assertion. For as an assertion it would conflict with itself. Even the assertion that there is no possible truth for man would be judged by the skeptical principle and could not stand as an assertion. Genuine skeptical doubt does not use the form of an assertion. It is an attitude of actually rejecting any certainty. Therefore, it can not be refuted logically. It does not transform its attitude into a proposition. Such an attitude necessarily leads either to despair or cynicism, or to both alternately. And often, if this alternative becomes intolerable, it leads to indifference and the attempt to develop an attitude of complete unconcern. But since man is that being who is essentially concerned about his being, such an escape finally breaks down. This is the dynamics of skeptical doubt. It has an awakening and liberating function, but it also can prevent the development of a centered personality. For personality is not possible without faith. The despair about truth by the skeptic shows that truth is still his infinite passion. The cynical superiority over every concrete truth shows that

truth is still taken seriously and that the impact of the question of an ultimate concern is strongly felt. The skeptic, so long as he is a serious skeptic,
is not without faith, even though it has no concrete content.

The doubt which is implicit in every act of faith is neither the methodological nor the skeptical doubt. It is the doubt which accompanies every risk. It
is not the permanent doubt of the scientist, and it is not the transitory doubt
of the skeptic, but it is the doubt of him who is ultimately concerned about a
concrete content. One could call it the existential doubt, in contrast to the
methodological and the skeptical doubt. It does not question whether a
special proposition is true or false. It does not reject every concrete truth,
but it is aware of the element of insecurity in every existential truth. At the
same time, the doubt which is implied in faith accepts this insecurity and
takes it into itself in an act of courage. Faith includes courage. Therefore,
it can include the doubt about itself. Certainly faith and courage are not
identical. Faith has other elements besides courage and courage has other
functions beyond affirming faith. Nevertheless, an act in which courage accepts risk belongs to the dynamics of faith.

This dynamic concept of faith seems to give no place to that restful affirmative confidence which we find in the documents of all great religions, including Christianity. But this is not the case. The dynamic concept of faith is
the result of a conceptual analysis, both of the subjective and of the objective
side of faith. It is by no means the description of an always actualized state
of the mind. An analysis of structure is not the description of a state of
things. The confusion of these two is a source of many misunderstandings
and errors in all realms of life. An example, taken from the current discussion
of anxiety, is typical of this confusion. The description of anxiety as the
awareness of one's finitude is sometimes criticized as untrue from the point
of view of the ordinary state of the mind. Anxiety, one says, appears under
special conditions but is not an ever-present implication of man's finitude.
Certainly anxiety as an acute experience appears under definite conditions.
But the underlying structure of finite life is the universal condition which
makes the appearance of anxiety under special conditions possible. In the
same way doubt is not a permanent experience within the act of faith. But
it is always present as an element in the structure of faith. This is the difference between faith and immediate evidence either of perceptual or of logical
character. There is no faith without an intrinsic "in spite of" and the courageous affirmation of oneself in the state of ultimate concern. This intrinsic
element of doubt breaks into the open under special individual and social
conditions. If doubt appears, it should not be considered as the negation of
faith, but as an element which was always and will always be present in the
act of faith. Existential doubt and faith are poles of the same reality, the state
of ultimate concern.

The insight into this structure of faith and doubt is of tremendous practical importance. Many Christians, as well as members of other religious

groups, feel anxiety, guilt and despair about what they call "loss of faith." But serious doubt is confirmation of faith. It indicates the seriousness of the concern, its unconditional character. This also refers to those who as future or present ministers of a church experience not only scientific doubt about doctrinal statements—this is as necessary and perpetual as theology is a perpetual need—but also existential doubt about the message of their church, e.g., that Jesus can be called the Christ. The criterion according to which they should judge themselves is the seriousness and ultimacy of their concern about the content of both their faith and their doubt. . . .

I.   THE INTELLECTUALISTIC DISTORTION
OF THE MEANING OF FAITH

Our positive description of what faith is implies the rejection of interpretations that dangerously distort the meaning of faith. It is necessary to make these implicit rejections explicit, because the distortions exercise a tremendous power over popular thinking and have been largely responsible for alienating many from religion since the beginning of the scientific age. It is not only the popular mind which distorts the meaning of faith. Behind it lie philosophical and theological thoughts which in a more refined way also miss the meaning of faith.

The different distorted interpretations of the meaning of faith can be traced to one source. Faith as being ultimately concerned is a centered act of the whole personality. If one of the functions which constitute the totality of the personality is partly or completely identified with faith, the meaning of faith is distorted. Such interpretations are not altogether wrong because every function of the human mind participates in the act of faith. But the element of truth in them is embedded in a whole of error.

The most ordinary misinterpretation of faith is to consider it an act of knowledge that has a low degree of evidence. Something more or less probable or improbable is affirmed in spite of the insufficiency of its theoretical substantiation. This situation is very usual in daily life. If this is meant, one is speaking of *belief* rather than of faith. One believes that one's information is correct. One believes that records of past events are useful for the reconstruction of facts. One believes that a scientific theory is adequate for the understanding of a series of facts. One believes that a person will act in a specific way or that a political situation will change in a certain direction. In all these cases the belief is based on evidence sufficient to make the event probable. Sometimes, however, one believes something which has low probability or is strictly improbable, though not impossible. The causes for all these theoretical and practical beliefs are rather varied. Some things are believed because we have good though not complete evidence about them; many more things are believed because they are stated by good authorities. This is the case whenever we accept the evidence which others accepted as sufficient for belief, even if we cannot approach the evidence directly (for example, all events of the past). Here a new element comes into the picture, namely, the trust in the authority which makes a statement probable for us. Without such trust we could not believe anything except the objects of our immediate experience. The consequence would be that our world would be infinitely smaller than it actually is. It is rational to trust in authorities which enlarge our consciousness without forcing us into submission. If we use the word "faith" for this kind of trust we can say that most of our knowledge is based on faith. But it is not appropriate to do so. We believe the authorities, we trust their judgment, though never unconditionally, but we do not have faith in them. Faith is more than trust in authorities, although trust is an element of faith. This distinction is important in view of the fact that some earlier theologians tried to prove the unconditional authority of the Biblical writers by showing their trustworthiness as witnesses. The Christian may believe the Biblical writers, but not unconditionally. He does not have faith in them. He should not even have faith in the Bible. For faith is more than trust in even the most sacred authority. It is participation in the subject of one's ultimate concern with one's whole being. Therefore, the term "faith" should not be used in connection with theoretical knowledge, whether it is a knowledge on the basis of immediate, prescientific or scientific evidence, or whether it is on the basis of trust in authorities who themselves are dependent on direct or indirect evidence.

The terminological inquiry has led us into the material problem itself. Faith does not affirm or deny what belongs to the prescientific or scientific knowledge of our world, whether we know it by direct experience or through the experience of others. The knowledge of our world (including ourselves as a part of the world) is a matter of inquiry by ourselves or by those in whom we trust. It is not a matter of faith. The dimension of faith is not the dimension of science, history or psychology. The acceptance of a probable hypothesis in these realms is not faith, but preliminary belief, to be tested by scholarly methods and to be changed by every new discovery. Almost all the struggles between faith and knowledge are rooted in the wrong understanding of faith as a type of knowledge which has a low degree of evidence but is supported by religious authority. It is, however, not only confusion of faith with knowledge that is responsible for the world historical conflicts between them; it is also the fact that matters of faith in the sense of ultimate concern lie hidden behind an assumedly scientific method. Whenever this happens, faith stands against faith and not against knowledge.

The difference between faith and knowledge is also visible in the kind of certitude each gives. There are two types of knowledge which are based on complete evidence and give complete certitude. The one is the immediate evidence of sense perception. He who sees a green color sees a green color and is certain about it. He cannot be certain whether the thing which seems to him green is really green. He may be under a deception. But he cannot doubt that he sees green. The other complete evidence is that of the logical and mathematical rules which are presupposed even if their formulation admits different and sometimes conflicting methods. One cannot discuss logic without presupposing those implicit rules which make the discussion meaningful. Here we have absolute certitude; but we have no reality, just as in the case of mere sense perception. Nevertheless, this certitude is not without value. No truth is possible without the material given by sense perception and without the form given by the logical and mathematical rules which express the structure in which all reality stands. One of the worst errors of theology and popular religion is to make statements which intentionally or unintentionally contradict the structure of reality. Such an attitude is an expression not of faith but of the confusion of faith with belief.

Knowledge of reality has never the certitude of complete evidence. The process of knowing is infinite. It never comes to an end except in a state of knowledge of the whole. But such knowledge transcends infinitely every finite mind and can be ascribed only to God. Every knowledge of reality by the human mind has the character of higher or lower probability. The certitude about a physical law, a historical fact, or a psychological structure can be so high that, for all practical purposes, it is certain. But theoretically the incomplete certitude of belief remains and can be undercut at any moment by criticism and new experience. The certitude of faith has not this character. Neither has it the character of formal evidence. The certitude of faith is "existential," meaning that the whole existence of man is involved. It has, as we indicated before, two elements: the one, which is not a risk but a certainty about one's own being, namely, on being related to something ultimate or unconditional; the other, which is a risk and involves doubt and courage, namely, the surrender to a concern which is not really ultimate and may be destructive if taken as ultimate. This is not a theoretical problem of the kind of higher or lower evidence, of probability or improbability, but it is an existential problem of "to be or not to be." It belongs to a dimension other than any theoretical judgment. Faith is not belief and it is not knowledge with a low degree of probability. Its certitude is not the uncertain certitude of a theoretical judgment.

II.   THE VOLUNTARISTIC DISTORTION
OF THE MEANING OF FAITH

One can divide this form of the distorted interpretation of faith into a Catholic and a Protestant type. The Catholic type has a great tradition in the Roman Church. It goes back to Thomas Aquinas, who emphasized that the lack of evidence which faith has must be complemented by an act of will. This, first of all, presupposes that faith is understood as an act of knowledge with a limited evidence and that the lack of evidence is made up by an act of will. We have seen that this way of understanding faith does not do justice to the existential character of faith. Our criticism of the intellectualistic distortion of the meaning of faith hits basically also the voluntaristic distortion of the meaning of faith. The former is the basis of the latter. Without a theoretically formulated content the "will to believe" would be empty. But the content which is meant in the will to believe is given to the will by the intellect. For instance, someone has doubts about the so-called "immortality of the soul." He realizes that this assertion that the soul continues to live after the death of the body cannot be proved either by evidence or by trustworthy authority. It is a questionable proposition of theoretical character. But there are motives driving people to this assertion. They decide to believe, and make up in this way for the lack of evidence. If this belief is called "faith," it is a misnomer, even if much evidence were collected for the belief in a continuation of life after death. In classical Roman Catholic theology the "will to believe" is not an act which originates in man's striving, but it is given by grace to him whose will is moved by God to accept the truth of what the Church teaches. Even so, it is not the intellect which is determined by its content to believe, but it is the will which performs what the intellect alone cannot do. This kind of interpretation agrees with the authoritarian attitude of the Roman Church. For it is the authority of the Church which gives the contents, to be affirmed by the intellect under the impact of the will. If the idea of grace mediated by the Church and motivating the will is rejected, as in pragmatism, the will to believe becomes willfulness. It becomes an arbitrary decision which may be supported by some insufficient arguments but which could have gone in other directions with equal justification. Such belief as the basis of the will to believe is certainly not faith.

The Protestant form of the will to believe is connected with the moral interpretation of religion by Protestants. One demands "obedience of faith," following a Paulinian phrase. The term can mean two different things. It can mean the element of commitment which is implied in the state of ultimate concern. If this is meant, one simply says that in the state of ultimate concern all mental functions participate—which certainly is true. Or the term "obedience of faith" can mean subjection to the command to believe as it is given in prophetic and apostolic preaching. Certainly, if a prophetic word is accepted as prophetic, i.e., as coming from God, obedience of faith does not mean anything other than accepting a message as coming from God. But if there is doubt whether a "word" is prophetic, the term "obedience of faith" loses its meaning. It becomes an arbitrary "will to believe." Yet one may describe the situation in a more refined way and point to the fact that we are often grasped by something, e.g., Biblical passages, as expressions of the objectively ultimate concern, but we hesitate to accept them as our subjective ultimate concern for escapist reasons. In such cases, one says, the appeal to the will is justified and does not ask for a willful decision.

This is true; but such an act of will does not produce faith—faith as ultimate concern is already given. The demand to be obedient is the demand to be what one already is, namely, committed to the ultimate concern from which one tries to escape. Only if this is the situation can obedience of faith be demanded; but then faith precedes the obedience and is not the product of it. No command to believe and no will to believe can create faith.

This is important for religious education, counseling and preaching. One should never convey the impression to those whom one wants to impress, that faith is a demand made upon them, the rejection of which is lack of good will. Finite man cannot produce infinite concern. Our oscillating will cannot produce the certainty which belongs to faith. This is in strict analogy to what we said about the impossibility of reaching the truth of faith by arguments and authorities, which in the best case give finite knowledge of a more or less probable character. Neither arguments for belief nor the will to believe can create faith.

III.   THE EMOTIONALISTIC DISTORTION
OF THE MEANING OF FAITH

The difficulty of understanding faith either as a matter of the intellect or as a matter of will, or of both in mutual support, has led to the interpretation of faith as emotion. This solution was, and partly is, supported from both the religious and the secular side. For the defenders of religion it was a retreat to a seemingly safe position after the battle about faith as a matter of knowledge or will had been lost. The father of all modern Protestant theology, Schleiermacher, has described religion as the feeling of unconditional dependence. Of course, feeling so defined does not mean in religion what it means in popular psychology. It is not vague and changing, but has a definite content: unconditional dependence, a phrase related to what we have called ultimate concern. Nevertheless, the word "feeling" has induced many people to believe that faith is a matter of merely subjective emotions, without a content to be known and a demand to be obeyed.

This interpretation of faith was readily accepted by representatives of science and ethics, because they took it as the best way to get rid of interference from the side of religion in the processes of scientific research and technical organization. If religion is mere feeling it is innocuous. The old conflicts between religion and culture are finished. Culture goes its way, directed by scientific knowledge, and religion is the private affair of every individual and a mere mirror of his emotional life. No claims for truth can be made by it. No competition with science, history, psychology, politics is possible. Religion, put safely into the corner of subjective feelings, has lost its danger for man's cultural activities.

Neither of the two sides, the religious and the cultural, could keep this well-defined covenant of peace. Faith as the state of ultimate concern claims the whole man and cannot be restricted to the subjectivity of mere feeling. It claims truth for its concern and commitment to it. It does not accept the situation "in the corner" of mere feeling. If the whole man is grasped, all his functions are grasped. If this claim of religion is denied, religion itself is denied. It was not only religion which could not accept the restriction of faith to feeling. It was also not accepted by those who were especially interested in pushing religion into the emotional corner. Scientists, artists, moralists showed clearly that they also were ultimately concerned. Their concern expressed itself even in those creations in which they wanted most radically to deny religion. A keen analysis of most philosophical, scientific and ethical systems shows how much ultimate concern is present in them, even if they are leading in the fight against what they call religion.

This shows the limits of the emotionalist definition of faith. Certainly faith as an act of the whole personality has strong emotional elements within it. Emotion always expresses the involvement of the whole personality in an act of life or spirit. But emotion is not the source of faith. Faith is definite in its direction and concrete in its content. Therefore, it claims truth and commitment. It is directed toward the unconditional, and appears in a concrete reality that demands and justifies such commitment.

MIRACLES

DAVID HUME
Of Miracles

Though experience be our only guide in reasoning concerning matters of fact; it must be acknowledged, that this guide is not altogether infallible, but in some cases is apt to lead us into errors. One, who in our climate, should expect better weather in any week of JUNE than in one of DECEMBER, would reason justly, and conformably to experience; but it is certain, that he may happen, in the event, to find himself mistaken. However, we may observe, that, in such a case, he would have no cause to complain of experience; because it commonly informs us beforehand of the uncertainty, by that contrariety of events, which we may learn from a diligent observation. All effects follow not with like certainty from their supposed causes. Some events are found, in all countries and all ages, to have been constantly conjoined together: Others are found to have been more variable, and sometimes to disappoint our expectations; so that, in our reasonings concerning matter of fact, there are all imaginable degrees of assurance, from the highest certainty to the lowest species of moral evidence.

A wise man, therefore, proportions his belief to the evidence. In such conclusions as are founded on an infallible experience, he expects the event with the last degree of assurance, and regards his past experience as a full *proof*

OF MIRACLES   From "An Enquiry Concerning Human Understanding" in *Essays, Moral, Political and Literary* by David Hume, edited with preliminary dissertations and notes, by T. H. Green and T. H. Grose. Volume II. London, Longmans, Green, and Co., 1875.

of the future existence of that event. In other cases, he proceeds with more caution: He weighs the opposite experiments: He considers which side is supported by the greater number of experiments: To that side he inclines, with doubt and hesitation; and when at last he fixes his judgment, the evidence exceeds not what we properly call *probability*. All probability, then, supposes an opposition of experiments and observations, where the one side is found to overbalance the other, and to produce a degree of evidence, proportioned to the superiority. A hundred instances or experiments on one side, and fifty on another, afford a doubtful expectation of any event; though a hundred uniform experiments, with only one that is contradictory, reasonably beget a pretty strong degree of assurance. In all cases, we must balance the opposite experiments, where they are opposite, and deduct the smaller number from the greater, in order to know the exact force of the superior evidence.

To apply these principles to a particular instance; we may observe, that there is no species of reasoning more common, more useful, and even necessary to human life, than that which is derived from the testimony of men, and the reports of eye-witnesses and spectators. This species of reasoning, perhaps, one may deny to be founded on the relation of cause and effect. I shall not dispute about a word. It will be sufficient to observe, that our assurance in any argument of this kind is derived from no other principle than our observation of the veracity of human testimony, and of the usual conformity of facts to the reports of witnesses. It being a general maxim, that no objects have any discoverable connexion together, and that all the inferences, which we can draw from one to another, are founded merely on our experience of their constant and regular conjunction, it is evident, that we ought not to make an exception to this maxim in favour of human testimony, whose connexion with any event seems, in itself, as little necessary as any other. Were not the memory tenacious to a certain degree; had not men commonly an inclination to truth and a principle of probity; were they not sensible to shame, when detected in a falsehood: Were not these, I say, discovered by *experience* to be qualities, inherent in human nature, we should never repose the least confidence in human testimony. A man delirious, or noted for falsehood and villany, has no manner of authority with us.

And as the evidence, derived from witnesses and human testimony, is founded on past experience, so it varies with the experience, and is regarded either as a *proof* or a *probability*, according as the conjunction between any particular kind of report and any kind of object has been found to be constant or variable. There are a number of circumstances to be taken into consideration in all judgments of this kind; and the ultimate standard, by which we determine all disputes, that may arise concerning them, is always derived from experience and observation. Where this experience is not entirely uniform on any side, it is attended with an unavoidable contrariety in our judgments, and with the same opposition and mutual destruction of argument as in every other kind of evidence. We frequently hesitate concerning the reports of others. We balance the opposite circumstances, which cause any doubt or uncertainty; and when we discover a superiority on any side, we incline to it; but still with a diminution of assurance, in proportion to the force of its antagonist.

This contrariety of evidence, in the present case, may be derived from several different causes; from the opposition of contrary testimony; from the character or number of the witnesses; from the manner of their delivering their testimony; or from the union of all these circumstances. We entertain a suspicion concerning any matter of fact, when the witnesses contradict each other; when they are but few, or of a doubtful character; when they have an interest in what they affirm; when they deliver their testimony with hesitation, or on the contrary, with too violent asseverations. There are many other particulars of the same kind, which may diminish or destroy the force of any argument, derived from human testimony.

Suppose, for instance, that the fact, which the testimony endeavours to establish, partakes of the extraordinary and the marvellous; in that case, the evidence, resulting from the testimony, admits of a diminution, greater or less, in proportion as the fact is more or less unusual. The reason, why we place any credit in witnesses and historians, is not derived from any *connexion*, which we perceive *a priori*, between testimony and reality, but because we are accustomed to find a conformity between them. But when the fact attested is such a one as has seldom fallen under our observation, here is a contest of two opposite experiences; of which the one destroys the other, as far as its force goes, and the superior can only operate on the mind by the force, which remains. The very same principle of experience, which gives us a certain degree of assurance in the testimony of witnesses, gives us also, in this case, another degree of assurance against the fact, which they endeavour to establish; from which contradiction there necessarily arises a counterpoise, and mutual destruction of belief and authority. . . .

But in order to encrease the probability against the testimony of witnesses, let us suppose, that the fact, which they affirm, instead of being only marvellous, is really miraculous; and suppose also, that the testimony, considered apart and in itself, amounts to an entire proof; in that case, there is proof against proof, of which the strongest must prevail, but still with a diminution of its force, in proportion to that of its antagonist.

A miracle is a violation of the laws of nature; and as a firm and unalterable experience has established these laws, the proof against a miracle, from the very nature of the fact, is as entire as any argument from experience can possibly be imagined. Why is it more than probable, that all men must die; that lead cannot, of itself, remain suspended in the air; that fire consumes wood, and is extinguished by water; unless it be, that these events are found agreeable to the laws of nature, and there is required a violation of these laws, or in other words, a miracle to prevent them? Nothing is esteemed a miracle, if it ever happen in the common course of nature. It is no miracle that a man, seemingly in good health, should die on a sudden: because such a kind of death, though more unusual than any other, has yet been frequently observed to happen. But it is a miracle, that a dead man should come to life; because that has never been observed, in any age or country. There must, therefore, be a uniform experience against every miraculous event, otherwise the event would not merit that appellation. And as an uniform experience amounts to a proof, there is here a direct and full *proof*, from the nature of the fact, against the existence of any miracle; nor can such a proof be destroyed, or the miracle rendered credible, but by an opposite proof, which is superior.[1]

The plain consequence is (and it is a general maxim worthy of our attention), 'That no testimony is sufficient to establish a miracle, unless the testimony be of such a kind, that its falsehood would be more miraculous, than the fact, which it endeavours to establish: And even in that case there is a mutual destruction of arguments, and the superior only gives us an assurance suitable to that degree of force, which remains, after deducting the inferior.' When any one tells me, that he saw a dead man restored to life, I immediately consider with myself, whether it be more probable, that this person should either deceive or be deceived, or that the fact, which he relates, should really have happened. I weigh the one miracle against the other; and according to the superiority, which I discover, I pronounce my decision, and always reject the greater miracle. If the falsehood of his testimony would be more miraculous, than the event which he relates; then, and not till then, can he pretend to command my belief or opinion.

PART II

In the foregoing reasoning we have supposed, that the testimony, upon which a miracle is founded, may possibly amount to an entire proof, and that the falsehood of that testimony would be a real prodigy: But it is easy to shew,

---

[1] Sometimes an event may not, *in* itself, *seem* to be contrary to the laws of nature, and yet, if it were real, it might, by reason of some circumstances, be denominated a miracle; because, in fact, it is contrary to these laws. Thus if a person, claiming a divine authority, should command a sick person to be well, a healthful man to fall down dead, the clouds to pour rain, the winds to blow, in short, should order many natural events which immediately follow upon his command; these might justly be esteemed miracles, because they are really, in this case, contrary to the laws of nature. For if any suspicion remain, that the event and command concurred by accident, there is no miracle and no transgression of the laws of nature. If this suspicion be removed, there is evidently a miracle, and a transgression of these laws; because nothing can be more contrary to nature than that the voice or command of a man should have such an influence. A miracle may be accurately defined, *a transgression of a law of nature by a particular volition of the Deity, or by the interposition of some invisible agent.* A miracle may either be discoverable by men or not. This alters not its nature and essence. The raising of a house or ship into the air is a visible miracle. The raising of a feather, when the wind wants ever so little of a force requisite for that purpose, is as real a miracle, though not so sensible with regard to us.

that we have been a great deal too liberal in our concession, and that there never was a miraculous event established on so full an evidence.

For *first*, there is not to be found in all history, any miracle attested by a sufficient number of men, of such unquestioned good-sense, education, and learning, as to secure us against all delusion in themselves; of such undoubted integrity, as to place them beyond all suspicion of any design to deceive others; of such credit and reputation in the eyes of mankind, as to have a great deal to lose in case of their being detected in any falsehood; and at the same time, attesting facts, performed in such a public manner, and in so celebrated a part of the world, as to render the detection unavoidable: All which circumstances are requisite to give us a full assurance in the testimony of men.

Secondly. We may observe in human nature a principle, which, if strictly examined, will be found to diminish extremely the assurance, which we might, from human testimony, have, in any kind of prodigy. The maxim, by which we commonly conduct ourselves in our reasonings, is, that the objects, of which we have no experience, resemble those, of which we have; that what we have found to be most usual is always most probable; and that where there is an opposition of arguments, we ought to give the preference to such as are founded on the greatest number of past observations. But though, in proceeding by this rule, we readily reject any fact which is unusual and incredible in an ordinary degree; yet in advancing farther, the mind observes not always the same rule; but when anything is affirmed utterly absurd and miraculous, it rather the more readily admits of such a fact, upon account of that very circumstance, which ought to destroy all its authority. The passion of *surprize* and *wonder*, arising from miracles, being an agreeable emotion, gives a sensible tendency towards the belief of those events, from which it is derived. And this goes so far, that even those who cannot enjoy this pleasure immediately, nor can believe those miraculous events, of which they are informed, yet love to partake of the satisfaction at second-hand or by rebound, and place a pride and delight in exciting the admiration of others.

With what greediness are the miraculous accounts of travellers received, their descriptions of sea and land monsters, their relations of wonderful adventures, strange men, and uncouth manners? But if the spirit of religion join itself to the love of wonder, there is an end of common sense; and human testimony, in these circumstances, loses all pretensions to authority. A religionist may be an enthusiast, and imagine he sees what has no reality: He may know his narrative to be false, and yet persevere in it, with the best intentions in the world, for the sake of promoting so holy a cause: Or even where this delusion has not place, vanity, excited by so strong a temptation, operates on him more powerfully than on the rest of mankind in any other circumstances; and self-interest with equal force. His auditors may not have, and commonly have not, sufficient judgment to canvass his evidence: What judgment they have, they renounce by principle, in these sublime and mysterious subjects: Or if they were ever so willing to employ it, passion and a heated imagination disturb the regularity of its operations. Their credulity encreases his impudence: And his impudence overpowers their credulity. . . .

Thirdly. It forms a strong presumption against all supernatural and miraculous relations, that they are observed chiefly to abound among ignorant and barbarous nations; or if a civilized people has ever given admission to any of them, that people will be found to have received them from ignorant and barbarous ancestors, who transmitted them with that inviolable sanction and authority, which always attend received opinions. When we peruse the first histories of all nations, we are apt to imagine ourselves transported into some new world; where the whole frame of nature is disjointed, and every element performs its operations in a different manner, from what it does at present. Battles, revolutions, pestilence, famine, and death, are never the effect of those natural causes, which we experience. Prodigies, omens, oracles, judgments, quite obscure the few natural events, that are intermingled with them. But as the former grow thinner every page, in proportion as we advance nearer the enlightened ages, we soon learn, that there is nothing mysterious or supernatural in the case, but that all proceeds from the usual propensity of mankind towards the marvellous, and that, though this inclination may at intervals receive a check from sense and learning, it can never be thoroughly extirpated from human nature. . . .

I may add as a *fourth* reason, which diminishes the authority of prodigies, that there is no testimony for any, even those which have not been expressly detected, that is not opposed by an infinite number of witnesses; so that not only the miracle destroys the credit of testimony, but the testimony destroys itself. To make this the better understood, let us consider, that, in matters of religion, whatever is different is contrary; and that it is impossible the religions of ancient ROME, of TURKEY, of SIAM, and of CHINA should, all of them, be established on any solid foundation. Every miracle, therefore, pretended to have been wrought in any of these religions (and all of them abound in miracles), as its direct scope is to establish the particular system to which it is attributed; so has it the same force, though more indirectly, to overthrow every other system. In destroying a rival system, it likewise destroys the credit of those miracles, on which that system was established; so that all the prodigies of different religions are to be regarded as contrary facts, and the evidences of these prodigies, whether weak or strong, as opposite to each other. According to this method of reasoning, when we believe any miracle of MAHOMET or his successors, we have for our warrant the testimony of a few barbarous ARABIANS: And on the other hand, we are to regard the authority of TITUS LIVIUS, PLUTARCH, TACITUS, and, in short, of all the authors and witnesses, GRECIAN, CHINESE, and ROMAN CATHOLIC, who have related any miracle in their particular religion; I say, we are to regard their testimony in the same light as if they had mentioned that

MAHOMETAN miracle, and had in express terms contradicted it, with the same certainty as they have for the miracle they relate. This argument may appear over subtile and refined; but is not in reality different from the reasoning of a judge, who supposes, that the credit of two witnesses, maintaining a crime against any one, is destroyed by the testimony of two others, who affirm him to have been two hundred leagues distant, at the same instant when the crime is said to have been committed. . . .

Upon the whole, then, it appears, that no testimony for any kind of miracle has ever amounted to a probability, much less to a proof; and that, even supposing it amounted to a proof, it would be opposed by another proof; derived from the very nature of the fact, which it would endeavour to establish. It is experience only, which gives authority to human testimony; and it is the same experience, which assures us of the laws of nature. When, therefore, these two kinds of experience are contrary, we have nothing to do but substract the one from the other, and embrace an opinion, either on one side or the other, with that assurance which arises from the remainder. But according to the principle here explained, this substraction, with regard to all popular religions, amounts to an entire annihilation; and therefore we may establish it as a maxim, that no human testimony can have such force as to prove a miracle, and make it a just foundation for any such system of religion.

I beg the limitations here made may be remarked, when I say, that a miracle can never be proved, so as to be the foundation of a system of religion. For I own, that otherwise, there may possibly be miracles, or violations of the usual course of nature, of such a kind as to admit of proof from human testimony; though, perhaps, it will be impossible to find any such in all the records of history. Thus, suppose, all authors, in all languages, agree, that, from the first of JANUARY 1600, there was a total darkness over the whole earth for eight days: Suppose that the tradition of this extraordinary event is still strong and lively among the people: That all travellers, who return from foreign countries, bring us accounts of the same tradition, without the least variation or contradiction: It is evident, that our present philosophers, instead of doubting the fact, ought to receive it as certain, and ought to search for the causes whence it might be derived. The decay, corruption, and dissolution of nature, is an event rendered probable by so many analogies, that any phænomenon, which seems to have a tendency towards that catastrophe, comes within the reach of human testimony, if that testimony be very extensive and uniform.

But suppose, that all the historians who treat of ENGLAND, should agree, that, on the first of JANUARY 1600, Queen ELIZABETH died; that both before and after her death she was seen by her physicians and the whole court, as is usual with persons of her rank; that her successor was acknowledged and proclaimed by the parliament; and that, after being interred a month, she again appeared, resumed the throne, and governed ENGLAND for three years: I must confess that I should be surprized at the occurrence of so many odd circumstances, but should not have the least inclination to believe so miraculous an event. I should not doubt of her pretended death, and of those other public circumstances that followed it: I should only assert it to have been pretended, and that it neither was, nor possibly could be real. You would in vain object to me the difficulty, and almost impossibility of deceiving the world in an affair of such consequence; the wisdom and solid judgment of that renowned queen; with the little or no advantage which she could reap from so poor an artifice: All this might astonish me; but I would still reply, that the knavery and folly of men are such common phænomena, that I should rather believe the most extraordinary events to arise from their concurrence, than admit of so signal a violation of the laws of nature.

But should this miracle be ascribed to any new system of religion; men, in all ages, have been so much imposed on by ridiculous stories of that kind, that this very circumstance would be a full proof of a cheat, and sufficient, with all men of sense, not only to make them reject the fact, but reject it without farther examination. Though the Being to whom the miracle is ascribed, be, in this case, Almighty, it does not, upon that account, become a whit more probable; since it is impossible for us to know the attributes or actions of such a Being, otherwise than from the experience which we have of his productions, in the usual course of nature. This still reduces us to past observation, and obliges us to compare the instances of the violation of truth in the testimony of men, with those of the violation of the laws of nature by miracles, in order to judge which of them is most likely and probable. As the violations of truth are more common in the testimony concerning religious miracles, than in that concerning any other matter of fact; this must diminish very much the authority of the former testimony, and make us form a general resolution, never to lend any attention to it, with whatever specious pretence it may be covered. . . .

I am the better pleased with the method of reasoning here delivered, as I think it may serve to confound those dangerous friends or disguised enemies to the *Christian Religion*, who have undertaken to defend it by the principles of human reason. Our most holy religion is founded on *Faith*, not on reason; and it is a sure method of exposing it to put it to such a trial as it is, by no means, fitted to endure. To make this more evident, let us examine those miracles, related in scripture; and not to lose ourselves in too wide a field, let us confine ourselves to such as we find in the *Pentateuch*, which we shall examine, according to the principles of those pretended Christians, not as the word or testimony of God himself, but as the production of a mere human writer and historian. Here then we are first to consider a book, presented to us by a barbarous and ignorant people, written in an age when they were still more barbarous, and in all probability long after the facts which it relates, corroborated by no concurring testimony, and resembling those fabulous accounts, which every nation gives of its origin. Upon reading this book, we find it full of prodigies and miracles. It gives an account of a state of the world and of human nature entirely different from the present: Of our fall from that state: Of the age of man, extended to near a thousand years: Of the destruction of the world by a deluge: Of the arbitrary choice of one people, as the favourites of heaven; and that people the countrymen of the author: Of their deliverance from bondage by prodigies the most astonishing imaginable: I desire any one to lay his hand upon his heart, and after a serious consideration declare, whether he thinks that the falsehood of such a book, supported by such a testimony, would be more extraordinary and miraculous than all the miracles it relates; which is, however, necessary to make it be received, according to the measures of probability above established.

What we have said of miracles may be applied, without any variation, to prophecies; and indeed, all prophecies are real miracles, and as such only, can be admitted as proofs of any revelation. If it did not exceed the capacity of human nature to foretel future events, it would be absurd to employ any prophecy as an argument for a divine mission or authority from heaven. So that, upon the whole, we may conclude, that the *Christian Religion* not only was at first attended with miracles, but even at this day cannot be believed by any reasonable person without one. Mere reason is insufficient to convince us of its veracity: And whoever is moved by *Faith* to assent to it, is conscious of a continued miracle in his own person, which subverts all the principles of his understanding, and gives him a determination to believe what is most contrary to custom and experience.

P. NOWELL-SMITH
Miracles—The Philosophical Approach [1]

I

Mr Lunn throws down the gauntlet, several gauntlets, to the "modernist"; but it is not on behalf of modernism that I intend to take up his challenge. I shall confine myself solely to the question of miracles, and to one aspect only of this many-sided problem. First let me indicate the extent of my agreement with Mr Lunn:

P. Nowell-Smith (1914–), born in England, is currently teaching at York University in Ontario. He is the author of several philosophical works, most notably *Ethics*.

MIRACLES—THE PHILOSOPHICAL APPROACH, A REPLY TO MR. ARNOLD LUNN   From *The Hibbert Journal*, Vol. 48, July 1950. Reprinted by permission of the author and the Hibbert Trustees.

[1] A reply to Mr Arnold Lunn's article "Miracles—The Scientific Approach," *Hibbert Journal*, April 1950, itself a reply to an article by Professor H. Dubs contributed in January 1950.

(*a*) I am in full agreement with him about the value of controversy and about the need, in controversy, for sticking to accepted definitions. One can prove anything with sufficient elasticity or watering down of terms.

(*b*) The problem must be attacked with an open mind, that is to say with a mind not disposed to reject evidence because it conflicts with some preconceived theory. I have known a very distinguished physicist to explain that Dr Rhine's experimental results in "parapsychology" must be false because such things just cannot happen. The parallel which Mr Lunn adduces between this attitude and that of the Church towards Galileo is apt.

(*c*) I hold no brief for the Euhemerising attitude of some modernists. I do not altogether agree that it is illogical to accept what seems credible in the gospel stories and to reject the miracles, when the evidence is the same for both. It seems to me that we are sometimes entitled to accept part of a witness' story and reject another part. But I will not quarrel with Mr Lunn over this, since I reject Euhemerism myself for other reasons. Nevertheless, I must protest that to reject the thesis that Jesus was a man on to whom fabulous stories have been foisted is not to prove the Christian view that he was a Man-God. As Mr Lunn knows, there is the alternative theory that he was always a God and that the growth of the gospel stories is not the progressive deification of a man but the progressive humanisation of a God. However, Mr Lunn was explicitly attacking the modernist view, and it is not fair to criticise him for not fighting his battle on two fronts at once. I mention this point solely as an illustration of Mr Lunn's tendency to treat a convincing refutation of one view as a proof of another which is not the only possible alternative, a tendency of which I shall produce a more important example later.

So much for my agreement with Mr Lunn. Whether modernists commit the fallacies of bad definition, the closed mind and Euhemerism I shall not presume to say. Let it suffice that they are fallacies; and now let us turn to miracles.

To put my cards on the table at once, I have no intention of trying to refute Mr Lunn's explanation of miracles, since he has put it beyond the bounds of possible refutation. But I do not think that it *explains* and I am at a loss to understand it. In particular, I am at a loss to understand the distinction of the "natural" and the "supernatural" of which he makes so much in his explanation of miracles, but which he does not explain in its turn. But before coming to my main point I shall first summarise Mr Lunn's argument and put out of the way two minor points. Mr Lunn's main argument is as follows:

(*a*) A miracle is defined as "an event above or contrary to or exceeding nature which is explicable only as a direct act of God."

(*b*) Miracles certainly occur. (There is plenty of evidence for them, if only people will bother to investigate it instead of rejecting miracles out of hand.)

(c) Miracles are "evidence provided by God to demonstrate the existence of a divine order."

(d) Therefore we must believe that reality is not "co-terminous with the natural order" and must answer in the negative the momentous question "whether all phenomena recorded and witnessed by man are due to purely natural causes, such as the actions of the human will or physical causes." Moreover, it is on the authority of the scientists themselves "that we declare that a particular phenomenon is inexplicable as the effect of natural agents and must therefore be ascribed to supernatural agents."

Before coming to my main point, I have two objections to make to this thesis: the first will certainly be familiar to Mr Lunn and he has probably answered it elsewhere; the second is more important. In the first place, every religion has its own stock of miracles, some of which are as well attested as the Christian miracles. Would Mr Lunn deny that these miracles occurred? And, if he does, must it not be from some arbitrary standpoint such as he himself condemns? If he is willing to accept them, must there not be some flaw in the argument by which the devotees of other religions prove the existence of their Gods from such evidence? And might not this flaw appear also in the Christian case? Or are we to accept the God of Muhammad and the whole Greek and Hindu Pantheons?

My second, and more serious, point is that Mr Lunn *defines* "miracle" in such a way that, whatever scientists may say, it can well be doubted whether miracles have in fact occurred. If any scientist has said that a certain phenomenon "is inexplicable as the effect of natural agents and must *therefore* be ascribed to supernatural agents," he is not speaking as a scientist, but as a philosopher; and whatever authority he may have in his own scientific field he is by no means a safe guide here. We may trust him, as a trained observer, accurately to describe the phenomenon; we may believe him when he says that no scientific method or hypothesis known to him will explain it. But to say that it is inexplicable as a result of natural agents is already beyond his competence as a scientist, and to say that it must be ascribed to supernatural agents is to say something that no one could possibly have the right to affirm on the evidence alone. Mr Lunn defines a miracle, not merely as an event "exceeding nature," but also as one *which is explicable only as a direct Act of God.* But to say that a phenomenon is a direct act of God is to offer an explanation, not to report its occurrence. Let us accept all the evidence for miracles; what this evidence shows is that extraordinary phenomena occur, and it is only in this sense that the evidence forces us to admit that miracles occur. If we define "miracle" in the way that Mr Lunn does, we could only be forced to admit the occurrence of miracles by means of some *argument*, such as Mr Lunn himself offers. Mr Lunn has, in short, smuggled his explanation of these phenomena into the evidence for them, and this he has no right to do. Evidence must be kept distinct from explanatory theory; otherwise, in accepting the evidence, we are already committed to accepting the theory. But, no matter how strange an event someone reports, the statement that it must have been due to a supernatural agent cannot be a part of that report.

II

As I have said, my main difficulty is to understand Mr Lunn's distinction between the "natural" and the "supernatural." There is, first, a certain inconsistency in his use of these terms. At one point he regards God's intervention as analogous to that of human beings. It "does not violate the laws of nature but modifies some of the laws of nature by a process analogous to that by which the human will influences nature." Here the human will is held to be, in some sense "non-natural," if not supernatural. (Otherwise the analogy has no point.) "Natural" comes near to meaning "physical" or even "material." But in the next paragraph the actions of the human will are treated, along with "physical causes" as natural; so that the phrase "natural order" cannot be regarded as co-terminous with the domain of physical science.

It is true that some scientists claim that, in the end, all explanation will turn out to be physical. I do not propose to examine this claim as it is irrelevant. Mr Lunn must be intending to attack a different thesis, namely, that all phenomena will ultimately admit of a natural explanation. It is vital, therefore, that he should let us clearly understand what he means by this phrase.

Mr Lunn's belief that "natural" explanations cannot be given seems to me to rest on an unstated, and therefore unexamined assumption as to the nature of natural science. He seems to believe that science is committed to certain definite *theories* and to the use of certain definite *concepts*—for instance, the concepts of matter and motion. But surely this is a mistake. Scientific theories are continually being overthrown; the scientific vocabulary is continually being revised and enriched. For example, "Energy" does not mean for a scientist to-day what it meant for Newton; still less what it meant for Aristotle. In addition to explaining more and more with its existing battery of concepts and theories, science may advance by developing radically new concepts. The concept of gravity was unknown to Galileo and that of an electric charge unknown to Newton; and it is for this reason that if Newton himself said that such and such an event was inexplicable I should take leave to doubt him. Let us grant that Mr Lunn has a right to say, on the authority of "scientists," that no scientist can at present explain certain phenomena. It does not follow that the phenomena are inexplicable by scientific methods, still less that they must be attributed to supernatural agents.

It might be argued that I am cheating here by using the term "science" in such a loose way that it can be used to cover any type of explanation. But this is not so. Science is committed, not to definite theories or concepts, but to a certain *method* of explanation. I do not say that this must be the only method; but I do not see what other there can be.

I may be doing Mr Lunn an injustice in saying that he regards science as committed to definite theories and concepts rather than committed to a certain method. But so many of his points, both good and bad, seem to me to follow from this assumption that I cannot but attribute it to him. In the first place, his strictures on the absence of *Zetesis* in the attitude of some scientists seem to me to presuppose this view (as does the absence of *Zetesis* itself). It is true that some scientists refuse to admit any explanations that are not couched in terms of the orthodox scientific concepts of to-day; and it is also true that this is a mistake, a blindness fitly compared with that of Galileo's opponents. Mr Lunn says: "All evidence for such (*i.e.* supernatural) agencies must, on modernist assumptions, either be explained here and now as the result of natural causes or be referred to the science of the future to interpret in accordance with modernist preconceptions." But there is an ambiguity here that must, I think, arise from the mistaken view of science that I have attributed to Mr Lunn. If he means that, according to the modernists, science must either be able to explain everything here and now or be able, in the future, to explain everything *in terms now current*, he is right to object. But there is still the possibility that science may be able, in the future, to offer an explanation which, though couched in quite new terms, remains strictly scientific. And I shall try to show later that this is the only possible alternative to saying that *no* explanation is possible. Thus the breakdown of all explanations in terms of present-day science does not, as Mr Lunn thinks, immediately force us outside the realm of the "natural"; and we can only think that it does so if we make the mistake of equating "science" with a certain set of theories. An explanation would still be "natural" if it made use of quite different terms, provided that its method was scientific. If this be conceded, it is difficult to understand Mr Lunn's distinction between the "natural" and the "supernatural." For the problem is not whether science can explain everything in current terms, but whether the explanation of miracles requires a method quite different from that of science. Unless this latter thesis is proved, it is hard to see why miracles should be called "supernatural."

III

If the notion of the "natural" is unclear, that of a "miracle" is no less so; and that in spite of Mr Lunn's explicit definition. At times he holds that a miracle is "above, contrary to or exceeding nature"; at others he holds that, in performing miracles, God does not violate natural law. I find it hard to reconcile these two views; at least the words "contrary to" must go; and with them the analogy between Acts of God and human actions. Mr Lunn sees that a fieldsman who catches a cricket ball is not violating or suspending— (he is not even modifying)—the law of gravity. And if God's interventions are analogous to those of human agents, they conform to natural laws. In this case they are in principle predictable (however great the difficulties may be in practice); and the word "supernatural" loses its force.

It might be argued that God's interventions are indeed "lawful"; but that they proceed according to laws which are not "natural laws"; but at this point the difference between a "natural" and a "supernatural" law cries out for explanation. There are many different kinds of scientific law—physical, chemical, biological, psychological, and so on. If supernatural law is another group alongside these, it is not necessarily unscientific. But in calling it "supernatural" Mr Lunn evidently means to imply that it is different, for example, from physical law in a way in which a physical law is not different from a biological law. Yet I cannot imagine what this difference would be. If it is a law, it must (a) be based on evidence; (b) be of the general type "Under such and such conditions, so and so will happen"; (c) be capable of testing in experience. And if it conforms to this specification, how does it differ from a natural law? The supernatural seems to dissolve on the one hand into the natural and on the other into the inexplicable.

And this is no *a priori* dogma; it follows from the nature of explanation. It is, I think, a failure to investigate what is involved in the notion of an explanation that leads Mr Lunn to leap at once into the supernatural. A scientific explanation is an hypothesis from which predictions can be made, which can afterwards be verified. It is of the essence of such an hypothesis— (a "law" is but a well-confirmed hypothesis)—that it should be capable of such predictive expansion. This is, incidentally, the burden of the old attack on *virtus dormitiva* and Bacon's "*tamquam virgo intacta, nihil parit.*" The type of explanation satirised by Molière and Bacon is futile because it merely repeats in learned jargon what has already been said in plain language in stating the phenomenon to be explained. A scientific explanation—any explanation—must do more than this. It must be capable of application to new phenomena. Now Mr Lunn's explanations are inevitably *ex post facto*; we can only recognise a miracle after it has occurred. Mr Lunn may reply that it is "illogical to exploit against an hypothesis consequences which are inevitable if that hypothesis is correct." Certainly; but my argument is not intended to show that Mr Lunn's hypothesis is false; it is intended to show that it is not an hypothesis at all. It is as if one were to say: "Certain events in the past were caused by boojums; but I cannot tell you on what principles boojums operate or what they will do in the future; my hypothesis inevitably involves this consequence." If anyone said this, we should have to treat his phrase "caused by boojums" as simply a special way of describing the phenomena, moreover a misleading way, since it looks like an explanatory hypothesis. But in fact it is not. In the same way, to say that God's interventions in the natural order are "lawful," but that we cannot use these laws for prediction is to retreat into an asylum of ignorance and to use the word "law" in a most paradoxical sense.

To illustrate this let me turn to the example of Leverrier, which Mr Lunn cites: "If Leverrier had assumed that the planetary order is a closed system he would never have discovered Neptune." True; and a valid argument against the exaggerated orthodoxy which Mr Lunn and I both condemn and also against *a priori* proofs in the Hegelian manner of the number of planets that there must be. But the analogy with explanations in supernatural terms is invalid. For Leverrier discovered Neptune, not merely by saying "the planetary system is not closed; there is something outside." He showed how the aberrations in the orbits of other planets could be accounted for; and his explanation involved a prediction that if astronomers examined a certain quarter of the sky they would find a new planet. And lo! it was so. It is here that the analogy breaks down; for Mr Lunn's "explanation" involves saying: "Known laws and factors will not explain this phenomenon; there must be something outside; but I cannot tell you what this is or how it operates." An explanation must explain *how* an event comes about; otherwise it is simply a learned (or a tendentious) name for the phenomenon to be explained.

Moreover, the new entity postulated by Leverrier was not of an altogether unknown type; it was another planet assumed to obey the known laws. I am prepared to allow Mr Lunn much more than this (at least for the purpose of this discussion), and to admit that the present hypotheses of science can never be expanded to cover miraculous phenomena; that we may require new concepts and new laws. What I reject is the theory of science which makes it possible to claim that any phenomenon is essentially inexplicable, the leap to "supernatural agencies," and the view that such agencies in fact explain the phenomena. If miracles are "lawful" it should be possible to state the laws; if not, the alleged explanation amounts to a confession that they are inexplicable.

IV

Having said that miracles must be attributed to supernatural agencies, Mr Lunn goes on to claim that they are "evidence provided by God to demonstrate the existence of the divine order." But what, in detail, can they prove? If we can detect any order in God's interventions it should be possible to extrapolate in the usual way and to predict when and how a miracle will occur. To expect accurate and detailed predictions would be to expect too much. But we must be able to make some predictions, however vague. Otherwise the hypothesis is not open either to confirmation or refutation. As far as

I can see, we are limited to saying that God has in the past intervened in such and such a way. If Mr Lunn would say more than this, I would ask how his method differs from that of a scientist. We would be faced, not with the supernatural, but with a new department of the natural, a department that might be as strange as electrical phenomena once were. But if he confesses that no predictions can be made, is not the phrase "Act of God," which is introduced in order to explain miracles, in fact but a synonym for "the miraculous"? We are back at the *virtus dormitiva* type of explanation. If "Christ is risen" implies "Christ is supernatural," we are entitled to ask what *other* attributes, besides rising from the dead, "supernatural" connotes. We shall then be in a position to see whether a being that rises from the dead necessarily or probably has those attributes. Mr Lunn passes from unusual or abnormal events (for which there is evidence) to the miraculous, from the miraculous to the supernatural and from the supernatural to God. He cannot mean each successive phrase to be a mere synonym for the previous one; each step in the argument is intended to explain the last and to add something more. But, to make use of an old-fashioned way of putting this, we have no right to postulate in the cause any power greater than what is necessary to produce the effect. The difficulty with the argument from miracles, as with other arguments for the existence of God, is that it is first claimed that certain evidence requires us to postulate an unknown X; we then call this X "God" and we then claim to have proved the existence of a being endowed with characteristics by no means warranted by the original evidence. Now science too does this. The gravitational theory says much more than is necessary to describe the fall of an apple. But we can test the truth of this "more" by predicting how other bodies will behave. It is the absence of such a test for supernatural explanations that makes them at once unscientific and also non-explanatory.

It might be argued that I am in effect begging the question because my thesis amounts to saying that the phrase "supernatural explanation" is a contradiction in terms. To assume this is tantamount to assuming that all explanation must be scientific. Now I certainly would not claim to be able to prove this dogma. To do so I should have to appeal to some premise that would be equally unacceptable. All I can do is offer Mr Lunn a challenge. Let him consider the meaning of the word "explanation" and let him ask himself whether this notion does not involve that of a law or hypothesis capable of predictive expansion. And then let him ask himself whether such an explanation would not be natural, in whatever terms it was couched, and how the notion of "the supernatural" could play any part in it. If he objects that I am in effect conceding his point by offering so very wide a definition of "natural," my reply would be:

> By all means; I do not wish to quarrel about words. I will concede your supernatural, if this is all that it means. For the supernatural will be nothing

but a new field for scientific inquiry, a field as different from physics as physics is from psychology, but not differing in principle or requiring any non-scientific method.

The supernatural is either so different from the natural that we are unable to investigate it at all or it is not. If it is not, then it can hardly have the momentous significance that Mr Lunn claims for it; and if it is it cannot be invoked as an explanation of the unusual.

PAUL TILLICH
Revelation and Miracle

The word "miracle," according to the ordinary definition, designates a happening that contradicts the laws of nature. This definition and the innumerable unverified miracle stories in all religions have rendered the term misleading and dangerous for theological use. But a word which expresses a genuine experience can only be dropped if a substitute is at hand, and it does not seem that such a substitute has been found. The New Testament often uses the Greek word *sēmeion*, "sign," pointing to the religious meaning of the miracles. But the word "sign" without a qualifying addition cannot express this religious meaning. It would be more accurate to add the word "event" to "sign" and to speak of *sign-events*. The original meaning of miracle, "that which produces astonishment," is quite adequate for describing the "giving side" of a revelatory experience. But this connotation has been swallowed by the bad connotation of a supranatural interference which destroys the natural structure of events. The bad connotation is avoided in the word "sign" and the phrase "sign-event."

While the original naïve religious consciousness accepts astounding stories in connection with divine manifestations without elaborating a supranaturalistic theory of miracles, rationalistic periods make the negation of natural laws the main point in miracle stories. A kind of irrationalist rationalism develops in which the degree of absurdity in a miracle story becomes the measure of its religious value. The more impossible, the more revelatory! Already in the New Testament one can observe that, the later the tradition, the more the antinatural element is emphasized over against the sign element. In the postapostolic period, when the apocryphal Gospels were produced, there were no

REVELATION AND MIRACLE   From *Systematic Theology,* Volume I, by Paul Tillich. Copyright 1951 by The University of Chicago Press. All rights reserved. Copyright 1951 under the International Copyright Union. Reprinted by permission of The University of Chicago Press and the Estate of Paul Tillich.

checks against absurdity. Pagans and Christians alike were not so much interested in the presence of the divine in shaking and sign-giving events as they were in the sensation produced in their rationalistic minds by antirational happenings. This rationalistic antirationalism infected later Christianity, and it is still a burden for the life of the church and for theology.

The manifestation of the mystery of being does not destroy the structure of being in which it becomes manifest. The ecstasy in which the mystery is received does not destroy the rational structure of the mind by which it is received. The sign-event which gives the mystery of revelation does not destroy the rational structure of the reality in which it appears. If these criteria are applied, a meaningful doctrine of sign-events or miracles can be stated.

One should not use the word "miracle" for events which create astonishment for a certain time, such as scientific discoveries, technical creations, impressive works of art or politics, personal achievements, etc. These cease to produce astonishment after one has become accustomed to them, although a profound admiration of them may remain and even increase. Nor are the structures of reality, the *Gestalten*, the qualities, the inner *teloi* of things miracles, although they always will be objects of admiration. There is an element of astonishment in admiration, but it is not a numinous astonishment; it does not point to a miracle.

As ecstasy presupposes the shock of nonbeing in the mind, so sign-events presuppose the stigma of nonbeing in the reality. In shock and stigma, which are strictly correlated, the negative side of the mystery of being appears. The word "stigma" points to marks of disgrace, for example, in the case of a criminal, and to marks of grace, for example, in the case of a saint; in both instances, however, it indicates something negative. There is a stigma that appears on everything, the stigma of finitude, or implicit and inescapable nonbeing. It is striking that in many miracle stories there is a description of the "numinous" dread which grasps those who participate in the miraculous events. There is the feeling that the solid ground of ordinary reality is taken "out from under" their feet. The correlative experience of the stigma of nonbeing in the reality and the shock of nonbeing in the mind produces this feeling, which, although not revelatory in itself, accompanies every genuine revelatory experience.

Miracles cannot be interpreted in terms of a supranatural interference in natural processes. If such an interpretation were true, the manifestation of the ground of being would destroy the structure of being; God would be split within himself, as religious dualism has asserted. It would be more adequate to call such a miracle "demonic," not because it is produced by "demons," but because it discloses a "structure of destruction" (see Part IV, Sec. I). It corresponds with the state of "being possessed" in the mind and could be called "sorcery." The supranaturalistic theory of miracles makes God a sorcerer and a cause of "possession"; it confuses God with demonic structures in the mind and in reality. There are such structures, based on a distortion of genuine manifestations of the mystery of being. A supranaturalistic theology which employs patterns derived from the structure of possession and sorcery for the sake of describing the nature of revelation in terms of the destruction of the subjective as well as of objective reason is certainly intolerable.

The sign-events in which the mystery of being gives itself consist in special constellations of elements of reality in correlation with special constellations of elements of the mind. A genuine miracle is first of all an event which is astonishing, unusual, shaking, without contradicting the rational structure of reality. In the second place, it is an event which points to the mystery of being, expressing its relation to us in a definite way. In the third place, it is an occurrence which is received as a sign-event in an ecstatic experience. Only if these three conditions are fulfilled can one speak of a genuine miracle. That which does not shake one by its astonishing character has no revelatory power. That which shakes one without pointing to the mystery of being is not miracle but sorcery. That which is not received in ecstasy is a report about the belief in a miracle, not an actual miracle. This is emphasized in the synoptic records of the miracles of Jesus. Miracles are given only to those for whom they are sign-events, to those who receive them in faith. Jesus refuses to perform "objective" miracles. They are a contradiction in terms. This strict correlation makes it possible to exchange the words describing miracles and those describing ecstasy. One can say that ecstasy is the miracle of the mind and that miracle is the ecstasy of reality.

Since neither ecstasy nor miracle destroys the structure of cognitive reason, scientific analysis, psychological and physical, as well as historical investigation are possible and necessary. Research can and must proceed without restriction. It can undercut the superstitions and demonic interpretations of revelation, ecstasy, and miracle. Science, psychology, and history are allies of theology in the fight against the supranaturalistic distortions of genuine revelation. Scientific explanation and historical criticism protect revelation; they cannot dissolve it, for revelation belongs to a dimension of reality for which scientific and historical analysis are inadequate. Revelation is the manifestation of the depth of reason and the ground of being. It points to the mystery of existence and to our ultimate concern. It is independent of what science and history say about the conditions in which it appears; and it cannot make science and history dependent on itself. No conflict between different dimensions of reality is possible. Reason receives revelation in ecstasy and miracles; but reason is not destroyed by revelation, just as revelation is not emptied by reason.

R. G. SWINBURNE
Miracles [1]

In this article I wish to investigate whether there could be strong historical evidence for the occurrence of miracles, and contrary to much writing which has derived from Hume's celebrated chapter "Of Miracles", I shall argue that there could be. I understand by a miracle a violation of a law of Nature by a god, that is, a very powerful rational being who is not a material object (viz., is invisible and intangible). My definition of a miracle is thus approximately the same as Hume's: "a transgression of a law of nature by a particular volition of the Deity or by the interposition of some invisible agent".[2] It has been questioned by many biblical scholars whether this is what the biblical writers understood by the terms translated into English 'miracle'. I do not propose to enter into this controversy. Suffice it to say that many subsequent Christian theologians have understood by 'miracle' roughly what I understand by the term and that much medieval and modern apologetic which appeals to purported miracles as evidence of the truth of the Christian revelation has had a similar understanding of miracle to mine.

I shall take the question in two parts. I shall enquire first whether there could be evidence that a law of nature has been violated, and secondly, if there can be such evidence, whether there could be evidence that the violation was due to a god.

First, then, can there be evidence that a law of nature has been violated? It seems natural to understand, as Ninian Smart [3] does, by a violation of a law of nature, an occurrence of a non-repeatable counter-instance to a law of nature. Clearly, as Hume admitted, events contrary to predictions of formulae which we had good reason to believe to be laws of nature often occur. But if we have good reason to believe that they have occurred and good reason to believe that similar events would occur in similar circumstances, then we have good reason to believe that the formulae which we previously believed to be the laws of nature were not in fact such laws. Repeatable counter-instances do not violate laws of nature, they just show

R. G. Swinburne (1934–), a senior lecturer in philosophy at the University of Hull, is the author of *Space and Time* and the forthcoming *An Introduction to Confirmation Theory*. His recent book, *The Concept of Miracle*, provides a more detailed discussion of points made in the article reprinted here.

MIRACLES   From *The Philosophical Quarterly*, Vol. 18, No. 73, October 1968. Reprinted by permission of the author and *The Philosophical Quarterly*.

[1] I am most grateful to Edgar Page and Christopher Williams for their helpful criticisms of an earlier version of this paper.
[2] David Hume, *An Enquiry Concerning Human Understanding*, ed. L. A. Selby-Bigge (Oxford, 2nd ed., 1902), p. 115, footnote [in *Philosophy of Religion: Selected Readings*, p. 387].
[3] Ninian Smart, *Philosophers and Religious Truth* (London, 1964), Ch. II.

propositions purporting to state laws of nature to be false. But if we have good reason to believe that an event E has occurred contrary to predictions of a formula L which we have good reason to believe to be a law of nature, and we have good reason to believe that events similar to E would not occur in circumstances as similar as we like in any respect to those of the original occurrence, then we do not have reason to believe that L is not a law of nature. For any modified formula which allowed us to predict E would allow us to predict similar events in similar circumstances and hence, we have good reason to believe, would give false predictions. Whereas if we leave the formula L unmodified, it will, we have good reason to believe, give correct predictions in all other conceivable circumstances. Hence if we are to say that any law of nature is operative in the field in question we must say that it is L. This seems a natural thing to say rather than to say that no law of nature operates in the field. Yet E is contrary to the predictions of L. Hence, for want of a better expression, we say that E has violated the law of nature L. If the use of the word 'violated' suggests too close an analogy between laws of nature and civil or moral laws, that is unfortunate. Once we have explained, as above, what is meant by a violation of a law of nature, no subsequent confusion need arise.

The crucial question, not adequately discussed by Smart, however, is what would be good reason for believing that an event E, if it occurred, was a nonrepeatable as opposed to a repeatable counter-instance to a formula L which we have on all other evidence good reason to believe to be a law of nature. The evidence that E is a repeatable counter-instance would be that a new formula L^1 fairly well confirmed by the data as a law of nature can be set up. A formula is confirmed by data, if the data obtained so far are predicted by the formula, if new predictions are successful and if the formula is a simple and coherent one relative to the collection of data.

Compatible with any finite set of data, there will always be an infinite number of possible formulae from which the data can be predicted. We can rule out many by further tests, but however many tests we make we shall still have only a finite number of data and hence an infinite number of formulae compatible with them.

But some of these formulae will be highly complex relative to the data, so that no scientist would consider that the data were evidence that those formulae were true laws of nature. Others are very simple formulae such that the data can be said to provide evidence that they are true laws of nature. Thus suppose the scientist's task is to find a formula accounting for marks on a graph, observed at (1, 1), (2, 2), (3, 3), and (4, 4), the first number of each pair being the x co-ordinate and the second the y co-ordinate. One formula which would predict these marks is x = y. Another one is $(x - 1)$ $(x - 2)(x - 3)(x - 4) + x = y$. But clearly we would not regard the data as supporting the second formula. It is too clumsy a formula to explain four observations. Among simple formulae supported by the data, the simplest is the best supported and regarded, provisionally, as correct. If the formula survives further tests, that increases the evidence in its favour as a true law.

Now if for E and for all other relevant data we can construct a formula L^1 from which the data can be derived and which either makes successful predictions in other circumstances where L makes bad predictions, or is a fairly simple formula, so that from the fact that it can predict E, and L cannot, we have reason to believe that its predictions, if tested, would be better than those of L in other circumstances, then we have good reason to believe that L^1 is the true law in the field. The formula will indicate under what circumstances divergencies from L similar to E will occur. The evidence thus indicates that they will occur under these circumstances and hence that E is a repeatable counter-instance to the original formula L.

Suppose, however, that for E and all the other data of the field we can construct no new formula L^1 which yields more successful predictions than L in other examined circumstances, nor one which is fairly simple relative to the data; but for all the other data except E the simple formula L does yield good predictions. And suppose that as the data continue to accumulate, L remains a completely successful predictor and there remains no reason to suppose that a simple formula L^1 from which all the other data and E can be derived can be constructed. The evidence then indicates that the divergence from L will not be repeated and hence that E is a non-repeatable counter-instance to a law of nature L.

Here is an example. Suppose E to be the levitation (viz., rising into the air and remaining floating on it) of a certain holy person. E is a counter-instance to otherwise well substantiated laws of mechanics L. We could show E to be a repeatable counter-instance if we could construct a formula L^1 which predicted E and also successfully predicted other divergences from L, as well as all other tested predictions of L; or if we could construct L^1 which was comparatively simple relative to the data and predicted E and all the other tested predictions of L, but predicted divergences from L which had not yet been tested. L^1 might differ from L in that, according to it, under certain circumstances bodies exercise a gravitational repulsion on each other, and the circumstance in which E occurred was one of those circumstances. If L^1 satisfied either of the above two conditions, we would adopt it, and we would then say that under certain circumstances people do levitate and so E was not a counter-instance to a law of nature. However, it might be that any modification which we made to the laws of mechanics to allow them to predict E might not yield any more successful predictions than L and they [might] be so clumsy that there [would be] no reason to believe that their predictions not yet tested would be successful. Under these circumstances we would have good reasons to believe that the levitation of the holy person violated the laws of nature.

If the laws of nature are statistical and not deterministic, it is not in all cases so clear what counts as a counter-instance to them. How improbable does an event have to be to constitute a counter-instance to a statistical law? But this problem is a general one in the philosophy of science and does not raise any issues peculiar to the topic of miracles.

It is clear that all claims about what does or does not violate the laws of nature are corrigible. New scientific knowledge may force us to revise any such claims. But all claims to knowledge about matters of fact are corrigible, and we must reach provisional conclusions about them on the evidence available to us. We have to some extent good evidence about what are the laws of nature, and some of them are so well established and account for so many data that any modifications to them which we could suggest to account for the odd counter-instance would be so clumsy and *ad hoc* as to upset the whole structure of science. In such cases the evidence is strong that if the purported counter-instance occurred it was a violation of the laws of nature. There is good reason to believe that the following events, if they occurred, would be violations of the laws of nature: levitation; resurrection from the dead in full health of a man whose heart has not been beating for twenty-four hours and who was, by other criteria also, dead; water turning into wine without the assistance of chemical apparatus or catalysts; a man getting better from polio in a minute.

So then we could have the evidence that an event E if it occurred was a non-repeatable counter-instance to a true law of nature L. But Hume's argument here runs as follows. The evidence, which *ex hypothesi* is good evidence, that L is a true law of nature is evidence that E did not occur. We have certain other evidence that E did occur. In such circumstances, writes Hume, the wise man "weighs the opposite experiments. He considers which side is supported by the greater number of experiments".[4] Since he supposes that the evidence that E occurred would be that of testimony, Hume concludes "that no testimony is sufficient to establish a miracle, unless the testimony be of such a kind, that its falsehood would be more miraculous, than the fact which it endeavours to establish".[5] He considers that this condition is not in fact satisfied by any purported miracle, though he seems at times to allow that it is logically possible that it might be.

One wonders here at Hume's scale of evidence. Suppose two hundred witnesses claiming to have observed some event E, an event which, if it occurred, would be a non-repeatable counter-instance to a law of nature. Suppose these to be witnesses able and anxious to show that E did not occur if there were grounds for doing so. Would not their combined evidence give us good reason to believe that E occurred? Hume's answer which we can see from his discussion of two apparently equally well authenticated miracles is—No. But then, one is inclined to say, is not Hume just being bigoted, refusing to face facts? It would be virtually impossible to draw up a table showing how many witnesses and of what kind we need to establish the occurrence of an event

[4] *Op. cit.*, p. 111.   [5] *Op. cit.*, p. 116.

which, if it occurred, would be a non-repeatable counter-instance to a law of nature. Each purported instance has to be considered on its merits. But certainly one feels that Hume's standards of evidence are too high. What, one wonders, would Hume himself say if he saw such an event?

But behind Hume's excessively stringent demands on evidence there may be a philosophical point which he has not fully brought out. This is a point made by Flew in justification of Hume's standards of evidence: "The justification for giving the 'scientific' this ultimate precedence here over the 'historical' lies in the nature of the propositions concerned and in the evidence which can be displayed to sustain them . . . the candidate historical proposition will be particular, often singular, and in the past tense. . . . But just by reason of this very pastness and particularity it is no longer possible for anyone to examine the subject directly for himself . . . the law of nature will, unlike the candidate historical proposition, be a general nomological. It can thus in theory, though obviously not always in practice, be tested at any time by any person".[6]

Flew's contrast is, however, mistaken. Particular experiments on particular occasions only give a certain and far from conclusive support to claims that a purported scientific law is true. Any person can test for the truth of a purported scientific law, but a positive result to one test will only give limited support to the claim. Exactly the same holds for purported historical truths. Anyone can examine the evidence, but a particular piece of evidence only gives limited support to the claim that the historical proposition is true. But in the historical as in the scientific case, there is no limit to the amount of evidence. We can go on and on testing for the truth of historical as well as scientific propositions. We can look for more and more data which can only be explained as effects of some specified past event, and data incompatible with its occurrence, just as we can look for more and more data for or against the truth of some physical law. Hence the truth of the historical proposition can also "be tested at any time by any person".

What Hume seems to suppose is that the only evidence about whether an event E happened is the written or verbal testimony of those who would have been in a position to witness it, had it occurred. And as there will be only a finite number of such pieces of testimony, the evidence about whether or not E happened would be finite. But this is not the only testimony which is relevant—we need testimony about the character and competence of the original witnesses. Nor is testimony the only type of evidence. All effects of what happened at the time of the alleged occurrence of E are also relevant. Far more than in Hume's day we are today often in a position to assess what occurred by studying the physical traces of the event. Hume had never met Sherlock Holmes with his ability to assess what happened in the room from the way in which the furniture lay, or where the witness was yesterday from

---

[6] Antony Flew, *Hume's Philosophy of Belief* (London, 1961), pp. 207 ff.

the mud on his boot. As the effects of what happened at the time of the occurrence of E are always with us in some form, we can always go on examining them yet more carefully. Further, we need to investigate whether E, if it did occur, would in fact have brought about the present effects, and whether any other cause could have brought about just these effects. To investigate these issues involves investigating which scientific laws operate (other than the law L of which it is claimed that E was a violation), and this involves doing experiments *ad lib*. Hence there is no end to the amount of new evidence which can be had. The evidence that the event E occurred can go on mounting up in the way that evidence that L is a law of nature can do. The wise man in these circumstances will surely say that he has good reason to believe that E occurred, but also that L is a true law of nature and so that E was a violation of it.

So we could have good reason to believe that a law of nature has been violated. But for a violation of a law of nature to be a miracle, it has to be caused by a god, that is, a very powerful rational being who is not a material object. What could be evidence that it was?

To explain an event as brought about by a rational agent with intentions and purposes is to give an entirely different kind of explanation of its occurrence from an explanation by scientific laws acting on precedent causes. Our normal grounds for attributing an event to the agency of an embodied rational agent A is that we or others perceived A bringing it about *or* that it is the sort of event that A typically brings about and that A, and no one else of whom we have knowledge, was in a position to bring it about. The second kind of ground is only applicable when we have prior knowledge of the existence of A. In considering evidence for a violation E of a law of nature being due to the agency of a god, I will distinguish two cases, one where we have good reason on grounds other than the occurrence of violations of laws of nature to believe that there exists at least one god, and one where we do not.

Let us take the second case first. Suppose we have no other good reason for believing that a god exists, but an event E then occurs which, our evidence indicates, is a non-repeatable counter-instance to a true law of nature. Now we cannot attribute E to the agency of a god by seeing the god's body bring E about, for gods do not have bodies. But suppose that E occurs in ways and circumstances C strongly analogous to those in which occur events brought about by human agents, and that other violations occur in such circumstances. We would then be justified in claiming that E and other such violations are, like effects of human actions, brought about by agents, but ones unlike men in not being material objects. This inference would be justified because, if an analogy between effects is strong enough, we are always justified in postulating slight difference in causes to account for slight difference in effects. Thus if because of its other observable behaviour we say that light is a disturbance in a medium, then the fact that the medium, if it exists, does not, like other media, slow down material bodies passing through it, is not by itself (viz., if there are no other disanalogies) a reason for saying that the light is not a disturbance in a medium, but only for saying that the medium in which light is a disturbance has the peculiar property of not resisting the passage of material bodies. So if, because of very strong similarity between the ways and circumstances of the occurrence of E and other violations of laws of nature to the ways and circumstances in which effects are produced by human agents, we postulate a similar cause—a rational agent, the fact that there are certain disanalogies (viz., we cannot point to the agent, say where his body is) does not mean that our explanation is wrong. It only means that the agent is unlike humans in not having a body. But this move is only justified if the similarities are otherwise strong. Nineteenth-century scientists eventually concluded that for light the similarities were not strong enough to outweigh the dissimilarities and justify postulating the medium with the peculiar property.

Now what similarities in the ways and circumstances C of their occurrence could there be between E (and other violations of laws of nature) and the effects of human actions to justify the postulation of similar causes? Suppose that E occurred in answer to a request. Thus E might be an explosion in my room, totally inexplicable by the laws of nature, when at the time of its occurrence there were in a room on the other side of the corridor men in turbans chanting "O God of the Sikhs, may there be an explosion in Swinburne's room". Suppose, too, that when E occurs a voice, but not the voice of an embodied agent, is heard giving reasonable reasons for granting the request. When the explosion occurs in my room, a voice emanating from no man or animal or man-made machine is heard saying "Your request is granted. He deserves a lesson". Would not all this be good reason for postulating a rational agent other than a material object who brought about E and the other violations, an agent powerful enough to change instantaneously by intervention the properties of things, viz., a god? Clearly if the analogy were strong enough between the ways and circumstances in which violations of laws of nature and effects of human action occur, it would be. If furthermore the prayers which were answered by miracles were prayers for certain kinds of events (e.g., relief of suffering, punishment of ill-doers) and those which were not answered by miracles were for events of different kinds, then this would show something about the character of the god. Normally, of course, the evidence adduced by theists for the occurrence of miracles is not as strong as I have indicated that very strong evidence would be. Violations are often reported as occurring subsequent to prayer for them to occur, and seldom otherwise; but voices giving reason for answering such a request are rare indeed. Whether in cases where voices are not heard but the occurrence of a violation E and of prayer for its occurrence were both well confirmed, we would be justified in concluding that the existence of a god who brought E about is a matter of whether the analogy is strong enough as it stands. The question of exactly when an analogy is strong enough to justify an inference based on it is a difficult one. But my only point here is that if the analogy were strong enough, the inference would be justified.

Suppose now that we have other evidence for the existence of a god. Then if E occurs in the circumstances C, previously described, that E is due to the activity of a god is more adequately substantiated, and the occurrence of E gives further support to the evidence for the existence of a god. But if we already have reason to believe in the existence of a god, the occurrence of E not under circumstances as similar as C to those under which human agents often bring about results, could nevertheless sometimes be justifiably attributed to his activity. Thus, if the occurrence of E is the sort of thing that the only god of whose existence we have evidence would wish to bring about if he has the character suggested by the other evidence for his existence, we can reasonably hold him responsible for the occurrence of E which would otherwise be unexplained. The healing of a faithful blind Christian contrary to the laws of nature could reasonably be attributed to the God of the Christians, if there were other evidence for his existence, whether or not the blind man or other Christians had ever prayed for that result.

For these reasons I conclude that we can have good reason to believe that a violation of a law of nature was caused by a god, and so was a miracle.

I would like to make two final points, one to tidy up the argument and the other to meet a further argument put forward by Hume which I have not previously discussed.

Entia non sunt multiplicanda praeter necessitatem.—Unless we have good reason to do so we ought not to postulate the existence of more than one god, but to suppose that the same being answers all prayers. But there could be good reason to postulate the existence of more than one god, and evidence to this effect could be provided by miracles. One way in which this could happen is that prayers for a certain kind of result, for example, shipwreck, which began "O, Neptune" were often answered, and also prayers for a different kind of result, for example, success in love, which began "O, Venus" were also often answered, but prayers for a result of the first kind beginning "O, Venus", and for a result of the second kind beginning "O, Neptune" were never answered. Evidence for the existence of one god would in general support, not oppose, evidence for the existence of a second one since, by suggesting that there is one rational being other than those whom we can see, it makes more reasonable the postulation of another one.

The second point is that there is no reason at all to suppose that Hume is in general right to claim that "every miracle . . . pretended to have been wrought in any . . . (religion) . . . as its direct scope is to establish the particular system to which it is attributed; so has it the same force, though more indirectly, to overthrow every other system. In destroying a rival system it likewise destroys the credit of those miracles on which that system was established".[7] If Hume were right to claim that evidence for the miracles of one religion was evidence against the miracles of any other, then indeed evidence for miracles in each would be poor. But in fact evidence for a miracle "wrought in one religion" is only evidence against the occurrence of a miracle "wrought in another religion" if the two miracles, if they occurred, would be evidence for propositions of the two religious systems incompatible with each other. It is hard to think of pairs of alleged miracles of this type. If there were evidence for a Roman Catholic miracle which was evidence for the doctrine of transubstantiation and evidence for a Protestant miracle which was evidence against it, here we would have a case of the conflict of evidence which, Hume claims, occurs generally with alleged miracles. But it is enough to give this example to see that most alleged miracles do not give rise to conflicts of this kind. Most alleged miracles, if they occurred, would only show the power of god or gods and their concern for the needs of men, and little else.

My main conclusion, to repeat it, is that there are no logical difficulties in supposing that there could be strong historical evidence for the occurrence of miracles. Whether there is such evidence is, of course, another matter.

[7] *Op. cit.,* pp. 121 ff.

Aquinas' view of faith may be usefully compared with a somewhat similar view to be found in John Locke, *Concerning Human Understanding,** Book 4, Chapters 18 and 19 (Dover, 1959). A good discussion of the classical view of revelation is Etienne Gilson, *Reason and Revelation in the Middle Ages* * (Scribner's, 1938). Versions of the second view of faith discussed in the introduction may be found in Karl Barth, *Dogmatics in Outline* * (Harper, 1959), in Abraham Heschel, *God in Search of Man, A Philosophy of Judaism* * (Farrar, 1965), and in Søren Kierkegaard, *Concluding Unscientific Postscript* * (Princeton University Press, 1941). For an excellent presentation of the third view of faith, see John Hick, *Faith and Knowledge* (Cornell University Press, 1941). Issues connected with "the will to believe" and the ethics of belief are discussed in W. K. Clifford, "The Ethics of Belief," *Lectures and Essays* (Macmillan, 1901) and Van A. Harvey, "Is There an Ethics of Belief?" *Journal of Religion,* 49 (1969). The essays in Sidney Hook, ed., *Religious Experience and Truth,* Part 2 (New York University Press, 1961) are somewhat uneven in quality but do provide a good introduction to many of the philosophical issues connected with the topic of faith and revelation.

For a brief presentation of the classical doctrine of miracles, see St. Thomas Aquinas, *Summa Theologica,* Part 1, Question 105, Articles 6, 7, and 8, and the first part of Part 2, Question 113, Article 10. A readable and lively defense of the traditional position may be found in C. S. Lewis, *Miracles* * (Macmillan, 1963). Some of the more significant recent papers on miracles are Paul Dietl, "On Miracles," *American Philosophical Quarterly,* 5 (1968), R. G. Holland, "The Miraculous," *American Philosophical Quarterly,* 2 (1965), Alastair McKinnon, "Miracles and Paradox," *American Philosophical Quarterly,* 4 (1967), and Guy Robinson, "Miracles," *Ratio,* 9 (1967). Ninian Smart also devotes some attention to miracles in *Philosophers and Religious Truth* * (Macmillan, 1970). And a very good discussion of this subject is R. G. Swinburne, *The Concept of Miracle* * (St. Martin's Press, 1971).

* Available in paperback.

RELIGIOUS
LANGUAGE

W hen religious thinkers make the statement "God loves His creatures," they believe that they are saying something that is true. Throughout history, many critics of theism have considered the assertion either false or not known to be true; in recent times, however, critics have often maintained that what is asserted is meaningless. The first readings in this section consider the charge that statements about God are meaningless and examine some of the replies that have been made to this charge. For those philosophers who have decided that statements about God are meaningful, there is still the problem of explaining how they are meaningful and what, in particular, they mean. The selection by William Alston focuses attention on this latter problem, while E. L. Mascall and Paul Tillich each sketch theories concerning the meaning of religious discourse.

Antony Flew challenges the meaningfulness of statements about God on the grounds that the believers who make these statements are unable to specify what events, should they happen, would show that the statements are false. If there is nothing whatever that, should it happen, would convince the believer that God does not exist or does not love us after all, then the assertion that God loves us is empty of content and says nothing at all. This portion of Flew's argument seems plausible. If a statement does not rule out anything, then it cannot tell us anything very significant. But we need to clarify Flew's challenge. Suppose God suddenly started to hate us. A believer might well say that if that happened it would follow that the statement "God loves His creatures" is false. It seems, then, that the believer can specify something—God's hating us—which, should it happen, would show that God does not love His creatures. Flew, of course, would not be impressed. His challenge to the believer is not to specify just any event, but to specify an empirical event, some occurrence in the world that we all experience which, if it happened, would show that God does not love us. Of course, once this is made clear, it is less clear that the believer's inability to do this shows that "God loves His creatures" is meaningless. Still, if God's love for His creatures is compatible with absolutely any conceivable empirical event happening in the world, the claim that God loves us seems to be emptied of any real significance (so far as our lives in this world are concerned). Suppose, however, the theist simply says that there are empirical happenings which, if they occurred, would show that "God loves His creatures" is false. Is that sufficient, or must he also be able to specify those events? Is it reasonable to require that he be able to do so? For the theist may believe that God's love does rule out the occurrence of certain empirical events and that no human being is in the position of knowing just what those events are. Therefore, is his assertion "God loves His creatures" empirically meaningful after all?

Mitchell, Matthews, and Hick reply to the general issue raised by Flew's challenge and press several points in addition to those mentioned above.

Hick, for example, develops the notion of "eschatological verification"—experiences of events after bodily death—and endeavors to show that the existence of the theistic God is verifiable by such experiences. Hare, however, tries to avoid Flew's challenge by suggesting that religious language may be understood as expressing what he calls *bliks* rather than statements. A *blik* is neither verifiable nor falsifiable but may (in some sense) be right or wrong and may make a considerable difference to one's beliefs and conduct. It is doubtful, however, that Hare's concept of a *blik* is sufficiently clear to provide a way out for the theist. Furthermore, as Flew notes in response to Hare, the theist certainly intends "God loves His creatures" to express a statement.

For those who hold that religious statements about God are meaningful, there is the problem of explaining how they can be meaningful and what they mean. Within the theistic tradition, God is viewed as an immaterial being. Accordingly some theologians have distinguished between predicate expressions which in their primary meaning refer either to parts of a body (for example, the verbs *hand* or *face*) or to activities impossible without a body (for example, *walking* or *drinking*) and predicate expressions which in their primary meaning refer to properties of the mind or to mental activities (for example, *wise, just, merciful,* or *loving*). Expressions of the first kind cannot be predicated *properly* (that is, with their primary meaning) of God. For, since God does not have a body, to apply them properly to Him would result either in contradiction or nonsense. Thus, such expressions may be predicated of God only metaphorically. Expressions of the second kind, it is felt, can be predicated properly of God; moreover, it is generally pointed out that the properties designated by *just, wise,* and so on, occur in God in the highest possible degree—thus God is said to be infinitely just, infinitely wise.

Some philosophers have rejected this view because they think that expressions like *just* or *merciful*—no less than expressions like *hand* or *walking*—involve, as part of their meaning, a reference to bodily behavior. Even if this claim is too strong, it does seem that the criteria we use in determining whether an individual is forgiving or just do include bodily behavior—what one says and how he behaves. Perhaps, then, when these terms are applied to God they are to be understood as carrying their normal meaning but not the features surrounding their normal use—for example, the criteria on which we judge when it is appropriate to apply them—which involve any reference to bodily behavior. In the selection by Alston, this approach to religious language is dubbed the "whittle-down explanation" and subjected to a number of criticisms. Alston's basic objection is that such a view takes these expressions out of the framework within which we know how to use them without providing any new framework for understanding them.

Mascall endeavors to explain how religious statements can be meaningful by developing the Theory of Analogy. According to this theory, predicate expressions like *just* and *merciful* do not have the same meaning when applied to creatures as they do when applied to God. Nor are they used in an entirely different sense, as, for example, the term *bank* is used to mean both a financial institution and the ridge of earth bordering a river. That is, terms like *just* and *merciful* when used of God and creatures are used neither *univocally* (with the same meaning) nor *equivocally* (with a purely different meaning); they are, according to the theory, used *analogously*. The two sorts of analogous predication most important for this theory of religious language are analogy of attribution and analogy of proportionality. A classical example of the former is the application of the term *healthy* to both the man and his complexion. As Mascall explains this sort of analogy, the same term is applied to both the man and his complexion because of a certain relation between a healthy man and a healthy complexion—namely, the latter is a sign of the former. Health belongs primarily to the man and only secondarily to his complexion. But when we say "God lives" and "that man lives," what is the relation between the life of God and the life of that man? Mascall follows tradition and bases the analogy on the causal relation. Since God causes life in his creatures, He has life in whatever way He must have in order to create life in man. The difficulty with this view, as Mascall notes, is that it leaves us in the dark as to the nature of the Divine Life, for all it strictly implies is that God causes life in man. Another difficulty, not mentioned by Mascall, is that the term *cause* as applied to both finite things and to God presumably would have to be elucidated by the theory as well. And we could not use the causal relation between causal activity in God and causal activity in man in order to explain how the term *cause* is meaningfully applied to God.

Mascall also sees difficulties with analogy of proportionality as a basis for understanding the application of predicates to God. According to this form of analogy, life belongs properly to both God and man. But *life* does not denote in God what it denotes in man for the sort of life God has is determined by the kind of being He is and the sort of life man has is determined by the kind of being he is. One major difficulty with this view is that since God's essence is unknown, we. are unable to know or understand the kind of life God has. Mascall suggests that a satisfactory explanation of religious meaning would require a combination of both the analogy of attribution and the analogy of proportionality.

Tillich presents a radical theory of the meaning of religious language. His theory is radical because, unlike those who support the analogy theory and the "whittle-down explanation," Tillich identifies God not with a supreme being, but with what he calls "being-itself" or "ultimate reality." For philosophical reasons, Tillich holds that every existing being (including the Supreme Being, if there is one) exists only by virtue of participating in being-itself (ultimate reality), and being-itself is not a particular being at all. And for religious reasons, he identifies God with ultimate reality. Hence, God, properly speaking, is being-itself. What then of the theistic God, the Supreme Being? In Tillich's view, God (conceived of as the Supreme Being) is a religious symbol. What is *it* a symbol of? Like other religious symbols (sacred trees, statues, and so forth), God (conceived of as the Supreme Being) is a symbol of God (being-itself).

The radical nature of Tillich's view of religious discourse about God is a logical consequence of his view that God is not *a* being, even the Supreme Being, and of his view that predicate expressions are logically tied (by virtue of their primary meaning) to beings. Hence, no religious term—even the religious term *God*—can be applied literally to God (being-itself). All religious language is symbolic.

Religious symbols, on Tillich's view, are distinguished from nonreligious symbols on two grounds: first, in terms of what the symbol points to, and second, in terms of the attitudes and feelings the symbol evokes. Religious symbols point to ultimate reality (being-itself) and are the objects of ultimate concern—that is, religious symbols are viewed as infinitely important and holy. In Tillich's view, the religious symbol manifests true holiness (ultimate reality, being-itself) to us. The great problem of religion is the tendency to identify true holiness with the religious symbol that mediates it. When this happens the symbol in question becomes idolatrous.

The careful reader will note that Tillich does not explicitly distinguish between linguistic and nonlinguistic symbols. His remarks seem directed primarily toward nonlinguistic symbols. What, then, is his account of religious statements such as "God is living" and "God is merciful"? Given his view of God, it is clear that he must regard them as symbolic statements about being-itself. If so, just what do these statements say about being-itself? Tillich's answer to this question is to provide "translations" of religious, symbolic statements into philosophical statements about being-itself. Thus concerning the predicate *life*, Tillich remarks:

> Life is the actuality of being, or, more exactly, it is the process in which potential being becomes actual being. But in God as God there is no distinction between potentiality and actuality. Therefore, we cannot speak of God as living in the proper or nonsymbolic sense of the word life. We must speak of God as living in symbolic terms. . . . God lives in so far as he is the ground of life.[1]

The major points made in this excerpt are that *life* in its primary meaning is tied to the realm of beings and, therefore, can be applied to God (being-itself) only symbolically and that the meaning of "God lives" can be explained as "God is the ground of life."

Some of the objections to Tillich's theory of religious statements about

[1] Paul Tillich, *Systematic Theology,* Vol. I (University of Chicago Press, 1951), p. 242.

God should be mentioned here. First, according to his own theory, no positive statement about God (being-itself) can be true and nonsymbolic. Therefore, if true, the statement "God is the ground of life" is also symbolic. The implication is that Tillich's theory does not itself break out of the web of symbols. Moreover, if to interpret or explain what is meant by a symbolic or metaphorical statement s is to produce another statement, s', which expresses in nonsymbolic terms essentially what s expresses in symbolic terms, it follows that it is impossible using Tillich's theory ever to explain or interpret any religious statement about God. Second, critics of Tillich point out that, when they make such statements, religious thinkers certainly intend to be talking about a supreme being, and not about a metaphysical absolute like being-itself. Can we then be representing the meaning of their utterances if we explicate them in terms of metaphysical statements about being-itself?

W. L. R.

MEANING AND VERIFICATION

ANTONY FLEW, R. M. HARE,
AND BASIL MITCHELL
Theology and Falsification

ANTONY FLEW

Let us begin with a parable. It is a parable developed from a tale told by John Wisdom in his haunting and revelatory article 'Gods'.[1] Once upon a time two explorers came upon a clearing in the jungle. In the clearing were growing many flowers and many weeds. One explorer says, 'Some gardener must tend this plot'. The other disagrees, 'There is no gardener'. So they pitch their tents and set a watch. No gardener is ever seen. 'But perhaps he is an invisible gardener.' So they set up a barbed-wire fence. They electrify it. They patrol with bloodhounds. (For they remember how H. G. Wells's *The Invisible Man* could be both smelt and touched though he could not be seen.) But no shrieks ever suggest that some intruder has received a shock.

The contributors to this discussion represent the style of analytical philosophy that emerged in England following World War II. Antony Flew is a professor at the University of Keele, Staffordshire. R. M. Hare and Basil Mitchell teach at Oxford University.

THEOLOGY AND FALSIFICATION   Reprinted with permission of The Macmillan Company and SCM Press Ltd. from *New Essays in Philosophical Theology*, edited by Antony Flew and Alasdair MacIntyre. First published in 1955 by SCM Press Ltd.

[1] *P.A.S.*, 1944–5, reprinted as Ch. X of *Logic and Language*, Vol. I (Blackwell, 1951), and in his *Philosophy and Psychoanalysis* (Blackwell, 1953).

No movements of the wire ever betray an invisible climber. The bloodhounds never give cry. Yet still the Believer is not convinced. 'But there is a gardener, invisible, intangible, insensible to electric shocks, a gardener who has no scent and makes no sound, a gardener who comes secretly to look after the garden which he loves.' At last the Sceptic despairs, 'But what remains of your original assertion? Just how does what you call an invisible, intangible, eternally elusive gardener differ from an imaginary gardener or even from no gardener at all?'

In this parable we can see how what starts as an assertion, that something exists or that there is some analogy between certain complexes of phenomena, may be reduced step by step to an altogether different status, to an expression perhaps of a 'picture preference'.[2] The Sceptic says there is no gardener. The Believer says there is a gardener (but invisible, etc.). One man talks about sexual behaviour. Another man prefers to talk of Aphrodite (but knows that there is not really a superhuman person additional to, and somehow responsible for, all sexual phenomena).[3] The process of qualification may be checked at any point before the original assertion is completely withdrawn and something of that first assertion will remain (Tautology). Mr. Wells's invisible man could not, admittedly, be seen, but in all other respects he was a man like the rest of us. But though the process of qualification may be, and of course usually is, checked in time, it is not always judiciously so halted. Someone may dissipate his assertion completely without noticing that he has done so. A fine brash hypothesis may thus be killed by inches, the death by a thousand qualifications.

And in this, it seems to me, lies the peculiar danger, the endemic evil, of theological utterance. Take such utterances as 'God has a plan', 'God created the world', 'God loves us as a father loves his children'. They look at first sight very much like assertions, vast cosmological assertions. Of course, this is no sure sign that they either are, or are intended to be, assertions. But let us confine ourselves to the cases where those who utter such sentences intend them to express assertions. (Merely remarking parenthetically that those who intend or interpret such utterances as crypto-commands, expressions of wishes, disguised ejaculations, concealed ethics, or as anything else but assertions, are unlikely to succeed in making them either properly orthodox or practically effective.)

Now to assert that such and such is the case is necessarily equivalent to

---

[2] Cf. J. Wisdom, 'Other Minds', *Mind*, 1940; reprinted in his *Other Minds* (Blackwell, 1952).
[3] Cf. Lucretius, *De Rerum Natura*, II, 655–60,

> Hic siquis mare Neptunum Cereremque vocare
> Constituet fruges et Bacchi nomine abuti
> Mavolat quam laticis proprium proferre vocamen
> Concedamus ut hic terrarum dictitet orbem
> Esse deum matrem dum vera re tamen ipse
> Religione animum turpi contingere parcat.

denying that such and such is not the case.[4] Suppose then that we are in doubt as to what someone who gives vent to an utterance is asserting, or suppose that, more radically, we are sceptical as to whether he is really asserting anything at all, one way of trying to understand (or perhaps it will be to expose) his utterance is to attempt to find what he would regard as counting against, or as being incompatible with, its truth. For if the utterance is indeed an assertion, it will necessarily be equivalent to a denial of the negation of that assertion. And anything which would count against the assertion, or which would induce the speaker to withdraw it and to admit that it had been mistaken, must be part of (or the whole of) the meaning of the negation of that assertion. And to know the meaning of the negation of an assertion, is as near as makes no matter, to know the meaning of that assertion.[5] And if there is nothing which a putative assertion denies then there is nothing which it asserts either: and so it is not really an assertion. When the Sceptic in the parable asked the Believer, 'Just how does what you call an invisible, intangible, eternally elusive gardener differ from an imaginary gardener or even from no gardener at all?' he was suggesting that the Believer's earlier statement had been so eroded by qualification that it was no longer an assertion at all.

Now it often seems to people who are not religious as if there was no conceivable event or series of events the occurrence of which would be admitted by sophisticated religious people to be a sufficient reason for conceding 'There wasn't a God after all' or 'God does not really love us then'. Someone tells us that God loves us as a father loves his children. We are reassured. But then we see a child dying of inoperable cancer of the throat. His earthly father is driven frantic in his efforts to help, but his Heavenly Father reveals no obvious sign of concern. Some qualification is made—God's love is 'not a merely human love' or it is 'an inscrutable love', perhaps—and we realize that such sufferings are quite compatible with the truth of the assertion that 'God loves us as a father (but, of course, . . .)'. We are reassured again. But then perhaps we ask: what is this assurance of God's (appropriately qualified) love worth, what is this apparent guarantee really a guarantee against? Just what would have to happen not merely (morally and wrongly) to tempt but also (logically and rightly) to entitle us to say 'God does not love us' or even 'God does not exist'? I therefore put to the succeeding symposiasts the simple central questions, 'What would have to occur or to have occurred to constitute for you a disproof of the love of, or of the existence of, God?'

R. M. HARE

I wish to make it clear that I shall not try to defend Christianity in particular, but religion in general—not because I do not believe in Christianity,

---

[4] For those who prefer symbolism: $p \equiv \sim\sim p$.
[5] For by simply negating $\sim p$ we get p: $\sim\sim p \equiv p$.

but because you cannot understand what Christianity is, until you have understood what religion is.

I must begin by confessing that, on the ground marked out by Flew, he seems to me to be completely victorious. I therefore shift my ground by relating another parable. A certain lunatic is convinced that all dons want to murder him. His friends introduce him to all the mildest and most respectable dons that they can find, and after each of them has retired, they say, 'You see, he doesn't really want to murder you; he spoke to you in a most cordial manner; surely you are convinced now?' But the lunatic replies 'Yes, but that was only his diabolical cunning; he's really plotting against me the whole time, like the rest of them; I know it I tell you'. However many kindly dons are produced, the reaction is still the same.

Now we say that such a person is deluded. But what is he deluded about? About the truth or falsity of an assertion? Let us apply Flew's test to him. There is no behaviour of dons that can be enacted which he will accept as counting against his theory; and therefore his theory, on this test, asserts nothing. But it does not follow that there is no difference between what he thinks about dons and what most of us think about them—otherwise we should not call him a lunatic and ourselves sane, and dons would have no reason to feel uneasy about his presence in Oxford.

Let us call that in which we differ from this lunatic, our respective *bliks*. He has an insane *blik* about dons; we have a sane one. It is important to realize that we have a sane one, not no *blik* at all; for there must be two sides to any argument—if he has a wrong *blik*, then those who are right about dons must have a right one. Flew has shown that a *blik* does not consist in an assertion or system of them; but nevertheless it is very important to have the right *blik*.

Let us try to imagine what it would be like to have different *bliks* about other things than dons. When I am driving my car, it sometimes occurs to me to wonder whether my movements of the steering-wheel will always continue to be followed by corresponding alterations in the direction of the car. I have never had a steering failure, though I have had skids, which must be similar. Moreover, I know enough about how the steering of my car is made, to know the sort of thing that would have to go wrong for the steering to fail —steel joints would have to part, or steel rods break, or something—but how do I know that this won't happen? The truth is, I don't know; I just have a *blik* about steel and its properties, so that normally I trust the steering of my car; but I find it not at all difficult to imagine what it would be like to lose this *blik* and acquire the opposite one. People would say I was silly about steel; but there would be no mistaking the reality of the difference between our respective *bliks*—for example, I should never go in a motor-car. Yet I should hesitate to say that the difference between us was the difference between contradictory assertions. No amount of safe arrivals or bench-tests will remove my *blik* and restore the normal one; for my *blik* is compatible with any finite number of such tests.

It was Hume who taught us that our whole commerce with the world depends upon our *blik* about the world; and that differences between *bliks* about the world cannot be settled by observation of what happens in the world. That was why, having performed the interesting experiment of doubting the ordinary man's *blik* about the world, and showing that no proof could be given to make us adopt one *blik* rather than another, he turned to backgammon to take his mind off the problem. It seems, indeed, to be impossible even to formulate as an assertion the normal *blik* about the world which makes me put my confidence in the future reliability of steel joints, in the continued ability of the road to support my car, and not gape beneath it revealing nothing below; in the general non-homicidal tendencies of dons; in my own continued well-being (in some sense of that word that I may not now fully understand) if I continue to do what is right according to my lights; in the general likelihood of people like Hitler coming to a bad end. But perhaps a formulation less inadequate than most is to be found in the Psalms: 'The earth is weak and all the inhabiters thereof: I bear up the pillars of it'.

The mistake of the position which Flew selects for attack is to regard this kind of talk as some sort of *explanation*, as scientists are accustomed to use the word. As such, it would obviously be ludicrous. We no longer believe in God as an Atlas—*nous n'avons pas besoin de cette hypothèse*. But it is nevertheless true to say that, as Hume saw, without a *blik* there can be no explanation; for it is by our *bliks* that we decide what is and what is not an explanation. Suppose we believed that everything that happened, happened by pure chance. This would not of course be an assertion; for it is compatible with anything happening or not happening, and so, incidentally, is its contradictory. But if we had this belief, we should not be able to explain or predict or plan anything. Thus, although we should not be *asserting* anything different from those of a more normal belief, there would be a great difference between us; and this is the sort of difference that there is between those who really believe in God and those who really disbelieve in him.

The word 'really' is important, and may excite suspicion. I put it in, because when people have had a good Christian upbringing, as have most of those who now profess not to believe in any sort of religion, it is very hard to discover what they really believe. The reason why they find it so easy to think that they are not religious, is that they have never got into the frame of mind of one who suffers from the doubts to which religion is the answer. Not for them the terrors of the primitive jungle. Having abandoned some of the more picturesque fringes of religion, they think that they have abandoned the whole thing—whereas in fact they still have got, and could not live without, a religion of a comfortably substantial, albeit highly sophisticated, kind, which differs from that of many 'religious people' in little more than this, that 'religious people' like to sing Psalms about theirs—a very natural and proper thing to do. But nevertheless there may be a big difference lying behind—the difference between two people who, though side by side, are walking in different directions. I do not know in what direction Flew is walking; perhaps he does not know either. But we have had some examples recently of various ways in which one can walk away from Christianity, and there are any number of possibilities. After all, man has not changed biologically since primitive times; it is his religion that has changed, and it can easily change again. And if you do not think that such changes make a difference, get acquainted with some Sikhs and some Mussulmans of the same Punjabi stock; you will find them quite different sorts of people.

There is an important difference between Flew's parable and my own which we have not yet noticed. The explorers do not *mind* about their garden; they discuss it with interest, but not with concern. But my lunatic, poor fellow, minds about dons; and I mind about the steering of my car; it often has people in it that I care for. It is because I mind very much about what goes on in the garden in which I find myself, that I am unable to share the explorers' detachment.

BASIL MITCHELL

Flew's article is searching and perceptive, but there is, I think, something odd about his conduct of the theologian's case. The theologian surely would not deny that the fact of pain counts against the assertion that God loves men. This very incompatibility generates the most intractable of theological problems—the problem of evil. So the theologian *does* recognize the fact of pain as counting against Christian doctrine. But it is true that he will not allow it—or anything—to count decisively against it; for he is committed by his faith to trust in God. His attitude is not that of the detached observer, but of the believer.

Perhaps this can be brought out by yet another parable. In time of war in an occupied country, a member of the resistance meets one night a stranger who deeply impresses him. They spend that night together in conversation. The Stranger tells the partisan that he himself is on the side of the resistance—indeed that he is in command of it, and urges the partisan to have faith in him no matter what happens. The partisan is utterly convinced at that meeting of the Stranger's sincerity and constancy and undertakes to trust him.

They never meet in conditions of intimacy again. But sometimes the Stranger is seen helping members of the resistance, and the partisan is grateful and says to his friends, 'He is on our side'.

Sometimes he is seen in the uniform of the police handing over patriots to the occupying power. On these occasions his friends murmur against him: but the partisan still says, 'He is on our side'. He still believes that, in spite of appearances, the Stranger did not deceive him. Sometimes he asks the Stranger for help and receives it. He is then thankful. Sometimes he asks and does not receive it. Then he says, 'The Stranger knows best'. Sometimes his friends, in exasperation, say 'Well, what *would* he have to do for you to admit that you were wrong and that he is not on our side?' But the partisan refuses to answer. He will not consent to put the Stranger to the test. And sometimes his friends complain, 'Well, if *that's* what you mean by his being on our side, the sooner he goes over to the other side the better'.

The partisan of the parable does not allow anything to count decisively against the proposition 'The Stranger is on our side'. This is because he has committed himself to trust the Stranger. But he of course recognizes that the Stranger's ambiguous behaviour *does* count against what he believes about him. It is precisely this situation which constitutes the trial of his faith.

When the partisan asks for help and doesn't get it, what can he do? He can (*a*) conclude that the Stranger is not on our side or; (*b*) maintain that he is on our side, but that he has reasons for withholding help.

The first he will refuse to do. How long can be uphold the second position without its becoming just silly?

I don't think one can say in advance. It will depend on the nature of the impression created by the Stranger in the first place. It will depend, too, on the manner in which he takes the Stranger's behaviour. If he blandly dismisses it as of no consequence, as having no bearing upon his belief, it will be assumed that he is thoughtless or insane. And it quite obviously won't do for him to say easily, 'Oh, when used of the Stranger the phrase "is on our side" *means* ambiguous behaviour of this sort'. In that case he would be like the religious man who says blandly of a terrible disaster 'It is God's will'. No, he will only be regarded as sane and reasonable in his belief, if he experiences in himself the full force of the conflict.

It is here that my parable differs from Hare's. The partisan admits that many things may and do count against his belief: whereas Hare's lunatic who has a *blik* about dons doesn't admit that anything counts against his *blik*. Nothing *can* count against *bliks*. Also the partisan has a reason for having in the first instance committed himself, viz. the character of the Stranger; whereas the lunatic has no reason for his *blik* about dons—because, of course, you can't have reasons for *bliks*.

This means that I agree with Flew that theological utterances must be assertions. The partisan is making an assertion when he says, 'The Stranger is on our side'.

Do I want to say that the partisan's belief about the Stranger is, in any sense, an explanation? I think I do. It explains and makes sense of the Stranger's behaviour: it helps to explain also the resistance movement in the context of which he appears. In each case it differs from the interpretation which the others put upon the same facts.

'God loves men' resembles 'the Stranger is on our side' (and many other significant statements, e.g. historical ones) in not being conclusively falsifiable. They can both be treated in at least three different ways: (1) As provisional hypotheses to be discarded if experience tells against them; (2) As significant articles of faith; (3) As vacuous formulae (expressing, perhaps, a desire for reassurance) to which experience makes no difference and which make no difference to life.

The Christian, once he had committed himself, is precluded by his faith from taking up the first attitude: 'Thou shalt not tempt the Lord thy God'. He is in constant danger, as Flew has observed, of slipping into the third. But he need not; and, if he does, it is a failure in faith as well as in logic.

ANTONY FLEW

It has been a good discussion: and I am glad to have helped to provoke it. But now—at least in *University*—it must come to an end: and the Editors of *University* have asked me to make some concluding remarks. Since it is impossible to deal with all the issues raised or to comment separately upon each contribution, I will concentrate on Mitchell and Hare, as representative of two very different kinds of response to the challenge made in 'Theology and Falsification'.

The challenge, it will be remembered, ran like this. Some theological utterances seem to, and are intended to, provide explanations or express assertions. Now an assertion, to be an assertion at all, must claim that things stand thus and thus; *and not otherwise*. Similarly an explanation, to be an explanation at all, must explain why this particular thing occurs; *and not something else*. Those last clauses are crucial. And yet sophisticated religious people—or so it seemed to me—are apt to overlook this, and tend to refuse to allow, not merely that anything actually does occur, but that anything conceivably could occur, which would count against their theological assertions and explanations. But in so far as they do this their supposed explanations are actually bogus, and their seeming assertions are really vacuous.

Mitchell's response to this challenge is admirably direct, straightforward, and understanding. He agrees 'that theological utterances must be assertions'. He agrees that if they are to be assertions, there must be something that would count against their truth. He agrees, too, that believers are in constant danger of transforming their would-be assertions into 'vacuous formulae'. But he takes me to task for an oddity in my 'conduct of the theologian's case. The theologian surely would not deny that the fact of pain counts against the assertion that God loves men. This very incompatibility generates the most intractable of theological problems, the problem of evil'. I think he is right. I should have made a distinction between two very different ways of dealing with what looks like evidence against the love of God: the way I stressed was the expedient of qualifying the original assertion; the way the theologian usually takes, at first, is to admit that it looks bad but to insist that there is—there must be—some explanation which will show that, in spite of appearances, there really is a God who loves us. His difficulty, it seems to me, is that he has given God attributes which rule out all possible saving explanations. In Mitchell's parable of the Stranger it is easy for the believer to find plausible excuses for ambiguous behaviour: for the Stranger is a man. But suppose the Stranger is God. We cannot say that he would like to help but cannot: God is omnipotent. We cannot say that he would help if he only knew: God is omniscient. We cannot say that he is not responsible for the wickedness of others: God creates those others. Indeed an omnipotent, omniscient God must be an accessory before (and during) the fact to every human misdeed; as well as being responsible for every non-moral defect in the universe. So, though I entirely concede that Mitchell was absolutely right to insist against me that the theologian's first move is to look for an *explanation*, I still think that in the end, if relentlessly pursued, he will have to resort to the avoiding action of *qualification*. And there lies the danger of that death by a thousand qualifications, which would, I agree, constitute 'a failure in faith as well as in logic'.

Hare's approach is fresh and bold. He confesses that 'on the ground marked out by Flew, he seems to me to be completely victorious'. He therefore introduces the concept of *blik*. But while I think that there is room for some such concept in philosophy, and that philosophers should be grateful to Hare for his invention, I nevertheless want to insist that any attempt to analyse Christian religious utterances as expressions or affirmations of a *blik* rather than as (at least would-be) assertions about the cosmos is fundamentally misguided. *First*, because thus interpreted they would be entirely unorthodox. If Hare's religion really is a *blik*, involving no cosmological assertions about the nature and activities of a supposed personal creator, then surely he is not a Christian at all? *Second*, because thus interpreted, they could scarcely do the job they do. If they were not even intended as assertions then many religious activities would become fraudulent, or merely silly. If 'You ought *because* it is God's will' asserts no more than 'You ought', then the person who prefers the former phraseology is not really giving a reason, but a fraudulent substitute for one, a dialectical dud cheque. If 'My soul must be immortal *because* God loves his children, etc.' asserts no more than 'My soul must be immortal', then the man who reassures himself with theological arguments for immortality is being as silly as the man who tries to clear his overdraft by writing his bank a cheque on the same account. (Of course neither of these utterances would be distinctively Christian: but this discussion never pretended to be so confined.) Religious utterances may indeed express false or even bogus assertions: but I simply do not believe that they are not both intended and interpreted to be or at any rate to presuppose assertions, at least in the context of religious practice; whatever shifts may be demanded, in another context, by the exigencies of theological apologetic.

One final suggestion. The philosophers of religion might well draw upon George Orwell's last appalling nightmare *1984* for the concept of *double-think*. '*Doublethink* means the power of holding two contradictory beliefs simultaneously, and accepting both of them. The party intellectual knows that he is playing tricks with reality, but by the exercise of *doublethink* he also satisfies himself that reality is not violated' (*1984*, p. 220). Perhaps religious intellectuals too are sometimes driven to doublethink in order to retain their faith in a loving God in face of the reality of a heartless and indifferent world. But of this more another time, perhaps.

GARETH B. MATTHEWS
Theology and Natural Theology

A person, seasoned with a just sense of the imperfections of natural reason, will fly to revealed truth with the greatest avidity, while the haughty dogmatist, persuaded that he can erect a complete system of theology by the mere help of philosophy, disdains any further aid and rejects this adventitious instructor. To be a philosophical sceptic is, in a man of letters, the first and most essential step towards being a sound, believing Christian. . . .
(David Hume, *Dialogues Concerning Natural Religion*, Part XII)

Doubtless many readers of Hume's *Dialogues Concerning Natural Religion* disregard this concluding comment of Philo's on the grounds that it is a mere sop to the pious. Hume was presumably not himself a "sound, believing Christian." And we have independent evidence that he was anxious about how the public would receive his devastating critique of natural theology. So it is reasonable to suppose that he made some effort to sugarcoat his conclusion and that having Philo offer the concluding remark quoted above was part of this effort.

I am not here interested, however, in whether Hume was sincere or not. Instead I am interested, simply for its own sake, in the position he has Philo take. The position is this. Natural theology, i.e., theology that appeals only

Gareth B. Matthews (1929–   ) is a professor of philosophy at the University of Massachusetts. His major writings have been in the areas of medieval philosophy and the philosophy of religion.

THEOLOGY AND NATURAL THEOLOGY   From *The Journal of Philosophy*, Volume LXI, No. 3, January 30, 1964. Copyright 1964 by The Journal of Philosophy, Inc. Reprinted by permission of the author and *The Journal of Philosophy*.

to reason and to general experience and not at all to revelation as the basis for its conclusions, is impotent. At best it can establish with only low probability doctrines of quite vague import. Its results are so modest as to be indistinguishable from the conclusions of skepticism or agnosticism. To have been shown that this is the case or to have discovered it for oneself is to have learned the real importance of revelation. Revealed religion is not the unlearned man's substitute for natural theology. Rather, natural theology is the counterfeit of revelation. One who is taken in by natural theology, therefore, fails to understand what religious belief really is. The person Philo calls "a man of letters" is precisely the one who might be taken in by natural theology. Therefore, "to be a philosophical sceptic is, in a man of letters, the first and most essential step towards being a sound, believing Christian."

I want now to single out one thesis from Philo's position and give it a name. That thesis is the proposition that natural theology cannot either confirm or disconfirm the truths of divine revelation. I shall call the view stated by that proposition *theological nonnaturalism*.

Philo arrives at theological nonnaturalism by applying philosophical skepticism to the arguments of natural theology. But there is another important route to the same goal. "I believe," says Luther in his *Small Catechism*, "that by my own reason or strength I cannot believe in Jesus Christ, my Lord, or come to him." With just this consideration in mind the contemporary Swiss theologian, Karl Barth, insists that

> God is knowable to us in His grace, and because in His grace, only in His grace. For this reason [the church] can make no use of natural theology with its doctrine of another kind of knowability of God.[1]

I should point out that Barth's statement, like Luther's, expresses an article of faith. It can be given a justification in terms of other articles of faith. But it is not the conclusion of a set of philosophical arguments. So, whereas Philo arrives at theological nonnaturalism by philosophical argumentation, Barth holds it by faith.

From a theological point of view, Philo's position is synergistic. That is, Philo supposes that a man can make a real contribution to his own salvation by disabusing himself of the illusions of natural theology. Barth denies this. "The illusion that we can disillusion ourselves," he writes (169), "is the greatest of all illusions." Nevertheless, and in spite of their great differences, Barth and Philo are both theological nonnaturalists.

I

I have begun this paper with a delineation of theological nonnaturalism; but my purpose is neither to defend nor to attack that view as such. What I wish to do instead is to examine a notion about theology and natural theology

[1] *Church Dogmatics* (Edinburgh: Clark, 1957), vol. II (1), p. 172.

which seems to enjoy wide contemporary approval. I shall examine it by testing it out on theological nonnaturalism. What I have in mind is the notion that it must be natural theology, or at least the willingness to engage in natural theology, that gives religious beliefs the meaning they are thought to have. If this notion is correct, then clearly theological nonnaturalism would rob religious beliefs of the meaning they are thought to have. In the discussion to follow I wish to examine several arguments which purport to show that it does just this.

Let us consider first a line of argument Antony Flew presents in his much discussed little piece, "Theology and Falsification." [2] Flew makes use of a general principle about what is required for a putative assertion to be a genuine assertion; his principle could be expressed this way:

(1) An alleged assertion is a *bona fide* assertion if, and only if, the person making the assertion is prepared to specify what conceivable turn of events would be incompatible with it and what conceivable evidence would count against its truth.

Of course (1) is a cousin, albeit several times removed, of the old Verification Criterion of Meaning. However, (1) is a much more reasonable principle than the Verification Criterion. In fact a survey of the considerable literature that Flew's piece has inspired suggests that hardly anyone would want to attack (1) directly. We are not here interested in (1) for its own sake, however; we are interested only in the bearing of (1) upon natural theology.

Suppose that a person holds a given doctrine as a revealed truth—without any appeal to natural theology. Flew does not demand that the doctrine be thrown out on grounds of insufficient evidence. But he does insist that the believer be able to specify some conceivable evidence that would tend to count against the truth of the doctrine and some conceivable turn of events that would be incompatible with it. If the believer maintains that no conceivable turn of events is incompatible with the doctrine and no conceivable evidence would count against its truth, Flew will answer that, since obviously nothing is ruled out by the doctrine, to assert it is to make no assertion at all. If, however, the believer accedes to Flew's demand, he will end up, it seems, making an appeal to natural theology. For he will specify what events, if they happen, and what evidence, if it were found, would tend to disconfirm the doctrine. Moreover, in specifying what would tend to disconfirm the doctrine, he may be also specifying what, by its absence, would tend (in appropriate circumstances) to support or give credence to it. So natural theology might either disconfirm or confirm the theological doctrine.

Consider an example. If one were to say that the doctrine that God made all living things is incompatible with the synthetic production of living cells

[2] *New Essays in Philosophical Theology,* edited by A. Flew and A. MacIntyre (New York: Macmillan, 1955), pp. 96–99.

in a laboratory, then the repeated failure over a long period of time of skilled biochemists to produce living cells in a laboratory would tend to support the theological doctrine; and success in their effort would, of course, falsify it.

The demand for at least disconfirmability in a *bona fide* theological assertion thus envelops, it would seem, a demand for either a modicum of natural theology or else no theology at all. It is not that Flew will not let us believe something on insufficient evidence. His idea is rather that we cannot believe something immune to counterevidence; for in such a case there is nothing to believe.

One might object that I have not shown Flew's demand to be a demand for natural theology or no theology, since I have not shown that, according to him, theological assertions must be open to disconfirmation from natural, as opposed to revealed, theology. In fact Flew is not explicit on this point. However, if his challenge to theology is not taken to include an implicit demand for a bit of natural theology, it will pose no threat at all to the believer. Let me explain what I mean.

Consider one of Flew's two sample theological claims, the claim that God loves us. Flew wants to know what conceivable turn of events is incompatible with this claim and what conceivable evidence would count against its truth. Flew supposes that a sophisticated believer will say that no conceivable evidence would count against its truth and no conceivable turn of events is incompatible with it. But surely even (or especially) the most sophisticated believer can say that evidence that, e.g., God is really jealous of us human beings (cf. Carl Gustav Jung's *Answer to Job*) or that God hates us would tend to count against the truth of the claim that God loves us. Of course evidence of this sort would have to come either from a new revelation or from the reinterpretation of accepted revelation.

Interestingly, none of Flew's fellow symposiasts answers his challenge in this fashion. So we cannot be absolutely sure what Flew's reaction would be. Nevertheless, I am quite confident that Flew would be unimpressed with such a rejoinder. For he is not interested in the claim that God loves us *per se*; he is interested in it only as a sample theological claim. His broader question is, "Are theological assertions *bona fide* assertions?" If I respond to his challenge by talk of evidence that God is jealous of human beings or even hates us, I am introducing further theological statements. Quite clearly Flew would want to call these into question in just the same way he questioned the original theological claim. The only way to satisfy Flew would thus be to introduce conceivable disconfirming evidence or a conceivably incompatible state of affairs that could be described in purely *nontheological* terms (i.e., without reference to God or His love, purpose, grace, etc.). To do that would be, of course, to engage in natural theology.

It is clear then that, unless Flew's challenge to theology is taken to include a demand for a modicum of natural theology, (*a*) the believer will have no trouble meeting the challenge and (*b*) Flew will not be able to use his challenge as a test for whether theological assertions are, *per se, bona fide* assertions. But it is also clear that (1) is really an insufficient basis for demanding that theology be backed by natural theology. What Flew needs for that job is something more like this:

> (1a) An alleged *theological* assertion is a *bona fide* assertion if, and only if, the person making the alleged assertion is prepared to specify in *nontheological* terms what conceivable turn of events would be incompatible with it and what conceivable evidence would count against its truth.

However, (1a) is much less appealing than (1). For (1) is based upon a rather plausible general conception of what it is to make an assertion, whereas (1a) singles out theology and demands that theological assertions, if they are *bona fide* assertions, must have clear nontheological consequences. This might be a reasonable demand if we had already established that, e.g., geometrical assertions have clear nongeometrical consequences, that physical assertions have clear nonphysical consequences, that ethical assertions have clear nonethical consequences, etc. But in the absence of any such established conclusions, (1a) appears to be discriminatory against theology.

Could (1a) be supported nevertheless? One way to try would be to argue that, unless theological statements have clear nontheological consequences, the believer is not free to buttress his claims by appeal to natural phenomena like the starry heavens above, the first cuckoo in spring, or—more generally and abstractly—the regularity of nature. However, we must not forget that we embarked on this discussion of Flew as a way of determining whether natural theology is needed to give meaning to theological claims. To suppose simply that a believer will want finally to appeal to natural theology anyway renders our inquiry trivial. So this way of supporting (1a) makes Flew's challenge to theology irrelevant as a way of showing that natural theology is required to give meaning to religious beliefs. Moreover, I know of no way of supporting (1a) that does not share the same weakness.

II

A persistent agnostic sympathetic to Flew might be quite dissatisfied with my argument in the last section. He might be worried about what, if anything, a theological claim such as the claim that God loves us has to do with ordinary goings-on in the world we all inhabit—agnostic and believer alike. In this world babies are born, sometimes healthy, sometimes diseased or deformed. In this world people die, sometimes after long and happy lives, sometimes after very short and perhaps very painful ones. In this world there is sunshine and rain, drought and flood, bumper crops and famine, etc. The agnostic wants to know whether the claim that God loves us has anything to do with all this. Are some conceivable configurations of these "natural" elements ruled out by the claim that God loves us, or not? If not, then, since

God is "Lord of Heaven and Earth," [3] His love for us cannot amount to much. For unless the fact that He loves us rules out some conceivable developments in the world which both agnostic and believer live in and recognize, the claim that God loves us seems to be emptied of significance. If, on the other hand, this claim is incompatible with some conceivable configurations of "natural" elements, then evidence that such a configuration were actually present would tend to falsify the claim that God loves us. And thus the believer would become involved in doing natural theology.

I can make this last point quite general.

(2) A given claim is either compatible with all conceivable states of affairs in the empirical world, or it is not. If it is not, then it could be confirmed or disconfirmed by empirical evidence. If it is, then in making the claim, one is saying nothing about what comes to pass in the empirical world.

As we have seen, the theological nonnaturalist is a believer who supposes that theological doctrines are not subject to empirical confirmation and disconfirmation. According to (2), such a person would have to say that theological doctrines are compatible with all conceivable states of affairs in the empirical world and so say nothing about the empirical world.

No doubt the theological nonnaturalist would be unhappy with such a conclusion. Of course he might be quite happy to allow that *some* theological doctrines say nothing about the empirical world (e.g., the Christian doctrine that God is three-in-one). But surely he must think that other theological doctrines (e.g., the Christian doctrine that God loves His children) do say something about the empirical world and what goes on in it. But how can he, if he is to remain a theological nonnaturalist?

I think he must grasp firmly one horn of the dilemma. To be sure, a given claim either is compatible with all conceivable states of affairs in the empirical world or it is not. But suppose it is not. It would follow that the claim is subject to empirical confirmation and disconfirmation *only if we knew which conceivable states of affairs it is incompatible with*. Certainly one can understand that a given claim is incompatible with some conceivable states of affairs without claiming to know what the incompatible states are. But then, the agnostic may protest, the claim is no longer an empirical claim; for without knowing what states of affairs are incompatible with the claim, we could not conceivably falsify it empirically—we should not know what to look for. Precisely. This is just what the theological nonnaturalist supposes. The world, he thinks, proceeds according to God's providence. But our understanding of God's providence—and God's providence, let us not forget, is thought to govern both earthly life and eternity as well—is too limited for us to know just what empirical states of affairs are ruled out by the claim that He loves us.

---

[3] I put this point somewhat informally in order to avoid the traditional terminology of natural theology ('God's omnipotence', 'omniscience', etc.).

The agnostic will doubtless remain dissatisfied. Why, he may want to know, is one supposed to be comforted by the doctrine that God loves us if one cannot specify a single empirical calamity or set of calamities incompatible with the claim that God loves us? Why indeed? Because, I suppose, one has faith. "For I am persuaded," wrote St. Paul,

> . . . that neither death, nor life, nor angels, nor principalities, nor powers, nor things present, nor things to come, nor height, nor depth, nor any other creature, shall be able to separate us from the love of God, which is in Christ Jesus our Lord (Romans 8:38–9).

The theological nonnaturalist should thus insist that (2) be modified as follows:

(2a) A given claim is either compatible with all conceivable states of affairs in the empirical world or it is not. If it is not, *and we know what at least one of the states of affairs is with which it is incompatible*, then it could be confirmed or disconfirmed by empirical evidence. However, if it is compatible with all conceivable states of affairs in the empirical world, then in making the claim, one is saying nothing about what comes to pass in the empirical world.

Let us agree to suppose, the agnostic may reply, that the claim that God loves us is incompatible with some conceivable states of affairs in the empirical world—we know not which. Without knowing what the states are, or at least what some of them are, the claim still says nothing about what comes to pass in the empirical world.

The theological nonnaturalist's reply is, of course, this: The claim that God loves us says about every happening in the world that, given all relevant information about God and His plans, about us and the world, this happening is consistent with God's love.

III

A sophisticated agnostic may remain dissatisfied. Normally, he may say, the concept of love is an empirical concept. That is, normally there are ways of confirming or disconfirming the claim that x loves y. And even when there are not, as, for example, when a suitor's beloved dies suddenly without giving evidence of her feelings, we at least know what it would be like to have confirming or disconfirming evidence (e.g., a diary entry, the report of a confidante sworn to secrecy, etc.).

The theological nonnaturalist wants to construe the claim that God loves us as a nonempirical claim—not just in the weak sense that we do not as a matter of fact have any satisfactory empirical evidence pro or con—but in the strong sense that we cannot conceive of empirical evidence that could really confirm or disconfirm the doctrine in question. But the effect of this move is to change the concept of love—the agnostic continues—so that, when linked to God, the concept of love is nonempirical. This nonempirical concept of love takes its meaning from the contexts in which God's love is spoken of (e.g., the scriptures, the liturgy, etc.). And it is quite distinct from the ordinary empirical concept.

The encouragement people receive from the doctrine of God's love is, therefore—according to the agnostic—quite delusory. That encouragement comes from associating the empirical concept with the nonempirical one. The association is natural enough, for we use the word 'love' to express both. But, where 'love' has a nonempirical meaning, there is nothing reassuring in the least about the claim that God loves us.

With this set of considerations in mind it may be tempting for the believer to appeal to a doctrine of analogy to connect the nonempirical concept of Divine love to the empirical concept of human love. I do not wish to comment here upon the value of doctrines of analogy in general. But I do wish to say that appeal to analogy is a poor way for the theological nonnaturalist to try to avoid the difficulty stated above. For if we suppose that the concept of God's love is a nonempirical concept linked by analogy to the empirical concept of human love, we must either make good on this claim by trying to specify roughly the respects in which Divine love is like human love or else the assertion of analogy is quite unhelpful. If we do specify the respects in which the analogy applies, we shall by this means either give the theological concept a certain empirical content or not. If we do, then the theological nonnaturalist will have to give in to the request for natural theology after all. If we do not, then the criticism above still applies.

The theological nonnaturalist is well advised, then, to resist the enticements of analogy [4] and to challenge the agnostic's argument on a more basic level. Let us review that argument. An ordinary claim that, say, Edward loves Wally, is an empirical claim. According to the theological nonnaturalist, the claim that God loves His children is a nonempirical claim. If this is so, says the agnostic, then it must be that the term 'love' is being used in the two cases to express two different concepts—an empirical concept of love and a nonempirical concept of love. But once we realize this the claim that God loves us is no longer comforting.

The crucial move in this argument is the move from noting that one love claim is empirical, the other nonempirical, to the conclusion that the term 'love' in the two propositions must *therefore* express two different concepts of love. Why should we suppose this? Do we want to say that whenever a single term goes to make up both an empirical and a nonempirical proposition, it expresses two different concepts? Presumably we should not want to say this for the syncategorematic or logical terms (e.g., 'and', 'if', 'not', etc.). But what about categorematic terms? I think the answer is clearly no. The claim that

---

[4] This is in fact what Karl Barth does; cf. *op. cit.*, pp. 63–128.

all cubes have twelve edges is not, I take it, an empirical claim; but the claim that all Susan's building blocks are cubes is. Yet we should not want to say that we were dealing with two concepts of a cube, the one empirical, the other nonempirical. If we did, the inference from these two propositions to the conclusion that all Susan's building blocks have twelve edges would be invalid; it would depend upon an equivocation on 'cube'. But that is absurd.

I am not at all sure that one can specify good general rules for the proper individuation of concepts. But whether one can or not, clearly the implicit rule upon which this criticism of theological nonnaturalism is based will not do.

So the theological nonnaturalist is not forced by this argument to suppose that God's love is completely different from human love. True, he wants to construe the claim that God loves us as a nonempirical claim. But this is not because he considers God's love to be completely different from human love. It is because, not knowing what the pain and sorrow of this world mean in the light of eternity, we cannot use empirical data about what happens in the world as evidence for or against God's love. It is a mistake, then, to speak of the concept of Divine love (or justice or goodness, etc.) as being a distinct and nonempirical concept of love (or justice, etc.). To be sure, God's love may be thought to be more perfect than any human love. But to say that it is more perfect is a way of saying that God loves us more perfectly than we can love Him or other people. We need not suppose that two distinct concepts are involved. Indeed, in saying that God loves us more perfectly than human beings love one another we are suggesting that only one concept of love is involved.

I am aware that some Christian theologians have offered reasons for insisting that God's love, justice, goodness, wisdom, etc. are radically different from human love, justice, etc. For one reason or another the theological nonnaturalist may wish to agree. My point is simply that his nonnaturalism does not force him to any such conclusion.

My arguments in this paper ought not to be viewed as a philosophical defense of theological nonnaturalism. I should question whether a philosophical defense of that view is either appropriate or possible.

What I have been trying to do is rather to use theological nonnaturalism to call into question a quite plausible notion about the importance of natural theology to theology generally. I have taken up arguments intended to establish three different, but related, theses. According to the first thesis, which I took from Flew, theological assertions are not *bona fide* assertions unless they are open to disconfirmation by natural theology. According to the second, theological assertions say nothing about what goes on in the empirical world unless they are open to conceivable confirmation and disconfirmation by natural theology. According to the third, concepts like love, when they are set in theological contexts, lose the meaning the believer supposes they have unless the theological doctrines in which they appear are made con-

firmable and disconfirmable by natural theology. What these three theses
have in common is the notion that it *must be* natural theology, or at least the
willingness to engage in natural theology, that gives theological doctrines the
meaning they are thought to have. In criticizing the arguments which purport to establish these three theses I have been trying to justify my own
belief that the notion they have in common is wrong.

JOHN HICK
Theology and Verification

To ask "Is the existence of God verifiable?" is to pose a question which is too
imprecise to be capable of being answered.[1] There are many different concepts of God, and it may be that statements employing some of them are
open to verification or falsification while statements employing others of
them are not. Again, the notion of verifying is itself by no means perfectly
clear and fixed; and it may be that on some views of the nature of verification the existence of God is verifiable, whereas on other views it is not.

Instead of seeking to compile a list of the various different concepts of God
and the various possible senses of "verify," I wish to argue with regard to one
particular concept of deity, namely the Christian concept, that divine existence is in principle verifiable; and as the first stage of this argument I must
indicate what I mean by "verifiable."

I

The central core of the concept of verification, I suggest, is the removal of
ignorance or uncertainty concerning the truth of some proposition. That p is
verified (whether p embodies a theory, hypothesis, prediction, or straightforward assertion) means that something happens which makes it clear that
p is true. A question is settled so that there is no longer room for rational

THEOLOGY AND VERIFICATION   From *Theology Today*, Volume XVII, No. 1, April, 1960. Reprinted by permission of *Theology Today* and the author.

[1] In this paper I assume that an indicative sentence expresses a factual assertion if and only if the
state in which the universe would be if the putative assertion could correctly be said to be true
differs in some experienceable way from the state in which the universe would be if the putative
assertion could correctly be said to be false, all aspects of the universe other than that referred to
in the putative assertion being the same in either case. This criterion acknowledges the important
core of truth in the logical positivist verification principle. "Experienceable" in the above formulation means, in the case of alleged subjective or private facts (*e.g.,* pains, dreams, after-images, etc.),
"experienceable by the subject in question" and, in the case of alleged objective or public facts,
"capable in principle of being experienced by anyone." My contention is going to be that "God
exists" asserts a matter of objective fact.

doubt concerning it. The way in which grounds for rational doubt are excluded varies, of course, with the subject matter. But the general feature common to all cases of verification is the ascertaining of truth by the removal of grounds for rational doubt. Where such grounds are removed, we rightly speak of verification having taken place.

To characterize verification in this way is to raise the question whether the notion of verification is purely logical or is both logical and psychological. Is the statement that p is verified simply the statement that a certain state of affairs exists (or has existed), or is it the statement also that someone is aware that this state of affairs exists (or has existed) and notes that its existence establishes the truth of p? A geologist predicts that the earth's surface will be covered with ice in 15 million years time. Suppose that in 15 million years time the earth's surface *is* covered with ice, but that in the meantime the human race has perished, so that no one is left to observe the event or to draw any conclusion concerning the accuracy of the geologist's prediction. Do we now wish to say that his prediction has been verified, or shall we deny that it has been verified, on the ground that there is no one left to do the verifying?

The range of "verify" and its cognates is sufficiently wide to permit us to speak in either way. But the only sort of verification of theological propositions which is likely to interest us is one in which human beings participate. We may therefore, for our present purpose, treat verification as a logico-psychological rather than as a purely logical concept. I suggest, then, that "verify" be construed as a verb which has its primary uses in the active voice: I verify, you verify, we verify, they verify, or have verified. The impersonal passive, it is verified, now becomes logically secondary. To say that p has been verified is to say that (at least) someone has verified it, often with the implication that his or their report to this effect is generally accepted. But it is impossible, on this usage, for p to have been verified without someone having verified it. "Verification" is thus primarily the name for an event which takes place in human consciousness.[2] It refers to an experience, the experience of ascertaining that a given proposition or set of propositions is true. To this extent verification is a psychological notion. But of course it is also a logical notion. For needless to say, not *any* experience is rightly called an experience of verifying p. Both logical and psychological conditions must be fulfilled in order for verification to have taken place. In this respect, "verify" is like "know." Knowing is an experience which someone has or undergoes, or perhaps a dispositional state in which someone is, and it cannot take place without someone having or undergoing it or being in it; but not by any means every experience which people have, or every dispositional state in which they are, is rightly called knowing.

[2] This suggestion is closely related to Carnap's insistence that, in contrast to "true," "confirmed" is time-dependent. To say that a statement is confirmed, or verified, is to say that it has been confirmed at a particular time—and, I would add, by a particular person. See Rudolf Carnap, "Truth and Confirmation," Feigl and Sellars, *Readings in Philosophical Analysis,* 1949, pp. 119 f.

With regard to this logico-psychological concept of verification, such questions as the following arise. When A, but nobody else, has ascertained that p is true, can p be said to have been verified; or is it required that others also have undergone the same ascertainment? How public, in other words, must verification be? Is it necessary that p could in principle be verified by anyone, without restriction, even though perhaps only A has in fact verified it? If so, what is meant here by "in principle"; does it signify, for example, that p must be verifiable by anyone who performs a certain operation; and does it imply that to do this is within everyone's power?

These questions cannot, I believe, be given any general answer applicable to all instances of the exclusion of rational doubt. The answers must be derived in each case from an investigation of the particular subject matter. It will be the object of subsequent sections of this article to undertake such an investigation concerning the Christian concept of God.

Verification is often construed as the verification of a prediction. However, verification, as the exclusion of grounds for rational doubt, does not necessarily consist in the proving correct of a prediction; a verifying experience does not always need to have been predicted in order to have the effect of excluding rational doubt. But when we are interested in the verifiability of propositions as the criterion for their having factual meaning, the notion of prediction becomes central. If a proposition contains or entails predictions which can be verified or falsified, its character as an assertion (though not of course its character as a true assertion) is thereby guaranteed.

Such predictions may be and often are conditional. For example, statements about the features of the dark side of the moon are rendered meaningful by the conditional predictions which they entail to the effect that if an observer comes to be in such a position in space, he will make such-and-such observations. It would in fact be more accurate to say that the prediction is always conditional, but that sometimes the conditions are so obvious and so likely to be fulfilled in any case that they require no special mention, while sometimes they require for their fulfillment some unusual expedition or operation. A prediction, for example, that the sun will rise within twenty-four hours is intended unconditionally, at least as concerns conditions to be fulfilled by the observer; he is not required by the terms of the prediction to perform any special operation. Even in this case, however, there is an implied negative condition that he shall not put himself in a situation (such as immuring himself in the depths of a coal mine) from which a sunrise would not be perceptible. Other predictions, however, are explicitly conditional. In these cases it is true for any particular individual that in order to verify the statement in question he must go through some specified course of action. The prediction is to the effect that if you conduct such an experiment you will obtain such a result; for example, if you go into the next room you will have such-and-such visual experiences, and if you then touch the table which you see you will have such-and-such tactual experiences, and so on. The content of the "if" clause is of course always determined by the particular subject matter. The logic of "table" determines what you must do to verify statements about tables; the logic of "molecule" determines what you must do to verify statements about molecules; and the logic of "God" determines what you must do to verify statements about God.

In those cases in which the individual who is to verify a proposition must himself first perform some operation, it clearly cannot follow from the circumstances that the proposition is true that everybody has in fact verified it, or that everybody will at some future time verify it. For whether or not any particular person performs the requisite operation is a contingent matter.

II

What is the relation between verification and falsification? We are all familiar today with the phrase, "theology and falsification." A. G. N. Flew and others,[3] taking their cue from John Wisdom,[4] have raised instead of the question, "What possible experiences would verify 'God exists'?" the matching question, "What possible experiences would falsify 'God exists'? What conceivable state of affairs would be incompatible with the existence of God?" In posing the question in this way it was apparently assumed that verification and falsification are symmetrically related, and that the latter is apt to be the more accessible of the two.

In the most common cases, certainly, verification and falsification are symmetrically related. The logically simplest case of verification is provided by the crucial instance. Here it is integral to a given hypothesis that if, in specified circumstances, A occurs, the hypothesis is thereby shown to be true, whereas if B occurs the hypothesis is thereby shown to be false. Verification and falsification are also symmetrically related in the testing of such a proposition as "There is a table in the next room." The verifying experiences in this case are experiences of seeing and touching, predictions of which are entailed by the proposition in question, under the proviso that one goes into the next room; and the absence of such experiences in those circumstances serves to falsify the proposition.

But it would be rash to assume, on this basis, that verification and falsification must always be related in this symmetrical fashion. They do not necessarily stand to one another as do the two sides of a coin, so that once the coin is spun it must fall on one side or the other. There are cases in which verification and falsification each correspond to a side on a different coin, so that one can fail to verify without this failure constituting falsification.

Consider, for example, the proposition that "there are three successive sevens in the decimal determination of π." So far as the value of π has been

---

[3] A. G. N. Flew, editor, *New Essays in Philosophical Theology*, 1955, Chapter VI.

[4] "Gods," *Proceedings of the Aristotelian Society*, 1944–45. Reprinted in A. G. N. Flew, editor, *Logic and Language*, First Series, 1951, and in John Wisdom, *Philosophy and Psycho-Analysis*, 1953.

worked out, it does not contain a series of three sevens, but it will always be true that such a series may occur at a point not yet reached in anyone's calculations. Accordingly, the proposition may one day be verified, if it is true, but can never be falsified, if it is false.

The hypothesis of continued conscious existence after bodily death provides an instance of a different kind of such asymmetry, and one which has a direct bearing upon the theistic problem. This hypothesis has built into it a prediction that one will after the date of one's bodily death have conscious experiences, including the experience of remembering that death. This is a prediction which will be verified in one's own experience if it is true, but which cannot be falsified if it is false. That is to say, it can be false, but *that* it is false can never be a fact which anyone has experientially verified. But this circumstance does not undermine the meaningfulness of the hypothesis, since it is also such that if it be true, it will be known to be true.

It is important to remember that we do not speak of verifying logically necessary truths, but only propositions concerning matters of fact. Accordingly verification is not to be identified with the concept of logical certification or proof. The exclusion of rational doubt concerning some matter of fact is not equivalent to the exclusion of the logical possibility of error or illusion. For truths concerning fact are not logically necessary. Their contrary is never self-contradictory. But at the same time the bare logical possibility of error does not constitute ground for rational doubt as to the veracity of our experience. If it did, no empirical proposition could ever be verified, and indeed the notion of empirical verification would be without use and therefore without sense. What we rightly seek, when we desire the verification of a factual proposition, is not a demonstration of the logical impossibility of the proposition being false (for this would be a self-contradictory demand), but such weight of evidence as suffices, in the type of case in question, to exclude rational doubt.

III

These features of the concept of verification—that verification consists in the exclusion of grounds for rational doubt concerning the truth of some proposition; that this means its exclusion from particular minds; that the nature of the experience which serves to exclude grounds for rational doubt depends upon the particular subject matter; that verification is often related to predictions and that such predictions are often conditional; that verification and falsification may be asymmetrically related; and finally, that the verification of a factual proposition is not equivalent to logical certification—are all relevant to the verification of the central religious claim, "God exists." I wish now to apply these discriminations to the notion of eschatological verification, which has been briefly employed by Ian Crombie in his contribution to *New Essays in Philosophical Theology,*[5] and by myself in *Faith and Knowledge.*[6] This suggestion has on each occasion been greeted with disapproval by both philosophers and theologians. I am, however, still of the opinion that the notion of eschatological verification is sound; and further, that no viable alternative to it has been offered to establish the factual character of theism.

The strength of the notion of eschatological verification is that it is not an *ad hoc* invention but is based upon an actually operative religious concept of God. In the language of Christian faith, the word "God" stands at the center of a system of terms, such as Spirit, grace, Logos, incarnation, Kingdom of God, and many more; and the distinctly Christian conception of God can only be fully grasped in its connection with these related terms.[7] It belongs to a complex of notions which together constitute a picture of the universe in which we live, of man's place therein, of a comprehensive divine purpose interacting with human purposes, and of the general nature of the eventual fulfillment of that divine purpose. This Christian picture of the universe, entailing as it does certain distinctive expectations concerning the future, is a very different picture from any that can be accepted by one who does not believe that the God of the New Testament exists. Further, these differences are such as to show themselves in human experience. The possibility of experiential confirmation is thus built into the Christian concept of God; and the notion of eschatological verification seeks to relate this fact to the logical problem of meaning.

Let me first give a general indication of this suggestion, by repeating a parable which I have related elsewhere,[8] and then try to make it more precise and eligible for discussion. Here, first, is the parable.

Two men are travelling together along a road. One of them believes that it leads to a Celestial City, the other that it leads nowhere; but since this is the only road there is, both must travel it. Neither has been this way before, and therefore neither is able to say what they will find around each next corner. During their journey they meet both with moments of refreshment and delight, and with moments of hardship and danger. All the time one of them thinks of his journey as a pilgrimage to the Celestial City and interprets the pleasant parts as encouragements and the obstacles as trials of his purpose and lessons in endurance, prepared by the king of that city and designed to make of him a worthy citizen of the place when at last he arrives there. The other, however, believes none of this and sees their journey as an unavoidable and aimless ramble. Since he has no choice in the matter, he enjoys the good

---

[5] *Op. cit.,* p. 126.

[6] Cornell University Press, 1957, pp. 150–62.

[7] Its clear recognition of this fact, with regard not only to Christianity but to any religion, is one of the valuable features of Ninian Smart's *Reasons and Faiths* (1958). He remarks, for example, that "the claim that God exists can only be understood by reference to many, if not all, other propositions in the doctrinal scheme from which it is extrapolated" (p. 12).

[8] *Faith and Knowledge,* pp. 150 f.

and endures the bad. But for him there is no Celestial City to be reached, no all-encompassing purpose ordaining their journey; only the road itself and the luck of the road in good weather and in bad.

During the course of the journey the issue between them is not an experimental one. They do not entertain different expectations about the coming details of the road, but only about its ultimate destination. And yet when they do turn the last corner it will be apparent that one of them has been right all the time and the other wrong. Thus although the issue between them has not been experimental, it has nevertheless from the start been a real issue. They have not merely felt differently about the road; for one was feeling appropriately and the other inappropriately in relation to the actual state of affairs. Their opposed interpretations of the road constituted genuinely rival assertions, though assertions whose assertion-status has the peculiar characteristic of being guaranteed retrospectively by a future crux.

This parable has of course (like all parables) strict limitations. It is designed to make only one point: that Christian doctrine postulates an ultimate unambiguous state of existence *in patria* as well as our present ambiguous existence *in via*. There is a state of having arrived as well as a state of journeying, an eternal heavenly life as well as an earthly pilgrimage. The alleged future experience of this state cannot, of course, be appealed to as evidence for theism as a present interpretation of our experience; but it does suffice to render the choice between theism and atheism a real and not a merely empty or verbal choice. And although this does not affect the logic of the situation, it should be added that the alternative interpretations are more than theoretical, for they render different practical plans and policies appropriate now.

The universe as envisaged by the theist, then, differs as a totality from the universe as envisaged by the atheist. This difference does not, however, from our present standpoint within the universe, involve a difference in the objective content of each or even any of its passing moments. The theist and the atheist do not (or need not) expect different events to occur in the successive details of the temporal process. They do not (or need not) entertain divergent expectations of the course of history viewed from within. But the theist does and the atheist does not expect that when history is completed it will be seen to have led to a particular end-state and to have fulfilled a specific purpose, namely that of creating "children of God."

The idea of an eschatological verification of theism can make sense, however, only if the logically prior idea of continued personal existence after death is intelligible. A desultory debate on this topic has been going on for several years in some of the philosophical periodicals. C. I. Lewis has contended that the hypothesis of immortality "is an hypothesis about our own future experience. And our understanding of what would verify it has no lack of clarity." [9] And Morris Schlick agreed, adding, "We must conclude that im-

---

[9] "Experience and Meaning," *Philosophical Review*, 1934, reprinted in Feigl and Sellars, *Readings in Philosophical Analysis*, 1949, p. 142.

mortality, in the sense defined [i.e. 'survival after death,' rather than 'never-ending life'], should not be regarded as a 'metaphysical problem,' but as an empirical hypothesis, because it possesses logical verifiability. It could be verified by following the prescription: 'Wait until you die!' " [10] However, others have challenged this conclusion, either on the ground that the phrase "surviving death" is self-contradictory in ordinary language or, more substantially, on the ground that the traditional distinction between soul and body cannot be sustained.[11] I should like to address myself to this latter view. The only self of which we know, it is said, is the empirical self, the walking, talking, acting, sleeping individual who lives, it may be, for some sixty to eighty years and then dies. Mental events and mental characteristics are analyzed into the modes of behavior and behavioral dispositions of this empirical self. The human being is described as an organism capable of acting in the "high-level" ways which we characterize as intelligent, thoughtful, humorous, calculating, and the like. The concept of mind or soul is thus not the concept of a "ghost in the machine" (to use Gilbert Ryle's loaded phrase [12]), but of the more flexible and sophisticated ways in which human beings behave and have it in them to behave. On this view there is no room for the notion of soul in distinction from body; and if there is no soul in distinction from body, there can be no question of the soul surviving the death of the body. Against this philosophical background the specifically Christian (and also Jewish) belief in the resurrection of the flesh, or body, in contrast to the Hellenic notion of the survival of a disembodied soul, might be expected to have attracted more attention than it has. For it is consonant with the conception of man as an indissoluble psycho-physical unity, and yet it also offers the possibility of an empirical meaning for the idea of "life after death."

Paul is the chief Biblical expositor of the idea of the resurrection of the body.[13] His view, as I understand it, is this. When someone has died he is, apart from any special divine action, extinct. A human being is by nature mortal and subject to annihilation by death. But in fact God, by an act of sovereign power, either sometimes or always resurrects or (better) reconstitutes or recreates him—not, however, as the identical physical organism that he was before death, but as a *soma pneumatikon* ("spiritual body"), embodying the dispositional characteristics and memory traces of the deceased physical organism, and inhabiting an environment with which the *soma pneumatikon* is continuous as the *ante-mortem* body was continuous with our present world. In discussing this notion we may well abandon the word "spiritual," as lacking today any precise established usage, and speak of

---

[10] "Meaning and Verification," *Philosophical Review*, 1936, reprinted in Feigl and Sellars, *op. cit.*, p. 160.

[11] E.g. A. G. N. Flew, "Death," *New Essays in Philosophical Theology;* "Can a Man Witness his own Funeral?" *Hibbert Journal*, 1956.

[12] *The Concept of Mind*, 1949, which contains an important exposition of the interpretation of "mental" qualities as characteristics of behavior.

[13] I Cor. 15.

"resurrection bodies" and of "the resurrection world." The principal questions to be asked concern the relation between the physical world and the resurrection world, and the criteria of personal identity which are operating when it is alleged that a certain inhabitant of the resurrection world is the same person as an individual who once inhabited this world. The first of these questions turns out on investigation to be the more difficult of the two, and I shall take the easier one first.

Let me sketch a very odd possibility (concerning which, however, I wish to emphasize not so much its oddness as its possibility!), and then see how far it can be stretched in the direction of the notion of the resurrection body. In the process of stretching it will become even more odd than it was before; but my aim will be to show that, however odd, it remains within the bounds of the logically possible. This progression will be presented in three pictures, arranged in a self-explanatory order.

First picture: Suppose that at some learned gathering in this country one of the company were suddenly and inexplicably to disappear, and that at the same moment an exact replica of him were suddenly and inexplicably to appear at some comparable meeting in Australia. The person who appears in Australia is exactly similar, as to both bodily and mental characteristics, with the person who disappears in America. There is continuity of memory, complete similarity of bodily features, including even fingerprints, hair and eye coloration and stomach contents, and also of beliefs, habits, and mental propensities. In fact there is everything that would lead us to identify the one who appeared with the one who disappeared, except continuity of occupancy of space. We may suppose, for example, that a deputation of the colleagues of the man who disappeared fly to Australia to interview the replica of him which is reported there, and find that he is in all respects but one exactly as though he had travelled from say, Princeton to Melbourne, by conventional means. The only difference is that he describes how, as he was sitting listening to Dr. Z reading a paper, on blinking his eyes he suddenly found himself sitting in a different room listening to a different paper by an Australian scholar. He asks his colleagues how the meeting had gone after he ceased to be there, and what they had made of his disappearance, and so on. He clearly thinks of himself as the one who was present with them at their meeting in the United States. I suggest that faced with all these circumstances his colleagues would soon, if not immediately, find themselves thinking of him and treating him as the individual who had so inexplicably disappeared from their midst. We should be extending our normal use of "same person" in a way which the postulated facts would both demand and justify if we said that the one who appears in Australia is the same person as the one who disappears in America. The factors inclining us to identify them would far outweigh the factors disinclining us to do this. We should have no reasonable alternative but to extend our usage of "the same person" to cover the strange new case.

Second picture: Now let us suppose that the event in America is not a sudden and inexplicable disappearance, and indeed not a disappearance at all, but a sudden death. Only, at the moment when the individual dies, a replica of him as he was at the moment before his death, complete with memory up to that instant, appears in Australia. Even with the corpse on our hands, it would still, I suggest, be an extension of "same person" required and warranted by the postulated facts, to say that the same person who died has been miraculously recreated in Australia. The case would be considerably odder than in the previous picture, because of the existence of the corpse in America contemporaneously with the existence of the living person in Australia. But I submit that, although the oddness of this circumstance may be stated as strongly as you please, and can indeed hardly be overstated, yet it does not exceed the bounds of the logically possible. Once again we must imagine some of the deceased's colleagues going to Australia to interview the person who has suddenly appeared there. He would perfectly remember them and their meeting, be interested in what had happened, and be as amazed and dumbfounded about it as anyone else; and he would perhaps be worried about the possible legal complications if he should return to America to claim his property; and so on. Once again, I believe, they would soon find themselves thinking of him and treating him as the same person as the dead Princetonian. Once again the factors inclining us to say that the one who died and the one who appeared are the same person would outweigh the factors inclining us to say that they are different people. Once again we should have to extend our usage of "the same person" to cover this new case.

Third picture: My third supposal is that the replica, complete with memory, etc. appears, not in Australia, but as a resurrection replica in a different world altogether, a resurrection world inhabited by resurrected persons. This world occupies its own space, distinct from the space with which we are now familiar. That is to say, an object in the resurrection world is not situated at any distance or in any direction from an object in our present world, although each object in either world is spatially related to each other object in the same world.

Mr. X, then, dies. A Mr. X replica, complete with the set of memory traces which Mr. X had at the last moment before his death, comes into existence. It is composed of other material than physical matter, and is located in a resurrection world which does not stand in any spatial relationship with the physical world. Let us leave out of consideration St. Paul's hint that the resurrection body may be as unlike the physical body as is a full grain of wheat from the wheat seed, and consider the simpler picture in which the resurrection body has the same shape as the physical body.[14]

In these circumstances, how does Mr. X know that he has been resurrected or recreated? He remembers dying; or rather he remembers being on

---

[14] As would seem to be assumed, for example, by Irenaeus (*Adversus Haereses,* Bk. II, Ch. 34, Sec. 1).

what he took to be his death-bed, and becoming progressively weaker until, presumably, he lost consciousness. But how does he know that (to put it Irishly) his "dying" proved fatal; and that he did not, after losing consciousness, begin to recover strength, and has now simply waked up?

The picture is readily enough elaborated to answer this question. Mr. X meets and recognizes a number of relatives and friends and historical personages whom he knows to have died; and from the fact of their presence, and also from their testimony that he has only just now appeared in their world, he is convinced that he has died. Evidences of this kind could mount up to the point at which they are quite as strong as the evidence which, in pictures one and two, convince the individual in question that he has been miraculously translated to Australia. Resurrected persons would be individually no more in doubt about their own identity than we are now, and would be able to identify one another in the same kinds of ways, and with a like degree of assurance, as we do now.

If it be granted that resurrected persons might be able to arrive at a rationally founded conviction that their existence is *post-mortem*, how could they know that the world in which they find themselves is in a different space from that in which their physical bodies were? How could such a one know that he is not in a like situation with the person in picture number two, who dies in America and appears as a full-blooded replica in Australia, leaving his corpse in the U.S.A.—except that now the replica is situated, not in Australia, but on a planet of some other star?

It is of course conceivable that the space of the resurrection world should have properties which are manifestly incompatible with its being a region of physical space. But on the other hand, it is not of the essence of the notion of a resurrection world that its space should have properties different from those of physical space. And supposing it not to have different properties, it is not evident that a resurrected individual could learn from any direct observations that he was not on a planet of some sun which is at so great a distance from our own sun that the stellar scenery visible from it is quite unlike that which we can now see. The grounds that a resurrected person would have for believing that he is in a different space from physical space (supposing there to be no discernible difference in spatial properties) would be the same as the grounds that any of us may have now for believing this concerning resurrected individuals. These grounds are indirect and consist in all those considerations (*e.g.,* Luke 16:26) which lead most of those who consider the question to reject as absurd the possibility of, for example, radio communication or rocket travel between earth and heaven.

IV

In the present context my only concern is to claim that this doctrine of the divine creation of bodies, composed of a material other than that of physical matter, which bodies are endowed with sufficient correspondence of characteristics with our present bodies, and sufficient continuity of memory with our present consciousness, for us to speak of the same person being raised up again to life in a new environment, is not self-contradictory. If, then, it cannot be ruled out *ab initio* as meaningless, we may go on to consider whether and how it is related to the possible verification of Christian theism.

So far I have argued that a survival prediction such as is contained in the *corpus* of Christian belief is in principle subject to future verification. But this does not take the argument by any means as far as it must go if it is to succeed. For survival, simply as such, would not serve to verify theism. It would not necessarily be a state of affairs which is manifestly incompatible with the non-existence of God. It might be taken just as a surprising natural fact. The atheist, in his resurrection body, and able to remember his life on earth, might say that the universe has turned out to be more complex, and perhaps more to be approved of, than he had realized. But the mere fact of survival, with a new body in a new environment, would not demonstrate to him that there is a God. It is fully compatible with the notion of survival that the life to come be, so far as the theistic problem is concerned, essentially a continuation of the present life, and religiously no less ambiguous. And in this event, survival after bodily death would not in the least constitute a final verification of theistic faith.

I shall not spend time in trying to draw a picture of a resurrection existence which would merely prolong the religious ambiguity of our present life. The important question, for our purpose, is not whether one can conceive of after-life experiences which would *not* verify theism (and in point of fact one can fairly easily conceive them), but whether one can conceive of after-life experiences which *would* serve to verify theism.

I think that we can. In trying to do so I shall not appeal to the traditional doctrine, which figures especially in Catholic and mystical theology, of the Beatific Vision of God. The difficulty presented by this doctrine is not so much that of deciding whether there are grounds for believing it, as of deciding what it means. I shall not, however, elaborate this difficulty, but pass directly to the investigation of a different and, as it seems to me, more intelligible possibility. This is the possibility not of a direct vision of God, whatever that might mean, but of a *situation* which points unambiguously to the existence of a loving God. This would be a situation which, so far as its religious significance is concerned, contrasts in a certain important respect with our present situation. Our present situation is one which in some ways seems to confirm and in other ways to contradict the truth of theism. Some events around us suggest the presence of an unseen benevolent intelligence and others suggest that no such intelligence is at work. Our situation is religiously ambiguous. But in order for us to be aware of this fact we must already have some idea, however vague, of what it would be for our situation to be not ambiguous, but on the contrary wholly evidential of God.

I therefore want to try to make clearer this presupposed concept of a religiously unambiguous situation.

There are, I suggest, two possible developments of our experience such that, if they occurred in conjunction with one another (whether in this life or in another life to come), they would assure us beyond rational doubt of the reality of God, as conceived in the Christian faith. These are, *first*, an experience of the fulfillment of God's purpose for ourselves, as this has been disclosed in the Christian revelation; in conjunction, *second*, with an experience of communion with God as he has revealed himself in the person of Christ.

The divine purpose for human life, as this is depicted in the New Testament documents, is the bringing of the human person, in society with his fellows, to enjoy a certain valuable quality of personal life, the content of which is given in the character of Christ—which quality of life (*i.e.* life in relationship with God, described in the Fourth Gospel as eternal life) is said to be the proper destiny of human nature and the source of man's final self-fulfillment and happiness. The verification situation with regard to such a fulfillment is asymmetrical. On the one hand, so long as the divine purpose remains unfulfilled, we cannot know that it never will be fulfilled in the future; hence no final falsification is possible of the claim that this fulfillment will occur—unless, of course, the prediction contains a specific time clause which, in Christian teaching, it does not. But on the other hand, if and when the divine purpose *is* fulfilled in our own experience, we must be able to recognize and rejoice in that fulfillment. For the fulfillment would not be for us the promised fulfillment without our own conscious participation in it.

It is important to note that one can say this much without being cognizant in advance of the concrete form which such fulfillment will take. The before-and-after situation is analogous to that of a small child looking forward to adult life and then, having grown to adulthood, looking back upon childhood. The child possesses and can use correctly in various contexts the concept of "being grown-up," although he does not know, concretely, what it is like to be grown-up. But when he reaches adulthood he is nevertheless able to know that he has reached it; he is able to recognize the experience of living a grown-up life even though he did not know in advance just what to expect. For his understanding of adult maturity grows as he himself matures. Something similar may be supposed to happen in the case of the fulfillment of the divine purpose for human life. That fulfillment may be as far removed from our present condition as is mature adulthood from the mind of a little child; nevertheless, we possess already a comparatively vague notion of this final fulfillment, and as we move towards it our concept will itself become more adequate; and if and when we finally reach that fulfillment, the problem of recognizing it will have disappeared in the process.

The other feature that must, I suggest, be present in a state of affairs that would verify theism, is that the fulfillment of God's purpose be apprehended *as* the fulfillment of God's purpose and not simply as a natural state of affairs. To this end it must be accompanied by an experience of communion with God as he has made himself known to men in Christ.

The specifically Christian clause, "as he has made himself known to men in Christ," is essential, for it provides a solution to the problem of recognition in the awareness of God. Several writers have pointed out the logical difficulty involved in any claim to have encountered God.[15] How could one know that it was *God* whom one had encountered? God is described in Christian theology in terms of various absolute qualities, such as omnipotence, omnipresence, perfect goodness, infinite love, etc., which cannot as such be observed by us, as can their finite analogues, limited power, local presence, finite goodness, and human love. One can recognize that a being whom one "encounters" has a given finite degree of power, but how does one recognize that he has *un*limited power? How does one observe that an encountered being is *omni*present? How does one perceive that his goodness and love, which one can perhaps see to exceed any human goodness and love, are actually infinite? Such qualities cannot be given in human experience. One might claim, then, to have encountered a Being whom one presumes, or trusts, or hopes to be God; but one cannot claim to have encountered a Being whom one recognized to be the infinite, almighty, eternal Creator.

This difficulty is met in Christianity by the doctrine of the Incarnation—although this was not among the considerations which led to the formulation of that doctrine. The idea of incarnation provides answers to the two related questions: "How do we know that God has certain absolute qualities which, by their very nature, transcend human experience?" and "How can there be an eschatological verification of theism which is based upon a recognition of the presence of God in his Kingdom?"

In Christianity God is known as "the God and Father of our Lord Jesus Christ." [16] God is the Being about whom Jesus taught; the Being in relation to whom Jesus lived, and into a relationship with whom he brought his disciples; the Being whose *agape* toward men was seen on earth in the life of Jesus. In short, God is the transcendent Creator who has revealed himself in Christ. Now Jesus' teaching about the Father is a part of that self-disclosure, and it is from this teaching (together with that of the prophets who preceded him) that the Christian knowledge of God's transcendent being is derived. Only God himself knows his own infinite nature; and our human belief about that nature is based upon his self-revelation to men in Christ. As Karl Barth expresses it, "Jesus Christ is the knowability of God."[17] Our beliefs about God's infinite being are not capable of observational verification, being beyond the scope of human experience, but they are susceptible

---

[15] For example, H. W. Hepburn, *Christianity and Paradox,* 1958, pp. 56 f.
[16] II Cor. 11:31.   [17] *Church Dogmatics,* Vol. II, Pt. I, p. 150.

of indirect verification by the removal of rational doubt concerning the authority of Christ. An experience of the reign of the Son in the Kingdom of the Father would confirm that authority, and therewith, indirectly, the validity of Jesus' teaching concerning the character of God in his infinite transcendent nature.

The further question as to how an eschatological experience of the Kingdom of God could be known to be such has already been answered by implication. It is God's union with man in Christ that makes possible man's recognition of the fulfillment of God's purpose for man as being indeed the fulfillment of *God's* purpose for him. The presence of Christ in his Kingdom marks this as being beyond doubt the Kingdom of the God and Father of the Lord Jesus Christ.

It is true that even the experience of the realization of the promised Kingdom of God, with Christ reigning as Lord of the New Aeon, would not constitute a logical certification of his claims nor, accordingly, of the reality of God. But this will not seem remarkable to any philosopher in the empiricist tradition, who knows that it is only a confusion to demand that a factual proposition be an analytic truth. A set of expectations based upon faith in the historic Jesus as the incarnation of God, and in his teaching as being divinely authoritative, could be so fully confirmed in *post-mortem* experience as to leave no grounds for rational doubt as to the validity of that faith.

There remains of course the problem (which falls to the New Testament scholar rather than to the philosopher) whether Christian tradition, and in particular the New Testament, provides a sufficiently authentic "picture" of the mind and character of Christ to make such recognition possible. I cannot here attempt to enter into the vast field of Biblical criticism, and shall confine myself to the logical point, which only emphasizes the importance of the historical question, that a verification of theism made possible by the Incarnation is dependent upon the Christian's having a genuine contact with the person of Christ, even though this is mediated through the life and tradition of the Church.

One further point remains to be considered. When we ask the question, "To *whom* is theism verified?" one is initially inclined to assume that the answer must be, "To everyone." We are inclined to assume that, as in my parable of the journey, the believer must be confirmed in his belief, and the unbeliever converted from his unbelief. But this assumption is neither demanded by the nature of verification nor by any means unequivocably supported by our Christian sources.

We have already noted that a verifiable prediction may be conditional. "There is a table in the next room" entails conditional predictions of the form: if someone goes into the next room he will see, etc. But no one is compelled to go into the next room. Now it may be that the predictions concerning human experience which are entailed by the proposition that God exists are conditional predictions and that no one is compelled to fulfill those conditions. Indeed we stress in much of our theology that the manner of the divine self-disclosure to men is such that our human status as free and responsible beings is respected, and an awareness of God never is forced upon us. It may then be a condition of *post-mortem* verification that we be already in some degree conscious of God by an uncompelled response to his modes of revelation in this world. It may be that such a voluntary consciousness of God is an essential element in the fulfillment of the divine purpose for human nature, so that the verification of theism which consists in an experience of the final fulfillment of that purpose can only be experienced by those who have already entered upon an awareness of God by the religious mode of apperception which we call faith.

If this be so, it has the consequence that only the theistic believer can find the vindication of his belief. This circumstance would not of course set any restriction upon who can become a believer, but it would involve that while theistic faith can be verified—found by one who holds it to be beyond rational doubt—yet it cannot be proved to the nonbeliever. Such an asymmetry would connect with that strain of New Testament teaching which speaks of a division of mankind even in the world to come.

Having noted this possibility I will only express my personal opinion that the logic of the New Testament as a whole, though admittedly not always its explicit content, leads to a belief in ultimate universal salvation. However, my concern here is not to seek to establish the religious facts, but rather to establish that there are such things as religious facts, and in particular that the existence or nonexistence of the God of the New Testament is a matter of fact, and claims as such eventual experiential verification.

WILLIAM P. ALSTON
The Elucidation of Religious Statements

It is generally recognized that talk about God stands in need of clarification. In this paper I shall address myself not directly to that task of clarification, but to the prior task of determining how such clarification is to be carried out.

William P. Alston (1921–   ) taught for a number of years at the University of Michigan and is currently a professor of philosophy at Rutgers University. He is the author of *Philosophy of Language* and has written extensively in the areas of philosophy of language and philosophy of mind.

THE ELUCIDATION OF RELIGIOUS STATEMENTS   From *The Hartshorne Festschrift: Process and Divinity,* edited by William L. Reese and Eugene Freeman. Reprinted by permission of The Open Court Publishing Co., La Salle, Illinois.

I

Consider the following statements:

(1) God made the heavens and the earth.
(2) God watches over the affairs of men.
(3) God has commanded us to love our neighbors.
(4) God forgives the sins of those who truly turn unto Him.
(5) God spoke to the prophets in days of old.
(6) God has comforted me in my distress.
(7) God will guide me in whatever I undertake.

It is no accident that this list is made up exclusively of action-sentences; they are the crux of the problem. It is essential for any religion, with the possible exception of extreme mystical sects and highly intellectualized fringe groups like Humanism, that God make effective contact with His worshippers and vice versa. This involves thinking of God as acting toward us and reacting to our actions. Moreover the other sorts of statements we make about God, e.g., attribute-statements, depend on action statements for their meaning. To call God merciful is to imply that He will sometimes perform acts of forgiveness. To call Him wise or just implies that His decisions, commands, judgments will exhibit wisdom or justice. God's freedom consists in the independence of His actions from any external compulsion.

These sentences are puzzling in a way that sentences about tables and chairs are not. We know perfectly well how to handle furniture-sentences in the contexts in which they are commonly used. It is only their "analysis" in some abstruse philosophical sense which is puzzling. But sentences about God are likely to seem strange even in their native habitat. In the course of using them in religion we are apt to become baffled over what implications they have, what they exclude or do not exclude, and how they are appropriately supported or attacked. It is the primary, garden variety sort of understanding that needs attention. Therefore what I want to ask is: how can one give an adequate account of what is meant by such a sentence?

II

It might seem that the task of elucidation falls into two parts, corresponding to subject and predicate. We need to make clear Who these statements are about (to Whom 'God' refers), and what is being said about Him (what 'made' or 'forgives' means in this context). With respect to any particular sentence these jobs are no doubt distinguishable. In (1) e.g., 'Who is God?' can't raise just the same problem as 'What does 'made' mean here?' They could receive the same answer only if the initial answer to the first question could be 'The maker of heaven and earth'. And to answer it in this way would be to interpret (1) as saying 'The maker of heaven and earth made heaven and earth'. Nevertheless over the long haul the questions merge. Although with respect to (1) we cannot answer 'Who is God?' by 'The maker of heaven and earth', we can only answer by using some other such phrase, 'the most perfect being', 'the father of our Lord Jesus Christ', 'He Who spoke to the prophets'; and these phrases raise exactly the same problems as the predicate terms 'is the most perfect being', 'is the father of our Lord Jesus Christ', and 'spoke to the prophets'. That is, the problem of explaining the subject-term is identical with the problem of explaining the meaning certain key predicate terms have when used in conjunction with this subject-term. It could be otherwise only if one could teach someone Who God is by means other than the citation of descriptive phrases, e.g., by pointing or in some way getting the pupil to notice the object. As there is no reliable way of determining whether an individual is noticing God at a given time, this method is not available.

III

In explaining "God forgives our sins" it is natural to begin with talk about men forgiving each other. Indeed this is what we always do when we teach a child to talk about God. We presuppose that he already knows what it is to speak of men forgiving, making, speaking, or comforting; if he doesn't, we see to it that he learns. Is there any alternative? Could we teach a child to talk about God before he has learned to talk about men? Only if we could do something like pointing to instances where God is forgiving, speaking, or making. And this seems impossible, for the reason mentioned in the last paragraph. In fact, the problem is even more acute here. To ostensively define the predicates we would need not only a reliable way of determining that a person was noticing God at a particular time, but also a reliable way of determining that he was noticing a particular activity of God. Otherwise there would be no reason to suppose that he was attaching the right meaning to the word.

Is this impossibility a matter of fact or of logic? Let us see whether we can envisage a state of affairs in which it would be possible. Let us suppose that I could tell whether someone is having an experience of the sort I would call an experience of the presence of God, without having to rely on the person's report that he is having such an experience. How I would tell is not important. It might be by a certain unique bodily attitude and demeanor. Or it might be that I had discovered that certain mental states or combinations of mental states for which there are objective criteria—e.g., humility, receptivity, or despair—are regularly correlated with that sort of experience. And now suppose that I teach a child to say 'God is forgiving me' every time I notice that he is having such an experience; and let us further assume that the child does not yet know how to talk of men forgiving each other, or indeed how to talk of men acting on each other in any way at all. If these conditions were satisfied, could I then teach a child to talk about God without having to depend on his mastery of talk about men? I fear not. From this instruction the child would simply have learned to use the words, 'God is forgiving me' to report, or express, a certain state of mind. It would be like learning to say 'God damn' to express irritation. Even if he is taught a whole range of God-sentences, he will have no basis for regarding the constant recurrence of 'God' as anything more than a reflection of a generic similarity in the experiences. He would miss the point. This brings out the way in which the objective reference of God-sentences is borrowed from the prior application of their predicate terms to human beings. We can use 'Jones has forgiven me' to talk about something objective, because we have public tests of its truth or falsity. It is our prior mastery of this sort of sentence that leads us to give 'God has forgiven me' an objective reference too, even in the absence of such tests. Take away the human model, and we are left, even in the conditions we are imagining, with an expression of a state of mind.

IV

Thus we get, and must get, the terms we apply to God from our talk about men. This is the first principle of religious semantics. And the second is equally important: in talk about God these terms no longer have their primary or literal meaning; their sense as well as their application has shifted. This is a familiar point, but lest familiarity breed contempt for the complexities involved, I want to consider it with some care.

Just how the senses differ depends on the ground rules for the particular religion, sect, or theology. A great many Christian theologians have felt called upon to deny that God exists in time. Mystical philosophies like the Vedanta deny that any distinctions at all can be made in God; this doctrine is found in a weakened form in Aquinas and other orthodox Christian theologians. Using these denials it is easy to show that action terms change their sense when applied to God. Surely it is logically necessary for a human command, supervision, or pardon to take time for its performance, and for a man's commanding to be distinguishable from his forgiving. But this is too easy. The rules look tailor-made for the occasion. In fact these denials, I believe, have been foisted onto the Judeo-Christian tradition by a coalition of mystics and speculative philosophers for purposes of their own, purposes which have little basis in religious thoughts, actions, attitudes, and feelings of most devout souls of this or any other tradition. In order to assure relevance to conceptions actually entertained in religious activity, I shall base my discussion on the very widespread denial that God has a body.

When I say 'My mother forgave me', I imply, or presuppose, that she performed some appropriate overt action, i.e., some action which could be publicly observed, i.e., would have been observed by any normal observer who was on the scene. There is no specific action, or sort of action, which I imply that she performed. It is not necessary that she said "I forgive you", or indeed that she said anything at all. Her forgiveness may have taken the form of a reassuring smile or a pat on the cheek. But if nothing of the sort took place, then she did not forgive me. I might still say "She has forgiven me in her heart". This does not imply that any appropriate overt action has taken place, or even that it will. She might conceivably go to her grave without betraying the fact that she has forgiven me, and continuing to act as if she still holds it against me. But it does imply that she might perform an overt act of the appropriate sort, and that she will do so in the absence of special reasons to the contrary. Thus it implies that it makes sense to talk of her performing such acts and that I would recognize them if they were performed.

Essential connections with bodily activity are found in other predicates from our initial list. 'Speaks' is a very clear case. If I say 'Smith spoke to me this morning' I certainly imply that Smith produced sounds which could be heard by any person with normal hearing who was close enough; and the standards for 'close enough' cannot be made impossibly strict. If other non-deaf people in the vicinity didn't hear anything, then Smith didn't really speak to me. I was 'hearing things'.

Clearly when we apply such predicates to an immaterial God, no such implications hold. I can say 'God has forgiven my sins' without being prepared to specify any utterance, embrace, or smile equally perceivable by all bystanders; I may say 'God has spoken to me' and stubbornly hold onto it in the face of a failure by others in the vicinity to hear anything. Nor would I be thought unreasonable, or deficient in understanding, in doing so. (It will be noted that I have shifted from general to particular God-sentences; e.g., from 'God forgives the sins of those who truly turn unto Him' to 'God has forgiven my sins'. But this is quite proper. I certainly cannot understand what it is for God to forgive sins in general, or in certain sorts of conditions, unless I understand what it would be for God to forgive my sins or your sins.)

All this comes out implicitly in ordinary religious instruction. The child who asks where God is, what He looks like, when He is coming, etc., is told that God can't be seen nor heard, nor is He located anywhere, because He is a pure spirit. What is not usually clearly recognized is the problem this raises. We begin by using 'makes', 'forgives', etc., as if we were using them in their familiar senses in which they apply to parents and neighbors, in order to give information about another person who is, unfortunately, out of sight. Then we stack the cards (or rather the cards are stacked by the nature of religion) so as to make these senses inapplicable. This raises, or should raise, the question: Then in what sense are these terms being used? Now obviously this sense, though different from the literal sense, is derived from it and has some continuity with it. Divine forgiving is more like human forgiving than it is like human commanding. That is the point of the necessity of the literal sense as a starting point. Hence the problem can be put: In just what way does the theological use of the term deviate from its 'anthropological' use? I now want to consider how one might go about answering this question.

v

At this point we might do well to turn to other cases where terms are given a derivative, non-literal use, and where we know how to handle the situation. The whole spectrum of metaphorical and figurative uses, so prominent in our discourse, plain and fancy, presents cases which fit this bill.
Consider:

> He blew his top.
> There is a power vacuum in the Middle East.
> Religion has been corroded by the acids of modernity.

Clearly 'blew . . . top' is being used here in a way derivative from its literal employment with respect to steam engines and oil wells. How could we go about explaining to a puzzled listener what is meant? There are at least three ways:

(1) Provide a literal way of saying the same thing, i.e., a way which does not involve using any terms in a derivative sense. "He suddenly became violently angry".

(2) Make explicit the features common to the top blowing off a boiler and a man becoming violently angry, i.e., the features which are common to the two senses of the term and make the derived sense appropriate. In this case they would include vigorous random motion, explosive sounds, a sudden discharge of energy.

(3) Simply point out or describe a situation where the term would be used in the derivative sense, and instruct the pupil to find the common features. This is how the sensitive reader grasps fresh metaphors in poetry.

For talk about God (1) and (3) are not available, and for basically the same reason. (3) is out because, as we have seen, there are no reliable ways of showing someone a case of God forgiving, commanding, or making. We can *describe* such a case, but that involves using words in the way we are trying to explicate. (1) is out because there can be no literal way of talking about God. And this is because the impossibility of ostensively defining any theological term leaves us no alternative to deriving its theological use from a non-theological use. Of course we can define some theological terms by means of others. Thus we can define "omnipotent" by "able to perform any act". But again the definiens contain words used in just the way about which we are trying to get clear. We can even introduce new terms, e.g., "divine", "holy", which have their primary application to God; the theological use of these terms is not derivative from their non-theological use. But like 'God', their use has to be explained in some way, and it seems that this can be done only by bringing in words whose primary use is elsewhere. This recourse can be delayed, but only delayed, by using other special theological terms which raise the same problem. 'Divine' means holy. And 'holy' means, in part, numinous. But now 'numinous' (or some further member of the series) will have to be explained, as Rudolf Otto does, by bringing in a lot of words which have a primary meaning elsewhere—'mysterious', 'powerful', etc. . . . The situation can be exhibited more clearly by talking in terms of uses rather than words. Any theological use of a word is derivative from a non-theological use of *some* word; derivative just in the sense that the former cannot be taught without employing the latter. This is enough to invalidate method (1), an essential condition of which is that there be some way of saying the same thing which does not raise the same sort of problems.

VI

This leaves (2). Is there any way in which we can specify the components of the literal sense of 'forgives' which carry over to the theological sense? When we remove all the bodily activity involved in forgiving, commanding, etc., what is left? Perhaps a correlated mental state. We must tread carefully here. It has often been assumed that every deliberate action is the outward expression of a private mental action, which is the real core of the performance and to which the overt behavior is an inessential accompaniment. Thus when I say 'I forgive you', my utterance is simply the outward manifestation of the real forgiving which is taking place behind the scenes. Or at the least, every deliberate or intentional action is prefaced by a volition to perform that action. Since this view has been decisively criticized by Gilbert Ryle and others, I shall not appeal to any such ghostly doubles of overt actions. But in the flush of victory over these hoary prejudices we should not lose sight of the fact that there commonly are private mental states accompanying overt actions, and that there is some pattern to these accompaniments. Volitions are psychological myths, but *sometimes* an action is preceded by a non-publicly observable decision, intention or resolution to perform the act. Acts of forgiveness and comforting are *often* accompanied by feelings of sympathy, compassion, and tenderness, and by private resolutions not to hold a grudge. Commands are *often* privately rehearsed before their official promulgation and are often issued in a stern frame of mind. Faced with the task of interpreting these words as applied to an immaterial being it is tempting to retreat to these private accompaniments and suppose that they are what is being asserted to go on. Thus 'God has forgiven X's sins' would mean something like 'God has said to Himself 'I forgive X's sins', God feels compassion toward X, and God does not feel grudges or resentments against X'. 'God watches over the affairs of men' would mean

'God has experiences which correspond exactly to what is going on in the world'. 'God commands us to love our neighbors' would mean 'God privately rehearses the command: Love thy neighbor as thyself'. I shall henceforth refer to this mode of explanation as the 'whittle-down method'.[1]

This sort of interpretation is less grotesque in some places than in others. It is not obviously absurd to think of God's judgments on my acts, or his knowledge of what I am doing (Divine knowledge involves some *very* thorny problems which I cannot go into here.) as consisting solely in private conscious states. But this obviously won't do for making, forgiving, commanding, and watching over. Forgiving me can't just consist in feeling well disposed and not feeling resentment, nor does watching over human affairs simply consist in registering sensations of what is going on. If these acts are to retain their religious point, they must involve some contact with the worshipper. God's private feelings and soliloquies are not enough. They must get through somehow to the human being. The former might be enough for a deist, who simply makes a formal assent to the existence of God and passes on, but it is woefully inadequate to an actually functioning religion. Pure thought thinking itself is of no use to religion, whatever attractions it may have for speculation.

No doubt this can be patched up. Where some impact on the worshipper is involved in what we mean by 'God . . .', we can introduce a reference to such impacts into our explanation. Thus 'God has forgiven me' means not only that God has private mental states like those which accompany human acts of forgiving, but also that I have feelings of release from guilt, of being accepted, of a profound peace, etc., i.e., feelings like those I have when a man has forgiven me. And part of which is meant by 'God has spoken to me' will be that I have experiences something like those I typically have when a man for whom I have a very high regard speaks to me, e.g., hearing a voice speak with authority, being seized with a sudden conviction, having a sudden sense of illumination, etc. Of course no one of these experiences has to be present. And even an open-ended class of experiences has a very loose connection with the divine action. I may say 'God has forgiven me' when nothing like this happens. ("I know that God has forgiven me, for the Bible promises that He will forgive those who truly turn unto Him, but I still feel dreadfully oppressed and guilty. What is wrong?") But we can admit exceptional cases while continuing to insist that the presence for the most part, of experiences of this sort is part of what is meant by 'God has forgiven me'. If people did not often have such experiences when they said 'God has forgiven me', the concept of divine forgiveness would be quite different. Compare this with the meaning of 'sad'. It is logically possible for a person to be sad without looking droopy, acting in a lethargic manner,

---

[1] This term was suggested to me by some remarks of I. M. Crombie. See *New Essays in Philosophical Theology,* ed. A. Flew and A. MacIntyre (London: SCM Press, 1955), p. 122.

speaking quietly, brooding, etc. But it is not logically possible for people, *as a rule*, to be sad without exhibiting behavior of this sort. If a man consistently said 'I feel sad' when he was acting exuberant, we would conclude that he did not know the meaning of 'sad'.

VII

But patching up the account is futile. The whole approach is defective in very fundamental ways. To bring these out I shall ask whether one who had been given this instruction would be able to use 'God forgives the sins of those who truly turn unto Him'. Suppose the following questions are raised

(1) How can I know whether this is true?
(2) How can I tell whether I really believe this?
(3) How do I go about truly turning unto Him?
(4) Why should I truly turn unto Him? Why should I care whether God has forgiven my sins?

Has the instruction provided a basis for answering these questions?
  (1) Answers that might be given to (1) are

> A. On the authority of the Bible.
> B. You can't know, at least not now. Now you can only believe. You will know this to be the case only by the long range consequences of your actions. If, e.g., you humbly confess your sins now, and then lead a blissful existence after death, that will show that this statement is true, or at least be very strong evidence in its favor.
> C. The only way one can know is by directly experiencing God's forgiveness. If you have not experienced it, proofs are of no avail; if you have, they are not needed.
> D. This question cannot arise. There is no such thing as knowing this. When we utter this sentence we are simply expressing a sense of being forgiven, a sense of cosmic acceptance. We are expressing this feeling by telling a story about a supreme person. There is no point in asking how we know this is really so. The only questions are whether one has this feeling and whether this story is a good expression of it.

Does the whittle-down explanation help the pupil to choose between these answers? I can't see that it does. Its impotence is underlined by the fact that any of the respondents could have accepted the whittle-down explication. Each could have agreed that, as he talks about God, God's forgiveness is like a man's forgiveness only with respect to certain private mental states and certain typical feelings in the forgiven. Their divergences develop beyond this point. They all take the same basis from the literal use of the word, but then they do very different things with it, e.g., make predictions about the future course of experience, express a state of feeling, or report what one perceives (or thinks he perceives). It is *these* differences that are responsible for their diverse responses to the demand for justification. And the salient fact is that these differences cannot be expressed by drawing further similarities or dissimilarities between human and divine forgiveness. It is not that the person who maintains answer "C" thinks divine forgiveness is like, or unlike, human forgiveness in a way that doesn't agree with the person who offers answer "D". Their description of God's forgiveness might be couched in exactly the same terms. It is what they do with the whole description that differs. Just as two men might describe King Arthur in exactly the same terms, agree completely as to what he is like, while one meant to be giving an historically accurate account, the other to be creating or narrating a piece of fiction.

(2) What is it to believe that God forgives my sins if I truly turn unto Him? The whittle-down explanation would suggest that it simply consists in entertaining the emasculated concept which has been derived, perhaps along with a feeling of conviction. But surely having a religious belief involves more than this; and this approach gives no hint as to what that something more might be. It tells us what it isn't, viz., having the sort of sensory expectations which would be involved in believing that a man would forgive me under certain conditions. But it does nothing to replace these deletions. (It might seem that on this approach the belief would involve expecting feelings of release from guilt, etc. after one had humbly confessed. But, as we have seen, one can believe that God has forgiven one, even when no such feelings occur.)

(3) Our pupil will be at a loss when it comes actually to making the turn. The whittle-down approach gives no help here. How does one address an immaterial being? Why do it in one place, posture, or attitude rather than another? Should one make the address silently or aloud? Alone or in concert? However we do it, what constitutes it an address *to* God, rather than talking to ourselves or an imaginary conversation? The use of the word 'God' is not sufficient. I might use that word in an imaginary conversation. "But this isn't pretence. I firmly believe that God is aware of what I am saying." If God is omniscient, He is aware of everything that happens. This can't mark out certain utterances as being addressed to Him. "But I *intend* Him to hear these. They are directed to Him." This is where we started. What is it to direct a confession to Him? In functioning religions we find standard methods for doing this. Sometimes confessions are to be made through an authorized representative, sometimes with the accompaniment of certain gestures, sometimes in certain postures. But from the analogies exploited by the whittle-down method one could anticipate neither the existence nor the nature of these methods. The method fails to connect sentences about God to the religious activities which they both guide and reflect.

(4) A salient feature of the logic of 'God' is the impossibility of indifference. God is a matter of "passionate interest" (Kierkegaard), an object of

"ultimate concern" (Tillich). A man who says "Oh yes, I know God made and sustains me, judges me, and died for my sins to save me", then yawns and turns to the sports page, is not merely idiosyncratic. He is exhibiting a semantic failure, a misunderstanding of 'God'. His yawn pragmatically contradicts what he said, in the way one would contradict himself if he said, "We must all work together for the common good", while making a killing in wheat futures on the basis of inside information. To define 'God' in such a way as to leave concern an open question is to commit an analogue of what G. E. Moore calls the naturalistic fallacy in ethics. And the whittle-down method does just that. A set of disembodied conscious states, with or without a pure ego or soul substance, may or may not inspire passionate interest. It will probably leave all but the speculative quite unmoved. To be sure, one could hardly be indifferent to the feelings of release from guilt, etc., but this does not help. It is surely a perversion of religious belief to be interested in one's religious experiences, but not in what God does or is. The problem is to exhibit their relationship in such a way that we see how the interest aroused by the former is also directed on to the latter. The most the whittle-down method can do to bridge the gap between these twin privacies is to take the divine conscious state as the cause (in some mysterious way) of the human feelings. But this won't really do; for, as we have seen, religious people are often prepared to say that God has forgiven them when no such feelings are forthcoming, and the divine forgiveness does not lose its interest on these occasions.

VIII

These deficiencies all have a common root and all point in the same direction. The basic trouble is that in removing overt behavior from forgiving, commanding, etc. (and even more if we remove temporal sequence too) we have taken these terms out of the language game in which they primarily function without replacing it by another. In etherealizing these action concepts we snip off the rules which normally govern their use—rules which stipulate what is relevant evidence for an application of the term, what constitutes believing that the term applies in a certain case, in what contexts it is appropriate to use the term, to what attitudes, if any, an application of the term commits one, etc. So long as we merely explain God's forgiveness, as being like human forgiveness except that there is no bodily activity, we have taken away an essential condition of the literal use of 'forgives' without indicating what is to be put in its place. At this point we have but a fragment of a meaning. We don't yet know how to use 'God has forgiven my sins'—we don't know what would count for or against its truth, what sorts of implications it has, or what to do about it.

There are other ranges of discourse in which similar problems arise, e.g., scientific explanations couched in terms of unobservable entities conceived by analogy with observable ones. Psychoanalytic theory is a good example. We find Freud saying things like:

> At the very beginning all the libido is accumulated in the id, while the ego is still in process of formation or far from robust. Part of this libido is sent out by the id into erotic object—cathexes, whereupon the ego, now growing stronger, attempts to obtain possession of the object-libido and to force itself upon the id as a love-object.[2]

It is clear that this cannot be construed literally. The ego and the *id* are not different persons. We can hardly suppose that conflicts between the ego and *id* might take the form of a fist-fight, nor can we picture the ego making eyes at the *id*, or the *id* making a pass at the ego. Then what is being said? We could try to explain it by the whittle-down method. The *id* is like a lustful brute, but without a body, and not even a glimmer of reason, etc. The ego is like a prudent business man, except for analogous restrictions. We can picture each as a cartoonist's model in which all personality functions but one have atrophied. This gives us a picture, but we still don't know what to do with it. We don't know how to test the statement, when to say that this attraction has taken place, what role it might have in the formation of neuroses, etc. For that we must go beyond similarities and differences, and depict the use to which the picture is put, the rules which govern that use. We must make explicit the sort of behavior which is to be expected in particular cases when this attraction does or does not take place; we must specify some way of (at least roughly) measuring the amount of energy possessed by the ego or *id* at a particular time. Until such jobs are done, we are merely amusing ourselves with fables.

It seems that the whittle-down method is effective when both literal and non-literal use belong to the same "language-stratum" (Waismann). This is the case with 'He blew his top' and 'There is a power vacuum in the Middle East'. The same *sort* of checks and tests, implication patterns, etc., hold for both 'That boiler blew its top' and 'Jones blew his top'; for example, both can be tested by observing the individual in question. Since they carry over from the primary to the derivative use they don't have to be explicitly mentioned in making the transition. We can confine ourselves to spelling out detailed differences between boilers blowing their tops and men blowing their tops. But when we go from an observable human being to a non-observable sub-system of the psyche, or from an embodied action to an action of a purely immaterial being, the usual sort of rules is no longer applicable, and we are forced to put something in their place explicitly. An immaterial person isn't simply another kind of person in the way a disagreeable or a talented person is, or even in the way a power vacuum is a different kind of vacuum from an air vacuum.

[2] Freud, *The Ego and the Id*, tr. J. Riviere (London: Hogarth Press, 1927), p. 65.

IX

The way forward is clear. By drawing analogies we get a picture, with taboos against using it in familiar ways. What is needed is a positive description of the ways in which it is to be used. More specifically the theistic picture could be, and has been, put to the following uses:

(1) Explanation of facts in the natural world.
(2) Matrix for predictions of the future course of events.
(3) Expression of feelings and attitudes.
(4) Imaginative presentation of moral ideals.
(5) Report of what is perceived in religious experience.
(6) Guide to worship.

This list is not complete. Furthermore it is obvious that these items are not necessarily mutually exclusive. But it serves as an indication of the diversity with which we are confronted. What we must do is to trace out in detail the various ways in which religious statements function in one or another of these dimensions. Clarification of talk about God awaits progress on this task.

THE ANALOGY THEORY

E. L. MASCALL
Analogy

Is it possible, we therefore ask, for statements expressed in human language to mean anything when made about God—that is to say, are theological statements meaningful or meaningless? (The relevance of this discussion to the questions raised by the logical positivists will be immediately clear to those who have any acquaintance with their works.) Starting from a famous distinction made by Aristotle,[1] we remark that, even within the realm of discourse about finite beings, one and the same word, when applied to two things, sometimes bears the same sense in both applications and sometimes different ones. In the former case it is used *univocally* (συνονύμως), as when Carlo and Fido are both called dogs. Even if Carlo is a great Dane and Fido a Pomeranian, we mean the same thing about each of them when we call them both *dogs*; the characteristics in each that distinguish Carlo as a Dane

E. L. Mascall (1905–   ) is an Anglican theologian and a professor of historical theology at King's College, the University of London. His major writings include *He Who Is, Existence and Analogy,* and *Words and Images.*

ANALOGY   From *Existence and Analogy* by E. L. Mascall. Reprinted by permission of Longman Group Limited and Archon Books.

[1] *Categories,* I. It is true that in this text Aristotle mentions only univocity and equivocity, though elsewhere he makes considerable use of the notion of analogy. Cajetan remarks *à propos* of this text that logicians (in contrast to philosophers) call analogy of attribution equivocation (*De Nom. Anal.,* cap. ii, no. 19).

from Fido as a Pomeranian, while they cannot be found in their totality except in dogs, are additional to caninity as such. But sometimes we use words purely equivocally (ὁμωνύμως), as when we apply the word "mug" both to a drinking utensil and to the victim of a fraud. (The neglect of this distinction can lead to unfortunate consequences, as the choirboys found who were starting a cricket team, when they asked the vicar for one of the bats which the verger had led them to believe were in the belfry.) But in addition to these two uses, it is alleged, a word is sometimes applied to two objects in senses that are neither wholly different nor yet wholly the same, as when we say that Mr. Jones and Skegness are both healthy, the former because he *enjoys*, and the latter because it *induces*, health; in this case we are said to use the term "healthy" *analogically* (ἀνάλογως).

At first sight the introduction of this mode of predication might seem to be unnecessary and trivial, and certainly Aristotle did not accord to it anything like as much attention as the scholastics do. We might be tempted to suppose that analogy is only a dignified kind of univocity, and that it is quite sufficient to say that the healthiness of Mr. Jones and the healthiness of Skegness are merely two ways of being healthy, just as the Danishness of Carlo and the Pomeranianity of Fido are merely two ways of being canine. Or, alternatively, we might go to the other extreme and say that analogy is only equivocity in sheep's clothing, that to enjoy health and to induce health are two altogether different activities and that only for the sake of economy in words can there be any justification for using the same term "healthy" *tout court* to denote them both. Furthermore, it might be asked, even if we admit this *tertium quid* of analogy, can we ever be quite sure when it applies? When we say that Mr. Jones is alive and that an oyster is alive, is the difference between the life of Mr. Jones and the life of the oyster something additional to a quality, namely life, which is found univocally in both, as the Danishness of Carlo and the Pomeranianity of Fido are additional to their common caninity? Or, on the other hand, is the life which is attributed to Mr. Jones and to the oyster, as the scholastics would say, an analogical perfection, contracted to each subject not by external *differentiae* but by different internal modes of participation? Can one possibly settle this kind of question? Can we even give the distinction any real meaning?

Now, so long as we are merely considering qualities and properties of finite beings, the introduction of analogical discourse, in addition to univocal and equivocal, might well appear to be an unnecessary and artificial complication. There are, however, two instances in which it—or something like it—seems to be unavoidable, namely when we are discussing transcendentals and when we are discussing God. And it is worth noting that, in Christian thought, it is precisely the necessity of talking about God that has given rise to the great development which the doctrine of analogy has undergone. Let us consider these instances in order.

The transcendentals, in scholastic thought, are those six primary notions—

ens, res, unum, aliquid, verum and *bonum*—which, because of their very universality, refuse to fall in any of the Aristotelian categories, but cut across them all.[2] The last five ultimately reduce to the first, so it will be sufficient to consider that. What, then, is meant by the analogy of being? Why is it denied that being is univocal? Simply because there is nothing outside being by which it could be differentiated. When we say that Carlo and Fido are both dogs, the word "dog" means precisely the same when applied to each of them; the differences that distinguish them as dogs are, as we have seen, extrinsic to caninity as such. But when we say that Carlo and Fido are both *beings*, the differences that distinguish them as beings cannot be extrinsic to being as such, for being, in its altogether universal reference, must embrace everything, including differences; if differences were not instances of being, they would be non-existent, and then no two things could be distinct from each other. So the scholastics tell us, being is not a genus,[3] since there is nothing outside it which could act as a differentia to it, to subdivide it into species; nevertheless everything is an instance of being, and being is differentiated by its own inherent analogical variety. To be is to be in a certain way, and the way is the very heart of the being. So the whole order of beings, of *entia*, from the triune Deity down to the speck of dust and the electron, consists of nothing more and nothing less than analogical instances of being: self-existent being and dependent being, actual being and possible being, substantial being and accidental being, real being and notional being, not in any pantheistic or monistic sense, as if being were some kind of cosmic material, a metaphysical modelling-clay appearing now in this shape and now in that, but in the far more profound sense that every being must *be*, and must be in some determinate way, and—the theist will add—in the sense that the way in which it has being depends in the last resort upon its relation to the self-existent Being which is the prime analogate of all.

Now what is true about beings as such in their relation to one another must be true *a fortiori* about finite beings in their relation to the God who is self-existent Being. If being is not a genus, then the supreme Being transcends all genera, and the principle of analogy, which we have seen applies even between creatures when they are considered as they participate in the transcendentals, will apply with even greater force when creatures are brought

---

[2] It should be noted that they are called transcendentals because they transcend the categories. This is not the meaning which the word "transcendent" has when applied to God to indicate that he transcends the realm of finite being. Nor is it the meaning that "transcendental" has for Kant: "I apply," he says, "the term *transcendental* to all knowledge which is not so much occupied with objects as with the mode of our cognition of these objects, so far as this mode of cognition is possible *a priori*" (*Critique of Pure Reason*, Introduction, ch. vii, trans. Meiklejohn). Cf. Garrigou-Lagrange, *Dieu*, p. 200, *n*. 1.

[3] R. G. Collingwood surprisingly asserts that for the traditional metaphysics being is the *summum genus* of which the ten Categories are species; in consequence he has little difficulty in arguing that there cannot be a science of pure being (*Essay in Metaphysics*, pp. 9, 10 f). What Aristotle actually thought will be found in *Met.* B., 998b.

into comparison with the altogether transcendent God and when God is spoken about in words whose meaning is derived from their application to finite things. Here, if anywhere, the distinction between the *perfectio significata* and the *modus significandi* will hold; here, if anywhere, will the classical definition of analogy apply, namely that it is the application of a concept to different beings in ways that are simply diverse from each other and are only the same in a certain respect, *simpliciter diversa et eadem secundum quid.*[4] It is noticeable that St. Thomas does not deny that analogues are equivocal but only that they are purely so.[5]

Let us now proceed to consider in more detail this classical doctrine of analogy. The precise classification of the various types of analogy that can be distinguished is to this day a matter of considerable controversy; the method that I shall adopt will, however, bring out the salient points.

II

In the first place, we may distinguish between analogy *duorum ad tertium* and analogy *unius ad alterum*; this is the fundamental distinction made by St. Thomas in both the *Summa Theologica* and the *Summa contra Gentiles.*[6] Analogy *duorum ad tertium* is the analogy that holds between two beings in consequence of the relation that each of them bears to a third (the analogy considered is, it must be noticed, between the *two*; the *tertium* only comes in as something in the background to which they are both related). For example, if the adjective "healthy" is applied both to Skegness and to the complexion of Mr. Jones who lives there, this double attribution of the adjective can only be seen to be legitimate if it is grasped that in its strict and primary application the adjective applies neither to Skegness nor to the complexion but to Mr. Jones. It is he who is (in the scholastic sense) *formally* healthy and is the *prime analogate.* His complexion is healthy only in the sense that it is a *sign* of health in him, Skegness is healthy only in the sense that it *induces* health in him (or in others like him); we cannot rationally

---

[4] This is the Thomist definition of analogical discourse. For the Suarezians, however, with their conceptualist bias and the consequent sharp line drawn between thought and the extra-mental thing, an analogical concept applies to different beings in ways *simpliciter eadem et diversa secundum quid.*

[5] *Hoc modo aliqua dicuntur de Deo et creaturis analogice, et non aequivoce pure neque univoce (S. Theol.,* I, xiii, 5c). We may compare the well-known statement of the Fourth Lateran Council that "between the creator and the creature no likeness can be discerned without a greater unlikeness having to be discerned as well" (*inter creatorem et creaturam non potest tanta similitudo notari quin inter eos major sit dissimilitudo notanda,* cap. ii; Denzinger-Bannwart, *Enchiridion,* 11th ed., no. 432). It is easy to see what this means, but it would be difficult to defend it as a precise philosophical statement, as it appears to assume that likeness and unlikeness are two different species of a measurable genus. One can validly say that two objects are less alike in one respect than they are in another, but to say that they are less alike in one respect than they are *unlike* in another does not seem to be strictly intelligible.

[6] *S. Theol.,* I, xiii, 5c; *S.c.G.,* I, xxxiv.

justify the attribution of the same predicate "healthy" to things as diverse as a complexion and a seaside town except by referring them both to human beings to whom the predicate formally and properly belongs.

This type of analogy can, however, have little or no application to the case where we are attributing the same predicate to God and to a creature, for there is no being antecedent to God to whom the predicate can apply more formally and properly than it applies to him. We therefore pass to the other type of analogy, analogy *unius ad alterum*, which is founded not upon diverse relations which each of the analogates bears to a third, but upon a relation which one of them bears to the other. And this type of analogy itself subdivides into two.

The former of these sub-types is that which is known as analogy of *attribution* or of *proportion*, analogy *unius ad alterum* in the strict sense. In this case the predicate belongs formally and properly to one of the analogates (which is thus not merely *an* analogate but is the *prime* analogate), and only relatively and derivatively to the other. Thus it is by an analogy of attribution or proportion that Mr. Jones and his complexion are both described as healthy; health is found formally and properly in Mr. Jones, and his complexion is described as healthy only because it bears a certain relation to his health, namely the relation of being a sign of it. In its theological application, where the analogates concerned are God and a creature, the relation upon which the analogy is based will be that of creative causality; creatures are related to God as his effects, by all those modes of participation by the creature in the perfection of its creator which are indicated, for example, by the Thomist Five Ways. Thus when we say that God and Mr. Jones are both good or that they are both beings, remembering that the content which the word "good" or "being" has for us is derived from our experience of the goodness and the being of creatures, we are, so far as analogy of attribution is concerned, saying no more than that God has goodness or being in whatever way is necessary if he is to be able to produce goodness and being in his creatures. This would not seem necessarily to indicate anything more than that the perfections which are found formally in various finite modes in creatures exist *virtually* in God, that is to say, that he is able to produce them in the creatures; it does not seem to necessitate that God possesses them formally himself. (In the case of Mr. Jones, of course, his complexion did indicate his formal possession of health, but there is, literally, all the difference in the world between the relation between two analogates in the finite realm and that between God and a creature.) Analogy of attribution certainly does not exclude the formal possession of the perfections by God, but it does not itself ascribe it to him. The mode in which the perfection which exists in the secondary analogate also exists in the prime analogate will depend on the relation between them; and if this relation is merely that the latter analogate is the *cause* of the former, the possession by the latter of a perfection that exists formally in the former will not, so far as the present mode of analogy is concerned, be necessarily anything more than a virtual one. Creatures are good (formally but finitely), God is the cause of them and of all that they have, therefore the word "good" applied to God need not mean any more than that he is able to produce goodness.[7] It is at this point that the second sub-type of analogy comes to the rescue.

This is analogy of proportionality, also called analogy *plurium ad plura*. In it there is a direct relation of the mode in which a perfection is participated to the being by which it is participated, independently of any relation to a prime analogate. (There may be a prime analogate, and indeed some would maintain that there must be,[8] but it does not come in at this stage.) A spurious, though sometimes useful, form of this type of analogy is *metaphor*, in which there is not a formal participation of the same characteristic in the different analogates but only a similarity of effects. Thus, to take a classic example, the lion is called the king of the beasts because he bears to savage animals a relation similar to that which a king bears to his subjects, but no one would assert that kingship is to be found formally in the lion. Again, God is described as being angry, because his relation to the punishments which he imposes is similar to that which an angry man has to the injuries which he inflicts, but no one (at least, no scholastic philosopher) would say that anger was to be found formally in God.[9] In the strict sense, an analogy of proportionality implies that the analogue under discussion is found formally in each of the analogates but in a mode that is determined by the nature of the analogate itself. Thus, assuming that life is an analogous and not a univocal concept, it is asserted that cabbages, elephants, men and God each

[7] It is important to observe that we are not arguing that the formal possession of goodness by creatures does not *prove* that goodness is formally in God; the argument is not here on the metaphysical but merely on the linguistic and logical plane. All that is asserted is that if the only analogy between God and creatures was analogy of attribution then the word "good" applied to God would not necessarily *mean* any more than that goodness was in God virtually. *In fact* the metaphysical relation of the world to God implies analogy of proportionality as well, and it is at this latter stage that the formal attribution of goodness to God becomes clear.

[8] Thus Garrigou-Lagrange writes: "It is not necessary here to mention the principal analogate in the definition of the others, but there nevertheless always is a prime analogate. In metaphorical analogy of proportionality, it is the one to which the name of analogue belongs in the strict sense. In strict analogy of proportionality, the principal analogate is that which is the higher cause of the others: the analogical similitude that exists in this latter case is always based on causality; it exists either between the cause and the effect or between the effects of the same cause" (*Dieu*, p. 532, *n*. 3). This last remark seems to imply the assertion that will be made later on: that in its theological application analogy of proportionality needs to be reinforced by analogy of attribution; Garrigou-Lagrange does not, however, explicitly make the assertion. We may add here, as a point of terminology, that the word "analogue" (*analogum*) refers to the common predicate (or common quality or transcendental signified by it), while the word "analogate" (*analogatum*) refers to the various subjects to which it is attributed, or to its diverse modes in them. An alternative nomenclature refers to the analogue as *analogum analogans* and the analogate as *analogum analogatum*.

[9] A further example of purely metaphorical proportionality is provided by Canning's celebrated epigram:

> Pitt is to Addington
> As London is to Paddington.

possess life formally (that is each of them is, quite literally and unmetaphorically, *alive*), but that the cabbage possesses life in the mode proper to a cabbage, the elephant in that proper to an elephant, the man in that proper to a man, and finally God in that supreme, and by us unimaginable, mode proper to self-existent Being itself. This is commonly expressed in the following quasi-mathematical form, from which, in fact, the name "analogy of proportionality" is derived: [10]

$$\frac{\text{life of cabbage}}{\text{essence of cabbage}} = \frac{\text{life of elephant}}{\text{essence of elephant}}$$

$$= \frac{\text{life of man}}{\text{essence of man}} = \frac{\text{life of God}}{\text{essence of God}}$$

We must, however, beware of interpreting the equal sign too literally. For the point is not that the life of the cabbage is determined by the essence of the cabbage in the *same* way as that in which the life of the man is determined by the essence of the man, but that the way in which cabbage essence determines cabbage life is proper to cabbagehood, while the way in which the human essence determines human life is proper to manhood. But at this point various objections rapidly spring to the mind.

In the first place, it may be asked, has not the remark just made landed us in an infinite regress? We began by denying the univocity of the identity,

$$\text{life of cabbage} = \text{life of man,}$$

and substituted for it the proportionality:

$$\frac{\text{life of cabbage}}{\text{essence of cabbage}} = \frac{\text{life of man}}{\text{essence of man}}$$

But we now have denied that the equal sign in this latter equation really signifies equality and have substituted for it a proposition which, in quasi-mathematical form, can be written as follows:

---

[10] "Let magnitudes which have the same proportion (λόγος) be called proportional (ἀνάλογον)" (Euclid V, Def. 6). For the sake of clarity it may be useful to indicate by a diagram the classification of analogy which I have adopted:
 I. Analogy *duorum ad tertium*.
 II. Analogy *unius ad alterum*.
   (i) Analogy of attribution or proportion, strictly *unius ad alterum*.
   (ii) Analogy of proportionality, *plurium ad plura*
      (*a*) in loose sense (metaphor)
      (*b*) in strict sense.
  Slightly different classifications may be found in Garrigou-Lagrange, *Dieu*, p. 351; Maquart, *Elem. Phil.*, III, ii, p. 36.

$$\frac{\text{way in which life of cabbage is determined by essence of cabbage}}{\text{essence of cabbage}}$$

$$= \frac{\text{way in which life of man is determined by essence of man}}{\text{essence of man}}$$

And again we shall have to remember that the equal sign means not identity but similarity, and shall now have to write:

$$\frac{\text{way in which way-in-which-life-of-cabbage-is-determined-by-essence-of-cabbage is determined by essence of cabbage}}{\text{essence of cabbage}}$$

$$= \frac{\text{way in which way-in-which-life-of-man-is-determined-by-essence-of-man is determined by essence of man}}{\text{essence of man}}$$

and so *ad infinitum*.

To put this more briefly, if we write L for "life of" and E for "essence of," *c* for "cabbage" and *m* for "man," and use A/B to signify "determination of A by B," we began by denying Lc = Lm, and put in its place

$$Lc/Ec = Lm/Em;$$

then we said that what we really meant was

$$(Lc/Ec)/Ec = (Lm/Em)/Em;$$

then we found that for this we should have to substitute

$$[(Lc/Ec)/Ec]/Ec = [(Lm/Em)/Em]/Em.$$

The next stage will be

$$\{[(Lc/Ec)/Ec]/Ec\}/Ec = \{[(Lm/Em)/Em]/Em\}/Em,$$

and so we shall go on for ever, at each successive stage denying progressively more complicated relationships between cabbages and men, and never managing to assert a relationship which we shall not immediately have to deny. And at the end of it we shall have nothing but a series of negations:

$$Lc \neq Lm,$$
$$Lc/Ec \neq Lm/Em,$$
$$(Lc/Ec)/Ec \neq (Lm/Em)/Em,$$
$$[(Lc/Ec)/Ec]/Ec \neq [(Lm/Em)/Em]/Em, \qquad \text{etc.}$$

Our proportionality has completely collapsed, and all we are left with is the fact that cabbages have nothing in common with men except the fact that, for no valid reason, men have described them both as being alive. In fact, the introduction of analogy as a *via media* between univocity and equivocity has turned out to be nothing more than an imposing piece of mystification. This is the first objection of which we must take account; it is obviously a serious one. It strikes, not in particular at the analogical application of terms to God, but to analogical predication as such. I shall not attempt a full reply until I have stated another objection which is concerned with the specifically theological case, but I shall offer a few observations in passing.

First, then, we may remark that the objection, while on the surface plausible, has something of the appearance of a conjuring trick. It brings to mind two somewhat similar feats of philosophical legerdemain. The first is Lewis Carroll's *What the Tortoise said to Achilles*.[11] In this problem, which its originator did not perhaps intend to be taken as seriously as it really demands, Achilles maintained that, if two premisses A and B logically implied a conclusion Z, then anybody who saw this and also accepted A and B as true would have to accept Z as true also. The tortoise objected that this would only be the case if he accepted a further proposition C, namely that if A and B are true then Z must be true. Achilles was thus forced to modify his original assertion, so that it now took the form "Anyone who accepts A, B and C as true must accept Z as true also." But again the tortoise objected that this involved the acceptance of another proposition D, which was that, if A and B and C are all true, Z must be true as well. And so on for ever! This corresponds, of course, to the well-known fact that the principle of inference is incapable of formal symbolic statement within the logical calculus to which it applies.[12] A logical system cannot, as it were, operate under its own steam, without help from outside; we shall derive from this fact a pointer towards the solution of our present problem. The other puzzle to which I wish to refer is one which its originator took much more seriously: I mean Mr. F. H. Bradley's famous argument that relations are illusions.[13] It is, he urged, of the essence of a relation to unite terms, but how is each term united to the relation? It can only be by another relation, but if so, what unites the term to this? To make the first relation intelligible we have to presuppose an infinite sequence of relations antecedent to it, and none of these is yet intelligible. Hence, Mr. Bradley concluded, relations are mere illusion. Lord Russell has caustically remarked that if Bradley's argument were valid it would prove that chains are impossible—and yet they exist.[14] Dr. C. D. Broad has dealt with Bradley's problem in some detail. He takes as an instance of it the fact that A is father of B. "Here," he writes,

---

[11] *The Complete Works of Lewis Carroll*, pp. 1104 f.

[12] Cf. B. Russell, *The Principles of Mathematics*, pp. 16, 35, where explicit reference is made to Lewis Carroll's puzzle.

[13] *Appearance and Reality*, I, ch. iii.   [14] *Outline of Philosophy*, p. 263.

"we have a perfectly intelligible statement, involving the non-formal [15] relation of *fatherhood*. At the next stage we get the fact that A is referent to
fatherhood, and the fact that B is relatum to *fatherhood*. The 'relations'
introduced at this stage are purely formal. At the next stage we get the fact
that A is referent to *referent to*, that *fatherhood* is relatum to *referent to*,
that *fatherhood* is referent to *referent to*, and that B is relatum to *referent to*.
Thus no new 'relations' are introduced at this or any subsequent stage. The
fact that at every stage after the first the relating relations are purely formal
and are merely repeated shows that we are now embarked on the self-evidently
impossible task of explaining, by means of particular relational judgments,
that general relational form which is presupposed by all relational judgments
whatever." [16] We might, in fact, say that, while it is of the essence of relations
to unite terms, they are not themselves terms in this context (though, of
course, in another context they may become terms, as when we pick out two
relations, or a relation and a term, and ask what is the relation between
them). Similarly, in the case of analogy of proper proportionality, we might
reply to our objector that we are simply concerned with the fact that essences
determine their qualities, and that the truth of this is not in the least affected
by the fact that they can only do this if they also determine the way in which
they determine their qualities, and the way in which they determine the way
in which they determine their qualities, and so on to the crack of doom.
Ce n'est que le premier pas qui coûte.

Such a reply would, I think, go a very long way, though I am doubtful
whether it is altogether sufficient. For the fact remains that we have denied
that our equal signs really stand for equality and we have not indicated anything definite that they do stand for. Can we in some way re-establish this
bond that we have broken? Clearly we cannot by analogy of proportionality,
but I shall suggest that we can by analogy of attribution, and that the two
types of analogy, while either in separation is insufficient, can in combination
do what is required.[17] But this is an anticipation. I will pass on now to con-

---

[15] "Formal," for Broad and all the modern logicians, means "purely logical," "having no reference
to particular concrete individual entities." This is very different from the scholastic use of the
word.

[16] *Examination of McTaggart's Philosophy*, I, p. 86.

[17] It may be interesting to see how Dr. A. M. Farrer deals with this difficulty. For him "this
proportionality claims to hold between four terms, and not two relations. We are not saying,"
he continues, " 'The way in which the divine intelligence is related to the divine existence resembles the way in which the creaturely intelligence is related to the creaturely existence' for
that is exactly what we have to deny. The way in which the several aspects of the divine being
(e.g. intelligence) have their synthesis into one, itself differs from the way in which the several
aspects of the creaturely being have their synthesis into one, *as* the divine being itself differs
from the creaturely. What we are saying is completely different, viz. 'Divine intelligence is
appropriate to divine existence as creaturely to creaturely' " (*Finite and Infinite*, p. 53, italics in
original).

Dr. Farrer's first point seems to me to be valuable, at least as denying *equality* of relations; in
this respect the older mathematical notation for proportionality, $a : b :: c : d$, might be less mis-

sider the second objection, which is specially concerned with analogical discourse about God.

III

Let us therefore see what happens when we attribute life both to a creature and to God; any other perfection which can be formally predicated of God would, of course, do as well. Analogy of proportionality asserts:

$$\frac{\text{life of man}}{\text{essence of man}} = \frac{\text{life of God}}{\text{essence of God}}$$

Now, the objector urges, even if the first objection has been successfully overcome, so that we have no longer to bother about the fact that the equal sign does not indicate an exact identity of relationship, our formula will not in fact tell us in what sense life is to be predicated of God. For the essence of God is as little known to us as is his life; indeed his life is, formally considered, identical with it. Our equation has therefore two unknowns and cannot be solved. Nor can we get out of our difficulty by comparing essence with existence and saying that the essence of a being will correspond to, and be determined by, the act in virtue of which it exists:

$$\frac{\text{essence of man}}{\text{existential act of man}} = \frac{\text{essence of God}}{\text{existential act of God}}$$

---

leading than the more modern $\frac{a}{b} = \frac{c}{d}$. But I do not think any scholastic would deny that proportionality was *some* sort of relation between two relations or would reduce it simply to a polyadic relation uniting four terms. Dr. Farrer himself in the quotation above seems, by italicizing the word *"as,"* to admit the equal sign at a subsequent stage and, while denying

$$\frac{\text{divine intelligence}}{\text{divine existence}} = \frac{\text{human intelligence}}{\text{human existence}},$$

to be asserting

$$\frac{\text{synthesis of aspects in God}}{\text{being of God}} = \frac{\text{synthesis of aspects in creature}}{\text{being of creature}},$$

but I cannot think that this was his intention. He has previously said that the formula "presupposes that intelligence can be attributed to God, and declares how it is to be understood when it is attributed to him and not to the creature, viz. as differing from its creaturely mode with a difference analogous to that by which the divine existence differs from the creaturely. And so it presupposes also the 'proportion' between the two 'existences.'" He goes on to say: "Proportion logically underlies proportionality, but this need not mean that we originally entertain the notion of the proportion 'divine existence/creaturely existence except as the foundation for a proportionality; the two are distinguished by philosophical analysis only." The proportion now mentioned is, it will be noticed, not either of the proportions that form the two sides of the proportionality, but the proportion between a term on one side and a term on the other. This seems to be in line with my assertion that, in the relation of God to creatures, analogy of proportionality and of attribution (proportion) are interlocked. Dr. Farrer continues: "The natural use of the proportion is inseparable from that of the proportionality, as the apprehension of the very fact of the divine being is inseparable from some apprehension of its mode."

Once again, both the terms on the right-hand side are unknown. Sheer agnosticism seems to be the outcome. What reply can we make?

Some scholastic philosophers, of whom Garrigou-Lagrange is one, claim to answer this objection, while remaining in the realm of analogy of proportionality, by denying that there are two unknown terms on the right-hand side. This last-mentioned writer, for example, taking the analogy

$$\frac{\text{creature}}{\text{its being}} = \frac{\text{first cause}}{\text{its being}}$$

asserts that only the fourth term is in fact unknown. "We have," he says, "(1) *the very confused concept of being in general,* which a child possesses from the moment of its first intellectual knowledge, (2) *the concept of finite being,* of which we know positively the finite mode and which is nothing else than the essence of the things that we see, stones, plants, animals, etc., (3) *the concept of analogous being,* imperfectly abstracted from the finite mode . . . ; it is a precision of the first very confused concept possessed by the child, and the metaphysician acquires it by recognizing that the formal notion of being does not in itself include the finite mode which accompanies it in the creature, (4) *the concept of the divine being,* the cause of created beings. These latter," he continues, "not having in their essence the reason of their existence, require a cause which exists of itself. In the concept of the divine being, the divine mode is expressed only in a negative and relative way, e.g. as non-finite or as supreme being. What is positive in this analogical knowledge of God is what God has that is proportionally common to him and the creature." [18] Again, he writes, "*being* designates *that which* has relation to existence; this relation is implied in the very nature of that which exists and it is essentially varied according as it is necessary or contingent. The created essence in its inmost entity is altogether relative to its contingent existence, which it can lose; the uncreated essence is conceived only relatively to that necessary existence with which it is identified. . . . Analogous perfections are thus not pure relations. They are perfections which imply in the creature a composition of two correlative elements, potentiality and act, but which in God are pure act. Our intelligence conceives that they are realized more fully according as they are purified of all potentiality; in God they exist therefore in the pure state. We thus see that there are not two unknowns in the proportionalities set up by theology." [19]

For this distinguished French Dominican, therefore, the third term in the formula is given us as that in which essence and existence are identical, and this gives us a limited and analogical, but nevertheless genuine, knowledge of the fourth term, while remaining within the realm of analogy of propor-

[18] *Dieu,* p. 541.   [19] Ibid., p. 542.

tionality.[20] We can transfer the notion of any perfection from a finite being to God, remembering that the difference of mode is that which corresponds to the difference between a being whose essence involves merely a possibility of existence and one whose essence involves existence of necessity. Of course, we do not know positively what the mode of the perfection in God is; to demand that would be to demand a quidditative knowledge of the divine essence and to abolish analogy altogether in favour of univocity. We are given all that we have a right to ask for; the comparison of the finite and the infinite modes of perfection is based on a comparison of the relations to existence which are proper to finite essence and to the divine essence respectively.

Now all this seems very satisfactory so far as it goes, but does it go far enough? Is it sufficient simply to base the comparison of the finite and infinite modes of a perfection upon a comparison of the finite and infinite modes of the essence-existence relation, without bringing in an explicit reference to the concrete relation which the creature has to God? There are indeed traces in Garrigou-Lagrange's own discussion of an awareness of the need of this further step; the very form in which he writes the formula last quoted suggests this. For he does not describe the finite being as a being in whom essence does not necessarily involve existence, but as a "creature"; and he does not describe God as a being whose essence necssarily involves existence, but as the "first cause." "In these equations," he writes, "two created terms are known directly, one uncreated term is known indirectly *by way of causality* and we infer the fourth term which is known indirectly in a *positive* manner as regards what is analogically common with creatures and in a *negative* and relative manner as regards its proper divine mode." [21] And the first cause and the creature are directly related by the relation of creation, which thus, as it were, cuts horizontally across the analogy of proportionality with an analogy of attribution.[22] The equal sign does not, as we have seen earlier, express a

---

[20] Penido's answer to the objection (*Rôle de l'Analogie*, pp. 136 f.) rests upon his assertion previously noticed (p. 96, *n.* 1, *supra*) that no use of analogy is necessary in the mere demonstration of the *existence* of God. Thus, in the proportionality,

$$\frac{\text{essence of creature}}{\text{existential act of creature}} = \frac{\text{essence of God}}{\text{existential act of God}},$$

the fourth term is not unknown; it is already given to us as self-existence, *ipsum esse subsistens*, existence not really distinct from essence. Thus, whereas for Garrigou-Lagrange the *third* term is given to us *in* and *through* the analogy, for Penido the *fourth* term is given to us *prior to* the analogy; thus he writes, "L'analogie . . . n'apparait pas *explicitement* au début de notre marche vers Dieu, elle ne s'occupe pas de la question 'an sit', elle n'entre en jeu que lorsqu'il s'agit du 'quomodo sit'" (*Rôle*, p. 138). I cannot help feeling that at this point Penido is nearer the truth.

[21] *Dieu*, p. 543 (first set of italics mine).

[22] Garrigou-Lagrange himself writes: "If the analogy of being is formally an analogy of proportionality it is virtually an analogy of attribution, in the sense that if, *per impossibile*, being did not belong intrinsically to the creature it could still be extrinsically attributed to it, in so far as the creature is an effect of the prime Being" (*Dieu*, p. 541, note). It is the word "virtually" in this passage from which I am disposed to dissent. Penido lays great stress upon the "mixed" nature of the analogy between God and the world (*Rôle de l'Analogie*, p. 134 *et al.*).

mathematical identity, but, on the other hand, the two sides of the formula are not left in complete separation. They are bound together by an analogy of attribution *unius ad alterum*, of the creature to God in the case which we have just been considering. In the cases considered earlier, where the two sides of the formula both refer to finite beings, the linking analogy is an analogy *duorum ad tertium*, which holds in view of the fact that each of the analogates is in an analogy of attribution *unius ad alterum*, of itself to God. The figure below may help to make this plain.[23]

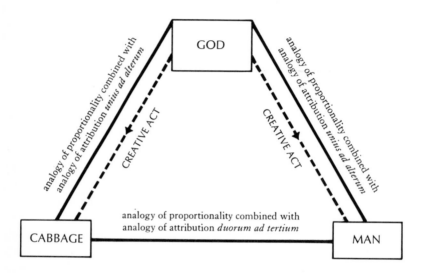

The conclusion would thus seem to be that, in order to make the doctrine of analogy really satisfactory, we must see the analogical relation between God and the world as combining in a tightly interlocked union both analogy of attribution and analogy of proportionality. Without analogy of proportionality it is very doubtful whether the attributes which we predicate of God can be ascribed to him in more than a merely virtual sense; without analogy of attribution it hardly seems possible to avoid agnosticism. Which of the two forms of analogy is prior to the other has been, and still is, a hotly debated question among scholastic philosophers.

---

[23] It should here be noted that analogy *duorum ad tertium* is itself an instance of analogy of attribution.

THE SYMBOL THEORY

PAUL TILLICH
Religious Symbols and Our Knowledge of God

The fact that there is so much discussion about the meaning of symbols going on in this country as well as in Europe is a symptom of something deeper. I believe it is a symptom of two things, something negative and something positive. It is a symptom of the fact that we are in a confusion of language in theology and philosophy and related subjects which has hardly been surpassed in any time in history. Words do not communicate to us anymore what they originally did and what they were invented to communicate. This has something to do with the fact that our present culture has no clearing house such as medieval scholasticism was, and Protestant scholasticism in the 17th century at least tried to be, and philosophers like Kant tried to renew. We have no such clearing house and this is the one point in which I am in sympathy with the present day so-called logical positivists or symbolic logicians or logicians generally. They at least try to produce a clearing house. My only criticism is that this clearing house is a very small room, perhaps only a corner of a house, and not a real house. It excludes most of life. But it could become useful if it increased in reach and acceptance of realities beyond the mere logical calculus. The second point which I want to make is that we are in a process in which a very important thing is being rediscovered: namely,

RELIGIOUS SYMBOLS AND OUR KNOWLEDGE OF GOD   From *The Christian Scholar*, Volume 38, No. 3, September, 1955. Reprinted by permission of The National Council of the Churches of Christ and the Estate of Paul Tillich.

that there are levels of reality of great difference, and that these different levels demand different approaches and different languages: that not everything in reality can be grasped by the language which is most adequate for mathematical sciences; the insight into this situation is the most positive side of the fact that the problem of symbols is taken seriously again.

I

I want to proceed in my own presentation with the intention of clearing concepts as far as I am able. And in order to do this I want to make five steps, the first of which is the discussion of "symbols and signs." Symbols are similar to signs in one decisive respect: both symbols and signs point beyond themselves to something else. The typical sign, for instance the red light of the corner of the street, does not point to itself but it points to the necessity of cars stopping. And every symbol points beyond itself to a reality for which it stands. In this, symbols and signs have an essential identity—they point beyond themselves. And this is the reason that the confusion of language with which I started this lecture has also conquered the discussion about symbols for centuries and has produced confusion between signs and symbols. The first step in any clearing up of the meaning of symbols is to distinguish it from the meaning of signs.

The difference which I see as a fundamental difference between them is that signs do not participate in any way in the reality and power of that to which they point. Symbols, although they are not the same as that which they symbolize, participate in its meaning and power. The difference between symbol and sign is the participation in the symbolized reality which characterizes the symbols, and the non-participation in the "pointed-to" reality which characterizes a sign. For example, letters of the alphabet as they are written, an "A" or an "R" do not participate in the sound to which they point; on the other hand, the flag participates in the power of the king or the nation for which it stands and which it symbolizes. There has, therefore, been a fight since the days of William Tell as to how to behave in the presence of the flag. This would be meaningless if the flag did not participate as a symbol in the power of that which it symbolizes. The whole monarchic idea is itself entirely ununderstandable, if you do not understand that the king always is both: on the one hand, a symbol of the power of the group of which he is the king and on the other hand, he who exercised partly (never fully, of course) this power.

But something has happened which is very dangerous for all our attempts to find a clearing house of the concepts of symbols and signs. I have experienced this in three seminars which I have had in Columbia University with my philosophical colleagues there. The mathematician has usurped the term "symbol" for mathematical "sign," and this makes a disentanglement of the confusion almost impossible. The only thing we can do is to distinguish different groups, signs which are called symbols, and genuine symbols. The mathematical signs are signs which are wrongly called symbols. Let me again say something about language. Language is a very good example of the difference between signs and symbols. Words in a language are signs for a meaning which they express. The word "desk" is a sign which points to something quite different—namely, the thing on which my paper is lying here and at which I am looking and which hides me partly from you. This has nothing to do with the word "desk", with these four letters. But there are words in every language which are more than this, and in the moment in which they get connotations which go beyond something to which they point as signs, then they can become symbols; and this is a very important distinction for every speaker. He can speak almost completely in signs, reducing the meaning of his words almost to mathematical signs, and this is the absolute ideal of the logical positivist. The other pole of this is the liturgical or the poetic language where words have a power through centuries, or more than centuries. They have connotations in situations in which they appear so that they cannot be replaced. They have become not only signs pointing to a meaning which is defined, but also symbols standing for a reality in the power of which they participate.

II

Now I come to my second consideration dealing with the functions of symbols. The first function is implied in what I have already said—namely, the representative function. The symbol represents something which is not itself, for which it stands and in the power and meaning of which it participates. This is a basic function of every symbol, and therefore, if that word had not been used in so many other ways, one could perhaps even translate "symbolic" as "representative," but for some reason that is not possible. If the symbols stand for something which they are not, then the question is, "Why do we not have that for which they stand directly? Why do we need symbols at all?" And now I come to something which is perhaps the main function of the symbol—namely, the opening up of levels of reality which otherwise are hidden and cannot be grasped in any other way.

Every symbol opens up a level of reality for which non-symbolic speaking is inadequate. Let me interpret this or explain this in terms of artistic symbols. I resisted for many years the temptation to call works of art symbolic for the simple reason that there is a special artistic style which we call symbolistic and which produces only bad works of art. For this reason I disliked the idea of saying that works of art are symbolic. But in the meantime, the more I tried to enter into the meaning of symbols, the more I was convinced that it was a function of art to open up levels of reality; in poetry, in visual art, and in music, levels of reality are opened up which can be opened up in no other way. Now if this is the function of art, then certainly artistic creations have symbolic character. You can take that which a landscape of Rubens, for instance, mediates to you. You can not have this experience in any other way than through this painting made by Rubens. This landscape has some heroic character; it has character of balance, of colors, of weights, of values, and so on. All this is very external. What this mediates to you cannot be expressed in any other way than through the painting itself. The same is true also in the relationship of poetry and philosophy. The temptation may often be to confuse the issue by bringing too many philosophical concepts into a poem. Now this is really the problem; one cannot do this. If one uses philosophical language or scientific language, it does not mediate the same thing which is mediated in the use of really poetic language without a mixture of any other language. This example may show what I mean by the phrase "opening up of levels of reality." But in order to do this, something else must be opened up—namely, levels of the soul, levels of our interior reality. And they must correspond to the levels in exterior reality which are opened up by a symbol. So every symbol is two-edged. It opens up reality and it opens up the soul. Here I could give the same example—namely, the artistic experience. There are people who are not opened up by music, or who are not opened up by poetry, or more of them (mostly in Protestant America) who are not opened up at all by visual arts. The "opening up" is a two-sided function—namely, reality in deeper levels and the human soul in special levels.

If this is the function of symbols then it is obvious that symbols cannot be replaced by other symbols. Every symbol has a special function which is just *it* and cannot be replaced by more or less adequate symbols. This is different from signs, for signs can always be replaced. If one finds that a green light is not so expedient as perhaps a blue light (this is not true, but could be true), then we simply put on a blue light, and nothing is changed. But a symbolic word (such as the word "God") cannot be replaced. No symbol can be replaced when used in its special function. So one asks rightly, "How do symbols arise, and how do they come to an end?" As different from signs, symbols are born and die. Signs are consciously invented and removed. This is a fundamental difference. "Out of which womb are symbols born?" I would say out of the womb which is usually called today the "group unconsicous" or "collective unconscious," or whatever you want to call it—out of a group which acknowledges, in this thing, this word, this flag, or whatever it may be, its own being. It is not invented intentionally; and even if somebody would try to invent a symbol, as sometimes happens, then it becomes a symbol only if the unconscious of a group says "yes" to it. It means that something is opened up by it in the sense which I have just described. Now this implies further that in the moment in which this inner situation of the human group to a symbol has ceased to exist, then the symbol dies. The symbol does not "say" anything any more. In this way, all of the polytheistic gods have died; the situation in which they were born, has changed or does not exist any more, and so the symbols died. But these are events which cannot be described in terms of intention and invention.

III

Now I come to my third consideration—namely, the nature of religious symbols. Religious symbols do exactly the same thing as all symbols do—namely,
they open up a level of reality, which otherwise is not opened at all, which is
hidden. I would call this the depth dimension of reality itself, the dimension
of reality which is the ground of every other dimension and every other
depth, and which therefore, is not one level beside the others but is the
fundamental level, the level below all other levels, the level of being itself, or
the ultimate power of being. Religious symbols open up the experience of
the dimension of this depth in the human soul. If a religious symbol has
ceased to have this function, then it dies. And if new symbols are born, they
are born out of a changed relationship to the ultimate ground of being, i.e.,
to the Holy.

The dimension of ultimate reality is the dimension of the Holy. And so
we can also say, religious symbols are symbols of the Holy. As such they
participate in the holiness of the Holy according to our basic definition of a
symbol. But participation is not identity; they are not themselves *the* Holy.
The wholly transcendent transcends every symbol of the Holy. Religious symbols are taken from the infinity of material which the experienced reality gives
us. Everything in time and space has become at some time in the history of
religion a symbol for the Holy. And this is naturally so, because everything
that is in the world we encounter rests on the ultimate ground of being.
This is the key to the otherwise extremely confusing history of religion. Those
of you who have looked into this seeming chaos of the history of religion in
all periods of history from the earliest primitives to the latest developments in
California, will be extremely confused about the chaotic character of this
development. But the key which makes order out of this chaos is comparatively simple. And the key is that everything in reality can impress itself as a
symbol for a special relationship of the human mind to its own ultimate
ground and meaning. So in order to open up the seemingly closed door to
this chaos of religious symbols, one simply has to ask, "Which is the relationship to the ultimate which is symbolized in these symbols?" And then they
cease to be meaningless; and they become, on the contrary, the most revealing creations of the human mind, the most genuine ones, the most powerful
ones, those who control the human consciousness, and perhaps even more
the unconsciousness, and have therefore this tremendous tenacity which is
characteristic of all religious symbols in the history of religion.

Religion, as everything in life, stands under the law of ambiguity, "ambiguity" meaning that it is creative and destructive at the same time. Religion
has its holiness and its unholiness, and the reason for this is obvious from
what I have said about religious symbolism. Religious symbols point symbolically to that which transcends all of them. But since, as symbols, they
participate in that to which they point, they always have the tendency (in
the human mind, of course) to replace that to which they are supposed to

point, and to become ultimate in themselves. And in the moment in which they do this, they become idols. All idolatry is nothing else than the absolutizing of symbols of the Holy, and making them identical with the Holy itself. In this way, for instance, holy persons can become god. Ritual acts can take on unconditional validity, although they are only expressions of a special situation. In all sacramental activities of religion, in all holy objects, holy books, holy doctrines, holy rites, you find this danger which I like to call demonization. They become demonic in the moment in which they become elevated to the unconditional and ultimate character of the Holy itself.

IV

Now I come to my fourth consideration—namely, the levels of religious symbols. I distinguish two fundamental levels in all religious symbols: the transcendent level, the level which goes *beyond* the empirical reality we encounter, and the immanent level, the level which we find *within* the encounter with reality. Let us first look at the first level, the transcendent level. The basic symbol on the transcendent level would be God himself. But we cannot simply say that God is a symbol. We must always say two things about him: we must say that there is a non-symbolic element in our image of God—namely that he is ultimate reality, being itself, ground of being, power of being; and the other, that he is the highest being in which everything that we have does exist in the most perfect way. If we say this we have in our mind the image of a highest being, a being with the characteristics of highest perfection. That means we have a symbol for that which is not symbolic in the idea of God—namely "Being Itself." It is important, and I think more than important, to distinguish these two elements in the idea of God. Thus all of these discussions going on about God being a person or not a person, God being similar to other beings or not similar, these discussions which have a great impact on the destruction of the religious experience through false interpretations of it, could be overcome if we would say, "Certainly the awareness of something unconditional is in itself what it is, is not symbolic." We can call it *"Being Itself,"* *esse qua esse, esse ipsum*, as the scholastics did. But in our relationship to this ultimate we symbolize and must symbolize. We could not be in communication with God if he were only "ultimate being." But in our relationship to him we encounter him with the highest of what we ourselves are, *person*. And so in the symbolic form of speaking about him, we have both that which transcends infinitely our experience of ourselves as persons, and that which is so adequate to our being persons that we can say, "Thou" to God, and can pray to him. And these two elements must be preserved. If we preserve only the element of the unconditional, then no relationship to God is possible. If we preserve only the element of the ego-thou relationship, as it is called today, we lose the element of the divine—namely, the unconditional which transcends subject and object and all other polarities. This is the first point on the transcendent level.

The second is the qualities, the attributes of God, whatever you say about him: that he is love, that he is mercy, that he is power, that he is omniscient, that he is omnipresent, that he is almighty and all this. These attributes of God are taken from experienced qualities we have ourselves. They cannot be applied to God in the literal sense. If this is done, it leads to an infinite amount of absurdities. This again is one of the reasons for the destruction of religion through wrong communicative interpretation of it. And again the symbolic character of these qualities must be maintained consistently. Otherwise, every speaking about the divine becomes absurd.

A third element on the transcendent level is the acts of God. For instance, when we say, "He has created the world," "He has sent his son," "He will fulfill the world." In all these temporal, causal, and other expressions we speak symbolically of God. And I would like here to give an example in which the four main categories of our finitude are combined in *one* small sentence: "*God has sent his son.*" Here we have in the word "has" temporality. But God is beyond *our* temporality, though not beyond every temporality. Here is space; "sending somebody" means moving him from one place to another place. This certainly is speaking symbolically, although spatiality is in God as an element in his creative ground. We say that he "has sent," [meaning] that he has caused something. In this way God is subject to the category of causality. And when we speak of him and his Son, we have two different substances and apply the category of substance to him. Now all this, if taken literally, is absurd. If it is taken symbolically, it is a profound expression, the ultimate Christian expression, of the relationship between God and man in the Christian experience. But to distinguish these two kinds of speech, the non-symbolic and the symbolic, in such a point is so important that if we are not able to make understandable to our contemporaries that we speak symbolically when we use such language, they will rightly turn away from us, as from people who live still in absurdities and superstitions.

Now consider the immanent level, the level of the appearances of the divine in time and space. Here we have first of all the incarnations of the divine, different beings in time and space, divine beings transmuted into animals or men or any kinds of other beings as they appear in time and space. This is often forgotten by those within Christianity who like to use in every second theological proposition the word, "incarnation." They forget that this is not an especially Christian characteristic, because incarnation is something which happens in paganism all the time. The divine beings always incarnate in different forms. That is very easy in paganism. This is not the real distinction between Christianity and other religions. Let me say something here, about the relationships of the transcendent to the immanent level just in connection with the incarnation idea. Historically, one must say that preceding both of them was the situation in which the transcendent and immanent were not distinguished. In the Indonesian doctrine of "Mana," that divine mystical power which permeates all reality, we have some divine presence which is both immanent in everything as a hidden power, and at the same time transcendent, something which can be grasped only through very difficult ritual activities known to the priest. Out of this identity of the immanent and the transcendent the gods of the great mythologies have developed in Greece and in the Semitic nations and in India. There we find incarnations as the immanent element of the divine. The more transcendent the gods become, the more incarnations of personal or sacramental character are needed in order to overcome the remoteness of the divine which develops with the strengthening of the transcendent element.

And from this follows the second element in the immanent religious symbolism namely, the sacramental. The sacramental is nothing else than some reality becoming the bearer of the Holy in a special way and under special circumstances. In this sense, the Lord's Supper, or better the materials in the Lord's Supper, are symbolic. Now you will ask perhaps, "only symbolic?" That sounds as if there were something more than symbolic namely, "literal." But the literal is not more but less than symbolic. If we speak of those dimensions of reality which we cannot approach in any other way than by symbols, then symbols are not used in terms of "only" but in terms of that which is necessary, of that which we *must* apply. Sometimes, because of nothing more than the confusion of signs with symbols, the phrase "only a symbol" means "only a sign." And then the question is justified. "Only a sign?" "No." The sacrament is not only a sign. And in the famous discussion between Luther and Zwingli, in Marburg in 1529, it was just this point on which the discussion was held. Luther wanted to maintain the genuinely symbolic character of the elements, but Zwingli said that the sacramental materials, bread and wine, are "only symbolic." Thus Zwingli meant that they are only signs pointing to a story of the past. Even in that period there was semantic confusion. And let us not be misled by this. In the real sense of symbol, the sacramental materials are symbols. But if the symbol is used as *only* symbol (i.e., only signs), then of course the sacramental materials are more than this.

Then there is the third element on the immanent level. Many things, like special parts of the church building, like the candles, like the water at the entrance of the Roman Church, like the cross in all churches, especially Protestant churches, were originally only signs, but in use became symbols. I call them sign-symbols, signs which have become symbols.

v

And now I come to my last consideration—namely, the truth of religious symbols. Here I must distinguish a negative, a positive, and an absolute statement. First the negative statement. Symbols are independent of any empirical criticism. You cannot kill a symbol by criticism in terms of natural sciences or in terms of historical research. As I said, symbols can only die if the situation in which they have been created has passed. Symbols are not on a level on which empirical criticism can dismiss them. I will give you two examples, both connected with Mary, the mother of Jesus, as Holy Virgin. Here you have first of all a symbol which has died in Protestanism by the changed situation of the relation to God. The special, direct, immediate relationship to God, makes any mediating power impossible. Another reason which has made this symbol disappear is the negation of the ascetic element which is implied in the glorification of virginity. And as long as the Protestant religious situation lasts it cannot be reestablished. It has not died because Protestant scholars have said, "Now there is no empirical reason for saying all this about the Holy Virgin." There certainly is not, but this the Roman Church also knows. But the Roman Church sticks to it on the basis of its tremendous symbolic power which step by step brings her nearer to Trinity itself, especially in the development of the last decade. If this should ever be completed as is now discussed in groups of the Roman Church, Mary would become co-Saviour with Jesus. Then, whether this is admitted or not, she is actually taken into the divinity itself. Another example is the story of the virginal birth of Jesus. This is from the point of view of historical research a most obviously legendary story, unknown to Paul and to John. It is a late creation, trying to make understandable the full possession of the divine Spirit of Jesus of Nazareth. But again its legendary character is not the reason why this symbol will die or has died in many groups of people, in even quite conservative groups within the Protestant churches. The reason is different. The reason is that it is theologically quasi-heretical. It takes away one of the fundamental doctrines of Chalcedon, viz., the classical Christian doctrine that the full humanity of Jesus must be maintained beside his whole divinity. A human being who has no human father has no full humanity. This story, then, has to be criticized on inner-symbolic grounds, but not on historical grounds. This is the negative statement about the truth of religious symbols. Their truth is their adequacy to the religious situation in which they are created, and their inadequacy to another situation is their untruth. In the last sentence both the positive and the negative statement about symbols are contained. Only a few words about the absolute statement about the truth of religious symbols. I said that religion is ambiguous and that every religious symbol may become idolatrous, may be demonized, may elevate itself to ultimate validity although nothing is ultimate but the ultimate itself; no religious doctrine and no religious ritual may be. I believe that if Christianity claims to have a truth superior to any other truth in its symbolism, then it is the symbol of the cross in which this is expressed, the cross of the Christ. He who himself embodies the fullness of the divine's presence sacrifices himself in order not to become an idol, another god beside God, a god into whom the disciples wanted to make him. And therefore the decisive story is the story in which he accepts the title "Christ" when Peter offers it to him. He accepts it under the one condition that he has to go to Jerusalem to suffer and to die; that means to deny the idolatrous tendency even with respect to himself. This is at the same time the criterion of all other symbols, and it is the criterion to which every Christian church should subject itself.

Interesting discussions of the problems and theories concerning the meaning and verification of religious discourse are Frederick Ferre, *Language, Logic and God* * (Harper, 1969), William Blackstone, *The Problems of Religious Knowledge* * (Prentice-Hall, 1963), Basil Mitchell, ed., *Faith and Logic* (Humanities Press, 1958), Ian Ramsey, *Religious Language* * (Macmillan, 1963), R. B. Braithwaite, *An Empiricist's View of the Nature of Religious Belief* (Ridgeway Books, 1955), and Alvin Plantinga, *God and Other Minds* (Cornell University Press, 1967).

Major sources of the analogy theory are St. Thomas Aquinas, "The Names of God," *Summa Theologica*, Part 1, Question 12, Articles 1–12, and Cajetan, *The Analogy of Names* (Duquesne University Press, 1959). A recent attempt to structure the analogy theory along new lines is James F. Ross, "A New Theory of Analogy: The Nature and Presuppositions of Analogy," *Proceedings of the American Catholic Philosophical Association*, 44 (1970).

Works by Paul Tillich that deal with his symbol theory of religious objects and religious discourse are "The Religious Symbol" and "The Meaning and Justification of Religious Symbols" in Sidney Hook, ed., *Religious Experience and Truth* (New York University Press, 1961). See also his *Dynamics of Faith* * (Harper, 1958). For an analysis and evaluation of Tillich's theory, consult William P. Alston, "Tillich's Conception of a Religious Symbol" in *Religious Experience and Truth* (previously cited) and William L. Rowe, *Religious Symbols and God: A Philosophical Study of Tillich's Theology* (University of Chicago Press, 1968).

* Available in paperback.

A	2
B	3
C	4
D	5
E	6
F	7
G	8
H	9
I	0
J	1